SAP R/3 Process-Oriented Implementation

Related titles published by Addison-Wesley:

ABAP/4 Programming the SAP R/3 System   Bernd Matzke

SAP R/3 System: A Client/Server Technology   Rüdiger Buck-Emden and Jürgen Galimow

SAP R/3 Administration   Liane Will, Christine Heinger, Frank Strafsenburg and Rocco Himmer

Gerhard Keller
Thomas Teufel

SAP R/3 Process-Oriented Implementation

Iterative Process Prototyping

Translated by Audrey Weinland

 Addison Wesley Longman

Harlow, England • Reading, Massachusetts • Menlo Park, California
New York • Don Mills, Ontario • Amsterdam • Bonn • Sydney • Singapore
Tokyo • Madrid • San Juan • Milan • Mexico City • Seoul • Taipei

Addison-Wesley Longman Limited
Edinburgh Gate
Harlow
Essex, CM20 2JE
England

and Associated Companies throughout the World.

Translated by Audrey Weinland
Typeset in Times by 58
Printed and bound in Great Britain by Biddles Ltd, Guildford and King's Lynn.

First printed 1998. Reprinted 1998

ISBN 0-201-924706

British Library Cataloguing-in-Publication Data
A catalogue record for this book is available from the British Library

"We are our customers' servants,
because an innovation without a meaningful use
is worthless."

Introduction

Process design plays a pivotal role in management and organization science. The implementation of DP systems is an attempt to support the results of process design in enterprises with integrated information processing.

From a historical perspective, the push to develop EDP concepts originated with manufacturers of hardware and software. They created new prospects for the efficient use of EDP, which businesses could and wanted to use. As a result, EDP-oriented research developed as well. As the first order of business, EDP requirements were derived from real-world operations, and specifications were drawn up. In the 1970s, for example, DP suppliers tried to provide optimal support for the requirements of individual function areas, but they paid little attention to the interdependencies between each functional area and preceding or subsequent areas. Closed hardware architectures only allowed development of software solutions that were closely tied to the operating system. Incompatibilities between DP systems from various suppliers led to systems known as *standalone systems*. The proprietary systems that were available had a counterproductive effect on the targeted objective of *taking advantage of the benefits of integration* and could only meet some of the function requirements.

In the 1980s, this situation began to cause *CIM* (Computer Integrated Manufacturing) *ruins* for the user. One important reason for this development was that, while the use of information systems conceived primarily for function brought out the functional organization prevailing in most enterprises, traditional organization structures required information systems that were organized according to classic functionality to handle their tasks. This development resulted in:

- disconnected process chains in the enterprise

- a large number of organizational interfaces

- a large number of interfaces between DP systems

Increased decoupling of hardware and software constituted the first step in the dismantling of proprietary DP systems. Integrated database systems and networks emerged, which were meant to solve the integration problems of the 1970s. The ability for different company departments to access the same database was meant to achieve the goal of making data created in one area immediately available to all other areas. Redundancy-free, easy-access structuring was meant to have the following effects:

- improve the completeness and accuracy of data

- ensure that data was up to date for all operational areas

- eliminate multiple entries of the same data

- avoid errors

- reduce costs for making changes

- shorten information transfer times

The development of conceptual data models was intended to solve the data redundancy and data consistency problems endemic in enterprises. Entire armies of scientists and practitioners plunged into enterprise data modelling according to Chen's entity relationship approach. The business application data models that they created did sensitize suppliers and users to the need to include data structure aspects in the consideration of interfaces and integration relationships, but they did not bring about a definitive breakthrough where software selection was concerned. Also, due to their complex notation, they were accessible mainly to a small circle of business science and computer science experts, they often resembled internal chip design, and they were limited in their ability to represent the end user's requirements.

The deficiencies in the data models prompted some scientists to address the fundamental question of how to set up model and company architectures (e.g., CIM Open System Architecture). One group of tool manufacturers used the functional deficiencies present in the standard software of the 80s as a starting point for developing computer-supported tools for software development – Computer Aided Software Engineering (CASE). Methods oriented towards information technology, such as Structured Analysis (SA), Structured Analysis/Real Time (SA/RT), Structured Analysis and Design Technique (SADT), program flowcharts, Petri nets, function trees, etc., were incorporated into these tools to describe functional and procedural aspects.

Lack of a user-friendly interface, insufficient integration with the physical implementation, no consideration for organizational change, and cumbersome handling limited the CASE tools' ability to be used to a small number of information-technology-oriented users. Lack of understanding on the part of information technology engineers of the operational requirements of end users, as well as inadequate knowledge about business solutions (such as those which numerous SAP customers have brought into the R/3 System) frequently resulted in a new set of ruins in an enterprise – so-called *CASE ruins*.

The practitioners' approach, which was to use CASE tools in a customer's company to automatically produce a software solution from a relatively large description of business requirements, failed. The scientists' approach, which was to provide an architecture for general software development projects, remained in its infancy. Moreover, the fact that there were so many possible business solutions in practice led to a situation in which the research scientists, who often worked in isolation, floundered when it came to *business process design* and were unable to work out sufficiently practicable design recommendations.

With the development of client/server solutions for business applications, such as SAP AG's R/3 System, new approaches emerged for organizational design in enterprises. These new design possibilities, however, also increased the complexity of the decision making that is part of creating information processing concepts supported by DP.

At the same time, trends in information technology (IT) and management caused a shift away from optimization of divisions and towards general business process design that concentrated on the most important net value added chains. The data-oriented approach of the 1980s moved out of the spotlight, and the design of business processes became the focus of attention. *Process owners*, who are responsible for the handling of entire processes, were often used in practice. In requirements analysis, too, discussion shifted away from technical details and moved more towards business problems. The technology – client/server system, database, network, for example – was accepted as a quasi-standard.

The development prompted SAP, at the end of 1992, to wrap up discussion about methods for representing business processes and quickly start developing the contents of the R/3 System's processes. Selected examples were presented at the international computer fair CeBIT '93, and the business audience's overwhelmingly positive response reinforced the path that SAP had chosen. The R/3 reference processes were delivered in succession, along with Releases 2.1, 2.2 and 3.0 of R/3, respectively. The current Reference Model, part of Release 3.x, is available in English and German. It includes processes for the following business areas (application components):

- Logistics
  - Sales and Distribution
  - Materials Management
  - Production Planning
  - Project System
  - Quality Assurance
  - Plant Maintenance
- Accounting
  - Financial Accounting
  - Assets Accounting
  - Investment Management
  - Controlling
- Human Resources
  - Personnel Administration and Payroll

– Personnel Planning and Development

Information system modelling was the purview of a small group of experts. Business process design, on the other hand, requires communication between IT suppliers, IT management, organization planners and end users across company divisions. It also requires that representatives from different areas, such as business management science, engineering, business engineering, computer science and information science, engage in dialogue.

These days, it is nearly impossible to implement efficient business process handling without using appropriate information technology. Just as telephones and televisions are everyday consumer goods in private households, industrial enterprises cannot get by in today's information age without information technology, for example data processing equipment and communication services (telefax, telex, America Online, sending of electronic messages using electronic mail over the Internet). While technological development and innovation forge ahead in dramatic leaps and enable new types of processing, in most enterprises, the business concepts for business process handling are still characterized by the paradigm of Taylorism. The thought processes and actions of employees in enterprises that follow the Taylor principle (according to which each person is responsible for optimizing his own area along with its tasks and information), and the structuring of enterprises according to the Taylor principle (i.e. division of tasks into planning activities, monitoring activities and executing activities), prevent enterprises from implementing integrated business processes. On the other hand, the increasingly dynamic nature of markets (in which things that are *state of the art* today are already outdated tomorrow, for example LP records and CDs, roller skates and inline skates, hot-metal typesetting and phototypesetting in the printing industry, electromagnetic data transfer (coaxial cables) and data transfer using optical fibre (fibre-optic cables), typewriters and computers, carburettors and fuel injection motors) requires quick and flexible action. Customizing products according to the customer's desires and manufacturing at the lowest possible costs to undercut current market prices, all the while retaining the necessary quality, are requirements that an enterprise must meet today in order to stay alive in the supplier market.

To meet the requirements mentioned, many enterprises spend time designing and optimizing business processes that will be supported by an information system. These enterprises must address four important questions:

- What are the main business processes that we use to generate profit?
- How should these business processes be designed?
- Which employees are responsible for them?
- Which production technology, communications technology and information technology do they require?

Information technology, as the supporter of integrated business processes, plays a significant role in this process. On the road towards DP-supported business process handling, the question now arises of how to implement this project. In the real world, two imposing problems emerge in the design of business processes:

- In many enterprises, existing business processes are not transparent, and responsibilities are unclear.

- The business processes provided by DP suppliers, especially those provided by software manufacturers, are often not clear to potential customers and are usually difficult to understand as a whole.

This book demonstrates how to design business processes and handle them with software by the world's leading supplier of business application software – SAP AG's R/3 System. In this context, business process means the meaningful linking together of parts into a whole process with the objective of creating something *new* when the entire process is executed, that is, value is added for the customer, for which the customer pays an appropriate price. This creation of value is therefore called the *net value added chain*.

The contents of this book are divided into five sections. *Section A* presents the various trends in business process design. Business process design is surrounded by the magical triangle of *corporate planning*, *technology selection* and *organization design*, *specifically the qualification-related planning of human resources*. For this reason, the first section presents an overview of the most important developments in these three areas. It demonstrates that while business process design may focus on one of these three points in the beginning, neglecting to work out some form of cooperation with the two neighbouring areas can lead to inadequate implementation or failure of the entire concept. The basic developments are put into concrete terms by an in-depth discussion of the selected approaches, which deal with aspects of business process design in a more-or-less developed fashion. The approaches range from those that are discussed in management science (for example, cybernetics), to those that deal with the integrated use of information and production technologies (for example, *Computer Integrated Manufacturing*) or with the use of information technologies (for example, *Continuous System Engineering*). The conclusion gives an overview of the *changes in software* from the suppliers' point of view, and it demonstrates the principal kinds of support that enterprises can demand in the future from software manufacturers when planning information processing concepts.

Section B deals with the fundamental concepts of process design. The authors are of the opinion that one should first look for solutions that are available on the software market, before starting custom development. Of course, both paths assume that an enterprise has clarified to the greatest extent possible what its objectives are and what its main path should be towards a solution. An enterprise must also decide, while weighing costs against benefits, to what extent any presupposed *software supplier dependency* is outweighed by the risk of *employee dependency*, with its attendant upkeep and maintenance costs. (After all, there are supposedly still a few isolated enterprises that, for example, propagate their own text processing program, for "strategic reasons".) Selecting the best possible solution available on the software market requires that the software manufacturers describe their solutions in their entirety, yet clearly and comprehensibly. The first part of Section B – Chapter 2 – presents an overview of the application packages offered as business solutions by the leading software manufacturer – the business solutions of SAP AG's R/3 System.

Business situations are generally explained using verbal descriptions, tabular representations and graphic models. Depending on the objective and the problem, on one hand, and the user's level of knowledge, on the other, one or the other of these forms of description may be more suitable. Due to the multitude of variants provided for describing business phenomena, even the form of description undergoes a selection process. For this reason, readers who want an overview of the most prevalent methods and their corresponding book and periodical references can find one in Chapter 3 of Section B.

The description leads into the graphic form of description that SAP AG provides for the presentation of R/3 processes. The methodological bases for the R/3 reference processes, and how the R/3 processes are handled, are mentioned in Chapter 4. Just as, at a crosswalk signal, the symbol showing a person walking means "cross", while the symbol showing a person standing means "do not cross", each of the different symbols in the R/3 Reference Process Model has a meaning, which is explained in that chapter. Anyone wanting to skip the scientific explanation of the individual elements can refer to the overview graphic showing the symbols, definitions and examples.

Section C introduces the capabilities of the tools provided by SAP for implementing and using the R/3 System. These tools can be used to set up individual application areas, such as Sales and Distribution, where they can be used to design individual function areas. In meaningful combinations, however, you can also use them to plan entire net value added chains, for example, from order processing, through production, goods movement, delivery processing and invoicing, on down to payment processing. Standard software implementation belongs to the general class of procedures that demonstrate a goal-oriented method for solving a problem. These can be divided into project management procedures, such as those implemented by corporate consultants in corporate planning projects, organization development projects and human resources development projects; software development procedures; and software implementation procedures. The different approaches are portrayed briefly in Chapter 5, which is also where the reader interested in more detail will find the corresponding technical literature.

In contrast to these phase-oriented methods, Chapter 6 in Section C presents an approach for process-oriented R/3 planning that is based on a cybernetic model, in which iterative jumps occur.

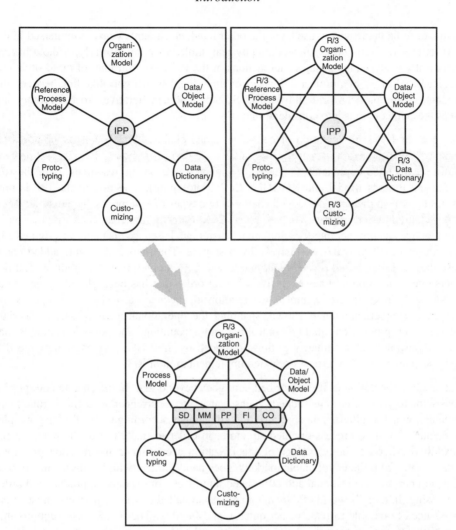

Fig. I.1: Elements and links in Iterative Process Prototyping (IPP)

In this context, Iterative Process Prototyping (IPP) means choosing the appropriate tool depending on the customer's objective. The conceptual interconnection of various resources allows the customer to navigate to the information he desires based on his problem(s). The resources needed for IPP are explained, the main links between the individual resources are portrayed, and the use of IPP is demonstrated on the basis of the following task: *Implement R/3 in a process-oriented manner.* Based on experience gained in workshops, the integration and use of each of the IPP tools is made tangible using a sample R/3 reference process, "RFQ processing". Special emphasis is placed on highlighting the links between the *model world* and the *system world*, i.e. between the R/3 Reference Process Model and the R/3 System. This is because it is not unusual for the results created by consulting firms in a business model world to remain unused in the rest of an R/3 implementation, or to be inadequately used. On the other hand, consultants who are immersed in the SAP-oriented system world often begin physical implementation too early, without having sufficiently analysed the business interactions of the R/3 System. Either of these situations can lead to disaster in a project's finances or time line. The network-like link between the contents of the model world and the R/3 System world in Iterative Process Prototyping takes these interactions into consideration early on.

The goal of IPP is the creation of net value added chains. While Section C focuses on explaining the procedures for using IPP, *Section D* describes the result of an IPP process and the associated application of the R/3 System. Based on the resources used, the R/3 Reference Process Model and R/3 IDES (R/3 Prototyping), a section of the IPP is presented to explain the net value added chains of two types of enterprises. The first net value added chain describes a *lot-size manufacturer with direct sales*, i.e. an enterprise that plans and produces its product line for anonymous customers based on planned sales figures and sells the goods it provides exclusively from storage. The second net value added chain describes an *order-based assembly manufacturer*, i.e. an enterprise that produces and delivers one of its product lines exclusively for an order that has been placed by an actual customer. Using concrete examples, the relationship between a business concept and its DP-related implementation is shown, spanning the operational areas of sales, materials management, production, quality, controlling and accounting. The possible solutions that are demonstrated refer primarily to those provided by SAP AG; they show how the IPP approach can be used for process-oriented implementation of R/3.

But process orientation as it is described here goes beyond that. In the end, an enterprise's consistent focus on net value added chains causes it to surrender its refined, functional structure, which capitalizes on specialization advantages according to the Taylor principle, in favour of a more process-oriented structure, in order to make use of the potential for flexibility. After all, the advantage of specialization according to the function principle, which stems from the era of stable markets, goes hand in hand with the disadvantage of a high number of organizational and DP-related interfaces, for example in product and order processing. In today's world of dynamic markets, so-called consumer markets, most enterprises need to be able to react or act quickly and flexibly. The R/3 System supports this capability. Reducing the number of organizational interfaces, on the other hand, is the responsibility of the enterprises and their employees. One prerequisite for implementing the IPP concept is that processes must be transparent, comprehensible and malleable. For this reason, Section D is arranged in such a way that the conceptual structure (structure of the process flow) of a process always appears on the left-hand side, beginning with a verbal description, while the corresponding solution in the R/3 System appears on the right-hand side. The left-hand side thus serves as a business description, while the right-hand side serves as a description of the R/3 System. It is the authors' hope that the contents displayed as examples in Section D will help lead the way as we enter a new era, the engineering of business processes.

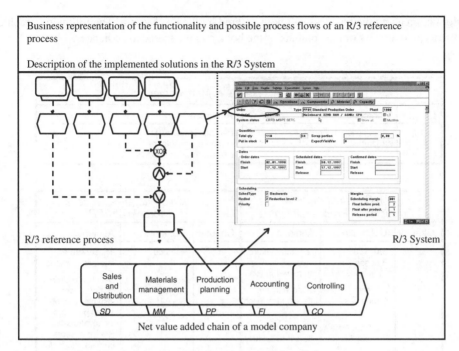

Business representation of the functionality and possible process flows of an R/3 reference process

Description of the implemented solutions in the R/3 System

R/3 reference process

R/3 System

Sales and Distribution	Materials management	Production planning	Accounting	Controlling
SD	MM	PP	FI	CO

Net value added chain of a model company

Fig. I.2: Link between the business world and the system world

The Iterative Process Prototyping approach, which is demonstrated on the basis of practical experience, makes several important developments possible in the overall software market. If the software industry managed to set standards to allow the substitution of certain subcomponents, as in the automobile industry, one could imagine that under certain conditions, different users' business software solutions could, for example, communicate with each other without a special interface having to be developed for each individual case. For another thing, one could imagine down the road that individual processes provided by different software manufacturers could be combined at the customer site to form net value added chains. Knowing how to set up net value added chains, however, will require consultants who have different qualifications, and will necessitate a different training curriculum. Some ideas for this are listed in *Section E*.

This book is meant for business-oriented readers who deal with the planning, implementation and use of business application systems. It may also provide ideas to decision makers who want to be involved in the design of net value added chains in general, and specifically in the use of the R/3 solution spectrum. Consultants in the areas of business (re-)engineering and process-oriented software implementation, as well as project team members working on R/3 implementation projects, are shown how to design net value added chains with the R/3 System, especially in Chapters 6, 7, 8 and 9. Readers who are more scientifically oriented, such as professors, trainers and students, can acquire a foundation in process design theory in Chapters 3, 4 and 5. Chapter 1 details the major discussions and developments related to the design of business processes. Chapter 2 provides information about the business solutions offered by the R/3 System. The following graphic presents an overview of the contents of the book and the intended audiences.

Section A: Trends in Management	
Chapter **Contents**	**Audience**
1 (R)Evolutionary corporate structures	Decision makers, corporate consultants, those with an interest in science

Section B: Fundamental Principles of Process Design			Section C: Iterative Process Prototyping (IPP)		
Chapter	**Contents**	**Audience**	**Chapter**	**Contents**	**Audience**
2	SAP R/3 Release 3.x	Decision makers, anyone interested in R/3	5	Methods	Those with an interest in science
3	Modelling companies	Those with an interest in science	6	Network paradigm in IPP	Decision makers, corporate consultants, organization planners, those interested in R/3, professors, trainers, students
4	R/3 Reference Process Model	Those with an interest in science			

Section D: Net Value Added Chains	
Chapter **Contents**	**Audience**
7 Structure of the model companies	Decision makers, corporate consultants, organization planners, those interested in R/3, professors, trainers, students
8 Model company *Lot-size Manu-facturer with direct Sales*	Decision makers, corporate consultants, organization planners, those interested in R/3, professors, trainers, students
9 Model company *Order-based Assembly Manufacturer*	Decision makers, corporate consultants, organization planners, those interested in R/3, professors, trainers, students

Section E: Future Prospects	
Chapter **Contents**	**Audience**
10 T-oriented consulting and hypermedia-based training	Decision makers, corporate consultants, organization planners, those interested in R/3, professors, trainers, students

Fig. I.3: Structure of this book

Preface

Designing business processes in order to remain competitive is an essential task for many enterprises. For one thing, there is the corporate challenge of determining which business processes should be handled in which form. Then one must determine which employees should perform these processes with which resources. Next to *performing business processes*, the key to balancing corporate risk is *planning the right business processes*.

Our experience has shown that designing business processes is often a not-so-trivial problem, both for R/3 customers and for us. We must often make decisions under a blanket of uncertainties because information is not transparent, and basic conditions are continually changing. A lot of discussion centres around the creation of operational processes. In our opinion, if business processes were documented sufficiently, it would and should be possible to refer to the experiences of other enterprises during such discussions.

Many such processes, driven by very different customer requirements, are physically implemented in the R/3 System. In creating the R/3 Reference Process Model, SAP AG's goal has been to portray in graphic format the business processes implemented in the R/3 System, along with all of their variations, and support the customer's decision-making process during business process design. We used the R/3 Reference Model and the R/3 System to demonstrate how to create and use business processes with them. Based on frequently requested customer requirements, we created and tested two model enterprises as an example, and presented them in this book.

The success of this work is due in large part to the support of our colleagues. We were able to tap the experience of subject-matter experts from many different areas in our information network. For their helpfulness in the design and testing of the model enterprises, we would like to extend thanks to Helmut Bartsch, Michael Bauer, Susanne Becker, Dagmar Brauch, Robert Cummings, Anke Gerhard, Dragan Grujic, Dirk Guttzeit, Frank Eck, Peter Flensberg, Jürgen Kniephof, Dennis Ladd, Andreas Lietschulte, Andreas Pfadenhauer, Arvind Prasad, Werner Wolf, all of whom are with SAP AG, and Daniel Malt, who is with the Plaut Controlling Systems Company. Thanks also to subject-matter experts Susanne Donald, Alan Prouse, Jürgen Röhricht and Werner Dilzer.

We would like to thank our colleague Stefan Meinhardt, as well as Tom Curran from the company TCManagement, who kept us on the right path with their critical reflection and encouraged us numerous times to bring this project to fruition. We would also like to thank Bernhard Hochlehnert and Stephan Magura for their valuable editing tips and hints. Thanks also to Martina Kuntschner and Tomas Wehren from Addison Wesley for their editorial revision of this work. And, of course, we would like to express our gratitude to the translators who made this English edition of our book possible: Stephen Healy, Martina Kuntschner, and especially Audrey Weinland.

A special "thank you" goes to our wives and children, who gave up their family vacations in 1996 and suffered our absence on many a weekend.

Introduction

In addition to our colleagues, who established the knowledge base for the creation of this book by making the R/3 System a reality, we would like to thank all those who, with their treasure trove of experience and their knowledge, communicated their needs to us and for whom we wrote this book – *the R/3 users*.

St. Leon-Rot and Spaichingen, Germany   *Dr Gerhard Keller*
January 1997   *Thomas Teufel*

Contents

Introduction

Section A   Trends in Management

1   (R)Evolutionary Enterprise Structures.. 1

1.1	Developments in business	3
1.1.1	The influence of global markets	3
1.1.2	Changing values in corporate culture	3
1.1.3	New horizons: alliances on a virtual basis	4
1.2	Technological developments	7
1.2.1	Client/Server	9
1.2.2	Object orientation	11
1.2.3	Multimedia	15
1.2.4	Data highway on the Internet	20
1.3	Organizational developments	24
1.3.1	Taylor's influence on organizations in America	24
1.3.2	Nordsieck's influence on organizations in Germany	27
1.4	Paradigms for business process design	30
1.4.1	Computer integrated manufacturing	30
1.4.2	Logistics	32
1.4.3	Lean Management	35
1.4.4	Simultaneous engineering	37
1.4.5	Net value added chains	39
1.4.6	Business transformation	41
1.4.7	Cybernetics	42
1.4.8	Workflow management	45
1.4.9	Continuous system engineering	48
1.4.10	Business (re)-engineering	51
1.5	Continuous business (quality) engineering with SAP	54
1.5.1	Risks in business process design	54
1.5.2	Process orientation and object orientation	56
1.5.3	Business processes as componentware	58

Section B   Fundamental Principles of Process Design

2   SAP R/3 – Release 3.x **64**

2.1   R/3 basis architecture 64
2.2   R/3 applications... 67
2.2.1   Accounting 68
2.2.2   Logistics 75
2.2.3   Human Resources Management... 95
2.3   Other R/3 services 99

3   Enterprise Modelling **109**

3.1   Models... 109
3.2   Architectures 112
3.2.1   Computer Integrated Manufacturing – Open System Architecture......... 113
3.2.2   Architecture of integrated information systems 116
3.2.3   Semantic object model 119
3.2.4   Knowledge Acquisition and Documentation Structuring 122
3.2.5   Object-Oriented Information Engineering 126
3.3   Methods.. 130
3.3.1   IT-oriented methods 130
3.3.2   Methods oriented towards business management science 137

4   The R/3 Reference Process Model **145**

4.1   Basic terminology regarding business process.................................... 145
4.2   Event-controlled process chains (EPC)... 150
4.3   Formal description of the EPC 158
4.3.1   Basics 158
4.3.2   General model 158
4.3.3   Control flow 164

Section C   IPP for Designing Net Value Added Chains

5   Procedures **169**

5.1   Procedures in project management 170
5.2   Procedures in software engineering 174
5.3   Procedures in software implementation 179
5.3.1   The BPI phase concept... 179
5.3.2   AcceleratedSAP 184

6   Cybernetics in Iterative Process Prototyping (IPP) **189**

6.1   IPP structure 189

Contents

6.1.1   R/3 Reference Process Model 190
6.1.2   R/3 Organization Model 193
6.1.3   R/3 Object/data Model 196
6.1.4   R/3 Prototyping 198
6.1.5   R/3 Customizing 200
6.1.6   R/3 Data Dictionary 203
6.2   Iterative paths in IPP 206
6.2.1   From process to Prototyping 207
6.2.2   From process to Organization Model 208
6.2.3   From process to Customizing 209
6.2.4   From process to Data Model 210
6.2.5   From process to Data Dictionary 211
6.2.6   From Prototyping to Organization 212
6.2.7   From Prototyping to process 213
6.2.8   From Prototyping to Customizing 214
6.2.9   From Prototyping to Data Model 215
6.2.10   From Prototyping to Data Dictionary 216
6.2.11   From Organization Model to Prototyping 217
6.2.12   From Organization Model to process 218
6.2.13   From Organization Model to Customizing 219
6.2.14   From Organization Model to Data Model 220
6.2.15   From Organization Model to Data Dictionary 221
6.2.16   From Customizing to process 222
6.2.17   From Customizing to Prototyping 223
6.2.18   From Customizing to Organization 224
6.2.19   From Customizing to Data Model 225
6.2.20   From Customizing to Data Dictionary 226
6.2.21   From Data Model to process 227
6.2.22   From Data Model to Customizing 228
6.2.23   From Data Model to Organization 229
6.2.24   From Data Model to Prototyping 230
6.2.25   From Data Model to Data Dictionary 231
6.2.26   From Data Dictionary to process 232
6.2.27   From Data Dictionary to Organization 233
6.2.28   From Data Dictionary to Data Model 234
6.2.29   From Data Dictionary to Prototyping 235
6.2.30   From Data Dictionary to Customizing 236
6.3   Project implementation with IPP 237
6.3.1   Identification of the process areas 240
6.3.2   Selection of the process modules in the process areas 250
6.3.3   Process analysis using the IPP method 252
6.3.4   The customer's net value added chain 271

Section D   Net Value Added Chains

7   Structure of the Model Companies..**275**

    7.1   IPP for model structure 275
    7.2   Model company: lot-size manufacturer with direct sales...................... 277
    7.3   Model company: order-based assembly manufacturer........................... 280
    7.4   Interaction of the two model companies 282

8   Value Chain of a Lot Manufacturer with Direct Selling **285**

    8.1   Process: Sales planning 290
    8.1.1   Business background.. 290
    8.1.2   SAP-specific description 290
    8.1.3   Using the process 291
    8.1.4   Navigation information 291
    8.2   Process: Sales and operations plan processing..................................... 298
    8.2.1   Business background.. 298
    8.2.2   SAP-specific description 298
    8.2.3   Using the process 301
    8.2.4   Navigation information 302
    8.3   Process: Cost and revenue element processing 310
    8.3.1   Business background.. 310
    8.3.2   SAP-specific description 310
    8.3.3   Using the process 311
    8.3.4   Navigation information 311
    8.4   Process: Cost centre processing 316
    8.4.1   Business background.. 316
    8.4.2   SAP-specific description 316
    8.4.3   Using the process 317
    8.4.4   Navigation information 317
    8.5   Process: Activity type processing 322
    8.5.1   Business background.. 322
    8.5.2   SAP-specific description 322
    8.5.3   Using the process 323
    8.5.4   Navigation information 323
    8.6   Process: Cost centre planning with flexible standard costing 326
    8.6.1   Business background.. 326
    8.6.2   SAP-specific description 326
    8.6.3   Using the process 330
    8.6.4   Navigation information 331
    8.7   Process: Cost centre plan closing.. 340
    8.7.1   Business background.. 340
    8.7.2   SAP-specific description 340
    8.7.3   Using the process 341
    8.7.4   Navigation information 341

Contents

8.8	Process: Material master processing for costing	354
8.8.1	Business background	354
8.8.2	SAP-specific description	354
8.8.3	Using the process	357
8.8.4	Navigation information	357
8.9	Process: Preliminary costing with quantity structure	364
8.9.1	Business background	364
8.9.2	SAP-specific description	364
8.9.3	Using the process	365
8.9.4	Navigation information	365
8.10	Process: Profitability planning	376
8.10.1	Business background	376
8.10.2	SAP-specific description	376
8.10.3	Using the process	377
8.10.4	Navigation information	379
8.11	Process: Material master processing PP	388
8.11.1	Business background	388
8.11.2	SAP-specific description	390
8.11.3	Using the process	392
8.11.4	Navigation information	393
8.12	Process: Material BOM processing	398
8.12.1	Business background	398
8.12.2	SAP-specific description	401
8.12.3	Using the process	404
8.12.4	Navigation information	405
8.13	Process: Work centre processing	410
8.13.1	Business background	410
8.13.2	SAP-specific description	410
8.13.3	Using the process	413
8.13.4	Navigation information	413
8.14	Process: Routing processing	420
8.14.1	Business background	420
8.14.2	SAP-specific description	424
8.14.3	Using the process	428
8.14.4	Navigation information	429
8.15	Process: Transfer of results to demand management	438
8.15.1	Business background	438
8.15.2	SAP-specific description	438
8.15.3	Using the process	439
8.15.4	Navigation information	439
8.16	Process: Demand management	444
8.16.1	Business background	444
8.16.2	SAP-specific description	447
8.16.3	Using the process	452
8.16.4	Navigation information	453

Contents

8.17	Process: MPS – Single-item processing	460
8.17.1	Business background	460
8.17.2	SAP-specific description	460
8.17.3	Using the process	462
8.17.4	Navigation information	463
8.18	Process: Material requirements planning – Total	468
8.18.1	Business background	468
8.18.2	SAP-specific description	470
8.18.3	Using the process	482
8.18.4	Navigation information	483
8.19	Process: Purchase requisition processing	488
8.19.1	Business background	488
8.19.2	SAP-specific description	488
8.19.3	Using the process	490
8.19.4	Navigation information	491
8.20	Process: Material master processing MM	496
8.20.1	Business background	496
8.20.2	SAP-specific description	496
8.20.3	Using the process	499
8.20.4	Navigation information	499
8.21	Process: Vendor master data processing	504
8.21.1	Business background	504
8.21.2	SAP-specific description	505
8.21.3	Using the process	506
8.21.4	Navigation information	507
8.22	Process: Purchase order processing	510
8.22.1	Business background	510
8.22.2	SAP-specific description	511
8.22.3	Using the process	513
8.22.4	Navigation information	513
8.23	Process: Credit master data processing	518
8.23.1	Business background	518
8.23.2	SAP-specific description	518
8.23.3	Using the process	520
8.23.4	Navigation information	521
8.24	Process: Invoice processing with reference (posting)	528
8.24.1	Business background	528
8.24.2	SAP-specific description	528
8.24.3	Using the process	532
8.24.4	Navigation information	533
8.25	Process: Goods receipt processing with PO reference	540
8.25.1	Business background	540
8.25.2	SAP-specific description	541
8.25.3	Using the process	544
8.25.4	Navigation information	545

Contents

8.26	Process: Material master processing QM	550
8.26.1	Business background	550
8.26.2	SAP-specific description	551
8.26.3	Using the process	553
8.26.4	Navigation information	553
8.27	Process: Inspection lot creation for GR from purchase order	556
8.27.1	Business background	556
8.27.2	SAP-specific description	558
8.27.3	Using the process	562
8.27.4	Navigation information	563
8.28	Process: Inspection lot completion for goods movement	568
8.28.1	Business background	568
8.28.2	SAP-specific description	569
8.28.3	Using the process	571
8.28.4	Navigation information	571
8.29	Process: Invoice processing with reference (release)	578
8.29.1	Business background	578
8.29.2	SAP-specific description	578
8.29.3	Using the process	581
8.29.4	Navigation information	581
8.30	Process: Automatic vendor payment	584
8.30.1	Business background	584
8.30.2	SAP-specific description	584
8.30.3	Using the process	586
8.30.4	Navigation information	587
8.31	Process: Planned order conversion	596
8.31.1	Business background	596
8.31.2	SAP-specific description	596
8.31.3	Using the process	597
8.31.4	Navigation information	597
8.32	Process: Creation of production order	602
8.32.1	Business background	602
8.32.2	SAP-specific description	603
8.32.3	Using the process	606
8.32.4	Navigation information	607
8.33	Process: Production order preliminary costing	616
8.33.1	Business background	616
8.33.2	SAP-specific description	616
8.33.3	Using the process	617
8.33.4	Navigation information	617
8.34	Process: Release of production order	622
8.34.1	Business background	622
8.34.2	SAP-specific description	622
8.34.3	Using the process	623
8.34.4	Navigation information	623

Contents

8.35	Process: Execution of production order	628
8.35.1	Business background	628
8.35.2	SAP-specific description	629
8.35.3	Using the process	631
8.35.4	Navigation information	631
8.36	Process: Goods issue for production order	636
8.36.1	Business background	636
8.36.2	SAP-specific description	636
8.36.3	Using the process	637
8.36.4	Navigation information	637
8.37	Process: Completion and confirmation of production order	642
8.37.1	Business background	642
8.37.2	SAP-specific description	643
8.37.3	Using the process	645
8.37.4	Navigation information	645
8.38	Process: Goods receipt processing from production	652
8.38.1	Business background	652
8.38.2	SAP-specific description	652
8.38.3	Using the process	653
8.38.4	Navigation information	653
8.39	Process: Overhead calculation	658
8.39.1	Business background	658
8.39.2	SAP-specific description	659
8.39.3	Using the process	660
8.39.4	Navigation information	661
8.40	Process: Determine WIP	668
8.40.1	Business background	668
8.40.2	SAP-specific description	668
8.40.3	Using the process	669
8.40.4	Navigation information	669
8.41	Process: Variance calculation	674
8.41.1	Business background	674
8.41.2	SAP-specific description	674
8.41.3	Using the process	675
8.41.4	Navigation information	675
8.42	Process: Settlement of production order	680
8.42.1	Business background	680
8.42.2	SAP-specific description	680
8.42.3	Using the process	681
8.42.4	Navigation information	681
8.43	Process: Transfer of production variances	686
8.43.1	Business background	686
8.43.2	SAP-specific description	686
8.43.3	Using the process	687
8.43.4	Navigation information	687

Contents

8.44   Process: Customer contract processing 690
8.44.1   Business background 690
8.44.2   SAP-specific description 692
8.44.3   Using the process 693
8.44.4   Navigation information 693
8.45   Process: Customer contract release order processing 698
8.45.1   Business background 698
8.45.2   SAP-specific description 698
8.45.3   Using the process 699
8.45.4   Navigation information 699
8.46   Process: Delivery processing 706
8.46.1   Business background 706
8.46.2   SAP-specific description 707
8.46.3   Using the process 712
8.46.4   Navigation information 713
8.47   Process: Goods issue processing 718
8.47.1   Business background 718
8.47.2   SAP-specific description 718
8.47.3   Using the process 722
8.47.4   Navigation information 723
8.48   Process: Customer master data processing 726
8.48.1   Business background 726
8.48.2   SAP-specific description 726
8.48.3   Using the process 727
8.48.4   Navigation information 727
8.49   Process: Billing 732
8.49.1   Business background 732
8.49.2   SAP-specific description 733
8.49.3   Using the process 737
8.49.4   Navigation information 737
8.50   Process: Billing document transfer and evaluation 742
8.50.1   Business background 742
8.50.2   SAP-specific description 742
8.50.3   Using the process 743
8.50.4   Navigation information 743
8.51   Process: Automatic customer payment 748
8.51.1   Business background 748
8.51.2   SAP-specific description 748
8.51.3   Using the process 749
8.51.4   Navigation information 749
8.52   Process: Cost centre analysis 758
8.52.1   Business background 758
8.52.2   SAP-specific description 758
8.52.3   Using the process 758
8.52.4   Navigation information 759

Contents

8.53	Process: Profit centre reporting	766
8.53.1	Business background	766
8.53.2	SAP-specific description	766
8.53.3	Using the process	767
8.53.4	Navigation information	767
8.54	Process: Analysis of profitability	772
8.54.1	Business background	772
8.54.2	SAP-specific description	772
8.54.3	Using the process	773
8.54.4	Navigation information	773

9 Value Chain of an Order-Related Assembly Manufacturer 779

9.1	Process: Standard order processing	782
9.1.1	Business background	782
9.1.2	SAP-specific description	785
9.1.3	Using the process	792
9.1.4	Navigation information	793
9.2	Process: Contract release order	802
9.2.1	Business background	802
9.2.2	SAP-specific description	802
9.2.3	Using the process	803
9.2.4	Navigation information	803

Part E   The Future

10 T-Oriented Consultancy and Hypermedia-Based Training 809

List of R/3 Abbreviations 817

References 823

Index 843

Trademark Notice

The following are trademarks or registered trademarks of their respective companies:
Microsoft Project, Powerpoint, Word, Excel, Windows and Windows NT, Microsoft
Corporation; Pentium, Intel Corporation; Unix, licensed through X/Open Company Ltd.;
Open VMS, Digital Equipment Corporation; OS Motif, Open Software Foundation;
OS/2 PM and Presentation Manager, International Business Machines Corporation;
Macintosh, Apple Computers Inc.; Java, Sun Microsystems; COMPACT II, Vivitar
Corporation (copyright 1998). We have been unable to trace the owners of the following:
APT, EXAPT and MPE/IX, and would be grateful for any information that will enable us
to do so.

Section A
Trends in Management

"He who questions everything will be able to change nothing,
because he no longer has a stable foundation.
He who questions nothing will be able to change nothing.
Innovations cause changes, changes can be
the basis for innovations."

1   (R)Evolutionary Enterprise Structures

As we step into the information age at the turn of the millennium, paradigms are shifting in a fundamental way in the area of operational structures. While some authors view enterprises as open, socio-technical and goal-oriented systems (cf. Grochla 1982, pp. 1–22; cf. Ferstl/Sinz 1993, pp. 59–65) based on decision-oriented and system-oriented business management science, other authors understand enterprises as living systems, comparable to those one finds in biology, for example (cf. Capra 1992, pp. 307–309). In this latter context, enterprises are analyzed the way living systems are analyzed: as organisms, social systems and ecosystems (cf. Luhmann 1991).

According to this latter paradigm, one cannot assume that a corporation can be planned, analyzed, and controlled entirely rationally in a given situation. Instead, when you look at the overall picture, there are soft factors that must be taken into account, such as social competence, cybernetics, employee participation, etc., in addition to the hard economic factors, in order to better meet changing market requirements. It is also becoming increasingly clear in many businesses that market-driven requirements cannot adequately be met with the thought processes traditionally applied in planning and control or with the separation of decision making from performance.

"With the growing complexity of our living conditions and the heightened dynamics of change, the gap is widening considerably between required reaction times and the time needed by organizations, which are growing ever more complex" (Bleicher 1992, p. 122).

Regardless of the differing opinions, successful systems must strive for harmonious cooperation between *business strategy*, *organizational strategy* and *technological strategy*, to ensure that these concepts do not work against each other within the enterprise.

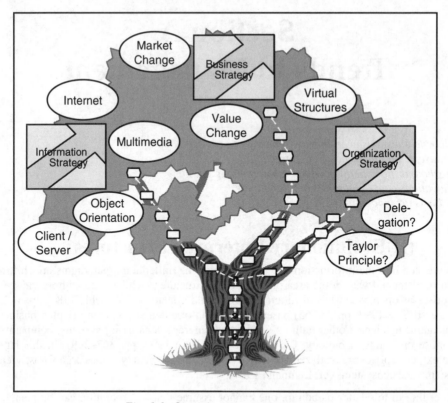

Fig. 1.1: Organic corporate structures

1.1 Developments in business

In the future, managers will no longer be judged on the basis of their technocratic authority, but on the basis of their ability to create rules and order instantaneously. Dynamism in global markets and changes in world views will lead to increasing development of decentralized, flexible structures that operate independently and with an awareness of decision making and responsibility issues.

1.1.1 The influence of global markets

The opening of Eastern European and Asian markets goes hand in hand with the globalization of business. The mobility of capital across political and national boundaries, which did not previously exist to the same extent, is one of the cornerstones of success for economies striving for progress. These new market players share the following traits: they have at their disposal a large workforce, part of which is very well trained, and they can provide inexpensive production locations. This places the global economy as a whole in a continual restructuring mode, putting pressure especially on established industrial nations. The process is intensified by rapid advances in the computer industry, which have drastically shortened the adaptation periods for structural change, which used to be comparatively long. In addition to individual businesses and their partners, more and more industrial locations are in competition with each other. So the emphasis is now predominantly on the dynamic environmental conditions that put pressure on enterprises to act quickly. Some of these conditions are the merging of multinational economic regions (NAFTA, EC), the dismantling of protectionist measures (GATT), and the improved application of information technology.

Businesses in western industrial nations have recognized that the policy of walling themselves off against unavoidable changes in the employment landscape is counterproductive and, in the long run, has serious disadvantages. They have also recognized that once positions in the global market have been lost, they can rarely be regained, due to all of the negative consequences in growth and the labour market. On the other hand, recent developments show that countries that stand up and face the challenge of competition in the global markets early on, as eastern Asia has done, experience the largest growth and success rates.

Since it is also an illusion to believe that one can catch up with low-wage countries simply by lowering the wage level and deregulating, it becomes necessary to fundamentally change the orientation of one's business strategy.

1.1.2 Changing values in corporate culture

It is generally true that "... every reality model (paradigm) must at some point necessarily, just when it has become successful, reach its limit; this manifests itself in the fact that more and more interactions emerge that it can no longer explain" (Lutz 1995, p. 159).

Corporate structures, which until now have been predominantly hierarchical in accordance with the Taylorist model, are no longer a match for the dynamism of global markets. In processes organized according to the principle of the division of labour, the focus is on the costs of highly specialized manufacturing and general market prices. Function-oriented, hierarchical organizations require rigid information flows, and they lead to long lead times for internal and external orders, as well as coordination problems at each interface point. This organizational principle was designed for relatively constant environmental conditions. New competitors and new products, however, create new service relationships that negate well-established, proven marketing practices. In general, change is no longer slow and predictable. Instead, it is rapid, irregular and disjointed. In the course of changing from an industrial society to an information society, customer requirements for products are also developing in a new direction. Thanks to increased market transparency due to the availability of complete information, the customer has a larger selection when it comes to products and services. Many markets, therefore, are changing from sellers' markets to buyers' markets. Together, these developments are causing a shift in the net value added, for everything from material production to services, directly at the customer's site. Another important task for the supplier is to integrate the customer in the entire net value added process, especially in cases where a large amount of customer-specific information is needed to perform a service. Efforts to create a systematic method for measuring customer satisfaction, and the introduction of efficient management of complaints, both attest to the fact that customer proximity has become the most important success factor in *customer integration* (cf. Kleinaltenkamp 1996, pp. 13–24; cf. Günter 1996, pp. 57–71). At the same time, production of high-quality goods and the attendant orientation towards customer requirements demand a high level of adaptability and condensed production life cycles. For this reason, there is a noticeable trend towards producing distinctive goods based on standard products (cf. Jacob 1995). This can be achieved only by concentrating on those operational processes that give customer use the highest priority and that cross traditional organizational boundaries. This is the basis for the conclusion that all processes in a corporation can be handled more efficiently if they are viewed in their entirety.

The adoption of new management paradigms which for the most part are based on the east-Asian model (for example, gaining competitive advantage by forming strategic corporate alliances) can also be seen as a sign of adaptation to the dynamic environment. This is based on the view that a corporation is a living organism that can adapt to environmental influences in an evolutionary or mutative way, to ensure its own survival. In the future, it will be lean organizations that concentrate on core competencies and that focus on their customers and their employees that will survive. Although corporate development is not necessarily determined by technological conditions, historical developments show that the *state of technology* can be the key to opening up new market segments. Increased use of rapidly developing information networks, such as the Internet, is creating a new dimension of cooperation across traditional business boundaries.

The globalization of the marketplace and the complexity of today's products demand the creation of new management concepts, to enable businesses to be more independent in their selection of locations and more flexible in product development. The management paradigm in which organizations are designed according to the concept of virtual corporations can provide a fresh start for enterprises in these new conditions.

1.1.3   New horizons: alliances on a virtual basis

Current information and communication technology enables enterprises to join together to form *virtual corporations*. This cooperation is temporary and may involve independent companies, vendors and customers who want to work on a project together. The term *virtual* signifies a parallel to virtual memory technology in computer science, in which a logical address space is created with the help of physical main memory and cache memory. Simulating a sufficiently large memory area lets you avoid having to expand the usually limited main memory. Similarly, setting up virtual connections does not require additional resource allocation. A temporary, location-independent network is formed out of loosely linked components that stay in contact with each other through a common communication system. This extensive use of telecommunications systems is also the fundamental thing that differentiates virtual corporations from traditional joint ventures. In contrast to other forms of cooperation, there is no underlying group contract, and there is no need to found a new company. A virtual corporation, therefore, has the advantage that is so important in competition: flexibility, because it can build small teams of experts depending on the market situation and the customer requirements. These teams combine the problem-specific core competencies of the individual participants. This know-how includes more than just a command of product technology and process technology. Core competencies are enterprise-specific; they provide problem solutions that are superior relative to the competition and that can be applied in more than one business area. The special thing about them is that only their combination in a dynamic network (cf. Miles/Snow 1986, pp. 62–73; cf. Malone/Rockart 1991, pp. 140–147; cf. Malone/Rockart 1993, pp. 37–56) can trigger their synergistic effect. It is rare that all of the capabilities required to execute a project in a way that appropriately addresses its requirements are available in a single enterprise; the result is a need to link complementary core competencies (cf. Scholz 1996, pp. 27–34).

"The empowerment of employees, combined with the cross-disciplinary nature of virtual products, will demand a perpetual mixing and matching of individuals with unique skills" (Davidow/Malone 1992, p. 198).

During the start-up phase, things are simplified by the fact that no new legal status must be found for the new partnership. In addition to eliminating start-up costs for production, the period of time before introduction of the product is shortened. Conversely, the risk is distributed among all participants. The team members meet to discuss the project in video conferences, without time-wasting travel, and work on the order together. So, based on these strategic success factors, partners around the world can melt together into a kind of symbiosis, just like ecosystems.

Currently, one most often finds this scenario employed in the multimedia industry and in the production of hardware and software in the computer industry. Virtual partnering allows mid-level businesses, especially, to act like a corporation when dealing with the customer and thereby gain access to their traditional markets.

In the end, taking advantage of the synergistic effect of a virtual corporation has a large impact on the structure of the workforce. A certain level of inhibition still exists when it comes to building virtual teams, mainly due to emerging labour law problems, brought about by telecommuting, and accident and insurance coverage issues. Until these issues can be resolved in detail, mutual agreements must serve as substitutes. For this reason, many of the managers of this new type of corporation are expected to have a high level of emotional competence and an affinity for building trust. The importance of the confidence level is particularly evident when one looks at things from an organizational point of view: there is no hierarchy, no organization chart, and there are no divisions with well-defined job descriptions. This alone demonstrates that these are not static structures. Instead, over the course of their existence, they pass through numerous process phases. That is also why one cannot understand virtual corporations by thinking in terms of classical organizational structure. Rather, one must view them as a business process and, consequently, as a process organization.

Taken together, the subprocesses that each core competency implements make up a virtual business process. This process is characterized by an optimum net value added in terms of the following factors: time, cost and quality. A special feature of this process is its variable nature, which guarantees adaptability during the start-up phase of a virtual corporation. This means that a subprocess must build on a standard that defines the combination and communication interface to the outside.

There is no definitive answer to the question of where potential partners can find each other to form virtual corporations. In addition to the traditional methods for making contacts, it is generally possible for an *information broker* to find the desired core competencies and bring them together when required. In another scenario, partners can find each other over the Internet, in a cooperation brokerage (cf. Hoffmann *et al.* 1996, pp. 35–41). In the end, what matters is not where virtual corporations are formed, but rather the fact that the market interdependencies described here are forcing them to be created. It is up to each participant whether or not to remain in a virtual corporation, assuming they can achieve increased profitability by doing so.

1.2 Technological developments

The beginnings of data processing were already evident in the 17th century. Between 1623 and 1641, Wilhelm Schickard (1592–1635) and Blaise Pascal (1632–1662) developed the first mechanical calculators, which were able, using cogs, to recreate the decimal system's method of carrying tens (cf. Stahlknecht 1995, pp. 472–479). The next innovation was the punch card, which was used in conventional data processing until the 1960s. As early as 1805, J. M. Jacquard (1752–1834) was using punch cards to control weaving looms. Also based on the punch card principle was the electromechanical punch card machine built eighty years later by Hermann Hollerith (1860–1929), which was named the *Hollerith machine*, after its inventor. In this punch card machine, the data was coded on cardboard, i.e. punch cards, and the program was controlled using control panels and plug-in connections. The Hollerith machine was first used in the US census in 1890 (cf. Ganzhorn 1986, pp. 25-47).

Another advance in the development of data processing was brought about by the first relays and electron tubes. Konrad Zuse built the first calculating machine in which numbers and commands were represented in a purely binary fashion, and the arithmetic-logic unit and the memory unit consisted of electromagnetic relays. John von Neumann created a concept in which, for the first time, function commands to the calculating machine could be coded and stored in the machine's memory. Before then, command signals had always come from the outside by way of control panels or punch cards. In the new concept, the program commands, as well as the data to be processed, were coded in binary, entered and stored. This allowed the program, like the other data, to be changed. Certain commands also made program branching that depended on intermediate results possible.

In 1955, the electron tube was replaced by transistors, ushering in the second generation of computers. The advantages of transistors, such as reduced generation of heat, less tendency to malfunction, smaller size, and the use of magnetic memory (magnetic core memory) as the main memory, which could be read and written to using electrical impulses, encouraged the expansion of data processing, although at this point computers were still very expensive and very large, room-filling devices.

In the third computer generation, around 1960, transistors were replaced by circuit technology. IBM built their first family of computers, which were controlled by an operating system. IBM's goal when they created this *family* was for one program to be able to run on different systems, so that a separate program did not have to be written for every computer system (cf. Stahlknecht 1995, pp. 503–509).

At this point in their development, computers were already being used in industry, but only by very large enterprises, who used them to electronically process highly standardized operations, such as payroll accounting and accounts receivable/payable accounting in the personnel and finance divisions. Operation and maintenance had to be done by experts. Input and output of data were manual and centralized. The focus was on processing large volumes of data, supporting operational tasks, and automating individual, structured, routine activities (cf. Scharfenberg 1993, pp. 9–19).

The 1970s brought with them a quantitative improvement in hardware. Integrated circuits gave way to logic chips, and instead of magnetic core memory, memory chips were used for main memory. This sped up the processing times of computers considerably. At the same time, software began to gain importance for data processing. In order to standardize the development of software to the point where one could achieve high quality and streamline the software creation process, methods were developed in the 1970s for structured system and program development. These methods included, for example, the fundamentals of structured programming, the principle of step-by-step refinement, and reduction in the number of external interfaces (cf. Schulz 1992, pp. 14–19). In addition, the first standard software packages for business applications were developed and implemented. This gave the user the advantage of not having to pay for costly in-house development of software. For the vendor, standard software had the advantage of being marketable to different buyers, not to mention that it could run on various computers with different operating systems.

Another mark of this time was the move from batch processing to interactive processing. In batch processing, the data to be processed was gathered into a single job and then processed without any further action on the part of the user. When processing ended, the user was presented with the results, for example a list. The end user was thus excluded from the processing process. The introduction of the first terminals brought an input and output medium directly to employees' workstations. This made dialogue processing, i.e., interactive processing between the user and the computer, possible. On the other hand, it also created competing goals within enterprises. Users wanted response times that were as short as possible, which required extensive computing capacity, while data processing managers wanted optimal usage of this expensive computing capacity.

The first microcomputer (ALTARI 8800) in 1975 opened up new possibilities and created new potential for data processing. In a continuation of the development of transistors, circuits and logic chips, this microcomputer contained an 8-bit processor. A processor is a functional unit in a digital computing system that contains the arithmetic-logic unit and the control unit on a single silicon chip (cf. Schneider 1991, p. 641). This development not only caused prices for computers to fall while performance and reliability improved, but it also meant that the room-filling giants of earlier days could be miniaturized, opening the door to their use as individual workstations.

At the same time that data processing was expanding in business, local networks were being developed that could link microcomputers together to form internal computing networks. Since the end of the 1980s, networking of electronic systems across great distances using powerful transmission networks has been growing. The linking of computers across great distances is made possible by WAN (wide area network). Technological standards such as ISO/OSI (International Standard Organization/Open Systems Interconnection) have been created. This international standards organization includes standardization committees from more than fifty countries. The goal of their standardization efforts is to enable electronic data exchange between computers and terminals by different manufacturers and between DP applications, to create open communication systems.

Electronic data processing has become an international information technology due to, among other things, the international dissemination of ISDN (Integrated Services Digital Network), satellite communication and the Internet (to which many developments will surely be linked in the future), leading towards the international *data highway*. There are four developments in the information sector that greatly influence the creation of business relationships and their related business processes today and will continue to do so in the future. These are:

■ client/server

■ object orientation

■ multimedia

■ the Internet

1.2.1 Client/Server

In general terms, the *client/server model* is an architecture in which an electronic EDP application is divided into one part that is used by an individual user (client, front end), which runs on the user's end system, and another part that is used by all users (server, back end). The idea is to achieve the most optimal usage possible of the system resources involved. Integrating the advantages of multi-user host computers (department computers, central computers) with the client/server model allows the individual functions of an application to be carried out by the system that is best suited for that task. The result is maximum performance, flexibility and economy. This division of roles in an application into service-requesting parts (clients) and service-providing parts (servers), however, is invisible to the user. The functions available on the server system (for example, database server, print server, communication server) can be called by different clients (cf. Plattner 1991, pp. 102–109).

In the 1970s, all of the larger computer manufacturers developed extensive concepts for computer network architectures. These include a precise specification of the functions to be carried out by the network's components during data transfer. Such concepts were first implemented for the architecture of hierarchically structured, proprietary internal networks with a powerful central computer. Proprietary means closed; the interfaces and data transfer procedures were standardized for the manufacturer's own devices and programs only. In the 1980s, when data processing began to be decentralized due to the implementation of department computers and workstations as well as the globalization of the economy, open or opened computing concepts for local and external areas emerged, in which communication control is decentralized to a great extent. In the modern ideal of distributed data processing, computers of all kinds and from any manufacturer can work together in a client/server architecture without any problems and across any distances (cf. Vaskevitch 1993, pp. 7–66).

A preliminary definition for client/server can be found in Svobodova, who describes client/server as follows: "The client/server model of distributed computing is a structuring concept which can be identified in many different distributed systems. Clients and servers are active modules communicating through messages" (Svobodova 1985, p. 485).

Decentralization is also the reason why more and more mainframe applications are being modified to work in a client/server architecture, and why new programs are being developed in this format. It seems logical to move tasks from the large, comparatively expensive host computers used to date (depending on configuration, this would be the central computer or a department computer) to cheaper, but powerful-enough workstations. Client/server architectures are essentially based on the view that a distinction can be made between different layers in an application program. This makes it possible, despite centralized data storage, to give the end user simple and quick access to data and to minimize the load on the network. Since part of the processing must be done by the client, not all of the information, for example the screen setup, must be sent over the network (cf. Buck-Emden/Galimow 1996, pp. 27–108; cf. Stahlknecht 1995, pp. 152–158; cf. Hansen 1992, pp. 425–431 and pp. 740–741).

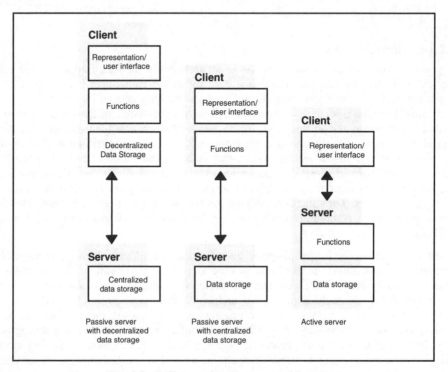

Fig. 1.2: Different client/server architectures

In one commonly held view, the software structure consists of the following layers:

- data storage

- application-specific functions and/or application logic

- user interface

Depending on how the individual layers are distributed between the server and the client, one speaks of an active or a passive server. It is also possible to use centralized data storage or to split data storage between client and server as well. Next to the ability to use all of the available resources enterprise-wide, the major benefits of this structure include better allocation of workstation-based tasks and better ability to delegate responsibilities to decentralized locations. Improved flexibility over centralized systems (for example, expansion capability) and overall lower hardware costs should also not be overlooked.

With the implementation of a client/server architecture, enterprises can look forward to the following improvements:

▪ Avoidance of performance bottlenecks and the long response times associated with them, which can occur, for example, when central computers are overloaded

▪ Introduction of superior business applications due to a computer configuration that has been optimized for the enterprise

▪ Configuration of heterogeneous computer networks in which certain specialists, for example particular database servers, take on specific tasks

▪ Implementation of more ergonomic user interfaces

▪ Breakdown of the hierarchical structures required by central computers in favour of a flat information structure (cf. Plattner 1991, pp. 102–109)

Aside from benefiting from the advantages of client/server architecture, which are related to decentralization and networking, the system as a whole generally attains a higher level of complexity. In particular, the demands on the system administrator increase, since he or she is confronted with a number of potentially possible combinations of hardware, database and application software systems. When planning the entire information processing concept, one must also watch for possible consistency problems due to the redundant data storage that is sometimes necessary, i.e. creating a logically integrated database when data storage is physically distributed.

In view of the facts that 1) workstation performance capacity is continually increasing, 2) less and less expensive and more and more powerful network connections are becoming available, and 3) the number of standards in the areas of communication and system platforms is increasing, the potential for use of this architecture is far from exhausted. Changing corporate structures that demonstrate integrated business processes and that are organized into independently-operating company departments divided according to markets, as well as the increasing desire to integrate currently isolated PC solutions into the enterprise's global data processing scheme are evidence of the trend towards decentralization and distributed processing.

1.2.2 Object orientation

In the last few years, object orientation has developed into a cure-all in the software industry, as the *artificial intelligence* and *computer-aided software engineering* paradigms did in the past. Object orientation is not, however, in any way an innovation of the software industry; as early as the 1920s, business management was discussing object orientation in relation to the structuring of organizations along business lines (for example, by market, region or product group). The features of object orientation were not really formalized, however, until the area of software development appropriated the idea. The fundamentals are briefly discussed in the next section, followed by a description of the individual directions in which object orientation is moving.

In the process of perception, humans impose a subjective structure on unstructured and amorphous sensory impressions, set time and space limitations, and combine certain facts into objects. Along the way, we assign attributes to these objects, set limits, and recognize relationships between different objects (cf. Wiegert 1995, pg. 1–3). Object orientation uses terms and basic concepts that are based on human perception of the physical world.

The central term in object orientation is object. "An object is a manifestation of perception, recognition, or thought" (Achtert 1995, p. 30). An object has information and a behaviour associated with it. Other objects can use the behaviour of this object to receive or change this information (cf. Jacobson *et al.* 1995, p. 48). Information is stored in the object's attributes, the behaviour in the methods, which the environment can call up. In this way, all of the relevant, but only a portion of all possible, characteristics of the related physical object are represented. "An object is an information carrier that has one status, which can change over time, and whose reaction to certain messages (incoming messages to an object) is predefined. An object has attributes (characteristics), such as size, quantity, etc., which describe the current status of the object" (König/Kundt 1994, p. 105).

High hopes have been placed on object orientation for simplifying reusability of existing systems and designs. The idea is that objects should be self-contained and widely usable, allowing them to be linked together into various combinations. Object orientation is meant to support the basic concepts of abstraction, classification, data and function encapsulation, message exchange, hierarchy building, and encapsulation.

■ *Abstraction*
The principle of abstraction basically involves ignoring those aspects of a thing that are not relevant to a problem at hand, in order to concentrate on the important things.

■ *Classification*
Classification is a basic principle of object orientation in which the common features of different objects are distilled and the objects are then combined into a class. A class is, therefore, "a set of objects with at least one common feature" (König/Kundt 1994, p. 106), and it describes physical objects with the same characteristics or features, for example, the *customer* class (cf. Taylor 1995, pp. 32–42).

■ *Data and function encapsulation*
Data structures represent object statuses, and functions are applied to this data. Until now, data structures and functions were modelled and/or implemented separately. One of the basic concepts of object orientation involves encapsulating the data and methods that belong to one object or one class in that object or class. In the process, the characteristics of the class instances, the data and the methods are determined, as well as interfaces to other objects.

■ *Message exchange*
Access to individual objects is gained by exchanging messages. Messages can trigger a procedure or operation at the receiving object and may cause a change in status. In this case, the reaction of the receiving object depends not only on the message, but also on its current status.

■ *Hierarchy building*
With the help of generalization and specialization, as well as aggregation, hierarchical structures can be built between classes.

■ *Inheritance*
In inheritance, characteristics of the upper-level class (superclass) are made available

to all of its subordinate classes (subclass). "The principle of inheritance makes it possible to create a variant of a class without modifying the class itself (...)" (König/Kundt 1994, p. 107). If a class is an instantiation of at most one superclass, this is called single inheritance. If, however, a class can be the instantiation of several classes and can inherit the characteristics of several classes, this is called multiple inheritance.

When you examine the term object orientation and the concepts behind it a little more closely, five different current trends emerge (cf. Pagé 1996, pp. 27–56).

- *Object-oriented programming*
  The beginnings of object orientation surfaced in programming languages. One of the precursors of object-oriented programming languages was Simula, a language developed in the 1960s (cf. Jacobson *et al.* 1995, p. 45). Current examples of object-oriented programming languages include Smalltalk, C++, Eiffel and ABAP/4OO. Some of these languages were developed as object-oriented languages from the start (for example, Smalltalk). In the case of other, so-called hybrid languages, an existing language was expanded to accommodate object-oriented concepts (for example, C++). In object-oriented programming, the data and the related functions for one logical unit are combined. Data represents the inner statuses of objects. The data can only be retrieved or changed using messages. This is called data encapsulation. The sending object can either keep its status until the called object sends back the results of the procedure call, or it can, after depositing the message, continue immediately in parallel with its own processing (cf. König/Wolf 1993, pp. 881–884). The internal structure and operations of an object are not visible to the outside world (information hiding, or the principle of secrecy).

- *Object-oriented database systems*
  In traditional databases, for example, in common relational databases, you can represent only *flat* data structures. To create complex structures, you must perform costly manipulation operations (cf. Schaschinger 1993, p. 34). This has caused problems especially in engineering science applications (for example, CAD, CIM) (cf. Keller/Baresch 1990, pp. 17–22). In object-oriented databases you can represent more complex data structures directly, and in the process, integrate structural and behavioural aspects into database objects. Data and the operations that can be applied to it are not stored separately. In contrast to traditional database systems, in object-oriented databases, the goal is to store not only the object data, but also the associated procedures. You can also store the class hierarchy structures in such a database (cf. Lüscher/Straubinger 1996, p. 81). In an object-oriented database, complex structures are represented like networks. Objects do not directly contain subordinate objects, but refer to them using pointers instead. Object-oriented databases, however, are not yet fully mature and are based on a theoretical foundation that is not as comprehensive as that of traditional relational databases (cf. Dittrich/Geppert 1995, pp. 8–23).

- *Object-oriented analysis and design techniques*
  At the end of the 1980s, object-oriented analysis and design techniques were developed that one can use to analyse the demands that an application area places on a system and develop an implementation (cf. Lüscher/Straubinger 1996, pp. 41–47). The draft, frequently called the design, adapts the logical system structure to the physical software structure. The transition from analysis to design is smooth. The methods

build on concepts from information modelling, object-oriented programming languages and knowledge-based systems (cf. Coad/Yourdon 1996, pp. 48–49). Some of them were derived from object-oriented programming languages, such as the methods by Coad/Yourdon, Martin/Odell, Booch, Wirfs-Brock, and Rumbaugh. In other cases, structured methods were expanded to include object-oriented concepts, for example the methods by Ferstl/Sinz and Shlaer/Mellor (cf. Coad/Yourdon 1996; cf. Martin/Odell 1992; cf. Booch 1991; cf. Wirfs-Brock *et al.* 1990; cf. Rumbaugh *et al.* 1991; cf. Ferstl/Sinz 1991; cf. Shlaer/Mellor 1988). Numerous diagramming techniques have been developed in the area of object-oriented analysis and design methods that make it possible to represent structural and behavioural aspects. Common ones are structograms, transition diagrams, interaction diagrams and event diagrams (cf. Martin/Odell 1996, pp. 27–32).

■ *Object-oriented user interfaces*
Text-based user interfaces, in which the user communicates with the system by entering a text command, are increasingly being replaced by graphical user interfaces. In these, symbols are used to display the available objects, while menus display the operations that can be used on them. The user no longer must concentrate on entering text for the desired operation, but needs only to select an object, after which the possible actions that can be performed on that object are displayed. For this reason, this kind of user interface is also called an object-oriented user interface. In addition to displaying the data in a user-friendly manner, object-oriented user interfaces offer the possibility of improved compression as well as individual editing of data, which help support the user in his or her effort to manage complex tasks (cf. Keller 1993, pp. 147–150).

■ *Object-oriented organizational structures*
Responsibility-oriented organizations and process-oriented organizations have traditionally been structured according to function. Tasks and areas of responsibility in industrial plants, such as production planning, quality assurance and plant maintenance, were kept strictly separate, while in production, resources with which the same routines were carried out were combined according to the workshop principle. Capacities were bundled together so that they could be used to their fullest potential. This division, however, severed connected processes, and the interfaces that resulted led to losses due to friction. Another problem was that the individual employee could no longer see how his activities fitted into the process as a whole. The result was long lead times, which can no longer meet today's demands for flexibility.

In contrast to this, object-oriented organizational structures attempt to align areas of responsibility and resources with objects, for example products or groups of products. So in production, for example, resources needed for the creation of product groups or part families are combined physically and organizationally into something known as manufacturing centres. Automation technology, with its CNC machines, flexible manufacturing cells and flexible manufacturing systems, provides the manufacturing basis for this type of organizational structure. The advantages of short lead times and increased flexibility can only be realized, however, if not only the operational tasks, but also the planning activities, such as production planning, production resource/tool (PRT) management and quality assurance, are handled in a decentralized fashion, and centralized control tasks are moved into the manufacturing islands as well (cf. Keller 1993, pp. 162–166).

The advantages of short lead times and increased flexibility will only become reality, however, if object orientation is implemented everywhere in the organizational structure, at all levels. In addition to implementing manufacturing islands at the lowest level, this can be done using an organization along business lines and/or creating divisions at the management level. At the planning level, planning centres can be implemented, which take over all of the technical and business planning tasks. In an organization with a traditional division of labour, planning activities are divided among various departments, meaning EDP support is usually also divided among different systems. When a planning centre is set up, there is no division into design, production planning, costing, etc.; instead, the tasks are combined based on a product, a market, or a product/market combination. In a planning centre, it is also possible to integrate data and tasks across departments and to create a more continuous flow of information (cf. Keller 1993, pp. 166–186).

1.2.3 Multimedia

The first scientific step in the direction of the area known as multimedia came in the year 1945. In his article at the time, titled *As We May Think*, Vannevar Bush described *a mechanized device* that serves as *a personal library for storing information of all types*. This so-called *memex*, as in *memory extender*, would let you store *general information from books, periodicals and newspapers, as well as illustrations and photos* in a single storage area. Furthermore, this apparatus would manage *personal, user-specific data, such as handwritten notes and correspondence*. Starting with the way the human brain works, i.e. associative thinking, Bush developed a concept for linking many different kinds of information units using associative indexing: *The process of linking two topics together is the main issue*. This gives the user the opportunity to link related units with paths he or she has chosen or to use predefined paths (cf. Bush 1945, pp. 101–108).

Due to the technological situation at that time, Bush's development never became a reality. His vision, however, comes fairly close to the concept of hypertext, despite the fact that it was based on information storage on microfilm and not on the idea of electronic data processing using computer architectures.

Behind this concept lies the idea of nonsequential or nonlinear writing. Originally established in the 1960s by Nelson, this methodology, which involves linking certain information units together using *links* (paths), did not gain a foothold until the proliferation of powerful computers. At the time, Nelson built a prototype of an *executable system for hypermedia publications*, called Xanadu. The goal was to build an *electronic library that was accessible world-wide (...) with freely accessible information units* (Nelson 1995, pp. 31-32; cf. Conklin 1987, p. 23).

Other milestones on the road to multimedia were the conception and development of an open hyperdocument system (OHS), as well as the implementation and marketing of this system. Related to OHS is the creation of a knowledge base with stored hyperdocuments which, as multimedia files, support networking and a multitude of object types. Engelbart, who is considered the father of this concept, characterizes it as follows: "The hyperdocument system should enable flexible, on-line collaborative development, integration, application, study and reuse of (...) knowledge" (Engelbart 1995, p. 30). He also turned his idea of an open document architecture into reality. With the oN-Line System (NLS) implemented in the 1960s at the Stanford Research Institute (SRI), and its commercial successor, AUGMENT, executable systems were available for the first time (cf. Engelbart 1995, p. 30). NLS proved its usefulness, too. It served as a work environment for scientists at SRI, where plans, reports, design studies, programs, documentation and notes could be stored and linked with cross references. In a nutshell, it created a consistent office and workflow environment for software engineers who were working together on projects (cf. Conklin 1987, pp. 22–23). Here, too, the fundamental concept of hypertext is evident.

Following these developments in research, purely commercial systems appeared in the 1980s, such as Hypercard and Toolbook, for creating hyperbased applications. Current trends in this area are systems called authoring tools. These are characterized by powerful functionality. Using certain tools, you can create interactive information and kiosk systems, computer based training (CBT) learning environments, and World Wide Web applications.

Multimedia is generally seen from various angles in the literature. Riehm, for example, sees multimedia as *mixed media plus interaction* (cf. Riehm/Wingert 1995, p. 198). Buford speaks of the simultaneous use of media formats that are linked to each other within a computer system. He makes a distinction between discrete and continuous media (cf. Buford 1994, pp. 4–5). Wolff expands on this approach by using a multimedia system as a starting point. By this he means *computer-based information systems whose user interfaces* exhibit *several different information carriers (media)*. Such a system "is characterized by the computer-controlled, integrated representation, processing, storage and transmission of independent, multimedia information" (Wolff 1993, p. 9).

The examples mentioned above demonstrate the different approaches: it is clear that a single, comprehensive definition must be found. In his work, Steinmetz delivers a complete and qualitative outline that begins with a characterization of multimedia systems: "A multimedia system is characterized by computer-supported, integrated creation, manipulation, display, storage, and communication of independent information that is coded in at least one continuous (time-dependent) and one discrete (time-independent) medium" (Steinmetz 1993, p. 19).

This highlights two tendencies in the discussion about multimedia. A distinction is made between the application itself and the system on which such an application is processed.

The former is characterized by the integration of different, but discrete and continuous, media formats, such as text, graphics, and photos and/or audio and video (cf. Gibbs/Tschritzis 1995, p. 15). Related to this is the special problem multimedia applications have with orientation and navigation in relation to the user interface. Examples of such applications are CBT, information systems, World Wide Web browsers and online newspapers (cf. Steinmetz/Sabic 1996, pp. 19–22; cf. Steinmetz 1993, p. 401).

A multimedia system must process these applications and the media they contain. Information processing in the multimedia sense comprises integrated creation, manipulation, that is, *personalization* by the user, display, storage, and exchange over communication networks. In this context, then, integration means creating time-, space-, and content-based synchronization relationships between these information units (cf. Steinmetz 1993, pp. 14–16). From a technical point of view, this results in requirements in the following areas: data compression of audio and video data, optical storage technologies, computer architecture, databases, communication networks, operating systems, and programming (cf. Steinmetz/Sabic 1996, pg. 8–22).

All multimedia applications start with the concept of hypertext, which is characterized by the following feature: "The fundamental idea of hypertext is that information units, in which objects and processes (...) are represented textually, graphically, or audiovisually, can be manipulated flexibly using links" (Kuhlen 1991, p. 13).

Two characteristics emerge here: the manipulation of different information units and their linking in a network. Manipulation here means that the user is able to include certain hypertext modules in new contexts and thereby create his or her own, personalized links. Linking the module in a network hides the character of the nonlinear structure; the user can navigate in the information space along the linked units. Basically, in such an information space, i.e., in a multimedia application and system, the user moves on three levels (cf. Kuhlen 1991, p. 125), namely:

- at the system level, as regards functional and hardware-dependent circumstances

- at the content level, as regards the actual information that is contained in the nodes

- at the structural level when determining suitable navigation and access paths and making use of orientation tools

For the description of a (hyperbased) network, points 2 and 3 are of particular importance. Their elements can be classified according to their functions: a distinction is made between objects that contain the information in question coded in a media format and can be selected directly and other objects. The former are defined in the literature as nodes and/or information units. Also worth mentioning are the actual connections between the information units, which are described using the term "link". Links start and end inside nodes, where they are integrated in the media interface as icons or highlighted text, depending on their specification. In technical terminology, they are called anchors (cf. Kuhlen 1991, p. 77; cf. Conklin 1987, pp. 33–41; cf. Nüttgens *et al.* 1993, p. 630).

The fundamental relationship between information units, links and anchors is illustrated in the graphic that follows. The graphic shows how the individual technical components of a multimedia application are related to each other. You can see nine units from various types of media, which sit between the implemented connections in the form of ten links, and you can see their start and end points within the media objects (anchors). The media formats used in this example are mainly of the textual kind, but at least one audio and one video recording are integrated in the information base's network.

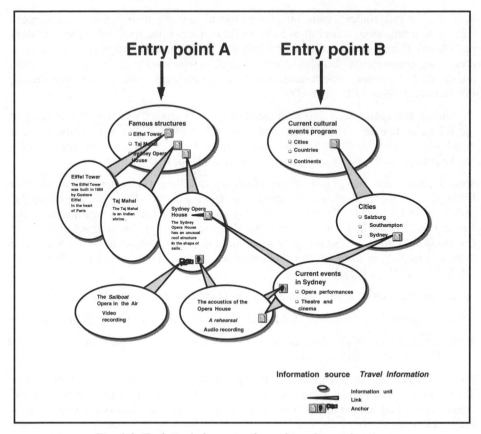

Fig. 1.3: Technical elements of a multimedia application

The elements that define a multimedia application, namely the information unit and the link, are examined here in terms of their characteristics, form and creation.

■ *Information units*

Within the framework of the hypertext concept, nodes embody "ideally (...) the smallest information unit addressable by the user" (Nüttgens *et al.* 1993, p. 631). According to Kuhlen, information units are used for "processing and usage of information" (Kuhlen 1991, p. 79). In the process, an author's ideas are transformed into objects in a multimedia format. In traditional books, headings, sections and paragraphs are used to impose a structure and to distinguish individual areas. In a linear medium such as text in a book, the user can determine the context of a particular area immediately. To do so, he looks for previous or subsequent passages and/or directly follows the reading path in a linear fashion to build comprehension. Applications based on hypertext and other multimedia do not provide a single context in the sense that linear media do. Usually, there are several branching opportunities available at every node. The user must be supported in his quest for knowledge. This is achieved using a certain selection and distribution of the nodes and/or using higher-level navigation structures. Although the scope and content of a node cannot be fixed, they must be coordinated with regard to the situation of the person searching for information. In the process of fragmenting knowledge to create information units, certain technical principles must be followed. *Labelling* nodes provides support. Part of this is the *assignment of a name or title* that also clarifies for the user the character of the node behind it. The user should be able to form a picture of the information that can be expected. Beyond this, linking to the information surrounding the node is important, i.e. examination and consideration of the context (cf. Kuhlen 1991, p. 88). Context means the semantic and cognitive relationships between individual nodes. It is the result of their being connected by links.

■ *Links*

Linking is the fundamental idea behind hypertext and hyperbased applications (cf. Kuhlen 1991, p. 99). Links serve to connect information units. They have start and end points, in the form of anchors. Among other things, links are distinguished by their direction and type. There are unidirectional and bidirectional connections. The latter allow navigation from a starting node to a target node and back along the same path. Unidirectional connections allow the selection of only certain information units from a starting point, in a single direction (cf. Kuhlen 1991, p. 104; cf. Nüttgens *et al.* 1993, pp. 631–632). Furthermore, links can be divided into two classes. Kuhlen distinguishes reference links and structural links.

– *reference links*

These do not follow the idea of a hierarchical structure. They only chain together units for the purpose of associative navigation, such as linking keywords in two different pieces of text. They are based on the principle of association. Association is the term used to describe the causal linking of ideas. Their job is to link essentially different information that has a common *denominator*. An example of this is the link between information about the current programme of the Sydney Opera and data about famous buildings such as the Taj Mahal in an electronic travel information system. Both nodes, the opera programme node and the historical architecture node, belong to different data domains, but they are linked together by association and the keyword *sights* (cf. Ginige *et al.* 1995, p. 26).

– *structural links*

These impose hierarchical and semantic structures. They are used for organizing information units within a single data domain. They link superordinate and subordinate nodes, such as the entries in a table of contents and the underlying objects, and/or semantically linked objects at the same level (cf. Conklin 1987, pp. 33–41). This structuring of information units actually runs contrary to the *hyper idea*, i.e., the idea of nonlinearity and navigation by association. However, such a display mirrors familiar thought structures and general reading behaviour, namely the process of working one's way from the general to the specific (cf. Kuhlen 1991, p. 106).

Structural links, in turn, are divided into two subclasses. Semantic links refer to the contents of nodes and groups of nodes. They provide meta information in the form of registers, tables of contents, and global and local overviews. Argumentative links are not really used for hierarchical organization in the sense of a table-of-contents-type graduation of information; instead, they are used to solve complex questions and problems in a predefined pattern and web of relationships. One can generally make out elements such as thesis, argument, proof, trigger or target event. These positions are embodied by information units. The goal of argumentative linking is to determine the relationships of positions using clearly defined links with particular labels. The degree of interdependence can also be illustrated using coloured signs, etc. (cf. Kuhlen 1991, p. 119). Such types of links support the user at the point of navigation already, because the user can recognize familiar and recurring structures.

When creating and implementing the types of links discussed above, one must find a middle ground between the associative and the semantic–argumentative formats. The former is associated with independent, free navigation in the information space, but it also implies disadvantages in orientation within the information base in view of the user model. Predefined, controlled links literally show the user the way in the beginning. One must find a use that is appropriate for the content relationships between the information units and user behaviour.

Multimedia applications will experience ever-broader distribution, particularly in light of the exchange of information over the Internet, which, linked to the front-end computer, operates as the system platform. Information providers will have to meet certain standards. Not quantity, but quality should be the focus where a need for information is concerned. "The use of information lies in its selection, not in its volume, lies in its relevance, not in its transmission speed" (Vester 1995, p. 14).

The advantages of the hyper principle, namely the ability to provide individual information units *in small chunks* and to enable associative branching between these by linking them in a network, contribute, among other things, to a meaningful exchange of information.

1.2.4 Data highway on the Internet

The *Internet* is the largest data network in the world, with currently more than nine million computers linked to it. At the end of the 1950s, a data network was developed in the US for the military, to ensure the secure transmission of information. When the ARPA NET was introduced in universities, the network infrastructure was expanded to include research use, until, in 1977, several networks joined together to form the Internet. In 1993, the development of the World Wide Web (WWW) by the core research centre CERN in Geneva, Switzerland, laid the groundwork for the increasing globalization of the Internet. With the entry of online services in 1996, commercial use of the Internet began (cf. Klute 1996; cf. Schneider 1995, pp. 263–271; cf. Regional Computer Centre for Lower Saxony 1996).

The Internet is a decentralized global network that links individual local networks together. Data is transmitted directly or indirectly over terminal points (nodes), which are linked together over dedicated or switched lines in such a way that the linked computers can communicate without limitation. The reason for the growing importance of the Internet is the increasing capabilities of the transmission lines, such as LAN (Local Area Network) or ATM (Asynchronous Transfer Mode). In the Internet, the data streams are divided into independent packets. This enables many computers to use a common single line and simplifies network management. Lost packets are automatically requested again, so that high transmission security is guaranteed. The language of the Internet is the same for all platforms (Unix, mainframe, PC, laptop, etc.); it is the TCP/IP transmission protocol. Participants are uniquely identified by an IP address (for example, 129.13.99.4) or by a name based on function (for example, www.stanford.edu). Although most Internet services require TCP/IP connections, e-mail and news transfer is also possible from other networks that were developed at the same time the Internet was being developed. Unlike classical centralized networks, the Internet's amorphous structure allows it to be expanded indefinitely, although it still often bumps up against its limitations in transmission speeds.

The Internet's range of capabilities includes the following services:

- *Telnet*
  Dialogue access to distant computers with access authorization (for example, library catalogues, databases, etc.)

- *FTP*
  File transfer for transmission (copying) of files between Internet computers

- *E-mail*
  Exchange of written news world-wide in a matter of seconds. E-mail is possible between all authorized Internet participants.

- *News*
  Automatic mechanism for distribution (bulletin board), accessible to all, for discussions, notices, and solutions to problems on various topics

- *Chat and video conferencing*
  Chat enables users to communicate online in written form. The same is possible in audio-visual format in video conferencing.

- *World Wide Web (WWW)*
  The WWW, with its enormous growth rate, is the star of the Internet services. The WWW is a multimedia- and hyperlink-based information system, with a graphical user interface, that is used for scientific and commercial purposes. It, too, is based on client/server architecture, which enables information on distant servers to be brought to the client and displayed regardless of platform. The basis of this technology is the centralized storage on Web site servers that are formatted with the text layout language HTML (Hyper Text Markup Language), and their display by local presentation browsers. With the help of world-wide links (hyperlinks) between documents, the user can navigate through different provider pages. He or she can also call up hypermedia services directly with a URL address (Uniform Resource Locator, such as http://www.servername.de) and display them. The communication between client and server is controlled by the HTTP (Hyper Text Transport Protocol) protocol. Furthermore, programs based on the Internet language Java can be executed through the World Wide Web. With the help of these tools, Web pages are increasingly being supplemented with multimedia such as sound, graphics and video animation.

In the future, more and more services that will go beyond pure information-providing will be moved into this open network infrastructure (for example, software installations, sales of goods and services, etc.). The WWW has provided a basis for the growing commercial use of the Internet, from which enterprises can address both customers and their own employees. This *electronic commerce* is divided into three types of customer/vendor relationships (cf. Zencke 1996, pp. 19–24):

▪ *Business to business, between employees from different enterprises*
Business-to-business scenarios often have the characteristics of interactive EDI (Electronic Data Interchange) transactions.

▪ *Intranet between employees within a single enterprise*
The term *intranet* encompasses EDP applications that use modern Web technologies to create internal information and communication systems. The same cross-platform standards are used (TCP/IP, HTML, Java, etc.), and the integration of various Internet services is supported. Use of intranets extends from electronic company news, company manuals and project information systems to new front ends for existing commercial and technical applications. Having a uniform communication system at an internal and external level reduces administrative effort and lays the foundation for effective security concepts.

▪ *Consumer to business, between end users and vendors*
In its *electronic marketplace*, the Internet offers all imaginable branches of business the technical opportunity to handle their goods and service traffic quickly and inexpensively. For example, one can present a product line to a potential customer in an electronic catalogue on the WWW in order to receive customer orders online. This avenue for sales offers several advantages. For the customer, the availability of the product line around the clock plays an important role. Beyond that, the World Wide Web offers the customer simple handling in a graphical user interface, with a great depth of information, that does not require special courses or long periods of training. Search engines simplify the extraction of information. In the future, growing international content and continually expanding selection will heighten the attractiveness of the network for customers. For the vendor, a new avenue for sales with relatively low costs has opened up. Multimedia marketing pitches can reach potential customers around the world any time of day or night, with increasingly easier network access for broad layers of the population, thereby expanding target groups. Furthermore, product information in electronic catalogues can be updated regularly. In the areas of customer order entry and payment transactions, growing automation will increase the efficiency of these business processes, as well.

Nevertheless, the commercial success of the Internet depends on several basic conditions. The legal foundation and security standards for doing business are the most important challenges that *electronic commerce* faces. Data transfer using the TCP/IP protocol usually involves many nodes, meaning that the open network architecture cannot guarantee the security of the packets. The following areas of risk must be taken into consideration:

▪ Authentication guarantees the true identity of the business partner. It prevents the manipulation of data under a false name.

▪ Message integrity during data transfer prevents intentional alterations (for example, quantity specifications in an order).

▪ Nonarguability uses digital signatures or auditing to create an obligation between network participants and transactions they have executed (for example, to avoid random order placement).

■ Privacy guarantees that transmitted data remains inaccessible to third parties, a basic requirement for payment transactions and protection of data privacy (for example, credit card numbers or basic customer data).

Which measures to take depends on the security requirements and the volatility of the data in the Internet application in question. Security measures are already being offered at the browser level, while data transfers are being monitored using protocol-based means (closed user groups). In payment transactions, security standards (for example SET – Secure Electronic Transaction) are ensuring that credit card numbers are being encrypted, and messages are being encoded with cryptographic procedures at their entry point and decoded at their exit point. Other measures affect access to and exit from the Internet, or the security of the computers themselves. Other technologies that could be used are screening routers (monitoring network traffic/filtering), application gateways (firewalls), and network separation (cf. Welz 1996, pp. 14–15).

These challenges will have an important effect on the continued development of the Internet and its ability to hold its ground as a new technology in the corporate environment, as well.

1.3 Organizational developments

Organizational developments must be judged in historical context. The goal of an organization is generally to have a number of people process complex tasks and subsequently bring them together to achieve a result. Although the division of labour was a fact of life as far back as the building of the pyramids, the development of industrial division of labour can presumably be traced back to Adam Smith (1723–1790), who separated the manual labor for the production of needles into individual work steps and made one specialist responsible for each step (cf. Smith 1988). By perfecting the manual labour substeps, each participant could increase his or her workload, and production as a whole could be increased a hundredfold. The fundamental idea of *Smith's division of labour and specialization* was based on the assumption that the division of labour would increase the skill level of each individual and would avoid unnecessary adjustment time for each individual when moving from one work step to another. In his work in 1832, Charles Babbage (1729–1871) seized on Smith's beginnings and explained the advantages that businesses could gain in terms of labour costs by separating work steps into simple activities. One reason given for dividing (complex) manual labour tasks into simple substeps was that one could then employ cheap labourers, because they were unskilled (cf. Babbage 1832). Over the course of industrialization both in the US and in Germany, Smith's idea was supplemented with the concept of separation of planning activities and executing activities.

The rise of mass production; the centralization of output in factories, and the growth in company size associated with this; as well as the suspicious view that management held of rising labour costs accompanied a development at the end of the 19th century that was strengthened by the division of labour and the separation of planning and executing activities. This era of industrialization found its way into organizational theory and practice under the heading *scientific management*. In this period, people trained in engineering sciences developed polished accounting systems, methods for process planning, and a series of wage and incentive systems for the sake of more efficient factory planning. The delegation and decentralizing of management's planning tasks to a group of engineers, the separation of related work steps in the factory into their smallest elements, and the analytical observation of these in time and motion studies made possible the rise of a new layer of managers in enterprises: the planners and controllers.

1.3.1 Taylor's influence on organizations in America

We shall name Frederic Winslow Taylor (1856–1915) and his work as the protagonist of this development (cf. Taylor 1911). Taylor's works focused on improvements in production. These were improvements in tools (for example, the invention of high-quality steel in 1899) and machine tools on the one hand, and improvements in the production cycle on the other. Taylor's idea was to impose the experimental methods of science on industry. These experimental methods consist of observing the physical world, analysing it, and determining which essential factors could be brought together to form a synthesis, then testing and checking this synthesis. The appropriate laws were derived and generalized from practical experience, although one must take into consideration that Taylor was at that time himself a business owner and represented the interests of free enterprise. Taylor's work consists of so-called principles, a method, and a doctrine.

According to the principles, it is the responsibility of the manager or managers to gather all of the traditional knowledge, which used to belong only to the individual workers. They should then classify the experiences, establish rules, laws and formulas based on the knowledge, and use these to help the workers in their daily jobs. In total, the principles consist of four types of duties for business managers:

- Management develops a science for each individual work element, in order to analyse the current division of labour down to the smallest detail. The goal is to do away with job evaluations, which are no more than the sum of rules of thumb and estimated values. As a result, each of the worker's actions must be preceded by management actions.

- Management chooses the *most fitting* (most productive) workers for every activity on the basis of a scientific study. Management trains, schools and educates the worker. The choice of activities and continued education is no longer left up to employees.

- The principle of *cordial agreement* between management and workers is applied, so that management can turn its scientific principles into practice with the help of the workers.

- Responsibility and work are distributed evenly in such a way that management takes on the work for which it is better suited than the worker, freeing the worker from the burden of responsibility.

As his method, Taylor develops a four-level concept and provides tools for putting it into practice.

- He recommends executing a detailed job analysis of the work to be done by the employee, to obtain a *scientific routine*. When working out which procedure is the best, it is important to listen to the employees.

- The *scientifically optimum speed* should be determined using the following three techniques:

  - The people scientifically determined to be most capable should be selected.

  - The staff should be rigorously integrated into the operation, to preclude any resistance to *advanced training*.

  - The optimal working speed should be determined with the help of a stopwatch. The time studies necessary for this are performed by students.

- He recommends individual work, because it is only through this that man can place all of his pride in the work.

- The agreement of the workers to this scientific method should be secured with a piecework rate system that is 20 – 60% higher than the general wage level.

In addition to his principles and methods, a description of Taylor's view of man is of central importance to understanding Taylorism. Taylor describes his opinions about working people and their relationships in enterprises in his doctrine. Taylor claims:

- The goal of man is to achieve (material) wealth. The happiness of man lies in consumption, which leads to more production.

- The basis of wealth is the efficiency of human work, so a maximum level of wealth can only come as a result of maximum productivity.

- Many workers have the bad habit of dawdling, which must be combated. Reasons for this are that workers believe that increased production will result in unemployment, an inefficient wage system, and the wasting of energy due to unscientific working methods.

- Senseless quarrels over the division of the net value added must be stopped by increasing it. The goal is to achieve close cooperation between management and employees. For this, both *partners* must change their attitudes and arrive at a *cordial agreement*. Furthermore, Taylor is convinced that in every business that is run according to this scientific method, all labour representation (union) is superfluous, since the wages paid there will already be higher than those demanded by the union.

- He divides the work in enterprises into head work and hand work, that is, separation of mental and physical labour, and classifies the workers into a first (ambitious and productive employees) and a second category (lazybones, weaklings, shirkers).

- Taylor assumes that the normal person is driven solely by personal ambition, which can be encouraged with good wages.

According to Taylor's view, there is basically no difference in designing machines and human labour. The goal of the systematic study of work processes was to minimize the number of personnel needed, to eliminate dead time, and to set up standard values for reasonable performance. The methods he developed led to noticeable economic success. In 1907, the automobile manufacturer Henry Ford (1863–1947) used the time and motion studies performed and the wage structure in industrial production to design assembly line production, and Taylor himself carried over the experiences made in production to management activities in the manufacturing area. In this case, he developed a differentiated system of planning, monitoring and instruction functions, which he called the *function master system* (cf. Kieser/Kubicek I 1978, pp. 116–141; cf. Kieser 1995, pp. 57–89). The idea of using the division of labour as a means of streamlining and improving efficiency in business not only influenced the division of logically linked processes, but also had a significant effect on the organizational plan. The individual, disassembled activities were assigned to task owners, who were grouped into various performance-oriented departments and included in a hierarchical structure. Accordingly, the Frenchman Henri Fayol in 1916, i.e., at the time of Taylor's scientific business management, centred his work around task structure (formation of departments) and the coordination of the business as a whole, and summed up his experiences in fourteen general management principles (cf. Fayol 1916).

The technology-oriented view of man that Taylor had, and the consequences of the division of labour, such as absenteeism, strikes, etc., led at the beginning of the 1920s to a study in the US whose results strongly questioned the idea that people could be planned the way machines are planned. And so we discovered, through the movement described as the human relations approach, that members of an organization do not behave in a purely self-centred fashion, and that social and psychological factors such as social prestige, self-respect, job satisfaction, etc., can have just as much importance as compensation (cf.

Burisch 1973, pp. 44–51; cf. Frese 1992; cf. Kieser/Kubicek II 1978, pp. 7–40; cf. Kieser 1995 along with the various contributions to organizational theory included there; cf. Mayo 1946; cf. Roethlisberger/Dickson 1939).

1.3.2   Nordsieck's influence on organizations in Germany

Just as Taylor's *Scientific Business Management* can be seen as having a formative influence on the study of organizations in America, in addition to the behavioural and human-oriented approaches, a concept of organizational structure was developed in Germany that has its roots in the works of Fritz Nordsieck. In this case, too, however, the results of the organizational analysis are fundamentally dependent on the point of view of the organization theory chosen. The abundance of *schools of thought* and *directions* in organization theory makes it exceedingly difficult to achieve a uniform classification (cf. Frese 1988; cf. Grochla 1978; cf. Hill *et al.* 1989; cf. Kieser/Kubicek I 1978).

German organization science is characterized by different approaches. In the institutional organization view, institutions as social systems are the focus. In this view, mainly socio-logical and social-psychological aspects are examined. Business organization studies are characterized by the instrumental organization view. Here, the organization is understood as a system of formal rules that should guarantee the efficient performance of tasks by people and machines. Behavioural rules are defined for people working in the enterprise, and function rules are set for objects. In addition, in the instrumental organization view, the activity of the organizer is included, as well.

In the study of business organizations, the task plays a dominant role in the design of corporate structures, leading over time to shifts in the emphasis in the research. Nordsieck, who can be considered the founder of business organization studies in the German-speaking world, focused on the operational task in his work in the 1930s (cf. Nordsieck 1932). Both the observation of organization studies from the point of view of the task and Nordsieck's differentiation between responsibility-oriented organization and process-oriented organization had a formative influence on subsequent German research on organizations. For Nordsieck, responsibility-oriented organization means the recording of structure relationships, while process-oriented organization means the observation of processes in the operation. While the design of responsibility-oriented organization focuses on the division of the operation into task-based, functional units and their coordination, process-oriented organization focuses on the physical and temporal structuring of the work processes and motions necessary to complete a task. The design of responsibility- and process-oriented organizations follows the principles of breaking down (task combinations or work combinations) and combining. The procedure for analysis and synthesis in organization design was taken up by Kosiol in 1962 and integrated in an organization(al) concept that is still valid today (cf. Kosiol 1962). According to this concept, as in Nordsieck's, the formulation and definition of the task is the starting point for organizational design in an enterprise.

Kosiol defines tasks as "goal setting for purposeful human handling..." (Kosiol 1962, p. 43). He divides the task into different defining features that concurrently form the elements of a task (cf. Kosiol 1962, pp. 41–79). Specifically, these are:

- *Activity (how?)*
  The type of activity that will complete the task is called an activity.

- *Task object (on what?)*
  The task object is the object on which the performance is to be carried out.

- *Person responsible for the task (who?)*
  The person responsible for the task is the person or group who must execute the task.

- *Material (using what?)*
  The material describes the tools that are needed to successfully carry out the task.

- *Location (where?)*
  The location describes the physical place where the task is to be carried out.

- *Time (when?)*
  The specification of time determines at which point the steps for fulfilling the task are to be carried out.

As part of task analysis, the object is to break down these tasks into subtasks according to specific criteria. This analysis is an experience-supported process that continues until the breakdown into elementary tasks is complete. Every subtask carries out part of its superordinate task. As part of the task synthesis, the subtasks that have been identified are then combined into objectified and basically people-independent positions (position creation). Afterwards, the positions created are assigned to those responsible for the task (staff members). The complement to this more statically oriented view of organizations is the (work) analysis and (work) synthesis of processes. Kosiol calls work analysis "extended achievement-based task analysis" (Kosiol 1962, p. 189). In this case, the specified subtasks are broken down into the smallest work elements and, as part of work synthesis, combined into complex process chains.

In their work, Nordsieck and Kosiol emphasize that responsibility-oriented and process-oriented organization are two sides of the same coin, and that the separation undertaken by them is purely analytical, to allow them to better examine the complex topic of organizational structure. It is, however, just as clear that the emphasis lies on the structure of responsibility-oriented organization, with which we will begin here. Responsibility-oriented organization as a representation of the enterprise structure provides the framework, in which the temporal and physical regulation of process flow is then coordinated. The dominance of responsibility-oriented organization with its resulting overweighted consideration of structural and hierarchical aspects ultimately led to the breakdown of logically connected tasks and their substeps in German research and in practice. In 1983, Gaitanides criticized this dominance in his publication entitled *Process Organization*, because, according to the Kosiolistic view, in the case of a given degree of division of labour, process structuring came after position creation. "After position creation, position-spanning overall processes and their internal process structure are no longer explicitly considered in work synthesis" (Gaitanides 1983, p. 62).

If one looks at the prevailing organizational structure in real life, it is evident that in most enterprises Taylor's basic idea (cf. Taylor 1911) is dominant both in the structure of the organization and in the minds of the employees. Both organizational interfaces in the overall task processing on the one hand, and function-oriented or department-oriented thinking and handling on the other, are a result of this development. In the case of process handling, different responsibilities and rights, such as for an order or a product, lead to different behaviour patterns in the individuals involved. So, for example, a sales employee sees the sales order handling process from the view of *turnover maximization*, the development manager sees it from the point of view of *technology optimization*, the production manager sees it from the point of view of the *production utilization ratio*, and the controlling experts see it from the point of view of *cost minimization*.

Eventually, with employee behaviour that is not always rational due to insufficient information about the big picture, these differing objectives lead to a situation in which the employees involved work counterproductively. In the concept presented above, a department-based optimization of costs leads to an increase in transaction costs.

The expanding globalization and dynamization of markets, however, are requiring that costs and order processing times be reduced throughout all enterprises in all branches of industry. Increasing demands for flexibility and quality require close proximity to the market and to customers, in order to be able to react to or act on changes quickly and efficiently. In an attempt to master these new market requirements, business-area-driven and business-process-driven organizational structures that inherently contain a potential for changing the organization in their systems are moving into the spotlight.

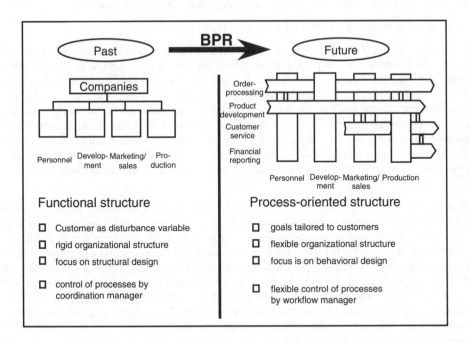

Fig. 1.4: Customer-oriented organization structure (source: Keller/Popp 1995, p. 44)

1.4   Paradigms for business process design

The approaches developed in the last few years for designing business-process-oriented corporate structures have various names. All of the approaches focus not on individual functions, but on logically connected processes. A select number of approaches that build on a process-oriented paradigm are described in more detail in the sections that follow.

1.4.1   Computer integrated manufacturing

The term *computer integrated manufacturing* identifies a concept from the real world that deals with integrated information processing for business and technical tasks in an industrial plant. The discussion about this term was started at the beginning of the 1970s by J. Harrington (cf. Harrington 1973). He defines the essential elements of computer integrated manufacturing as follows:

- computer-aided design – computer-supported engineering design

- computer-aided manufacturing – computer-supported machines and manufacturing plants

- computer-aided quality assurance – computer-supported quality control

- production planning – computer-supported planning

The first publications on this topic in the German-speaking world stem from Maier-Rothe and Lederer, both of whom placed the emphasis on coordinated work with modern computer technologies (cf. Maier-Rothe *et al.* 1983; cf. Lederer 1984). Grabowski, too, in 1983 placed the emphasis of his CIM view on the technical areas of computer-aided design and manufacturing. For the first of these, he accentuates geometric design, i.e. the creation of engineering design drafts and drawings; for the second, he emphasizes production processing, i.e. the physical alteration of materials using manufacturing procedures like milling, cutting, drilling and lathing (cf. Grabowski 1983). In 1984, Spur narrowed this view of CIM down to the manufacturing side of an industrial plant, computer-aided manufacturing (cf. Spur 1984).

Parallel to the ongoing discussion at the time, in 1983 Scheer published a model for computer-integrated manufacturing that encompassed, on the one hand, the business side of sales, materials management, economy of time and capacity, production scheduling, on down to control of shipping, and, on the other hand, the technical areas of product drafting, design, work scheduling, programming of machines, production implementation, on down to plant maintenance and quality assurance (cf. Scheer 1983). Furthermore, Scheer shifted the focus from primarily technological observation to logical design of the information flow. The rigorous alignment of the information flow to transaction chains must be supported by the application-independent organization of data and by small self-controlling groups (cf. Scheer 1990, pp. 14–16). Based on the views described above, the following points emerge from the discussion on computer-integrated manufacturing:

- Implementation of EDP plays an important role.

- Redundancy-poor storage of enterprise data is targeted, to avoid inconsistent data sets.

- Process-oriented design of the information flow is a goal, to minimize the number of interfaces in the process-oriented organization.

- Integrated information processing for the different applications is essential for minimizing the number of information interfaces.

- Logically and technically coordinated enterprise architecture is necessary to support speedy access to information.

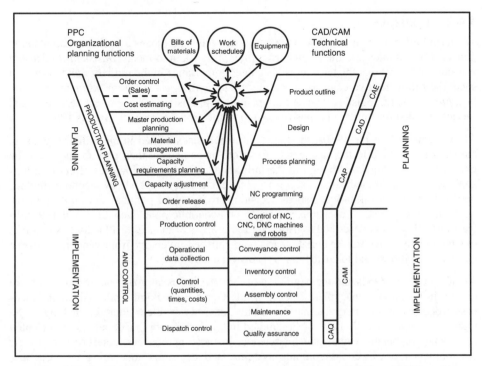

Fig. 1.5: Computer integrated manufacturing model (source: Scheer 1990, p. 2)

In order to give the different views of CIM a common basis, the Ausschuß für wirtschaftliche Fertigung (cf. AWF 1985) in 1985 published a recommendation for direction that had a wording similar to Scheer's. The AWF considers CIM to be the integrated implementation of EDP in all areas associated with production. Integration of technical and organizational functions is to be achieved through the use of a common, department-spanning data set. The CIM concept includes the application of computer-aided design, computer-aided planning, computer-aided manufacturing, computer-aided quality assurance, and production planning and control. Consequently, CIM consists of the following two broad areas:

- PPC, the order handling chain with the planning tasks of quantity, time and cost planning, as well as the consideration of the accompanying business and organizational data

■ CAD/CAM, the product creation chain with the technical tasks of product development, manufacturing and assembly (production), and the creation of geometrically descriptive and manufacturing-related data

This industry-heavy definition has been expanded by various authors into the terms computer-integrated business, computer-aided industry and computer-integrated enterprise, but at its core, it still embodies the interpretation postulated by Scheer and the AWF (cf. Bullinger *et al*. 1987; cf. Venitz 1990, p. 57; cf. Scheer 1990, p. 17).

1.4.2 Logistics

The term *logistics* originates from the Greek stem *lego* and means to think, to calculate, to ponder. Carried over into the English root *logic*, it is taken to mean *consistent thinking*. It was not until 1780 that the term logistics gained importance in the military sector, where it spent the following two centuries denoting the *activities necessary for military provision of supplies*. There, logistics included the planning, provision and use of the resources and services needed for military purposes, to support the armed forces (cf. Bartels 1980).

At the beginning of the 1960s, the logistical experiences gained in the military sector in the US were applied to the business sector. Both areas have at their core the need for the transportation of goods, although in the military sector the term logistics refers to troops and goods, while in the business sector it refers exclusively to goods. A second difference lies in the fact that military logistical decisions are based on political and military goals, while business logistical decisions are based on economic objectives (cf. Pfohl 1996). In the 1970s, Bowersox described logistics as "the process of managing all activities required to strategically move raw materials, parts, and finished inventory from vendors, between enterprise facilities, and to customers" (cf. Bowersox 1974, p. 1).

At the end of the 1960s and the beginning of the 1970s, this approach was examined more closely in business management science in the German-speaking world. All of the business processes of an enterprise that dealt with materials were considered to belong to the logistics area of research. Logistics is studied in the decision-oriented and system-oriented approaches of business management science. In those approaches, enterprises and their environment are viewed as complex systems, and decisions concerning the structure, control and regulation of business systems are analyzed (cf. Kirsch 1971; cf. Pfohl 1980).

The discipline known as *business logistics* is comparable to business sales management, financial management or production management. It is a part of business management science and deals with the description, explanation and design of processes in social systems. The range of logistical systems to be examined depends on the number and type of participants involved. Accordingly, they can be subdivided into (cf. Bäck 1984; cf. Kirsch 1971; cf. Pfohl 1996):

■ *Macrologistics*
  Macrologistical systems comprise subareas of economics. This includes, for example, the planning of transportation systems (road networks, railroad networks, aviation networks) and location planning for social institutions (schools, kindergartens, hospitals).

■ *Micrologistics*
  Micrologistical systems are seen from an individual business point of view. The limits

of micrologistical systems are influenced, for example, by a business's legal status and market relationships to customer and vendor. The focus is on analysing the intraorganizational relationships of enterprises. Examples of micrologistical consideration are planning the vehicle fleet of a company or public institution, route planning for a disposal business, or handling patients in a hospital.

■ *Metalogistics*
The object of metalogistical systems is to analyse interorganizational relationships between different business units. The issue is cooperation between several organizations that are linked by the flow of goods. An example of this is when an enterprise transfers its entire supply of safety parts to a carrier specializing in transports.

The goal of business logistics is to implement business-related design, control and regulation of the material and information flow in an enterprise. The things that can be designed include relationships from the vendor, over the enterprise, and down to the customer. In a larger sense, it is the task of logistics to ensure the availability from the vendor, over the enterprise, of goods in a certain place, at a certain time, and in the right quantity. In a more narrow sense, the task of logistics is the transportation, storage and sorting of materials (cf. Bloech 1984, p. 6).

The starting point for the practical application of logistics in enterprises was, in the 1970s, the supply of materials to production. Today, the term logistics comprises the regulation of service processes and includes the coordination of the flow of materials, information and production across department boundaries. In general, logistics includes the tasks of designing:

■ delivery relationships with the customer

■ procurement relationships with the vendor and the corresponding warehousing of raw materials, operating supplies and fuel

■ the production process, including the planning of transport paths and storage of intermediate and finished products

Classically, the task areas of logistics are divided into procurement, production or internal logistics, and sales or distribution logistics (cf. Pfohl 1996, pp. 171–215). It is the job of sales logistics to design, manage and control an enterprise's flow of goods on or onto the market. The goal is to deliver the requested goods to the customer in a timely manner while minimizing warehousing and transportation costs. Sales logistics includes activities ranging from inquiry and quotation processing, to order handling and control, delivery and invoicing, on down to financial accounting, which checks that payment is entered in an orderly fashion. Depending on the type of enterprise, sales logistics may look like this:

■ It may be temporally decoupled from procurement and production logistics, for example in the case of a made-to-stock manufacturer who produces goods for anonymous customers (washing machines, televisions).

■ It may be linked directly with production logistics, for example in the case of a supplier who manufactures order-based products from stored raw materials.

■ It may be linked directly with procurement and production logistics, for example in the case of an automobile manufacturer who configures the cars he offers for each individual customer and whose procured parts are delivered according to the just-in-time principle.

Production logistics has the task of ensuring the optimal provision of semi-finished products at the individual stages of the production process. The focus here is on the physical design of the material flow. In addition to the transport and warehousing steps mentioned above, as well as the actual manufacture and assembly of components and assemblies into a commercially viable product, this includes the following:

■ production planning, with an eye towards capacities, quantities and resources

■ production control, that is, the logistical process flow between machines and the logistical control of individual machines

The more automated an enterprise's production is, the more closely operational logistics is linked with manufacturing.

In industrial plants, procurement logistics must ensure that the raw materials, operating supplies and fuel needed by production are brought in sufficient quantities and at the right point in time. In businesses, procurement logistics must ensure that the products desired by potential customers are made available as quickly as possible, with minimal warehousing and transport costs. It includes the following tasks:

■ determining requirements and materials planning

■ monitoring delivery dates and quantities

■ monitoring quality, packaging, transport and delivery standards

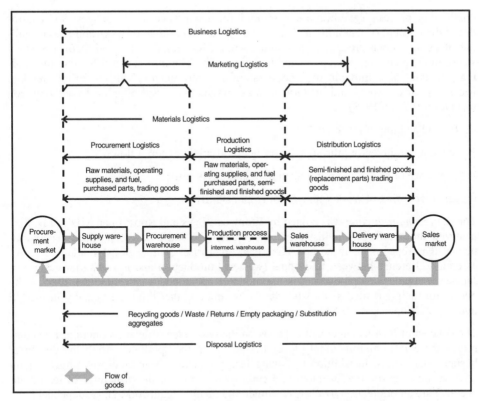

Fig. 1.6: Flow of goods in enterprise logistics (source: Pfohl 1996, p. 18)

1.4.3 Lean Management

Lean Management is a form of enterprise management, introduced primarily by Japanese firms, who use this concept to produce goods and services of a quality that meets the customer's needs, at a low cost. The term *lean* essentially means slim, thin or wiry, and it incorporates the philosophy of *avoidance of waste*.

Closely tied to the concept of lean management is the concept of lean production. In the broadest sense, the origins of lean production can be traced back to Henry Ford, who regarded the continual improvement of the flow principle as the essence of his production successes. Although, in Ford's view, people were divided into two groups, planning employees and executing employees, the lean philosophy in its current form is based on consensus building between autonomous partners. For this second approach, Kurt Lewin developed a teamwork concept at the beginning of the 1930s at the Research Centre for Group Dynamics of the Massachusetts Institute of Technology (MIT).

An extensive implementation was attempted in the real world after World War II by Tai-ichi Ohno. Ohno was looking for a solution to protect the Toyota company, which was in arrears at the time, from bankruptcy. Observations at the Ford company in Detroit, which had two large material warehouses and a high number of under-employed and overqualified employees, gave him the inspiration for making necessary changes. So he introduced the concept of autonomous teams that had a broad range of tasks and responsibilities at Toyota. Lean production is based on multi-functional teams and teamwork at all stages in the planning, production and logistics chain. The idea is that following the guiding principles of communication, cooperation and coordination will create the freedom necessary for creativity and, in turn, increase productivity. Specifically, lean production includes (cf. Ohno 1988):

■ frugal handling of resources

■ reduction of inventory through the design of efficient material flow

■ avoidance of errors and minimization of sources of error

■ self-monitoring of work with a lot of responsibility

The term *lean production* was coined by Womack, Jones and Roos. In an MIT study, they analyzed the automobile industry and researched the successes of production environments in European, Japanese and American enterprises in the global marketplace. An essential difference between traditional (western) production and the new (far eastern or Japanese) approach to production is the mode of operation, which they identified as the reason for the great success of Japanese firms, among other things, especially in the US market (cf. Womack *et al.* 1992).

The concept of lean management expands on the basic idea of lean production. It encompasses the entire enterprise and places the people in the spotlight during the design of business operations. In addition to having lean production, lean enterprises have a joint relationship to customers, vendors and employees. Some of the principles of lean management are an orientation towards customer and quality, teamwork, and independent and careful planning of all of an employee's activities. Bösenberg/Metzen name five ideas that are central to the concept of lean management – which in its basic form can be seen as a counter concept to Taylorism – (cf. Bösenberg/Metzen 1993, pp. 40–66) as follows:

■ *Proactive thinking: positive energy*
In the short term, proactive thinking is the prompt reaction to current problems, and in the long term it is an optimistic attitude towards progress and success. In practice, you can combine creative optimism and proactivity in management by having managers focus on their own possible actions and on those of the employees.

■ *Sensitive thinking: willingness to change*
Sensitivity means taking in information with the senses and including feelings and moods, in addition to hard (technological, business) facts, when making decisions. This type of critical and open thinking should make it possible to detect disturbances earlier, and should engender a willingness to change the status quo and make improvements.

■ *Holistic thinking: department-spanning and market-spanning integration*
A lean enterprise should know that the control, design and development of an enterprise is a complex, holistic and environment-based process, the result of which it cannot determine and influence by itself. The virtues of holistic thinking are respect and patience on the one hand, and cybernetics on the other, i.e an enterprise is viewed as an autonomous social organism that has its own dynamics.

■ *Potential thinking: tapping all resources*
   Tapping all resources requires a comprehensive view of all of the capacities in the entire process flow. This includes the procurement, production and marketing chain, i.e. from the acquisition of raw materials all the way down to the customer's use of the product.

■ *Economical thinking: avoiding all waste*
   In lean enterprises, waste is defined in such a way that not all net value added activities and capital expenditures are seen as wasteful. The idea is to use as few resources as possible and as many as necessary. Lean management assumes that buffering, storing and building up reserves not only engenders costs, but also hides the real problems and thus hinders the development of new capacities.

1.4.4   Simultaneous engineering

Simultaneous engineering concentrates on the technical tasks of an industrial plant; its goal is to shorten the time and costs for development by making parallel work steps in the development and design process, while simultaneously retaining the quality standards demanded by the marketplace. According to this concept, one should begin with subsequent engineering activities when enough information is available from the preceding activities, but the activities have not yet been completely finished. The focus here is on working as early as possible with documents that are still not entirely ready, to reach the *time to market*. Closely related to simultaneous engineering is concurrent engineering, in which several designers work on a single problem in a team. Concurrent engineering emphasizes the efficient distribution of a task among several people and bringing together the partial solutions (cf. Eversheim 1989; cf. Grabowski *et al.* 1992, pp. 125–130).

The starting point for simultaneous engineering was the sequentially executed activities in company departments that were organized according to function, which could no longer meet today's required development times. In many markets, such as automotive, high tech and electronics, engineering and construction, etc., the shortening of the product life cycle in recent years has triggered pressure to design and introduce new products more quickly (cf. Bullinger/Wasserloos 1990).

Simultaneous engineering was originally seen as an approach for organizational design in the engineering area. Trust and cooperation among all of the departments involved in creating a product, and the performance of various development activities in parallel, should abolish the classical organizational separation of development, design, work scheduling, programming and quality assurance.

In enterprises that are organized traditionally, according to Taylor and Fayol's function principle, an idea for a product is often born in the market research department. The development department then creates a rough sketch of the product, which is subsequently developed in more detail by the designer and the technical draftsman. When the design drawing is released, the work scheduling department and/or work planning puts together the bill of materials for production, taking into consideration the basic manufacturing conditions, i.e. the plant and the manufacturing technology available. Based on the bill of materials they produce, the work plan is created, i.e. the instructions for the sequence of the individual manufacturing steps. The material and machinery data then serves as a basis for the costing that must be performed, i.e. determining the costs for manufacturing the product. Finally, the production department checks the possible manufacturing implementations in detail, and the quality assurance department plans the corresponding measures for ensuring and checking quality.

Enterprises organized according to the simultaneous engineering principle follow the idea of project organization and put organizationally separated employees together in a team for a defined period of time. Grabowski *et al.* name three essential goals of the simultaneous engineering approach (cf. Grabowski *et al.* 1992, pp. 131–134):

- Improvement in quality, because a competent team can detect errors by individual engineers early on, and products with short development times tend to be more likely to incorporate up-to-date technology.

- Reduction of the development and lead times for a product, because a team of experts from different areas will consider various aspects of the market (for example, price and shape), development (for example, physical and mechanical procedures), and production (for example, power of the machine) early on. Also, the best compromise possible will be found between the economic and the ecological standpoints, and having an interdisciplinary team will improve the information flow and shorten communication gaps.

- Reduction of development costs, because team building will usually highlight potential errors earlier and thus reduce the number of unnecessary error correction processes to a minimum.

Simultaneous engineering is now being viewed as an integration concept that incorporates product-oriented and information-system-oriented aspects, in addition to the design of processes in interdisciplinary teams. The former includes the use of CAD, CAP and CAQ systems, as well as planning systems for controlling the design process (cf. Grabowski *et al.* 1992; cf. Hahn/Schramm 1992). The latter includes the methodical instruments for product planning, design and analysis for manufacturing and assembly (cf. Pahl/Beitz 1986, pp. 47–410). Essential factors for successful simultaneous engineering include considering the product development process across departments and parallelizing tasks, as well as integrating customers and vendors early on in the development process.

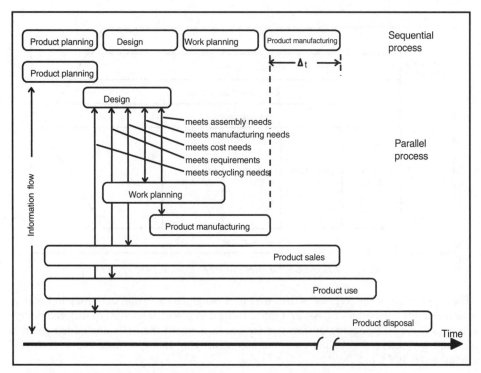

Fig 1.7: Reduction of development time through simultaneous engineering
(source: Grabowski et al. 1992, p. 133)

1.4.5   Net value added chains

The term *value chain* can be traced to Porter. According to him, a value chain is made up of nine company activities, which contribute to the manufacturing and increased value of a product, and a profit margin. It represents the total value of a product. Since usually something new or a net value added is developed or tapped by implementing a value chain approach, the term net value added chain is also often used. Value chain and net value added chain are used synonymously here. The company activities are divided into primary activities, which are linked directly to manufacturing, sales and customer service, and secondary activities, which support the primary activities.

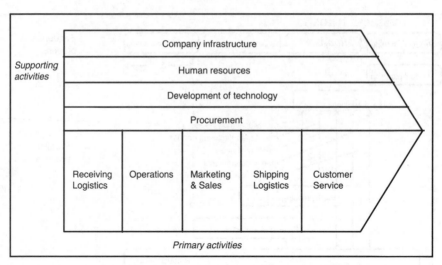

Fig. 1.8: Value chain model (source: Porter 1985, p. 37)

"The value chain disaggregates a firm into its strategically relevant activities in order to understand the behaviour of costs and the existing and potential sources of differentiation" (Porter 1985, p. 33). Seeing business processes in terms of the net value added chain is also an "approach for visualizing current and identifying future competitive advantages" (Brandstetter 1993, p. 87).

An enterprise's net value added chain is part of a comprehensive value system that consists of the vendor's net value added chains, the sales systems, and the customers. The net value added chain can thus be viewed at two different levels: at the branch level, you see the value chain system of an entire branch. An enterprise's value chain is embedded between the value chains of its suppliers and those of its consumers. "The relevant level for constructing a value chain is a firm's activities in a particular industry (the business unit)" (Porter 1985, p. 36).

At the business level, there is a subdivision into the most important functional areas along the physical material flow. Mayer, for example, defines a net value added chain as a series of workstations in production where an order can be carried out in its entirety (cf. Mayer 1994). The net value added chain is a refining process across different levels "in which the output of one operational subprocess performs preliminary work for the subsequent processes" (Brandstetter 1993, p. 91). "Accordingly, during an analysis of the performance specific to that enterprise, the preliminary work that flows into the production process is excluded from consideration, because it is the result of previous manufacturing processes, one's own actions have little influence on it" (Brandstetter 1993, p. 90).

Küffmann takes an expanded view of the value chain model, going beyond business activities, and points out the importance of the value chain model for planning and designing information systems. "This approach keeps one from planning isolated, individual activity groups of supported information systems and contributes to the meaningful design of integrated, department-spanning information systems" (Küffmann 1994, p. 22).

1.4.6 Business transformation

Business transformation is a management approach that encourages considering an enterprise as a whole from technological and psychological points of view. Enterprises are seen as living organisms, with their own consciousness, body, and links to the environment and the soul. This concept was drawn primarily from practical experience, supported by numerous examples (cf. Davidson 1995; cf. Gouillart/Kelly 1995). The approach has four dimensions:

- *Reframing*
  Reframing means changing an enterprise's self-image and management's notions about their own employees. The goal is to cultivate the motivation and engagement of employees. In this phase, you define an enterprise-wide vision, which you turn into a system of goal setting and measurements. Based on these, you then define the appropriate measures to take.

- *Restructuring*
  The goal of restructuring is to ensure competitiveness through lean corporate structures. First, you build a business model that is oriented towards net value added, i.e. you create net value added chain models and perform resource allocations. Afterwards, you adapt the physical infrastructure, i.e. the network of operational equipment and other fixed assets, to the work processes. You also restructure processes (classical reengineering) and establish permanent learning and optimization groups (bio-reengineering).

- *Revitalizing*
  Revitalizing takes a look at the links between an enterprise and its environment. Its main ideas are to achieve a customer focus, i.e. to identify and satisfy customer requirements (for example, developing appropriate products), to develop new business areas by bringing together capabilities and resources that are often available in the enterprise but scattered, and to attempt to make quantum leaps by implementing technology (especially information technology).

- *Renewing*
  Renewing includes educating, promoting and motivating employees, to increase the enterprise's know-how and adaptability. You do this by creating incentive systems, i.e. linking the payment system with performance data, encouraging individual learning and continued professional education, and implementing organizational planning and development that allows the enterprise to continually adjust to changing environmental conditions.

Davidson sees business transformation (Davidson 1993, p. 21) as having the long-term goal of changing the enterprise, i.e. redefining existing core processes as well as forging ahead into new business areas with new products and services. In contrast to Gouillart and Kelly, Davidson divides the business transformation concept into three independent phases, not four dimensions.

The aim of the first phase is to achieve a high level of operational performance, measured in productivity, run speeds, quality, and so on, by automating and reengineering. For this reason, this phase focuses on internal processes. The second phase concentrates on expanding the core business and the relationships with customers through new products and services. In phase three, these expansions can lead to the creation of separate business areas, or even new enterprises. Davidson calls the first phase micro reengineering and all of the phases together macro reengineering, which, in addition to optimizing existing operations, seeks to transform the current enterprise into a new enterprise over the long term.

Gouillart and Kelly's business transformation concept is not an entirely new management concept. Rather, it is a comprehensive, overall view of existing concepts. Instead of targeting partial optimization of these disciplines, which are normally considered separately, it strives to achieve an overall optimum. The interested reader, however, is given no methods or tools to accompany him along the way. The changes within the enterprise are supposed to run in parallel. This is in contrast to Davidson's distinct phase concept. He does not view an enterprise as a biological organism, either, nor does he consider any psychological aspects.

Both approaches, however, emphasize the importance of management in implementing the business transformation concept. Gouillart and Kelly are convinced that business transformation currently presents the primary challenge and is the most important, if not the only, task for corporate management (Gouillart/Kelly 1995, p. 19). Other things they have in common are customer orientation, working out a vision (not mandatory in Davidson's approach) (cf. Davidson 1993, p. 22), and developing new business areas.

1.4.7 Cybernetics

In the course of world-wide activities, quantum leaps in the business, technological and socio-political environment, as well as increasingly fierce competition, the participants in the areas named are running up against more-and-more complex situations. When divided into simple, complicated and complex problems, the latter are characterized by a number of dynamic elements and a continual changing of connections, interactions and circumstances. Examples of such complex problems are strategic decision processes, the building of an early warning system, or activities in international markets (cf. Probst 1992, pp. 22–41).

Because of the complexity of the areas mentioned, the question arises as to how one can avoid incorrect or incomplete approaches, which were created by a centrist point of view, when making future decisions. To address this question, in the mid-1980s Gomez, Probst and Ulrich developed a model for solving complex problems. It is based on the following three elements: understanding of the *components of holistic cybernetics*, the *methodology of cybernetics* for solving complex problems, and the *fundamental ideas of holistic management*. The basic idea is to start with networks when solving problems.

The first element, *components of holistic cybernetics*, puts forward the criteria to be used for examining complex problems and their environment. These include *sum and part, interconnectivity, openness, complexity, order, control* and *development* (cf. Probst/Gomez 1993, pp. 7–8).

Embedded in these components, the *methodology of cybernetics* emerges, which presents six steps, from delimiting and analyzing problems to planning and implementing strategies (cf. Probst/Gomez 1993, pp. 8–20).

■ *Step 1: Setting goals and modelling the problem situation*

- *system*
  Recording and recognizing the situation in terms of its connections, relationships and interactions. In order to achieve a comprehensive delimitation, it is necessary to include different interest groups, institutions and dimensions.

- *result*
  Delimited problem situation, premises for beginning the solution process.

■ *Step 2: Analyzing the stages of development of the effect*

- *system*
  Creating a representation of the situation, recording influences and connections, examining the progress of the effect, the behaviour over time, and the intensity of influences.

- *representation*
  Network technology with objects as nodes and qualifying and directed links, influence matrix or *paper computer* (cf. Vester 1980), intensity matrix.

- *result*
  Basic relationships in network format, qualified and temporal behaviour, relationship between exertion of influence and influenceability (intensity).

■ *Step 3: Recording and interpreting possible courses for change*

- *system*
  Finding independent units and building subnetworks (scenarios) within the network, simulating development paths and possible behaviours, evaluating the consequences.

- *representation*
  Expanded network with delimited areas.

- *result*
  Information about the basic scenario as well as the behaviour of the subnetworks in terms of self-support, cooperation and dependence.

■ *Step 4: Clarifying the possibilities for control*

- *system*
  Identifying values that can be controlled and values that cannot be controlled, as well as the indicators for success of control interventions, characterizing network objects according to their behaviour.

- *representation*
  Expanded network with structured objects.

- *result*
  Possibilities for influence and the resulting changes in the network.

■ *Step 5: Planning strategies and measures*

   – *system*
   Drafting a design and control strategy, imagined simulation.

   – *result*
   Problem solution, concrete project design that includes all network objects.

■ *Step 6: Implementing the solution to the problem*

   – *system*
   Using a project group, creating a monitoring information system, sensitizing and
   increasing the capability for self-control.

Due to its comprehensive approach, this methodology should make it possible to avoid examining only partial views and following a purely linear procedure when solving complex problems. It should be noted here that the steps mentioned above are not performed in isolation or in sequence. Rather – according to the nature of complex problems, which are also characterized by strong interconnectivity and interdependence of their input values – the individual steps must be seen in connection. Every unit of the methodology of cybernetics is influenced by the results of the other or remaining units. The graphic that follows illustrates the individual steps of the methodology and highlights their relationships. The examples presented in the book by Probst/Gomez show how to implement such an approach in practice (cf. Probst/Gomez 1993). For examples, refer to the articles *Strategische Führung eines Zeitschriftenverlages* (cf. Probst/Gomez 1993, pp. 23–39) and *Vernetztes Denken bei der Markteinführung neuer Produkte* (cf. Meister 1993, pp. 145–161).

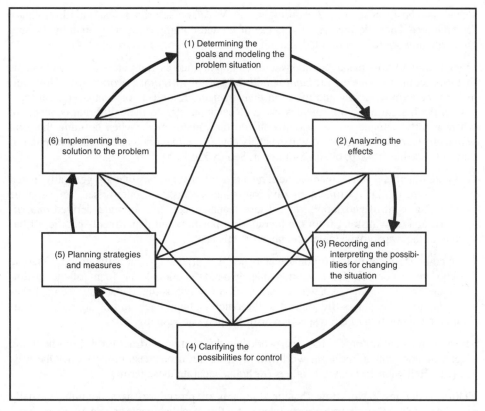

Fig. 1.9: The basic steps in the methodology of cybernetics
(source: Probst 1992, p. 26)

1.4.8   Workflow management

A successful implementation of the process-oriented design approach presupposes the availability of suitable information and communication technologies that can guarantee comprehensive, yet flexible support of operational process flows. In this context, something called a workflow management system represents a potential solution. These systems enable active support of department-spanning process flows on the basis of a graphical process flow specification.

The *workflow management* area is part of the research area of computer-supported teamwork, or CSCW – *computer supported cooperative work*, which deals in general with computer support for cooperative work (cf. Krcmar 1992). The research goal of CSCW is to improve cooperation between humans responsible for tasks in an organization by taking advantage of information and communication technologies (cf. Hasenkamp/Syring 1994).The idea is to make cooperation between humans responsible for tasks more efficient and flexible, but also more humane and social. Ergo, the work sciences and psychology contribute to the continued development of this research area, in addition to computer science and business science. Accordingly, CSCW can be described as an interdisciplinary research area that is defined less by its use of up-and-coming technology than by the specific type of work to be supported, namely *cooperative* work (cf. Syring 1994).

In general, workflow management systems can be defined as computer-supported systems that support the *management* (*planning and control*) of *workflows* (*work steps*). However, as both the term *workflow* and the term *management* are objects of controversial discussion in the literature, both terms deserve a closer look, due to their different concepts of where workflow management systems should be implemented. When defining the term *management*, one basically distinguishes between a *functional* and an *institutional* point of view (cf. Staehle 1994, p. 69; cf. Steinmann/Schreyögg 1990, p. 6).

- In the functional sense, management means a set of functions that are generally linked to control of the fulfilment of division-of-labour tasks in enterprises, for example planning, control and monitoring. These management functions are derived *analytically*, and they abstract from the hierarchical position and department-specific affiliation of the respective people who perceive this task.

- In contrast, the term institutional management is oriented towards the group of people who are responsible for executing management functions. The focus of the institutional approach is the *empirical* recording of all activities that a manager accomplishes in day-to-day business. In contrast to the functional approach, in this approach the hierarchical position of the respective manager plays an essential role.

The numerous definitions of the term workflow differ at an abstract level. For one thing, several authors equate the term workflow with the term business process (cf. Oberweis 1994; cf. Heilmann 1994), while others explicitly separate these terms.

Heilmann defines a workflow (business process or procedure) as a delimited, usually division-of-labour-based process that leads to the establishment or use of operational output (cf. Heilmann 1994). Jablonski goes on to specify that workflows can correspond to processes and process elements as well as process steps. The emphasis in all of these views is on the dynamic flow of the process from its initiation to its completion (cf. Jablonski 1995). What seems interesting here is the thesis, which claims that workflow does not necessarily assume the use of computers, but can also proceed with traditional means such as documents, files and conventional resources.

A workflow is generally brought into existence by a trigger. This can be, for example, an event in the form of a customer order, the attainment of a point in time, or the end of a time period. A workflow usually consists of process steps (actions, activities, tasks) that can, in turn, be subdivided – if necessary at several levels. Furthermore, a workflow ends with an explicit conclusion in the form of one or more results or a cancellation.

Workflow management (activities management in the case of Jablonski 1995) is described by Heilmann as a combination of modelling, analysis and simulation, control, and logging of arbitrary business processes with varying degrees of detail. Understood this way, workflow management covers a broad spectrum of implementation – from corporate modelling and reorganization to the control of daily routine work at the computer.

Accordingly, workflow management proceeds in the following cycle: the starting point is the modelling (definition) of the actual state of an existing procedure type (business process), followed by an analysis of its strengths and weaknesses. Animation and simulation of the process flow of a sample procedure can point to additional analysis steps. The analysis/animation subcycle can be run through repeatedly, until a sufficiently optimized procedure type is reached (dependent on the procedure attribute values selected and on the importance of the procedure for the enterprise). The sample procedure is controlled using the *re*modelled procedure type. The last branch of the cycle, logging the process flow of the sample procedure, contains the results, which can be used later for revisions or for renewed analysis.

According to Heilmann, workflow management can occur at three different levels. At the *strategic level*, the idea is to redesign core processes of the enterprise that are decisive for the degree of fulfilment of the critical success factors. At the *tactical level*, parts of core processes, as well as the supporting sideline processes, are modelled, analyzed and reorganized, while at the *operational level*, selected, easy-to-understand processes are analyzed as procedure types and improved. Top-down processing of the implementation levels is recommended, but, from a pragmatic point of view, should not be mandatory (cf. Heilmann 1994).

Numerous workflow management systems have been developed in the last few years, both in science and in the commercial area, some of which differ drastically in their functionality (cf. Jablonski 1995). The work of the Workflow Management Coalition – a standardization body consisting of manufacturers from all areas, which is attempting to develop uniform interfaces and consistent terminology in a workflow context – demonstrates, however, that it is possible to pinpoint some standard functions that are supported by a majority of these systems, despite the heterogeneous nature of the different workflow products.

Jablonski divides the demands on workflow management systems into practical (for example, functional, operational, behaviour-based, information-based, organizational, etc.) and technical (historical, transactional, etc.) modelling aspects, with a subset of the practical aspects having already been taken into consideration in the modelling of the process flow view or of the dynamic aspects of business processes (cf. Jablonski 1995).

- *Functional aspect*
  The functional aspect represents the logical processing units (workflows). A logical processing unit represents a complete unit from a practical and technical point of view.

- *Operational aspect*
  The operational aspect is implemented by applications. The applications furnish the real functionality in a workflow and are referenced by elementary workflows. Applications can be divided into two classes: *program* and *free application*. Free applications are not implemented by the workflow management system, but rather by the executor (cf. agents or organizational aspect) of a workflow.

- *Behaviour-based aspect*
  The behaviour-based aspect of a workflow is defined by the control flow between workflows and applications. Next to the basic constructs already implemented in programming languages, such as sequences (serial execution), conditional branching (alternative execution) and unconditional branching (parallel execution) and loops, additional, more complex control flow constructs are required to specify the control flow between workflows. For this reason, workflow management systems need to support

application-specific definition of macros. Examples of macros are the optional execution of workflows, repetition, and series.

■ *Information-based aspect*
In workflow management, where data management is concerned, one generally draws a distinction between control data, which the workflow management system defines, manages and checks, and production data, which is managed by applications and therefore cannot be checked by a workflow management system.

■ *Organizational aspect*
The organizational aspect of a workflow characterizes the organizational plan connections in an enterprise that are relevant for workflow. Both the organization structure, which consists of organizational objects and relationships, and the population that represents an enterprise's employees are specified. Organizational objects are grouped into agents and non-agents. Agents are all physical elements, such as machines, people, and server processes. The group of non-agents includes all virtual objects such as roles, divisions and teams. Agents are the ones who execute a workflow and must be taught by the workflow management system about tasks to be performed (notification). Because there are often several agents that could execute one task, these must also be synchronized by the workflow management system.

■ *Historical aspect*
The historical aspect covers the logging of a workflow's execution data. In addition to providing support in error situations (analogous to logging transactions in the database area), logging can optimize the workflow management system.

■ *Transactional aspect*
The transactional aspect consists of the use of expandable transaction models in workflow management systems. Like the use of the transaction concept in database management systems, these are meant to guarantee detailed and persistent execution of workflows.

1.4.9 Continuous system engineering

Business activity and its environment are both extremely dynamic in nature. Added to this are continual rapid developments in information processing technology, which in turn have an effect on organizational process flows. *Continuous system engineering* (CSE) assumes that all of these dependencies and potentials can be balanced or utilized only by a continuous process of adaptation (cf. Thome/Hufgard 1996).

The concept of continuous system engineering includes the business-related integration of organization and information and is based on a procedure for developing and maintaining an enterprise's competitiveness through adaptation in information processing and organization. The goal of CSE is to support the design of operational business processes and enable continuous adaptation. This is evident in the following seven theses of the authors (cf. Thome/Hufgard 1996, pp. 6–7).

■ The implementation of information systems in enterprises is generally too long and too costly, because organizational changes and problems in the development of information processing are unnecessarily linked together.

- Software libraries are a new form of standard business application software that encompasses almost all generally occurring business tasks and alternatives and that allows dynamic adaptation, that is, the changing of system settings even while the operation is running (cf. Hufgard 1994).

- Modern information system solutions should build as much as possible on software libraries. In-house development should be used only for those task areas in which an enterprise wants to distinguish itself from the competition through information processing. Special functions that it does not make sense to realize in standard software must be programmed internally.

- Implementing standard application software as the basis of a new information system should thus be restricted at first to exchanging the programs implemented to date for the new software library. Organizational changes during the changeover make sense only if they can be realized without severe problems for the enterprise, they utilize the potential of the software library, and they obviously present an improvement for all those involved.

- Organizational revolution, which, for example, is promoted by business process reengineering, should not be linked to the introduction of the software library, because this only causes unnecessary burdens and delays the changeover.

- All of the organizational improvement ideas that result from a fundamental rethinking of the corporate structure should be taken over step by step into the structural setup of the software library and at the same time be introduced into the operational process flow.

- Incremental improvement of information processing in organizations, known as continuous system engineering, generally leads to a higher-quality design of processes in operations than do the sporadic efforts expended with new information processing solutions in the name of implementing new process flows.

Continuous system engineering, however, can only be implemented realistically if two basic conditions are met for overcoming the justifiable objections that have been presented up to this point. For one thing, organizational change is not allowed to trigger costly software development or modification of the standard application software. For another, the description of the enterprise's organizational requirements must be carried out quickly and in a form that is usable specifically for the software implementation process.

Developments in the last two years have made it possible to meet these two demands. For one thing, a software library must have on hand nearly all of the software solutions necessary for organization changes related to operations. These solutions need only be selected correctly and incorporated into, or put in place of, the sections of the overall system that are already actively in use. For another, for targeted navigation, a system based on fundamental business knowledge must be able to take the goals of the operational functions and transform them into the software library default settings necessary for this.

The software library provides all of the modules needed for machine support of most business functionality. The problem therefore no longer consists of describing the tasks of the operational process flow that can be supported, modifying them with relation to implementing information processing systems, and then developing appropriate programs.

Instead, the process flow consists of identifying and classifying the dominant task areas in operations, to make it possible to identify and assign suitable library components for these (cf. Hufgard 1994, pp. 2–213; cf. Thome/Hufgard 1996, pp. 39–51).

The rash assumption that operations would simply be *electrified* this way and there would be no need to carry out an organizational improvement phase according to business process reengineering is false. The classification of business processes does not lead to blind adherence to operational activities that may have been handed down. It is more a matter of bringing out the essential functions that are truly necessary within the scope of the operation's purpose. These process flows which are characteristic of operational events can be described in business terms and can be clearly specified. This means that there is a fundamentally correct procedure for them, as well. The degree to which such a procedure can be automated in a real enterprise depends on the status of information technology and is determined by the software library's program design.

This is not to say that all enterprises must have the same process flow structure. The huge number of different settings in a software library, together with their innumerable combinations, make it possible to take into consideration the individual characteristics of the operational structure and its market situation. The end of the implementation process becomes the beginning of the improvement process. The enterprise, which acquires a stable information processing solution in a relatively short time, thus gains the employee capacity and the stored know-how that the software library contains. It then uses these to recognize weaknesses in the operational process flow and obtain an improved overall solution by changing the current software settings or incorporating other functionality from the library environment.

This has the following advantages over the normal procedure; for example, according to a phase model and business process reengineering (cf. Thome/Hufgard 1996, pp. 75–88):

- Operations run under stable, automated information processing after just a short modification and installation phase.

- The software library allows the enterprise to change functionality at any time, which in the method used previously would have required lengthy programming and possibly even led to incompatibilities.

- The current documentation about the level of organization and information processing reached in the most recent adaptation process provides an excellent starting point for reviewing previously stored knowledge, for continued improvement of the operational process flow.

- In connection with the software library, which was developed for structural integration, the business knowledge base of the tool protects against wrong decisions.

And so once again, in accordance with its original task, the software becomes the link between the functionality of the hardware, which cannot be changed over the medium term, and the continual changes in operational process flow requirements. Although this happens in an entirely different way than through configuration, it also happens in a much more stable form, because the responsibility for new development is not placed on an individual, isolated program development team, and the software itself is implemented in a development process that must meet standards for high quality.

1.4.10 Business (re-)engineering

Business reengineering has become the passing millennium's buzzword in management and industry circles. As a vision of management on the one hand and for organizational design on the other, the business reengineering concept is meant to be used as a strategic instrument for maintaining an enterprise's competitiveness. When you analyze the concept a little more closely, you see that, essentially, this is a new term for a classic business task – optimizing process flow organization.

Business reengineering, or business process reengineering, can be thought of as the task of recombining business tasks, which increasing specialization and hierarchy formation have broken down, into coherent business processes. A business process should contain primarily tasks that, taken together, create value for the customer. Therefore, a business process can generally be defined as a sequence of activities that requires input of one or more different pieces of detailed information, material or other resources, and that creates a value for the customer as a result. If one follows the approach of the founders Hammer and Champy (cf. Hammer/Champy 1994), one must also take into consideration, as the second paradigm of business reengineering next to consistent process orientation, the radical changing of business processes. This raises the question in business of whether to adopt the procedure as dogmatism or use this recommendation as motivation in the search for *best business practices* (cf. Brenner/Keller 1995; cf. Zencke 1994, pp. 63–76).

Hammer and Champy claim that business reengineering is not possible in small steps (cf. Hammer/Champy 1994, p. 13). According to their vision, an enterprise should throw all of their old principles overboard and work out a new concept, an enterprise model that is oriented towards business processes. They define business reengineering as "fundamental rethinking and radical redesign of enterprises or essential company processes" (Hammer/Champy 1994, p. 48). In this context, business processes mean tasks that, taken together, create a value for the customer. The goal of this kind of business reengineering is improvements in orders of magnitude. It is not simple improvements in departments that are pursued, but quantum leaps for the enterprise, and according to Hammer and Champy, this requires destruction of the old and creation of the new. The authors explain this fundamental rethinking using basic questions such as "Why do we do the things we do? Why do we do them the way we do them?" (Hammer/ Champy 1994, pp. 48–49). Furthermore, they emphasize that during business reengineering an enterprise must first determine what needs to be done, then determine afterwards how to implement this plan. Hammer and Champy describe radical redesign as a split from the past, its structures and its procedures, in order to find entirely new ways to do work. They do not, however, describe in detail how radical redesign should be achieved in individual enterprises. According to the authors, there are no general instructions for this. They restrict their discussion to descriptions of:

- typical characteristics of redesigned business processes

- participants in reengineering

- possible brainstorming techniques

- other characteristics that are often mentioned when participants are surveyed

- an approach for convincing the enterprise's employees of the need for redesign

- several practical examples

According to Hammer and Champy, the following typical characteristics can be observed when redesigning business processes. Instead of combining tasks into complex processes, as was done in the past, business reengineering emphasizes simple processes, to make cost reduction, flexibility, quality and service possible.

This has consequences for responsibility-oriented and process-oriented organization. For example, several positions may be combined so that a single employee, if possible, oversees and is responsible for one whole process. Departments must be restructured into process teams, and multi-layered hierarchy must be replaced by flat organization. According to the authors, information technology also plays a major role, because the use of new technologies makes new working methods possible and supports the design of processes. For example, all of an enterprise's employees can access up-to-date information simultaneously with centralized databases. The advantages of this new responsibility-oriented and process-oriented organization are:

- Employees make their own decisions, resulting in vertical compression of the responsibility-oriented organization.

- Overhead costs are reduced.

- There are fewer delays in the work process flow.

- Reactions to changing requirements are faster.

- Coordination costs are reduced, because the individual work process steps are carried out in a natural order.

- The need for monitoring and control is diminished, because you no longer check process flows and rules – it's the result that matters.

Hammer and Champy's procedure uses a top-down approach. According to Hammer and Champy, the idea and motivation for business reengineering must come from the highest level of management in the enterprise and must also be directed from there. For implementation, Hammer and Champy recommend two messages be given to company management. The goal is to win employee support for the redesign and implementation of business processes.

The first message reads: *Reason to Act* (cf. Hammer/Champy 1994, p. 191). It begins by laying out the business environment, including the business context, business problems and market demands, then moves to a diagnosis of the situation, and finally points to the possible consequences. This should explain to each employee the reasons for the enterprise's situation and present already envisioned solutions as the logical next step.

The second message, the *Vision* (cf. Hammer/Champy 1994, p. 197), describes the goals to be pursued, both quantitative and qualitative. These should, however, be objectives and evaluation values that can be measured, so that the success of business reengineering can also be measured objectively.

After company management has convinced the employees of the need for business reengineering, it is necessary to figure out which business processes are most urgently in need of reorganization. By establishing the sequence of business processes that have the most weak spots, such as too many interfaces, redundant data or wasted time, Hammer and Champy verge on contradicting their own thesis that business reengineering cannot be accomplished in a step-by-step fashion. As soon as the processes to be organized have been determined, process teams can start investigating redesign options. The authors suggest three techniques for enhancing the creativity of the process teams.

The first technique is *applying one or more principles* (cf. Hammer/Champy 1994, p. 174), for example the principle that all of the tasks of a process must be completed by one employee. The questions that result from this, such as *How would the person in question proceed, and what sort of support would he need?* (cf. Hammer/Champy 1994, p. 186) encourage new ideas for redesign.

The second technique is *identifying and refuting assumptions* (cf. Hammer/Champy 1994, p. 186). Both aspects (identifying and refuting) result in new possibilities for designing the process.

The third technique they suggest is *searching for possible creative uses for information technologies* (cf. Hammer/Champy 1994, p. 187). One can find new ways to divide labour using modern communication and processing capabilities such as workflow management systems, distributed databases and electronic mail systems.

Several characteristics mentioned by participants in redesign are:

■ One need not be an expert.

■ It may actually be advantageous to be an outsider.

■ The process should always be seen from the customer's point of view.

The characteristics mentioned here are advantageous for participants in business reengineering, because the goal is to separate oneself from the past and follow entirely new paths. Once the process team has agreed on a redesign variant, it is time to implement the idea in the enterprise. This is the most difficult part. Hammer and Champy, however, do not give any instructions for this; they just provide examples of business reengineering projects in enterprises (cf. Hammer/Champy 1994, pp. 173–204).

1.5 Continuous business (quality) engineering with SAP

Business reengineering (cf. Hammer/Champy 1994), business process reengineering (cf. Towers 1994), process innovation (cf. Davenport 1993), change management (cf. Doppler/Lauterburg 1994) and business process optimizing (cf. Scholz 1994) have become buzzwords in German and Anglo-American literature that neither managers nor scientists may overlook. When you examine the focal point of these different approaches, at their common core all of their contributions deal with the design of business processes. The goal is to design business processes in such a way that they meet the market-induced demands for increased flexibility and quality, as well as for reduced run time and costs. It is also important that the business processes implemented be integrated. The approaches spurred by real-world experience pursue, in more or less pronounced form, the implementation of flexible and market-based organization structures in enterprises. In most cases, however, these variable organization structures cannot act efficiently without corresponding DP support. If one assumes that a DP system is part of the operational information system, then the market's demand for flexibility in the enterprise must also be met by the DP system if it is not to be counterproductive.

1.5.1 Risks in business process design

As ever more powerful information systems become available, more demands are placed on the users of these systems. The increase in scope and complexity brought about by the implementation of integrated business processes increases the importance of criteria such as comprehensibility, correctness, user friendliness, reliability, flexibility, documentation and maintainability (cf. Meyer 1990).

When designing business processes, enterprises must usually decide whether to develop the application software themselves or build on solutions available in the DP supplier market. The goal of developing custom software is to meet the customer's requirements exactly. Often, however, custom software has the problems of being too error-prone, not sufficiently maintainable, and not ready on time (cf. Chroust 1992). The variable that is most problematic and difficult to foresee is not the time needed to do in-house development, but rather the period of time that development capacities must be available. In this regard, Schaschinger speaks of something called the *application jam* (cf. Schaschinger 1993). Baumgartner names the following factors as its causes (cf. Baumgartner 1990):

- the high level of complexity that business requirements demand from software systems
- the difficulty of setting correct and complete requirements at the beginning of the project
- the difficulty of taking changes into consideration in the software development process
- insufficient consideration of the user's requirements
- neglect of development and programming standards
- lack of reuse of software components

For this reason, there has for a while now been a trend in business towards implementing integrated standard software. One of the main goals of using standard software is to reduce the costs for personnel, software development, training and maintenance. Other benefits that are anticipated from the use of integrated standard software are:

- protection of the integrity of business data

- immediate availability of all business data to all employees

- department-spanning view of the business events and objects to be processed in the operation, for example requests, purchase orders, invoices, etc.

- more flexible modification of business process flows, within the range of solutions provided by the software supplier

The need to replace existing DP systems in favour of integrated standard software has steadily increased over the past few years. The costs, for example, to develop and maintain a software system tailored for an enterprise have risen more than the costs for a comparable standard solution from a software supplier.

These days, integrated standard software such as the R/3 System offers a generic problem solution and can be implemented in comparable areas in different enterprises. Integrated standard software supports several operational application areas, such as sales, materials management, production, financial accounting, controlling, and human resources. This minimizes the number of different programs from different manufacturers in the enterprise. The individual areas are implemented as applications, and these access a common logical database. This allows business processes to be performed in an integrated manner across department boundaries and automated to the highest degree possible. Reasons for implementing integrated standard software include:

- When development resources are tight, it is possible to concentrate on an enterprise's core competencies (cf. Scholz/Vrohlings 1994).

- The software vendor's business knowledge, which is conveyed through the standard software among other things, makes it possible to implement the latest business developments.

- When the organization structure within an enterprise changes, it is possible with the help of the standard software to react flexibly to new structures (cf. Zencke 1994).

- Because the product has been tested in the field for many years, standard software has achieved a high degree of maturity, which can be seen as insurance of the applications' quality and stability.

- The modular structure of the software enables step-by-step implementation and, consequently, gradual introduction of an enterprise's employees to the standard software.

- The use of standard software can reduce in-house development to a minimum. Creation of expensive and costly-to-develop custom software is eliminated.

- Because most of the maintenance of standard software is performed by the manufacturer, a majority of the maintenance costs are eliminated for enterprises that use it.

- The acquisition of integrated standard software is also the acquisition of flexibility, because it is possible to change program process flows through parameters and thus achieve a customer-specific adaptation (cf. Mertens *et al.* 1991, pp. 569–588).

▩ Standard software is an open system. It is usually independent of the EDP platforms used.

1.5.2   Process orientation and object orientation

The central question of the role of information technology these days is whether new software systems are built on an architecture that can properly handle the continuous organizational changes in an enterprise. On the other hand, one cannot let these changes lead to uncontrolled growth of parallel information systems that are not coordinated in the enterprise, otherwise the productivity gains that are the goal of IT implementation will not be achieved. If it seems as though these days a contradiction is often articulated between *business process design* as a paradigm for the enterprise and *object orientation* as a paradigm for software development, this is due to an error in thinking or is part of some trend-based prejudice (cf. Zencke 1994, pp. 63–76; cf. Zencke 1996, pp. 6–9).

In traditional architectures, purchasing systems, inventory management systems and financial accounting systems were born out of function requirements. In many enterprises, these *function-oriented* application modules led to an internal complexity that could no longer be controlled due to the many program interfaces, while the implementation of these kinds of IT systems cemented function-oriented organization structures.

The main task of *integrating* such systems in an enterprise was left mostly to the user. With the R/2 System, SAP early on offered a highly integrated system for *handling different business processes with a single system*, in which an accounting document is created automatically, for example, or data is automatically written in a cost accounting record. The price for this reduction in *external* (operational) complexity, however, was higher *internal* (program-related) complexity.

According to the object orientation paradigm, the user will in the future choose, from a multitude of objects which he can obtain from one or more software manufacturers, those objects that he needs for his task. The objects are encapsulated, that is, they contain all of the methods and communication interfaces relevant for the object type in question, not just standardized and prescribed ones. The user then composes his individual business processes from this variety of available object methods – without the straightjacket of business management science knowledge or of globally tested organizational process flows. A paradise? Unfortunately not. In this method, the egotism of individual people carrying out the functions will dominate the project work. The resulting business process will not be lean, nor will it deal responsibly with the resources. A lengthy agreement process will be needed to ensure the business-related integrity of the data.

A comparison of the current process and/or object models that describe standard software shows at once that processes are nothing more than navigation through object methods of different objects. These days, the user has a right to this kind of navigation, just as the user of a good travel guide has a right to itinerary suggestions, and the user of a good restaurant has a right to menu suggestions. No, object orientation does not solve the user's problems in terms of efficient and quick software implementation. At most, it solves the problem of finding optimal solutions for the individual functions (= object methods), which has moved into the background.

Object orientation, with its encapsulating and communication methodologies could, however, become a solution for developers' problems of complexity. In this respect, object orientation is certainly an indication of a software manufacturer's capability for evolutionary innovation and of their continued commercial competitiveness. Furthermore, object orientation is a requirement for changes in the software industry: reduction in the number of manufacturing levels, as well as diversification in finished product manufacturers (= process vendors) and system vendors (= object vendors), as has been observed in the last few years in the automobile industry.

We software developers have grown accustomed to writing software aimed at meeting the demands of efficient and integrated handling of business processes instead of purely for the paradigms of ingenious software architectures. Of course, software architectures have not in any way become simpler; with respect to the user, however, they take a back seat to the user's all-consuming interest in the process flow. Newer management strategies, lean management, customer orientation and process ownership, have accelerated this development. Universal, integrated and efficient support of comprehensive and standardized business process chains has replaced the most optimal solution possible of a multitude of individual functions. If the user builds on generic software components, he gains standardized solutions that he can, of course, adapt to his needs to various extents, i.e. flexibly. Standardized solutions always contain a bit of process-oriented organization that has been recommended by business management science and/or has proven itself in practical experience. The user no longer receives just a piece of software, but rather adaptable process-oriented organization. And so, hidden in the *good old Trojan horse* of software, insights from business management science sneak into those enterprises that do not afford themselves a business management staff.

Just as in the automobile industry, the user is dependent on optimal coordination of the system components. After all, they provide him with business processes for navigation through object methods. And only in this combination can the user experience progress.

If one thinks about the possible business processes of the potential customer from the user's point of view, a huge danger becomes evident. In principle, the processes are endless, and they must be completely variable in their detailed form because of market requirements. Every enterprise wants to design the processes in such a way that they fit the *market segment*, the *customer segment* or the *product group* optimally. Now, from the user's point of view, it would be no less than a historic mistake to use the business processes as a starting point and program each one individually. If a process change were to occur, something that is practically inherent in the system in modern organization structures, we would be faced once again with the dilemma of *line-of-business systems*, as we were ten years ago. *Optimal support of one or fewer selected processes of a line of business* – that are rigidly programmed – can meet the current requirements. If the business changes, the enterprises are blocked by their *own* process flows and are unable to integrate new processes.

It is exactly this dilemma – *covering different, variable business processes* with a *flexible, open application architecture* – that must be overcome using integrated DP systems with modern designs. In addition to using relational databases and the client/server architecture (cf. Plattner 1993, pp. 923–938; cf. Kagermann 1993, pp. 273–280) as the main fundamental technology, as well as offering open integration modules (Business Application

Programming Interface – BAPI) for linking third-party products, such systems must be familiar with centralized *business objects*. These business objects, such as *purchase orders*, *goods receipt documents* and *financial accounting documents*, can have various forms in the R/3 architecture. Depending on the business process context, for example, a purchase order in the R/3 system can be a *normal purchase order*, a *scheduling agreement* or an *outline agreement*, and it can *reference a purchase requisition* or be *assigned to an account*. Parameter setting for such business objects, which are encapsulated business-wise, makes it possible to represent different business processes with a *single* system. The internal architecture of the R/3 System is structured in such a way that these essential business objects know which business methods they need, and that these business objects can be called, putting them in a position to integrate based on context, according to the customer's desired business process chain.

1.5.3   Business processes as componentware

Integrated standard software systems exhibit a high degree of complexity, because they link together different, independent business processes. In order to do justice to the specific requirements of enterprises, a flexible, adaptable system architecture is necessary that allows adjustment of the software to business-specific requirements. This flexibility has two dimensions:

- flexibility in terms of the adaptability of the standard software to the demands of various enterprises

- flexibility in terms of the adaptability of an enterprise's system configuration over time. This aspect includes the structural and behavioural adaptation of the application system. In this context, structural adaptation means changing the organization structure of the enterprise, for example by adding new products or business areas. Behavioural adaptation means changing or adding functionality to the application system, for example modifications to the process-oriented organization undertaken as part of business reengineering projects.

One way to implement this flexibility is to provide standard software modules that can be *individually* combined into application systems. Thome/Hufgard use the term *standard software library* for this (cf. Thome/Hufgard 1996, p. 43). Modularizing application systems provides an important means for controlling complexity. Denert defines modularization as the "subdivision into parts of a system to be developed" (Denert 1991, p. 212). For example, at its highest level, SAP's R/3 System consists of the Financial Accounting, Asset Accounting, Sales and Distribution, Production Planning, and Human Resources modules. The formation of such components must meet a series of general requirements. Fundamental in this context is the requirement for maximum internal coherence and minimal external linking (cf. for general module-building criteria, for example, Denert 1991, pp. 213–214; cf. Myers 1975).

In the literature, application systems that consist of combinations of different modules are often called componentware. Componentware means application modules that are combinable into an executable system using the three steps of selection (finding and choosing), modification (adapting and expanding), and combination (cf. Mili *et al.* 1995). A series of tasks are linked to this approach:

■ *Finding application system components*
To be able to reuse application system components, search mechanisms must be available. It is often difficult in large component catalogues to find reusable modules (cf. Bellinzona *et al.* 1995; cf. Convent/Wernecke 1994).

■ *Constructing application systems*
Construction means the assembly of application system components into finished application systems (cf. Nierstrasz/Meijler 1995; cf. Keller/Popp 1996). This involves combining, integrating, testing and documenting the isolated application system components in a meaningful way.

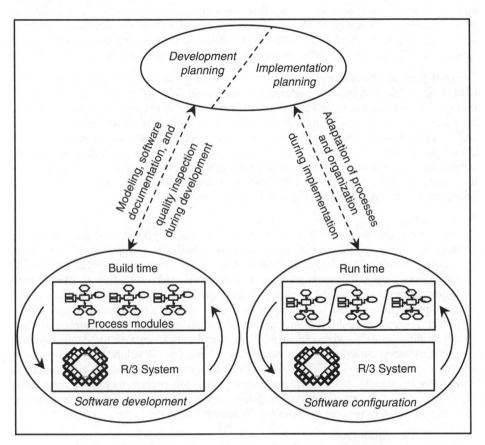

Fig. 1.10: General development plan for componentware

■ *Granularity of application system components*
Generally, application system components can be created at different levels of granularity. For example, an application system component may be a button on a screen or a module for material availability check (cf. Meyer 1996). Choosing the appropriate abstraction level is important for being able to implement the potential software composition.

Various authors suggest a division-of-labour-based software industry in this regard (cf. Kythe 1996; cf. Cleaveland *et al.* 1996). On one side the developers of application system components, whose task is to create reusable application system modules, and on the other side the product developers, who are responsible for assembling the application system modules. A prerequisite for this would be the development of a standard for linking application system components. Some progress has already been made in this area (cf. Kythe 1996).

Besides examining the possibilities for physically linking one or more application systems, business process design includes discussions of the logical business sense of linking scenarios. Such descriptions can be found in the software suppliers' model components, and they document the process flow variants for a corresponding business task to be supported. The business process model thus becomes the link between reality on the one hand and the application system on the other. This results in far-reaching demands on the arrangement of the process modules, which are explained more in the following section.

The configuration of the model components must meet certain basic requirements to make it possible to combine them into integrated business models and connect them to application system components. In addition to the requirements that are generally placed on business process modelling (cf. Fahrwinkel 1995), the following section examines the reusability, expandability and adaptability aspects of models. These characteristics are discussed particularly in connection with the discussion on forming application systems by combining prefabricated components, with the emphasis being on program modules. In the context of linking models and application systems, these characteristics also play a central role in the configuration of business process modules.

■ *Reusability*
The term *reusability* describes the feature of business process modules that allows them to be used partially or completely in the creation of business-specific business process modules. This feature is fundamental for the concept described, because the models are supposed to be implemented as *reusable application designs*. These application designs are created by linking process modules. The essential prerequisite for reuse is the process module's ability to be found. Since the user cannot completely re-model the process modules to link them to the application system, prefabricated process modules must be stored in such a way that the user can find the components he needs. A series of representation mechanisms have been developed for this purpose. You can find an overview of the various methods for finding reusable components in Zendler (cf. Zendler 1995). Implementation of reusable process modules is imperative for linking to the application system. There are three dimensions for judging the reusability of business process modules (cf. Goldberg/Rubin 1995):

– *inherent reusability*
suitability of a process model's internal characteristics for reuse

– *domain reusability*
suitability of a process model for reuse in a particular application domain or in a certain area of research

– *organizational reusability*
support for reuse through a systematic process of reuse

■ *Adaptability*

The process modules are provided by manufacturers of standard software. They must usually be adapted to the requirements of the enterprise. There are two kinds of adaptation, parameter setting, or modification, and the addition of new components while using existing components. The emphasis is on the modification of existing components. These modifications cannot really be performed 100% freely. It is therefore the job of the standard software manufacturer to provide the knowledge about interdependencies needed to supervise the modifications. Possible modifications to process modules would be:

- selection of certain subnetworks of the model

- changes to the sequence

- addition to/removal of interfaces to other process modules

■ *Expandability*

Expandability represents a special form of model adaptation, in which additional elements are added to the process modules without changing the existing behaviour. In this case, too, various possibilities are conceivable in principle. For one thing, any changes to the models could be permitted. This would guarantee the greatest possible flexibility of the process modules, which would, however, endanger the consistency of the business process model. So it is necessary to find a suitable compromise between maximum flexibility and maximum consistency of the model. For the specialization of process modules, the completeness of the process modules is the central feature, because it is an important prerequisite for linking to application system components. When configuring process modules, completeness can be viewed in three dimensions:

- *based on the requirements of the domain*
  Process modules describe a complete subtask of a business process. All of the functions that can be assigned to this subtask in this area of specialty must be contained in the process module. Furthermore, each process module must specify completely which process modules there are that make sense as precursors or subsequent modules in this business context. Because the requirements of the domain cannot be formalized, the completeness of the process model in relation to the tasks cannot be validated analytically.

- *based on the functions of the application system*
  In this view, a process module is complete if it contains all of the functions of the application system that logically belong to the subtask described in the process module. A module that is complete in this sense is imperative for linking the process modules to the application system. Which individual assignments should be undertaken is described in detail on the basis of model companies in Chapters 8 and 9.

- *based on the different parameter settings of the application systems*
  Within the framework of linking to application systems, process modules serve as the basis for setting parameters of application system components. All of the alternative parameter settings of the application system component must be represented in the process module. Only then can the selection of a particular parameter setting based on the modification of the process modules take place.

The objective of linking is to configure the application system based on the model. Business-specific configuration of the process module adapts the application system to the requirements. The task of the process module thus consists of displaying the variable behaviour characteristics of the corresponding application system component. This includes both control of the business process by the application system and description of individual functions of the application system by the module.

The initial stage of model-based configuration (cf. Zencke 1996, pp. 6–9) consists of representing the similarities between processes as representation of the model and processes as physical implementation, for example the R/3 System. After the contents of the R/3 System and the essential methodical prerequisites are described in Chapters 2 through 5, Chapter 6 demonstrates how the model world corresponds to the physical implementation, using the R/3 Reference Model and the R/3 System as an example.

Section B
Fundamental Principles of
Process Design

„Make it as simple as possible, but not simpler."
(Albert Einstein)

In 1972, five former IBM employees founded SAP Ltd, with the goal of developing and marketing standard application software. SAP stands for **S**ystems, **A**pplications and **Prod**ucts in data processing. In 1988, SAP Ltd went public and became a joint-stock company, SAP AG. The function-oriented R/2 software system for mainframe applications was followed by the R/3 System, which was based on client/server technology. In fiscal year 1995, the corporation posted sales of DM 2.7 billion and showed an annual net profit of DM 405 million. With over 8000 employees, it is one of the largest and fastest-growing international software houses.

SAP AG has over 5000 customers in over 40 countries and, with 5200 R/3 and 2200 R/2 installations, is one of the leading producers of standard software in the world.

1979 was the year the software system R/2 (R for realtime, i.e. realtime processing) was born. R/2 is standard software for business mainframe applications. It has a modular structure, and its comprehensive business functionality enables a high degree of integration. Even after the introduction of R/3, the R/2 System continues to be maintained and developed. According to SAP's plans, it will continue to be updated and its functionality expanded even after the turn of the millennium.

The R/2 System currently includes the following components:

- RA   Assets Accounting
- RF   Financial Accounting
- RK   Cost Accounting
- RK-P   Projects
- RM-INST   Plant Maintenance
- RM-MAT   Materials Management
- RM-PPS   Production Planning and Control
- RM-QSS   Quality Assurance
- RP   Human Resources

▨ RV   Sales and Distribution

In 1992, SAP introduced another standard business software package, the R/3 System, which is based on client/server architecture and can run on different hardware platforms with different operating systems and different databases.

2   SAP R/3 – Release 3.x

The *R/3 System* stands out because of the comprehensive business performance it provides, its high degree of modularity with simultaneous integration of individual modules, its support for international requirements with appropriate country-specific functionality (for example, payroll accounting in different countries due to different laws and tax systems), and its multilingualism, as well as its ability to run on different hardware platforms (cf. Buck-Emden/Galimow 1996, pp. 109–155).

The R/3 System is based on a three-level client/server architecture and can be divided into two task areas: basis tasks and business application tasks. The job of the basis layer is to make the business applications independent of the system interfaces of the operational, database and communication systems, and to ensure high-performance handling of the business transactions. The application layer contains the implemented solutions provided to support the business requirements of enterprises.

2.1   R/3 basis architecture

The *basis architecture* of the R/3 System is characterized by the following features:

▨ *Scalability*
   Scalability means that applications can run on computers of various sizes. Using a multi-level client/server architecture makes it possible to separate the application logic, the presentation and the database in the R/3 System. In a three-level R/3 configuration, separate computers are used for the presentation, the application and the database. The database computer can then serve several application servers, and a presentation computer can access different application servers. Other configurations are possible, however, as the following figure shows (cf. Plattner 1993, pp. 923–937; cf. SAP – R/3 Software-Architecture 1994, pp. 1.1–2.25).

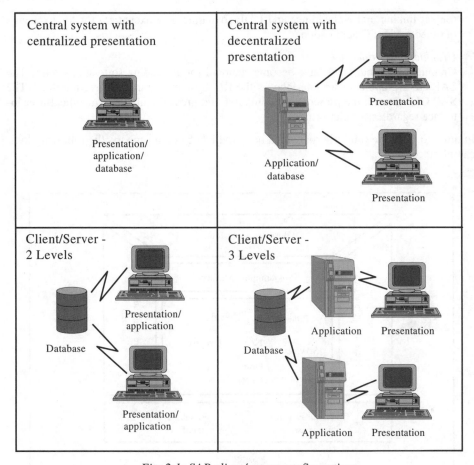

Fig. 2.1: SAP client/server configurations

■ *Portability*
Portability means the extent to which a software solution can be implemented on different hardware and operating system platforms. The R/3 System can run on all major Unix operating systems, on Open VMS, MPE/IX and Windows NT. In addition, the presentation using the SAP GUI (graphical user interface) can run on various front ends, such as Windows, OS Motif, OS/2 PM and Macintosh.

■ *Openness*
Openness in a software solution means the extent to which a standard software package on the market allows external applications to be integrated with standardized interfaces. Data and function integrity in the R/3 System are ensured through the support of international standards for interfaces, such as TCP/IP (transmission control protocol/Internet protocol) as the network communication protocol, RFC (remote function call) as the open programming interface, CPI-C (common programming interface – communication) for program-to-program communication, SQL (structured query language) and ODBC (open data base connectivity) for access to the database, and OLE

(object linking and embedding) and DDE (dynamic data exchange) for the exchange of objects with PC applications.

■ *Graphical user interface*
Graphical user interfaces have become standard for all leading software systems. The SAP GUI (graphical user interface) is the R/3 System's graphical user interface. The SAP GUI runs on the presentation computer and provides an almost identical user interface regardless of platform.

In order to fulfil the four criteria named here, the R/3 System supports the following logical interfaces.

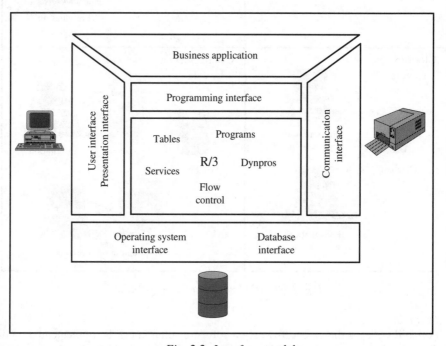

Fig. 2.2: Interface model

■ *Operating system interface*
The operating system interface of the R/3 System must work closely with various operating systems, such as Unix or Windows NT, for communication, data management and storage management. For this reason, there are different versions of it for different operating systems.

■ *Database interface*
The database interface implements the modifications necessary for accessing the different relational database systems.

■ *Presentation interface*
The presentation interface supports the system-independent portion for the software in

use on the presentation computer, such as OSF/Motif, Presentation Manager, Windows 3.1, Windows 95, Windows NT or Apple Macintosh.

- *User interface*
  System-dependent elements such as windows, menu bars and scroll bars are defined in the user interface.

- *Programming interface*
  The programming interface contains the basis technologies that substantially determine the structure of SAP applications.

  - *SAP SQL* is a special SAP version of SQL used for access to relational databases.

  - *EXEC SQL* is a variant of SQL that enables direct access to the database.

  - *Function modules* are reusable ABAP/4 modules, accessible anywhere in the system, that are stored in a central library.

  - *Remote function call* is the protocol for cross-system and system-internal access to function modules.

- *Communication interface*
  The communication interface contains the procedures for electronic exchange of information between different R/3 Systems and between R/3 Systems and non-SAP systems. In this case, too, the data exchange supports current standards, such as:

  - CPI-C (Common Programming Interface – Communication)

  - EDI (Electronic Data Interchange)

  - OLE (Object Linking and Embedding)

  - ALE (Application Link Embedding)

2.2   R/3 applications

The R/3 System consists of business application modules that can be used either individually or in sensible business combinations. SAP AG's delivery strategy involves delivering the complete system to the customer and activating on site the necessary functions and business processes based on the customer's requirements. The disadvantage of this strategy is that this requires some customers to have an oversized system configuration at the beginning of implementation. The advantage is that during the course of operations, it is easier to activate functionality from the existing pool of solutions than to continually undergo upgrades.

The sections that follow contain an overview of the R/3 System's business application modules, describing their capabilities. For detailed analyses, we refer to the documentation of SAP AG, which is specified in the individual chapters.

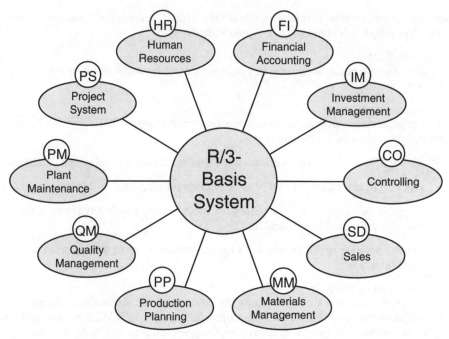

Fig. 2.3: Business application modules of the R/3 System

2.2.1 Accounting

Accounting deals with the value-based representation of business processes and is tasked with planning, controlling and checking the value flow in an enterprise. In accordance with the target group, accounting is divided into external and internal accounting. Internal accounting consists of cost and benefits accounting and is used to provide quantitative information to decision makers within an enterprise. External accounting is structured according to legal requirements and accommodates the commitment to openness towards external parties, particularly tax authorities and investors. Important components in the R/3 System for supporting accounting tasks are Financial Accounting, Investment Management, and Controlling.

a) Financial Accounting

The *Financial Accounting (FI)* module handles the functions of financial accounting and cash management. The principles of adequate and orderly accounting served as the most important basis for the design of this module. The software takes into consideration the legal requirements of the German-speaking world, the 1993 EU guideline for harmonizing the rendering of accounts, and it also meets non-European requirements such as those for the American rendering of accounts (cf. SAP – General Ledger Accounting 1996; cf. SAP – Legal Consolidation 1996; cf. SAP – Sub-Ledger Accounts 1996; cf. SAP – Asset Management 1995).

■ *Master Data*
The Master Data function area deals with setting up general ledger (G/L) accounts, i.e. establishing balance sheet accounts, as well as profit and loss accounts. The main organizational criterion is a chart of accounts, which is based on country-specific, but also enterprise-specific, criteria.

■ *G/L Accounting*
G/L Accounting has the task of supporting the representation of all of external accounting and thus of all accounts. All relevant business events must be collected in the general ledger, so that G/L Accounting can guarantee complete and reconciled accounting information at any time. G/L Accounting contains the customizable framework for the general ledger account, which automatically transfers all postings from subsidiary ledgers into the general ledger. Master data processes and planning processes must be carried out before actual postings or other activities that affect G/L account postings can be executed. G/L account postings can also be done across company codes. In an integrated R/3 System, the number of postings handled by this functionality is noticeably smaller, because G/L account postings from other applications are carried out directly in the general ledger. The year-end closing can be generated at any point in time. Closing tasks in G/L Accounting include monthly and yearly foreign currency valuation, recording of regroupings, and the generation of month-end and year-end closings.

■ *Accounts Receivable*
Both Accounts Receivable and Accounts Payable, which is described in the next section, support the user by automatically tracking open items and reconciling payment transactions. Account analyses, due date lists and flexible dunning are all part of this module's scope of functions. The user can determine the contents and the periodicity of payment notices, account statements, interest calculations and correspondence as desired. Accounts Receivable supports independent accounts receivable conto pro diverse (CPD) accounts receivable, branch accounts receivable, and purchasing co-op accounts receivable. Independent accounts receivable describes the handling of business events with customers who are deemed independent, that is, who do not have relationships to other customers. Supported functionality includes everything from issuing invoices to the customer on down to clearing the receivable for this customer. Between the issuance of an invoice and the clearing of the receivable, a down payment can be requested from the customer, and outstanding payment or down payment notices can be sent. Required payments and down payments can be automatically collected from customers who have provided a collection authorization, otherwise these are paid by the customer and must be assigned to the receivables on which they are based. CPD accounts receivable describes the handling of business events with customers who are not entered in the system as independent customers. Usually, only one business event is handled with these CPD customers, and no master data record is created. Branch accounts receivable describes the handling of business events with customers (branches) and their headquarters. Purchasing co-op accounts receivable encompasses the handling of business events with customers who have formed a co-op, but who have no headquarters to deal with payments, for example. Accounts receivable for these customers takes place with a so-called work list, which is used to determine who the customers are.

■ *Accounts Payable*

Accounts Payable describes the handling of business events with vendors who are deemed independent, that is, who do not have relationships to other vendors. Supported functionality includes everything from issuing of an invoice from a vendor on down to clearing the payable to this vendor. Between the issuing of the invoice and clearing of the payable, down payments can be demanded by the vendor, which are then paid automatically. Outstanding credit reminders can be sent. Required payments and down payments are paid automatically. CPD accounts payable describes the handling of business events with so-called one-time vendors. Branch accounts payable describes the handling of business events between vendors (branches) and their headquarters.

■ *Legal Consolidation*

The world-wide regulations for balancing accounts in corporate groups, as well as the specific regulations for admitting enterprises into capital markets, require the consolidation of legally independent subsidiaries and the creation of a consolidated financial statement. The subcomponent FI-LC deals with the possibilities for preparing and executing consolidations in a corporate group, which include mid-year closings and consolidations using plan values. Preparation for consolidation is usually the decentralized responsibility of the subsidiary in question. For this reason, this area of functionality describes how consolidation guidelines are to be implemented, how certain preparation activities should run decentralized, and finally, how information should be passed on to corporate headquarters. It is possible to enter certain individual financial statement data and other information decentrally, on a PC, and then pass it on to the R/3 System. This makes sense wherever there is no R/3 System in use and manual transmission would be too costly. Legal Consolidation itself describes the organization of consolidation, the maintenance of master data, the delimitation of the consolidated entity, the transfer of data, and the (automatic) consolidation measures.

■ *Asset Accounting*

Asset Accounting has the task of documenting all business events that are relevant to accounting that occur in relation to operational fixed assets. This subarea provides functions for meeting international legal regulations, as well as for company-internal management of fixed assets. In the R/3 System, Asset Accounting is carried out as subledger accounting. For one thing, this allows assets to be valuated in an orderly fashion on a balance sheet key date, and for another, it allows current information (for example, depreciation) to be determined and passed on to Controlling for planning purposes.

The master data that is important for Asset Accounting includes asset classes, group assets and fixed assets. Individual-entry and collective-entry functions are available for management (new asset, change). The valuation of fixed assets includes all depreciation types (normal depreciation, special depreciation, acquisition- and production-cost-reducing depreciation), as well as valuations for special purposes (revaluations, interest, insurable values). Postings can be divided into inventory postings, which are brought about by business events in the life cycle of a fixed asset, and value corrections, which reflect the periodic value changes of a fixed asset. Periodic processings refer to mid-year processes, which in turn affect business events in the life cycle of a large number of fixed assets, but also processes that deal with archiving, documentation, and their data exchange with Controlling. In addition, there are certain kinds of processing, such as physical inventory and year-end closing, that are carried out only once a year.

Lease handling provides functions that allow specific handling of leased assets as part of fixed assets. This includes, in particular, capitalization of leased assets based on the capital lease method, as well as handling of corresponding lease payments.

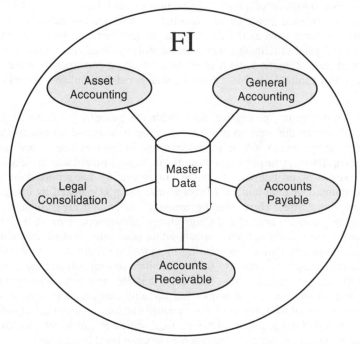

Fig. 2.4: Financial Accounting (FI) application module

b) Investment Management

The *Investment Management (IM)* module supports the accounting-related and controlling-related management of capital investment programmes and individual capital investment measures (cf. Dirks/Schöler 1996, pp. 212–219; cf. SAP – Investment Management 1995).

■ *Capital investment programmes*
  Capital investment programmes allow you to plan and control budgets across measures. The individual items at the lowest level of a capital investment programme can represent capital investment measures, but they can also be of a different nature (for example, maintenance orders). The user can select the hierarchical structure himself, which supports the various types of capital investment budgets of enterprises. Functions are available for structuring, planning and budgeting programmes. During the investment period, you can enter additions, returns and budget item transfers.

■ *Capital investment measures*
Capital investment measures are tangible investments that an enterprise makes in order to create a complex fixed asset for its own operational use. Depending on the measure being considered, functions from the Project System and Controlling (for example, internal orders) are used in this case. For purposes of settlement, it is also possible to access the functions from Asset Accounting at the end of the period. Generally, all of the measures are handled as projects or internal orders, if direct activation into fixed assets does not seem reasonable from a Controlling point of view due to the size of the measures. For purposes of parallel accounting-related handling, capital investment measures are assigned assets under construction, with the corresponding Controlling object always being used as the account assignment element. Functions for periodic settlement and final settlement support the identification of cost components that can be activated and automatic settlement of the asset under construction to the completed fixed asset. For capital investment projects, you can also calculate and capitalize interest.

Project-related measure processing deals with the processing of capital investment projects. As part of the creation of measures, project costs and schedules are planned. The corresponding award of a budget follows, and in this case a reference can be made back to a capital investment programme. If this capital investment project is part of a capital investment programme, then the corresponding budget availability can be checked against this total budget. Measure processing is initiated by *measure implementation*. From there, corresponding measures in certain areas such as Materials Management (purchase orders) and Controlling (funds reservation) are triggered. After the measures are carried out, the corresponding plans are updated and, if necessary, budgets are adjusted. Periodic processing includes especially those measures that are used to partially capitalize costs to the asset under construction and measures that ensure a settlement or capitalization of the costs that does justice to the origin before the end of measure processing. Additional functionality supports depreciation simulation and interest calculation. Closing of the measure consists of technical closing and accounting-related closing, which result in a final settlement, in which elements capitalized to assets under construction are reposted to completed fixed assets.

Single measure processing deals with processing of capital investment orders or internal orders. The orders are planned and budgeted as part of measure creation. Scheduling and differentiated cost planning are not included here. As with capital investment projects, a reference can be made back to a capital investment programme when the budget is awarded.

■ *Depreciation simulation*
For the development of depreciation, there are corresponding standard reports available for forecasting depreciation. In addition to capitalized fixed assets, it is also possible to include planned investments from Investment Management. Depreciation and interest planned in this manner can be transferred to Controlling through primary cost transfer.

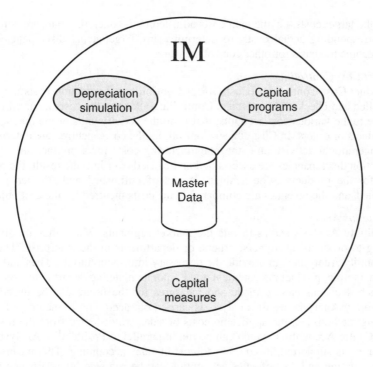

Fig. 2.5: Investment Management (IM) application module

c) Controlling

In the R/3 System, the application component *Controlling (CO)* is divided into Overhead Cost Controlling (CO-OM), Product Cost Controlling (CO-PC), and Profitability Analysis (CO-PA) (cf. Kagermann 1990, pp. 277–306; cf. Kagermann 1993, pp. 273–280; cf. Kagermann 1993, pp. 455–464; cf. Keller/Malt 1995, pp. 234–249; cf. Plattner 1987, pp. 58–81; cf. SAP – Overhead Cost Controlling 1996; cf. SAP – Product Cost Controlling 1996; cf. SAP – Profitability Analysis 1996; cf. SAP – Activity-Based Cost Controlling 1996).

■ *Overhead Cost Controlling*
   Overhead Cost Controlling includes the planning, control and checking of overhead costs, i.e. the costs that cannot be assigned directly to one cost object. Overhead Cost Controlling is divided into Cost Element Accounting, which documents which costs have been incurred in the enterprise, and Cost Centre Accounting, which records which costs were incurred and where in the enterprise they were incurred. Costs and activities can be allocated to the cost centres either directly or with internal activity allocation. Internal order processing represents the most detailed operational level of cost and activity allocation. Based on cost centre and order planning, all actual costs are allocated to the appropriate cost incurring parties, i.e. cost centres or overhead cost orders. In the course of allocating internal activities or orders, the actual costs are allocated further, to ensure that costs for internal activity exchange are also recorded. Fi-

nally, the target costs, i.e. the plan costs adjusted to the operating rate, are compared to the corresponding actual costs, to determine any target/actual discrepancies, which then become the basis for other control measures.

■ *Product Cost Controlling*
In Product Cost Controlling (Cost Object Controlling), production costs are planned, controlled and checked. Cost Object Controlling allocates the costs incurred in the enterprise to the various cost accounts, that is, to the activity units of the operation, such as products or orders. In Cost Object Controlling, the costs incurred are determined for each operational activity unit, the manufacturing costs for a product are calculated, production discrepancies are ascertained and carried over into the result, the minimum price for the products is determined, stocks of unfinished and finished goods are evaluated, and the revenues are compared to the costs incurred for the cost object.

■ *Profitability Analysis*
Profitability Analysis serves to rate the market segments, which may be divided according to products, customers, orders, or departments in the enterprise. The task of Profitability Analysis is to provide the necessary information to the sales and distribution, marketing, product management and corporate planning departments, on the basis of which decisions can be made and measures for the future can be introduced. In Profitability Analysis, results analysis is carried out according to the cost-of-sales accounting method, i.e., the applicable costs of sales are deducted from the revenue. In Profit Centre Accounting, which can be run in parallel to Profitability Analysis, period accounting is supported, in addition to cost-of-sales accounting. This means that period accounting and cost-of-sales accounting can be run side by side in the R/3 System. For its analyses, Profitability Analysis takes data from different areas of the system: for example, revenues and sales deductions from Sales and Distribution (SD), manufacturing costs from product costing, cost centre fixed costs and cost centre discrepancies from Cost Centre Accounting, special direct costs from Financial Accounting (FI), and order-specific and project-specific costs from Order and Project Settlement. The transfer and valuation of planned sales quantities into Sales and Revenue Planning allows you to determine planned revenues, as well as planned sales deductions and planned costs of goods manufactured.

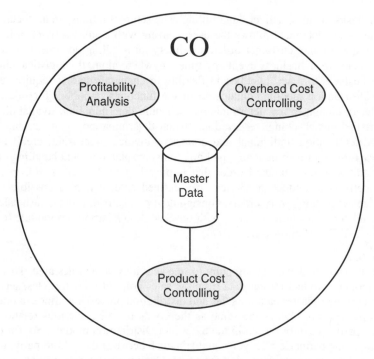

Fig. 2.6: Controlling (CO) application module

2.2.2 Logistics

Operational logistics includes the design of the material, information and production flow, from the vendor, through production, down to the consumer. If you implement the Logistics application modules provided in the R/3 System, you can plan, control and coordinate logistical processes across department boundaries, based on the integration of existing data and functions. The integration of the individual application modules in the R/3 System prevents unnecessary and time-consuming multiple entries when processing logistical business events. This integration also ensures that the value-related side of the business event is taken into consideration in the quantity-oriented processing steps, and therefore also the accounting requirements. Specifically, the Logistics application modules include Sales and Distribution, Materials Management, Production Planning and Control, Quality Management, the Project System, and Plant Maintenance.

a) Sales and Distribution

The application module *Sales and Distribution (SD)* supports all of the tasks necessary for executing activities in the labour market. Using the Sales and Distribution module, you can sell products to business partners and perform services. The data for the products, services and business partners are stored as master data and form the basis for all activities in sales and distribution processing. In addition to managing all of the market and product data necessary for a customer order, the Sales and Distribution module can be used to perform the tasks of sales, delivery and billing. The setup of a transparent document flow based on the sales document allows the user, starting with a sales activity, a request for quotation, a quotation, a customer order, a delivery, or a billing document, to determine the current status for a business event any time, anywhere along the logistical chain. This allows the business to react quickly and flexibly to changing market requirements. The Sales and Distribution module contains all of the functions important for sales, such as material determination, price determination, schedule determination, availability check, costing, credit limit checking, reservations, batch determination, order tracing, tax and condition determination, individual and collective invoice processing, credit and debit memo processing, returns processing, picking, transport planning, and handling of foreign trade. In addition to the standard order that is prevalent in the real world, in which an enterprise delivers a product or service on a defined date, it is also possible to handle outline agreements, third-party orders, consignment goods, rush orders, cash sales, rental contracts, and deliveries free of charge with the Sales and Distribution module (cf. SAP – SAP's Sales and Distribution system 1994).

■ *Master Data*
Master data serves as the starting point for the activities in the sales area. This includes the material or product master data from the sales point of view (articles, services), as well as customer master data for sales and distribution processing. Since in practice the sold-to party is not always the same as the goods recipient, various relationships to business partners can be stored in the Sales and Distribution module. So, for example, by defining the partner's role, you can distinguish between the sold-to party, the goods recipient, the invoice recipient, and the payer. Common master data, such as the material master and the customer master, is also used by other application modules. Financial Accounting's Accounts Payable accesses the appropriate customer master data, Materials Management and Production Planning and Control access the common part of the material master and add their own area-specific data to it. To support price determination, the condition technique can be used to take into consideration various material prices, surcharges and price reductions (customer discounts and quantity discounts), freight charges and sales tax. So by taking into consideration customer- and material-based settings, price determination can be executed almost entirely automatically in quotation processing and billing, for example.

■ *Sales*
Sales includes all activities from request for quotation (RFQ) processing, through quotation creation, on down to processing of all kinds of orders. Entered data in RFQ processing is automatically taken over into the quotation, and the corresponding item data, such as material, price and delivery date, are filled in by accessing the corresponding master data. This quotation may result in a single order or a longer-term customer relationship in the form of an outline agreement with appropriate special conditions. Outline agreements can be divided into contracts and scheduling agreements and are valid for a defined period of time. For contracts, quantities and prices are specified; for scheduling agreements, delivery dates are also specified. In order processing, the functions of price determination, availability check, credit limit check and delivery scheduling serve as a basis for the user to decide whether to accept or decline an order. With the data in sales documents as a basis, deliveries and bills can be created. Several sales documents, for example cash sales and rush orders, automatically trigger the creation of subsequent deliveries and bills.

■ *Shipping*
Shipping helps guarantee on-time and cost-saving retrieval and shipment of the articles agreed upon in a customer order. Because of the high degree of integration in the R/3 System, the data necessary for a delivery can be copied into a reference copy from order processing and processed with the goal of optimizing shipping. So, for example, material data, availability and delivery schedule can be retrieved from order processing. Incidentally, deliveries can also be created without reference to a customer order, in which case material determination, availability check and delivery scheduling take place directly in Shipping. In addition to determination, maintenance, and deadline monitoring of orders that are due, Shipping also handles picking, for example the collection of warehouse materials or articles for a delivery, transportation (disposition and transportation processing of transports, tracking and monitoring of transports, management of transportation means and resources as well as transport costs), creation of packaging and loading instructions, and creation, printout and transmission (for example, using Electronic Data Interchange) of shipping documents, under consideration, if necessary, of foreign trade requirements (management of export permits, notices to government agencies). At the end of delivery processing, material inventories are corrected, and the goods issue is performed. Furthermore, there is a change in values in Financial Accounting due to the change in inventory. Shipping activities can also be decentralized in the R/3 System, and picking can be performed by linking a warehouse management system.

■ *Billing*
In the Sales and Distribution module, order processing ends with billing. Billing supports the creation of invoices based on deliveries and services rendered, of credit and debit memos as part of complaint processing, and of proforma invoices. Bills can be created as individual invoices or collective invoices. So, for example, different deliveries based on different orders could be combined into a collective invoice, and the delivery items from one delivery could be split across several invoices. It is possible to create so-called invoice lists, for cases in which different sold-to parties have the same payer. The payer, for example the headquarters of a purchasing group that pays the invoices for its members, first takes over the payment based on the invoice list and then passes the invoice on to its members, possibly with a service charge. You can also process rebates in Billing, i.e., a customer is assured a discount within a certain period of time based on sales or revenue numbers. For a rebate payment that occurs after the defined period of time has expired, all of the relevant bills (invoices, credit and debit memos) are gathered in the R/3 System. Furthermore, invoices can be cancelled and assigned to other areas, for example Controlling, Project Management or Treasury. In any case, the bills and credit and debit memos that are created are passed on to Financial Accounting, which monitors receipt of payment.

■ *Sales Support*
Sales Support contains marketing- and sales-related information about customers, potential customers and partners, as well as competitors and their products. It supports sales and marketing department employees in market segmentation, business development and customer service. Sales Support helps the sales employee plan and execute direct mailing campaigns and sales activities. Direct mailing can be used, for example, to organize the mailing of product information or promotional gifts to various target

groups (customers, potential customers, contact persons). Sales activities can be used to store all interactions with a customer or potential customer in the R/3 System, for example, to make this information available to all field representatives for the purpose of preparing for other activities and to use it as the basis for quotations or orders.

■ *Sales and Distribution Information System*
The Sales and Distribution Information System is tightly linked with Sales Support. The Information System is used to gather, condense and evaluate data from sales. By entering different performance measures, you can use the system to recognize and assess changes in market circumstances and economic trends early on. By setting various views and levels of detail, you can obtain control, planning and guidance information for different decision levels. The Sales and Distribution Information System supports the analysis of performance measures according to various methods, for example ABC analysis, correlation curves, cumulative frequency curves and planned/actual comparisons. An early warning system is also built into the Information System. With the early warning system, you can define exception situations, in order to uncover and remove impending error situations. One of the things that can be specified, for example, is whether a critical situation should automatically trigger an e-mail or fax.

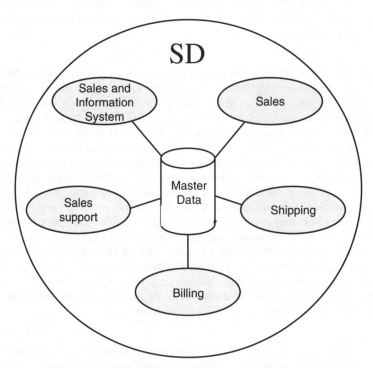

Fig. 2.7: Sales and Distribution (SD) application module

The integration of the Sales and Distribution module in the R/3 System is also assured across boundaries, for example with Materials Management, with Production Planning and Control, with Controlling and with Financial Accounting. In order processing, an availability check with regard to the stocks in the Materials Management module can be performed in the Sales and Distribution module. Delivery processing can create goods issues that are processed by the Materials Management module. Likewise, in order processing, the existing sales quantities of one or more customer orders can be transferred to the Production Planning and Control module as planned independent requirements to be produced. In demand management, the existing customer orders are then included in production planning and, if necessary, consumed against the quantities from planning. Furthermore, assembly orders for production can be created directly in the Sales and Distribution module. Another aspect of integration is the fact that, in order processing, the Sales and Distribution module can access the bills of materials from the Production Planning and Control module and retrieve from there corresponding values for price determination, availability checking and delivery date determination. If an enterprise's product line consists of one-piece products, the appropriate data from the Sales and Distribution module is passed on to Controlling for product costing purposes. During billing, the relevant objects in the Controlling module, for example profit centre postings, are automatically updated. During billing, the invoice amounts are automatically transferred, with the help of the condition technique, as revenues to the appropriate accounts in Financial Accounting, where the receipt of payment is monitored or open items are dunned, if necessary. By setting a posting block, you can temporarily hold back bills and credit and debit memos, for example if there are unresolved issues with the customer.

b) Materials Management

The Materials Management (MM) module contains functionality from procurement needs down to goods receipt, thus supporting the entire procurement cycle in an enterprise. All areas of materials management are supported, starting with requirements planning, determination of supply sources, vendor selection, ordering and purchase order monitoring, goods receipt processing, invoice processing, as well as planning and control of stocks in Inventory Management (cf. Sänger 1996, pp. 31–33; cf. SAP – Materials Management 1996).

■ *Master Data*
   In Materials Management, integral master data includes the material master, the vendor master, the bill of materials, and the conditions. From the Purchasing point of view, all of the purchasing-related data for raw materials, operating supplies and fuel, for example the replenishment lead time for a material, are of interest. In addition to data for ordering, the material master contains information for Inventory Management's goods movement postings and physical inventory and for the posting of invoices in Invoice Verification. The vendor master contains data on business partners from whom external materials or services are procured. In addition to the vendor number and address, important data includes, in particular, terms of delivery, terms of payment, sales order values and delivery times. Conditions can be used, for example, to represent tolls, delivery costs (freight charges), discounts, price/quantity scales (discounts depending on procurement quantities), surcharges and taxes.

■ *Material forecast*
The procurement process begins with requirements planning and material requirements planning. Reorder point planning, forecast-based planning and time-phased materials planning are supported. These use consumption values from the past (consumption-based planning) and take into consideration data relevant for decision making in planning, such as safety stock and delivery time. In the case of material requirements planning, a requirements explosion over a gross/net calculation is used to derive the date on which a material is to be delivered and in which quantity.

■ *Purchasing*
The Purchasing area is divided into external procurement of materials and services, determination of possible sales sources, and monitoring of goods deliveries or payments. The palette of functions ranges from creation of purchase requisitions to printing out of purchase order quantities and vendor outline agreements. Purchase requisitions are created either indirectly through material requirements planning or directly through manual entry. Purchase orders are created automatically, using existing data, and the items are assigned to the outline agreements. Price rules are created on the basis of quotation receipts; these rules serve as a foundation for deciding whether the quotation situation is sufficient for a purchase requisition or additional quotations are needed. Some of the monitoring procedures in Purchasing include vendor evaluation and monitoring of ordering activity. Basically, information about the current stocks, service level and delivery date ensures transparency in Purchasing. After a purchase order has been triggered, all of the order-related data is entered in the system in goods receipt. A material movement results in an update of the quantities through account determination.

■ *Inventory Management*
Material stocks are recorded in the system according to both quantity and value, with receipts and withdrawals, returns, transfers, and goods reservations being implemented. Inventory Management is characterized by realtime recording, which enables checking and correction in the material flow. This helps minimize the error rate. Additional functions include the balance sheet valuation method and physical inventory.

■ *Warehouse Management*
In Warehouse Management, you can define warehouse structure (high racks, block storage areas, etc.) and storage bin organization (fixed, chaotic). Based on this, you can call up from the system strategic suggestions for placement in storage, picking, and stock placement and removal.

■ *Invoice Verification*
After a delivery has been completed, the preparation of payment transactions must undergo invoice verification. The complete integration of master data makes it easier for the user to create an invoice. The system checks whether the planned values match the actual goods receipt, and if they do, it posts and releases for payment the incoming invoice. If tolerances are exceeded (with regard to quantity, price or date), potential payment of the incoming receipt is blocked.

■ *Logistics Information System*
Just like the Sales and Distribution (SD) module and the Production Planning and

Control (PP) module, Materials Management also provides information tools that can be used for decision support in materials management. Variable analyses can be called in the Logistics Information System and can be customized. They support the user in day-to-day business activities as well as in strategy development. In the Purchasing Information System, purchasing groups or delivery aspects are analyzed and quantified with meaningful key figures. In Inventory Controlling, posting documents are analyzed and characteristic values important to inventory management are derived (for example, with regard to capital lockup or timing of receipts and issues). A weak-point analysis is carried out using a graphic. Furthermore, the user can perform a vendor evaluation according to weighted criteria.

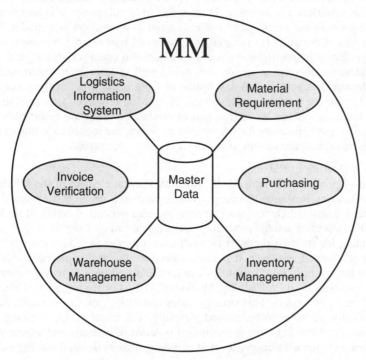

Fig. 2.8: Materials Management (MM) application module

c) Production Planning and Control

The *Production Planning and Control (PP)* module deals, within this logistics chain, with the quantity- and time-related planning of products to be manufactured, as well as the control of the production process flow. In addition to the corresponding functionality for master data maintenance, the Production Planning and Control module supports all of the quantity- and capacity-related steps for planning and control of production. This includes both different planning concepts, for example MRPII and Kanban, and different types of production, such as production by lot size, make-to-order production (variant production), repetitive manufacturing and process manufacturing (cf. SAP – Production Planning and

Control 1994; cf. SAP – Production Planning and Control – Process Industry 1995; cf. Weihrauch 1996, pp. 34–37).

▧ *Master Data*
The main master data, or basic data, for executing production planning and control includes material, bill of materials, routing, documents, production resources or tools, and work centres. Some of these, for example material, are also used by other modules. A material describes the output produced by a manufacturing company. This may be finished products, assemblies or components. There can be structural relationships between the produced output items, for example between a cylinder head and a motor (*cylinder head goes into the motor*). The superordinate and subordinate relationships between the different materials, along with their quantity specifications, are stored in the bill of materials. Furthermore, in manufacturing companies it is necessary to provide the geometrical specifications of a material to production as a model. In the R/3 System, this information is managed as documents, for example drawings. In addition to the geometrical specifications, a drawing can also contain technological specifications (measurements, cross-sections, views) as well as other notes (references, classification features). A routing is a description of the process flow for the production of a material or for the rendering of a service. Production resources are non-stationary operating facilities that can be used as part of production. They are assigned in the plans or orders to those processes for whose execution they are required. In this case, a work centre is an organizational unit in which work can be performed.

▧ *Sales and Operations Planning*
Sales and Operations Planning (SOP) is a fundamental element of the MRPII (MRPII = Manufacturing Resource Planning) planning concept, which is the basis for the R/3 PP system. Sales and Operations Planning includes general planning of mid- to long-term sales quantities and the production quantities resulting from them. It is possible to do planning for finished products in this phase. In order to reduce the number of objects to be planned, however, it is often more sensible at this planning level to work with product groups. Sales quantities can be calculated various ways, for example by transferring data from Profitability Analysis (CO-PA) or from the Sales and Distribution Information System. Furthermore, sales quantities can, for example, be forecast automatically, or they can be entered manually. The result of this planning level is a sales and operations plan that is reconciled in terms of capacity and whose values can be passed on to the next-deeper level of planning, namely demand management.

▧ *Master Planning*
Master Planning is divided into sections called Demand Management, Long-Term Planning, and Master Production Scheduling (MPS). In Demand Management, requirement quantities and dates are set for finished products and important intermediate products. The result of Demand Management is the demand programme, which consists of independent requirements. A distinction is made between planned independent requirements and customer independent requirements. Planned independent requirements are used for anonymous planning of production and procurement and are either entered directly by the MRP controller, determined through automatic forecasting, or copied from the previous planning level (Sales and Operations Planning). Customer independent requirements result from incoming sales orders. Long-Term Planning can

be used to create different versions of the demand programme and simulate their complete planning within the framework of requirements and capacity planning. After analyzing the results of this planning simulation, it is possible to replace the existing demand programme with a better version. Materials that have a lot of influence on an enterprise's net value added or that occupy critical resources can be marked as master schedule items and planned separately. The reduced scope of planning enables more frequent planning for these items and can thus lead to a reduction in inventory as well as improved material availability. Since Master Production Scheduling only considers the next-lower bill-of-material level, it is possible in the beginning to plan the master schedule items precisely, before the planning result has an effect on all of the production levels, thus creating more stable planning data.

■ *Material Requirements Planning*
It is the task of Material Requirements Planning to cover requirements using goods receipts, assuming they cannot already be handled with existing stocks. Beginning with independent requirements, the requirements of all subordinate assemblies are calculated (dependent requirements). The Material Requirements Planning process flow is an interplay between requirements and orders. To cover an independent requirement, a planned order is created. This planned order creates dependent requirements through the bill of materials; these requirements are in turn covered by planned orders, and so on. The interplay repeats itself until the lowest requirements planning level is reached. In the case of materials produced in-house, planned orders are transformed into production orders, and in the case of externally procured materials, they are transformed into purchase requisitions.

■ *Discrete Order Processing*
Actual production can be controlled using production orders. A production order determines which material should be produced at which work centre on which date. It also determines which resources must be used and how the costs incurred should be allocated. The process flow of production controlled with production orders involves everything from the opening and release of the order all the way to the actual production of the material. The production order is notified of the output produced, the goods issues of the materials withdrawn and the goods receipt of the finished materials are posted, and the costs incurred are allocated according to the specified rules.

Kanban is an alternative method of production control that dispenses with costly planning and production management. According to the principle of Kanban planning, a demand source obtains the materials it requires from containers in production. When a certain number of these containers are empty, the demand source notifies the source of its requirement with the help of an impulse (for example, a card (Japanese Kanban)); the source then controls its production itself (principle of self-controlling control cycles), which supposedly leads to reduced management and accounting costs. Kanban can be implemented in all of production or, for example, in combination with production orders, beginning at a certain level of production.

In the area of repetitive manufacturing, the run schedule header presents an instrument that meets the challenge of the realities of this type of production through simplified control and actual data entry of production. Because in repetitive manufacturing the product remains the same over a longer period of time, and its run through the work centres remains relatively constant, the complex construct of the production order is not used for control. Instead, put simply, one defines in a run schedule header only the production timeframe and the quantities to be produced in each of the time periods (run schedule quantities). In this method, there are also differences in the provision of materials and in the entry of actual data. In assembly processing, it is possible to create a production order or a planned order (a so-called assembly order) at the same time as a sales order. This direct link makes it possible to avoid performing the availability check in the sales order on the basis of the not-so-exact total replenishment lead time of the finished product and instead to execute it at the component level in the production order. The direct link between the production order and the sales order also allows data to be passed on to the sales order automatically, for example in the case of a delay in production or a reduction of the production quantity due to capacity bottlenecks. This makes exchange of current information with the customer possible.

■ *Continuous Order Processing*
The PP-PI application was developed for the needs of the process industry (chemical, pharmaceutical, food, and semi-luxury food industries). The R/3 MRPII planning concept was used and, in the area of production, production processing was expanded to include process manufacturing. This kind of processing differs from unit-based production in the following ways:

– Recipes are used instead of routings. Recipes can be restricted to certain lot sizes (specifically in the pharmaceutical industry) and must be prepared for production either electronically for one process control system, as a control recipe, or in text form on the screen as a so-called R/3 PI sheet.

– More attention is paid to resources, both technical, i.e. work centres or pools, and human, i.e. persons or groups of persons. In the case of technical resources (including intermediate storage and transport containers within the plant), any links that may exist (production lines), and their often exclusive use (for example, kettles) must be taken into account. In the case of personnel, qualification profiles are required (either by law or by internal rules) for certain production steps.

– Production is batch based, with batch documentation down to the so-called electronic batch record, in which an electronic process log automatically makes it possible to perform a batch trace for every raw material used.

– Parallel to production, expansive process coordination is necessary. Process messages from the process control systems, which may be different, must constantly be accepted and automatically processed in R/3. In addition to various monitors for monitoring the production process, these process messages serve as automatic replies about quantities, times, quality data and exception messages, as well as triggers for other external systems.

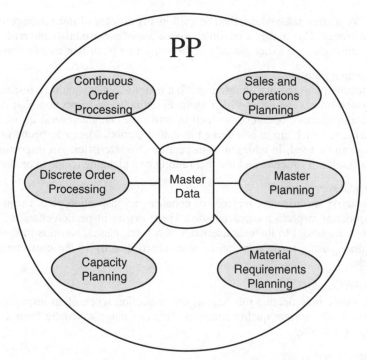

Fig. 2.9: Production Planning (PP) application module

d) Quality Management

The job of Quality Management (QM) is to ensure that both the processes themselves and the units processed in the processes meet the requirements that are placed on them everywhere in the logistical transaction chain (cf. SAP – Quality Management 1996).

▪ *Quality Planning*
  Quality Planning includes all of the functions necessary for maintaining QM-related basic data. Specifically, this means:

  – *material master*
    In the material master, QM data is stored in a QM-specific view; for example, which inspection types in general can be carried out for a material and which of these inspection types are active at the moment. It also specifies whether the material is to be handled in batches or not.

  – *inspection characteristics*
    Inspection characteristics indicate which features of an object are to be inspected and the results that should be expected. Inspection characteristics are contained in exactly one inspection plan.

  – *master inspection characteristics*
    In contrast to normal inspection characteristics, master inspection characteristics

are like master data and can thus be used in any number of inspection plans by way of reference. This makes it possible to generate where-used lists and replace master inspection characteristics globally in the inspection plans that contain them.

– *inspection plan*
Inspection plans specify, in reference to a material, what should be inspected, how, in which order, and using which tools. Essentially, an inspection plan consists of several inspection operations, which in turn may contain several inspection characteristics, which are to be checked in that operation. Master inspection characteristics can be used, in addition to inspection characteristics. An inspection plan is very similar in structure and use to a routing or a planning recipe in production.

– *material specification*
A material specification replaces or enhances an inspection plan, because it contains master inspection characteristics. These master inspection characteristics can, in turn, be linked to the characteristics of a batch class. Over this link, the results obtained during inspection can be transmitted directly to the characteristics of a batch.

– *dynamic modification rule*
A dynamic modification rule adjusts the inspection scope of an inspection characteristic to the current quality situation. This can range anywhere from a 100% inspection to a skip.

– *sampling procedure*
The sampling procedure specifies how the sample size is to be determined and how the inspection characteristic is to be evaluated. For example, an inspection rhythm may be specified.

– *sampling scheme*
With a sampling scheme, the inspection lot size can be determined according to the lot size.

■ *Quality Inspection*
The functionality of the Quality Inspection function area is based on quality planning and provides results for quality control. Quality Inspection determines whether the inspection lot, for example of a material, meets requirements with regard to the inspection characteristics stored in an inspection plan and/or a material specification. After an inspection lot has been created, an inspection plan and/or a material specification is selected, shop papers are created for the inspector, the inspection lot is checked, evaluated and closed, defects are entered in the system, and a usage decision is made. Afterwards, the material stocks found to be good are released, quality scores are calculated, the quality level based on the quality scores is updated, which can have an effect, for example, on the material or the material's vendor, and follow-up actions are triggered for the usage decision, for example a message is sent.

■ *Quality Control*
The Quality Control function area is based on the data maintained in Quality Planning, and it controls the quality inspections to be performed by reconciling the parameters of the quality inspections to be performed with the current quality level at all times. In

this way, reliable data can be gained for updating the quality level, and appropriate decisions can be made with regard to the usability of the inspected units. In the literature, quality control includes the processing of quality notifications, in addition to a corresponding information system.

■ *Quality Certificates*
A quality certificate certifies the use of certain manufacturing or work methods, the performance of inspections defined on the basis of laws, standards, customer specifications or other agreements, and, if applicable, flawless inspection results. Quality certificates are created for individual delivery items and are generally attached to the delivery. The certificate verifies that the delivered product (batch material) possesses the qualities listed in the certificate. In particular, the items can be checked for effects of things that might occur during storage or loading, such as sudden temperature changes, damage to the exterior covering, etc. Quality certificates refer to forms, which, in turn, can be linked to several certificate templates. These define the layout, format and contents. You can set up certificates individually by assigning them to a material, a product group, or a combination of material and customer.

■ *Quality Notifications*
Quality notifications are problem messages that are needed when the quality of goods or services is deemed to be deficient. Possible types of problem messages include, for example, notifications of defects with reference to a delivery or a customer complaint. In a quality notification, defects are entered and measures for dealing with them are specified. In addition, actions can be defined, which, in contrast to a task, do not have a status and cannot be assigned to a partner.

Fig. 2.10: Quality Management (QM) application module

e) Plant Maintenance

The *Plant Maintenance (PM)* module supports all of the functions associated with planning and processing of repair measures. Both scheduling of periodic maintenance and inspection measures and order placement for internal and externally procured repairs in case of unforeseen malfunctions can be supported with this module. Orders are analyzed according to type and urgency, the sequence of the orders and the responsibilities are determined, and scheduling and budgeting are carried out.

The Plant Maintenance and Service Management area deals with the management and maintenance of technical systems within the logistics chain. You can manage not only internal company systems, such as production systems, supply systems, disposal systems and transport systems, but also third-party systems, such as customer equipment.

Service handling is becoming increasingly important, because strategic enterprise goals, such as close relationships between customers and vendors, or long-term customer ties, can be attained with increased customer service. Sinking margins in sales and the profitable replacement parts business are bolstering this development. At the same time, increasingly strict regulations and manufacturers' liability are making it necessary to keep information about equipment that has been sold and the maintenance measures performed on it. A more detailed overview is also a must for making marketing decisions. In the R/3 System, this is achieved with the integration of logistics and accounting. All of the procedures in internal and external Plant Maintenance are automatically reflected in Cost Accounting, Materials Management, Financial Accounting, etc. The reasons for having a common system for internal plant maintenance and customer service are as follows (cf. Detering/Kienle 1996, pp. 38–41; cf. SAP - Plant Maintenance system 1995):

- Customer objects and internal objects are maintained by the same plant maintenance organization.

- Plant maintenance processing and internal customer service processing follow a similar course.

■ *Master Data*
The basic data needed for carrying out plant maintenance includes equipment, measuring points, functional locations and object linking. In this case, equipment means individual technical complex fixed assets that are managed as individual physical objects. Using functional locations, operational systems can be set up according to function-oriented, process-oriented or physical criteria. Measuring points are assigned to a functional location or to a piece of equipment and describe the physical or logical location for reading measuring points. They are necessary for determining intervals for plant maintenance measures. Using object linking, which can be set up between functional locations as well as between pieces of equipment, you can represent dependencies between elements of different systems.

■ *Preventive Maintenance*
Preventive Maintenance is used to secure a high degree of availability of production equipment over the long term. Preventive maintenance is the right tool for avoiding equipment breakdowns, which, in addition to the costs of repairs, often incur very high

ensuing costs due to non-production. Preventive maintenance is carried out and managed with the help of task lists, preventive maintenance plans, maintenance items and preventive maintenance strategies.

- *task lists*
  To describe recurring activities, you create task lists, in which you specify the individual work processes, the times needed and the resources required, for example work centres, production resources and tools.

- *preventive maintenance strategies*
  Scheduling rules for planned activities are stored as preventive maintenance strategies, which control the type and sequence of individual preventive maintenance packages.

- *maintenance items*
  Maintenance items determine on which objects (for example, functional locations, pieces of equipment, or assemblies) activities are to be performed. A maintenance schedule combines maintenance items for purposes of common scheduling. In addition to the strategy, it contains all of the data needed for scheduling the regular maintenance orders.

A preventive maintenance plan can be scheduled either according to the selected preventive maintenance strategy or with a manual maintenance call. In special cases, maintenance measures can also be inserted outside the usual maintenance cycle. All scheduled calls are documented in a scheduling log, which guarantees the ability to monitor deadlines at any time. Based on maintenance plan scheduling, when a preventive maintenance package is due, the regular maintenance orders for all of the maintenance items affected are automatically created. With rolling planning, for example, you always retrieve the orders for the next periods, so that an appropriate supply of work is always available. Regular maintenance orders contain only those operations of the maintenance items that are contained in the preventive maintenance package retrieved. Scheduling determines automatically both the deadline and the scope of the maintenance work required. When the order is released, the individual order items can be performed by internal plant maintenance organizations or by external service companies, the technical findings can be recorded, notification of the activities performed can be given, and the maintenance order can be settled internally, after confirmation.

■ *Maintenance Order Management*
Maintenance Order Management is divided into notifications, orders, confirmations, log, and capacity requirements and resource planning. In Plant Maintenance, unforeseeable events can occur in addition to planned activities. Such malfunctions or exception situations require quick reactions and are recorded and managed by a large notification system. A maintenance notification describes a technical exception situation for a reference object. All notifications represent a pool of measures for the plant maintenance organization to include in planning. Notifications serve both to initiate maintenance measures and to document technical confirmations. Notifications can be assigned to orders.

Maintenance measures are executed with a maintenance order. A maintenance order describes the type, scope, deadlines and resources for the execution of the measures, and it specifies the rules for account assignment and settlement. Order management is structured for flexibility. For one thing, detailed planning is possible, with deadlines, costs and technical facts, and for another, quick and simple direct opening of an order is possible. In the case of unplanned orders, the Plant Maintenance module makes it possible to open maintenance measures for elements of the equipment structure that are not yet detailed at this point. The actual objects affected are then specified later during confirmation. This makes it possible to react quickly to operational exception situations while simultaneously building a detailed maintenance log, which contains exact specifications about functional locations, pieces of equipment, or assemblies. Maintenance orders are created by:

– scheduling of preventive maintenance plans

– conversion of maintenance notifications into maintenance orders

– direct opening (without reference to notifications)

While a maintenance order is being processed, or after it has been processed, the associated notifications can be supplemented with confirmation information. A confirmation documents the measures carried out on a maintenance object. Additionally, other notifications can be created as a result of technical reviews and research into causes.

Maintenance logs are important for reasons of accountability, for planning of alternative investments, and for repetitive planning. A maintenance log consists of a usage log for the pieces of equipment and functional locations, a notification log, confirmation documentation, and a measure log for completed orders, including the resources used. This makes it possible to carry out a differentiated analysis that is object-specific, function-based or measure-based. Transparency in terms of the resources required by plant maintenance, as well as assurance of their functional and timely availability, are prerequisites for smooth plant maintenance operations. Capacity requirements are determined for the different work centres based on the maintenance orders. With every confirmation for a maintenance order, the capacity requirements are adjusted accordingly. The capacity requirements are automatically updated in the system for every order change or confirmation. Capacity levelling allows flexible balancing of capacity requirements and supply in every planning phase. Manual capacity levelling can be done with a planning table. In this case, the orders already dispatched to the work centre and the work supply are displayed. The resource planner can then choose the orders/procedures that should be processed in certain time periods.

■ *Service Management*
The Service Management area is divided into service agreements, installation management and call management. Objects to be maintained are often the object of numerous contracts. The service agreements section consists of functions for the conclusion and processing of service contracts, their billing and cancellation, and for the control of subsequent activities, as well as functions for warranty processing. Warranties can refer to the equipment as a whole or to individual maintenance assemblies. A master warranty type describes what the warranty covers. In the broadest sense, installation management deals with pieces of equipment and functional locations installed at the customer's site. In order to create the customer reference, you specify the data about the customer, the end customer and the operator, as well as the contact per-

son and the serial number in the master record of the functional location as well as in the equipment master record. This makes it easy to represent the exchange of equipment at the customer site using the installation/dismantling functions.

The call management section itself is divided into service notifications and service orders. Service notifications are used to record customer malfunction reports and contain the following important information: the location or equipment number, the desired repair date, the damage, and a contact person at the customer's site. The processing of a service order can be very different, depending on attenuating circumstances. Some influential factors are:

– plant maintenance in the service workshop or service at the customer site

– planning of service work or immediate execution and brief documentation for the log

– maintenance measure or repair

– quotation phase or maintenance measure that is not directly preceded by sales activities

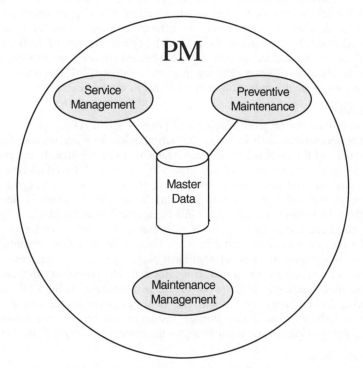

Fig. 2.11: Plant Maintenance (PM) application module

f) Project System

You can represent and manage projects with the Project System (PS) module. The system delves into the specific characteristics of projects in this case. Projects are customarily complex, unique, active for a limited time, and cost- or resource-intensive. They are subject to precise objectives between the ordering party and the contractor, with defined quality requirements, and they are usually of strategic importance (cf. SAP – Project System 1994).

Projects are most often linked to the operational process flow. A project-specific form of organization is necessary to implement them, which should be located somewhere between the affected departments. To be able to plan, monitor and control a project, the project goals and products must be precisely formulated and structured. In the Project System, the work breakdown structure and the network make this structure visible; they can be used in combination or alone. Data integration with other modules allows a project to be planned, executed and settled across applications. Examples of projects include the creation of a turn-key installation, the development of innovative products, and the conversion of production to a new type of technology.

Organizational planning determines the structures for the organization and control of the project and divides the project into individual, hierarchically aligned structural elements. The criteria for dividing the project may be different and depend on the type and complexity of the project, for example on the responsibility and structure of the departments or teams involved, or on production- and assembly-related connections. Process flow planning places the elements of setup planning in a time sequence. This determines, for example, which activities are dependent on each other and to what extent.

- *Master Data*
  Master data includes project-spanning and project-neutral setting of resources or repetitive project structures. It serves as the starting point for a precise description of the project goal and the resulting project achievements to be fulfilled. In the project definition, this goal is formulated within a mandatory framework for all objects, for example start date and end date, responsible person, etc. Links are also forged to other applications at this point. Afterwards, the work breakdown structure is developed. It places the achievements to be fulfilled in a hierarchical model with a user-specific degree of detail and forms the basis for organization and coordination. Labour, time and cost of a project are demonstrated in work breakdown structure elements (PSP elements) as an operational basis for additional planning steps. On this basis, costs and deadlines are determined, and a budget is allocated. The procedures in a network represent additional detailing of the work breakdown structure, as the PSP elements are assigned to it in an integrated fashion. The network determines the task sequence and time span. Labour, capacities, materials, resources and services are related to each other through procedures and relationships – the essential elements of the network.

- *Project Planning*
  Being able to meet the deadlines and cost targets for a project depends primarily on project planning. In general or detailed planning, all of the planning activities are recorded before the start of the project, although flexible modification is possible at any

time during the project. The project planning board serves as a graphic tool (it is based on the so-called Gantt chart); it allows manageable maintenance of project elements such as networks, procedures, etc. One of these project elements is cost projection, which is an important element for project planning. It serves as a basis for costing, budget allocation, and monitoring of cost deviations. In this case, as well, different levels of detail are supported in planning forms, for example cost-element-independent structure planning or unit costing. Likewise, any revenues that the project might realize due to sales of valuated materials and services can be anticipated in planning. Precise scheduling, which can be set manually or can be automatically derived from the network, takes care of the time aspect. By scheduling start and end dates for individual network elements, you can determine float and the critical path. Financial budgeting describes the planned expenditure of mid-term and long-term funds for each PSP element. Additional planning elements involve capacities (supply and demand) and materials and services (usage or manufacturing).

■ *Project Budgeting*
Project Budgeting is the predefined cost framework of a project within a particular time period. In contrast to cost planning, a budget is binding. While in the planning phase the costs must be estimated as exactly as possible, in the approval phase, the funds are allocated in the form of the budget. The budget can be either manually created or copied from Cost Planning. After planning is complete, the budget is released by a decision-making body and monitored over the life of the project. A purchase order that exceeds the budget, for example, triggers an automatic message to the responsible employee. The project leader can distribute the funds decentrally to the individual PSP elements, according to either the top-down or the bottom-up principle. You can update the budget to reflect unforeseen events, additional necessary measures, or increases in price by executing supplements, returns or transfer postings in the system. The user's budget management efforts are supported by an approval history, which logs the budget creation and update processes.

■ *Project Execution*
After a project has been released, the execution phase begins, in which a majority of the tasks to be executed are triggered from and confirmed within the project. This is done principally by other components (for example, purchase orders in Purchasing, material reservations in Inventory Management) and allocated to the project through a corresponding account assignment to a PSP element or an activity. Confirmations document the processing state of activities and activity elements in the network and can provide a prognosis for the continued process flow of the execution. During the execution, the exact current status is also determined and stored in the project for additional planning. In the end, this serves as an important control instrument for early recognition of trends. Actual values affect schedules, costs and revenues, finances, material and capacities. So, for example, in Material Requirements Planning, procurement can be automatically triggered when there is a need. Likewise, it is possible in Capacity Leveling to balance capacity underutilization and capacity overloads at work centres. After the project has been finished, the costs incurred are settled, with all project-related data being collected and evaluated in an accrual.

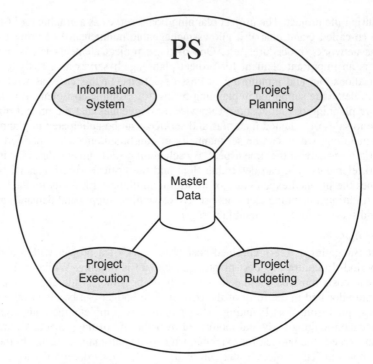

Fig. 2.12: Project System (PS) application module

■ *Information System*
The Information System is used for project analysis. The large amount of data that results from a project must be prepared in a current, transparent and comprehensive
fashion for the different information needs of those involved. Thus information can be
queried concerning the project status – the current status of the project in view of various influential factors – and the progress of the project. The Information System delivers data for determining factors such as the budget, costs and revenues, resources,
deadlines, etc., in various levels of detail. It allows the user to compare project or plan
versions and to analyze projects in a more compact form. These functions are supported by graphical analysis capabilities (for example, Gantt charts, portfolio graphics
etc.). The Cost Information System, for example, makes available hierarchical structures for multidimensional analysis of the budget, planned and actual values, and cost
element reports. The *Structure/Deadlines* Information System deals mostly with aspects of technical Controlling such as delay monitoring and work control. Using key
figures for qualifiable aspects of the project makes it possible to assess technical or
business performance quickly. On the other hand, the last item to be mentioned here,
progress analysis, does not look at the determining factors alone, but relates them to
actual performance.

2.2.3 Human Resources Management

The *Human Resources Management (HR)* area is divided into the areas of *Personnel Planning and Development (HR-PD)* and *Personnel Administration and Payroll Accounting (HR-PA)*. Personnel Planning and Development supports the strategic use of personnel by providing functionality that makes it possible for an enterprise to manage personnel systematically and qualitatively. Personnel Administration and Payroll Accounting combines all of the administrative and operational tasks of human resources management (cf. SAP – Human Resources Management 1995; cf. Seeger/Würth 1996, pp. 41–44).

■ *Organizational Management*
  Organizational Management describes the definition of the enterprise's organizational plan and the execution of personnel cost planning. An organizational plan contains an organizational structure (for example, matrix organization) in which the relationships between organizational units (for example, departments) are determined. General areas of activity in an enterprise can be described with jobs (for example, development leader). Positions, that is, individual, potential employees in the enterprise, can then be derived from these jobs (for example, development leader of the Personnel Administration area). A position can be specified by tasks and the work centre. The tasks describe the activities combined in the position, and the work centre describes the location where the activities are carried out. Personnel Cost Planning makes it possible to estimate the personnel costs that will be incurred in a certain period of time. Depending on the planning purpose and planning specifics, the basis for cost planning can be employees' planned pay, basic pay and/or concrete payroll accounting calculations. Varying the different input values (for example, pay scales, taxes) allows you to simulate different cost planning scenarios.

■ *Personnel Development*
  Personnel Development is used to reconcile the development goals of the enterprise and those of the employee. You can manage the employee's development in the enterprise using Career and Succession Planning. Personnel Development is based on career models, which demonstrate the different general career paths in an enterprise. An individual career plan is created by reconciling the employee's qualification profile with the requirement profiles of the positions in the chosen career model. You can also determine the further education and training measures necessary for the employee for that career model. It is also possible to determine appropriate successors for a particular position using a profile comparison.

■ *Workforce Planning*
  Workforce Planning deals with determining and scheduling the employees needed by an enterprise or a department to be able to carry out planned activities optimally. Work Schedule and Shift Planning enables person-related workforce planning for complete organizational units. You can schedule needed personnel capacity on the basis of days, taking into account work-related requirements and employee qualifications. As part of order-related workforce planning, employees can be assigned to so-called personnel orders depending on qualification and work load. A planning table provides an overview of employees' work loads and the load on work centres.

■ *Training and Event Management*

This component allows you to plan, prepare, execute and follow up on internal and external business events, such as training and continued education events, seminars, conventions and conferences. As part of this planning, you can define business event types, group them together, and combine them into a training programme using event contents, qualification prerequisites, and the kinds of resources needed (for example, types of rooms, types of instructors). Planning a specific business event consists of assigning the appropriate resources, scheduling, and setting prices. The result of this planning is a detailed business event catalogue. Putting on the event includes first and foremost managing the attendees, that is, prebooking, booking, rebooking, and cancelling participants for particular business events, as well as handling the resulting correspondence. Following up on a business event includes business event appraisal, assignment of the qualification earned to employees, and creation of the invoice and the confirmation of attendance for external attendees.

■ *Recruitment*

With this component, you can carry out the entire recruitment process, from creating open positions to filling them. The starting point for recruitment is a vacancy that affects a position to be filled and thus represents a workforce requirement. This workforce requirement can be met either internally or externally. In the case of external recruitment, the vacancy is announced in a job advertisement using various recruitment instruments (for example, the newspaper). Applications that are received may be related to a vacancy or may be spontaneous. Every application is automatically examined to see if the applicant has applied before or has previously worked for the enterprise. The applicant selection process occurs in two steps. In the first step, the general suitability of the applicant for the enterprise is checked. The applicant can be either rejected or assigned to various vacancies. In the second step, the suitability of the applicant for a specific vacancy is checked. Assignment to a vacancy can be supported by a comparison of the application's qualifications with the requirements profiles defined for a position in Human Resources Management. The current status of the application at any point in time is managed by the applicant status (for example, put on hold, rejected). The application process goes through a series of predefined applicant events (for example, entry of basic data, rejection of applicant). Different applicant actions (for example, sending a notice of receipt, invitation for an interview) can be triggered automatically, depending on the applicant status reached through the applicant event. Once the applicant has been hired, all of the relevant data can be copied directly into Personnel Administration.

■ *Time Management*

This component allows you to plan and calculate employee-specific personnel times and their book value, based on attendance and absence information. Time Management includes recording and analysis of all employee-related work time data and its preparation for Payroll Accounting. Work times and break times are represented with the help of a hierarchically structured work schedule. In a period work schedule (for example, Mon–Fri: early shift, Sat–Sun: off), a sequence of daily work schedules is determined for a particular period of time, independent of the calendar. These work schedules define the daily working times (for example, 5 a.m. – 2 p.m. (early shift)). Assigning a period work schedule to a calendar month results in an actual work schedule for that month. Assigning employee groups to work schedules determines the employees' planned working time. There are two ways to record time. In negative time recording, only the deviations from the prescribed work plan are recorded (for example, vacation, overtime, substitution). In positive time recording, all instances of attendance of the employees are recorded, as well, which makes time recording more flexible and more exact. In this case, however, in contrast to negative time recording, the recording of time data is not manual, but is carried out with linked external, automatic time recording systems or by transfer of data from plant data collection. The employees' recorded attendance and absence times are settled as part of time evaluation, although time evaluation is mandatory only for positive time recording. The results of time evaluation form the basis for subsequent payroll accounting.

■ *Incentive Wages*
The Incentive Wages component is used to record and analyze data for payment of piecework wages, premium wages and time wages. All types of wages in which the monthly wage is calculated on the basis of predefined performance parameters are called incentive wages. In the case of time wages, the actual work time worked is valuated using an appropriate hourly wage. In the case of piecework wages, the finished quantity of a product serves as the basis for wage calculation. Premium wages are characterized by the fact that, in addition to the quantity produced, other performance parameters can be taken into account with a premium formula. Incentive wages can be divided into individual incentive wages, in which the employee is paid only for his individual performance, and group incentive wages, in which an employee's pay depends on the performance of the group as a whole. Different time ticket types are available for recording incentive wage data, depending on the incentive wage type (for example, time wage tickets, premium wage tickets). The result of a wage ticket, the labour utilization rate (planned time/actual time) or the premium, is calculated from the planned data and the confirmed actual data. In addition to manual recording of the data, copying from confirmed orders in Production Planning and Control (PP) and automatic time ticket generation from Plant Data Collection (PDC) are also possible. Settlement of incentive wages is integrated with Payroll Accounting.

■ *Payroll Accounting*
Payroll Accounting is used to calculate employees' pay, taking into account national differences and determining factors of different countries. These include, for example, taxes, social security and retirement funds. Payroll Accounting describes the calculation of pay for the work performed by employees in an enterprise and consists of the following steps: salary structure definition, gross payroll accounting, net payroll accounting, and subsequent activities. Calculation of gross pay is based on the employee's payments, which are made up of basic pay, recurring payments and deductions, supplementary payments, and the working time data derived in Time Management. Basic pay means the fixed portion of earnings that is defined using wage types. An employee's basic pay can be changed by a pay scale reclassification, i.e. assignment of the employee to another pay scale group or pay scale level. Recurring payments and deductions are called additional, periodic portions of earnings (for example, Christmas bonus). Supplementary payments are one-time sums (for example, company anniversary payments). After gross pay is calculated, under certain conditions (for example, entering/leaving during the payroll period), a proportional reduction (monthly

factoring) is undertaken. Afterwards, various gross values are combined into assessment bases. Based on these assessment bases, tax and social security deductions, as well as other net deductions (for example, company insurance, garnishment), are made as part of net payroll accounting. The result of net payroll accounting is the net pay that is transferred to the employee's bank. Additional subsequent activities are required after execution of payroll accounting. These include, for example, preparation of statements regarding contributions paid for social security and employment tax notification.

■ *Travel Expenses*
The Travel Expenses component provides complete handling of the business aspects of a business trip, from the travel request and its approval, to the posting of travel expenses. When processing travel expenses, you can distinguish between trip data entry with a request and trip data entry after a completed trip. In the first of these variants, the employee submits a travel request, which must be approved by the responsible division. In connection with the creation of this travel request, it is possible also to submit a request for an advance, which can be paid directly. After the trip has been completed, the travel request and the additional travel data are updated. The approved trip is then forwarded to travel expense accounting. In the second variant, no trip data is entered, processed or approved until after the trip has been completed. Trip data can be divided into basic data (for example, trip destination, account assignment) and additional data (for example, receipts, stopovers). In travel expense accounting, the costs incurred can be settled on a per diem basis or on the basis of individual receipts. Travel expenses can be divided either across trips according to a general scheme, or on a trip-specific basis (overall trip, per stopover or per receipt), with account assignment being possible to cost centres, orders or projects. In the process, travel expense accounting takes into consideration country-specific individualities. The travel expenses calculated can be paid to the employee various ways (for example, through payroll accounting or through a payment program in Financial Accounting).

Fig. 2.13: Human Resources Management (HR) application module

2.3   Other R/3 services

In addition to the business application modules for support of the various task areas in an enterprise, SAP AG offers a number of other services. Some of these are software solutions that are tailored to particular branches of industry, others are various techniques for supporting different requirements. These include, for example, word processing, an archiving system, internal and external communication services (electronic mail within the system, and Electronic Data Exchange and links to the Internet outside the system). Furthermore, it is possible to navigate from a transaction to desired information in the R/3 System using various *online help tools*. SAP AG's *Workflow Management Concept* supports active linking of the transactions implemented in the R/3 System. For example, in order processing, this can be used to automatically create an order confirmation or invoice and send it using EDI. For smooth processing of day-to-day business, you can use the *Computer Centre Management System (CCMS)*, which monitors and controls the basis system. Using this system, for example, you can analyze at any moment if the data sets will lead to an overflow of the database if the business volume remains constant.

The *ABAP/4 Development Workbench* is the programming environment of the R/3 System and can be used as a separate product by the customer for developing custom software and carrying out modifications. The ABAP/4 Development Workbench supports the software development cycle with programming in the 4GL language ABAP/4, data access, network communication, and implementation of graphical user interfaces. As a supplement to the

ABAP/4 Development Workbench, you can undertake customized expansions of prede-fined interfaces, called Customer Exits, in the standard application (cf. Buck-Emden/Galimow 1996, pp. 157–190; cf. Matzke 1996; cf. SAP – ABAP/4 Development Workbench 1995).

Rounding out these SAP services is *Service & Support*, which offers world-wide, around-the-clock support for customers.

■ *Industry-specific application solutions*
For certain business areas, SAP has developed industry solutions that are based on the standard R/3 applications (cf. Buck-Emden/Galimow 1996, p. 205). These application solutions provide enterprises in that line of business with all of the advantages of a standard system (cf. SAP – Hospital System 1996; cf. SAP – Industry Solution for Banking IS-B 1995). The following *Industrial Solutions (IS)* are currently available or are in development:

– budgeting and financial planning for the public sector (IS-PS)

– hospital administration, with patient management and accounting as well as hospi-tal controlling (IS-H)

– subscription management and advertising management for publishers of newspa-pers and periodicals (IS-P)

– financial assets management for insurance and financial service organizations (IS-IS)

– industry solution for banks, with risk management, statutory reporting, and con-trolling (IS-B)

– industry solution for the oil industry for exploration, transport and distribution (IS-Oil)

– production planning and control for the process industry (PP-PI)

– merchandise management systems for retail, with article structures, distribution lo-gistics and point-of-sale systems (IS-RT)

– industry solution for utilities, with device management, house installation, proc-essing of meter reading data and accounting (IS-U)

The contents of these industry solutions will be demonstrated briefly here using the example of IS-B for banking, with risk management. In addition to the branch-of-industry-neutral components of the R/3 System, SAP offers additional solutions for the areas of controlling, risk management and external statutory reporting for the banking area. These solutions include other subcomponents such as interest rate risk, currency risk and other price risks, for example in the area of risk management. IS-B takes into consideration the growing importance of risk management, for example by making available additional information in the form of risk determination and valuation. These not only serve internal management as a basis for decision making, but they are also needed for statutory reporting, in order to meet legal requirements with respect to gov-ernment agencies. Due to the modular structure of the application, any bank can build on the industry solution and expand it to suit its own areas of concentration.

■ *Help tools in an R/3 transaction*

The R/3 System supports the user in a transaction with comprehensive help tools. The goal of online help is to make it easier for the user to use the system and to replace paper documentation. The system contains complete, function-related documentation, which is also available on CD-ROM. The R/3 System's online help is context-sensitive and is generally used from within a transaction, meaning that help text can be displayed from any screen. Three basic methods for use are supported:

– *F1* function key

– *F4* function key

– *Help* menu

F1 provides notes for fields or settings that are requested during input entry for a transaction and on which the cursor has been positioned with the mouse or the keyboard. F4 input help supports the user in the selection of an entry by displaying the possible values or information for an input field. Value documentation can take on different forms. For example, in the case of a small value range, the input possibilities may be displayed directly at the input field with a list field. If the number of choices is too large, the user can restrict the value range using a matchcode query (for example, restricting the values proposed for a customer number by using the name, street address, etc.). Using the *Help* item in the menu bar accesses the following kinds of information:

– *Expanded Help* describes application-related topic areas (for example, production planning), where the user can display detailed information for the work area in which he is currently working.

– The *R/3 Library* contains the complete contents of the documentation. Topic organization is intuitive.

– The *Glossary* serves as a reference tool for looking up business terms and SAP terminology.

– *Release Infos* provide information about functions and expansions that are new in a release.

– *Intro to R/3* supports users of the documentation CD with their first steps and, in addition to describing the individual areas of the R/3 System, displays notes for starting the system.

– *Help on Help* explains the various help tools available in the R/3 System.

Furthermore, the R/3 online help contains a hypertext system in which text modules are linked to one another through references or the glossary, and in which tools simplify the search for desired information. The navigation possibilities will be described briefly here on the basis of three examples.

1. navigation example

You can retrieve selection lists during data entry by using the F4 function key, or by clicking on the arrow icon to the right of a field. Some selection lists represent a Customizing check table, i.e. in this case you can only use the possible values presented in the list (for example, order types for a sales document or material group for materials). In the example shown, the selection list can be restricted with a matchcode and used to make a selection. If, for example, an employee wants to enter or change data for a material but does not know the material number, he or she can click on the arrow to the right of the material field or press the F4 key. A screen for performing a matchcode search then appears, offering various possibilities for restricting the range of values. In the example, the arrow to the right of the material group field has been activated, and a selection list with the existing material groups – for example, food, pharmaceuticals, metal – appears. Selecting the material group metal and clicking on the check mark on the bottom left causes the materials for the material group metal to appear.

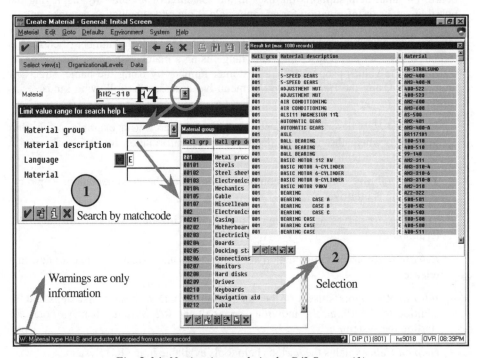

Fig. 2.14: Navigation tools in the R/3 System (1)

2. navigation example

If the user does not understand something during data entry, for example, if he wants to know what an MRP type is, he can use the F1 key (Help) to display a descriptive text for that item. If that is not sufficient for the user, he can navigate into the R/3 online documentation using the *Expanded Help* button. A link stored in the R/3 System then takes the reader exactly to the appropriate spot, in this case to the chapter on creating material master records.

Furthermore, every R/3 screen includes status information on the bottommost line, which displays warnings or error messages for the situation at hand. In the screen that follows, an example is displayed that includes a warning *W*, which tells the user important information about the transaction. The user can skip the warning by pressing Enter. If the system generates an error message, which is marked with an *E*, the user is stopped until he makes corrections. If the information displayed does not adequately explain the problem, the user can double click on the status bar to receive a more detailed description with a diagnosis. From this popup menu, he can, in turn, jump into the online documentation by clicking on the *Expanded Help* button. In addition, clicking on the *Technical Info* button causes technical information like the name of the main program to be displayed. Using the main menu name, you can look at the corresponding source code in the ABAP/4 Development Workbench and analyze it with the debugger. This troubleshooting is meant for identifying basic errors in the ABAP/4 source code later.

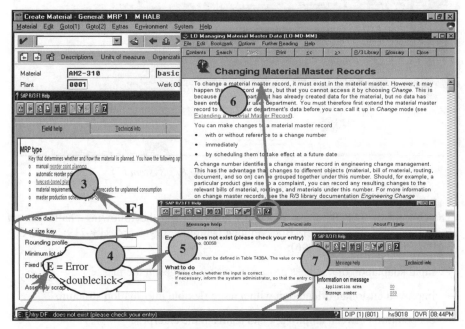

Fig. 2.15: Navigation tools in the R/3 System (2)

3. navigation example

You can call up the complete R/3 documentation about the individual application modules using the menu path *Help→Expanded Help*. You can read and print out the business descriptions by clicking on the individual areas.

The example shows the navigation from Materials Management to the Purchasing area. From there, the text *Create purchase order* has been displayed, which contains detailed descriptions for use. In addition, you can find the individual definitions for SAP terms in the Help menu in the form of a glossary list. To ensure that each release can be updated, SAP has stored information about each release in the system. This information can be reached by clicking on the *Release Infos* item in the Help menu.

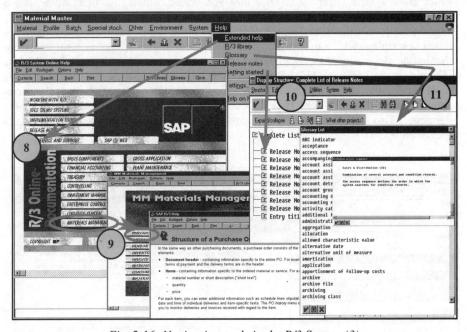

Fig. 2.16: Navigation tools in the R/3 System (3)

■ *SAP Business Workflow*

The concept of SAP Business Workflow aims to meet the following challenges (cf. Fritz 1994, pp. 277–286; cf. Buck-Emden/Galimow 1996, pp. 213–219; cf. SAP – SAP Business Workflow 1996):

– rapid adaptation of business process flows to changes in the market

– improved customer orientation with a more flexible information structure

– cooperation between employees and teams in the enterprise

– cooperation between suppliers, production, sales and customers

The Workflow Management system represents a concept for automating business processes. Using R/3 system functions, you can coordinate the work steps and the activities of the people involved in the process and link transactions freely.

The tasks of people and teams are determined and graphically represented in the Workflow Editor. Business objects and desktop object types are defined and linked to the corresponding methods, attributes and events the same way. For example, business objects (sales order, production order, material, invoice) are linked to operational process flows, to achieve integration between business transactions and objects. SAP Business Workflow supports various concepts:

– *work list management*
  Work list management is used to manage work lists, which can be assigned to employees or teams.

– *event management*
  Event management enables easily adjustable reactions to events.

– *deadline management*
  Deadline management is used to start escalation procedures automatically.

In the runtime environment, the process flow of workflow, as well as the execution of individual work steps, is monitored, for example deadline monitoring using the Work Item Manager. Characteristic data of the workflow can be displayed in an information system. Interfaces to other manufacturers are also available, so that workflows can be integrated into external applications as well using Application Programming Interfaces (APIs).

■ *Computer Centre Management System*
The Computer Centre Management System (CCMS) contains several tools that ensure the smooth operation of the SAP software in both centralized and distributed environments (cf. SAP – R/3 Software Architecture 1994; cf. Buck-Emden/Galimow 1996, pp. 142–150). These tools, known as management tools, support the following important tasks:

– software installation

– release upgrades

– system control

– system monitoring

– system optimization

– problem management

The CCMS is closely linked to the R/3 System with its business applications, to the operating system being used, and to the database management system and the network system. It guarantees uninterrupted operation of the R/3 applications. Furthermore, the graphically oriented work environment allows the system administrator to build his system management with a minimum of effort. The functions in CCMS can be divided into monitoring, control, and open interfaces.

System monitoring displays all of the relevant R/3 System performance data. With the help of performance monitoring, the alarm service and the performance database, bottlenecks in certain system resources can be recognized early and eliminated, with a monitoring environment allowing them to be displayed graphically. If, for example, threshold values for storage or CPU loads or paging rates are exceeded, alert monitors signal this audibly. Performance optimizing for the R/3 System can be introduced based on the log of all relevant performance data. System control includes control mechanisms for reliable operation of R/3. So, for example, the startups and shutdowns of systems and processes are documented in system management. CCMS also provides services for load distribution and for background processing.

■ *ABAP/4 Development Workbench*
As part of the R/3 System tools, the ABAP/4 Development Workbench basically provides the ability to develop custom software and to customize or expand function modules (cf. SAP – ABAP/4 Development Workbench 1995; cf. Buck-Emden/Galimow 1996, pp. 157–190).

The ABAP/4 programming language was developed specifically for business applications and integrated into the client/server architecture. For this reason, custom developments run on all operating systems, databases and presentation managers supported by R/3. With its expansive palette of functions, the ABAP/4 Development Workbench lightens the load of developers in routine tasks. The ABAP/4 Development Workbench contains several development tools for prototyping, testing and debugging, and these support the creation of custom components. These can be combined with the standard components in many ways in the ABAP/4 development environment. Changes in the application logic, however, are not recommended, because it can become very expensive to maintain changes to the standard software, for example during release updates. Two types of applications in particular can be implemented using ABAP/4:

– transaction applications

– database analyses (reporting)

Other important features of the ABAP/4 programming language are:

– event-oriented program development

– modularization of applications through the use of subroutines and function modules

– special language elements for business applications, for example for date calculation

– open programming interfaces based on OLE automation and Remote Function Call (RFC)

– independence from technical environments; both centralized and distributed client/server configuration

In addition to the programming possibilities in ABAP/4, the ABAP/4 Development Workbench also contains tools for modelling, for defining tables and data structures

(Data Dictionary), and for implementing graphical user interfaces (Screen Menu Painter). In the end, developers need not concern themselves with system-specific interfaces or low-level communication and distribution aspects in order to adjust applications created in the ABAP/4 Development Workbench to system types, database management systems or graphical user interfaces supported by SAP.

■ *Service & Support*
SAP R/3 Service & Support contains all of the services that make the implementation and availability of R/3 as optimal as possible for the customer. Provided are consultation, training and active information management (cf. SAP – R/3 Service & Support 1996). These services are also offered by certified partners of SAP AG, for example certified partners and system resellers.

Because it is a world-wide organization, the customer can begin by accessing local services, before queries are forwarded internationally to headquarters. Support consists of all services that are automatically specified in the licensing agreement with the purchase of an R/3 licence. These include all of the aspects of maintenance: software maintenance, help in case of malfunctions, and access to the Online Service System (OSS). Beyond the services purchased with a licence, additional services are offered that support the handling of the R/3 System and intensify its use. The specific services, such as workshops or check-and-monitoring services, are coordinated with the R/3 project phases and with each other, each service being usable at a different level of intensity.

Another aspect of R/3 Service & Support involves information management. Information for customers and partners is available in different media and can be queried in various levels of detail through customer identification. The quality of service is checked with certificates that are awarded to employees and partners. Based on customer requirements, the current standard is regularly checked, to preserve and improve the level of quality in consulting. Furthermore, practical experience from customer projects also flow into the Service & Support areas. Services that meet the customers' needs and are flexible are another aspect of SAP Service & Support, with the degree of service being tailored to the customer.

3 Enterprise Modelling

Enterprises can be thought of as open systems whose elements have numerous relationships both with each other and with the environment. „A system is a totality of elements, separate from the environment, that are linked to each other by relationships" (Schulte-Zurhausen 1995, p. 28). They are furthermore characterized by the fact that the elements exchange information while executing tasks. As part of the increasing penetration of DP, more and more enterprises are performing tasks and exchanging information with the help of computers. The computer-supported information system is thus an important part of the operational information system (cf. Grochla 1978, pp. 203–218; cf. Kieser/Kubicek 1978 II, pp. 77–104; cf. Ulrich 1989, pp. 19–26). The concurrent consideration of business and information technology aspects results in the fact that, within the planning and implementation of computer-supported, operational information systems, a complex task must be mastered over a longer period of time.

The real business world is characterized by complex problems and heterogeneity where terminology is concerned. Information technology, on the other hand, deals with clearly structured facts that must be uniquely and incontrovertibly defined. Programming languages were developed for this, but due to their special syntax, they are unsuitable for describing business facts. On the other hand, the DP systems that have been developed are supposed to support the user in the handling of tasks. So it must be possible to conceive of a tool that organization planners, DP planners and users can use to communicate and carry on discussions with each other. To overcome the discrepancy between the business world and the DP world, we turn to modelling. In modelling, we can increase transparency by abstracting to the most important components and relationships. Information content and comprehensibility should be equally important in modelling.

3.1 Models

Models are simplified representations of reality (cf. Eichhorn 1979, pp. 60–104). A distinction can be made between reality as it exists now and the future reality that is the target. Likewise, the aspects of isomorphism (structure is the same) and homomorphism (structure is similar) must be heeded in the building of models. In the case of models with the same structure, every object in the model world is uniquely assigned to an object in the real world, and the model that results displays the same complexity as the real world. In models with similar structures, every element and every relationship of a model is uniquely assigned to one element or one relationship in the real world, but not vice versa (cf. Schroeder 1990, pp. 425–432). People have always constructed models in the form of plans or sketches before realizing them. Over a thousand years ago, construction, for example the building of the pyramids, was first produced as small models. Today, people work with models in many disciplines. Architecture, shipbuilding, mechanical engineering, plant engineering and construction, and the automobile industry are all examples of this. While in these areas it is generally a rule that you do not proceed without first conceiving a construction plan or a model (engineering drawing, bill of materials, task list), in software development, the use of such models as a basis for the description of software is limited. Often, the solutions implemented in the code are described verbally, which in the case of software with over one hundred thousand lines of code can quickly lead to the problem of information overload.

These days, software systems are tasked with supporting integrated business processes in enterprises. This does not mean, however, that all of an enterprise's functions must automatically be performed by software. Enterprises are structured differently, depending on their branch of industry, their market segment, their size, their legal form, their organizational philosophy (autocratic or democratic, flat or vertical hierarchy), etc., and they must carry out different types of business processes.

This raises the question of what the real reference world actually is for business process models of standard software systems.

- Is it the real, existing software system with its scope and number of functions, which results in a multitude of processes?

- Is it the abundance of knowledge in business management science on the topic of business processes?

- Is it the business processes practised in a single enterprise or in a branch of industry? (cf. Keller/Schröder 1996, pp. 77–88)

Regardless of the theoretical answer to this question, it is possible to determine that modelling has the following goals:

- Models should make the elements and their relationships within a system transparent.

- Models should explain how a system functions.

- Models should support communication through consistent formalization.

One model that deals with the description of tasks that can be supported by data processing is the Kölner Integration Model (KIM), which was developed in the 1970s by Grochla and his coworkers (cf. Grochla *et al.* 1974). The goal was to reduce integration problems that arose in connection with data processing by using a descriptive model, which makes the factual links between different enterprise tasks visible. The main aspects of this model are the description and graphical depiction of the most important information processing tasks, as well as the data that goes into a task and the data that is created (input/output analysis or analysis of the information flow). To reduce complexity, the whole model is divided into planning tasks, implementation tasks and control tasks, and a task description list, a channel description list and a connector description list are presented for each of these submodels. The task description list is a directory of the tasks contained in the model and their contents. The relationship between the tasks presented and the relationship between a task and its inbound and outbound data contents are represented in graphical form as follows.

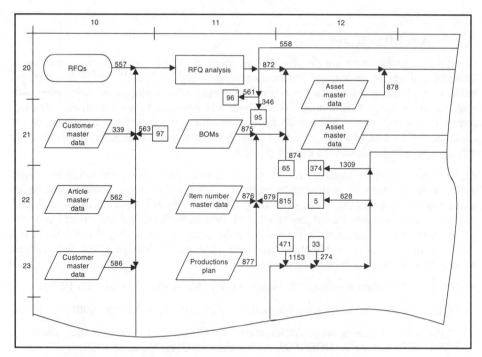

Fig. 3.1: Factual links in the Kölner Integration Model
(source: Grochla et al. 1974, insert 3)

So as not to increase the size of this quite complex model, connectors were conferred on the individual tasks that could be supported by DP. These are symbolized by squares (internal connectors) or circles (external connectors). The connectors represent tasks that are contained in a different submodel. In this way, they represent the links between the various submodels.

In all, the model consists of 332 individual tasks and about 1500 channels. The development and description of the model at the factual level make executing it interesting to this day for describing enterprise tasks that can be supported by DP, and their relationships.

Due to the notation, however, the relationships are not always clear in the representation. In particular, task flow in the sense of control flows is not represented. Cross-function relationships, however, can be made clear precisely through the information and task flow. In order to illustrate cross-function relationships, therefore, the information and task flow must be explicitly identified. In addition to integrating enterprise tasks, cross-function relationships should also be included when integrating DP systems.

3.2   Architectures

Questions of architecture are discussed from many diverse points of view in relation to planning and implementation of information systems. In 1972, SAP started developing a business application system. In the beginning, emphasis was placed on developing software for accounting. This solution, R/2, which was developed on a mainframe architecture, was expanded in the 1980s with applications for human resources management and logistics. At the end of the 80s, SAP began development on a three-layer client/server architecture, which reached the market in 1993.

At the same time as the suitable *architecture for application systems* was being discussed, in the 1980s, another discussion began regarding *model architectures*. Various approaches claim that they support the entire software product life cycle. In relation to this, a multitude of *procedure models* were described, and discussion flourished over which *descriptive elements* were necessary for representing the complete life cycle. What follows is a series of approaches to architecture that were published in the past few years, listed roughly in order of their historical emergence:

- IRDS – Information Resource Dictionary System (cf. ANSI 1989; cf. ISO 1990)

- IEM – Information Engineering Method (cf. Martin 1989; cf. Martin 1990)

- CIM-OSA – Open System Architecture for CIM (cf. Jorysz/Vernadat 1990; cf. ESPRIT Consortium AMICE 1993; cf. Kosanke 1993; cf. Kosanke 1996)

- AD/Cycle – Application Development Cycle (Mercurio *et al.* 1990; cf. Corzilius 1992)

- SOM – Semantic Object Model (cf. Ferstl/Sinz 1990; cf. Ferstl/Sinz 1993)

- KADS – Knowledge Acquisition and Documentation Structuring (cf. Hickman *et al.* 1990; cf. Keller 1993)

- ISM – Information Systems Methodology (cf. Olle *et al.* 1991)

- ESF – Eureka Software Factory (cf. Fernström 1991)

- ASEM – ATMOSPHERE System Engineering Model (cf. Obbink 1991)

- ARIS – Architecture for Integrated Information Systems (cf. Scheer 1991)

- CC RIM – Reference Model (cf. Gutzwiller 1994)

- BOS – Engineering Method (cf. Barengo *et al.* 1994)

- OOIE – Object-Oriented Information Engineering (cf. Martin/Odell 1995; cf. Martin/Odell 1996)

- PERA – Purdue Enterprise Reference Architecture (cf. Williams 1996)

- GERAM – Generic Enterprise Reference Architecture and Methodology (cf. Bernus/Nemes 1996)

Aside from their differences in terms of objectives, the approaches have a similar way of identifying and defining descriptive elements (representation tools or methods) and their relationships to each other, which are necessary for characterizing application systems. At the beginning of the 1990s, the discussion intensified with the introduction of the topic of Business Reengineering, and the point of view was expanded to include the entire enterprise, where process-related and organizational questions are particularly important. An *architecture* thus describes different levels, starting with an (operational or business) situation and ending with an executable information system. Using a set of rules, it defines the relationships between the levels, as well as the relationships between the elements within a level. In science, this set of rules is often called a meta model.

Today, a multitude of architectures exist in theory, but none of the model architectures has managed to become a standard in the real world. Likewise, the different architectures contain different descriptive languages for representing operational and informational content. As a result, a user can choose between different forms of representation. This degree of freedom leads to problems when business content is represented different ways to a user who is choosing an application system.

3.2.1 Computer Integrated Manufacturing – Open System Architecture

In the ESPRIT (European Strategic Programme for Research and Development in Information Technology) programme, the project *Computer Integrated Manufacturing – Open System Architecture (CIM-OSA)* was supported, with the goal of developing a reference model for CIM systems. Building on an open system architecture, this reference model allows you to support all of the phases of a CIM installation, from first draft to implementation, with a methodical procedure. The CIM architecture meets the following requirements (cf. Stotko 1989, pp. 9–15; cf. Macconaill 1990, pp. 140–143; cf. Panse 1990, pp. 157–164; cf. Vernadat 1992, pp. 189–204; cf. Kosanke 1993, pp. 113–141):

- covers the requirements of the manufacturing industry, regardless of branch, type of manufacturing, or size

- adaptable to changes in the environment and in production processes

- flexible organization with regard to structure and process flow in the entire enterprise

- realtime control of work routines

- optimal use of information technologies

- develops a reference framework for terminology, architectures and standardization plans

The project work of CIM-OSA includes the following two areas of concentration. One of the emphases is on enterprise modelling, which in its final form can be used to control and monitor daily business processes and to derive a planned concept from a given actual status. The second point of emphasis is on the establishment and storage of an integrated infrastructure, which is used to create the conditions under which the enterprise model created according to CIM-OSA rules can be used to control and monitor daily business needs. In enterprise modelling, a distinction is drawn between the three complementary levels, which represent different views of the object to be described, i.e. an enterprise:

■ *Architecture level*
This is divided into a generic level that is valid for all types of enterprises, a partial level that is valid for branches of industry or a group of similar enterprises, and an enterprise-specific (individual) level.

■ *Modelling level*
CIM-OSA uses a top-down approach. At the top level, the enterprise is described from a function point of view. At this level, the requirements are set in a generally understandable language. A technically oriented language in the intermediate layer adapts the requirements of the top layer to the interests of data processing and conveys them to a DP implementation model (third layer).

■ *View level*
In the CIM-OSA philosophy, a CIM system can be adequately described using the four different, complementary views of function, information, resources and organization. The tasks and subtasks of an enterprise are structured and described in the function view. Every enterprise function is described by the structure, by a function description, and, if the enterprise function is broken down into other enterprise functions, by a process flow. SADT-like representations (cf. Chapter 3.3) are specified to represent the *business processes* and the *enterprise activities*. In the information layer, all of the information objects are characterized. These can be CIM activities, data, monitoring information, resources or physical objects. These, too, are subdivided into other information elements if necessary. The information objects are described using the symbols of the ERM technique (cf. Chapter 3.3) and additional constructs. The resource layer is used to view, check and optimize all of the resources, such as employees and material, needed to complete a task from the function layer. Competencies are described in the organization layer. That is where it is determined who has access to the individual elements and who can change them. No descriptive elements are specified for these two views (cf. Jorysz/Vernadat 1990, pp. 144–167).

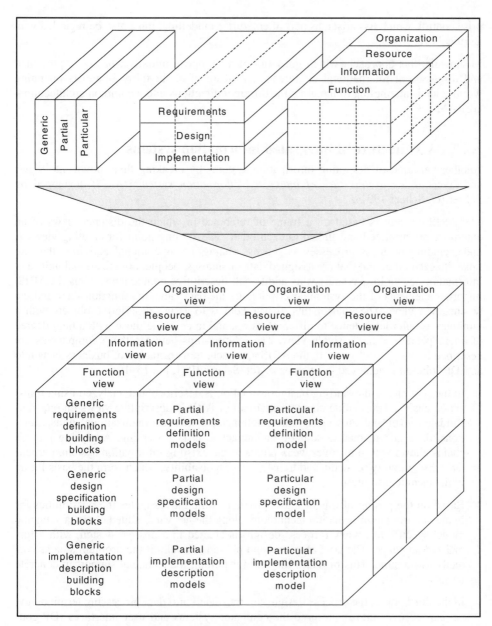

Fig. 3.2: The CIM-OSA framework (source: Panse 1990, p. 161)

If one takes a look at the demands of the CIM-OSA project, it is the measures for standardization and the establishment of a structure for systematic planning of CIM components in the enterprise, which go beyond technical aspects, that stand out as positive. Previous publications, however, have not yet shown consistency between the different views. The demand for planning and implementation of enterprises all the way down to enter-

115

prise control, which has arisen as part of enterprise modelling, must also be regarded with a critical eye.

Meanwhile, this approach, which grew out of a European initiative, has been presented and discussed at international conferences. A team of about thirty scientists operating world-wide is attempting to integrate the different directions into a common architecture – GERAM.

3.2.2 Architecture of integrated information systems

Another variation of designing information systems by breaking them down into views and layers is the *architecture of integrated information systems (ARIS)* developed by Scheer (cf. Scheer 1991).

The ARIS concept is based on a frame of reference in which the disjunct views of an enterprise are arranged and linked to each other. The starting point for creating views is understanding business processes as process chains, i.e. operational activities that are linked to each other and that are assigned data or statuses, people, organizational units and information technology resources as additional, descriptive components. Thus, in ARIS, important elements of the system description are the data view, the function view and the organization view. The goal of this view model is to assign descriptive objects with a minimum of interdependence to different views, and to combine those with a high degree of interdependence into a single view. The relationships between these components are described by the control view. In the ARIS approach, transformation of business facts into an EDP solution is achieved in five phases (cf. Scheer 1991, pp. 15–19):

- In the first phase, the starting business situation is described and analyzed using transaction chains. Transaction chains contain all of ARIS's descriptive views on one consolidated level and thus clarify the relationship between organizational units, functions, data, and manual, automatic or interactive task processing. Analyzing process chains allows you to uncover weak points in the existing information system, particularly discontinuity of media and transfers of responsibility, which form the basis for an initial technical solution.

- Based on the posing of this business problem, which investigates the possibilities for implementing the information technology along the net value added chain, a semantic model specific to a view (process design) is created in a process design, with a formalized language. The goal of the second phase is to delimit the problem area as correctly as possible. This provides the link for putting the technical support in concrete terms.

- In the third phase, the process designs are translated into data processing terminology, i.e. carried over into requests to the computer systems and user interfaces (DP concept), without, however, referring to a specific tool. There is no fixed link to the process design, i.e. the DP transformation can be adapted to recent developments without having repercussions on the process design. For this reason, the goal of this level and the following levels is to optimize the EDP system.

- It is not until the technical implementation in the fourth phase that coding of requirements as physical data structures using available hardware and software components (implementation) takes place.

■ Immediately after the system is implemented, the operation and maintenance phase begins.

Because the resource view specifies the basic conditions within the four views of an information system, each of these conditions is divided into three levels that correspond to the three development phases process design, DP concept, and implementation. In this case, the idea behind the division into levels is not to conceive a sequential procedure model, but rather to characterize different descriptive levels in relation to their proximity to information-related implementation within a project process flow. The software development process is characterized instead by a prototyping method, in which the phases described above are gone through one after another in a cyclical sequence. The DP concept and implementation levels are subject to much shorter life cycles than the process design. For this reason, the ARIS method description focuses on the process design, because a longer-term business know-how is stored there. The intended goal of dividing the modelling process into views and levels is to reduce complexity.

■ *Data view*

At the process design level, the descriptive language used is based mostly on the entity relationship model according to Chen and its expansions. Entity types and relationship types are combined under the term information object. All static information objects and structural relationships are recorded in the data view. It thus contains all of the statuses and events from the process chains that can be represented by data, such as a sales order and its status. In this way, a logical database of the application area is created, which is transported in the subsequent phases into the concrete implementation of a database system.

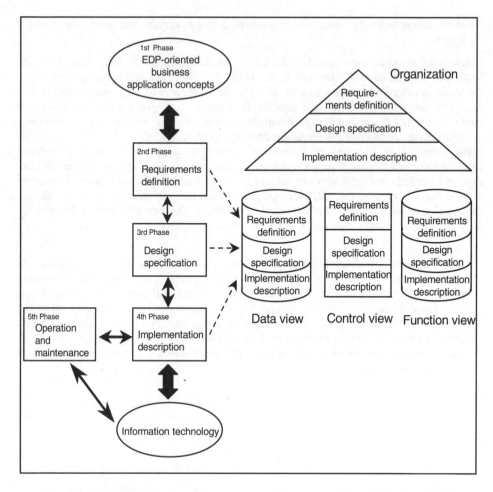

Fig. 3.3: ARIS phase and architecture concept (source: Scheer 1991, pp. 17/18)

■ *Function view*
   In this view, the information system is examined with regard to the sequence of functions and their formation of hierarchies in the form of function trees. The assumption
   is made that main functions, which support the business processes, can be broken
   down into subfunctions. So, for example, credit rating check is a part of order release.
   The function structure is static and does not provide any information about the sequence of the functions within a process. Process flows, on the other hand, can be represented in network diagrams or in very detailed structural diagrams. In addition, the
   specification of the processing form determines whether the function is executed
   automatically or interactively. At the subsequent levels, these descriptions are specified down to the program code. The function modules created this way are reusable in
   various business application areas, meaning that several function modules can belong
   to one business process and, vice versa, one function module can be used in several

business processes. The hierarchy-oriented structured analysis approach to modelling is used in this case, in addition to other possible descriptive methods (cf. Chapter 3.3).

- *Organization view*
  At the requirements level in the organization view, it is mainly user classes and organizational structures that are formed, which are linked in hierarchies or networks. A particular employee, for example, may belong to more than one production team. In the ARIS approach, the representation of the organization of an enterprise is illustrated with the help of a reporting structure, which contains organizational units, or people responsible for a task, and their links. Finally, the description of the ways users can access information system components serves at the implementation level to design the company network.

- *Control view*
  As the main component of the ARIS architecture, the control view defines a connection between the data, functions and organizational units, all of which were modelled separately. Even just the fact that functions describe the transformation or status transfer of data objects, and that these on their part receive intermediate results of processing in the shape of derivative information objects, shows that the data view and the function view cannot be created in isolation from each other. For this reason, the relationship between the partial views is recreated in this view. If a function is assigned several organizational units, this is represented in a function assignment diagram, which also specifies the processing form. The relationship between the function view and the data view is based on a control or monitoring flow along a sequence of events, which can be visualized easily, for example, in the form of *event-controlled process chains (EPC)*, which were developed by SAP AG (cf. Chapter 4). Process-flow-oriented aspects can be represented in the ARIS architecture with process chains or SADT-like representations, too. The attending data flow can be supplemented with the help of information flow diagrams; in this case, the connections between the functions show the information flow. Finally, the link between the data view and the organizational view is set in a data-level concept, which assigns the maintenance of the data to certain units at the organizational level. Scheer emphasizes that different methods can be arranged in the control view, but he does not completely specify how the consistency between the individual semantically different methods and the subdivided views can be ensured.

Over the last few years, the basic concept has been further developed for commercial purposes, and the resulting ARIS tool set (formerly known as the CIM Analyzer, the ARIS Analyzer, the ARIS Navigator and the ARIS Modeler) has been implemented in a number of projects to develop customized models and reference models, for example SAP AG's R/3 Reference Model (cf. Jost *et al.* 1991, pp. 33–64; cf. Jost 1993; cf. Nüttgens 1995, pp. 56–59; cf. Scheer 1996, pp. 71–78).

3.2.3 Semantic object model

The *semantic object model (SOM)* developed by Ferstl and Sinz is used for analysis and specification of operational information systems (cf. Ferstl/Sinz 1990, pp. 567–581). The scope of models in the SOM approach includes the performance view, the control view and the process flow view of a system of business processes. The performance view shows which operational services are being performed by business processes and which they order from each other. A control view specifies how the operational objects involved in the performance of services are being coordinated. The process flow view shows the event-controlled task execution within the objects.

The first thing that occurs in modelling is the delimitation of the enterprise from the environment. This section of reality is called the analysis area. It is in contact with particular objects in the environment through service and information relationships. Tasks are assigned to the analysis area objects, and at all levels viewed, they serve to attain the enterprise goal. As a result, the analysis area represents an open, goal-oriented system (cf. Ferstl/Sinz 1995, p. 211). The environment objects and the analysis area together form the object system, which contains the entirety of the reality to be represented and is thus the object of enterprise modelling. At the same time, the object system is broken down into subsystems on the basis of three criteria for delimitation:

■ Since a task can be performed on a physical object in the sense of an article or on an information object, a distinction is made accordingly, based on the object principle, between the basic system and the information system. All of the information relationships, such as data transfer, belong to the information system, while purely material relationships, such as flows of goods, belong to the basic system.

■ Tasks can basically be handled by people or machines. The assignment of tasks to the task-performer level therefore requires division into an automated and a nonautomated subsystem. Analysis area objects that belong equally to both subsystems are called partially automated.

■ In addition, task performance can be divided into individual sections according to the phase principle. The phases planning, control, and monitoring are assigned to the guidance system, and the performance of operational tasks is assigned to the performance system. Similar to the control cycle principle familiar from biology and electronics, the guidance system takes on the function of the controller, and the performance system takes on the role of the controlled system (cf. Ferstl/Sinz 1993, p. 5).

The automated portion of the information system in the analysis area, which can discern both the tasks of the guidance system and those of the performance system, is called the application system and is an important resource, next to people, for supporting business processes within the scope of modelling according to the SOM approach. The SOM approach distinguishes in the enterprise architecture between three model levels: enterprise plan, business process model, and application system specifications.

■ The enterprise plan describes from an external point of view the delimitation of the analysis area and determines net value added chains and success factors, in addition to strategic objectives.

■ Based on these standards, the business process level prepares solution procedures for DP-supported conversion, which belong to the internal view of the operational system.

■ At the third model level, on the basis of the second level, the automatable part of the business processes is examined in the form of a technical specification for application systems.

„This kind of overall model is an important resource for permanent, evolutionary adaptation and thus for preservation of the company's viability" (Ferstl/Sinz 1995, p. 212).

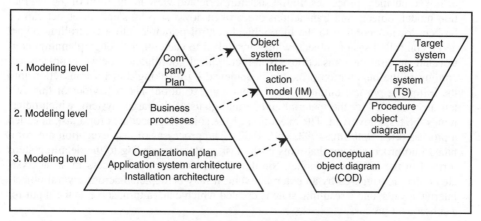

Fig. 3.4: Architecture of the semantic object model
(source: Ferstl/Sinz 1995, pp. 212/213)

These levels are integrated with the meta model (set of rules), which puts business process modelling on a common base and creates a relationship between the individual parts. A procedure for using the basic constructs, called the V Model, is described in the SOM approach (cf. Ferstl/Sinz 1991, pp. 477–491).

The method for the SOM approach represents the different levels from a behaviour- and structure-oriented point of view, according to the left and the right side. The V-shaped symbol is divided into three levels that correspond to those of the enterprise architecture. The distance between the two sides also means that the degree of modelling freedom in both points of view decreases, from top to bottom, as the application system is put in more and more concrete terms. The three levels are discussed here, with the model views of each level being created in coordination with each other.

■ At the first level, a line is drawn between the object system and the corresponding tasks in the target system. The former includes all of the structurally relevant characteristics of net value added chains from the analysis area. The target system determines the material and formal goals for this.. Material goals determine what will be done, and formal goals describe the corresponding rating criteria. A typical formal goal is cost minimization, to more closely determine the material goal of goods production. At this level, modelling is usually done in text form.

■ Based on this, at the second level, the structure is modelled from the performance view and the control view, and the process flow is modelled from the business process behaviour, and they are then refined on the basis of the hierarchical breakdown concept. The representation is illustrated in semi-formal fashion in diagrams. The permitted breakdown structures are derived using the production rules for object and transaction breakdown, so that the consistency and completeness of the model can be verified. Operational objects encapsulate structure and behaviour in the form of object-internal memory and the solution procedure for a task that is applied to it. They process performance or guidance packets, which are exchanged as an operational transaction over communication channels. Transactions are therefore the binding elements in a system of linked business processes. In the structure-oriented view in the form of the interaction model, objects and transactions are broken down step by step. An object can be broken down according to the hierarchical control principle into a controlling object and a controlled system object, which are linked to each other through planning, control and monitoring transactions. Non-hierarchical coordination between objects according to the negotiation principle is achieved by breaking down a transaction into the following phases: initiation, agreement and execution. The behaviour of this system is controlled by the material and formal goals of the target system, which determines the tasks involved. The execution of the solution procedures for a task is called a process (cf. Ferstl/Sinz 1993, pp. 54–57). The processes of task execution are combined into process-event diagrams in the task system, according to the detailing steps formed in the interaction model. Similar to Petri networks, a process in an analysis area object is triggered by an external event; it may be depicted across several object-internal events, and a resulting state is created which can, in turn, serve as the input for a subsequent process.

■ At the third level, under consideration of the information technology possibilities, the parts of the business process to be automated are outlined. The technical specification for an application system is developed from this; it consists of a conceptual object diagram and the process object diagram that builds on it. The representation of the conceptual objects is based on an object-oriented expansion of the *structured entity relationship model (SERM)* (cf. Sinz 1990, pp. 17–29; cf. Ferstl/Sinz 1993, p. 154) and includes conceptual object types from the application system and their information relationships. In the behaviour-oriented view, process object types determine the cooperation between conceptual object types during task execution.

In contrast to the sequence determined above, it is possible, for a reorganization or design of an enterprise's business processes, to take a different path, namely to begin with an actual-state analysis at the second level and then coordinate its results with the objectives of the enterprise plan. In this case, every business process is examined to see if it has reached its material goal for converting the enterprise plan.

3.2.4 Knowledge Acquisition and Documentation Structuring

The *Knowledge Acquisition and Documentation Structuring (KADS)* approach has the goal of simplifying the development of knowledge-based systems, with emphasis being placed on the modelling of the knowledge base (cf. Hickman 1989, pp. 12–56).

For enterprise modelling on a conceptual level, the first phase of the KADS approach, the construction of the conceptual model, is most important. This phase belongs at the epistemological level of knowledge representation and is the most developed within the project. It is divided into four layers that build on each other: domain, inference, task and strategy. Each of these describes a different view of the domain.

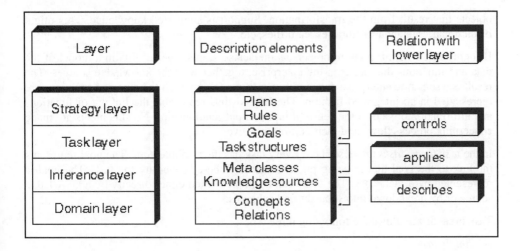

Fig. 3.5: The four views of the conceptual model (source: Wielinga et al. 1987, p. 106)

The *domain layer* is the starting point for modelling. In this layer, the unstructured knowledge of the domain is turned by the terms concept and relation into a shape that can, for example, be depicted in a semantic network and represented as a graph. The description has an existential nature, that is, the individual instances are described. The goal is to bring the domain into a shape that can be used for data processing. The concepts of the domain layer are standardized in the inference layer, i.e. divided into classes (meta-classes). In the task layer, procedural knowledge is described from the point of view of the goal. Descriptive elements are *task*, *goal* and *program*. The strategy layer serves to describe plans and strategies. The KADS approach suggest rules as a method for modelling plans, but it does not specify their syntax or semantics in any detail.

The individual model elements have been copied to the requirements for enterprise modelling as part of the formation of business processes and object-oriented organizational structures (cf. Keller 1993, pp. 103–306).

The verbally described layer technique of the KADS approach has been put into graphic form in order to represent different operational points of view. The lowest level of the conceptual model in the KADS approach corresponds to the existence of enterprise-specific facts in enterprise modelling. The knowledge about the enterprise is the starting point for all development in this case. When enterprise modelling begins, the description of operational facts (reality) is of an existential nature. They can be data or functions in the enterprise. In reality, data is stored in various files, folders, employees' memories, etc., and is partially visible and partially invisible. What is important is that the knowledge necessary for modelling is filtered out and brought into a cohesive structure.

In the *inference layer*, the enterprise's information objects are described as metaclasses, and the function types are described as knowledge sources. The function type has the attributes *input*, *output*, *method* and *support*. In method, the transformation procedure used is described verbally. Input, output and support represent metaclasses. Input describes the information objects that are transformed, and output describes the information objects that result from the transformation. Support is supported knowledge. This might be dictionaries, standards libraries, card files, etc.

Bringing in UDM information objects as metaclasses, this layer results in a model of the data and functions that occur in the enterprise, together with the knowledge sources. The result is a semantic enterprise data and function model in which the data and functions are represented in an integrated fashion. The UDFM thus represents the linking of functions and information objects in the sense of input/output relationships. No statements are made concerning process flows and their control, however.

In the *task layer*, *tasks* are described. Every task has the attribute *goal*. The goal represents the link to the goal that is being pursued and is to be achieved by the task. The goal is represented by a metaclass. The tasks can be implemented either directly by a knowledge source or by breakdown into subtasks and subgoals.

Task breakdown allows the following three types:

■ *Simple task*
  The simple task describes a goal-oriented view of the knowledge source. The simple task has a knowledge source and a metaclass as attributes. In this case, the knowledge source represents the implementation, and the metaclass represents the goal.

■ *Complex task with subtasks*
  In addition to having the metaclass assigned to it as a goal, this task also has meta-classes assigned to it as subtasks. Furthermore, the complex task with subtasks also has a *program* as an attribute. This contains a textual description of the sequence and the way in which the subtasks should be activated, and it defines the flow control at the task level.

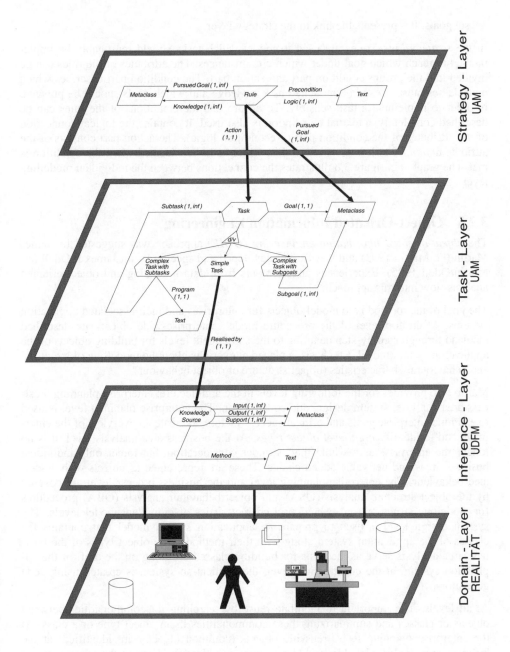

subgoals. It represents the link to the strategy layer.

In the *strategy layer*, rules are used to model which tasks should reasonably be implemented to reach which goal under which circumstances. The attributes of the rules can be divided into the groups condition part and action part. The condition part describes which metaclasses must already be modelled as knowledge and which goals should be pursued, in order to implement a task sensibly. To ensure that the conditions of the rules can be described completely, a textual description is also used. It contains the logical connection of the attributes of the condition part (precondition logic). The action part consists of the attribute *action*. A task is assigned to this, which is to be executed when the condition is met. The graphic in figure 3.6 illustrates the connections between the individual modelling levels.

3.2.5   Object-Oriented Information Engineering

The *object-oriented information engineering (OOIE)* approach was suggested by James Martin (cf. Martin 1993) and was further developed and specified with James J. Odell (cf. Martin/Odell 1995). Experiences and elements from data modelling and object-oriented analysis flow into this approach.

The goal of the method is to model objects for enterprises and their associated application systems. At the top level of the procedure model, enterprise-wide objects are described that lead through step-by-step detailing to the subsequent levels for building objects of the application system model. Emphasis is placed at every level on the modelling of structural and behavioural characteristics (object structure or object behaviour).

Martin also provides for the following levels in the architecture: enterprise planning, business area analysis, system design, and construction. The enterprise planning level is used to examine enterprise goals and critical success factors, to create an overview of the enterprise, and to identify *high-level object types*. At the business area analysis level, it is no longer the enterprise as a whole that is under consideration, but rather only individual business areas and net value added chains. These are represented as objects with associated behaviour. The enterprise planning level and the business process level are covered by the object structure analysis (OSA) and object behaviour analysis (OBA) procedures for modelling structural and behavioural characteristics of individual model levels. The system design level is used to prepare an application system model that contains the classes of the application system along with their methods. The object types of the business area analysis serve as the basis for building classes. Building on the draft of the application system, at the construction level, the application system is created using code generators.

At all levels, it is important to facilitate reuse by searching for commonalities between objects or classes and summarizing these commonalities in an object type or a class. At the enterprise planning level, reusable objects (common objects) are identified; at the business area analysis level, reusable processes are identified; and at the system design level, reusable procedures, user interfaces and methods are identified. Reuse is supported by a central model repository (cf. Martin 1993, pp. 245–257).

In the section that follows, the focus is on the first two levels, in order to work out the aspects relevant for business process design there. It should be noted beforehand that the relationships between the two levels occur through the specialization of products from the object flow diagram to object types from the object structure analysis and through the specification of activities from the object flow diagram through event diagrams from object behaviour analysis.

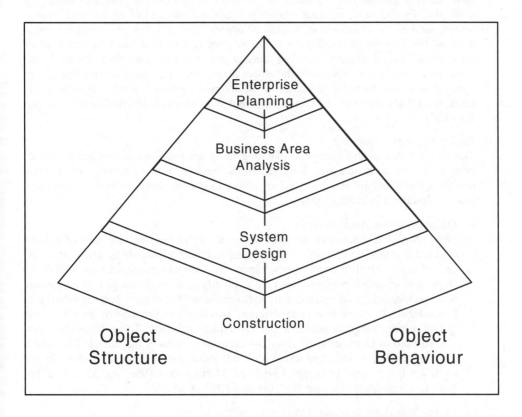

Fig. 3.7: Architecture for object-oriented information engineering
(source: Martin 1993, p. 244)

■ *Enterprise plan modelling*
  The goal of the enterprise planning level is to provide an overview for *top management*. The model of the enterprise plan should describe, in particular, goals and critical success factors (cf. Rockart 1982, pp. 3–13). Although the objects modelled at the enterprise planning level are closely linked to the strategic enterprise goals and critical success factors, the goals and critical success factors are not explicitly modelled. So the relationship between objects and goals or critical success factors is not obvious. Rather, the enterprise planning level provides an overview of the enterprise that is represented on the structure side by an object categorization and on the behaviour side by one or more object flow diagrams.

  One of the things that distinguishes Martin and Odell's approach is the object flow diagram. It simplifies the representation of success-determining business processes at

127

an overview level for strategic purposes as well as of the products that these processes produce and exchange. The object flow diagram represents products such as goods, semi-finished goods, and byproducts that are produced or consumed in an enterprise, along with the business processes (activities) that exchange the products. It thus demonstrates how products are produced and consumed by business processes within an enterprise. Furthermore, external consumers (external entities) of products are represented, such as the customers of a retail company. Subtypes can be formed for products and business processes. Similar to Porter's net value added chain approach, Martin and Odell also distinguish between primary activities and supporting activities. The latter are normally not depicted in the object flow diagram. Activities represent an external view of the business processes. If the internal view of a process is to be modelled, the OOIE approach falls back on event diagrams (cf. Martin/Odell 1996, pp. 109–129).

■ *Business process modelling*
The object types of the enterprise planning level are made more specific as object types of the business area analysis level. In the business process model, object types and their relationships are described in object diagrams, while behaviour of object types is described in event diagrams.

– *Object Structure Analysis (OSA)*
Object Structure Analysis comprises the modelling of the structure view of object-oriented systems in the form of object types and their relationships. The steps to be carried out to identify object types, super- and subtypes of object types, relationships, and so-called business rules are explicitly described in a procedure model. Subtype hierarchies (generalization) and composed-of structures (aggregations) can be modelled. In the case of generalization, two forms of breakdown (partition) are distinguished: complete partition and incomplete partition. These hierarchies can also be used to form detailed views as well as overviews of the model. The generalization technique described above is used to minimize the number of object types modelled (cf. Martin 1993, pp. 85–95; cf. Martin/Odell 1996, pp. 53–55). „This leads to a high level of reusability" (Martin 1993, p. 95).

– *Object Behaviour Analysis (OBA)*
The behaviour view of objects is modelled as part of Object Behaviour Analysis (OBA). State change diagrams and event diagrams are used for this. Objects can be in various states. A change in the state of an object is a change in its attribute values or a change in the object's relationships. It triggers an operation: operations lead to changes in states. Changes in states are depicted in state change diagrams.

In Martin and Odell's approach, a business process is modelled in something called *event diagrams*. The modelling elements in event diagrams are operations and event types. An event is an important change in the state of an object. The event types considered are the results of operations. An operation changes the state of an object. The relationships in event diagrams are known as trigger rules. Trigger rules call an operation when an event occurs. Operations are used on objects and can have prerequisites and subsequent conditions, which are formulated as rules. A prerequisite must be met before an operation can be executed, and a subsequent condition is met when the operation has been executed correctly. In addition, before an operation can be executed, the control condition must be met. The difference between the control condition and a prerequisite is that the prerequisite is independent of the application system, while the control condition is dependent on it. In the event that different events trigger one operation, the trigger rules are simply maintained together in the appropriate operation. Hierarchy formation is possible in this model, too: events can be partitioned into subevents, entire process flows can be combined into operations at a higher level (cf. Martin/Odell 1996, pp. 66–126).

The models described above are closely related. So, for example, an event is a change in the status of an object. That is the reason for the strong interdependence between event diagrams and state change diagrams. There are several ways to visualize them. The state change diagram, in particular, is useful for checking whether states and changes in states have been recorded correctly and *completely* in the event diagram.

3.3 Methods

Dividing and delimiting methods is just as difficult as uniquely characterizing architectures, because the literature contains contradictory statements. Therefore, methods are seen in the broadest sense as a collective term that includes both architecture and procedural aspects. On the other hand, methods are seen in the more narrow sense as being at the same level as procedures. Methods have a static-constructive character, while procedure models display a sequential structure within development. In the section that follows, the term method is used in the more narrow sense, i.e. the emphasis is on descriptive languages and representation tools (static-constructive character) (cf. Nüttgens 1995, pp. 5–68). The procedure aspect is examined in detail in Chapter 5.

In connection with the organizational description of enterprises and the characterization of application systems, there are a multitude of different approaches with all sorts of different methods. They can be differentiated as follows:

■ according to an emphasis on implementation in the phases of the application development process

■ according to the descriptive proximity to the information technology

■ according to the way a business problem is viewed

If one divides current methods into their most basic core elements, it becomes clear that emphasis is placed on structurally oriented or behaviourally oriented questions. And more or less data-oriented, function-oriented, task-oriented or organization-oriented aspects are taken into account, as well. In the following section, the methods are divided according to their origin in the sciences, namely information science and business management science. It should be noted at this point that the *data flow plan* and *program flow plan* methods attributed to business management science (cf. Chapter 3.3.2) can also be counted as IT-oriented methods. Furthermore, it is likely that in the course of increasing computerization in enterprises, the representation forms will continue to be mixed and expanded in one direction or another.

3.3.1 IT-oriented methods

Methods oriented towards information technology come from the world of clear, unambiguous, contradiction-free logic, which is analytically structured. The idea was to transform the extreme form of the binary state of active and deactive in computer systems into more semantic descriptive forms. The structural diagram developed by Nassi and Shneiderman must be seen as a first attempt to achieve this. The structural diagram contains the principles of sequencing, branching and recurrence (loop) (cf. Nassi/Shneiderman 1973, pp. 12–26). Likewise, the widely distributed data flow and program flow plans are among the first information system development methods. Several selected methods that deal with either structure-related aspects of information system design, behaviour-related aspects of information system design, or both, are described here.

■ *Entity Relationship Model*
   The *Entity Relationship Model (ERM)* was developed by Chen (cf. Chen 1976, pp. 9–36). The descriptive language developed by Chen has proven to be a suitable tool for

creating system-independent designs of database systems. Chen distinguishes between the following basic elements: entities, relationships and attributes. Entities are individual, identifiable examples of things, people or terms from the real world or the conceptual world. An entity is described by certain characteristics, for example:

- customer 4711, Smith Co., Hayward, CA 94545

- customer 4712, Meyer Corp., Cincinnati, OH 45230

Entities can be combined into classes. An entity type is specified for individual objects (entities) with common characteristics. They thus correspond to a combination of entities that are different, but similar due to certain characteristics. The entity type CUSTOMER, for example, includes all of an enterprise's customers. A relationship is a logical link between one, two or more entities, and a relationship type is a logical link between one, two or more entity types. Relationships or relationship types can exist only in connection with the appropriate entities or entity types. An example of a relationship is a real enterprise that buys a product. The process in which Customer 4711, the Smith Co., purchases the product 5813, car radios, in a particular quantity, represents a single relationship. In the semantic data model, where abstractions are created from individual instances in the real world, the fact that different customers purchase different products is represented as follows. The quantity of all relationships that represent a purchasing process between a customer and a product forms the relationship type BUYS. There can be different quantity relationships between entity types. The type of link, i.e. the frequency with which the elements occur in a relationship, is called cardinality. Attributes are characteristics of entity types. The entity type CUSTOMER, for example, can be described with the attributes customer number, customer name, address, etc. Attribute instances represent concrete values of the characteristics. They describe individual entities, i.e. facts in the real world.

Graphically, entity types are depicted as rectangles, while relationship types are shown as rhombuses. Attributes are displayed as circles or ellipses and are connected to entity or relationship types by a link. Attributes that identify the entity type, called key attributes, are underlined. The basic model has been expanded repeatedly in the past few years, for example to include the aspects of generalization and specialization, leading to numerous modifications (cf. Hars 1994, pp. 6–128; cf. Scheer 1990, pp. 23–43; cf. Seubert 1991, pp. 87–109; cf. Seubert *et al*. 1995, pp. 15–23; cf. Sinz 1990, pp. 17–29).

■ *Structured Analysis*
The starting point for the development of *Structured Analysis (SA)* was the idea of supporting the requirements analysis phase and the requirements definition phase of the software development process methodically. Until that point, functions were for the most part considered in isolation. It was de Marco's goal to show the relationships between the functions. So, unlike in ERM, where the analysis of the data structure is the focus, Structured Analysis looks at the data flow (cf. de Marco 1978, pp. 15–178; cf. Ward/Mellor 1985). Structured Analysis consists mainly of the following components: *data flow diagrams, data dictionary* and *mini specifications*. Data flow diagrams contain data flows (represented by arrows), processes or nodes (indicated by circles), files or data memory (represented by two straight lines running in parallel), sources and drains (represented by rectangles), AND links from data flows (shown as

stars), and OR links from data flows (shown as crosses). The data dictionary contains the definitions of the data flows, the components of the data flows, the files and the processes. The mini specifications, which are used for the actual description of the functions at the basic level, consist of a description of the results to be aimed for and the transformation rules that describe the conversion process from input data to output data.

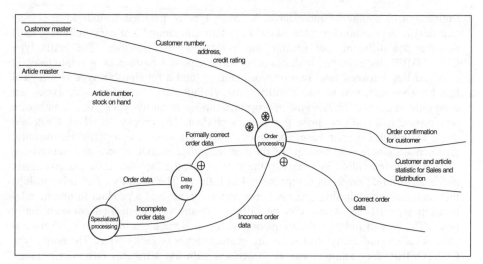

Fig. 3.8: Data flow in structured analysis for order processing
(source: Scheer 1990, p. 130)

Rounding out the example shown here, Structured Analysis provides hierarchical breakdowns of complex facts. At the top level, diagrams called *context diagrams* are created, which characterize the link to the environment. These are symbolized by rectangles. At the lowest level, the data flow diagrams are represented. Breaking down the process names or function names shown in the bubbles results in a hierarchical structure.

One weakness of Structured Analysis is the fact that it is limited to representing data flows and their associated functions. Various authors have therefore undertaken to expand the method to include representation of control flows, in order to meet the demands of realtime systems. Similar to the way data flows are described in data flow diagrams, the data dictionary and mini specifications, control flows are characterized by control flow diagrams, control flow specifications and the control dictionary. The expansion of Structured Analysis into Realtime-Representing Structured Analysis (SA/RT) makes it possible to represent both the data flow and the control flow. In order for the data flow diagrams and the control flow diagrams to correspond to each other, the identical subsystems are represented at each of the hierarchy levels in both diagrams. In general, however, it is also possible to represent both facts in a single diagram. The sequential process flow of the functions is not clearly visible in the control flow diagram, however. The different approaches to problem analysis used in SA/RT are not always clearly coordinated, for example ERM and status automation.

Likewise, no explicit distinction is drawn between the physical and the conceptual view in the representation of the data. Furthermore, the only place you can represent the environment is in the context diagram.

■ *Structured Analysis and Design Technique*
The *Structured Analysis and Design Technique (SADT)* (cf. Marca/McGrowan 1988, pp. 1–72) pursues a similar goal to *Structured Analysis*, namely to support the analysis and system design phase in the software development process.

The difference between SA and SADT is the point of view. While Structured Analysis places the emphasis on the role of a system's data flow, in SADT the focus is on the point of view of the beholder. The basic elements for the graphical description of a system are rectangles and arrows. In system representations, a distinction is made between a functional point of view and an information-object-oriented point of view.

In the functional view, an activity is represented in the rectangle. The input data is written on the left, inbound arrow, and the output data is written on the right, outbound arrow. The arrow pointing into the rectangle from below symbolizes the mechanism or the processor. It describes the transformation rule according to which the inbound data is converted to output data. The control data is shown as going into the rectangle from above. It controls in the sense of a control flow, or it has a controlling effect on the transformation process in the sense of environmental conditions. No distinction is made between the representation of the control flow and the environmental conditions, however. Except for the arrow that symbolizes the mechanism, the arrows characterize the interface between the activity shown in the rectangle and the environment. Just like SA, SADT provides for a reduction in complexity by breaking down the functions in a hierarchy diagram technique.

In the information-object-oriented view, the data is described in the rectangle. Starting from the rectangle, one observes which activity creates the data, which activity uses the data, and which activity has a controlling effect on the data. In this case, the mechanism describes the type of memory or data carrier.

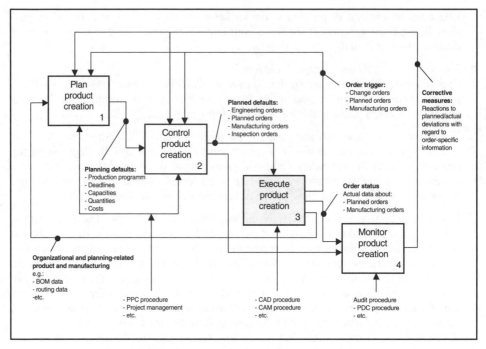

Fig. 3.9: SADT model of the product creation process
(source: Grabowski/Schäfer 1990, p. 255)

SADT makes it clear that activities and data should not be viewed separately. The control flow, however, is not clearly identified in the two submodels. The decision aspect and organizational facts are also neglected.

■ *Hierarchy of Input–Process–Output*
The *Hierarchy of Input–Process–Output Method (HIPO Method)* was developed by IBM in 1974/5. It is a graphical procedure for formalizing and illustrating program work steps. The emphasis is on support of the design phase of the software development process. The function-oriented view is the focus here. The HIPO Method consists of a construction diagram, in which functions are subdivided into subfunctions, and a level diagram, in which an algorithmic function description (process) and the input and output data are specified. The level diagrams are called overview diagrams or detail diagrams depending on their level of detail. They are uniformly structured as three-column tables. The input is shown on the left, the process is shown in the middle, and the output is shown on the right. As in Structured Analysis, the description of the level diagrams can also be called (simplified) mini specifications. The process flow between a function's individual processing steps can be represented by a control flow. The isolated consideration of individual functions, however, prevents the process-flow-dependent relationship between the functions from being visible. This method also fails to take into consideration decisions and organizational aspects (cf. Heinrich/Burgholzer 1991, pp. 78–84).

■ *Graphs with Results and Activities Interrelated*

The GRAI method was developed at the University of Bordeaux. The method is used to describe operational information and decision flows in production operations. It makes a distinction between a physical system and a production management system, which in turn is subdivided into a decision system and an information system. The physical system has the task of performing the transformation of the incoming flow of goods into other goods. The information system creates the link between the physical system and the decision system and shows the communication within the decision system. The GRAI method gives major importance to modelling of the decision system. The decision system has the task of actively controlling the production process. GRAI grids and GRAI networks are used for analysis and representation of decision relationships (cf. Doumeingts 1983, pp. 194–256).

Function Horizon/ Cycle	SALES	PLANNING	PROCUREMENT	PLANT MAINTENANCE	QUALITY
1.5 Y 1 Y				Determine maintenance measure and intervals	
1.5 Y 1 Mo		Determine production volume: quantity/ prod. Family/Mo			Determine quality assurance method and quality level
1 Y 1 Mo	Analyze customer requirements quantity/prod./Mo	Determine long-term production volume quantity/prod./D	Determine material requirements and process purchase order		
1 Mo 1 Mo	Adjust delivery date quantity/prod./Wk	Adjust production volume quantity/prod./Mo			
8 Wk 1 Wk	Determine weekly delivery plan quantity/prod./Wk	Determine production plan quantity/assembly/D			
<1 Mo 1 Wk		Monitor production			
2 Wk 1 Wk			Plan material header record quantity/assembly/D		
<5 D 1 Sh	Plan shipping quantity/prod./ customer/D	Create order sequences quantity/assembly/ machine	Prepare material header record quantity/assembly/D	Plan regular maintenance order	Samples and analyses
RT		Adjust order sequences quantity/ assembly/machine	Stock removal / Goods receipt and inspection	Maintaining	Measuring and inspecting

Y : Year   D : Day
Mo : Month   Sh : Shift
Wk : Week   RT : Realtime

Fig. 3.10: Example of a decision matrix (source: Bünz 1987, p. 45)

In a GRAI grid, decision cells are organized according to operational functions and temporal aspects, like the planning horizon and cycle, are organized in a two-dimensional aspect shown in Fig. 3.10. In that representation, the decision relationships are organized hierarchically in an overall structure. The goal is to show the decision relationships across function areas. The decision horizon specifies the time span that is followed for planning and for which a decision is valid. The planning cycle describes the time span between two planning points, i.e. the time intervals within which a decision is reached under normal circumstances. A double arrow between two decision cells symbolizes a decision flow, and a single arrow represents the transfer of information. The logical decision flow is not always clearly visible, however, due to the symbols used; it becomes clear only when one looks at the explanatory contents in the various decision cells. Likewise, the representation of the information flow shows only that an information flow exists; it does not show which information is being transferred. You use GRAI networks to specify decision process flows.

■ *Petri networks*
Petri networks are named for their creator (cf. Petri 1962, p. 1). Petri's goal is to describe as many phenomena as possible in information exchange and information transformation in a uniform and precise way. Petri networks originate in network theory and provide the ability to represent secondary, dynamic aspects by depicting the three logical process flow structures: sequence, selection and loop. Representing the behaviour of complex systems over time is therefore often the focus in the use of Petri networks. The precise mathematical orientation of this approach and the publications to date on the use of Petri networks exhibit similarities to digital and control techniques (cf. Starke 1990; cf. Busch 1989, pp. 822–838).

Petri networks are directed graphs. This refers to a set of nodes that are linked to each other with connecting lines (arrows). No node may be isolated, and no parallel arrows or double arrows may occur. The node types consist of two disjunct sets of elements. A distinction is made here between passive and active system components. Passive system components are shown as circles, and they describe the current state of a system node. Events represent the active system components and cause the crossover from an old state to a new state. They are symbolized by squares.

Petri networks can be divided into different classes of network types (cf. Reisig 1986, pp. 81–96; cf. Rosenstengel/Winand 1982, pp. 5–50; cf. Wendt 1989, pp. 169–183). For example, there are:

– *channel instance networks*
   A channel instance network shows the static view of a problem. The passive component is called the channel, and it represents information states, for example. The channel is shown as a circle. Instances, which are symbolized by squares, represent the active components of a system.

– *condition event networks*
   Condition event networks determine which conditions must be met before a particular event may occur. Conditions that have been met are marked, while conditions that have not been met remain unmarked. For an event to be able to occur, all of the conditions that point to that event must be marked.

– *position transition networks*
   Position transition networks, or predicate transition networks, represent the dynamic behaviour of a system. The position forms the passive part of the system. A capacity specification for a position specifies the maximum number of flags. The relationship at the arrow indicates how many flagging elements are transformed during a switching process. The transformation is accomplished with the transition, which represents the active components of the system. It thus changes a position's

flags. If there are fewer flags in one position than is specified on the link to the subsequent transition, the transition cannot switch. By continually changing the position's flags in each switching processes, you can depict the behaviour of a system over a period of time. Predicate transition networks, which have a variable extension, are an expansion of these networks (cf. Richter 1984, pp. 28–40).

The equally weighted consideration of active and passive components in Petri networks enables integrated consideration of a problem. Setting flags allows you to represent dynamic features of a system, although decisions and organizational facts are not explicitly identified in traditional Petri networks.

3.3.2   Methods oriented towards business management science

In function and task structuring, unique classification is more difficult, partially because the terms are used synonymously, and partially because they have different intentions. While the term task comes from organization science and generally follows its objectives, in DP terminology, the term function is often understood from the point of view of the transformation of input and output data. Task breakdown is reflected in task structure plans; function breakdowns are represented in hierarchy diagrams or function trees. The goal is to represent complex formations in a clear, static structure. For one thing, the task breakdown demonstrates which tasks (functions) are superordinate or subordinate to other tasks (functions). For another thing, it shows which tasks (functions) belong to which group (cf. Frese 1988; cf. Grochla 1978; cf. Kosiol 1962; cf. Nordsieck 1932). The question arises as to what the structuring criterion and the structuring level are. Starting with global enterprise tasks (functions), the tasks are broken down until they represent a process that can no longer be subdivided in a way that is meaningful in terms of business. These kinds of basic tasks (functions) are always executed in their entirety and thus have no alternatives. In the simplest case, the structural relationship may be a hierarchical structure, although often it is a network structure.

The following possibilities are conceivable for grouping tasks (functions). In a process-oriented grouping, the tasks (functions) that occur in a business (sub)process that is meaningful for business are grouped together. In an object-oriented grouping, all of the tasks (functions) that process a defined information object are grouped together. An execution-oriented grouping combines equal execution steps that are carried out on different information objects.

Organization-oriented approaches concentrate primarily on the consideration of responsibility-oriented organizational relationships in the enterprise. They are reflected in reporting structures. These describe the relationships that individual organizational units in an enterprise have to each other. Disciplinary relationship structures are often in the foreground. For one thing, the extent of centralization/decentralization is determined here; for another, coordination is determined. Both design parameters then determine the type of configuration, i.e. the horizontal and vertical structure of an enterprise (cf. Grochla 1978). Next to the disciplinary rules, however, technical or project-based assignments are becoming increasingly important for implementing leaner enterprise structures.

Business management science dealt with different methods of representation for describing organizations much earlier than information scientists did. In the design of enterprise structures, the term task plays a dominant role. Just like the consideration of organizational science from within a task, Nordsieck's distinction between responsibility-oriented organization and process-oriented organization has a formative influence on ongoing organization research in the German-speaking world.

The design of the responsibility-oriented organization and process-oriented organization follows the principle of breaking down (task complexes or work complexes) and putting them back together. The multitude of representation techniques that have come about in organization science as a result can generally be divided into:

- verbal representation techniques, for example oral lectures, presentations, written reports, organization directions

- tabular representation techniques, for example communication tables, communication matrixes, social matrixes

- graphical representation techniques, for example reporting structures, process flow diagrams, network diagrams, decision trees

The following graphics are used as tools for designing a process-oriented organization (cf. Nordsieck 1932; cf. Nordsieck 1972; cf. Kosiol 1962; cf. Grochla 1982; cf. Schmidt 1991):

- *Task structuring plan*
  In *task structuring plans*, the overall tasks are split into individual task parts, so that all of the tasks to be completed and their relationships can be understood (cf. Figure 3.11).

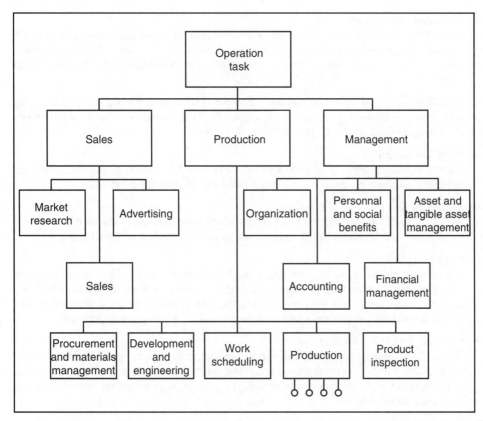

Fig. 3.11: Task structure (source: Nordsieck 1972, Illustration 3 of the appendix)

■ *Reporting structures*
Reporting structures are used to represent concrete department and position structure. They provide an important source of information about existing or planned structure solutions and specify both the existing and the planned structure of the enterprise at any point in time (actual vs. planned state).

■ *Position descriptions*
Position descriptions contain information about task distribution, responsibility distribution and skills distribution. Only predictable tasks can be described in these. They are also called function descriptions, functional specifications or task descriptions.

■ *Job indexes*
Job indexes record the name and number of available positions, as well as their salary classification.

■ *Function diagrams*
Using task structuring, you can record and represent transparently the task relationships between different positions. *Function diagrams* unify reporting structures and task structures and provide the ability to represent in detail additional facts related to responsibility-oriented organization.

- *Communication diagrams*
  Communication diagrams depict the overall results of communication tables, which are used for periodically examining individual positions. The task of communication diagrams is to record the general relationships and to overcome the position-based view.

Responsibility-oriented organizations are represented with work breakdown plans, verbal process flow descriptions, work centre descriptions, work instructions, and various process flow diagrams. Examples of process flow diagrams are:

- *Workflow tickets*
  Workflow tickets, also called process flow tickets or job tickets, record the processes belonging to a subprocess. One job ticket is usually written for every order.

- *Document flow descriptions*
  Using document flow descriptions, you can show the exchange of documents between the departments involved based on the work steps to be performed (see Figure 3.12).

- *Harmonograms*
  Harmonograms are used to represent complicated work flows. They are created by adding together several simple diagrams. These are process flow diagrams, which are meant to show how work processes of the same or similar type are controlled within the framework of a department and how the overall load looks in a department.

- *Gantt charts (or bar charts)*
  Gantt charts represent project flows in a two-dimensional system of coordinates. On the horizontal axis, you enter a time scale, and on the vertical axis you enter the names of those responsible for tasks or materials. You can then show the time needed by the individual capacities.

- *Data flow plans*
  Data flow plans are standardized methods for graphically representing input and output data in systems. They depict which data is necessary to carry out processing and which new data is created by processing. Data flow and program flow plans are commonly known as block diagrams.

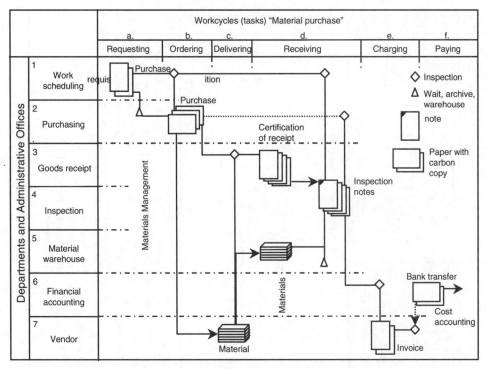

Fig. 3.12: Document flow representation
(source: Nordsieck 1972, Illustration 18 from the appendix)

■ *Program flow plans*
Program flow plans represent the sequence of processing steps, i.e. the temporal process flow of operations, as information-providing processes that depend on the available data.

■ *Enterprise/functions/tasks model*
The *enterprise/functions/tasks model* (*EFFM*) is used to describe the process flow sequence of tasks under consideration of the people responsible for the task, the resources, and the information objects required. The tasks are triggered by events, and the flow logic or the control flow is indicated with dotted lines. An important characteristic, next to the explicit identification of decisions, is the consideration of sequential, secondary (parallel) and alternative paths by way of corresponding link operators, as well as the differentiation of allocation aspects between the person responsible for the task (executor) and the information transmitter or information recipient (cf. Keller 1993, pp. 119–129).

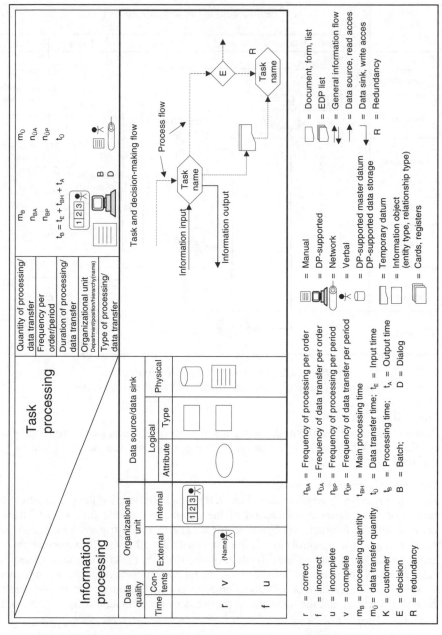

Fig. 3.13: Enterprise/functions/tasks model (source: Keller 1993, p. 126)

When one looks at the current methods with an eye towards the design of business processes, the following tendencies emerge. For one thing, many of the methods concentrate on the aspect of information flow, with the focus being on the question of which information is created where and to where this information is flowing. When aspects *relevant to business processes* are considered, for example the question of which functions are triggered when, it becomes clear that this aspect is either insufficiently handled, or that the current methods rapidly become complex and difficult to understand. In general, each the following deficiencies can be noted in the individual methods in more or less prominent form.

Many method designers tend to create different symbols with different meanings for different questions. The numerous symbols direct attention to methodical questions, while the business task of content-related business process design fades into the background. The organization of the symbols can often be determined by the user in practically any form he or she desires. This degree of freedom also leads to the fact that models created by different people are so entirely different in their organization that a content-based comparison is difficult to perform – at least for business models that have a meaningful content. Good models must ensure that there is a simple language available in addition to the symbols, so that even an inexperienced *business process designer* can quickly understand new business processes. Often, especially in business process design, missing naming conventions are an obstacle at the one extreme, while at the other extreme, abstract terms are an obstacle to implementing clearly interpretable business processes.

The heterogeneity presented above between the individual methods and the related deficiencies for methodical design of business processes led SAP, together with the Institute for Business Information Science in Saarbrücken, to develop a form of representation that can be used to represent business processes in a simple, clear, yet unambiguous manner.

4   The R/3 Reference Process Model

In the 1970s and 1980s, the focus was on the static view of information systems in information (data) and function models and on dynamic analysis in the form of data flow models, which were meant to uncover the high amount of discontinuity of media and organization and redundant task processing. Today, dynamic behaviour has moved into the foreground in the design of operational information systems. The stress is on process-oriented analysis (control flow analysis), whose goal is efficient design of the business relationships and interactions between the individual elements within consistent task processing. The representation of processes has been described as the job of process-oriented organization design since the beginning of the 1930s (cf. Nordsieck 1932), but because of the dominance of responsibility-oriented-organization-based design over the past sixty years, it was not until recently that it underwent a renaissance. In support of a behaviour-oriented view of operational information systems, a series of approaches have recently been developed whose goal is the design of operational process flows (business processes or processes).

4.1   Basic terminology regarding business process

In business management literature and in practice, it is not entirely clear what a process is and how it can be characterized. A process or business process (the word business in the term business process stands for types of enterprises; but it should also be noted that non-profit organizations, such as universities, hospitals, kindergartens, government agencies, etc. create processes) is generally defined „as a bundle of activities for which one or more inputs are needed and that creates a result of value for the customer" (Hammer/Champy 1994, p. 52). It has also been defined as a logically linked sequence of activities that are of measurable use to a process customer, contribute towards reaching enterprise goals, and are performed according to particular rules by operators (people) responsible for the tasks (cf. Davenport 1993, pp. 5–6; cf. Ferstl/Sinz 1993, pp. 589–592; cf. Gaitanides 1983, p. 65; cf. Hauser 1996, pp. 12–23; cf. Kosiol 1962, pp. 42–79; cf. Krickl 1994, pp. 19–20; cf. Striening 1988, p. 57). While some authors use business process and net value added chain synonymously, other authors consider a business process to be part of the net value added chain, which can cross organizational boundaries, such as department or enterprise boundaries (cf. Davenport/Short 1990, pp. 12–13). Still other authors classify business processes, for example Österle, who divides business processes into management processes, service processes and support processes (cf. Österle 1995, pp. 130–131).

As the different views suggest, a business process describes all of the activities whose execution brings about desired performance or planned performance by people responsible for the task, which is transferred to external customers (main processes) or internal customers (service processes) and represents a value for these. To execute a business process, information and materials are needed, and a result is created that is measurable. The following is a list of characteristics of a business process, for which the term net value added chain is used synonymously and for which in SAP terminology the term scenario is also used.

- Business processes are goal-oriented.

- Business processes create an added value that can be sold.

- Business processes are planned independent of the person responsible for the task and the allocation of resources, but are then adjusted to operating conditions.

- Generally, a business process comprises several tasks, which are coordinated in a goal-oriented fashion.

- A business process includes tasks that are usually processed by several people or departments.

- The object of business processes is the performance of operational services that lead to changes in objects such as sales orders, products, purchase orders, etc..

- The individual tasks of a business process are often networked and interdependent, that is, the end of one substep triggers another step or even other business processes.

- Business processes have a defined beginning and a defined end.

- Business processes have one or more locations where they are executed.

The scope of a business process depends entirely on the point of view of the designer and the user. With regard to the problem of identifying the length of a business process, Ferstl/Sinz differentiate between formal and technical features (cf. Ferstl/Sinz 1993, pp. 589–592). In the sections that follow, a business process is created by linking R/3 System processes. The following examples demonstrate sample business processes.

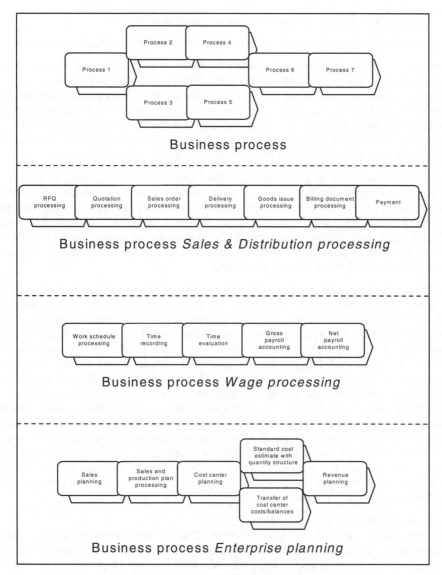

Fig. 4.1: Sample business processes

The terms reference model and reference process model are often used in connection with the creation of business processes, without a more precise definition of what is meant by reference. References in terms of model creation may refer to the following, for example:

■ business experience gathered on a large scale

■ experience gathered in a branch of industry on a large scale

■ a comparable enterprise and the business processes created there

■ business application software and the business process solutions implemented in it

Reference, which stems from the Latin word referre (to carry back, transfer, report), includes making a recommendation for an open question about something comparable. As explained in Chapter 3, *model* means to represent the objects for a specified problem, their features and relationships (static and dynamic relationships or structure and behaviour), in a simplified manner, by concentrating on the important things and their relationships and eliminating unimportant things. So a model also includes a generalization step, because you abstract from the individual circumstances of a particular unit of analysis.

Thus the construction of the term *reference model* and the objective pursued by it render it a contradictory term in itself, because on the one hand a concrete recommendation is supposed to be expressed, while on the other hand an operational fact is supposed to be represented in a simplified fashion. Due to the generalization aspect, reference models always include an aspect of insecurity, i.e. that in a concrete case of an operational situation, it will not function as desired. Reference models can reduce the insecurity of a business decision, but they can never entirely eliminate it.

A reference model is meant to be a generally valid model that can be used as a starting point for a solution and adjusted to the specific situation (cf. Jost 1993, p. 12). Standardized and competition-neutral process flows, such as those in Financial Accounting, can be taken over, and the enterprise can avoid unnecessary modelling work and profit from the experiences of other enterprises (cf. Brenner/Hamm 1995, p. 32). The characteristic features of a reference model, therefore, are the criteria of general applicability, reusability, and security with respect to implementation. The specification of the reference model should thus go so far that the models contained in it can also be used without changes as specific models for an enterprise (cf. Scheer *et al.* 1995, p. 430). The question remains, however, how to define change. Does *change* mean that the reference model must be taken over in the existing form and ergo also the information system that is to be implemented? Does change mean that new functions or processes are defined and modelled without assurance that the processes created can be performed with any information system in the world? The term change is therefore specified as follows in connection with the use of reference process models:

■ *Change in the sense of configuration*
  Change in the sense of configuration means that the user moves within the solution spectrum of a reference model and can select among alternative process paths. The range of reference process variants determines the number of possible solutions. By following the configuration approach from the reference model of a software vendor, for example the R/3 Reference Model, the user is assured that the configured solution can be implemented technically and that its future release capability and maintainability are ensured. The use of a reference model in the sense of configuration can have the following advantages for an enterprise:

  – Adapting already existing process flow structures that have been tested in the real world has time and quality advantages, as a working foundation exists from the beginning of the project.

- A prescribed process flow structure and the implementation of a tested method simplify training and communication between project employees and end users.

- The use of reference models allows rapid handling of non-critical processes or parts of processes and thus supports concentration on the strategically important or critical processes or parts of processes.

■ *Change in the sense of modelling*
Change in the sense of modelling means that the user creates individual solutions by adding new functions or processes and therefore moves outside the spectrum of solutions of a reference model. In addition to a technical comparison, the user must also perform a semantic comparison against a reference model if he intends to introduce standard software and the software vendor has published a reference model. On the other hand, he must evaluate the targeted solution directly in the software system.

The demand for people with entirely different job backgrounds and technical knowledge to be able to communicate using the R/3 Reference Model prompted SAP AG to establish the following premises:

■ *Define the elements that are absolutely necessary* for describing and representing business processes.

■ *Target a simple representation* by minimizing the number of symbols and the semantics behind them.

■ *Determine a framework for the logical and graphical order* of the business process elements, to achieve clear understanding of the process by all involved. Special value was placed on making it possible for the process model to be read and analyzed by people who did not participate in its creation.

■ *Create a structure for representing the model at different levels of detail*, to support user-driven navigation. A division of the reference model into different layers makes it possible for the customer to be trained quickly in its use. The depiction of scenarios and R/3 process modules in the form of event-controlled process chains (EPC) can be supported by four strategies (complete EPC, EPC without input/output, EPC without organizational unit, EPC without input/output and without organizational unit).

Between 1990 and 1992, SAP AG developed the *event-controlled process chain (EPC)* method to represent processes. EPC makes it possible to represent business processes in a simple, yet clear, manner (cf. Keller *et al.* 1992; cf. Keller 1993; cf. Keller/Meinhardt 1994; cf. Keller 1995, pp. 45–66; cf. Keller/Schröder 1996, pp. 77–88).

4.2 Event-controlled process chains (EPC)

With the help of modelling, it is possible to drastically simplify the design of operational process flows by abstracting complex facts. The goal of modelling is to increase the transparency of process-oriented organization relationships by concentrating on the components relevant to the analysis and their relationships. The following are the main questions considered in modelling using event-controlled process chains:

▪ When should something be done?

▪ What should be done?

▪ Who should do something?

▪ Which information is needed for this?

The basic principle of the event-controlled process chain method describes the sequential process flow of events and task (functions) or events and processes, and it has the following elements:

▪ *Event*, which describes when something is to be done (hexagon)

▪ *Task or function*, which describes what is to be done (rounded rectangle)

▪ *Organizational unit*, which describes who does something (oval)

▪ *Information objects (data)*, which describe which information is needed for successful processing of the task (rectangle)

The relationships between the elements are identified as follows:

▪ *Control flow*, which identifies the sequential business process flow (dotted-line arrow that points downward and links events with tasks (functions))

▪ *Information flow*, which specifies whether data is read, changed or written by a task (function) (solid arrow that points left from a task (function); can also be used for assignment of materials)

▪ *Organization assignment*, which specifies which organizational unit processes which task (function) or is responsible for which task (function) (solid line that points right from a task (function); can also be used for assignment of resources)

▪ *Link operator*, which specifies how the business process structure logic looks between events and tasks (functions). The different types of link operators are „and," „or" and „exclusive or". They can be combined. If several arrows exit a link operator, only one arrow may enter it (distributor), and if several arrows enter it, only one may exit it (connector).

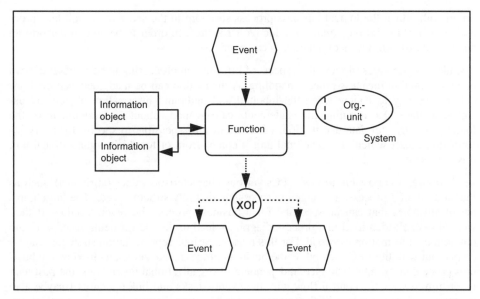

Fig 4.2: Basic structure of an EPC

Navigation between individual processes occurs with *common* events. To make business process links easily visible, especially on printed copies, there is the following solution:

■ *Process signs*, which point out the link from one process to another process (combines function and event symbol, with the function symbol in the foreground and the event symbol in the background)

With the EPC method, operational business processes can be described in their entirety. The goal is to represent the sequential dependencies of tasks (functions). The important thing is that the EPCs always begin with at least one starting event and end with at least one ending event. If needed, a process sign can be added as a supplement. An event-controlled process chain always consists of the following processes, at a minimum: event, function, information object, organizational unit, and the corresponding relationships (control flow). Depending on the variability, the necessary link operators are also included. Since functions are the active components in an enterprise, decisions are also made, in addition to the performance of an activity or the completion of a company task. In contrast to this, an event cannot make any decisions, which results in logical restrictions in the use of link operators.

The EPC method links data, tasks and organizations and is therefore the central element of Business Process Engineering. For example, in business process analysis, it is the consideration of the type of task processing and the transfer medium between sequential tasks that is of interest. In the real world, discontinuities in the business process chain, especially those caused by changes in media, are often an indication of process-oriented organization weaknesses. Another important element of EPC is the organizational assignment of tasks to operational operators or enterprise organizational units. In this case, a division or position can be assigned, making it possible to track a process across several organizational units. Since organization structures have often been formed according to criteria other than the logical business process structure in the sense of overall task processing, this can point out counter-productive structures. In order to be able to perform an analysis at different levels of detail, you can condense processes.

Just like task flow description, the aspects of information processing to be represented can be represented in business process handling. A distinction can be made between the logical and the physical view when the inbound and outbound information objects are assigned to the tasks, meaning that statements can be made about the assignment of the logical and physical data distribution. Furthermore, it is possible to specify for every information object which organizational unit it comes from or to which organizational unit it is to be sent.

Furthermore, it is possible to give EPCs various characteristic values (attributes), such as the duration of a process, a change in processing, quantity structures, etc. The large number of attributes that can be specified for a business process, however, would – if they were always all identified in a process diagram – lead to the viewer being faced with the problem of information overload. For this reason, various representation strategies can be carried out with the EPC method. If the business process analyzer wants to view the business process in its entire variance, independent of organizational restrictions, the best idea is for him to view the control flow with the events, tasks and link operators (maybe also the process signs) in a lean business process analysis first. If organizational questions are being handled, the organizational units should also be shown (for example, in the analysis of a workflow). If the object flow is being analyzed, the inbound and outbound information objects must be shown.

Name	Symbol	Definition
Event	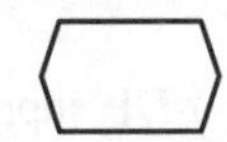	The event describes the entering of a state that causes a consequence.
Function	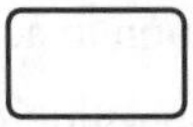	The function describes the transformation of an entry state to a target state.
Link operators	 XOR ∧ ∨	The link operator describes the logical links between events and functions or processes.
Control flow		The control flow describes the temporal dependencies of events and functions.
Process sign	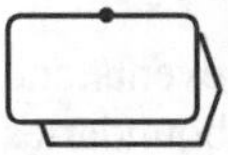	The process sign shows the link from one to another process (navigational aid).
Organizational unit	 System	The organizational unit describes the structure of a company. In the R/3 System the organizational unit is a system organizational unit or R/3 structural unit.
Information object	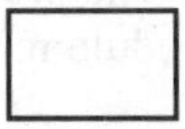	An information object is a representation of an object from the physical world (for example, business object, entity).
Information flow	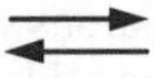	The information/material flow describes whether something is read from, changed in, or written to a function.
Assignment of system organizational units		The resource/organizational unit assignment describes which unit (employee) or resource processes the function.

Fig. 4.3: Elements of event-controlled process chains

The EPC method is the central element in business process design, because it shows the process flow structure and it also takes into consideration other aspects of organization and information design. Beyond this, depending on the enterprise's objectives, other things may be of interest in addition to the analysis of the *process model*, such as:

- analysis of the structural relationships of an information system (*data model* of the business objects, for example customer inquiry, sales order, customer delivery, or of the entities, for example invoice recipient, payer, competitor)

- analysis of responsibility-oriented organization relationships of an enterprise or DP-supported information system (*organization model*, for example business area, sector, sales area)

- analysis of the application area to be considered or of the application components offered by a software manufacturer (*application component model*, for example sales and distribution, sales, shipping, invoicing)

- analysis of the information flow relationships of a DP-supported information system (*information flow model*, for example in the R/3 System, the transfer of a customer document from the sales and distribution organization to accounts receivable)

- analysis of an enterprise's communication relationships (*communication model*, for example the sending of the message *start delivery processing* from sales and distribution to shipping)

The EPC supports the consistency between the other models and makes it possible to derive some of the aspects of these models from the EPC. An example is the integration between the process model and the object/data model as well as the organization model, as shown in Figure 4.4.

The EPC describes the sequential process flow of events and tasks (functions) or events and processes. The methodical setting of process boundaries across starting and ending events makes it possible to document processes as process modules that

- *have an internal structure*
  The internal structure shows the possible variations of a process module from the provider's view. Filtering out of the customer's desired functional requirements is achieved using reduction and selection techniques. The provider in this case shows the optional functions, but the usage of the process module remains assured despite deactivation.

- *have an external structure*
  The external structure shows the possible combinations of process modules from the provider's point of view. Customer-based net value added chains (scenarios) are created by combining process modules. The provider in this case shows the compatibility of the process modules being offered and thus provides a design framework for creating net value added chains that make business sense.

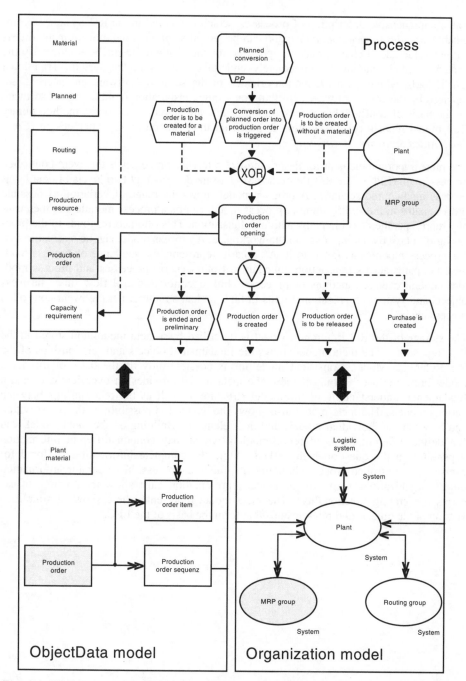

Fig. 4.4: EPC as connecting link in the R/3 Reference Model in an example from production

The comprehensive description of processes, which are stored in the R/3 System as combinable *modules* (*process modules*) and can be reused as process modules in many different net value added chains, makes it possible for the customer to analyze and verify the contents without having to immediately undertake settings in the system. Traditional CASE tools, which were production-oriented in the sense of software engineering, are replaced by the era of software configuration – quick installation (combining) of software on the basis of configurable process modules that are stored in a process module library (R/3 model repository). Installation is based on the principle of modular design (*Computer-Aided Software Assembly*).

The most important element for describing R/3 reference processes is the event-controlled process chain (EPC). The R/3 Reference Models are described at two levels of detail – as process module and scenario. A process model shows the range of variation of possible process paths in the R/3 System. A process model can be a process module and then usually represents the possible paths within a transaction. This often corresponds to the processing of a task by an employee in the workplace. A process model can be a scenario that has process modules assigned to it. A scenario represents the sequence of process modules, i.e. paths across transaction boundaries. Both scenario processes and process modules contain events, functions or processes, link operators, control flow links, business objects and system organizational units in their logical structure, i.e. the event-controlled process chain.

The storage of the R/3 Reference Model is described by a meta model and stored in the R/3 Repository. The meta model shows the fundamental objects and relationships of the R/3 Reference Model. Consistent modelling is possible only on the basis of this meta model From the user's point of view, the meta model provides an overview over and a fundamental understanding of the model structure as well as the relationships between various models. The meta model also shows the navigation possibilities that exist within and between the individual models and their elements. Building on the meta model, you can define different forms of representation, which may contain different information depending on the question being asked. While the complete information is stored for every event-controlled process chain (events, function/process, link operator, information object, organizational unit), the graphical representation must allow the creation of excerpts (generating functionality). The meta model represented here shows a simplified version of the objects and relationships that form the basis of the EPC.

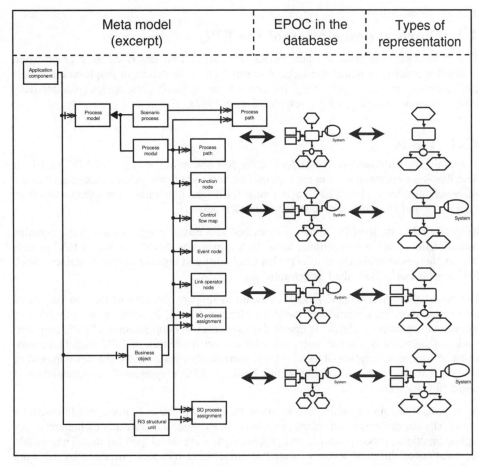

Fig. 4.5: Meta model for EPC structure and representation strategies

With the created process modules of the R/3 Reference Model, SAP guarantees internal consistency and external compatibility. The potential combination possibilities are displayed in a *process module library* and are identified by the starting and ending events that are the same in the various process modules. In addition to navigational support, the graphics also contain representations of process signs for orientation. The 800 existing process modules of the R/3 Reference Model in principle enable over 10000 possible combinations. The customer's task is to pick the provided process modules out of the process library based on his business requirements and arrange them according to his desired net value added chain (cf. Chapter 6).

4.3   Formal description of the EPC

The event-controlled process chain model (EPCM) can be described as a graph-based model that consists of nodes and links. A description of the syntax of graph-based models can be described either operatively, for example using graph grammars, or declaratively using description languages for graphs (cf. Simon 1992).

4.3.1   Basics

The section that follows presents a declarative description of the syntax of EPC models. It describes the elements used, i.e. the various link and node types. Afterwards, it defines the characteristics that a correct EPC model must fulfil. The illustration that follows shows an example of an EPC with all of the node and link types.

In its general form, the EPC model is described as a mixed graph. Such a graph contains both directional and nondirectional links. If, however, the „slim" version of EPC models is used, there is no assignment of organizational units and input or output containers. Such EPC models can be described as digraphs.

The syntax definition of EPC models is meant to support checking of the consistency of the process modules contained in the R/3 Reference Model. In addition, the provision of automated consistency checks supports the user-specific configuration of EPC diagrammatic representations. Furthermore, rules for correct modelling of EPC models are provided. A formal description of these rules is particularly important for the development of modelling tools. In the remainder of this book, an EPC diagrammatic representation is called EPC for short.

An important task in modelling of expansive business processes is managing the model's complexity. In the event-controlled process chain method, the concepts of hierarchically ranked functions, process macros and process signs were developed for this. They enable the creation of different levels of detail for describing business processes by allowing individual elements of an EPC to be described by another EPC. As in the R/3 Reference Model, in the following reference model, two hierarchy levels are distinguished. An EPC at the lower level is called a process module. The assigned EPC is also called a process EPC. Scenarios combine a series of process modules. The corresponding EPC is called a scenario EPC. The following section begins by presenting the general model of the EPC. Afterwards, it describes the rules that characterize a correct EPC.

4.3.2   General model

The following syntax defines the EPC model as an attribute-possessing, directional and connected graph. Abstractions are made from model features such as size, shape, colour and geometrical arrangement of the individual nodes, as well as the geometrical course of the links. A unique type and one or more attributes are assigned to every node and every link of the graph. The EPC model is defined as a 7-tuple.

$$EPCM = (Id, \nu, \kappa, \tau, \tau_\kappa, \alpha, \alpha_\kappa)$$

The following list explains the individual elements of the 7-tuple.

■ Id is the unique identifier of an EPC model.

■ v is the non-empty, finite set of nodes of an EPC. $3 \leq |v| < \infty$ is true, because an EPC consists of at least one starting event, one ending event, and one function.

■ κ is the link relationship, which describes the connections between the various types of nodes. κ is defined as $\kappa \subseteq v \times v$.

■ τ and τ_κ are representations that assign a type to every node or link.

■ α and α_κ are representations that assign attributes to every node or link type.

The representations τ and τ_κ are defined as follows:

$\tau: v \rightarrow$ {function, event, process sign, OR connector,

AND connector, XOR connector, hierarchically ranked

function, input container, output container, organizational unit}

$\tau_\kappa: \kappa \rightarrow$ {control flow link, information flow link, organization assignment link}

Directional links are used to describe the control flow and the information flow. Only the assignment of organizational units is done with simple links.

In order to be able to further specify the node set v, the terms adjacency list, input degree and output degree are introduced here.

A link (u,v) connects the nodes u and v, if $(u,v) \in \kappa :\Leftrightarrow u \rightarrow v$ is true. In this case, u is called the start node and v is called the end node of the link.

The *adjacency list* of a node v is the set

$$adj^+(v,t) = \{u \in v| (v,u) \in \kappa \wedge \tau_\kappa((v,u)) = t\}.$$

The amount of this set is the *output degree* $\gamma^+(v,t) = |adj^+(v,t)|$ of v. The definition of the input degree is analogous to this. The *input degree* of v is

$$\gamma^-(v,t) = |adj^-(v,t)| = |\{u \in v| (u,v) \in \kappa \wedge \tau_\kappa((u,v)) = t\}.$$

The incidence list for a node v is defined as the set of positive incident links $inz^-(v,t) = \{(u,v) \in \kappa| \tau_\kappa((u,v)) = t\}$. Analogous to the input degree of a node v, the following is true:

$i^-(v,t) = |inz^-(v,t)|$. Likewise, the set of initial nodes (negative incident links) and their number can be defined as

$i^+(v,t) = |inz^+(v,t)| = |\{(v,u) \in \kappa| \tau_\kappa((v,u)) = t\}|.$

For the description of the control flow of EPC models, the terms connection and path are introduced here.

A series $u_1, u_2, ..., u_n$ where $n \geq 0$ and $u_i \in v$, $u_i \neq u_j$, $i \neq j$, $i,j \in \{1,...,n\}$, $\tau(u_i) \in$ {AND connector, OR connector, XOR connector} is called a connection, if $u_1 \rightarrow \cdots \rightarrow u_n$. The shortened notation $u \xrightarrow{v} v$ is introduced for the existence of a connection between the nodes u and v, where $\tau(u)$, $\tau(v) \in$ {event, function, hierarchically ranked function, process sign}. This means that the node u is linked to the node v by a chain of connectors.

Furthermore, a series u_1, u_2, ..., u_n where $n \geq 0$ and $u_i \in v$, $u_i \neq u_j$, $i \neq j$, $i,j \in$ {1,...,n} is called a path, if $u_1 \rightarrow \cdots \rightarrow u_n$. The notation $u \xrightarrow{P} v$ serves as the abbreviated form. This means that the node u is linked to the node v by a chain of events, (hierarchically ranked) functions, process signs and connectors.

The adjacency list of a node v with regard to a connection to other nodes is

$$\text{adj}_V^+ (v) = \{u \in v|\, v \xrightarrow{V} u\} \text{ and analogously } \text{adj}_V^- (v) = \{u \in v|\, u \xrightarrow{V} v\}.$$

With the help of these definitions, the node set v of an EPC can be specified in more detail. The following individual sets are distinguished.

■ The set of functions F where $F = \{u \in v|\, \tau(u) = \text{function}\}$. $F \neq \varnothing$ is true, so every EPC possesses at least one function.

■ The set F_H of hierarchically ranked functions where $F_H = \{u \in v|\, \tau(u) = \text{hierarchically ranked function}\}$

■ E stands for the set of events:

$E = \{u \in v|\, \tau(u) = \text{event}\}$.

The set of events can be further divided into:

− the set of start events $E_S = \{u \in E|\, \bar{\gamma}(u, Kfk) = 0 \wedge \dot{\gamma}(u, Kfk) = 1\}$, where Kfk stands for a control flow link. Every EPC contains at least one start event. Therefore, $E_S \neq \varnothing$ is true.

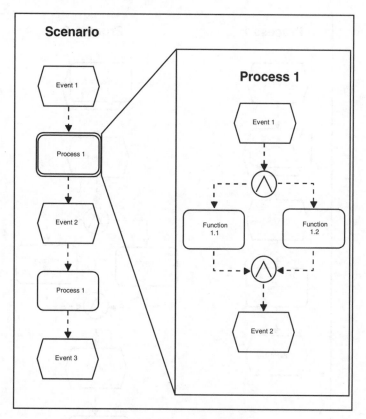

Fig. 4.6: Hierarchy building

- the set $E_{PS} = \{u \in E| \exists v \in V : \tau(v) \in \{$process sign, hierarchically ranked function$\}$ $\wedge u \in adj_V^+ (v)\}$ of start events for a subsequent or subordinate EPC

- the set of end events $E_E = \{u \in E| \dot\gamma(u,Kfk) = 1 \wedge \gamma^+(u, Kfk) = 0\}$. $E_E \neq \varnothing$ is true.

- the set $E_{PE} = \{u \in E| \exists v \in V : \tau(v) \in \{$process sign, hierarchically ranked function $\} \wedge u \in adj_V^- (v)\}$ of end events for a preceding or subordinate EPC

- the set E_N of internal events of an EPC

  $E_N = E \setminus (E_S \cup E_{PS} \cup E_E \cup E_{PE})$

- $P_N = \{u \in P| \gamma(u,Kfk) + \gamma^+(u,Kfk) = 1\}$ is the set of „normal“ process signs that point to a preceding or subsequent EPC.

161

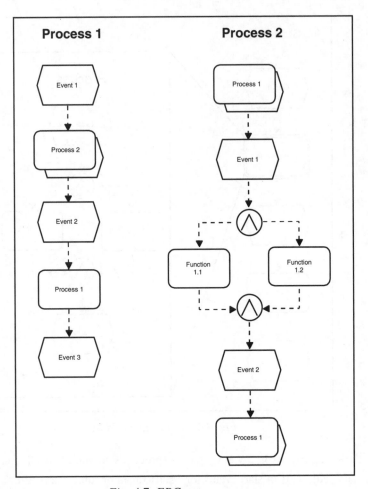

Fig. 4.7: EPC macro

- The set of connectors J can be divided into the set of joins and the set of distributors. The joins J_{AND}, J_{OR} and J_{XOR} are used to synchronize parallel process flows, whereas the distributors D_{AND}, D_{OR} and D_{XOR} divide a process flow into several process flows. The following are true:

- $J_{AND} = \{u \in v|\ \tau(u) = \text{AND connector} \wedge \gamma(u,Kfk) > 1 \wedge \gamma^{+}(u, Kfk) = 1\}$

- $J_{OR} = \{u \in v|\ \tau(u) = \text{OR connector} \wedge \gamma(u,Kfk) > 1 \wedge \gamma^{+}(u, Kfk) = 1\}$

- $J_{XOR} = \{u \in v|\ \tau(u) = \text{XOR connector} \wedge \gamma(u,Kfk) > 1 \wedge \gamma^{+}(u, Kfk) = 1\}$

- $D_{AND} = \{u \in v|\ \tau(u) = \text{AND connector} \wedge \gamma(u,Kfk) = 1 \wedge \gamma^{+}(u, Kfk) > 1\}$

- $D_{OR} = \{u \in v|\ \tau(u) = \text{OR connector} \wedge \gamma(u,Kfk) = 1 \wedge \gamma^{+}(u, Kfk) > 1\}$

- $D_{XOR} = \{u \in v|\ \tau(u) = \text{XOR connector} \wedge \gamma(u,Kfk) = 1 \wedge \gamma^{+}(u, Kfk) > 1\}$

■ $P = P_M \cup P_N = \{u \in v| \tau(u) = \text{process sign}\}$ stands for the set of process signs, where:

  – $P_M = \{u \in P| \gamma(u,\text{Kfk}) = 1 \wedge \gamma^+(u,\text{Kfk}) = 1\}$ is the set of process macros that reference a subordinate EPC

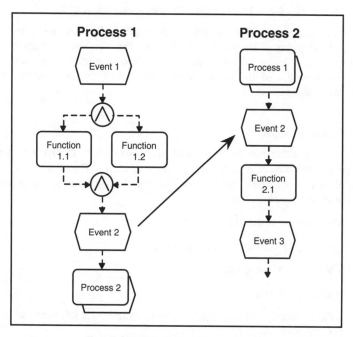

Fig. 4.8: EPC connections

■ $C_I = \{u \in v| \tau(u) = \text{input container}\}$ is the set of input containers. Because an EPC contains at least one function, and every function is assigned an input container, $C_I \neq \varnothing$ is true.

■ $C_o = \{u \in v| \tau(u) = \text{output container}\}$ stands for the set of output containers, where $C_o \neq \varnothing$.

■ $O = \{u \in v| \tau(u) = \text{organizational unit}\}$ is the set of organizational units.

The set $K = K_K \cup K_I \cup K_O$ of the links of an EPC is divided into control flow links K_K, information flow links K_I, and links for the assignment of organizational units K_O.

■ $K_K = \{(u,v) \in (B_1 \times E) \cup (E \times B_1) \cup (J \times J)\}$ where $B_1 = F \cup F_H \cup P \cup J$ and the following is true:

  $(u,v) \in K_K : \Leftrightarrow \tau_K((u,v)) = \text{control flow link}$. This makes the following control flow links invalid:

  – Kfk that link events to events

  – Kfk that link functions or process signs to functions or process signs

- $K_I = \{(u,v) \in (B_2 \times C_o) \cup (C_1 \times B_2) \cup (C_o \times C_1)\}$ where $B_2 = F \cup F_H \cup P$.

    $(u,v) \in K_I : \Leftrightarrow \tau_K((u,v)) =$ information flow link

- $K_o = \{(u,v) \in (F \times O) \cup (O \times F)\}$

    $(u,v) \in K_o: \Leftrightarrow \tau_K((u,v)) =$ organization assignment link

Based on this definition, it is possible to describe an EPC model in its entirety. For the following description of the control flow, the slim version of event-controlled process chains is used as a basis, which is used as the basis for the explanations in this book. A formal representation of the information flow and of the assignment of organizational units is not examined in detail.

4.3.3   Control flow

The control flow describes the sequential process flows of events, functions and process signs. For a better overview, assume $v_K = F \cup F_H \cup E \cup P \cup J$ is the set of control-flow-relevant elements of an EPC model. An EPC that is correct in terms of control flow must exhibit the following characteristics:

K1:   There are no isolated nodes, i.e.

$$\forall\, u \in v_K : \gamma^-(u,Kfk) + \gamma^+(u,Kfk) > 0.$$

K2:   There are no loops, i.e.

$$\forall\, u \in v_K : (u,u) \notin K.$$

K3:   (Hierarchically ranked) functions have exactly one inbound and one outbound control flow link, i.e.

$$\forall\, u \in F \cup F_H : i^-(u,Kfk) = 1 \wedge i^+(u,Kfk) = 1.$$

K4:   Events have exactly one inbound and/or one outbound control flow link, i.e.

$$\forall\, u \in E : (i^-(u,Kfk) = 1 \wedge i^+(u,Kfk) = 1) \vee u \in E_s \vee u \in E_E.$$

K5:   Process signs have only one inbound and/or one outbound control flow link, i.e.

$$\forall\, u \in P : (i^-(u,Kfk) + i^+(u,Kfk) = 1) \vee (i^-(u,Kfk) = 1 \wedge i^+(u,Kfk) = 1).$$

K6:   Connectors have either several inbound and one outbound control flow links or one
inbound and several outbound control flow links, i.e.

$$\forall\, u \in J : (i^-(u,Kfk) = 1 \wedge i^+(u,Kfk) > 1) \vee (i^-(u,Kfk) > 1 \wedge i^+(u,Kfk) = 1).$$

In the former case, the connector is called a distributor, and in the latter case, the connector is called a join.

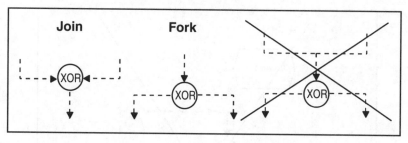

Fig. 4.9: Joins and distributors

K7: Connections between connectors are acyclical, i.e.

$$\forall\, u \in J : u \xrightarrow{v} v \Rightarrow u \neq v.$$

K8: Events are only linked to (hierarchically ranked) functions and process signs, i.e.

$$\forall\, u, v \in E \cup F \cup F_H \cup P : u \xrightarrow{v} v \wedge u \in E \Rightarrow v \in F \cup F_H \cup P.$$

K9: (Hierarchically ranked) functions and process signs are linked only with events, i.e.

$$\forall\, u, v \in E \cup F \cup F_H \cup P : u \xrightarrow{v} v \wedge u \in F \cup F_H \cup P \Rightarrow v \in E.$$

K10: Because events are not allowed to make decisions with regard to the continuation of
the process flow, no outbound connections are split off of events, i.e.

$$\forall\, e \in E,\, \forall\, u_1, u_2 \in F \cup F_H \cup P,\, u_1 \neq u_2,\, \forall\, w \in J :$$

$$e \xrightarrow{v} w \xrightarrow{v} u_1 \wedge e \xrightarrow{v} w \xrightarrow{v} u_2 \Rightarrow w \in D_{AND}.$$

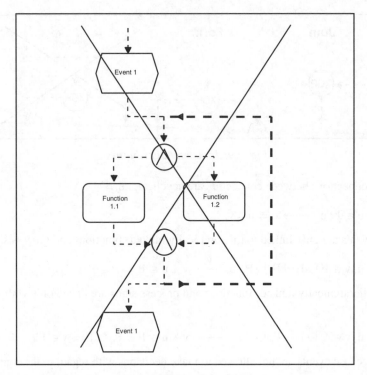

Fig. 4.10: Invalid cycles

K11: All events, (hierarchically ranked) functions and process macros are linked to a start event, i.e.

$$\forall\, u \in v_K \,\exists\, v_1,...,v_n \in v_K,\, n \in N_0 : v_1 \to \cdots \to v_n \to u \wedge v_1 \in E_{pg.}$$

K12: All events, (hierarchically ranked) functions and process macros are linked by a path to an end event, i.e.

$$\forall\, u \in v_K \,\exists\, v_1,...,v_n \in v_K,\, n \in N_0 : u \to v_1 \to \cdots \to v_n \wedge v_n \in E_E.$$

K13: There is at least one start event and at least one end event.

K14: Multiple links between two nodes are not allowed.

With the help of the rules described here, the consistency of EPC models can be analyzed. In this case, consistency means freedom from contradictions and coherence in the EPC models.

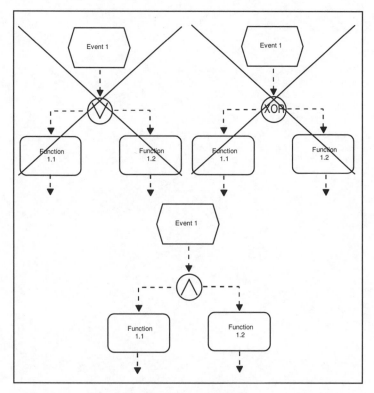

Fig. 4.11: Invalid connections

The consistency criteria described here for the most part describe the consistency of individual EPC models. Such criteria are identified as local consistency criteria. To check all of the models of a reference model, one must formulate global consistency criteria. An example is the existence of corresponding process signs. Every outbound process sign has a process sign in the called process that identifies the calling process. A formal description of the global consistency criteria will not be provided here.

Section C
IPP for Designing Net Value Added Chains

„There are always three opinions: yours, mine, and the right one."

5   Procedures

A procedure, often called a procedure model in the literature, is a phase concept with defined phase results in which the work steps or activities, the methods or description languages (cf. Chapter 3.3), and tools (resources) to be used are determined (cf. Küffmann 1994, p. 45). Furthermore, a procedure should also provide information about the temporal and logical sequence in which the individual activities are to be performed (cf. Jost 1993, pp. 12–13). The basic goal of a procedure model is to systematically structure the solution process for a complex task. This structuring results in easily comprehensible sections (the phases just mentioned), which enable step-by-step planning, execution, decision making and inspection (cf. Pomberger/Blaschek 1996, p. 17). A procedure model is therefore „one of the essential foundations for a division-of-labor-based, uniform, repeatable process flow" (Chroust 1992, p. 37).

According to Chroust, procedure models can be set up on different levels (cf. Chroust 1992, p. 39). Global procedure models describe a principle process flow structure and general guidelines (for example, major procedure steps in software development), reality-based procedure models define work steps in executable form (for example, the creation of a process description with the standardized rules of event-controlled process chains in the work step *describe process flow*), and atomic models are very much at implementation level and provide detailed and precise definitions of all data and process steps. Likewise, procedures can be viewed from different points of view. Nüttgens mentions, for one thing, analogies to the product life cycle for software systems, underscoring the division into phases for procedure models (cf. Nüttgens 1995, pp. 19–25). For another thing, Nüttgens and Kirchmer differentiate the following three levels for use of procedures, similar to enterprise planning:

- strategic information management or strategic information system planning

- project management and implementation or tactical and operational information system planning

- information system design or standard-software-oriented information system planning (cf. Nüttgens 1995, pp. 90–93 and 113–228; cf. Kirchmer 1996, pp. 47–63)

Procedures are used in many very different fields (cf. Burghardt 1988; cf. Daenzer/Huber 1992; cf. Schmidt 1991; cf. Schulte-Zurhausen 1995; cf. Sommerville 1992). In the following sections, an attempt is made to differentiate and describe procedures according to different areas of use and different purposes.

5.1 Procedures in project management

„The term project management includes all activities that deal with the organization of software manufacturing. These include subdivision of the manufacturing process, of the division of labor, and of communication" (Kimm *et al.* 1979, p. 289). Project management is not isolated, however, but must rather be seen as part of the overall development area (cf. Burghardt 1988, p. 11).

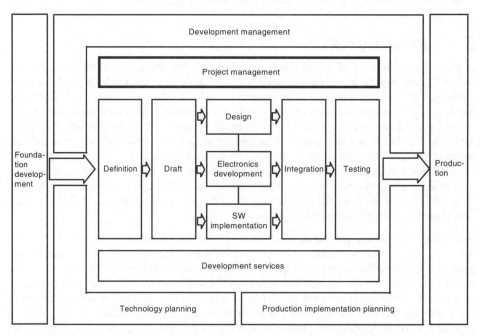

Fig. 5.1: Project management environment (source: Burghardt 1988, p. 11)

As visible in the illustration, above the project management for a project sits the development management of the area in question. „Individual project management receives from development-related management the decisive corner parameters for that area, just as vice versa development management draws its basic data from project management." (Burghardt 1988, p. 12).

Projects generally differ fundamentally from daily routine work and must therefore also be handled according to other points of view. „Projects are plans with a defined beginning and an end, that are characterized by a time limit, a relative newness and complexity, and by an interdisciplinary type of problem" (Schulte-Zurhausen 1995, p. 343). Daenzer and Huber define the term project management as a general term for all determining and strong-willed activities connected to the handling of projects. „The important thing here is not the activities that affect the problem to be solved itself, especially not the subject-matter contributions to the problem solution, but rather the management of the problem solving process." (Daenzer/ Huber 1992, p. 242).

According to the definition given above for a project, the idea is to ensure proper, on-time and cost-effective execution of projects through efficient project management. The procedure module according to Burghardt divides project flow into four main sections:

- project definition

- project planning

- project control

- project conclusion

Each of the project management tasks to be executed over the course of the project is assigned to these project sections. The relevant literature postulates various procedures in relation to this, which are oriented towards different paradigms. In most cases, there are no separate procedure models for project management. Instead, there are only explanations of tasks and contents of project management. So, for example, Schmidt and Schulte-Zurhausen structure the contents of project management into a *functional dimension* and an *institutional dimension*. Daenzer and Huber add to this classification a *personal*, a *psychological* and an *instrumental* dimension (cf. Schmidt 1991; Schulte-Zurhausen 1995; cf. Daenzer/Huber 1992).

The flow structure of a project, however, is always oriented towards the manufacturing process of the actual product, which is software production in our example. Procedures in software development, however, are part of the next chapter, so Burghardt's approach (cf. Burghardt 1988) is followed here, which is based on a separate procedure structure for the project.

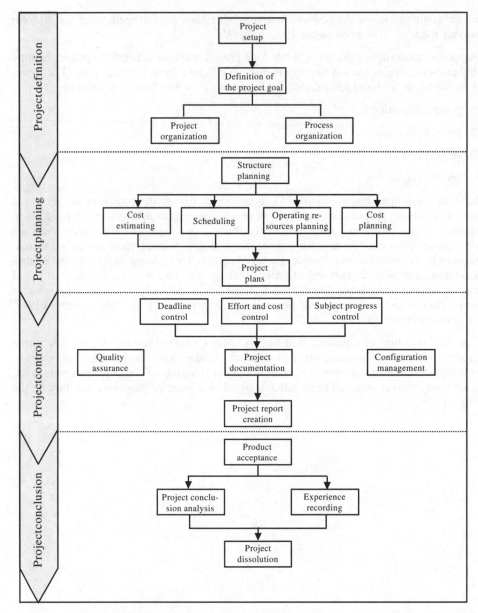

*Fig. 5.2: Project management tasks over the course of a project
(source: Burghardt 1988, p. 12)*

The project definition phase provides the foundation for the project. This phase includes:

■ establishment of the project

- definition of the project goal
- organization of the project
- organization of the process

The basics for all of the phases to follow are formed as part of *project definition*. The starting point in every project is the project proposal, which contains all of the relevant specifications for task description, cost and deadline goals, as well as responsibilities. Approving the project proposal creates the project order, thus establishing the project.

The next step involves complete and clear definition of the project goal. The project goal is documented by the contractor by way of a requirements catalogue or functional specifications. It is important to think beyond the current product requirements and already consider possible future changes to the product. The organizational prerequisites for the project are also created during project definition. In addition to choosing a type of organization, the designers must be named, and, finally, resource allocation must take place. The last section of this phase consists of determining the overall process-oriented organization of the development process. „This includes determining development phases, break points (milestones), development lines (baselines), and activity types" (Burghardt 1988, p. 13).

The *project planning* that follows includes task areas such as structure planning, effort estimation, scheduling, resource planning, cost planning, and the creation of project plans. The result of this phase is the project plans, which contain all of the results of the project planning. These plans include both plans for the organization, structuring and execution of the project and project plans for the deadlines, the planned effort, and costs.

After the planning documents have been created, actual project execution begins, accompanied by *project control*. Project control contains the following task areas:

- deadline control
- effort and cost control
- subject progress control
- quality assurance
- configuration management
- project documentation
- project report creation

Fulfilling the individual task areas is optional, and, depending on the type and scope of the project, can be done with different levels of intensity. For example, in larger projects, deadline control makes sense only with network technology. Furthermore, trend analyses may offer useful support in deadline control and in effort and cost control. Subject progress control is probably the most important, but also the most difficult, task for project leaders, because usually there are no direct ways to measure the progress of the subject matter. In this case, too, network technology can provide a lot of support. Project-accompanying and development-supporting quality assurance contains the tasks of quality planning, quality control and inspection. The goal is to produce high-quality products with minimal development costs through timely error prevention. Configuration management guarantees transparency and consistency in the multitude of individual parts in a system to be developed. All of the information about project events flows into the project documentation. This contains both the pure project plans and the project reports in which information about the current status is entered and compared to plan information. Project report creation delivers all of the relevant information to directly or indirectly involved instances and persons.

The final project section, *project conclusion*, contains the following steps:

- product purchase
- project completion analysis
- experience recording
- project dissolution

Project conclusion is introduced by product acceptance, in which the finished product must undergo an acceptance test, if possible at a location independent of development. The project conclusion analysis includes a final costing that, because it is created in the same procedure as preliminary costing and standard cost estimating, can provide informative insights into deviations that have occurred. It is advisable to record these and other similar results in experience recording, in order to be able to make good use of this knowledge in future projects. The last step in the project conclusion phase and thus in the project flow as a whole is project dissolution. As already mentioned above, a project is characterized by fixed start and end points. When these are reached, the project personnel can be transferred to new tasks, and the resources tied to the project can be directed to new projects (cf. Burghardt 1988, pp. 12–16).

5.2   Procedures in software engineering

Due to the high requirements for functionality, integration and distribution, industrial development of software systems requires large development projects. There is, however, debate about how the sequence of such projects should be handled and in which form of organization (macro organization) they should be handled, for example as a pure project organization, as a matrixed project organization, as an order-based project organization, and how the project teams (micro organization) should be structured, for example organization structures with centralized control, with decentralized control, or democratically decentralized (cf. Nüttgens 1995, pp. 167–175).

When manufacturing software, one encounters numerous difficulties, which can be traced back to, among other things, the complexity of business management and software as well as the tasks to be executed during the creation process. To ensure the quality of software, the following measures are recommended, which can be divided into three classes (cf. Pomberger/Blaschek 1996, pp. 9–15):

- Class of constructive measures, such as consistent use of methods in all phases of the development process, use of appropriate development tools, and consistent development documentation

- Class of analytical measures, such as systematic selection of suitable test cases and consistent logging of analysis results

- Class of organizational measures, such as the application of systematic procedures and institutionalization of quality assurance

„Developing high quality software with low costs is a demanding activity that is ultimately shaped by systematic procedure." (Xu 1995, p. 22). Therefore, an attempt was made to introduce engineering-style procedures into the software development process and to divide the process into phases for this purpose. The numerous variations of the phase concept that have been created assume the following six steps in their basic principles (cf. Kimm *et al.* 1979, pp. 18–19; cf. Pomberger/Blaschek 1996, p. 18; cf. Sommerville 1992, p. 5):

- problem analysis and planning

- system specification (requirements definition)

- system and component design

- implementation and component testing

- system test

- operation and maintenance

The phase concept assumes that for every phase there is a clear definition of the results the phase must produce. The subsequent phase can begin only when the preceding phase has been entirely completed. This strict sequential procedure is mirrored in the classical model of the software life cycle. „One associates the term *software life cycle* with the idea of a period of time in which the software product is developed and implemented, all the way to the end of its use" (Pomberger/Blaschek 1996, p. 18). Software engineering according to the software life cycle is based on turning „black boxes" into reality step by step. This is also called „top down decomposition".

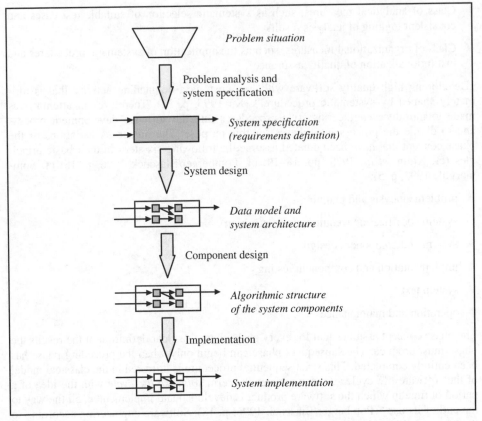

Fig. 5.3: Step-by-step turning into reality according to the software life cycle model
(source: Pomberger/Blaschek 1996, p. 21)

Two aspects are characteristic of the procedure pictured above. The system is first defined from the outside, which means that at first it describes only *what* the system or software should do. The internal structure of the software is consciously neglected in the beginning and is represented as grey boxes. In the subsequent phases, it is then illuminated step by step. „The phases are clearly delimited and should be exited only when the results have been accepted in a verification/validation step" (Pomberger/Blaschek 1996, p. 21). It is critical to note that such a method, which requires the conclusion of a planning step before the next step can be executed, leads to expensive software development due to the absence of feedback and coordination mechanisms.

Over time, very different variants of the phased model crystallized out of the experiences with classical software life cycle concepts. Characteristic for these models was the fact that they further subdivided the individual phases and furthermore that they paid attention to the interactions between the individual phases. Probably the most well known of these models, the waterfall model, is presented here as a representative of these models (cf. Boehm 1981, pp. 35–56).

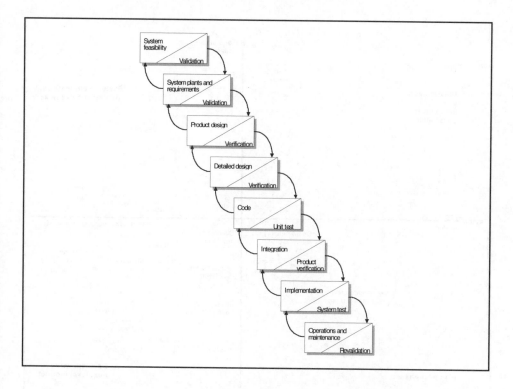

Fig. 5.4: The waterfall model (source: Boehm 1981, p. 36)

The waterfall model contains two important expansions when compared to the sequential software life cycle model:

■ The introduction of feedback between the development steps, with the simultaneous restriction that such feedback may occur only between two sequential phases. The goal of this procedure is to minimize *expensive* subsequent processing resulting from iterations that span several phases.

■ The integration of validation of phase results into the development process.

This approach softens the strict sequential procedure of the software life cycle and moves an incremental procedure into the foreground in its place. Repeated runthroughs, especially of the specification phase – „first as a prototype for experimental validation and quick correction and then as phase model" (Pomberger/Blaschek 1996, p. 24) – reduce the risk of a faulty or incomplete system specification.

Nüttgens places the procedure presented here in the category of traditional procedures. In addition, he makes a distinction between transformation-oriented procedures, which are characterized by an automated transition between design phase and implementation phase, and evolutionary procedures, which support incremental and prototyping-oriented development (cf. Nüttgens 1995, pp. 18–25). The spiral model and the Fontain model represent the class of evolutionary procedures (cf. Boehm 1988, pp. 64–72; cf. Henderson-Sellers/Edwards 1990, pp. 142–159).

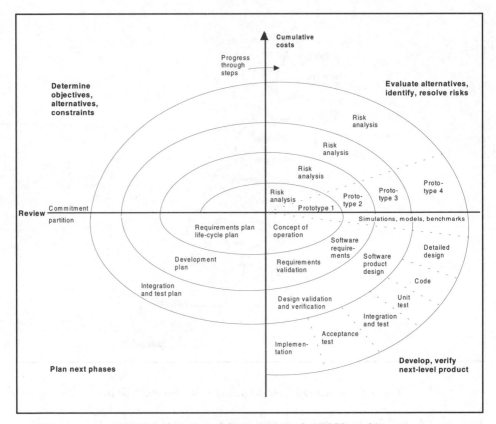

Fig. 5.5: Spiral model (source: Boehm 1988, p. 64)

In the case of the spiral model, every cycle leads to an executable system, so that the use of individual subsystems can be checked quicker. The spiral model is divided into four quadrants and describes software development as a sequence of iterative tasks. Development begins in the middle of the quadrant, and the steps *define goals and basic conditions*, *risk analysis*, *implementation* and *test* are run through in every cycle. In the first quadrant, the defined goals are specified with regard to alternative solution concepts and the prevailing influential factors or constraints for the development concepts. In the second quadrant, the solution alternatives at hand are evaluated using the various tools of prototyping, simulation, tests and inquiries. In the third quadrant, the individual requirements are further specified, and the product or the prototype is further developed. A cycle is concluded with a review of the targeted (sub)goals, and the transition to the first quadrant begins.

One advantage of this procedure is that an executable prototype is available after every cycle. This can be used for testing purposes with regard to feasibility and quality and can thus support project management. Because every cycle is considered a separate project, the stated goals of an overall design can be validated earlier, possible risks can be assessed better, and the potential for risk can be reduced.

5.3   Procedures in software implementation

There are various recommendations for installing standard software that are based more or less on the common basic steps of *corporate analysis, comparison of requirements to the capabilities of the application software, system implementation* and *monitoring of the productive system.* Where previously the focus was on so-called functional analyses, these days there is a growing trend towards considering the process orientation aspect (cf. Brenner/Hamm 1995, p. 32; cf. Österle 1995, p. 31). Despite consideration of the process idea, however, an extensive disjunct view of the individual steps is often in the foreground, although in the sense of process orientation the steps are highly networked and have interactions. This way of thinking, which probably resulted for practical reasons as an obvious simplification, leads to the fact that the networked state behind the process idea is insufficiently considered. For this reason, at this point there is often only a note that the steps to be executed can also be executed iteratively, without showing how and in what form said iteration occurs.

Next to phase orientation, most of the existing approaches are based on the concept of determining the customer's requirements in comprehensive analyses. Here, too, however, there is an increasing trend towards performing analyses on the basis of reference models provided by software vendors and consulting companies. The resources supplied for this, however, often leave open the question of how the reference models can be implemented efficiently and quality-assured. Furthermore, tool-based restrictions often lead to a focus on technical questions about tool handling, allowing the business requirements analysis for determining the needs of the user to recede into the background. Certainly, however, continued developments in the market for DP-supported implementation tools will increasingly include user-oriented requirements, moving the factual question of the implementation of standard software back into the foreground. The BPI phase concept and the 4 phase concept are described here as representatives of the phase-oriented approach for the implementation of standard software.

5.3.1   The BPI phase concept

In the *business-process-oriented implementation of standard software (BPI),* an attempt is made to emphasize and coordinate interfaces between strategic, tactical and operational implementation methods (cf. Kirchmer 1996, p. 47). The starting point is a comparison between representatives of strategic information system planning (cf. Wildemann 1990), tactical and operational information system planning (cf. Heinrich/Burgholzer 1990), and explicitly standard-software-oriented approaches (cf. Keller/Meinhardt 1994) represented by a DP-supported procedure (cf. Kirchmer 1996, p. 63).

In his analysis, Kirchmer points out the emphases of the approaches mentioned and, on this basis, develops a separate approach for business-process-oriented implementation of standard software. The strategic view serves as a basis, and a complete approach for information system planning is developed on this, without neglecting standard software aspects. The procedure for business-process-oriented implementation integrates the approaches quoted above and goes beyond these in partially explained aspects (for example, specification and putting into concrete form as part of implementation).

The procedure contains three business-process-oriented levels (BPLs) (cf. Kirchmer 1996, pp. 73–212). The BPL design, which is based on the enterprise strategy, serves as the starting point into BPI. It takes into account the branch-of-industry and corporate situation of the user enterprise and defines strategy objectives derived from this. Separate concept development, independent of the standard software, according to exclusively business-oriented points of view, is characteristic. In order to later adjust to the standard software specification, business process models that are drafted are kept at a general level and are brought in by the user enterprise at this level of detail for continued BPI.

Regardless of the strategic objectives, the manufacturer of standard software provides the equipment for the standard-software-based concept. The business aspects specified by the enterprise in the strategy-based BPL design are detailed on the basis of the standard software's process design. Putting things into concrete form is possible down to the transaction level of the standard software, so that you can design the usage of the software by the user enterprise optimally on the basis of a business concept. The process design mentioned includes the provision of reference models, which are typically general and well structured and can therefore be adjusted to enterprise-specific requirements. In general, a distinction is made between branch-of-industry and standard-software reference models, with the branch-of-industry reference model also supporting the enterprise's strategy concept.

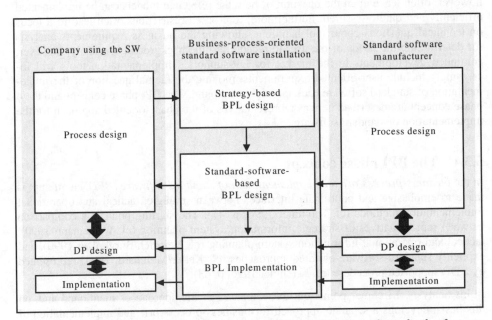

Fig. 5.6: Procedure for business-process-oriented implementation of standard software (source: Kirchmer 1996, p. 71)

From the two concepts, a measure catalogue is developed for implementing the final implementation, the BPL implementation. Typical questions deal with the DP design, implementation questions, or definitions of interfaces, to be able to copy existing data or ensure that the system is open towards external applications. BPI concept development is also oriented towards event-controlled process chains (cf. Chapter 4) with which the procedure is modelled at every BPL level.

■ *Strategy-based BPL design (cf. Kirchmer 1996, pp. 73–124)*
Starting with a goal definition, Kirchmer first formulates the general requirements for the concept for developing strategically oriented business processes. It should include enterprise-specific and branch-of-industry-specific aspects, be standard-software-neutral and business-oriented, and exhibit a low degree of concretization with a high degree of freedom.

The development process begins with the specification of a target system. All of the implementation activities are oriented towards this and have a supportive effect. As far as content is concerned, a competition strategy is set up for the user enterprise. In it, targeted goals such as cost leadership or concentration on emphases are formulated, and critical success factors (for example, increasing flexibility, reducing costs) are identified, from which concrete operational objectives regarding quantities, time frames and costs are subsequently developed. The number of goals that are set depends on the size and results of a current-state analysis of the enterprise in question.

Afterwards, business processes are defined at a general level of detail. They should model the enterprise completely as an overall system and should in the process include both indirectly affected as well as enterprise-spanning areas. The development may be based on a branch-of-industry reference model, if one is available. If this is the case, all of the functions or the underlying flow logic contained in it must be adjusted to the enterprise-specific requirements or supplemented to include missing business processes. The latter is the case, for example, if the range of products is not completely recorded in the branch-of-industry reference model, or the target system anticipates previously undefined function/goal relationships. Event-controlled process chains are used for the modelling.

The third step in working out strategically oriented business processes involves specifying individual information system views. The goal here is to figure out, on a modelling basis, the enterprise specifics that are used in the BPI to obtain competitive advantages. In order to enable comparison later with the standard software, and to minimize planning efforts, the level of detail should be kept as low as possible in this case, too. The process is oriented towards general data modelling methodology, starting with working out product data models and a function-level design, on down to deriving the models to be created in the organization view, the function view, the data view and the control view. The description is based on entity relationship models (ERM).

In order to retain comprehensible units for further use in the BPI, there is a fourth step: the breakdown of business processes. The main idea is to manage complexity by creating comprehensible process excerpts. The standard software already provides the user enterprise with predefined structures for corresponding DP-supported subsystems.

The step that pulls it all together between the enterprise concept and the standard software concept is related to the scope of the standard software implementation. The enterprise must determine, based on the previous steps, which processes the standard software shall support. Specifically, the enterprise must work out sensible implementation possibilities and ensure that the standard software fulfils the enterprise specifics. The potential need for custom development emerges in this stage of planning. Core activities include comparing the defined business processes or detail information models and the information models of the standard software, with subsequent evaluation of the comparison. Finally, determination of the implementation strategy concretizes the path from the actual situation to the planned situation, realizing the defined goals. First, a basic plan is created for the application software that identifies the vendor and the scope of the standard software package. Subsequent prioritizing of subprocesses is based on the different uses of the processes for implementing the strategic enterprise goal. Scheduling pinpoints a time frame for the implementation activities, to prepare additional phases of the BPI.

■ *Standard-software-based BPL design (cf. Kirchmer 1996, pp. 125–168)*
From the vendor side, a detailed process design flows into the BPI; the goal of this design is the transformation into reality of the business processes on the basis of the standard software. The standard-software-based BPL design, however, includes modules that are independent of DP technology, meaning that the level of detail is based solely on a subject area/business foundation. The transformation takes place at transaction level and screen level and is divided into five steps by Kirchmer.

First, you determine consistent definitions for technical terms. The goal is to synchronize terminology that is valid across the entire enterprise, to avoid misunderstandings, overlaps, and deviations between standard software vendors and user enterprises. On the basis of a technical term model, enterprise-specific technical terms are assigned to standard-software terminology.

The second step comprises supplementing the BPL design with material flow. On the basis of interfaces between the material flow and the information flow, relevant business processes, for example in the entire logistical area, must be optimized with respect to this aspect and taken into account during standard software implementation. The latter makes the necessary infrastructure available in the shape of an information system, to support interactive relationships between material flow and the attendant information exchange. The transformation occurs on the basis of material flow considerations.

These two preparatory steps are followed by the third step: specification of the BPL design at the transaction level in the standard software. This is oriented towards the specifications of the existing transaction structure. The strategic orientation must be guaranteed by the standard software, especially with regard to relevant detail models, or supplemental measures must be defined. The standard software reference model serves as the basis. On this foundation, process-relevant objects are represented in the standard software, and afterwards these objects are transformed into data structures. After additional, neutral data models have also been represented at data structure level, the complete process models are specified and arranged in the organizational plan according to the standard software transactions. This includes the assignment of organizational units analogous to a plant and warehouse structure.

From the process view, specification continues in the next step at screen level. Screen processing and data entry begin at the lowest hierarchy level and require reducing all degrees of freedom in strategy-based BPL design in such a way that the realization of the strategic goals is completely assured. Specification at screen level includes the selection of model excerpts and information system views, on the basis of which process models and data models are projected onto the screen level. With regard to the data models, authorization aspects such as access privileges and archiving times must then be specified. The last step in standard-software-based BPL design determines a migration strategy, in which the standard software implementation schedule is coordinated, differentiated according to DP-oriented and organization-oriented measures, to prepare for BPL implementation.

■ *BPL implementation (cf. Kirchmer 1996, pp. 169–201)*
Starting with the migration strategy that was worked out, and taking into consideration basic conditions, the standard software infrastructure is implemented, and the organization structure in the enterprise is rearranged in preparation for going live.

Typical DP-oriented measures affect hardware and software, as well as data-oriented measures and system tests. Specific actions include, for example, defining interfaces for data transfer or customizing. Organization-oriented measures affect the following areas: personnel, responsibility-oriented organization and process-oriented organization, as well as the work space concept. This is where activities such as training, system administration structuring, recruiting, and the arrangement of departments take place. Kirchmer's BPI ends with going live. The standard software is put into operation, and migration strategy measures are activated, with the implementation phase being accompanied by startup support. Kirchmer does emphasize, however, the importance of optimization and continuous monitoring of the standard software beyond the implementation phase.

In a continual improvement process, achievement of strategic goals can be ensured, and modifications due to new basic conditions can be taken into consideration in the shape of continual modifications. The latter can include both the defined target system and the strategy-based and standard-software-based BPL design. After the description of the individual BPI phases and the specification of each, Kirchmer models the BPI at three levels of detail. In addition, aspects of the requirements for the BPI concept are examined explicitly, such as the comparison of object-oriented and function-oriented points of view, integration aspects, decentralization of work processes, dynamic aspects, and the targeted inclusion of employees during the standard software implementation. At the end, Kirchmer looks to the future, where he sees runtime optimization concepts for running standard software systems gaining importance. Something known as IS management is supported on IS planning, which determines further development.

In his concept, Kirchmer refines the steps to be executed, from strategic planning to implementation. In his phase-oriented approach, however, he does not give any indication of practicability with respect to implementation time, implementation costs or implementation quality. Likewise, optimization of business processes comes up often, although in business management literature, optimization is regarded as a task that is anything but trivial, and that might even be impossible.

5.3.2 AcceleratedSAP

AcceleratedSAP (ASAP) is SAP's comprehensive implementation solution for streamlining R/3 projects. It is the process component of TeamSAP and was introduced in June ´96 and released for worldwide availability in June ´97. It is continuously being improved and updated by an international consulting team that collects very detailed feedback from SAP customers who already use it. AcceleratedSAP optimizes time, quality and efficient use of resources.

AcceleratedSAP – ASAP for short – is SAP's all-in-one solution for rapid implementation and ongoing optimization of R/3. The similarity to the common abbreviation for „as soon as possible" is, of course, no coincidence. Offering comprehensive, front-to-back support with tools, recommendations and checklists, it has all the answers to questions such as:

▪ How much will my project cost and how long will it take?

▪ How do I go about the implementation?

▪ How can I ensure quality?

▪ What tools can I use?

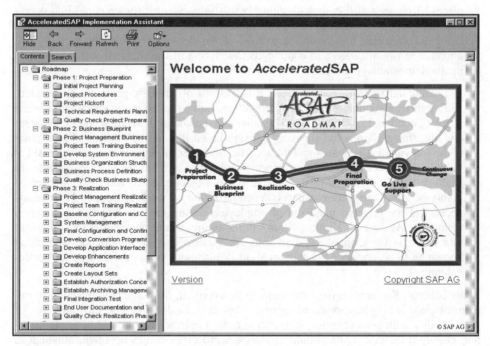

Fig. 5.7: ASAP Roadmap

AcceleratedSAP bundles the expertise gleaned from the countless R/3 implementation projects carried out over the past five years, and aims to offer you the best from these experiences. It is process-oriented throughout, and greatly streamlines the implementation procedure. In addition to the implementation tools contained in the R/3 Business Engineer in the R/3 System, it offers you instruments that up until now normally had to be created from scratch for every project – templates, examples and checklists. AcceleratedSAP includes a project plan in Microsoft Project®, and templates in PowerPoint® or Word® that cover all the issues typically dealt with by the steering committee, for example. An experienced consultant would probably have all these documents to hand. But what if you are planning your first R/3 implementation? AcceleratedSAP helps you think of everything – the first and most important step toward guaranteed quality. It focuses on the coordination of all elements that make an implementation successful:

■ *The Roadmap*

The Roadmap is a project plan with detailed descriptions about what, why and how certain activities are performed. It describes all activities in an implementation, makes sure that nothing is left out, and that project management plans well in advance for the execution of end-user training, for example. The Roadmap also includes the entire technical area to support technical project management and addresses things like interfaces, data conversions, and authorizations earlier than in most traditional implementations. It even includes printer setup – things that often proved to be difficult in the past. The Roadmap contains descriptions about what and why SAP does certain things. Wherever possible, the ASAP provides examples, checklists or templates as samples, for example, for a cutover plan. They are used as a starting point to avoid „reinventing the wheel". ASAP calls these things Accelerators. They are used in any type of implementation, even when you do not use all ASAP elements.

■ *Tools*

Tools include ASAP-specific tools to support project management, questionnaires for the business process consultants, and numerous technical guidebooks and checklists. The backbone in the R/3 System is, of course, the Business Engineer with all of its configuration tools.

■ *R/3 Services and Training*

R/3 Services and Training includes all consulting, education and support services, such as the hotline, EarlyWatch, remote upgrade, archiving, etc. These products help standardize certain consulting tasks so that they can be performed as quickly as possible

AcceleratedSAP is divided into the following phases:

■ *Project Preparation*

The Project Preparation phase is concerned with organizing the executive kickoff meeting and making all the organizational arrangements for the project team. Once the team has been chosen, they are trained in the AcceleratedSAP methodology, a rough project plan is drafted, and the hardware order is checked. The project starts officially with the kickoff meeting, which is attended by the project team, SAP consultants, and the customer's steering committee. Checklists and templates are of course available for all the activities in this phase – to make the work easier, and to ensure that nothing is overlooked. Based on an estimated project duration of six months, this phase would take between one and two weeks.

■ *Business Blueprint*

The aim of the Business Blueprint phase is to document your requirements. Interviews and workshops on the individual enterprise process areas, supported by questionnaires and graphical process chains from the R/3 Business Engineer, help you decide which R/3 business processes you need. Interfaces legacy data, and other technical matters are also covered. The R/3 processes are demonstrated using the International Demo and Education System (IDES), a version of the complete R/3 System that SAP offers to all customers for hands-on experience of the software. Together with the consultants, you create the Business Blueprint, a to-be business analysis that consists of written and pictorial representations of the company's structure and business processes. Once the blueprint has been approved, it becomes the central document in the project, and is used as the basis for all further activities. At the end of this phase, the project managers use the Business Blueprint to plan resources, check hardware requirements, and clear up any open issues. Again, based on an estimated project duration of six months, this phase would take three to four weeks.

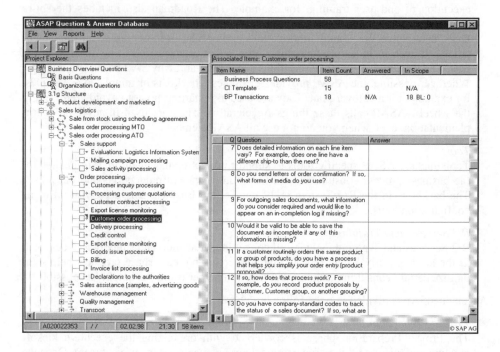

Fig. 5.8: Questions for the process „Customer order processing"

■ *Realization*

Based on the processes documented in the Business Blueprint, a baseline system is configured to match your company structure 100% and to cover 80% of your daily business processes. The system is configured and documented using the R/3 Business Engineer tools. The technical team sets up the system administration and plans the interfaces and data transfer. SAP consultants work together with the project team, so that they can apply the skills they've learned in the training courses. At the end of the phase, the customer project team presents the central business processes to a larger group of end users and decision makers, to verify that the blueprint has been implemented correctly. The customer system is not configured during the Business Blueprint phase, so that the system produced here – known as the baseline system – is the basis for the production system. There is no prototype that's discarded. Fine-tuning takes place during the Validation phase.

■ *Final Preparation*
The Final Preparation phase sees the consolidation of all the activities in the previous phases, and is aimed at readying the R/3 System and the company for production startup. This phase covers the final system tests, end-user training and migration of data to the new system. The conversion and interface programs are all checked, volume and stress tests are run, and user-acceptance tests are carried out. The first EarlyWatch session, which is designed to actively tune the R/3 System, often takes place at this point. To train end users, the project team trains key users utilizing a train-the-trainer method. The goals are to develop the expertise needed for day-to-day business and to promote end-user acceptance. Another purpose of this phase is to create a production-startup strategy. This plan specifically identifies the data-conversion strategy, internal audit procedures and end-user support (internal help desk). The final step is to sign off the system, to go live and switch on. This phase takes four to five weeks.

■ *Go live and support continuous change*
Immediately after going live, the system is reviewed to ensure that the business environment is fully supported. This means checking the business processes and technical parameters, and interviewing end users. In the last step, the business benefits of the new system are measured, to monitor the return on investment from the start. This can be followed by more phases aimed at further improving the processes.

Most of the project activities take place in the Blueprint phase. Iterative Process Prototyping is one analysis technique in this phase; its goal is to build customer-oriented net value added chains on the basis of the R/3 reference processes.

6 Cybernetics in Iterative Process Prototyping (IPP)

Cybernetics means using various instruments in a targeted fashion while taking into consideration the effects on adjacent areas or questions (cf. Chapter 1.4.7). The result of cybernetics in business process design for planning information systems and the associated implementation of standard software is that one leaves behind traditional phase concepts and, depending on the task at hand, uses the optimum information material. According to this point of view, it is sometimes even desirable in an early phase of the business process discussion, for example, to consider physical solutions as alternatives to a piece of software (see Chapter 6.3 regarding holding a workshop).

6.1 IPP structure

The goal of Iterative Process Prototyping (IPP) is the implementation of feasible business processes. This means that the enterprise needs an organization form and employees that can execute and control the desired processes. But the enterprise also needs information technology with which the processes can be executed consistently, quickly and with assured quality. First comes the planning of the optimum business process under basic economic, staffing and ecological conditions, and in the end there is the assurance that the planned business process can also be executed with the technology available on the market.

The availability of information technology in the marketplace makes it possible to use various resources at different levels of intensity in the selection process. Say, for example, that an enterprise needs a piece of software to be developed; in this case, it must think about building a consistent data structure. If an enterprise wants to install integrated standard software, the fundamental data structure and the degree of freedom it allows are prescribed by the software vendor. In this case, selection concentrates primarily on the aspects relevant to process flow, with the corresponding embedding in the organization. Often, however, an enterprise cannot meet all of its requirements with the standard software from a single vendor, meaning that it must in some cases connect other systems (for example, a system for controlling driverless transportation units in a high rack storage area) or custom-develop special tasks (for example, a marketing information system for planning portfolios for new market segments). To ensure that in these situations consistent integration with the standard system, which has been implemented to the greatest extent possible, is retained, the logical and technical data structures must be coordinated for data transfer, for example.

To support the different situations that an enterprise may find itself in when selecting and implementing standard software, SAP AG has developed various resources, whose most important contents are presented briefly in the sections that follow. Iterative Process Prototyping is active in the area of resources that can be considered to belong more to the conceptual, business level or more to the implemented, system level (cf. Teufel/Ertl 1995, pp. 22–24). The former of these two levels includes the models for R/3 reference processes, for R/3 organization, and for R/3 objects and R/3 data, while the latter of these levels includes the R/3 System (R/3 Prototyping with the model company IDES – International Demonstration and Education System, and the corresponding R/3 documentation), R/3 Customizing (Implementation Guide and parameter configuration), and the R/3 Data Dictionary.

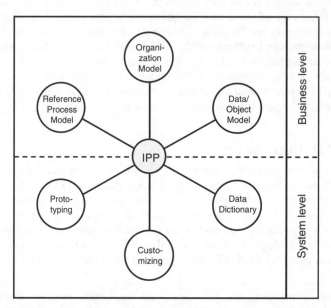

Fig. 6.1: Basic elements of Iterative Process Prototyping (IPP)

At the business level, the conceptual relationships are displayed as models in diagrams. The goal is to meet the demands for *simplicity* and *transparency* by concentrating on the central questions, such as „Which business processes does the enterprise need?", „Which organizational units are linked in what way?", „Which information is processed and how is it connected to other information?" The system level shows the physical or implemented world of the business requirements in the R/3 System. In this case, it is the demands for *completeness* and *feasibility* that are being addressed. Completeness refers to the scope of capabilities offered by the R/3 System, with all of its functional details (millions of lines of code and thousands of tables). Feasibility means that the R/3 System provides a highly integrated application software system with the guarantee that the solutions demonstrated in the model world (business level) can be carried out completely and in an integrated fashion with the R/3 System.

6.1.1 R/3 Reference Process Model

To simplify the representation of the process flows implemented in the R/3 System, SAP AG has represented the R/3 processes in graphic model images using the event-controlled process chain (EPC) method. The R/3 processes offered by SAP AG provide an extensive, integrated and function-spanning collection of operational business processes that occur often in practice and can be handled to the greatest extent possible automatically if one implements the complete R/3 System. The created R/3 processes are assigned to the business areas offered, such as sales and distribution, production, and financial management, allowing the user to enter the model world from his subject area.

The R/3 reference processes are used to represent the most important business process flows supported by the R/3 System. Each individual R/3 process usually shows one logically coherent task of a qualified staff person, for example processing of a purchase order, with determination of the least expensive material, vendor selection and purchase order monitoring, or order processing, with determination of price and delivery conditions, picking, and route planning. The semi-formal description of the EPC, i.e. defined symbols, allows the business contents of the R/3 System to be revealed in a *standardized communication language*. By linking processes together, it is possible to give the user an understanding of department-spanning processes and also to make transparent the interaction between operational functional areas. Determining and defining business terms makes it possible to reduce the multitude of terms used for the same thing (something one often encounters in practice) to a common *communication term*. This reduces unnecessary discussion caused by the use of different terms during teamwork in business process design.

The R/3 Reference Process Models are meant to address operational decision makers, administrators, planning engineers and qualified staff members in the business areas. With this objective in mind, the number of descriptive elements used (for example, showing a function as a rounded rectangle) is limited to those most necessary for understanding the flow logic that is feasible in business with the R/3 System, and the arrangement of the symbols used is standardized to support navigation that can be easily understood. Wherever possible, the language of users familiar with business was used to describe the contents of the symbols, and no technical abbreviations, which are used often in information science, were used as explanations. However, for the symbols containing business contents, in places where it makes sense to do so, the user is shown the links to the physically implemented R/3 System through specification of the transaction code (cf. Keller 1995, pp. 45–66).

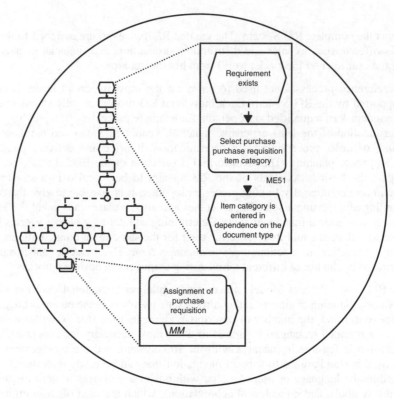

Fig. 6.2: R/3 reference process Purchase Requisition Processing (excerpt)

A process analysis begins with an analysis of the potential entry points. Although in the integrated R/3 System data transfer from one process to the subsequent process occurs automatically, it is useful in the requirements analysis to analyze any process links that may exist, in order to configure the customer-specific net value added chain based on this.

In the example at hand, an employee from the production department has manually reported a requirement for stock material, that is, the process begins with the starting event *Requirement exists*. In the next step, the item category for the stock material must be determined in the transaction, which is why the reference model contains a note for the corresponding transaction, ME51. Stock material is handled in the R/3 System with the item category NORMAL, which is defined in accordance with the document type (in this case, the document type is purchase requisition). In the next steps, the material to be requisitioned is specified, item detail data is entered, the source is determined, and the purchase requisition is automatically monitored in the R/3 System. In practice, purchase requisitions can be created by any number of management and production departments, which is why they are also linked in the R/3 System with any number of application areas, such as Production Planning and Control, Materials Management, Inventory Management, Sales and Distribution, etc. In addition to the manual requisition described here, purchase requisitions can be automatically created in these individual application areas on the basis of preceding processes, such as planned order conversion, material requirements planning, master production scheduling, production order creation, third-party order processing, network maintenance, etc. These different entry points are brought together in the process Purchase requisition assignment and given a release strategy for creation of a purchase order. Therefore, after the manual purchase requisition for stock material has been entered (see example), a reference is made to the subsequent process module „Assignment of purchase requisition."

Workshop question:
Which business possibilities does the R/3 reference process show?

6.1.2   R/3 Organization Model

Designing business processes with the goal of minimizing interfaces demonstrates that in addition to logical structuring of business processes for operational execution, it is necessary to include the assignment aspect, i.e. it is necessary to determine responsibilities for processing the business processes. Organizational assignment is influenced in operational practice by, among other things, the capabilities of the employees, the supporting machinery and, most importantly, the expert knowledge of the staff member, which is, in the end, a result of education and training. Just as one can make assumptions about the capacities of an employee based on job qualifications, it is necessary to coordinate the different performance pictures in an enterprise. In business theory and practice, several basic patterns have emerged in this context. For example, Marketing and Sales and Distribution carry out market-level tasks, Production deals with the manufacturing and assembly of products, Procurement concentrates on the tasks to be executed with vendors, goods receipts, etc. The interfaces between these basic patterns, which have evolved differently depending on the type of enterprise and branch of industry, require flexible design of the potential organizational assignments.

The R/3 System's basic organizational pattern mirrors the requirements to be met for the operational task areas Accounting, Logistics, and Human Resources Management; this pattern is identified in the R/3 Organization Model along with its essential R/3 structural elements and their relationships. In the area of Financial Management, the R/3 structural elements company code and business area serve to meet legal balance sheet requirements. In the R/3 System, the company code is a business organizational unit that is used to represent independent accounting units that conform to legal regulations. If an enterprise is active in several countries, this requires setting up one company code for each country. The business area is used to create internal balance sheets, as well as profit and loss calculations, and thus contains an enterprise's non-independent organizational and economic units (cf. SAP – General Ledger 1996, pp. 2.1–2.3).

Two of the main structural elements in Controlling are the organizational elements known as controlling area and operating concern. The controlling area represents an organizational unit in which complete, self-contained cost accounting with several cost centres can be performed. The controlling area is related to the bookkeeping-oriented units called company code and business area and the logistically oriented unit known as plant, meaning it also takes their requirements into consideration. So, for example, controlling area and company code are based on the same charts of accounts and currencies, with a controlling area being able to combine several company codes from a Controlling point of view. The operating concern is used to segment an enterprise's markets, the goal being to identify explicit results – i.e. costs and revenues – for individual segments (profitability analysis). Operating concerns can be designed flexibly, according to the market requirements, with regard to articles (products), sales areas and customers and can contain several controlling areas (cf. SAP – Overhead Cost Controlling 1996, p. 2.1; cf. Profitability Analysis 1996, pp. 2.1–2.5).

An important element for structuring logistics is the organizational element known as plant. It organizes the tasks for production and warehouse logistics and can be a physical production location or the logical combination of several locations in which materials are produced or materials or services are provided. For fulfilling logistical tasks, the planning and inventory management activities are defined here, meaning the production-relevant activities of production planning and control, materials management, inventory management and quality assurance are taken into account. Individual logistical tasks, for example material requirements planning and production order planning, which often occur at plant level, as well as planning and control functions, can be executed across plant boundaries. The plant is closely linked to the purchasing organization and the sales organization, which are used to structure external logistics tasks, i.e. sales and distribution logistics and procurement logistics tasks. The sales organization is responsible for the sales and distribution of materials or services with the corresponding conditions, etc.; the purchasing organization is responsible for the procurement of materials and services. Using the R/3 structural elements of Accounting and Logistics, as well as the flexible relationships represented in the R/3 System, you can represent all of the requirements for delivery and service traffic across plants, business areas and company codes (cf. SAP's Sales and Distribution System 1994, pp. 2.1–2.7; cf. SAP – Materials Management 1996, pp. 2.1–2.2).

While the R/3 organizational elements of Accounting and Logistics are used primarily for business structuring of tasks, the R/3 organizational elements of Human Resources Management are used to reflect pay- and management-related tasks. For one thing, the R/3 Organization Model contains the R/3 structural element known as organizational plan unit, which you can use to create any desired operational organization structures to define an enterprise's management and directors. The personnel area and the position are important R/3 organizational elements that should be mentioned here for administrative processing of Human Resources Management business tasks. The personnel area contains a delimited enterprise area that includes tasks relevant for personnel administration, time management and payroll accounting. The position contains a description of tasks, authorities and responsibilities, which are oriented towards established career paths, such as secretary, financial accountant, systems analyst, engineer/designer, etc.

By identifying the corresponding relationships, the R/3 Organization Model demonstrates the R/3 System's organizational design possibilities, i.e. the degrees of freedom related to the organizational plan. The goal is for the customer to represent his operational organization requirements in such a way that legal requirements are met (for example, year-end closing), reporting requirements are met (for example, balance sheet), and smooth and resource-saving process flow of a net value added chain is ensured (for example, quick reaction to the market or quality-assured manufacturing of a product). The customer's organizational requirements can be based on:

■ *Market and product structure*
(market segmenting based on similar markets, customers, products with profit responsibility)

■ *Business tasks*
(task structuring according to the business areas of sales and distribution, production, quality assurance, procurement, warehouse management, etc. – so-called functional structuring)

■ *Management structure*
(centralization or decentralization, with hierarchical, matrixed or project-based structuring of management, for example structuring into a central purchasing department or one local purchasing department per plant)

■ *Reporting requirements*
(open books requirement in a joint-stock company, profit margin report in a business area)

In the excerpt that follows, from the application area Materials Management, one of the main organizational units is the plant. In the first step, the meaning and the contents of the plant must be adjusted to fit the customer. Then, in the second step, it can be determined how many of these plants a customer needs in his enterprise. Although the quantity-based view takes precedence in Materials Management, in the integrated R/3 System, you can automatically monitor values at the same time. Of course, the corresponding relationships to the accounting units, such as company code and/or business area, must be set up for this to work. Within a plant, for example, the responsibilities for ordering and inventory management must be clarified. If the customer has defined a plant *A*, for example, then this plant can be assigned to only one company code; in other words, there exists a 1:M relation restriction.

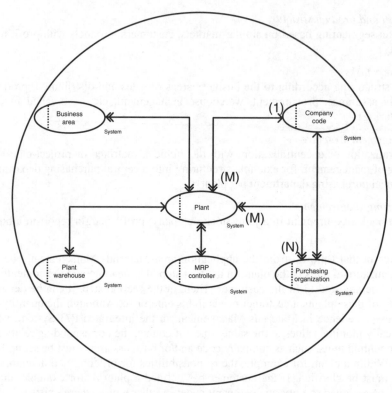

Fig. 6.3: R/3 Organization Model for Materials Management (excerpt)

Workshop question:
Which organization-related degrees of freedom or restrictions are prescribed by the R/3 System?

6.1.3   R/3 Object/Data Model

The R/3 Data Model describes the logical business objects that are needed to execute R/3 applications. The source of the graphical descriptive language is Chen's Entity Relationship Model, which is based on a simple notation of objects (entities) and their relationships. This simple representation, with its multiple uses, has the disadvantage, due to unlimited graphical arrangement of the symbols, that large models quickly become unclear, thus missing the point, which is to create a good overview for purposes of documentation and of ensuring consistency. The R/3 Data Model therefore has two supplemental rules, the alignment rule and the compression rule. The R/3 Data Model is logically built up from left to right, meaning it supports a particular rule for reading the model and thus represents a semantic in the shape of an existence dependency. The instances of the object types aligned to the left in the R/3 Data Model generally have a longer life than those aligned to the right in the data set. The interdependencies between the individual objects are documented with different types of arrows. Overall, the R/3 Data Model has about 3000 objects that are linked together (cf. Seubert *et al.* 1995, pp. 15–23).

Among these 3000 objects are some that are particularly important for business. The R/3 System contains 180 of these business-relevant objects, called business objects, which describe a comprehensive business connection in the R/3 System and without which the business application functionality could not exist. In Sales and Distribution, these important objects include, for example, the customer, the customer inquiry, the customer quotation and the customer scheduling agreement; in Production Planning and Control, for example, they include the sales and operations plan, the material requirement and the planned order; in Human Resources Management, these objects include, for example, the position, the skills and the business event type. The business objects are divided into objects that have a more structural character, such as plant, debtor, creditor, controlling area, operating concern and profit centre, and those that have more of an interchangeable character, such as material, bill of material, routing, purchase order and inspection plan. The more structural business objects can be divided into those that shape the ties to the outside world, for example customer, vendor, creditor, debtor, business partner, bank, and those that are used for internal business structuring in the R/3 System, for example plant, sales organization, purchasing organization and company code. To make it easier for the user to familiarize himself with the R/3 Data Models, the business objects are assigned to individual business subject areas, such as sales, purchasing, inventory management, etc. In the following illustration, selected business objects from the Purchasing subarea of Materials Management are listed. The relationships between the business objects are shown, and every individual business object can be expanded and its internal structure according to the ERM notation analyzed, for example the type and number of relationships.

In the example, the order makes it clear that a purchase requisition can precede the business object purchase order. The expanded business object purchase requisition is shown in the Structured Entity Relationship Model (SERM) representation. The entities purchase requisition and purchase requisition item characterize the purchase requisition document with its header and item data. Likewise, specialization (the black triangle) shows that a purchase requisition can occur in different variants (for example, subcontracting and stock transfer).

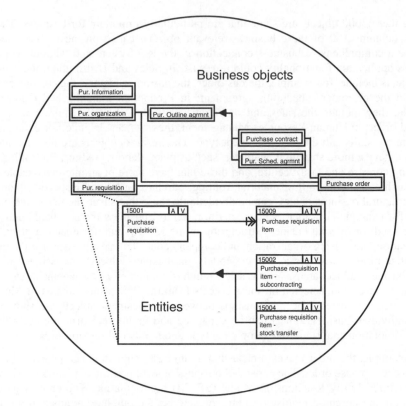

Fig. 6.4: R/3 Object Data Model for Purchasing (excerpt)

Workshop question:
What does the object/data structure for an application instance look like?

6.1.4 R/3 Prototyping

R/3 Prototyping means that the customer can look at and execute individual implemented processes in an executable R/3 System. To support this approach, SAP AG has developed a model company called *International Demonstration and Education System* (IDES), for which parameters have been set, and in which corresponding data has been stored for processing individual transactions for sales and training purposes (cf. Pfähler 1995, p. 20).

The model company contains an internationally active enterprise with several subsidiaries. The enterprise represents a multinational corporation with one corporate group in Europe and one in America. The corporate group in Europe includes companies in Germany, Great Britain, Portugal and Italy. The corporate group in America includes companies in the US and Canada. Each company has business areas for financial accounting and plants for handling materials management. For controlling, two cost centre structures have been created, which reference the European and the American company. The cost centre 1000 includes the companies from Germany, Great Britain, Italy and Portugal; the cost centre 2000 includes the companies from the US and Canada. The corporate group in Europe contains independent accounting units in the individual countries, i.e. independent companies, each with its own company code. The company codes for the US corporate group and the Europe corporate group are structured identically, so that the same examples can be used and shown to customers, supplemented with country-specific characteristics.

Stored in the IDES model company as a whole are process examples for processing different product groups and all kinds of enterprise areas. In Logistics, for example, you can view the implemented processes for discrete manufacturing, process-oriented and kanban-oriented manufacturing; in Accounting, you can view the processes for financial accounting, for overhead cost accounting, and for product costing; and in Human Resources Management, you can view the processes for personnel management, personnel planning and personnel development. IDES demonstrates, for example, the processing for the production of light bulbs (mass production), pumps and doors (order-related production), motorcycles and personal computers (sales-order production) and elevators (make-to-order production) in the R/3 System. For each of the process examples created in the IDES model company, you can see how the corresponding transactions are used. The goal is to gain familiarity with the transactions in the R/3 System and to understand the implemented flow logic. For purposes of introduction to and training in the use of the model company IDES, an instruction is stored for every transaction that shows the individual data entry steps for using that transaction. In addition, valid sample data is specified that can be used by the user during training. The processes implemented in IDES contain the current range of capabilities of Release 3.x of the R/3 System.

While in the graphic the R/3 reference processes usually show several processing paths, in R/3 Prototyping there is always exactly one goal-oriented path set for a single point in time. Under certain circumstances, however, it is possible to manually set additional paths in R/3 Prototyping, in addition to the modelled process alternatives of the R/3 Reference Process Model, because not all of the R/3 System's capabilities are represented in the model. While the links to the preceding and subsequent processes in the R/3 reference processes are explicitly identified by the common starting and ending events or by the process signs, the next step after a transaction is completed is not always explicitly shown in R/3 Prototyping.

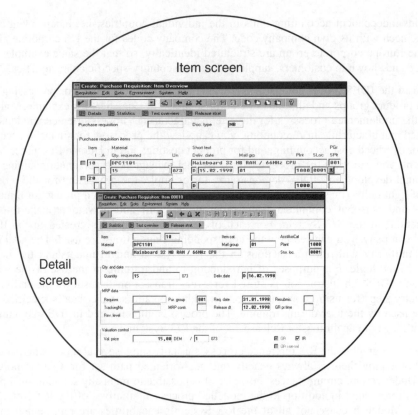

Fig. 6.5: Prototyping of a purchase requisition item

This example shows a section of the transaction for purchase requisition processing (ME51) implemented in the R/3 System. In R/3 Prototyping in this case, you would use a preset R/3 System with maximum functionality, possibly supplemented with master data and transaction data from IDES. If necessary, additional customer examples with the corresponding customer data could be created. In the example, based on the material DPC1101 from the model company IDES, the maximum input data that can be created for a purchase requisition item is shown in the item screen and the detail screen.

Workshop question:
What do the transaction and the sequence of screens look like in the R/3 System?

6.1.5 R/3 Customizing

R/3 Customizing makes it possible for the customer, based on his goals and requirements, to select and assign parameters to the processes he desires with the corresponding functionality, from the multitude of solutions offered for functions and processes. It is advantageous for the customer to be able, when implementing the flexible R/3 standard software, to execute consistently in the R/3 data architecture every instance created by Customizing. Furthermore, customer parameter settings occur within the R/3 System's predefined range of solutions, they do not pose problems in release updates, and they can be modified in the productive system to meet changing requirements (cf. Buck–Emden/Galimow 1996, pp. 241–245; cf. Görk 1996, pp. 28–29).

Before we elaborate on the central elements of Customizing, we shall demonstrate, by way of an analogy from the world of traffic control, the connection between the R/3 Reference Process Model, R/3 Prototyping and R/3 Customizing. A traffic planner must develop the best routes from one location to another location and present them to an authoritative body for a decision. In the process, he must plan, say, the kinds of roads (freeway, highway, country road, etc.) and traffic junctions (freeway on-ramp, interstate exchange, intersection, etc.) and their rights-of-way (traffic light or right-of-way signs). The traffic network is described in street maps, which show the possible driving routes. Like the street maps, the R/3 Reference Process Model shows the possible alternative routes that can be taken in the R/3 System to fulfil a task, for example order processing, purchase order processing, stock transfer, production execution, travel expense processing, business event planning, etc.

To prepare for a vacation or business trip, a motorist can, for example, obtain the necessary street maps at the AAA automobile club and ask the staff there to show him the route with the least traffic. The staff member may describe, for example, a possible detour due to a blocked street, a construction area along the route, or a toll road. By marking a travel route on the street map, the motorist receives a navigation (driving instruction) for his trip and lets himself be guided (controlled) by this. Similarly, R/3 Customizing supports the user in that parameters are set for a certain processing path, so that the staff member is given a favourable path for fulfilling his task. Say, for example, an enterprise is working with subcontracting in Purchasing; in this case, the reference is set in Customizing for purchase order processing to a goods issue for material provided. This manual setting of purchase order processing in Customizing has the effect of providing electronic navigation support, in that the desired path is controlled by the parameters (control data) set in Customizing.

The motorist starts his journey on the basis of the recommended route and thus, under the conditions that are most favourable for him, travels from his starting location (home) to his destination (vacation spot or business location). This corresponds to R/3 Prototyping (set-up R/3 System) in that, for example, a staff member, starting from a customer inquiry (starting location), creates a purchase order and sends it (destination). In R/3 Prototyping, a specific travel route is taken. Just as there are lots of motorists with different home towns and travel desires, there are many different customers with varied requirements to be supported by the R/3 System. To support the setting of the most favourable path for a staff member, R/3 Customizing contains documentation with recommendations for marking the desired route (Implementation Guide) and the capability to mark a specific route (parameter configuration).

For every parameter setting, the Implementation Guide shows the activities to be carried out to execute a transaction. The Implementation Guide explains why the activity is needed and what effects a setting has. Recommendations for settings are shown and, based on a type of instruction, the concrete steps to be performed for a setting are described. The R/3 Reference Guide contains all of the setting activities that are necessary for implementing the R/3 System in its entirety. Because this is not always required, the customer can configure an enterprise-specific Implementation Guide on the basis of the area he wants to have supported, such as Sales and Distribution, and the requirements needed there. Say, for example, the R/3 System is to be implemented in several areas by different project teams. In this case, the enterprise-specific Implementation Guide can be divided into the activities specific to each project (project-specific Implementation Guide). This can be condensed further by considering and entering in the first step settings for the activities known as mandatory activities.

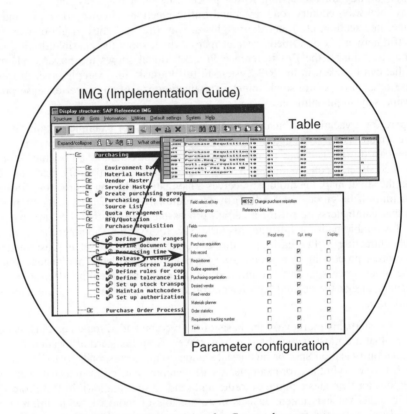

Fig. 6.6: R/3 Customizing for Create document type

In general, the R/3 System provides a selection of useful presettings for the most necessary settings. If a setting must be made for an activity, the R/3 implementor can do this by way of a business description using Customizing transactions. No knowledge is needed about the technical data storage of a business fact. The R/3 implementor does not have to know which transaction manipulates which tables with which fields, because the physical table structure is hidden by transactions that are business-oriented.

In the integrated R/3 System, data that has been recorded once is automatically made available to subsequent activities for processing. This data exists in the form of electronic documents, i.e. in the example of purchase requisition processing, a document type must first be defined. Customizing is structured in such a way that for each of the larger business application areas, for example Purchasing, Sales, Shipping, etc., the objects relevant to system settings are shown with the corresponding setting activities. The example shows the setting activities to be performed for a purchase requisition in Purchasing. Activating the step *Determine document type and number range* displays the corresponding setting table, which contains a selected set of preset document types. If the customer has special purchase requisition variants, he can in addition define custom document types. The second system setting in the example shows how parameters for the screen structure of a purchase requisition are maintained. In this Customizing case, the range of business solutions in the R/3 System is preset. It is up to the customer to define in which form a specific field should be used in the processing of the purchase requisition, for example optional entry of the desired vendor and MRP controller, and mandatory entry of the requisitioner.

Workshop question:
Which settings must be carried out to set up an R/3 transaction, and what choices are there?

6.1.6 R/3 Data Dictionary

The Data Dictionary is a central information source that contains the description of all of an enterprise's application data, as well as information about relationships between this data and the data's use in programs and screens. The descriptive data of a Data Dictionary is also called „meta data", because it represents data about data. Recently, building on the term Data Dictionary, the term Repository has established itself as part of software development and management (cf. Habermann/Leymann 1993, pp. 15–27).

The R/3 Data Dictionary or ABAP/4 Dictionary (cf. Buck–Emden/Galimow 1996, pp. 180–184; cf. Matzke 1996, pp. 17–25) answers the following core questions for users, developers and end users:

- What data is contained in the enterprise's database?

- What characteristics does this data have (name, length ...)?

- What is the relationship between the data objects?

These days, the relational data model is an important part of the R/3 System. At its core, it consists of two-dimensional tables, which contain all of the data and relationships. These tables, as well as data fields and database structures, are defined in the R/3 Data Dictionary.

Tables are elementary data fields without an internal structure. They are uniquely identified by a primary key and are isolated from each other. Access is possible regardless of the database structure, which ensures that data independence is retained. Access occurs through the specification of a table name, a primary key and a field name and is based on a query language such as SQL. Using foreign keys, it is possible to create links between tables.

A distinction is made between transparent tables, which in the R/3 System, for example, can also be used for other applications (for example, all customer data tables), and pooled tables or cluster tables, in which several smaller or internal tables are combined, buffered completely for capacity reasons.

In the R/3 System, tables are at first not physically present, but are logically defined in the ABAP/4 Dictionary with the help of meta data. In the dictionary, fields that are used in tables, dynpros (dynamic programs for controlling queries) and applications are described globally. Also described globally are help information that can be called up online and relationships between data elements using foreign keys.

Another important feature in relation to data changes in the ABAP/4 Dictionary affects the development environment. The architecture of the ABAP/4 Dictionary is completely integrated in the ABAP/4 Development Workbench and the R/3 development environment. When a table is called, it is not present as a physical table definition in the form of a database, but is rather regenerated when the ABAP/4 Dictionary is accessed and then stored in a database.

Despite having performance-inhibiting characteristics, this interpretive incorporation of the ABAP/4 Dictionary into the program flow has the following advantages:

- Tables can be displayed directly in the ABAP/4 editor; application programs can use table structures directly (integrated ABAP/4 Dictionary).

- Changes immediately and automatically have an effect on all affected applications (active ABAP/4 Dictionary).

Furthermore, it is possible to define something called views in the ABAP/4 Dictionary. Views are virtual tables in which the user can display application-based data. Only necessary fields are displayed; data can be combined. Field descriptors can be given names that differ from the original field names. Views support the formatting of data in reports or list screens.

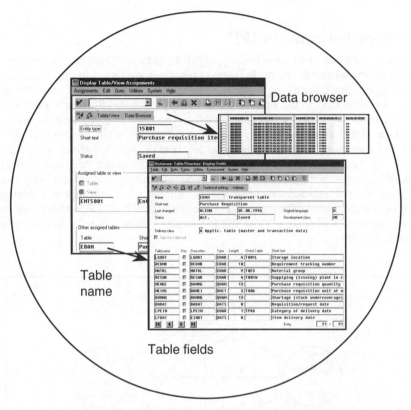

Fig. 6.7: R/3 table for purchase requisition item

This example presents the table associated with the purchase requisition, EBAN. By selecting the table name, you can jump into the data structure and analyze the individual table fields. The fields of this table contain master data and transaction data, whose type and length are described. Also specified is whether a field has a check table. This enables the application to directly check and reject an invalid entry. The data browser can be used to view the individual values in the database fields for monitoring.

Workshop question:
How is the table for an application object structured?

6.2   Iterative paths in IPP

The resources of Iterative Process Prototyping (IPP) presented here are linked together in a network of relationships. The business-level resources are linked to the resources of the technical system level, for example the R/3 Reference Process Model to the R/3 System. But they also have links at the same level, for example the R/3 Reference Process Model accesses elements of the R/3 Object/Data Model. The following section presents the possible links in Iterative Process Prototyping using the resources provided in SAP AG's R/3 System. For each possible link, the contents are first described, and the typical question that comes up during a feasibility study is formulated. Afterwards, the implementation of the link whose contents have been described is demonstrated using selected excerpts from the R/3 System. The question depends not only on the general existence of a relationship, but also on the direction of the relationship. Because the IPP method is based on six fundamental elements, which are always related in pairs, you end up with 30 navigation and combination possibilities.

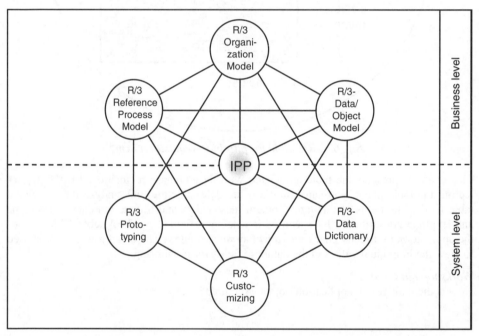

Fig. 6.8: Navigation paths (network) in Iterative Process Prototyping

6.2.1   From process to Prototyping

Graphic models can only ever show a simplified representation of the real world. The truth of the business solution, however, lies in the R/3 System. In the early analysis phase, it makes sense for the consultant to begin by explaining the business process alternatives in a simplified form based on the model depictions. The functions contained in the model can be the decision-making functions of a staff member, control functions that are set in Customizing, and/or application functions that appear on the screens. The important thing is not to get lost in individual fields of the R/3 System during this iterative jump, but rather to look first at only those aspects for which there is a model reference. In the example demonstrated, *Select purchase requisition item type*, navigation took place from the process model to the corresponding transaction, and the initial screen for *Create purchase requisition* appeared. On the system screen, under the item type, the list of the item types provided in the standard R/3 System can be displayed and discussed with the customer.

Workshop question:
Can we look at the demonstrated process in the R/3 System as an example?

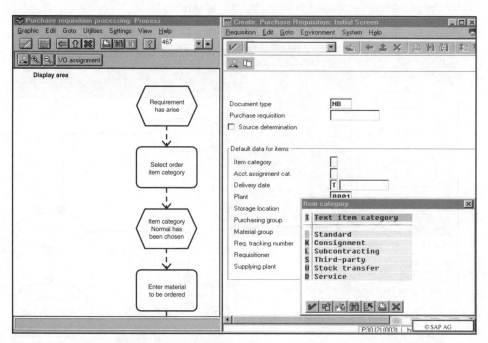

Fig. 6.9: Iterative path – from process to Prototyping

6.2.2   From process to Organization Model

Processes are executed by people with the help of information systems. The people, in turn, are part of an enterprise's responsibility-oriented organizational structure. In the case of guidelines for various branches of industry (chemical, pharmaceutical, food industry, safety parts for the automotive industry), it is necessary to define responsibilities for ensuring safety and quality requirements, such as those that have been defined by legislators or legitimate standardizing bodies. Likewise, certain basic conditions must be defined in the R/3 System for organizational arrangements. Therefore, the organizational units of the R/3 System that must be set are specified for every process, for example plant and purchasing organization for the process *Purchase requisition processing for stock material*. Furthermore, it is possible, for example, to make different groups of people responsible for purchased parts from different product groups or vendors. You define optional purchasing groups for this. An iterative jump into the Organization Model makes it possible to analyze the relationships there, allowing the organizational degrees of freedom or restrictions to be discussed early on.

Workshop question:
Which organizational constraints must be met for the process?

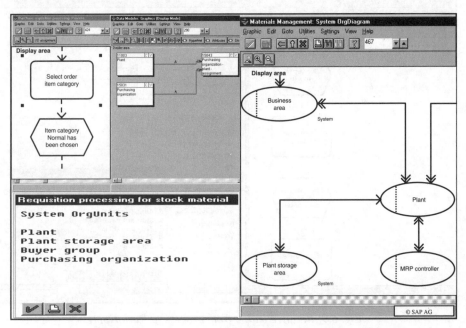

Fig. 6.10: Iterative path – from process to Organization Model

6.2.3   From process to Customizing

The solution paths demonstrated in the R/3 Reference Process Model can often be made more specific and, if necessary, expanded in Customizing. With an iterative jump into Customizing, the consultant can display the standard alternatives offered and discuss their usefulness with the customer. If he selects a standard Customizing parameter, the customer automatically becomes the recipient of integrity and consistency in the flow logic and does not need to deal with an analysis of tables and their relationships. In the example shown, the item category *Normal* is selected for the process *Purchase requisition processing*, that is, the subject is purchase requisitions for goods that must be procured externally. If the default values are insufficient for a customer's business area, new item categories can be defined, for example. In this case it will be necessary, however, to analyze the affected tables and their relationships at a later point in time, to check if the prescribed process or other related processes might need to be changed.

Workshop question:
Which possibilities are there for setting parameters for this process?

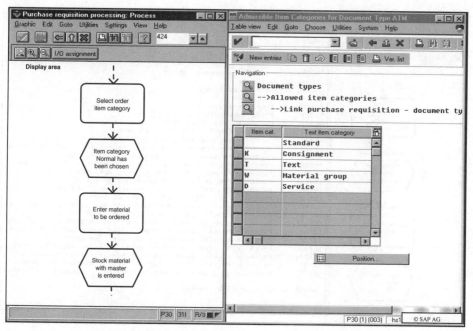

Fig. 6.11: Iterative path – from process to Customizing

6.2.4 From process to Data Model

In process consulting, both the analysis of necessary input information and the examination of possible variants (specialization) for an object are important. The specialization of an object influences the scope of variation of a process. So, for example, the purchase requisition item can refer to a subcontract or a stock transfer. If various processes are linked together, usually information is passed from the preceding process to the subsequent process. While in an integrated R/3 System these connections are automated to the greatest extent possible, if non-SAP systems are incorporated, it is absolutely necessary to view the data to be passed by undertaking an iterative jump from the Process Model into the Data Model. Because objects of the Data Model can, in turn, have additional relationships with each other, if an R/3 object is used for a non-SAP system, the logical predecessor relationships must be checked to ensure consistency.

Workshop question:
Which variants (specializations) are there for a function in the process?

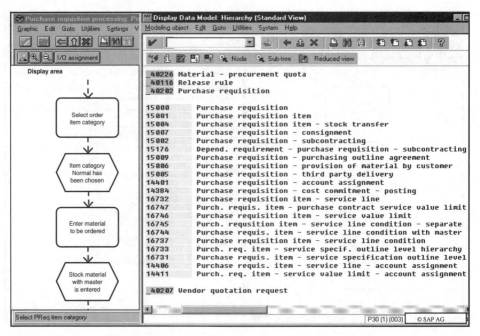

Fig. 6.12: Iterative path – from process to Data Model

6.2.5   From process to Data Dictionary

An iterative jump from the Process Model to the Data Model concentrates on the logical data structure; the goal of jumping from the Process Model to the Data Dictionary is to adjust the physical data structure of the field lengths. What is important, in relation to the key fields of the tables, is that there exist a complete equivalency between the SAP System and the non-SAP system. On the other hand, corresponding conversion programs must be written to protect the integrity. During IPP, however, the individual fields are not analyzed. Instead, the principal necessity of a connection to a non-SAP system is recorded with the activity *Execute field adjustment in the detailed analysis*. If an enterprise has not installed the R/3 System in all areas, such as not in production, and if purchase requisitions are created during production planning, the purchase requisition information must either be manually entered into the integrated R/3 System, or it can be transferred automatically through *batch input* after a preceding field adjustment.

Workshop question:
Does the enterprise need *batch input* for this process?

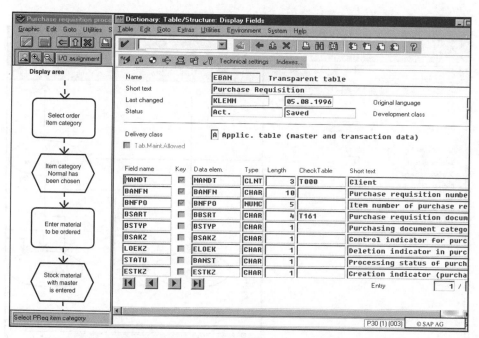

Fig. 6.13: Iterative path – from process to Data Dictionary

6.2.6   From Prototyping to Organization

At the beginning of a transaction, the organizational units of the R/3 System that are relevant for this processing step are displayed. In this case, it is important to differentiate which input data is mandatory and which is optional based on the enterprise's basic organizational conditions. When a sales order is created in Sales and Distribution, first the order type is determined and then the R/3 organizational units sales organization, distribution channel and division are specified. An iterative jump into the Organization Model allows the possible relationships between these three mandatory entries to be discussed early on with the customer. If the customer has defined different order types for different divisions, jumping into the Organization Model can point out conceptual inconsistencies, for example with the purchasing organization. The R/3 organizational units sales office and sales group are additional structuring criteria for order processing that can be used to specify responsibilities or to perform differentiated evaluations, for example to calculate sales numbers for different sales groups.

Workshop question:
Do the R/3 organizational units in this transaction have certain restrictions?

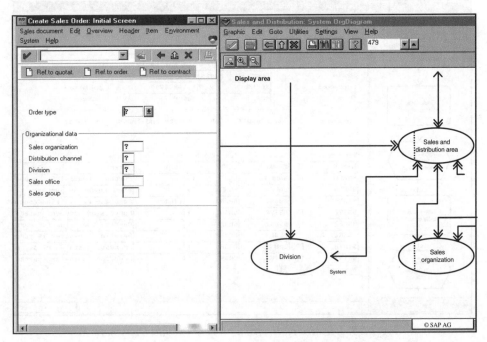

Fig. 6.14: Iterative path – from Prototyping to Organization

6.2.7   From Prototyping to process

From time to time, it is necessary in a requirements analysis to show the customer a physical process flow at transaction level. At the end of processing, this prototyping results in a physical result that is visible to the customer. Say, for example, that *Billing run* prototyping has created an invoice with a note. An iterative jump from a completed transaction to the corresponding logical place in the Process Model demonstrates the connections to the subsequent processes. By identifying the associated application component or application, this jump illuminates the networking in the system across transaction boundaries. Another aspect may be that during the use of the transactions all of the relevant fields are displayed. An iterative jump into the Process Model causes a business concentration on the most necessary things, since the graphic shows the overall logic in simplified form.

Workshop question:
Which logical subsequent process can be activated after the transaction ends?

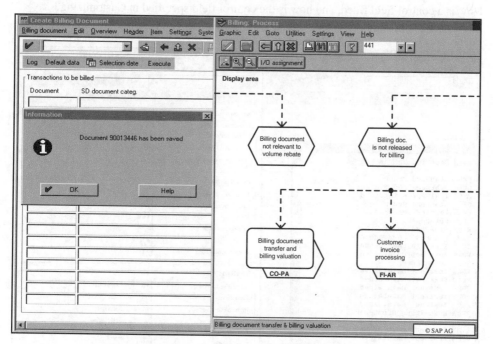

Fig. 6.15: Iterative path – from Prototyping to process

6.2.8   From Prototyping to Customizing

Usually, the document types, condition types and other control fields delivered with the standard system are sufficient. In individual cases, however, it can be necessary for the customer to add special things. The first thing to do is to check the provided capabilities to see if they can be used. If that is not sufficient, an iterative jump can show the customer how to create new control fields using Customizing. In the example at hand, the sales document types provided by SAP are demonstrated in Prototyping. The sales document types provided can be made more specific, for example, by assigning a document to a division or by activating a credit limit check. In the latter case, for example, you can determine if an exceeded credit limit should trigger only a warning, or if the delivery should be automatically blocked (indicator *C* in the right-hand screen). In the area of transaction flow, you can also determine the sequence of screens. It is also possible to create entirely new sales document types with the corresponding specification.

Workshop question:
How is a control field filled, and how is the control field specified in Customizing?

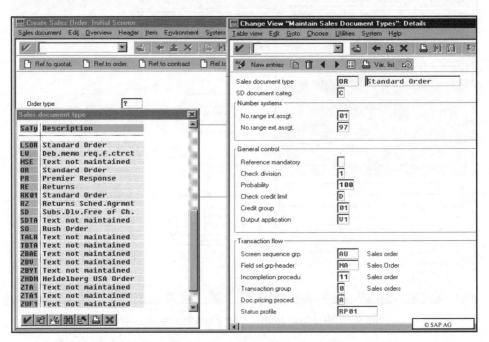

Fig. 6.16: Iterative path – from Prototyping to Customizing

6.2.9   From Prototyping to Data Model

In a field analysis within a transaction, the relevant fields are displayed without relationships in Prototyping. The possible degrees of freedom within a transaction can be demonstrated with an iterative jump into the Data Model. In the Data Model, you can analyze the relationships on the basis of either a graphic (in the form of an Entity Relationship Model) or a list. The example at hand in Prototyping for *Change cost centre* refers to the Data Model's main entity *cost centre*. For the cost centre, for example, it is necessary to define the responsibility, the business area and the currency. Based on the relationship list, it becomes clear that the business area is an optional entry, that is, a cost centre can be assigned to one business area, and a business area can contain several cost centres (relation of business area to cost centre is c:cn). On the other hand, a cost centre has a unique cost centre manager and works with one currency (relation of cost centre manager to cost centre is 1:cn).

Workshop question:
What relation do the individual fields of a transaction have to each other?

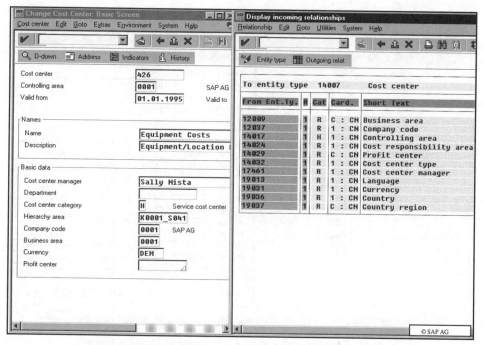

Fig. 6.17: Iterative path – from Prototyping to Data Model

6.2.10 From Prototyping to Data Dictionary

While the Reengineering approach is based on a complete reconception, in operational practice it is often the case that continual changing must be carried out based on existing information landscapes. In this case, the important thing is that existing data is incorporated, improved, and some of it is carried over into a new system landscape. For example, if the old cost centre structures should be retained from responsibility-oriented organizational measures, an iterative jump into the Data Dictionary is necessary to adjust the field types and field lengths for the attributes. With Prototyping, first you determine the fields that must be maintained in the R/3 System to build a consistent cost centre structure. If information is missing in the customer's data set, for example the profit centre group, the data must be created during data transfer. Furthermore, in the standard system there are usually additional fields, and in certain cases one must check which fields the customer will use in which form in the future.

Workshop question:
How should *batch input* be structured?

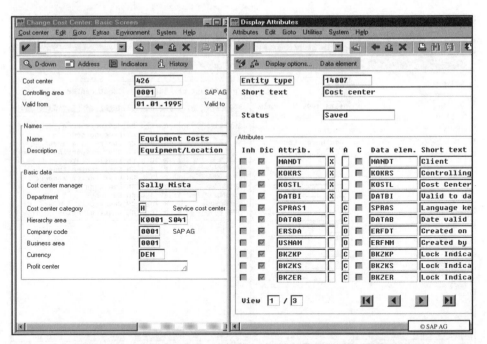

Fig. 6.18: Iterative path – from Prototyping to Data Dictionary

6.2.11 From Organization Model to Prototyping

The Organization Model shows the degrees of freedom of the R/3 System with the relations at type level; the executable system needs the organizational relationships to be determined in terms of the customer's concrete data. The example shows that if the customer wants several *divisions*, he must inevitably define several *sales areas*. Since a sales area, in turn, consists of the triple combination of *division, sales organization* and *distribution channel*, instances (values) must be created for these, too. The sales area is the automatic result of the triple combination. Once all of the organization values have been determined conceptually, you can test the consistency and completeness with an iterative jump into Prototyping. If a division has been determined, then when a material is used, for example from the bookkeeping view, the division must be specified in addition to the plant. To do this, one can look at the divisions defined earlier in Prototyping, assign the material, or, if necessary, define a new division in Customizing.

Workshop question:
Have the organizational instances been defined correctly in dependence on the relations allowed?

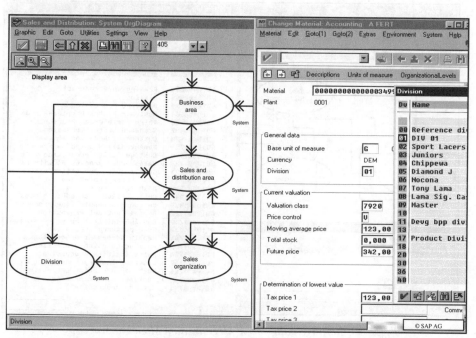

Fig. 6.19: Iterative path – from Organization Model to Prototyping

6.2.12 From Organization Model to process

Once the R/3 organizational units have been defined, the relevant processes for each organizational unit can be demonstrated through an iterative jump into the process view. The integrated storage of model information in the R/3 Repository allows jumping to occur automatically from the organizational units to the affected processes based on a where-used list. In the example at hand, the R/3 organizational unit *division* was selected from the Organization Model. Activating the division opens a selection screen with the selection choice *where-used list*, after which the process list is created. Furthermore, after this iterative jump, additional navigation steps can be taken through model integration. So, for example, by selecting a process, in this case standard order processing, you can analyze either individual attributes of the process (type of processing, pertinent transaction code, component to which it belongs, etc.) or the process structure (flow logic) in the EPC graphic.

Workshop question:
Which R/3 organizational unit is needed for which process?

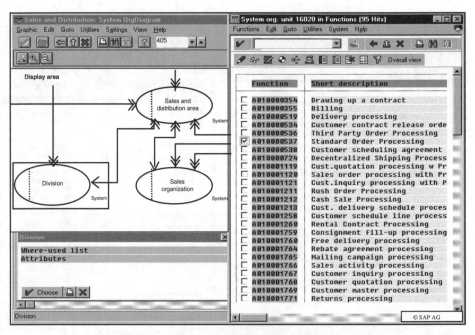

Fig. 6.20: Iterative path – from Organization Model to process

6.2.13 From Organization Model to Customizing

Once the R/3 organizational units have been analyzed and specified at type level, the next step is to set the parameter for the type and maintain the relationship tables through an iterative jump into Customizing. In the example at hand, it was defined that several shipping points should exist in a plant. One peculiarity in parameter setting is that a shipping point can be a physical location or a logical grouping of people who are responsible for shipping activities. The shipping point can furthermore be combined with shipping conditions (for example, frozen goods, chemical goods, etc., are transported with specially made trucks) and loading groups or loading tools (crane, forklift, assembly lines, etc.). When defining a shipping point, you can retrieve predefined values or set new parameter values, such as factory calendar, determination of pick/pack time and loading time, use of standardized address text, design of the picking list, type of transmission of the shipping documents, etc.

Workshop question:
Which possible parameter settings are there for an R/3 organizational unit?

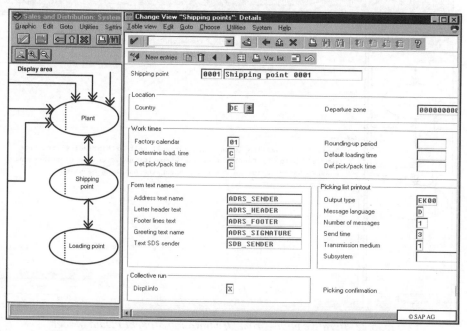

Fig. 6.21: Iterative path – from Organization Model to Customizing

219

6.2.14 From Organization Model to Data Model

The R/3 organizational units have an integrated relationship to the processes and are linked to operationally manageable entities of the Data Model, such as the material, the sales order, etc. Through an iterative jump from the Organization Model to the Data Model, it is possible for one thing to analyze the importance of the selected R/3 organizational units using their definition. A supplemental comment section provides the user additional support for using an organizational unit correctly in the R/3 System. In the example, you can see that a *sales organization* can be used to support market segmenting and that within a *sales organization*, various conditions can be defined for the market partner, i.e. the customer. An iterative jump into the Data Model graphic also allows you to view the preceding and subsequent entities for an R/3 organizational unit. So, for example, the sales organization has interdependencies with customer delivery.

Workshop question:
What understanding does the customer have of an R/3 organizational unit?

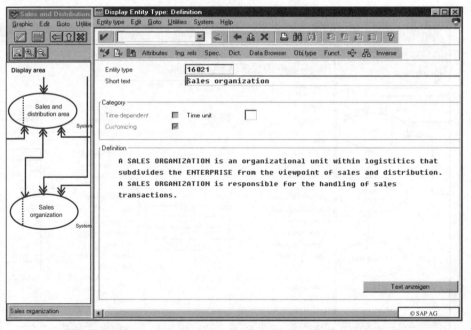

Fig. 6.22: Iterative path – from Organization Model to Data Model

6.2.15 From Organization Model to Data Dictionary

The logical R/3 organizational structures can be visualized with the help of the Organization Model. If the customer uses the R/3 System in its entirety to handle his business processes, analysis of the individual tables is not necessary. If, however, he would like to copy an existing organizational structure, for example a cost centre structure, an iterative jump over the Data Model into the Data Dictionary is necessary in order to check the individual physical tables there. An iterative jump from the Organization Model into the Data Dictionary based on the *cost centre* example makes it clear that the cost centre consists of the fields of two different physical tables, the cost centre master record, and the cost centre texts. Activating a table, for example CSKS for the cost centre master record, identifies the pertinent fields. So, for example, the table CSKS contains the specification of the fields for the business area, for the company code, the clearing methods, responsibility, currency key, etc.

Workshop question:
What do the table structures for an R/3 organizational unit look like?

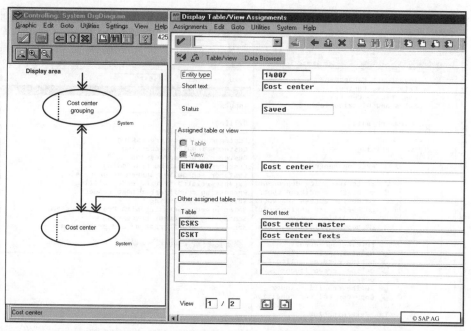

Fig. 6.23: Iterative path – from Organization Model to Data Dictionary

6.2.16 From Customizing to process

The Process Model describes the operational execution of one or more transactions. Customizing describes the path, i.e. which business settings must be made so that the selected process can be executed in the desired form. To provide support for the Customizing steps to be performed, an **Im**plementation **G**uide (IMG) is provided in a structure overview. In the example of customizing activities to be carried out for *price determination*, an iterative jump over the *price determination (16105)* entity of the Data Model can display a list of those processes in which price determination plays a role. It is also possible to increase the level of detail in the IMG to the point where one reaches individual business activities to be performed (represented by the flag symbol). From the individual activity, depending on the business situation, either a reference to a Customizing table can be made and the desired settings entered there, or the setting parameters can be selected.

Workshop question:
In which workflows (processes) do settings to be made have an effect, and what is that effect?

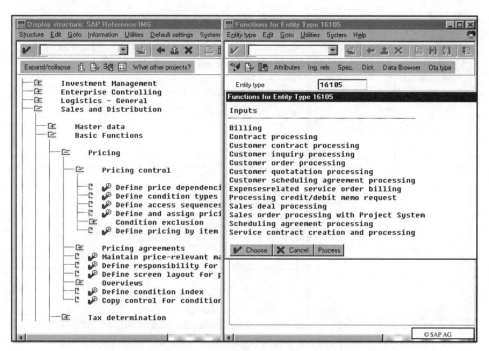

Fig. 6.24: Iterative path – from Customizing to process

6.2.17 From Customizing to Prototyping

The goal of Customizing is to customize the transactions to be used based on the customer's needs. In the example at hand, goods receipts with the movement type *101* are identified and differentiated as to whether the goods receipt should be posted to stock or assigned to an asset account, a cost centre or a project (Cns column). In the case of quantity-based entry of goods in Materials Management, an automatic account determination can be set for value-based updating in Financial Accounting in the background. This is done by defining so-called value strings. These determine which transaction keys are addressed depending on the *Cns* field. With the transaction key, the appropriate G/L account is determined and a line item is updated for every quantity-based movement. For example, in the case of a consumption posting, the line items for a *consumption account* (for the debit posting) and for a *balance sheet account* (for the credit posting) are created. An iterative jump from the executed Customizing activities to Prototyping allows the set system parameters to be tested. In the example, an accounting document is created for every movement type, and the accuracy of the posting records is checked.

Workshop question:
Are the Customizing parameters set correctly?

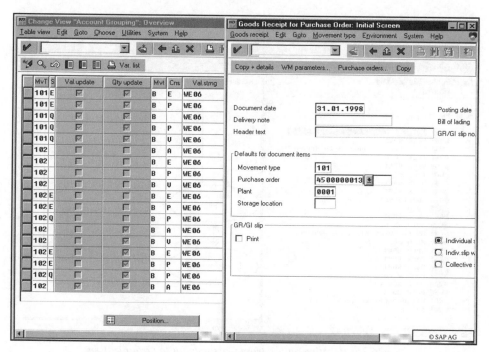

Fig. 6.25: Iterative path – from Customizing to Prototyping

6.2.18 From Customizing to Organization

Customizing of the R/3 organizational units is done in the Implementation Guide in the chapter titled *Global Settings*. In Customizing, that is where the relationships are demonstrated, based on structural representations. The example at hand presents the principal relationship between the purchasing organization and the plant. At the instance level (specification level), the corresponding plants and the purchasing organization to which they belong must then be determined. The relationships of the R/3 organizational units cannot, however, be varied as desired in every case. An iterative jump from Customizing into the Organization Model enables you to visualize the maximum number of combination possibilities that exist. The Organization Model shows that a purchasing organization can purchase goods for different plants, and that plants can procure goods over different purchasing organizations (m:n relationship). If the customer limits the existing combination possibilities in the R/3 Organization Model based on his enterprise's organizational structure, these restrictions must be taken into consideration in Customizing.

Workshop question:
Which restrictions must be taken into consideration in Customizing due to the R/3 organizational unit relationships?

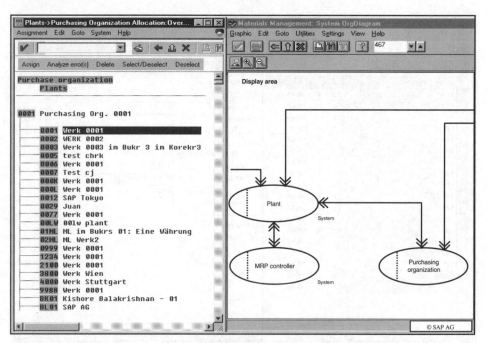

Fig. 6.26: Iterative path – from Customizing to Organization

6.2.19 From Customizing to Data Model

In Customizing, the set parameters are represented in list format. In the *Maintenance of order types* view, you can see that in the practical example at hand, the customer has numerous different business relationships that are represented by the individual order types. You can also see that the customer has specified the sales order document type *standard order* (SO), which is delivered as part of the standard R/3 System, and has declared this variant with the identifier *OR*. An iterative jump from Customizing into the Data Model allows you to display the variants of a document on the basis of the specializations, in this case the specialization for the sales order (for example, standard order, rush order, third-party order). When the sales order type is specified, a classification is performed that controls the further processing of the sales documents in the R/3 System. Here, the necessary input data is defined, in addition to the screen sequence. These are visible in the detail screen for each document type, and the conceptual relationships can be analyzed on the basis of the Data Model graphic by identifying the inbound relationships for a document type.

Workshop question:
Which conceptual relationships do the control parameters to be set in Customizing have?

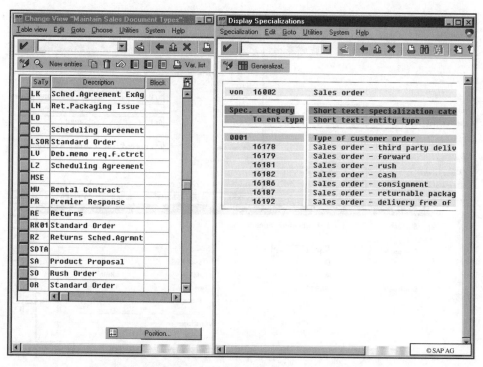

Fig. 6.27: Iterative path – from Customizing to Data Model

6.2.20 From Customizing to Data Dictionary

When switching to a new system, the question usually arises as to which master data and transaction data can be transferred in which format. Classic examples for this are the customer master, the vendor master and the material master, as well as the G/L accounts, which are the most standardized due to national guidelines. In the example at hand, there is a need to transfer the existing G/L accounts into the R/3 System. With the help of Customizing, the standardized charts of accounts, for example the industrial account framework and community account framework for Germany, or the chart of accounts for the USA, can be copied directly as a template. Additional, custom G/L accounts, however, must be reconciled with the structure of the Data Dictionary before being transferred. With an iterative jump into the Data Model, you can first determine the pertinent table SKB1 on the basis of the entity *G/L account*, then from there branch into the Data Dictionary. In the Data Dictionary, the data type CHAR, the field name SAP SAKNR, and the corresponding field lengths can then be determined and reconciled with the technical values of the customer's G/L accounts.

Workshop question:
How is mass data structured in Customizing?

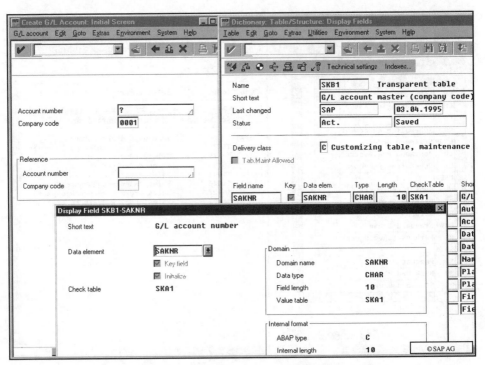

Fig. 6.28: Iterative path – from Customizing to Data Dictionary

6.2.21 From Data Model to process

For successful processing, employees need information or preceding decisions that can be recorded in an information document. For the structuring of a consistent information architecture, on the other hand, it is necessary to know which processes and, finally, which employees access which common information. If, for example, a process accesses certain information (object or entity) and changes the state of the object within processing, at run time it must be blocked for all other processes that could change the information. Due to the integration of the models in the R/3 Repository, you can, through an iterative jump from a selected entity of the Data Model (in the example, the entity *condition* with the number 16105), obtain a list of all of the processes that operate on it, represent all inbound and outbound information (input or output), and navigate from there into the desired process graphic. Within the process, it must then be determined which functions process the objects mentioned. In the example at hand, the *condition* plays a role especially in the function *Determine/transfer order prices/taxes*.

Workshop question:
In which processes is the object or the entity needed?

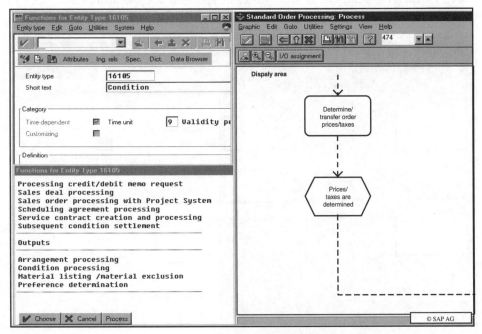

Fig. 6.29: Iterative path – from Data Model to process

6.2.22 From Data Model to Customizing

Objects can reference setup activities (IMG) in Customizing. The example demonstrates the logical relationship in the Data Model between *Purchasing organization* and *Vendor evaluation criteria*. A concrete evaluation of a vendor thus always references the validity of evaluation criteria in relation to one purchasing organization. An iterative jump into Customizing allows the *Vendor evaluation per purchasing organization* parameters to be demonstrated, as briefly explained in the following section on the basis of the organization *0001*. In the parameter *Best score*, the maximum number of points that can be achieved within a *purchasing organization* is specified. In the subcriterion parameters, you can record, for example, whether there is only one vendor for a material. By recording a key figure in the field *Share of business volume*, it is possible to determine which qualitative error is allowed for which sales, so that no complaint is sent to the vendor. In the audit you enter whether a plant-based audit is to be performed for each delivery, or whether a general audit is to be performed by calculating the mean value of the individual plant-based evaluations. Furthermore, for a complete evaluation, criteria must be determined for deadline and quantity reliability.

Workshop question:
Which logical relationships of the Data Model are specified in Customizing?

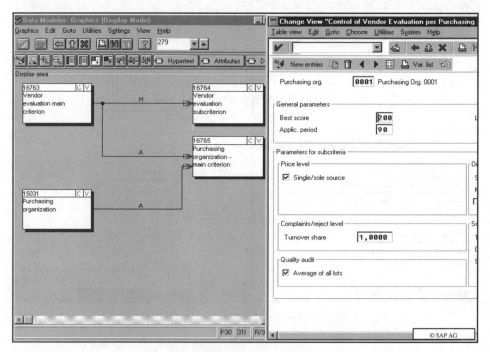

Fig. 6.30: Iterative path – from Data Model to Customizing

6.2.23 From Data Model to Organization

The Data Model shows objects and their structural relationships. These depict the logical table relationships of the R/3 System. The objects of the Data Model can be divided into „transfer objects" and „structure objects". Transfer objects are, for example, inquiries, sales orders, purchase requisitions, purchase orders, etc. They are characterized by the fact that they are passed through the enterprise in processing. Structure objects are, for example, the plant, the sales organization, the purchasing organization, etc. In the example at hand, the purchasing organization has relationships to the transfer objects outline agreement and purchase order, as well as to the structure object plant. An iterative jump into the Organization Model illuminates the R/3 organizational structure relationships between the plant and the purchasing organization, in this case an m:n relationship.

Workshop question:
Which entities of the Data Model have a responsibility-oriented organizational structure?

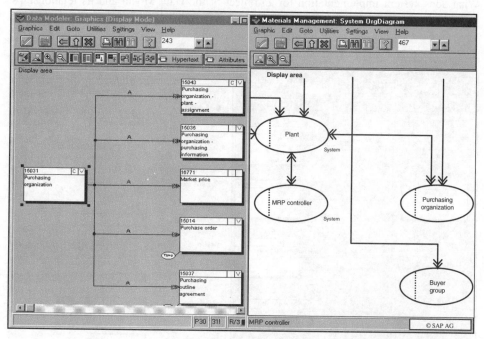

Fig. 6.31: Iterative path – from Data Model to Organization

6.2.24 From Data Model to Prototyping

R/3 processes operate on objects of the Data Model and represent a simplified view of R/3 transactions. As a result, the objects of the Data Model are also used in transaction processing. In the example at hand, the logical existence of the *Production order confirmation* is dependent on the *Production order*. An iterative jump into the R/3 transaction *Create confirmation for production order* allows this logical relationship to be tested as a prototype. While in the Data Model a reference is made to a general confirmation, it becomes clear in Prototyping that confirmation can have different variants (partial confirmation, final confirmation, automatic confirmation). An appropriate procedure is selected depending on the customer's desires and the existing production technology, etc. Furthermore, the yields and scrap quantities are specified, along with the causes for the scrap and possible rework. When the confirmation has resulted in Prototyping, the status is updated; in the Data Model, the only indication of this is a time symbol.

Workshop question:
What does system implementation for an object of the Data Model and its relationships look like?

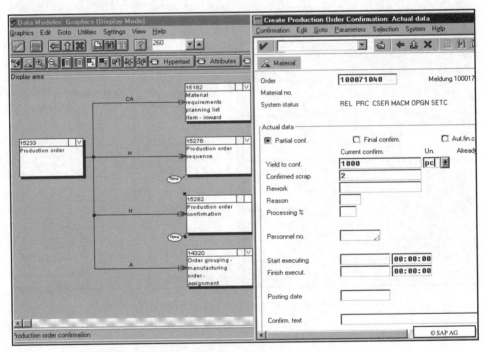

Fig. 6.32: Iterative path – from Data Model to Prototyping

6.2.25 From Data Model to Data Dictionary

The Data Model describes the logical structures of the R/3 System from the aspect of freedom from redundancy and consistency; the Data Dictionary describes the physical structures from the aspect of minimized redundancy, consistency and high-performance accessibility. An object of the Data Model can refer to one or more transparent tables of the Data Dictionary. It is possible, for one thing, to demonstrate from one object all of the relevant attributes of various tables, that is, to create a *view*. For another thing, it is possible, for each object (in the example, for the *production order*), to look at the individual tables with all of their attributes. Two tables of the Data Dictionary are assigned to the production order: AFKO for *order header data PPC orders*, and AUFK for *order master data*. An iterative jump from the Data Model into the Data Dictionary lets you analyze the individual fields of a table. An important field in every table of the Data Dictionary is the determination of the definition *delivery class*. In this case, SAP distinguishes whether a table is an application table, a Customizing table, a control table or a system table, for example.

Workshop question:
How is a logical object physically structured?

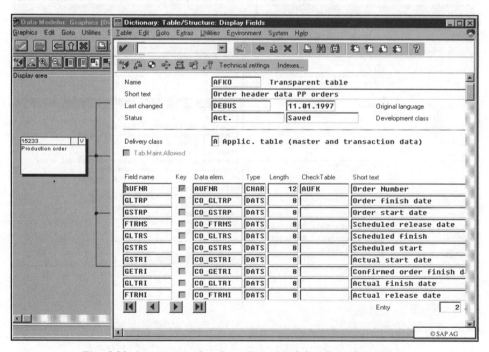

Fig. 6.33: Iterative path – from Data Model to Data Dictionary

6.2.26 From Data Dictionary to process

Successful processing requires input information, a trigger and a processor, i.e. a person, a machine, or both. Input data consists of objects from the Data Model, which in turn have a relationship to the Data Dictionary. A logical object can consist of several tables, such as the sales order, which consists of the three tables VBAK, VBKD and VEDA. If the integrated R/3 System is being used in its entirety, analysis in the Data Model and the Data Dictionary is not necessary. If, for example, however, sales orders are gathered daily by decentralized sales divisions using heterogeneous systems and fed into the R/3 System in a night run using *batch input* for planning and continued processing purposes, it is necessary to reconcile the relevant order fields of the non-SAP systems with the three SAP tables mentioned above. An iterative jump over the Data Model enables you to identify, based on the object sales order, all of the processes operating on the tables for which batch input is a precursor.

Workshop question:
Which tables of the R/3 System must be reconciled with an external system for successful processing?

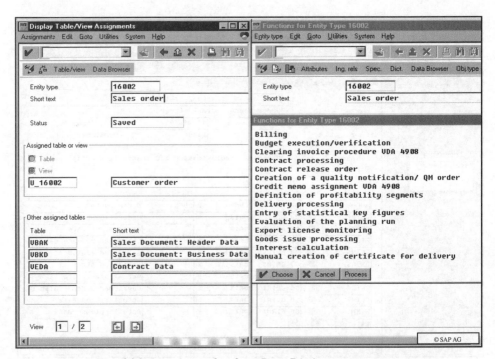

Fig. 6.34: Iterative path – from Data Dictionary to process

6.2.27 From Data Dictionary to Organization

The fields of a table can be classified according to various criteria. For example, they can be divided according to organizational, conceptual, country-specific or program aspects. The main organizational element for the object customer billing document is the organizational unit company code. Likewise, in the Data Dictionary one can see additional organizational details that have been specified, such as time recorded, name of staff person and change date. For the fields (in the Data Dictionary) of an object (in the Data Model) that are determined using the view technique, the processes operating on the object and the corresponding R/3 organizational units can be determined through the object. An iterative jump can list, for example, the processes relevant for the customer billing document, and from there it is possible to navigate into the respective R/3 organizational units. So the example shows that within billing document processing, next to the customer billing document, which is assigned to the company code, there are also other R/3 organizational units that are relevant.

Workshop question:
Which fields in the Data Dictionary are of an organizational nature?

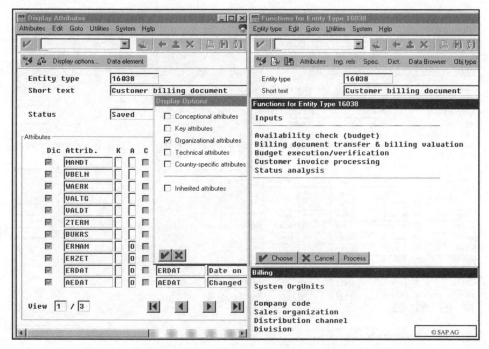

Fig. 6.35: Iterative path – from Data Dictionary to Organization

6.2.28 From Data Dictionary to Data Model

In the Data Dictionary, you can analyze the physical tables and their fields. Individual fields are linked to a check table, that is, a valid input range has been defined for these fields. Say, for example, a user wants to enter a particular purchasing organization (EKORG), *0004*, but only the purchasing organizations *0001* and *0002* are defined in the check table. In this case, the system points out the incorrect input. The physical tables can, in turn, have relationships to other tables. An iterative jump into the Data Model allows you to jump to the pertinent logical object (in the example, this is the purchase order). By way of the Dictionary assignment, you can determine for the object *purchase order* with the physical table EKKO (purchase order document header) which other physical tables are related. Likewise, through the relationships of the objects of the Data Model, you can achieve additional references to physical relationships of the Data Dictionary tables. Thus, the purchase order has relationships to the purchase order item with the table EKPO (purchasing document item) and to the purchase order/business partner assignment with the table EKPA (partner roles in Purchasing).

Workshop question:
What relationship do the tables of the Data Dictionary have to each other?

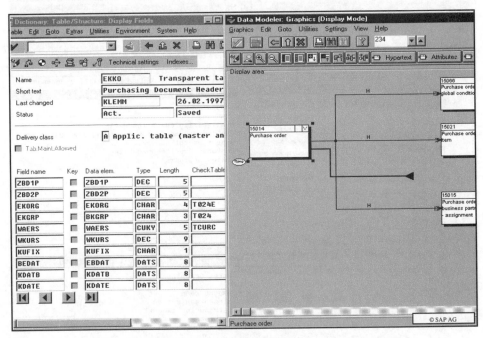

Fig. 6.36: Iterative path – from Data Dictionary to Data Model

6.2.29 From Data Dictionary to Prototyping

When structuring an efficient software system, the central question arises as to which information must be built up for integrated process flow and for purposes of ensuring consistency (hidden logic), and which information must be made transparent to a staff member for processing his operational business processes (Prototyping). If the specific values are to be calculated for an object of the Data Model, for example the purchase order, it is possible to look at all of the existing purchase orders and their respective transaction data in list form in the Data Dictionary. By selecting a document number, for example EBELN *4500011096*, you can display the individual fields for a data record. An iterative jump into Prototyping allows you to analyze the fields called short descriptions from the point of view of the staff member. Thus the short form MATNR in the Data Dictionary corresponds to the input field *Material* in the Prototyping transaction *Display purchase order*.

Workshop question:
On which screens do a table's fields appear?

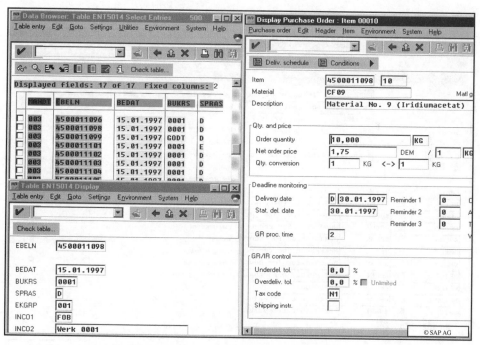

Fig. 6.37: Iterative path – from Data Dictionary to Prototyping

6.2.30 From Data Dictionary to Customizing

All of an application table's possible fields are listed in the Data Dictionary. It is not necessary, however, for all of these possibilities, for example in the application table purchasing document item (EKPO), to be used in their entirety by every customer or every staff member of a customer. An iterative jump from the Data Dictionary into Customizing makes it possible to divide the fields into four classes: mandatory entry, optional entry, display, and hide. Determining this field selection group depends on the respective transaction. In the transaction *Add purchase order* (ME21), the data, for example *price* and *price unit*, are mandatory entries for a staff member in the purchasing organization. In the transaction *Display purchase order* (ME23), these two fields are blocked for processing, to ensure, for example, that the staff member does not accidentally change the determined price during goods receipt. However, Customizing of these fields basically allows price data to be entered even when using ME23. To support settings that make business sense, these transactions are delivered in the R/3 System with preset values.

Workshop question:
For which fields of an application table are parameters set in what way for a transaction?

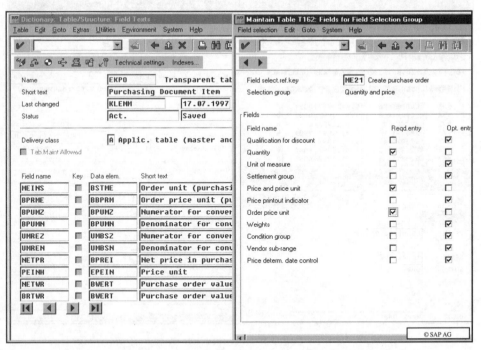

Fig. 6.38: Iterative path – from Data Dictionary to Customizing

6.3   Project implementation with IPP

The implementation of DP systems has its starting point in various situations of an enterprise, and different procedures are appropriate, depending on the question and the targeted goal. So, for example, the reason for an implementation may lie in organizational restructuring, the definition of a new market segment may require a new technology, or new technical capabilities may cause a change in an enterprise's information landscape. The process must also be oriented towards the customer's objective. If an enterprise wants, for example, to design its business processes while retaining its basic organizational structure, then the basic organizational conditions must be considered as the starting point in the project (organization-driven analysis). If an enterprise wants to improve its processing in a subarea, for example in sales, it makes sense to record the functional requirements in general and to start the project on the basis of the basic functional conditions (function-driven analysis).

Surely the most difficult case in a DP implementation arises when types of cross-department processing are to be analyzed and redesigned, and the type of organization used to date is under discussion (process-driven analysis). One of the difficulties lies in the fact that to design cross-department links, you must make transparent the subject knowledge of various groups with many different kinds of business and technical knowledge. Another difficulty, however, lies in the personal trepidation of employees that can result from restructuring and can lead to barriers in the project.

Regardless of the general tendencies mentioned above, the field of investigation must be generally delimited depending on the objective. The second step in the implementation of standard software involves selecting the modules of the software to be analyzed, for example selecting all of the modules needed to design production processing for a particular product set. Once the modules have been selected, they must be compared to the customer's requirements and adjusted to the customer's needs. Afterwards, the adjusted modules must be evaluated under consideration of the basic technological, organizational and personnel-related conditions, and a cost estimate must be produced to provide a basis for deciding the course of the rest of the project.

A case study (analysis of usage by a customer) should illuminate in which form the IPP technique can be used for this and which elements of the IPP are important in the R/3 implementation. The goal of the case study is to analyze the customer's order processing types and to investigate the possibility of processing with the R/3 System. The first part of the objective implies selection of the appropriate subject matter experts and active listening by the consultants to determine exactly what the customer-specific requirements are. Because every enterprise is unique in its specific type of processing due to technological, organizational and personnel-related circumstances, the wealth of variants of the R/3 System must be adjusted to the customer's specific requirements. By selecting the relevant functionality from the R/3 offering and deleting the functions not needed, SAP's proposed solution can be configured so that it is tailored for the customer. Each of the customer's various order processing types contains different net value added chains, which consist of configured R/3 process modules, which are selected according to the building block principle and placed into their sequence.

An IPP workshop starts by identifying the relevant process areas. First the areas are selected in which the customer wants to perform a net value added chain analysis using the IPP technique. In the analysis described below, the process areas selected were procurement logistics, production logistics, and sales and distribution logistics. In its R/3 Reference Process Model, SAP has predesigned processes that are used as process modules, to assemble the net value added chain. At this early point in time, the net value added chain is purely a sequence with standard R/3 System processes. It serves as a basis for the rest of the process analysis. According to the customer requirements, the predesigned R/3 reference processes are changed in the sense that their number is reduced. At the same time, the customer's individualities with regard to the individual function steps are recorded in a process in table format. Every individual process module needs a process analysis and, after completion, is configured for the customer as part of the net value added chain. The customer's net value added chain contains process sequences and parallels. If, in addition, there are non-SAP systems, these can be integrated into the customer's net value added chain, and the interfaces to the process modules of the R/3 Reference Model made clear. To define the requirements, the individual subject matter experts are brought together in the IPP workshop and, with the help of moderating techniques, the individual net value added chains are interactively analyzed. An efficient IPP workshop involves:

- 6–8 of the customer's employees and a moderator with knowledge of the respective branch of industry and R/3

- relevant R/3 reference models in printed format, for selecting the necessary functionality using highlighters

- R/3 System access and visual aid capabilities via LCD display, for the presentation of the business solution in the R/3 System

- 2–3 pin-up boards for the flexible arrangement of process modules, etc., using index cards, during structuring of a customer's net value added chain

- optional: a spreadsheet program for recording in a structured fashion the requirements that have open points during the workshop

- optional: depending on the scope of the analysis, additional consultants with specialized knowledge in various areas of logistics, financial accounting or human resources management.

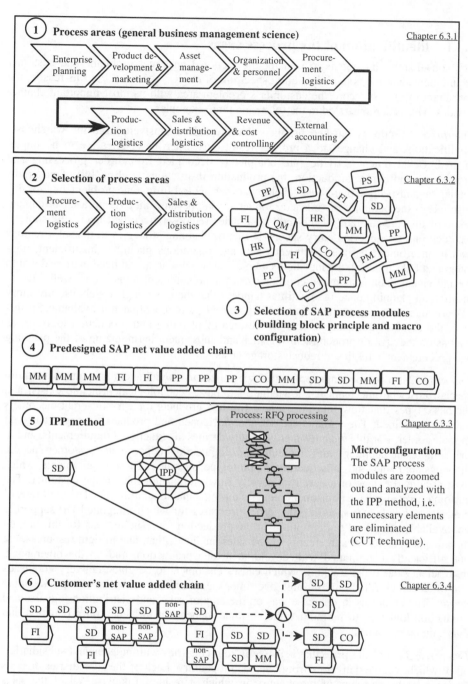

Fig. 6.39: Overall plan for the IPP workshop

6.3.1 Identification of the process areas

The consultant's first job is to transfer the recorded customer problems and customer requirements into the potential solution spectrum of the R/3 software. For this reason, the consultant must first record the customer's problem area with its most important characteristics. This is demonstrated in the following three examples.

Enterprise 1 produces finished products that are sold exclusively from the warehouse. Modifications and changes to a product result only when new series are to be implemented. Development activities are completely decoupled from order processing and production, and before production, the production instructions, such as bill of materials, routing, and inspection plan, are available in order-neutral form. One problem area for this customer is the planning of finished product stocks, because they tie up a lot of capital. Some of the forecast data of the individual sales regions is recorded manually, some is recorded on PC-supported entry sheets. Different planning strategies in the sales regions lead to insufficient harmony between sales and operations planning. Insufficient, non-integrated DP support in the logistical chain of sales, sales area, and headquarters down to the individual plants has grave consequences for procurement logistics, as well. Due to insufficient planning data, it sometimes happens that there is a high warehouse inventory of particular components, and particular procured parts are often not available. In this case, the focus of the analysis was on the area of planning and production logistics, as well as on the area of procurement logistics and subsequent harmonizing of the planning and procurement activities to reduce storage costs.

Enterprise 2 is a component supplier that specializes in providing components that require specialized electromechanical knowledge. The basic technological principle exists, and the basic types that flow into the various finished products for very different customers have been defined. The variants are defined, developed and produced in dependence on the sales order. For this the customer generally defines his functional requirements, and in the component supplier's development and engineering department, customer-specific drawings are made, and subsequently the prototype is created. These requirements, which exist at an early stage of a new run, usually flow into a pilot run for the customer. The customer may also have adjustment requests during a manufacturing run. The multitude of product- and customer-specific sales order processes for which integrated DP support is not available often lead to disruptions in the production run. The reasons for this are, on the one hand, technical agreements by the sales engineers that, due to tight resources, are not sufficiently coordinated with development and production, and on the other hand, insufficient sales order tracking, which causes customers to be given delivery go-aheads that often can be filled only through overtime, special shifts, etc. by involving a *deadline chaser*. The emphasis in this case was on the area of sales and distribution logistics and production logistics, to harmonize the customer-dependent influence on production and thus gain more control.

Enterprise 3 is an enterprise that is active in four countries with independent subsidiaries, all of which receive deliveries from one central country. Each of the subsidiaries does its business in the currency of the country in which it resides. Likewise, all of the sales documents must be created in the language of that country. The foreign subsidiaries use separate DP systems for processing their sales and distribution activities. Due to lack of

DP integration, all of the debtor transactions are first recorded in a list, after which real-time posting of the transactions to the appropriate G/L ledger can occur. Furthermore, the use of different program systems requires costly program maintenance that is limited by different programming techniques, data management and user interfaces. The emphasis of the analysis in this case was on the financial accounting area, where the goal is for creditor and debtor business transactions to be handled uniformly across country boundaries, as well as on the structure of enterprise-wide profitability analysis.

As support for the business area analysis, SAP AG offers something called process areas as an introduction. A process area depicts a business structure, which represents a homogeneous unit in the sense of process-oriented structuring. Similar process chains that can be traced back to a common, basic pattern are represented in a single process area. SAP AG provides the following process areas, among others, for arranging customer requirements in a specific area of analysis:

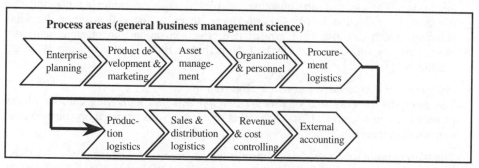

Fig. 6.40: Business process areas

■ *Process area: Enterprise planning*
Planning is used to set goals. By comparing actual events with planned events, you can identify deviations. These deviations can then serve as control signals, which you can use to take corrective action in process flows. The enterprise process area of *enterprise planning* is divided into the areas of strategic enterprise planning and operational enterprise planning.

The goal of strategic enterprise planning is to determine general mid-term and long-term planning data (1–5 years) for enterprise development. Operational planning is carried out periodically – usually annually – on the basis of the strategic corporate plan. A flexible standard for planned (performance and consumption) quantities and values derived from these occurs as part of operational enterprise planning. Planning occurs for clearly defined periods of time (usually one year). The goals of operational enterprise planning are:

– To undertake the planning-related design of the business future for a particular time period, including defining specific standards and goals. The (market) circumstances both within the enterprise and outside it, as well as strategic enterprise planning, must be taken into consideration.

- To create standards for controlling the course of business during the current accounting period. As part of dynamic planning, the standard goals can be adjusted to changed basic conditions.

- To check efficiency after closure of the accounting period, based on planned/actual or target/actual comparisons.

- To create a standard foundation for evaluating operational performance independent of incidental fluctuations.

The default values and degrees of goal achievement of the planning must be determined in cooperation and agreement with those responsible. The business activities in the individual enterprise areas cannot be effectively controlled or a satisfactory efficiency check achieved unless the planning is supported by them. The starting point for operational enterprise planning is the sales plan, which records which quantities are to be brought to market in the planning time frame, or the sales and distribution information system. The planned sales quantities are passed on to the production planning department in production logistics. Furthermore, there are dependencies on financial planning, which can also have a restrictive effect on production planning and cost centre planning (cf. Gälweiler 1990; cf. Hinterhuber 1989; cf. Kreikebaum 1989; cf. Staehle 1991).

■ *Process area: Product development and marketing*
The enterprise process area of *product development and marketing* consists of the planning of a new product based on market research results or based on concrete customer requirements.

The starting point for a new development is the *function search* of the product, derived from the requirements to be met by the product (*planning phase*). After the subsequent *working out of the principle*, the first creative drafts are conceived as part of the *product design*, before *drawing creation* (*preparation*). The entire engineering and design process is a procedure in which the engineering documents, which are the basis for future manufacturing, are created step by step, starting with a defined task. According to the VDI (Verein Deutscher Ingenieure, Association of German Engineers) guideline 2223, engineering and design is defined as follows: „engineering and design is the predominantly creative, knowledge- and experience-based, optimal-solutions-targeted conception of technical products, determination of their functional and structural buildup, and creation of production-ready documents" (Kühn 1980, p. 11).

In addition to the function search with the corresponding physical calculations, the area of product development also includes object description (material master), creation of engineering drawings and bills of materials, and management and information procurement activities necessary to carry out the development. *Product complexity* and *product standardization* have an important influence on the cost of these activities. The result of engineering and design activities serves as a basis for creating the basic data for production, such as the production bill of materials, the routing, the inspection plan and the standard cost estimate. Continual development of the product and the production procedure also occurs in the area of product development. Which department in an enterprise triggers the development of a product depends on various factors, such as the type of order placement. If a *customer* places an order directly with the enterprise, this planning step is often executed in the (technical) sales division. If the enterprise is working for an *anonymous market*, the impetus is often market research. The basic phases are:

a) specification of market or customer requirements

b) product development phase

- Stage 1: research into information needs

- Stage 2: development of procedures and tests

- Stage 3: feasibility check of the run (prototyping)

c) release/transfer to production

- of material master, recipe, bill of materials, routing, work centres

- of the documentation, engineering/change status (for example, new drawing), SOP – standard operating procedure (for example, certain protective clothing at a work centre, work instructions, handling instructions), quality control instructions

d) production run or repetitive manufacturing run

Phases 1 and 2 require close cooperation with the customer or the market or market research, and Phases 3 and 4 require coordination with production. In Phase 4, control of production is often incumbent on the employees of product development (cf. Backhaus 1990; cf. Böcker 1990; cf. Brockhoff 1988; cf. Pahl/Beitz 1986).

■ *Process area: Asset management*
The enterprise process area *asset management* brings together all of the business events that in the widest sense possible contribute to preparing and managing the necessary operating facilities (for example, buildings, machines, etc.) for an operational performance process. If you look at the life cycle of fixed assets, the business events can be distinguished by when they occur:

- *from before the investment decision until start-up*
  Before a decision is made to invest, preinvestment analyses are carried out with regard to the impending new or replacement investments. The sum of all planned investments is managed enterprise-wide in an investment programme that, from the planning phase, over the procurement/in-construction phase, to start-up, provides information about the credit limit used (percentage) of the approved investment budget with a planned/budgeted/actual comparison.

- *during the useful life of the fixed assets*
  During the useful life, a distinction is made between commercial and technical asset management.

Asset accounting includes the phase from the first acquisition of the fixed asset until its retirement. Between these two points in time, values are calculated for depreciation, interest and insurance. In addition to these considerations relating to financial policy, operational asset management includes all technical measures that are oriented towards projection, preparation, administration and maintenance (for example, maintenance and repair) of operating facilities (fixed assets). With today's increasing mechanization, which leads to high fixed costs in the area of fixed assets, a high degree of availability of the production assets is essential for efficient distribution of fixed costs. Expanded demands for quality assurance require more and more plan-based maintenance of production assets. In addition to this, legal requirements and public demands with regard to the importance of environmental protection and asset security have increased the importance of technology-oriented asset management. Specifically, this includes tasks for inspection (measures to determine the actual status), for maintenance (measures to preserve the planned status), and for plant maintenance (measures to recover the planned status) (cf. Adam 1989; cf. Männel 1988).

■ *Process area: Organization and personnel*
The task of operational *organization and personnel* has over the course of time changed from pure human resources management to include organizing functions, such as personnel development. At the same time, human resource tasks have gained importance in enterprises, because of their increasing importance for success and insurance of long-term existence. Personnel is organized quite differently in different enterprises. Internal organization is particularly dependent on the branch of industry and the size of the enterprise, the individual enterprise's development, and the attitude of management towards human resources. Human resources management must merge requirements with human performance, using knowledge about the numerous influences on people at work. The goals of human resources management are to provide the required work volume according to quantitative, qualitative, temporal and location-related demands, increase human performance, and satisfy social needs, both material and non-material. The functions of this enterprise process area are:

- *personnel organization*
  (job description, ergonomics, work centre grading, wage and salary structure)

- *personnel planning*
  (labour market, requirements planning, procurement planning, workforce planning, personnel development planning)

- *recruitment*
  (internal job description, temporary personnel, external job description, selection process, contract closing)

- *human resources management*
  (introduction, training, industrial law and social legislation, changes due to transfers, giving notice, terminations, transfer into retirement)

- *personnel development*
  (evaluations, operational employee suggestion system, wage and salary politics)

- *personnel education and training*
  (successor training, employee training, continued education)

- *social benefits*
  (child care, recreational activities, industrial safety)

Human Resources in the R/3 System enables the enterprise and management to process all of the above-mentioned human resource task areas in an integrated fashion. It contains all of the functions that are prescribed by law and by collective agreements, that are necessary for gathering personnel data, that support the very different methods of payroll accounting (different country specifications), and that simplify the entry, storage, retrieval, processing and display of personnel data (cf. Berthel 1991; cf. Bleicher 1981; cf. Bühner 1989; cf. Hentze 1991).

Process area: Procurement logistics
Incumbent on *procurement logistics* is the task of providing the enterprise with the necessary goods and services for performing work. One focus of procurement logistics is the needs-based and inexpensive provision of the necessary operating factors. In addition to procuring raw material and operating supplies, semi-finished products and trading goods, the tasks of procurement logistics include processing goods receipts with the corresponding inspection and warehousing activities, as well as checking incoming invoices and triggering corresponding payment. Efficient execution of these tasks targets price and cost goals, as well as product and quality goals, whose scope will be described here briefly.

In price politics, price zones are defined, and specific prices are negotiated for the goods and services, taking into consideration discounts and rebates. Discounts can be guaranteed, for example, if the materials are picked up directly at the vendor's location. Rebates can be guaranteed if goods are purchased from a vendor in a defined period of time with a value over a minimum value. Price politics is also influenced by the determination of conditions, such as terms of delivery and payment terms. If a vendor delivers too late, for example, a one-time contractual penalty may be agreed upon, or a percentage-based deduction from the purchase price that is dependent on exceeding of the delivery date. Furthermore, in addition to the price for goods, procurement logistics must also take into consideration alternative transport and storage costs, as well as customs fees when crossing borders. Closely linked to the planning of terms of delivery is the general orientation of business relationships with the vendor. For the structure of longer-term supply relationships, which occur often in the component supply industry, for example, close cooperation is required to reach an inventory-reducing procurement strategy. Low storage costs create room for liquidity for the enterprise, but can also lead to grave production problems in case of delivery difficulties due to a lack of safety stock.

In accordance with product politics, the breadth and depth of the procurement program, as well as the temporal demand for component goods, is determined. Type-related specification determines the procurement assortment and defines the requirements for functionality, shelf life and integratability of the component goods. Furthermore, product politics determines which materials should be manufactured in-house and which should be procured externally, and when a product manufactured in-house should be replaced by an externally procured material or vice versa. For example, if the capacity load is completely utilized, it may be necessary for the enterprise to place external orders to meet a customer delivery date. Timely procurement of materials depends on the requirement dates of production and/or the customers, as well as on the type of material staging, for example stocking, individual procurement, delivery synchronized with usage (cf. Grochla 1978; cf. Hartmann 1990).

■ *Process area: Production logistics*
Production logistics contains the tasks for performing work and thus describes the physical creation process of industrial products. Performing work in the narrower sense of manufacturing and assembly characterizes the processing of raw materials into semi-finished and finished goods. In the broader sense, it describes the planning, execution and control of the performance of work.

The starting point for production logistics is the activities of production programme planning, where the type, quantity and deadline of the products to be produced are determined. In planning of manufacturing and assembly orders, the quantities to be produced must be reconciled with the available capacity in production and released. When the production order is released, in addition to executing production, one must also execute the required activities for the provision of materials and the necessary semi-finished products within an enterprise. This includes internal stock transfer and transportation processes as well as the corresponding quality assurance measures, both during and after the production process.

The tasks of production logistics, as well as their contents and scope, are decisively influenced by the fundamental manufacturing procedures of production, for example milling cutting, lathing, drilling, welding and forging. A distinction must be made here between manually controlled machines and NC-controlled or CNC-controlled machines or highly integrated manufacturing systems in the machinery. The type of production and the production organization (manufacturing and assembly organization) also have a large effect on the production logistics tasks to be executed.

The production type is divided into mass production, large repetitive manufacturing, small repetitive manufacturing and make-to-order production. In the case of mass production, products that are different, but similar in terms of their starting material and processing method, i.e. products that are closely related in terms of production, are produced over a longer period of time. Schäfer uses the example of a screw factory, as well as the production of files and pliers (cf. Schäfer 1969, pp. 63–67). Mass production can also include the production of complex products, however, such as washing machines or televisions, as long as the customer cannot choose between individual variants of a product line. Closely related to mass production is large repetitive manufacturing. In this case, closely related products are produced the same way over a longer period of time. The product types are manufactured in large numbers of pieces, and the customer can choose between different variants within the type program. Examples of this are automobile manufacturers and the manufacturers of application-specific machine tools. Component supplier operations, too, with their repetitive business, belong to this group. Small repetitive manufacturing means that within a period of time, different products are manufactured in small editions. Production in small numbers of pieces requires, in contrast to make-to-order production, complete preparation of the sales-order-based, technical documents for production and assembly. Typical representatives are machine tool construction with customer-specific modifications, or component suppliers in what is known as the pilot run business. What is typical for make-to-order production is that the product is tailored to specific, individual needs and thus inevitably has 1 as its edition number at the end-product level. Examples of make-to-order production are large machine construction, special machine construction and shipbuilding.

The production organization describes the arrangement of machines in manufacturing and assembly. While, in manufacturing, the arrangement of individual manufacturing processes is also important, in addition to the object, the assembly organization is decisively determined by the flow of the object. The workshop principle is based on the physical grouping of machines and work centres according to similar functions or performances, which is expressed in the use of the same production methods. In the manufacturing centre concept, the processing stations are arranged according to the flow principle of the product being produced (object orientation). Here, in addition to object orientation, there is flexible handling during determination of the process sequences. In the flow principle, the work sequences are also arranged according to the flow principle, but the flow is equally strictly oriented towards the arrangement of the different operating facilities. The personal room for freedom is smaller here than in the manufacturing centre concept. In the construction site principle, the necessary production materials and employees must reach the object to the processed, for example the construction site, machinery or fixed asset (cf. Corsten 1991; cf. Glaser *et al.* 1991; cf. Gutenberg 1983; cf. Hackstein 1989; cf. Hoitsch 1985).

■ *Process area: Sales logistics*

Sales logistics deals with the tasks of performance utilization and thus organizes the business relationships in the market. The task of sales and distribution is to provide customers with the goods produced in the enterprise, or with the financial or other services offered by the enterprise. While the long-term-oriented tasks of sales planning, such as customer segment analysis, market research and product planning, are assigned to the enterprise process area of product development and marketing, sales logistics includes the planning and control of distribution channels, from advertisement, inquiry and quotation processing, sales order processing (including pricing), delivery processing (including picking and goods issue checking), invoicing, on down to checking of incoming payments.

The scope of and trigger for sales activities are influenced by the type of service provided in the market and the type of order placement. In the case of short-lived consumer goods, sales has the task of selling the service to wholesalers, who pass the product on to the end user. Due to the technical complexity of the product, long-lived consumer goods often require more detailed, personal consulting. Capital goods, for example machines that are used to manufacture products, often require a high degree of technical subject knowledge on the part of the customer as well as on the part of the supplier. While in the former case the customer receives a standard offer in the form of a price list, in the second case, the product is often configured on the basis of the customer's requirements, with the help of standardized basic components.

In the former case, the customer has a general overview of the product selection, based on, for example, standard catalogues, advertising materials, etc., and inquiry and quotation processing is not necessary. The customer orders from a direct shipper or a dealer, or buys it directly in a store with a cash purchase.

In the latter case, one must check whether the customer's configuration desires can be accommodated by the supplier's available services. If it is a standard configuration, it can often be delivered directly from the warehouse. If it is a customer-based make-to-order configuration, it must be planned, scheduled and assembled according to the customer's wishes. Therefore, simple price determination and determination of a delivery date must often be carried out in quotation processing.

Capital goods must often be planned in detail, and costing must often be performed in quotation processing. Especially in the area of special machine construction, the scope of quotation processing can make up the bulk of sales order processing. In this case, it is not unusual for a technical feasibility check to be required, in which technical documents, such as the engineering design drawings, must be created, and production-related restrictions such as machines, tools and devices must be checked for the possibility of usage (cf. Backhaus 1990; cf. Gutenberg 1979; cf. Meffert 1989; cf. Wöhe 1993).

■ *Process area: Revenue and cost controlling*
The task of the enterprise process area *revenue and cost controlling* is to provide an enterprise's decision makers with quantitative information. Provision of appropriate master data and basic data is followed by planning and recording of costs, and subsequently calculation of variances between planned and actual costs. Parallel to this, revenue and cost controlling occurs, in the narrow sense, as a type of reporting, which must provide the information for control measures to be taken in case deviations occur. Revenue and cost controlling can be divided into the tasks of overhead cost controlling, profitability analysis and product cost controlling.

Overhead cost controlling, whose goal is to plan, control and monitor overhead costs, includes cost element accounting, cost centre accounting, activity cost controlling and overhead cost orders. Building on cost centre and order planning, all actual costs are charged to the appropriate cost-incurring parties, such as cost centres or overhead cost orders, as part of overhead cost controlling. These actual costs can then be assigned to further accounts as part of internal activity allocation or order settlement, in order to appropriately document the internal exchange of services from a cost perspective. The planned costs (target costs), adjusted to the capacity utilization level, are subsequently compared to the corresponding actual costs. Deviations of the actual state from the planned or targeted state that have been identified are then subject to further control measures in Controlling.

Profitability analysis is used to evaluate market segments – divided into products, customers, sales orders, or any combinations of these into groups with regard to their revenue contribution or profit margin. The goal is to support the areas of sales and distribution, marketing, product management, and enterprise planning controlling and decision-making information. Costs and revenues are calculated according to the cost-of-sales accounting principle, that is, the pertinent costs of sales are deducted from the revenues as marginal costs or full costs. Fixed costs can be assigned either as percentages or in blocks, at any levels of revenue hierarchy. The evaluation terms (features) and values (value fields) for profitability analysis are defined as part of basic data management. Data can be taken over from various areas, for example:

– revenues and sales deductions from the sales and distribution system

– manufacturing costs from product costing

– cost centre fixed costs and deviations from overhead cost controlling or cost centre accounting

- special direct costs from financial accounting, materials management, or controlling

- order-specific or project-specific costs from order settlement or project settlement

As part of profitability analysis, it is possible to calculate planned revenues, planned sales deductions and planned manufacturing costs through automatic valuation of planned sales quantities. Beyond that, sales quantities can be transferred from profitability analysis to production planning, so that a production programme can be planned there.

Product cost controlling or cost object controlling provides important information for planning, controlling and monitoring product costs. Product cost controlling provides basic information for the business functions of pricing and price politics, inventory valuation, manufacturing cost controlling and profitability analysis. Product cost controlling contains the areas of product costing and cost object controlling. Product costing represents order-neutral cost object piece accounting for a material or an object of cost accounting. It is a tool for cost planning and price determination for materials and is used to calculate the manufacturing costs and costs of goods sold per product unit. In the case of a mass producer, product costing is handled in the form of a standard cost estimate. Cost object accounting assigns the costs incurred in an enterprise to the operation's service units (for example, products, sales orders) and is used to optimize the manufacturing costs of a product. Cost object accounting in the area of revenue and cost controlling includes the final costing of a cost object. Before final costing, cost object accounting takes place parallel to the quantity flow in the enterprise process area of production (preliminary costing and simultaneous costing) (cf. Horváth 1990; cf. Kilger 1987; cf. Weber 1991).

Process area: External accounting
Operational accounting is an instrument for business representation of relationships and processes. You obtain a basic systematization of operational accounting by dividing, according to the various information addressees, into internal and *external accounting*. The tasks of external accounting are essentially:

- *the accounting obligation*
  Only with the aid of functional accounting can an enterprise meet its legal accounting obligations (for example. § 238 HGB, Handelsgesetzbuch, German trade law) to report the net assets, payables and profit of the enterprise to enterprise owners, the Internal Revenue Service and creditors/lenders.

- *the information obligation*
  The enterprise provides information partially because of the legal requirement for openness (for example, §§ 325 ff. HGB in Germany), partially voluntarily, to give the interested public an idea of the overall business situation of the enterprise.

External accounting serves to meet the merchant's obligation to systematically provide itself with information and to render accounts to others, especially providers of outside capital and fiscal authorities. The essential parts of external accounting are financial accounting and year-end closing.

In business management science, the task of financial accounting is to record all business events that have triggered a change in an enterprise's assets or capital. These processes are identified on the balance sheet as a summarizing comparison of the assets and payables of an enterprise. In the centre of external accounting stands the annual creation of the balance sheet prescribed by legislators (for example, § 242 HGB in Germany). Also part of external accounting is the creation of the profit and loss statement. The profit and loss statement provides information about the yearly profits. It lists all expenses and income for the fiscal year in question and, at the end of the business year, it flows over the *annual net profit/annual deficit* post into the *stockholders' equity* position on the liability side of the balance sheet.

A distinction is made between the annual balance sheet and so-called special balance sheets. The corporate group balance sheet, for example, while also legally prescribed (for example, §§ 329 ff. AktG and §§ 290 ff. HGB in Germany), nevertheless represents a *comparison of assets and capital of all of the companies belonging to the consolidated entity of a corporate group, excluding double payments.* As a result, all business transactions and therefore also the resultant cash flows that are created from the relationship between a parent company and its subsidiaries must be eliminated from the corporate group balance sheet. Furthermore, additional special balance sheets can be created, for example the liquidation balance sheet, which represents a comparison of assets and capital to liquidation values when an enterprise is dissolved.

According to the concept described, the capabilities provided by the R/3 System that belong to this enterprise process area include the processes of G/L accounting, consolidation, and the special ledger (cf. Küting/Weber 1989; cf. Weber 1988).

6.3.2 Selection of the process modules in the process areas

In the case study demonstrated below, an R/3 System implementation is planned in the following process areas: procurement logistics, production logistics and sales logistics. The processes to be considered are selected on the basis of the process modules available in the R/3 Reference Model. This requires that the customer describe in general his field of business. In the discussion with workshop participants, the R/3 consultant must then work out an assignment to the process modules of the R/3 Reference Model. This involves stringing together the process modules in a rough order. This provisional net value added chain serves as the basis for the microconfiguration that follows (see Chapter 6.3.3). In the process module selection phase, the selected R/3 reference processes still include the maximum functionality and number of process alternatives possible.

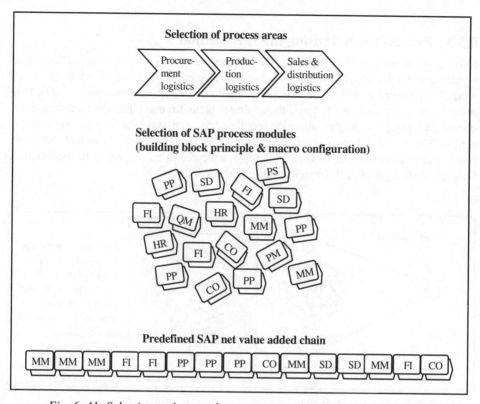

Fig. 6. 41: Selection and general arrangement of the R/3 process modules

6.3.3   Process analysis using the IPP method

Every process module of the predesigned SAP net value added chain is tested for implementability. To this end, the process modules are printed out and pinned to a board for all workshop participants to see, or they are handed out to each participant as a work template. In the discussion that follows, the available paths for every process module are discussed and compared to the customer requirements, and superfluous elements are discarded. The business discussion concerning elimination generally requires that, for every step in the process module, an iterative jump is executed in accordance with the problem, for example from the R/3 Reference Process to the R/3 Prototype.

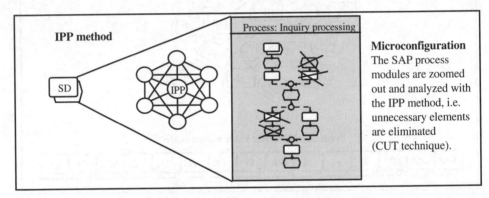

Fig. 6.42: Process analysis using the IPP method

The IPP method helps explain the various events and functions of an R/3 process module through the targeted use of the various R/3 tools. Say, for example, an R/3 consultant describes the function *Determine condition type* and poses the following question to the customer: "Which condition types do you need?" The customer first wants to find out what condition types are available in the R/3 System and suggests an iterative jump from the R/3 reference process into R/3 Customizing. In addition, the consultant could execute an iterative jump from the R/3 reference process into the R/3 System and, using IDES model data, show samples of R/3 documents in which condition types play a role. An iterative jump back into the R/3 reference process is appropriate if newly acquired information makes it possible to eliminate unnecessary events and functions (CUT technique), or if you want to examine the next process step after completing an analysis step. All of the results of this kind of process analysis are logged and recorded in table format for other project steps. The iterative process is demonstrated in detail below with an excerpt from a net value added chain that was analyzed in a workshop: *Sale from stock*. The description focuses on the process module *Inquiry processing*, which is presented in various excerpts (see dotted line in Figure 6.43). Each excerpt contains several substeps and ends with documentation of the results in table format.

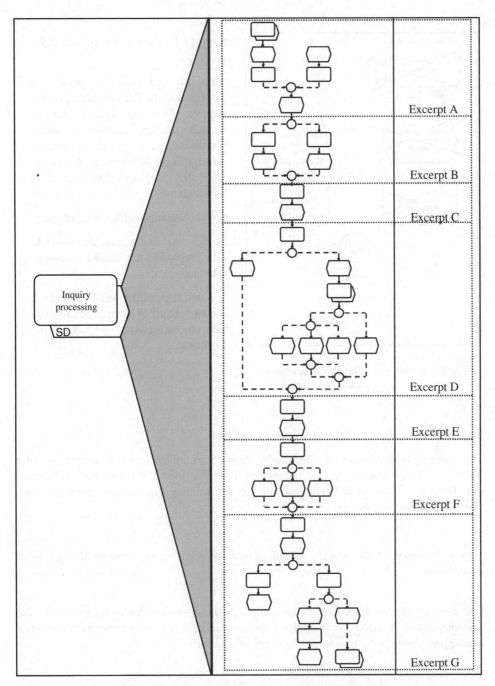

Fig. 6.43: Process analysis " Inquiry processing"

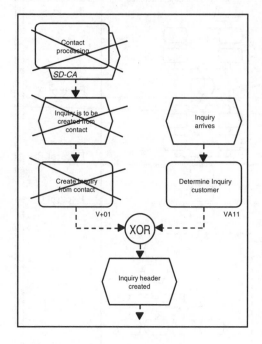

Step 1: Explain point of entry for process

Two principal points of entry are displayed in the R/3 reference process *Inquiry processing*. Queries can be created through preceding contact processing, or they can be entered directly in the R/3 System, for example if they are received in the mail or by telephone.

Step 2: Select possible points of entry

In the case study example, no field sales employees are needed to support sales activities.

For this reason, the left-hand branch showing point of entry through contact processing was deleted in the workshop.

Fig. 6.44: Process " Inquiry processing"
(Excerpt A)

Step 3: Analyze function *Determine Inquiry customer* (1)

The customer is identified in the Inquiry by the specification of a certain number. In order for this to work, however, this customer must first be defined in the customer master record. There is a separate R/3 reference process for defining the customer master record: *Customer master processing.*

Step 4: Inclusion of the process module *Customer master processing* in the net value added chain

The prerequisite that the customer be defined in the customer master record before the customer can be created in an operational process makes it necessary to position *Customer master processing* at the beginning of the net value added chain.

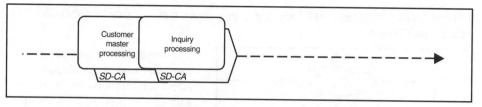

Fig. 6.45: Linking together the net value added chain

<u>Step 5:</u> Analyze function *Determine Inquiry customer* (2)

The customer number serves to identify the customer. In day-to-day business, however, it is not guaranteed that every customer will specify their assigned customer number when making an inquiry. In that case, the staff member can find the customer in the R/3 System using various criteria (matchcodes). You have the option, on the one hand, of executing an iterative jump into Prototyping to look at the various possibilities in the R/3 System, or, on the other hand, of analyzing which additional information is relevant for complete entry of an order header.

Workshop question:
Can we look at the implementation of *Determine Inquiry customer* in the R/3 System as a prototype?

When the *Inquiry processing* transaction (VA11) is called, the initial screen *Create Inquiry* appears. On this screen, an Inquiry type must first be specified. The Inquiry type defines the sales document, i.e. the document in Sales that is used for various business processes such as Inquiry processing, quotation processing, order processing and outline agreement processing. Furthermore, to activate the transaction, organizational data fields must also be specified, such as sales organization, distribution channel and profit centre.

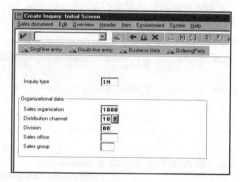

Fig. 6.46: Initial screen " Inquiry processing"

Workshop question:
What are the relationships between the necessary R/3 organizational units?

<u>Step 6:</u> Analyze R/3 organization structures for the transaction

Specification of the sales organization indicates who in Sales is responsible for certain products and services and who might be liable in relation to the customer. The distribution channel determines by which path, for example wholesale or retail, the goods will be distributed to the customer. If the customer's organization is structured as divisions, each with different terms of payment and back office processing types, it can be subdivided into different profit centres.

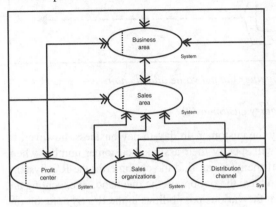

The organization model shows that the triple combination of sales organization, profit centre and distribution channel constitutes the sales area, that is, the sales area results automatically from the data entered. This lets you control, for example, that product spectrum A (CDs) is distributed through retailers and wholesalers, while product spectrum B (books) is restricted to wholesale distribution.

Fig. 6.47: Organization Model in Sales

Step 7: Analyze function *Determine Inquiry customer* (3)

Once the values have been entered in the initial screen, the screen for entering header and item data appears. In the example at hand, the customer was determined by activating the matchcode (see Step 5) in the field Sold-to party. Customer *Becker* has the customer number 1000 and lives in Berlin.

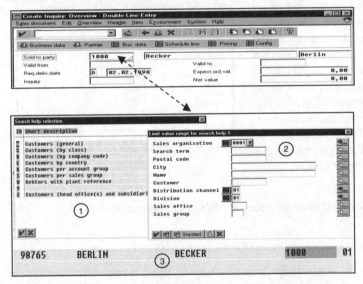

For the purpose of tracing Inquiries received, you can specify the expected order values and the period of validity of an Inquiry. These are of no further interest in this example, however. When the sold-to party has been determined, the event *Inquiry header created* is reached in the process.

Fig. 6.48: Prototyping " Inquiry header" and "Sold-to party" matchcode

<u>Step 8:</u> Record project activities for the function *Determine Inquiry customer*

The function *Determine Inquiry customer* in the standard R/3 System meets all of the customer requirements. The discussion revealed that the following organization structures provided in the R/3 System are not needed: *sales office* and *sales group*. In the future, inquiring parties will be classified using the ISO country code, which is supported by the R/3 System. One organizational point remains open: whether every first-time inquiring party should be entered as a one-time customer, for analyses or planning purposes.

Process: "Inquiry processing"							
Function	Actual/planned	Open questions	Organization	Interface	Responsible party	Date	Cost/Effort
1. Determine Inquiry customer	In future, Inquiry customers will be searched for using ISO country codes	One-time customer necessary?	Sales office, sales group not needed	Customer master (internal)	P. Miller	May 30	Standard

Fig. 6.49: Project activity plan (1)

<u>Step 9:</u> Analyze function *Determine Inquiry business partner*

In R/3 Customizing, different partner function types can be defined for every business partner, for example sold-to party, bill-to party and ship-to party. When the customer number is entered, the partner functions stored in Customizing are retrieved.

With an iterative jump to Customizing, the partner function types provided in the standard R/3 System can be analyzed, selected and, if necessary, supplemented, for example if the customer is an *interim purchaser* who processes the delivered goods further.

Workshop question:
Which partner function types are provided in the standard R/3 System?

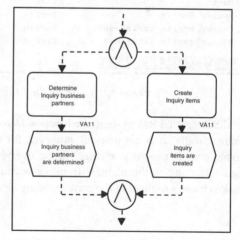

Fig. 6.50: Process " Inquiry processing"
(Excerpt B)

Step 10: Defining partner functions in Customizing

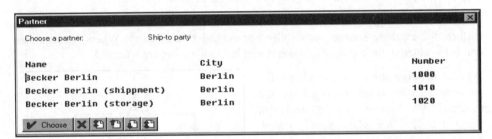

Funct	Description	Not changeable	Mandat.funct
SP	Sold-to party	☑	☑
CP	Contact person	☐	☐
BU	Buyer	☐	☐
KB	Credit rep.	☐	☐
KM	Credit manager	☐	☐
UN	Vendor	☐	☐
MD	partner	☐	☐
PE	sales employee	☐	☐

Fig. 6.51: Customizing business partner functions

In the standard R/3 System, parameters are set for more than 10 different partner functions that occur often in practice. In the process *Inquiry processing*, the sold-to party is declared as the identifier. In addition, in this example, the sold-to party has been defined as a mandatory function.

Step 11: Carry out the processing of the *partner functions* in Prototyping

In enterprises that diversify, there are often several ship-to parties. In this case, a selection screen appears in the application displaying the valid ship-to parties for the sold-to party. In the following case, the goods are to be shipped directly to the sold-to party *Becker* (1000).

Partner ✕

Choose a partner: Ship-to party

Name	City	Number
Becker Berlin	Berlin	1000
Becker Berlin (shippment)	Berlin	1010
Becker Berlin (storage)	Berlin	1020

✔ Choose ✕ 🗄 🗄 🗄 🗄

Fig. 6.52: Selecting the "ship-to party" in Prototyping

In the integrated R/3 System, the function *Determine Inquiry business partners* is executed automatically. It is not unusual, however, for the names and addresses of individual customer contact people to change. In the overview screen *Create Inquiry*, you can display and select any of the partners from the document header (i.e. for one sold-to party) and make changes to them in the corresponding detail screen.

Partner function		Partner	Name
☐ SP	Sold-to party	1000	Becker
☐ CP	Contact person	1	Martin Hansebergurk
☐ BP	Bill-to party	1000	Becker
☐ PY	Payer	1000	Becker
☑ SH	Ship-to Address	1000	Becker

All partners in the doc. header

Fig. 6.53: Application of the "Business partner used"

Step 12: Analyze function *Create Inquiry items*

From a business standpoint, Excerpt B is complete only when at least one item to be delivered has been specified, in addition to the business partner.

Workshop question:
Can we look at an Inquiry item in Prototyping?

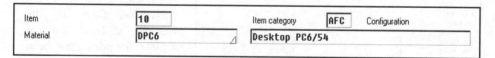

| Item | 10 | Item category | AFC | Configuration |
| Material | DPC6 | Desktop PC6/54 | | |

Fig. 6.54: " Inquiry item" in Prototyping

In the example, the material DPC6 was entered. The material master contains the information for the desired product. This is a configurable material (personal computer) that is identified by the particular item type AFC.

For every configurable material, you can specify different characteristics. You can differentiate according to country-specific conditions (for example, for electrical outlet, voltage, frequency), processor power and keyboard. After the material has been determined and configured through the

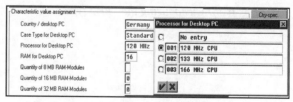

Fig. 6.55: "Configuration structure" in Prototyping

259

control of item type AFC, automatic pricing is carried out using the condition technique. Setting parameters for automatic pricing is done in Customizing. In the application, the salesperson can assign the gross prices PR00 for every material depending on the sales organization.

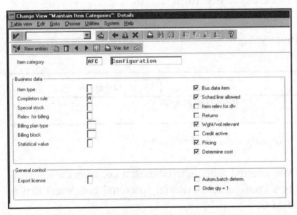

Fig. 6.56: "Configuration result" in Prototyping

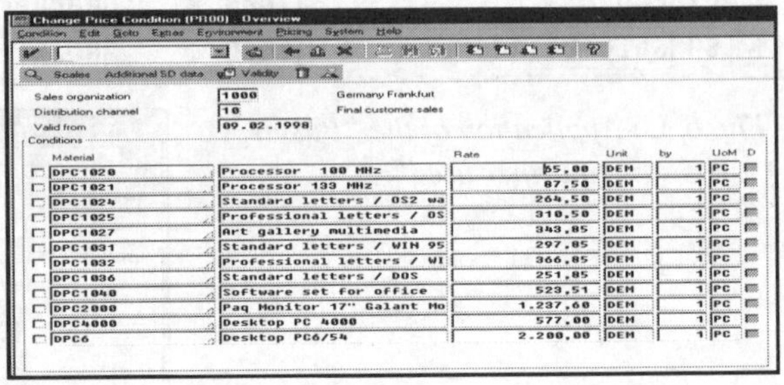

Workshop question:
What parameters can be set for the item type *AFC*?

Fig. 6.57: "Gross price maintenance" in Prototyping

Step 13: *Item types* in Customizing

Fig. 6.58: Customizing the "item type"

For Inquiry processing, you can specify for item type AFC which additional actions should follow in the transaction flow. In the example at hand, the parameter for pricing has been set to active. Because the possible parameter settings for the item type can apply to all sales documents in Sales (for example, quotation, outline agreement, order), additional valid entries are specified.

ItCa	Description	
TAB	Indiv.Purchase Orde	
TAC	VariantConfiguratio	
TAD	Service	
TAE	Explanation	
TAK	Make-to-order Prod.	
TAL	Ret.Packag.Shipment	
TAM	Assembly Item	
TAN	Standard Item	
TANN	Free of Charge Item	
TAO	Milestone billing	
TAP	Extent delivered	

Fig. 6.59: Selecting the "Customizing item types"

In this way, the *billing relevance* may be set in Customizing, although this is relevant for order processing, for the order item type TAN. In Inquiry processing in the standard R/3 System, the two item types AFN and AFC are provided, which serve for differentiation of normal and configurable material during further processing. The end of the discussion about the item type signals completion of Excerpt B of the process model.

Step 14: Inclusion of the process modules *Material master processing* and *Condition processing* in the net value added chain

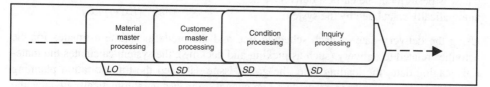

Fig. 6.60: Linking together the net value added chain

Step 15: Recording project activities for the functions *Determine Inquiry business partner* and *Create Inquiry items*

The customer's functional requirements can be represented completely in the standard R/3 System. It remains to be determined which item types with which parameter settings will be needed in the future.

Process: "Inquiry processing"							
Function	Actual/planned	Open questions	Organization	Interface	Respon-sible party	Date	Cost/ Effort
2. Determine Inquiry business partner	Set interim purchaser as new partner function type in Customizing	none		Customer master (internal)	P. Miller	May 30	Standard
3. Create Inquiry items	Use item type AFN in the standard R/3 System, copy old material numbers	Check whether in future configurable material should be offered (item type AFC)		Mat. master (internal) Condition processing (internal)	P.Miller, H. Smith	May 30	Standard

Fig. 6.61: Project activity plan (2)

<u>Step 16:</u> Analyze function *"Determine Inquiry schedule lines"*

It makes sense to use this function in those cases where it is possible to split an Inquiry into at least two partial deliveries.

Workshop question:
What do schedule lines look like in Prototyping?

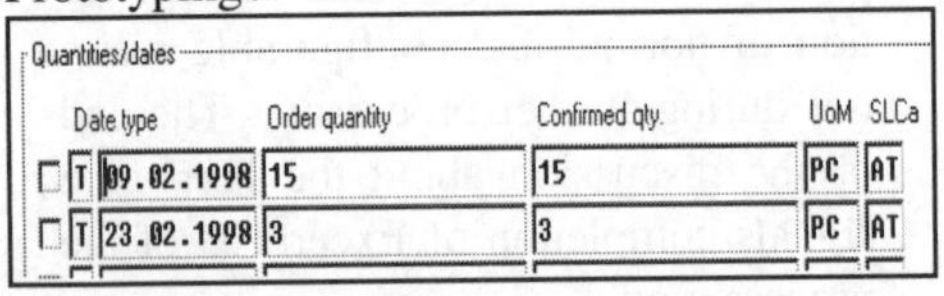

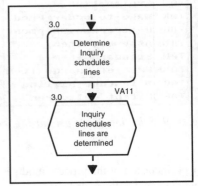

Fig. 6.62: *Process " Inquiry processing" (Excerpt C)*

Quantities/dates				
Date type	Order quantity	Confirmed qty.	UoM	SLCa
☐ T 09.02.1998 15		15	PC	AT
☐ T 23.02.1998 3		3	PC	AT

Fig. 6.63: "Schedule lines" in Prototyping

The first delivery date can be the deadline desired by the customer or, if an availability check is performed, the earliest delivery date automatically calculated by the system.

Using the delivery date of each schedule line and the predefined time estimates for the activities related to delivery (such as picking and packing), the system calculates the materials staging date, the loading date, the goods issue date and the transportation planning date. If the order quantity in a schedule line changes, the system automatically updates the confirmed quantity and executes another availability check and/or delivery scheduling.

<u>Step 17:</u> Recording project activities for the function *Determine Inquiry schedule lines*

Process: "Inquiry processing"							
Function	Actual/planned	Open questions	Organization	Interface	Respon-sible party	Date	Cost/ Effort
4. Determine Inquiry schedule lines	Standard	Clarification of information transfer into customer requirements planning			P. Miller	May 30	Depends on batch input

Fig. 6.64: Project activity plan (3)

<u>Step 18:</u>   Analyze function *Check processing type*

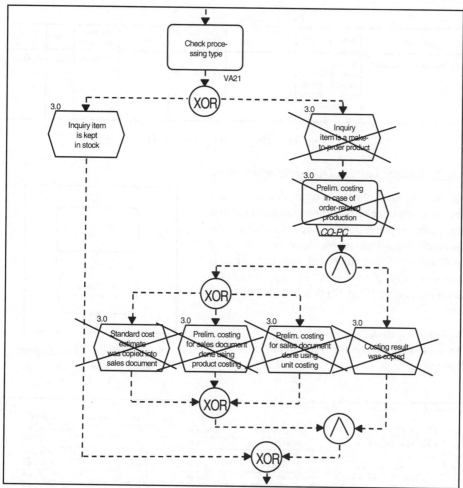

Fig. 6.65: Process " Inquiry processing" (Excerpt D)

In the function *Check processing type*, a determination is made whether the product is a standard one with all available costing data, which is usually kept in stock, and whether delivery to the customer is made from there, or whether it is a make-to-order product for which the appropriate costing data must be created before production. If it is a make-to-order product, the net value calculation described in Step 12 is, of course, unnecessary. In the case study example, the customer produces exclusively material kept in stock for a customer-anonymous market, i.e. the customer can choose only from the products offered on the market. For this reason, the entire right-hand branch that follows the function *Check processing type* in the process model is deleted.

<u>Step 19:</u> Record project activities for the function *Check processing type*

Process: "Inquiry processing"							
Function	Actual/planned	Open questions	Organization	Interface	Respon-sible party	Date	Cost/Effort
5. Check processing type	Manual de-cision function, material kept in stock is relevant				H. Smith	May 30	Standard

Fig. 6.66: Project activity plan (4)

<u>Step 20:</u> Analyze function *Determine order prices*

The R/3 System allows you to design pricing flexibly using a technique known as the condition technique, i.e. you can set different surcharges and discounts depending on the customer or on a combination of customer and material. This is necessary only if you want to supplement the automatic pricing (Step 12) that has already taken place.

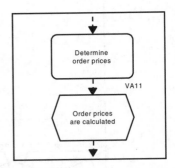

Workshop question:
Can we look at the condition technique in Prototyping?

Fig. 6.67: Process " Inquiry processing" (Excerpt E)

Conditions							DEM
CnTy	Name	Rate	Curr.	by	UoM	Cond.value	
☐ PR00	Price	2.200,00	DEM	1	PC		39.600,00
☐ ZA00	120 MHz CPU	448,00	DEM	1	PC		8.064,00
☐ ZA00	640 MB E-IDE hard di	256,00	DEM	1	PC		4.608,00
☐	Gross Value	2.904,00	DEM	1	PC		52.272,00
☐	Discount Amount	0,00	DEM	1	PC		0,00
☐	Rebate Basis	2.904,00	DEM	1	PC		52.272,00

Fig. 6.68: "Pricing" in Prototyping

When the desired product is specified, the price is automatically calculated in the R/3 System using the condition technique. In the example at hand, the condition type K007 was invoked afterwards, which ensures the customer a one-percent discount on the gross price.

Workshop question:
How are the condition types determined in Customizing?

Step 21: Analyze condition types in Customizing

In the standard R/3 System, the current price types (gross price, net price), taxes, surcharges and discounts are defined as condition classes. Taxes, for example, can be differentiated using various condition types, to take country-specific tax rates into account (local taxes in the US). Likewise, different surcharges and discounts can be defined that depend on the material ordered, the customer, or a combination of the two. The selected condition type K007 differentiates the surcharges and discounts according to agreements with the customer. In the detail screen of a condition type, you can use the calculation type to determine whether each respective surcharge or discount should be a fixed value or should be calculated as a percentage. You can also specify here that the condition applies to selected items only.

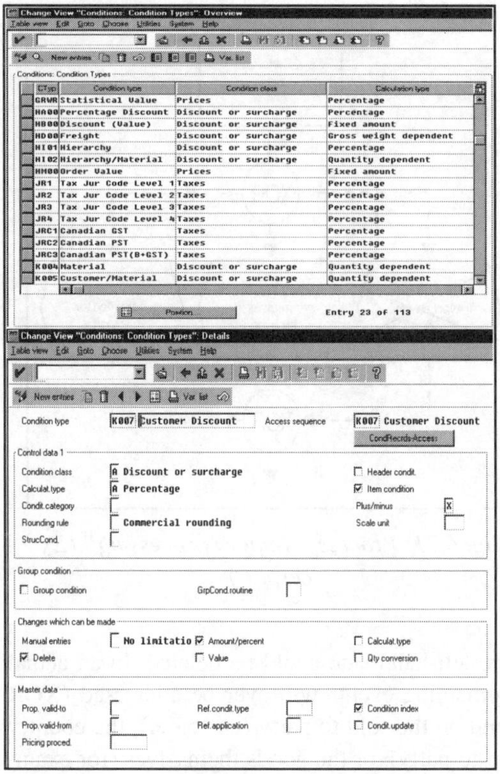

Fig. 6.69: "Condition types" in Customizing

Step 22: Record project activities for the function *Determine order prices*

Process: "Inquiry processing"							
Function	Actual/planned	Open questions	Organization	Interface	Respon-sible party	Date	Cost/Effort
6. Determine order prices	Sales price and condition types	Clarify handling of licensing fees and transfer risk	Sales organization	Condition processing	H. Smith	May 30	Standard

Fig. 6.70: Project activity plan (5)

Step 23: Analyze function *Perform export check*

This function is used in the R/3 System when the country of the ship-to party is different from that of the delivering plant. In this case, a determination is made whether the goods can be exported without a permit, whether they can be exported only with specific approval, or whether their exportation is forbidden as a rule. In the example at hand, the customer is exporting goods to different countries, some of which have different regulations. Since the goods are not military equipment, and the deliveries are not being made to embargo countries, an export licence is usually available, taking into consideration the legal conditions.

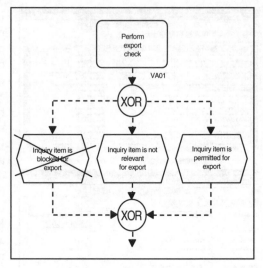

Fig. 6.71: Process " Inquiry processing" (Excerpt F)

In the workshop, therefore, the event on the left-hand side could be deleted. In an actual instance, of course, only one of the two remaining events will ever be addressed (XOR jump). The type of export licence can depend on the sold-to party (customer), the country to which the goods are being exported (ship-to party), or the goods themselves (for example, dangerous goods).

Workshop question:
Can we look at the possible parameter settings for *licence types*?

Step 24: Analyzing *export licence types* in Customizing

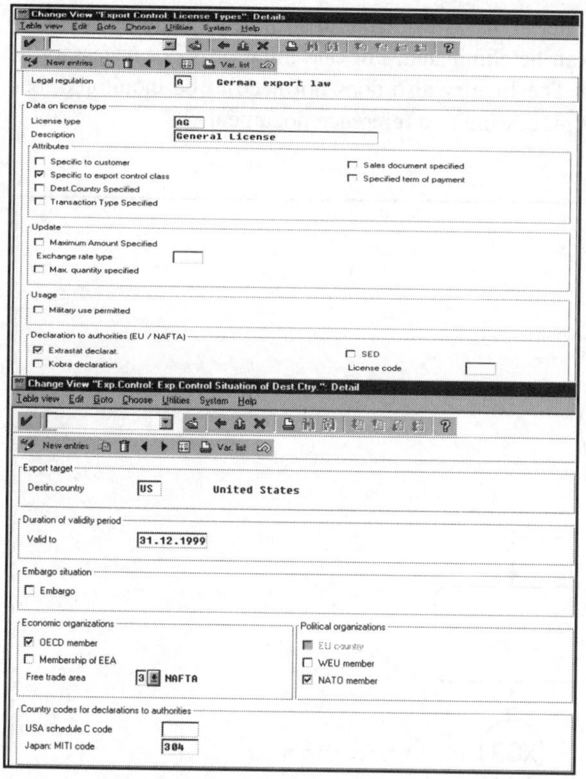

When defining licence types, you record the legal basis for the export regulations. In Germany, the standard is the Außenwirtschaftsgesetz (AWG) and the Außenwirtschaftsverordnung (AWV), while in the US, the standard is the Export Administration Act (EAA) and the Export Administration Regulations (EAR). For the AWV, you record in the parameter field *licence type* whether it is a general licence, an individual export licence, or a collective export licence. You also define the export-relevant information about the countries to which the goods are being delivered. In the example, the destination country is the US.

Fig. 6.72: Customizing the "licence types"

Step 25: Record project activities for the function *Perform export check*

Process: "Inquiry processing"							
Function	Actual/planned	Open questions	Organization	Interface	Responsible party	Date	Cost/Effort
7. Perform export check	Planned: definition of all license types for purposes of automating export check	Clarify export checks with legislative body		Material master, customer master	P. Jones (Export)	May 30	Standard

Fig. 6.73: Project activity plan (6)

<u>Step 26:</u> Analyze function *Edit/copy order text*

Since the customer offers a stock material that is available in sufficient quantities, individual activities in the process block can be eliminated. For one thing, it is not necessary to reject Inquiries or individual items. The Inquiry also does not need to be monitored, because it is copied directly into order processing as a reference document.

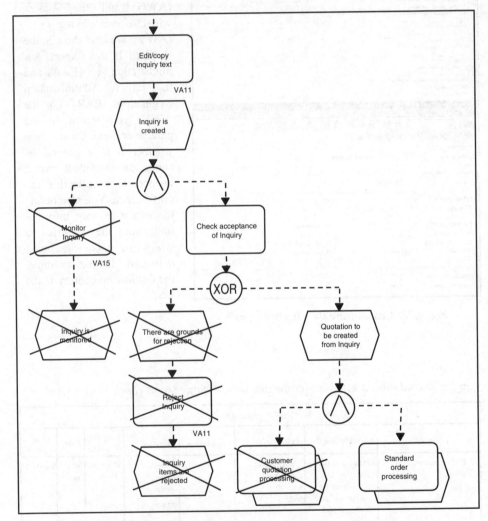

Fig. 6.74: Process " Inquiry processing" (Excerpt G)

Before an Inquiry is saved, it is possible to enter special comments at the header or item level. Each piece of text can be created as a text module in several languages with the help of SAP word processing. In subsequent processes, these texts can then be retrieved automatically from storage in the appropriate master records.

Workshop question:
What types of text are there in the application?

Step 27: Look at *text types* in the application

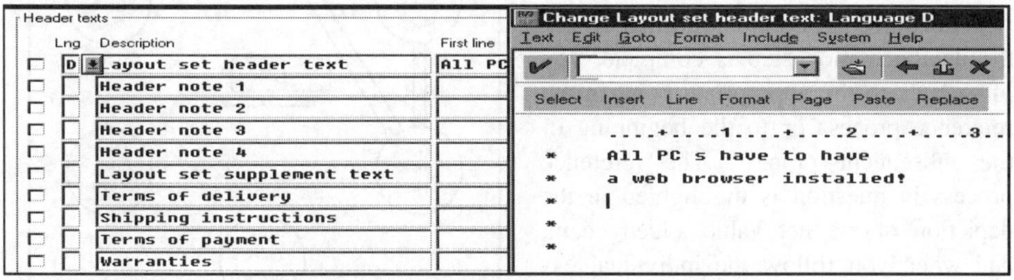

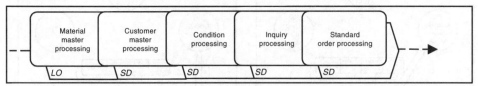

Fig. 6.75: Prototyping of the "text types"

For cases that occur often in practice, for example header notes, terms of delivery, or shipping instructions, corresponding text types are provided in the standard R/3 System.

Step 28: Inclusion of the process module *Standard order processing*

```
┌──────────┐ ┌──────────┐ ┌──────────┐ ┌──────────┐ ┌──────────────┐
│ Material │ │ Customer │ │Condition │ │ Inquiry  │ │  Standard    │
│ master   │ │ master   │ │processing│ │processing│ │order          │
│processing│ │processing│ │          │ │          │ │processing     │
└──────────┘ └──────────┘ └──────────┘ └──────────┘ └──────────────┘
    LO           SD           SD           SD            SD
```

Fig. 6.76: Linking together the net value added chain

Step 29: Recording project activities for the function *Edit/copy order text*

Process: "Inquiry processing"							
Function	Actual/planned	Open questions	Organization	Interface	Respon-sible party	Date	Cost/Effort
8. Edit/copy order text	Optional function	Determine text types and stan-dard texts		Standard order processing	H. Smith	May 30	Standard

Fig. 6.77: Project activity plan (7)

As a summary, the steps of the individual excerpts A through G of the IPP example demonstrated, *Inquiry processing*, are shown here. Each excerpt starts with the selected R/3 reference process and ends with documentation in table format. When the documentation step is complete, you jump back to the appropriate point in the reference process or to the beginning of the subsequent process. The reference process in question is highlighted in the depiction of the net value added chain, and when you follow the individual excerpts, you can see how the consistent, customer-oriented net value added chain grows.

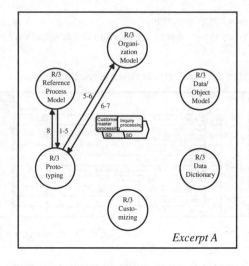

Excerpt A

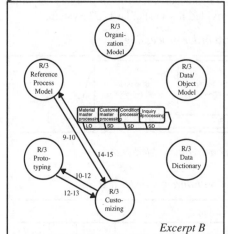

Excerpt B

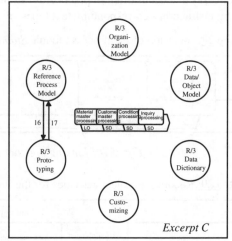

Excerpt C

Fig. 6.78a: Iterative jumps in the example " Inquiry processing" (I)

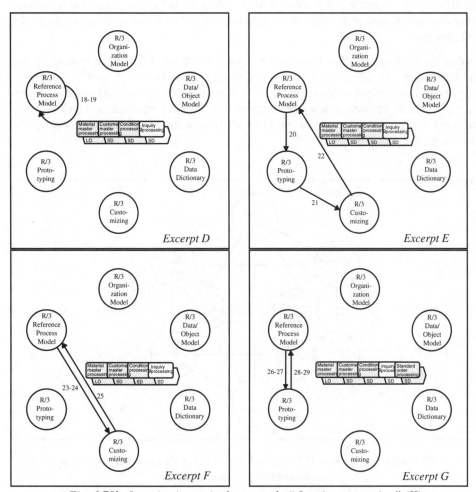

Fig. 6.78b: Iterative jumps in the example " Inquiry processing" (II)

6.3.4   The customer's net value added chain

The customer's objective, *Analysis of order processing types using standard software*, resulted in the following empirical results in the workshop. This discussion was based primarily on the R/3 reference processes, the R/3 System and R/3 Customizing. The R/3 Organization Model did not play a very important role in this case, because the organizational conditions had been predetermined to the greatest extent possible by the customer, and their general compatibility had been checked. The R/3 Object/Data Model and the R/3 Data Dictionary were not needed because the implementation analysis took place exclusively within the framework of the solution spectrum of the R/3 System's application software. In the workshop described here, the most frequent jump occurred from the R/3 reference process to the R/3 System, where the Customizing and master data settings of

271

the R/3 model company IDES were used. In addition, individual Customizing settings were undertaken, and some transaction data was created to facilitate visualization of the R/3 solution.

During the implementation of standard software, use of the R/3 Reference Process Model, the R/3 System (in this case, IDES), and Customizing under similar general conditions may result in deviations of plus or minus 5%. The importance of the Organization Model increases when corporate groups or enterprises with complex organizational structures are analyzed, while the importance of the Data Model and the Data Dictionary increases if custom software must be developed.

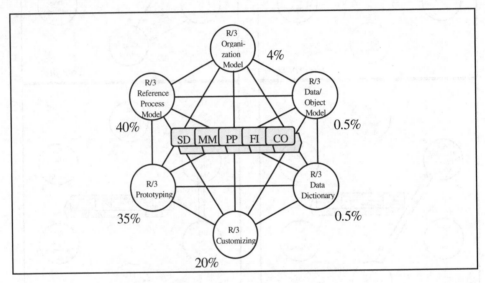

Fig. 6.79: Proportional use of IPP tools when designing the customer's net value added chain based on standard software

When performing an implementation analysis, one must take into consideration that the customer needs to be shown an incremental plan of action when replacing legacy software, and that, in practice, not all requirements can be covered with homogeneous application software. For this reason, it is important also to integrate non-SAP systems into the representation of the customer's net value added chain. It also becomes clear that certain process modules are interdependent and operate in sequence, while other process modules can operate in parallel. It is also possible for certain process modules to run detached from the main value-added business, for example returns processing.

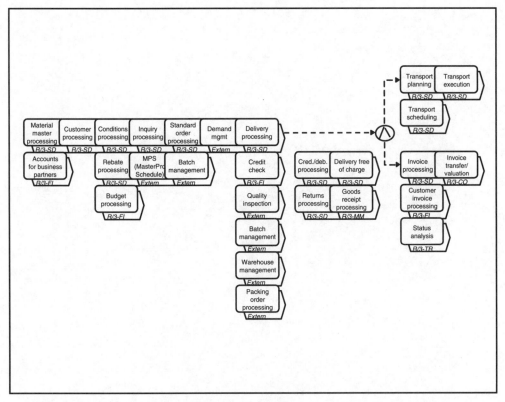

Fig. 6.80: The customer's net value added chain as a result of the IPP workshop

Section D
Net Value Added Chains

„Do it once, do it right."

7   Structure of the Model Companies

Iterative Process Prototyping (IPP) can be used in analysis to balance the customer requirements with the capabilities of a variant-rich and open standard software system, and it can also be used to help explain business solutions and their implementation in a software system.

7.1   IPP for model structure

If you use IPP to explain business content that has been implemented in a software system, the focus in process design is on the Reference Process Model and Prototyping. Therefore, in the following explanations, only the R/3 Reference Process Model and R/3 Prototyping are used and, in the appropriate explanatory sections, the links are shown.

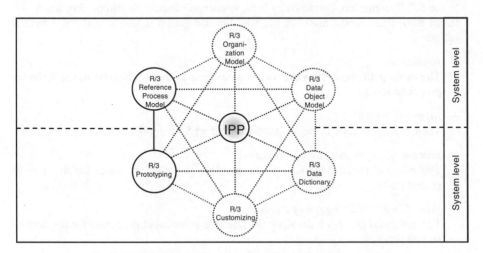

Fig. 7.1: IPP path in the representation of model companies

In the previous chapter, a small excerpt was extracted from a project as a demonstration, and based on an example, the use of the IPP method was shown. In the sections that follow, two net value added chains, each from different model companies, are presented that go beyond the operational process areas. Therefore, at the beginning of Chapter 8 and Chapter 9, overviews of the net value added chains are shown, and then every R/3 Reference Process Model used and configured for the model companies is described. The explanatory text describing the individual process modules is divided into the following sections:

■ *General business description*
The general description characterizes the process from the point of view of business management science, highlights the importance of the process in practice, and refers to the corresponding conceptual reference literature.

■ *General, SAP-oriented description*
The SAP-specific description reveals the solution spectrum of SAP's R/3 software and describes the myriad solutions of the process module stored in the R/3 System. The R/3 reference processes and the application descriptions for the R/3 System serve as the basis for this.

■ *Specific, process-oriented description*
Generally, an R/3 reference process contains several solution paths. Within this variety, the user can choose to follow one or more paths. Based on a case tested in the real world, a goal-oriented solution path is demonstrated (redlining) and verbally described.

■ *Navigation information*
In the R/3 System, too, connectivity is an important element for supporting users' different navigation needs. Some of the possible navigation methods in the R/3 System include:

– *menu path*
The menu path shows how the user can navigate in the R/3 System to reach the appropriate screen.

– *transaction code*
The transaction code is the program name of an SAP application.

– *process signs pointing into a process*
The inbound process links show the possible previous processes for the demonstrated process.

– *process signs pointing out of a process*
The outbound process links show the possible subsequent processes for the demonstrated process.

■ *Graphic representation of the R/3 reference process*
The business process flow of the individual R/3 reference process modules is represented as event-controlled process chains (EPC).

■ *Graphical representation of the R/3 application software*
In this case, the implementation is shown as user-oriented screens.

■ *Demonstration of the links*
The logical link is shown from a point in the configured R/3 reference process to the corresponding point in the data input screen of the R/3 application system. The path shown in the R/3 reference process has been tested with data in the R/3 System, and all demonstrated paths are thus viable in this form in the R/3 System (operationally executable process).

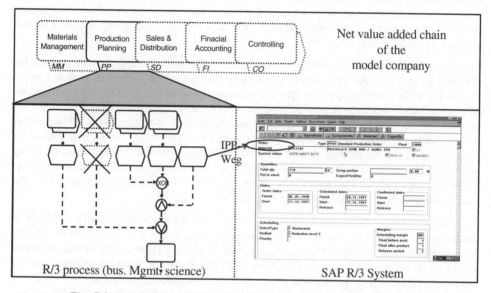

Fig. 7.2: Integration of business and information system technology

Before Chapters 8 and 9 demonstrate a general overview of the net value added chains and the detailed contents of the processes are shown, a general characterization of the two model companies and a demonstration of the business relationship between them, based on the *motherboard* product, are in order.

7.2 Model company: lot-size manufacturer with direct sales

The model company *Lot-size Manufacturer with Direct Sales* (Model Company A) offers standardized products that are included as build-in parts in other manufacturers' products. The individual customer has no direct influence over the standardized product or its functions, shape or size. The product offered is definitely influenced by the state of technology. Sales figures and product design are determined by management in cooperation with technically savvy staff members from the planning and production areas, as well as business-oriented staff members from the marketing and controlling areas and, in the accounting area, are retained on the market on the basis of demand. Model Company A thus defines its product spectrum independent of individuals outside the enterprise, and product engineering is customer-anonymous. The product engineering phase ends with the release of the build-in part as a salable product. So, before production of the salable build-in part begins, all of the supporting documents needed for production and assembly are on hand.

The decoupling, time-wise, of the product engineering phase in research and development and the sales order processing phase in the daily business of operations also has considerable influence on the design of production and assembly. A large amount of the same kind of products are produced, and the demand programme remains the same over an extended period of time. Changes in the process flow are primarily the result of substantial demand shifts in the individual market segments or the result of technically required model changes or model redesigns.

In one segment, the product palette offered includes the manufacture of motherboards for personal computers. Due to the multitude of different parts that go into it, such as central processing units (CPUs), resistors, diodes, transistors and chips, the product is characterized principally by a high degree of product complexity. Modularization of the complex product, which is technically possible, can simplify the bill-of-materials (BOM) structure, which also has an effect on the production flow and on purchasing. Production entails the preparation of the motherboard with its corresponding electrical circuits and soldering points and the mounting of the processor (CPU), the coprocessor, the working memory, the bus system, the cache memory, and other processors, transistors, diodes and resistors. The motherboards are manufactured in large lots.

To take advantage of the specialization benefits of machines, the in-house mechanical production is shaped by the workshop principle, and, in the area of assembly, highly automated, flexible production systems are used that have been designed and arranged according to the product and product flow principle (production-based process flow of product manufacturing). Production planning is done according to the American MRP II concept and includes the processes from sales and operations planning, demand planning, down to material requirements planning. Because material requirements planning is very costly due to the multitude of incorporated parts, the enterprise carries out master production scheduling for rough planning of production capacities and their loads. In this case, the scheduling consists of a two-phase planning procedure on the basis of the CPU and the working memory (RAM).

Orders for materials to be procured externally are activated on the basis of the results from production planning. In addition to the transistors, resistors and diodes, the various chips are procured from manufacturers who specialize in them. The procurement of valuable electronic parts, whose quality must be absolutely guaranteed, requires corresponding checks during goods receipt. For this reason, a quality inspection takes place for critical parts at goods receipt. One distinction is that invoices from vendors are sometimes received before the goods are received. These invoices remain blocked for payment until goods receipt and the subsequent quality inspection, which must have a positive result.

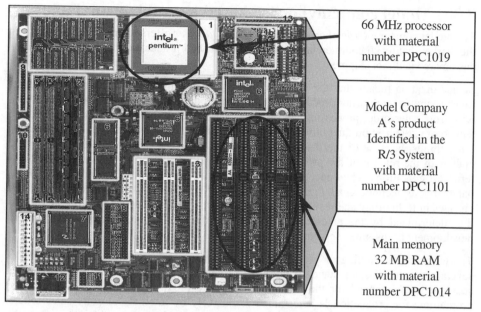

66 MHz processor with material number DPC1019

Model Company A´s product Identified in the R/3 System with material number DPC1101

Main memory 32 MB RAM with material number DPC1014

Fig. 7.3: Motherboard (source: Schüller/Veddeler 1996, p. 20)

The products completed in production, the various motherboards, are stored in the delivery warehouse, from where they are shipped to the customer. Delivering the product exclusively from the warehouse also causes a temporal decoupling of the sales activities from the procurement and production activities. An order is completed in its entirety in sales and distribution, without engineering documents or production-related documents having to be created when a sales order is received. The planning factor concentrates primarily on the picking and shipping of the product, with emphasis being placed on on-time delivery of the goods via the most efficient transportation method. Another unique aspect of doing business with the customer lies in the fact that Model Company A has signed contracts with its different customers, the manufacturers of personal computers. The planned volumes of sales of the individual motherboards are spelled out in the contract for each period of one year. The release order date and quantity, however, depend on the incoming PC orders by the customers of Model Company B. When the orders for motherboards are released, invoice processing and subsequent automatic payment take place in the R/3 System, in addition to delivery processing.

Accompanying the planning and production steps are preliminary costing and final costing. These require building a corresponding enterprise structure, including determining the cost elements and activity types, as well as the cost centres. When the production activities are complete, a cost centre and profit centre report is generated, and a profit analysis is performed, which is used as the basis for sales planning for the following year.

7.3   Model company: order-based assembly manufacturer

The model company *Order-based Assembly Manufacturer* offers standardized products on the market that reach commercial enterprises as finished products or are sent to individual customers via direct shipment.

Standardization means that the individual customer has no direct influence on the functions, shape or size during product development. Product development is decoupled time-wise from sales order processing, and its goal is to develop, based on the current state of technology, the best product possible from the technical, economic and ecological (among other things, because of the disposal costs) standpoint. The product development phase ends with the release of the prototypes, which have been tested sufficiently under long-term test conditions. The concept and design of a new product are determined predominantly by its technological feasibility. Generally, the catalyst for product changes are changes in technology and results of market research by the enterprise. The product line is thus determined by the enterprise as autonomously as possible, meaning that product development is customer-anonymous.

The temporal decoupling of product development from sales order processing provides several opportunities for standardization in production and assembly. So, for example, standard parts intended for the finished product are produced for storage. The demand programme for production is determined exclusively by internal company sales orders. The goal is to keep the production cycle constant for as long as possible. Therefore, the production documents are available in their entirety before production.

The customer's influence on sales order processing comes to bear in assembly of the finished product. So, for example, a customer-based assembler manufactures personal computers in different variants. Due to the combinable parts, such as housing, motherboard, main memory, graphics card, hard drive, floppy drive, CD-ROM drive, sound card, mouse, keyboard, monitor, speakers, fax/modem, various cables, etc., the final product is characterized by a high degree of product complexity.

In order to reduce the complexity, the enterprise has restricted the range of solutions that are technically possible to combinations that make realistic business sense, i.e. that are marketable, thereby reducing the number of product type variants. This allows the customer-based assembler to have the complete assembly instructions available before placing an order. In contrast to the situation with the model company *Lot-size Manufacturer with Direct Sales*, the customer can choose between numerous variants and thus has the feeling that a custom product is being produced based on his requirements. The customer's choices are not, however, based on the combinations that are technically feasible, but instead lie exclusively within the range of variants offered by the manufacturer.

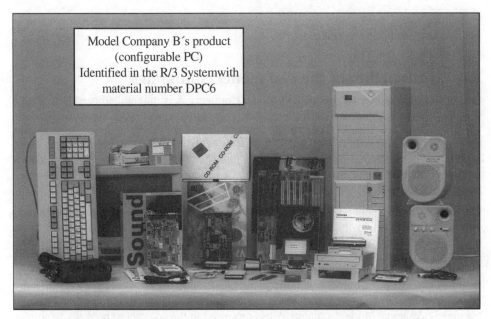

Model Company B's product
(configurable PC)
Identified in the R/3 Systemwith
material number DPC6

Fig. 7.4: Personal computer (source: Schüller/Veddeler 1996, p. 40)

In the case of the order-based assembly manufacturer, sales order processing is started by a customer's specific inquiry. For this, Model Company B has sent a catalogue to the potential customer showing the possible configurations, and the customer asks for a specific PC configuration according to the catalogue. Sometimes, an individual customer makes a direct inquiry without referencing the catalogue. In RFQ processing, a check is done to see if the desired configuration (for example, main memory with 32 MB of RAM or 40 MB of RAM; German, English or French keyboard; desktop or tower case; 17" or 20" monitor) can be produced. Afterwards, a price quote is generated based on the configured materials, with the corresponding surcharges or discounts, and an estimated delivery date is noted.

If the customer gives an order directly on the basis of the possible configurations listed in the catalogue, a sales application is generated, together with an exact delivery date, in sales order processing. The corresponding information for this is retrieved from the material master record, the BOM and the routing. Even if the customer does not influence the main assembly process, he nevertheless influences the planning dates for the individual components of the variants with his configuration wishes. For this reason, an availability check is performed for the individual materials in the BOM, in which the components' replenishment lead times are also stored. This is followed by the direct transformation of the sales order into a production order for assembly, as well as the creation of the necessary purchase requisitions.

Based on the contract established with Company A, the required motherboards are released. The motherboards are supplied directly to production, where assembly and quality inspection take place. Before delivery, the overall functionality of the personal computer is tested (process *Inspection lot to goods issue*), released for picking, and finally shipped to the customer. Side by side with the production and sales and delivery steps, cost object controlling and a profitability analysis are performed, to serve as the basis for the next planned sales and pricing policies.

7.4   Interaction of the two model companies

One of the main consumer products of Model Company A is the motherboard DPC 1101. It is described in the material master record and has a multi-level BOM structure. Individual BOM items are manufactured by the company itself, while the main master schedule items DPC1014 (32 MB RAM) and DPC1019 (66 MHz processor) are purchased from suppliers. The purchased parts are integrated into the motherboard DPC1101 in production order 60001007 and are transported from the production area into the delivery warehouse.

One of Model Company B's most important product lines includes personal computers, which are described in the material master record. One product has the identification number DPC6 (desktop PC). A desired configuration is received by telephone or written inquiry, and a quotation is sent to the customer. In the case at hand, a sales order is created afterwards with the number 60001012. The two model companies have an agreement that specifies that Model Company B (sold-to party nr. 1600) is to procure 10000 motherboards from Model Company A in the period between March 14 and December 21 (contractual agreement). Model Company A has promised in the contract to be ready to ship at any time during the specified period. The agreement causes the creation of a contract with the number 40000048 in the sales department of Model Company A and the creation of a quantity contract with the number 460000020 in Model Company B. Taking into consideration minimum safety stocks, the sales order 60001012 created in Model Company B causes a production order (assembly order) to be created directly for the personal computers to be assembled and a purchase requisition to be created for the motherboards to be procured externally. Referencing the purchase requisition and the contractual agreement, a release order is immediately triggered in Model Company B, and, as a result, customer contract release order processing is triggered in Model Company A. The element linking these interactions is the purchase order with the number 10002276. The finished motherboard DPC1101 is delivered to Model Company B via goods receipt processing of stock material and, once there, is directly incorporated in the production process, i.e. is built into the desktop PC (DPC6). Afterwards, the desktop PC is delivered to the customer via Model Company B's goods issue processing. The most important process module stations, along with the documents they generate, are presented in the following figure. They provide an overview of the business relationships between the model companies.

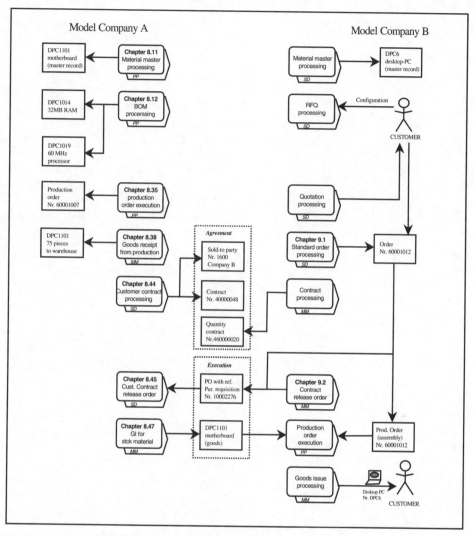

Fig. 7.5: Links between the model companies

8   Value Chain of a Lot Manufacturer with Direct Selling

"Progress in the areas of medicine and surgery is basically dependent on technological advances. New materials with new properties and new components, such as implants, instruments and equipment, are able to stand out successfully from their predecessors if they promise to provide substantial medical or economic benefits" (see Wintermantel/Ha 1996, p. IX). In the same way, progress in the world of business administration relies on technical innovations. The arrival of graphical user interfaces, for example, made it possible to handle more complex tasks. The developments in client/server technology and the success of the Internet and intranet have opened up new opportunities with regard to task distribution.

Bio-compatible materials are a prerequisite of the successful application of new technologies in medical science (see also Wintermantel/Ha 1996, pp. 1–24); the successful implementation of new software technologies in business administration necessitates *business-compatible software*. Just as a *cell* in medicine is the basic element of all forms of life, *maximum processes* can be seen as the essential elements in business administration. If a process fails to function productively in a company as defined by the requirements of the market, that company will in the long term drift into insolvency. Similarly, if a process that is fundamentally effective is supported by incompatible software, this counterproductiveness may also lead to a state of insolvency. If the process that has been developed is inappropriate to the market-induced requirements, even the best software will be in vain unless a solution is found to the basic problem. In the same way as the bio-compatible material helps to preserve living things in the wold of medicine, business-compatible software contributes towards the success of a company.

The starting point when considering bio-compatible materials is the cell with which a particular material is required to be compatible; the equivalent starting point in the area of business-compatible software is the maximum process. The importance of maximum processes as existence-preserving influencing factors is therefore explained below by comparing them with cells (see also Wintermantel/Ha 1996, pp. 25–36).

- *Cells versus maximum processes*
  A cell is a *universal element of all organisms* and the smallest unit capable of independent life. A maximum process is a *universal element of social organisms* and the smallest unit capable of independent life.

- *The structure of cells versus the structure of maximum processes*
  A cell has a *characteristic molecular and supramolecular structure*. Tissue, organs and whole organisms are made up of cellular units (e.g. cell membrane, cytoplasm, nucleus). A maximum process has a *characteristic singular and component-oriented structure*. Tasks, areas and whole companies are made up of process units (e.g. activities, events, information, organizational responsibilities).

■ *Cell functions versus maximum process functions*

A cell is an *open system, which constantly exchanges energy and other substances with its environment.* A cell maintains a dynamic equilibrium, safeguards the integrity of its environment and is capable of adapting to environmental changes. Its metabolism enables it to generate energy and growth. The cell exhibits internal and external movements in response to chemical and physical stimuli from its environment. A maximum process is an *open system, which constantly exchanges information and materials with its environment.* A maximum process maintains a dynamic equilibrium by responding to different types of received information with different kinds of adaptation (processing steps). The inherent variance of a maximum process thus enables it to adapt to different corporate situations. By generating consistent results, it ensures integrity in relation to the business environment.

■ *Cell multiplication versus maximum process multiplication*

Cell multiplication entails firstly an increase in the number and mass of the cells and secondly the transfer of information concerning their structure, function and auto-production. A cell's descendants are generally able to perform in the same way as the original cell. The genetic information of the majority of living things is carried by *deoxyribonucleic acid* (DNA). So-called RNA viruses are an exception. The germ plasm is usually present as a double strand. DNA is predominantly located in the chromosomes of the nucleus. It consists of three basic elements, namely deoxyribose (a saccharide), four organic bases (adenine, cyclosine, guanine and thymine) and phosphoric acid. These substances form a long-chain molecule with a structure resembling that of a rope ladder. The *rungs* are always formed by two of the organic bases, whereby the pairs are *not* produced arbitrarily. Adenine is always opposite thymine, while guanine is always opposite cyclosine. The sides can however be swapped around. The double strand rotates once about its own axis (360°) over the length of ten base pairs. The cells are able to read the *DNA recipe* from the order of the base pairs. The DNA forms the molecular building material for the genes – the germ plasm – in the chromosomes. The complete set of genes is transferred to all the cells in the body as a result of cell division. Since certain body cells may have different shapes and functions, however (e.g. muscle cells and nerve cells), the activity of certain genes must be blocked and that of other genes unblocked in order to form the various cell types.

Maximum processes and processes are created by human beings. They are based on the experience and know-how acquired as a result of business practice, training and the attitudes towards leadership that are innate in any person, i.e. a centralist or decentralist management style. Maximum processes are generally combined to form longer process sequences, and must be coordinated according to the prevailing division of labour while at the same time reducing transaction costs to a minimum. The inherited process design know-how refers firstly to the operational variance that is inherent in a maximum process, and that must be set or configured separately for each specific customer, and secondly to the time and logic arrangement of the configured maximum processes required to perform the overall corporate task. The maximum inheritance scope is derived from the variance of the maximum processes and the possible combinations of the maximum process link. The true inheritance is formed by the configured maximum process and the arrangement of selected maximum processes in a value chain on the basis of the corporate objectives.

The business administration requirements in the form of a maximum process and the corresponding software functionality in the form of a transaction, a function module or a group of transactions could be viewed as one base pair. The inheritance options incorporated in the software are thus mirrored in the parameterization options for the transaction and the possible transaction links. The true inheritance in the software consists of the transaction, which can be parameterized for the customer, and the software link for supporting business processes. Whereas the inheritance options of a maximum process mainly take account of the customer's knowledge of business practices, i.e. the branch of industry, market knowledge, production methods, etc., the options of a transaction are determined to a large extent by the range of services offered by the software vendor and the empirical experience of his employees. The software developers at SAP AG therefore incorporate the know-how of experienced and successful customers at an early stage, in order to ensure maximum adaptability.

As far as the true inheritance of data processing-based processes is concerned, on the one hand the congruence between the maximum processes and the transaction, etc. must be guaranteed, while on the other hand certain process paths and functions must be activated and others deactivated according to the operating constellation. If uncontrolled processes take place, i.e. mutations in medicine – usually accompanied by infections – the operational (inherited) process is no longer adequate to fulfil the set task. In the same way as only specific parts of the DNA are used for inheritance, only some (logical) maximum processes are relevant to a specific corporate situation. This is demonstrated below, taking two model companies as an example. Fig. 8.1, provides an overview of the links between the maximum processes. The name of the maximum process is shown in the centre of each box and the corresponding application or module in the R/3 System at the bottom. The value chain extends from Controlling through Production Planning and Control, Materials Management, Financial Accounting and Quality Management to Sales and Distribution and the subsequent final account in Controlling, i.e. the entire corporate cycle. The concrete links are described in the individual sections about each maximum process.

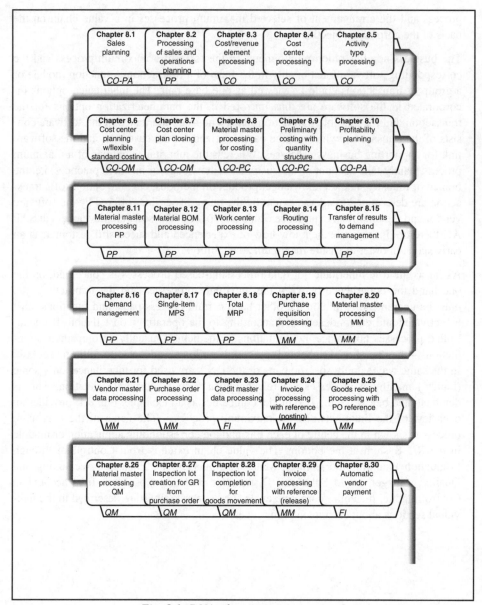

Fig. 8.1: DNA of a corporation – part 1

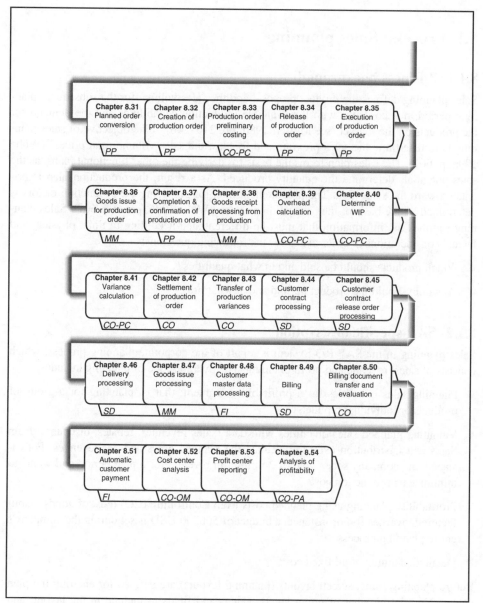

Fig. 8.1: DNA of a corporation – part 2

8.1 Process: Sales planning

8.1.1 Business background

Sales planning defines the product proposal and the sales volume for the subsequent planning period in accordance with the available production capabilities and the demand for the products on the market (see Meffert 1986, pp. 216–240). "The objective of sales planning is to determine the sales program and forecast the sales volumes and prices" (Wöhe 1996, p. 601). The sales plan forms the basis for deriving the other functional plans, as the sales potentials determine the quantity produced. As a result, the production plan is oriented toward the sales plan. The procurement plan for providing the production factors is determined on the basis of the production plan (see Wöhe 1996, pp. 595–607). Sales planning supplies the information that must be differentiated according to time, physical and factual considerations in order to answer the following questions:

- Which products should be sold and in what quantities?

- To whom should the product be sold and at what price?

8.1.2 SAP-specific description

Sales planning in the SAP R/3 System is a part of the corporate planning process, which consists of sales, revenue and profit planning. The overall scope of planning includes:

- Planning sales quantities for a profitability segment; that is, planning for a group of products or individual products

- Valuating planned sales quantities with data (sales revenues, rebates, discounts) from Sales and Distribution (SD) to calculate the planned gross and net revenues. For instance, the company sets a goal of 2 million in revenue for a plan period and wants to minimize its production costs

- Profitability planning using planned costs from Controlling (CO) (cost of goods manufactured, overhead). For instance, a budget of 500000 USD is set during the company's entire planning process

- Detailed planning of all fixed costs

Before planning starts, screen layouts (planning layouts) are defined for entering the plan values. You define what planning levels, values and fields to include in the layout, and specify how the screen is set up and where the different input fields are displayed. One row and one column are assigned to each input field based on its position on the entry screen. The contents of the input fields are determined by the entries you make in the rows and columns of the planning layout.

8.1.3 Using the process

The following components of planning are important for sales planning in Model Company A. You can plan data manually and automatically at any level and for as many levels as you require. A permanent planning level is not required. The system ensures that the data set always remains consistent, which means you can set up your own planning scenarios as you wish regardless of whether planning takes place at the lowest or highest level. Since planning is not linked to any particular time period, you can plan several fiscal years together and on a continuous basis.

Model Company A has so far created only one plan version. Plan versions let you store several sets of data for the same profitability segment. Using forecast models you can forecast plan values on the basis of existing reference data. Top-down distribution lets you distribute data from a higher planning level, for example the product group level, to the levels below it, the individual products. Plan data is distributed in the same manner as the selected reference data.

You can determine the structure of the characteristics and characteristic values you are planning for each plan version. During planning the system performs different checks against this structure.

You can transfer the planned sales volume to Sales and Operations Planning (SOP) per individual product or per product group. You can select any profitability segments (for example, all products in a division) and periods (posting periods and weeks) for transfer.

8.1.4 Navigation information

▪ *Menu path*
Accounting –> Controlling –> Profit. analysis –> Planning –> Change plan data

▪ *Transaction code*
KE11, KE1G, KEPP, KE1E

▪ *Ingoing processes in the R/3 Reference Model*
Sales planning
Preparation of sales and profitability planning

▪ *Outgoing processes in the R/3 Reference Model*
Sales planning
Profitability planning
Processing of sales and operations planning

Planning Types (Planning Layout)

Planning types are planning tables that can be created with the table painter. Planning types allow you to set up an individual, differentiated layout of your plan data. All planning layouts are based on a certain information structure. You can choose between a standard structure or an individually defined information structure. The range of structures available for planning data is almost infinite. Planning types, therefore, are the ideal tool for planning, saving and analyzing data. A planning type defines the layout of lines and the corresponding calculation rules in a planning table. The number of possible planning types is unlimited. Moreover, a planning type also defines a planning period. Enter the number of past and future periods you want to be shown in the planning table.

Value Columns

Value columns are defined using value fields, characteristics, attributes or formulas. You determine the profitability segments to be planned and the time frame to be used by choosing characteristics.

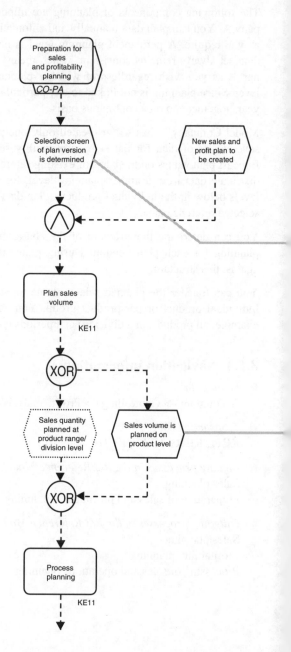

© SAP AG

292

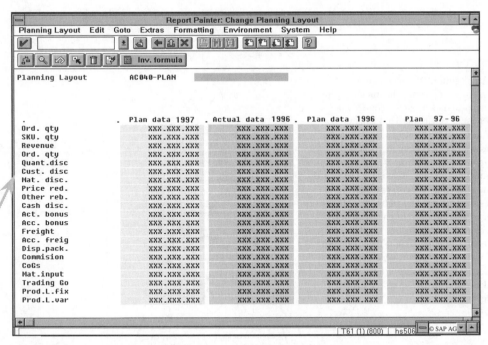

Fig. 8.2: Selection screen of sales planning

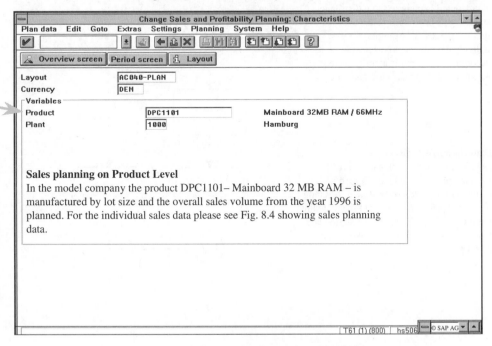

Fig. 8.3: Sales planning for the product DPC1101

Aggregation/Disaggregation

In complex planning hierarchies, you can plan data by either Top-Down Planning or Bottom-Up Planning functions. The system supports central as well as local planning with the aggregation and disaggregation functions. Aggregation is the procedure in which plan data is generated at an aggregated level by adding or copying the values of the reference data or by creating average values at a detail level. Disaggregation is the procedure in which plan data is generated on a detail level by distributing the values of the reference data at an aggregated level.

Top-Down Planning

Top-Down Planning lets you distribute summary planned objects (such as product ranges, for example) for individual products or customers according to automatic algorithms (e.g. actual quantity, actual sales quantities).

Plan Data in MS-Excel

In order to download plan data directly from the planning table to *Microsoft Excel,* choose *Go to* → Microsoft Excel. A dialog box then opens. Enter the path that contains the file *excel.exe*. Excel is then started and your plan data displayed. Save the data as an *excel* file.

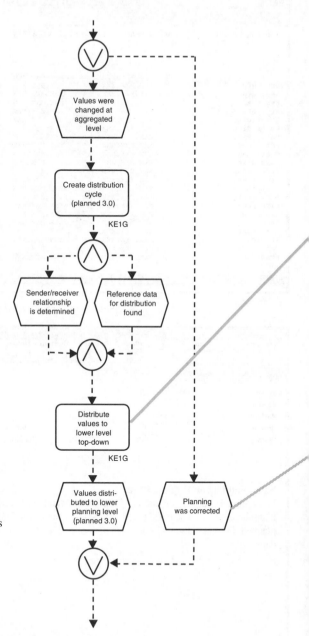

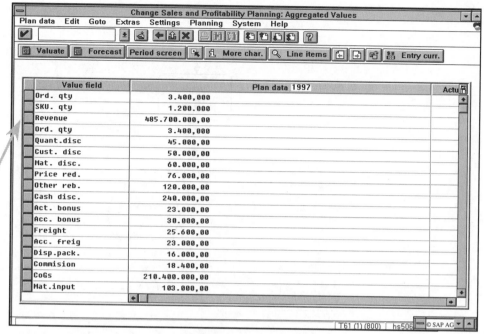

Fig. 8.4: Sales planning data

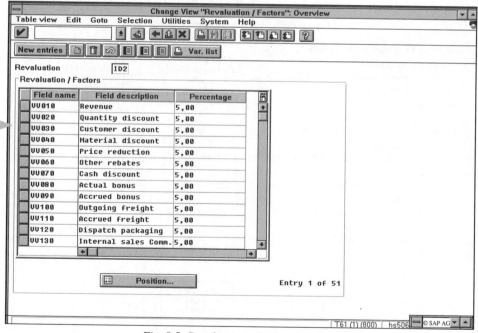

Fig. 8.5: Revaluation of sales planning data

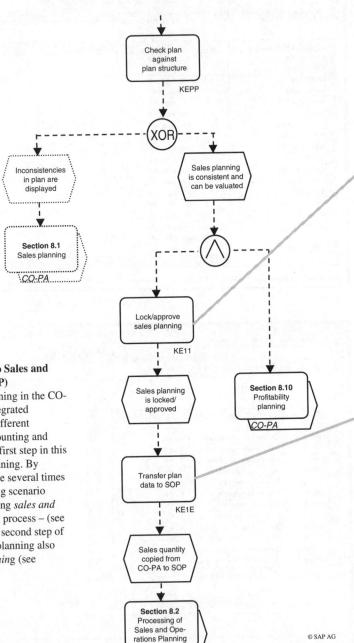

Transferring Plan Data to Sales and Operations Planning (SOP)

Sales and profitability planning in the CO-PA system is part of an integrated planning cycle that takes different operational budgets of accounting and logistics into account. The first step in this planning cycle is sales planning. By repeating the planning cycle several times you can make your planning scenario more accurate. The following *sales and operations planning (SOP)* process – (see Section 8.2) – explains the second step of this planning cycle. Sales planning also includes *profitability planning* (see Section 8.10).

© SAP AG

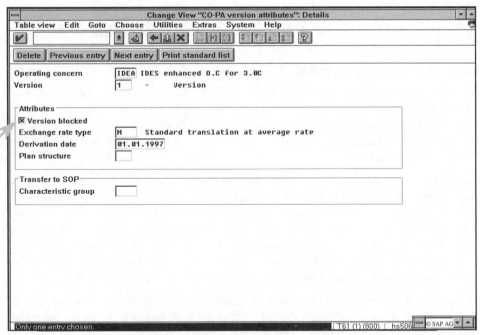

Fig. 8.6: Block sales planning

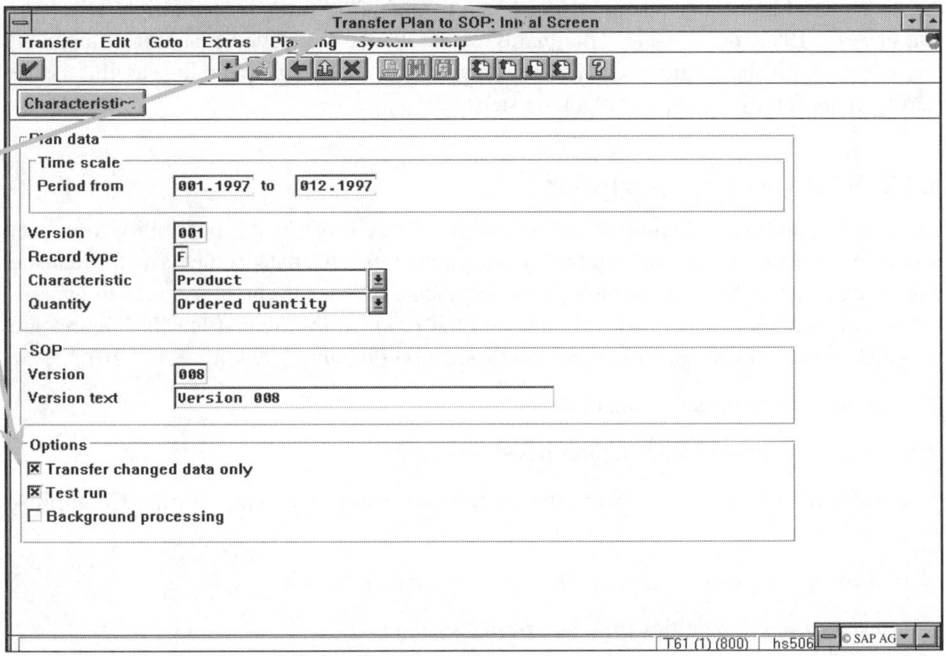

Fig. 8.7: Transfer plan to SOP

8.2 Process: Sales and operations plan processing

8.2.1 Business background

The main task of Sales and Operations Planning (SOP) is to determine the types and quantities of products to be produced and sold in the medium to long term. This comprises the cumulated requirement figures for product groups, end products and other saleable spare parts in the form of assemblies (e.g. electric motors) and individual parts (e.g. a clutch disc or a clip to fix an exhaust).

One aim is to obtain *planning data for production*, for example in the consumer goods industry or the food industry, and another is to obtain *rough planned sales quantities* based on market analyses or past data (e.g. existing customer orders), this data can then be compared with production quantities and capabilities (without exploding bills of material or scheduling routings) at, for example, plant level. Sales and Operations Planning is thus the connection between *market-oriented* sales planning on the one hand and production-oriented master production scheduling and demand management on the other.

In the case of non-integrated systems, a situation may arise where the sales forecasts or figures, which directly influence the subsequent areas of production control, materials management and human resource management, are not compared with the resources in production in time. This then often leads to the planned dates not being able to be reached due to material and other resources not being available on time or at the right time (see Glaser *et al.* 1991, pp. 37–44). The quality of the whole production planning component thus depends on the requirement figures obtained in this rough planning, as this is the starting point for all subsequent planning steps.

8.2.2 SAP-specific description

Sales and Operations Planning (SOP) in the R/3 System offers the possibility to collect data from various internal and external sources and to use this data as the basis for realistic business aims. The SAP production planning module offers various procedures to guarantee that the market-oriented sales figures and the production-oriented feasible figures are weighed up against each other (see SAP – Production Planning 1994, pp. 5.1–5.10):

- manual entry of the sales quantities

- automatic forecast of sales figures based on past values

- transfer of sales quantities from the profitability analysis planning in the Controlling module

- transfer of sales quantities from the Sales Information System

- transfer of sales quantities from an external system

Once the sales plan has been created, the next step is to create a rough-cut production plan using any of several methods.

- As in the sales plan, it is possible to enter the quantity to be produced manually.

- The quantities entered in the sales plan can be transferred 1:1 as the quantities to be produced.

- Stock quantities can be taken into consideration. First, existing stocks are deducted from the sales plan. The remaining quantity is taken as the quantity to be produced.

- It is possible to define so-called *target stock quantities* for products or product groups. In this case, production must be planned in such a way that this target stock quantity is produced in addition to the sales quantity.

- *Ranges of coverage* can be defined for products or product groups. If a company wants to guarantee that enough stocks are available to cover demand for 3 months and it sells, for example, 50 TV sets per day, it must have enough stock to cover sales of 50 sets per day over a period of 3 months. This is the minimum stock quantity that has to be guaranteed in production planning.

Due to the high amount of flexibility involved, SOP can be used for both rough-cut and detailed planning in logistics. The SOP functionality is based on the general concept of information structures used throughout the logistics applications. An *information structure* is a statistics file with operational data which can be based on past data (actual data) or future data (planned data). Information structures in logistics applications are used to accumulate data from the operative data in sales, purchasing, production, inventory management and quality management and to provide this data as the basis for analyses and evaluations in each of the areas concerned.

The data in an information structure can be processed in Sales and Operations Planning using various *planning methods*. Whereas planning is often carried out at product group level, which in the R/3 System can be carried cross-plant at various levels of a product group hierarchy using the techniques of aggregation (e.g. grouping together the planned figures for four countries for the product group containing vehicle A with 70–120 kW) and disaggregation (e.g. splitting the expected sales quantity of 300000 cars among the three production areas of Regensburg, Munich and Spartanburg/New Jersey), with Release 3.0 it is also possible to carry out planning more flexibly in the R/3 System using various characteristics such as sales organization, division or region. The material-independent planning using one characteristic or a combination of characteristics can, of course, also (still) be broken down to material level (for an individual product), as was the case in previous releases. The planning method determines how the existing relationships between the various planning levels of a planning hierarchy are kept consistent. The following planning methods exist in the R/3 System:

- Consistent planning

- Level-by-level planning

- Delta planning

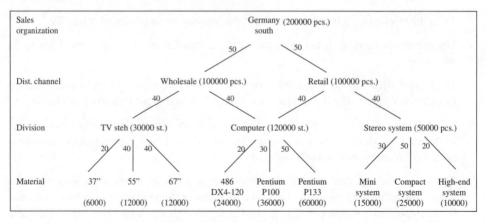

Figure 8.8: Planning hierarchy

In consistent planning, values are stored at the level of greatest detail. The individual planning levels are connected via the corresponding proportional factors and each change at one level automatically results in corresponding changes being made to the levels above and below it in the hierarchy according to the proportional factors. In the example above, for example, a change to the planned figures for the TV sets within the characteristic *division* from 30000 to 40000 pcs would result in the following changes. Firstly, the planned figures for the wholesale area would be increased to 110000 pcs and the aggregation within the sales organization *Germany south* would create a planned figure of 210000 pcs. As a result of automatic disaggregation (splitting) of the planned figures according to the percentage figures of the individual materials (37 cm, 55 cm and 67 cm TVs) the planned figures for the 37 cm TV would be increased to 8000 pcs, for the 55 cm TV to 16000 pcs. and for the 67 cm TV also to 16000 pcs.

In the case of level-by-level planning, the values for a characteristic are stored on each level. Here also, changes can be carried out at each level. The fact that the levels are independent of each other results in faster response times; it does not, however, automatically result in consistent data. The sum of the values of individual members of a planning hierarchy can therefore differ from the total of the highest node in the hierarchy. After each change, it is therefore necessary to cumulate the figures to each superior level in the hierarchy and disaggregate the figures to the next lowest level in the hierarchy using the proportional factors. The advantage of this is that data entered at one level can be checked and, if necessary, changed again, before it is aggregated or disaggregated.

Delta planning also results in the data entered at one planning level being automatically aggregated on higher levels in the hierarchy. Changes at a higher level, however, are not automatically disaggregated. If, for example, the planned figures for TVs are increased from 30000 pcs to 40000 pcs and this leads to the planned figures for the wholesale distribution channel being increased to 110000 pcs and those in sales organization *Germany south* being increased to 210000 pcs, the individual materials (37 cm, 55 cm and 67 cm TVs) still keep the old planned figures of 6000 pcs for the 37 cm TV, 12000 pcs for the 53 cm TV and 12000 pcs for the 67 cm TV. The difference of 10000 TVs, resulting from the increase from 30000 to 40000, is stored in the database at division level.

8.2.3   Using the process

The company starts the *Sales and Operations Planning* process with the events *Sales quantities* and *Production quantities long or medium term* which are integrated with the sales planning module in Controlling.

The first step is to define the *planning object*. The planning object can, as demonstrated in the example above, be a planning hierarchy with various characteristics (sales organization, distribution channel, division), a product group, i.e. a group of similar products (e.g. metal screws M5–M8 or washing machines, separated according to top or front loading), or an individual material (end product). A product group is said to be a multi-level product group if it contains other product groups. A product group is said to be a single-level product group if its members are all individual materials. The lowest level of a product group hierarchy always contains materials. A material can belong to several product groups. In our example, planning takes place for a single material.

In the R/3 System it is possible to have several *planning versions* for the same situation and to simulate the effects of each of the planning versions on production planning. Each planning version is stored under a planning version number with a short text. If several planning versions exist, the version first created is automatically set as the active version and can be set to inactive by the user if another version is to be used to carry out planning activities. The active planning version contains the data that is actually to be used; the inactive versions can be used to test various scenarios. Model Company A uses a strategy in which a range of coverage of at least 4 months is to be guaranteed. Secondly, the total target stock quantity, that is, the total number of boards to be delivered, is to be not less than 10000 in general and not under 25000 for certain customers.

Once the planning object and the planning version have been determined, the next step is to carry out planning. The company has decided to take the sales figures from the Controlling module. The production figures are taken over one to one from the sales figures provided by Controlling.

Within Sales and Operations Planning, it is possible to compare the planned production quantities with production capacity using the *planning table*. The planning table consists of a header and an input area. The header part shows which master data has been planned. This can be a planning hierarchy, a product group or a material. Furthermore, the header contains the name and short text of the planning version and an indicator showing whether the version is active or inactive. The input area is a matrix with rows and columns. The column on the left shows which figures (e.g. turnover, stocks, invoice amounts) are being planned, the column on the right shows the units relevant for each of the figures (e.g. currency, quantity). The area in the middle is used either to enter the values for the corresponding periods or to display the data for the periods taken from the Sales or Controlling Information Systems.

For the function *Create rough-cut production plan*, the company uses the standard planning table available in the R/3 System, which is structured as follows. The first line contains the planned sales quantities and the second line contains the planned production quantities. The stock level resulting from the sales and production quantities is displayed in the third line and the available range of coverage (how long the market can be supplied using a predefined minimum stock quantity) is displayed in the fifth line. Neither line 4 nor line 5 can be overwritten. If only sales quantities exist, you can generate the rough-cut production plan by entering the target stock level (line 4) or the target days' supply (line 6).

In Release 3.0, a correction of the rough-cut production plan and the capacity situation down to work centre level can be carried out at the same time on a two-part planning screen. In this way, the planner has the opportunity to compare the sales and operations plan with the capacity situation interactively. In the top part of the screen the key figures (in this case, the quantities) are displayed and can be changed. The bottom part of the screen contains the available capacity, capacity requirements and capacity load for each work centre involved in the production process. The comparison of planning and resource data takes place per period and the capacity load is expressed as a percentage figure. The monitoring of the capacity load is especially important as this shows a complete overview of the current situation. The capacity requirements caused by other materials or product groups not being planned here are also shown. In our example, the manufacture of a circuit board from beginning to end takes one hour. The first three steps in production are carried out at work centre 001, the last step at work centre 002. The production of 10 pcs (see Fig. 8.13) therefore needs a processing time of 5 hours, which results in a capacity load of 2% in period 1 (02.1997), given that 240 hours of available capacity exist. In the following period, 12 pcs have been planned, resulting in a processing time of 6 hours. The available capacity of 304 hours results in a capacity load of 2%.

The rough-cut plan can be corrected. This can be necessary if, for example, the resource load exceeds 100%. When processing has been carried out successfully, the messages *rough-cut production plan has been processed* and *Capacity leveling carried out are displayed*. If the requirement cannot be fulfilled in one period (even using overtime, having orders externally processed or purchasing from competitors for example), the remaining requirements are passed on to the next period and taken into consideration there.

Independent of the capacity load within a production period, the results produced by the *Sales and Operations Planning* process are transferred to the following process *Transfer of results to demand management*.

8.2.4 Navigation information

■ *Menu path*
Logistics –> Production –> SOP –> Planning –> For Material –> Create

- *Transaction code*
  MC 87

- *Ingoing processes in the R/3 Reference Model*
  Sales planning

- *Outgoing processes in the R/3 Reference Model*
  Transfer of results to demand management
  Cost centre planning with static standard costing
  Cost centre planning with flexible standard costing

Requirements for Transferring Data from Sales Planning (CO-PA)

Sales and Operations Planning (SOP) is integrated in Sales and Distribution and Profitability Analysis (CO-PA). Consequently, you have direct access to the quantities planned in CO-PA from Sales and Operations Planning. To copy data from CO-PA, the system requires the CO-PA field name and the CO-PA version. You can maintain a CO-PA field name for a product group in the master data of the product group's master record. This name establishes the link between the SOP product group and the desired CO-PA hierarchy level. If you execute this function for a single material, the CO-PA field name is predefined and cannot be changed. You can copy quantity key figures only. If the plant of the material or product group is specified in CO-PA, the data of this plant is copied. Otherwise, the system breaks down the quantities of the material or product group into plants using the settings made in the Customizing step "Define proportional distribution across plants".

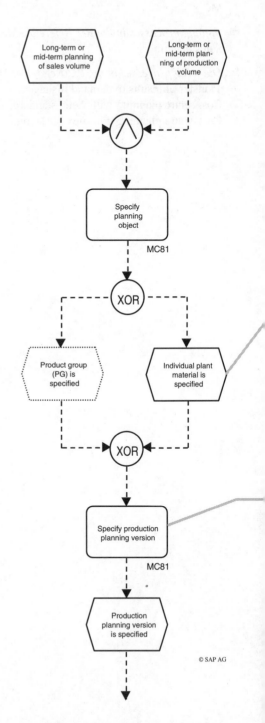

© SAP AG

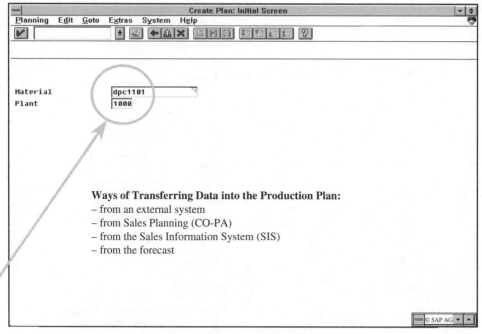

Fig. 8.9: Initial screen of SOP

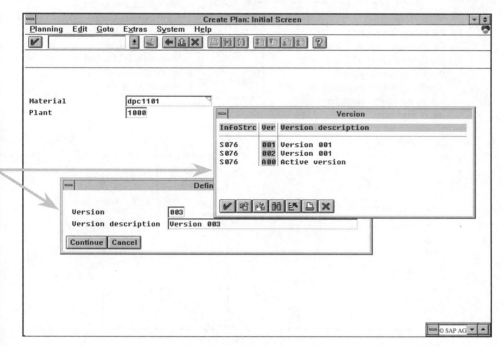

Fig. 8.10: Planning version of SOP

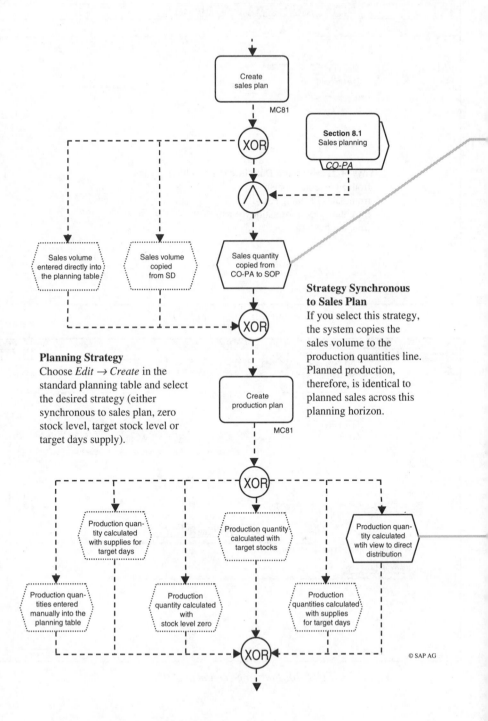

Planning Strategy

Choose *Edit → Create* in the standard planning table and select the desired strategy (either synchronous to sales plan, zero stock level, target stock level or target days supply).

Strategy Synchronous to Sales Plan

If you select this strategy, the system copies the sales volume to the production quantities line. Planned production, therefore, is identical to planned sales across this planning horizon.

© SAP AG

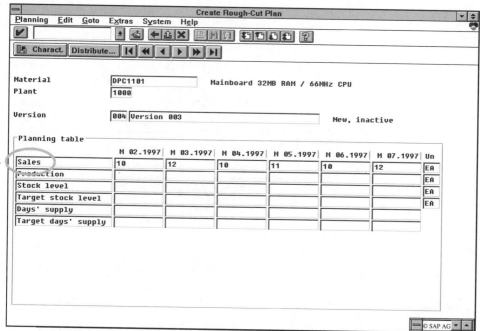

Fig. 8.11: Planning table with the sales data copied from CO

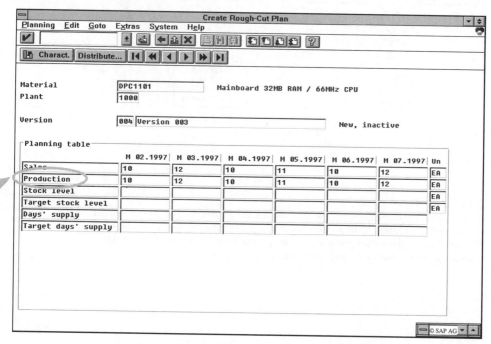

Fig. 8.12: Production data copied synchronously to sales plan

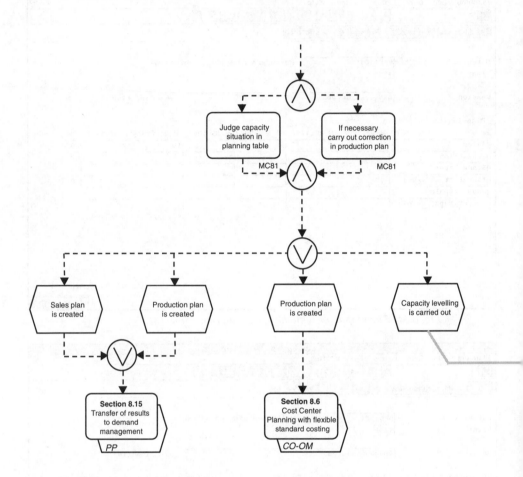

Loading Resources

In Sales and Operations Planning, you can compare the planned production requirements with the available capacities and adjust them if necessary. The example (see Fig. 8.14) shows how this function is activated in Customizing. The application *resource load* is activated by marking the *create capacity requirement* parameter.

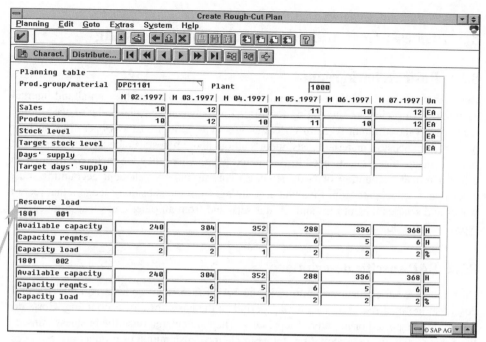

Fig. 8.13: Dependency of capacity on planning data

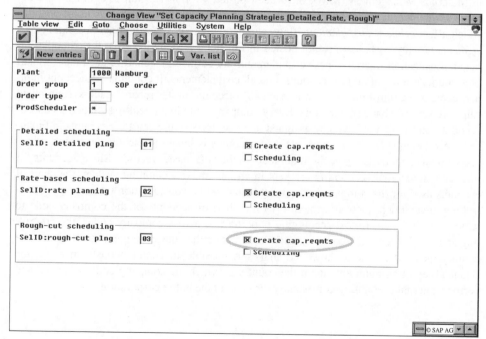

Fig. 8.14: Customizing of capacity planning

8.3 Process: Cost and revenue element processing

8.3.1 Business background

Businesses need to be able to manage and reconcile data from both external and internal accounting. Cost element accounting forms the link between financial and cost accounting. It represents the different types of costs that are incurred in a business operation, such as personnel expenses, material costs, depreciation and interest. Practical and economic reasons dictate that all costs need to be entered once, where they are incurred, in order to effect a proper accounting of cost elements. This means cost element accounting must receive and collect data from financial accounting, from the subsidiary ledgers that record wages and salaries, inventories and fixed assets, and from all other areas that produce any type of costing document.

8.3.2 SAP-specific description

Cost and revenue element accounting in the SAP R/3 System collects and classifies all costs that are incurred in an accounting period as the basis for cost accounting. Costs do not need to be posted or re-entered separately. They are entered once the business transactions that pertain to cost accounting, for example the consumption of production resources in Materials Management (MM), have been posted with an account assignment. An account assignment is a cost-bearing object: a cost centre, project or order. All cost postings which affect *primary cost elements* flow automatically to cost accounting. *Secondary cost elements* are any costs that are not posted in Financial Accounting (FI), for example imputed organization salaries. These cost elements are defined in a chart of accounts. A chart of accounts is a list of all G/L accounts and all cost elements. It contains the account number, name and control information in each G/L account master record. Each system client can have several charts of accounts. Every company code in a client is assigned a chart of accounts, and some may even be assigned to a country-specific chart of accounts in Financial Accounting (FI). The country chart of accounts is linked to the standard chart of accounts by using alternative account numbers in the G/L master records. Since accounts for internal and external accounting are kept in an integrated accounting system, the chart of accounts used for the company codes must be taken into consideration when creating controlling areas. Each controlling area uses the chart of accounts of the company code to which it is assigned. If cost accounting is performed across company codes, the controlling area and all company codes assigned to it must utilize the same chart of accounts. The country chart of accounts, however, makes it possible to simultaneously meet all the financial reporting requirements of the country in which the company code is located and perform internal accounting consistently throughout the entire corporation.

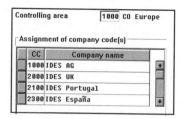

*Fig. 8.15: Controlling area –
company code (Customizing)*

Company codes 1000, 2000, 2100 and 2300, for example, are assigned to controlling area 1000 (see Fig. 8.15). The operational chart of accounts for these company codes is *INT*. This means that controlling area 1000 also uses chart of accounts *INT*.

8.3.3 Using the process

Because each primary cost element in Controlling (CO) corresponds to an account in the general ledger, you first need to create the G/L accounts in Financial Accounting (FI). In creating a G/L account, you specify a number, company code, and a name for it. Within the *Control* area, you determine whether the account is a balance sheet or income statement account and which group of accounts it belongs to. The *Account control* area of the G/L account shows the currency in which the account is kept, the tax codes that can be used in posting items to the account, and whether postings without tax can be made to the account. In the *Account management* area, you determine if the account is managed on an open item basis, if line items can be displayed in the account, and which accounting clerk is responsible for the account. The field status group you specify under Document Entry Control determines what fields to display during document entry and whether an entry is required or optional. Once the G/L account is created, you can create a primary cost element in Controlling (CO) by assigning it to a controlling area and entering a validity period and description for it (see Fig. 8.17). The cost element category on the basic screen of the cost element (see Fig. 8.17) is time-dependent and determines which transactions the cost element can be used for. Cost element type 1, for instance, specifies that the cost element is a primary cost from Financial Accounting (FI) and Materials Management (MM). Category 11, however, is for revenue postings.

8.3.4 Navigation information

▧ *Menu path*
Accounting –> Controlling –> Cost elements –> Master data –> Cost element –> Create primary/ Create secondary

▧ *Transaction code*
KA01, KS01, OB14, KAH1

▧ *Ingoing processes in the R/3 Reference Model*
G/L account master record processing

▧ *Outgoing processes in the R/3 Reference Model*
Activity type processing for overhead calculation
Processing internal orders

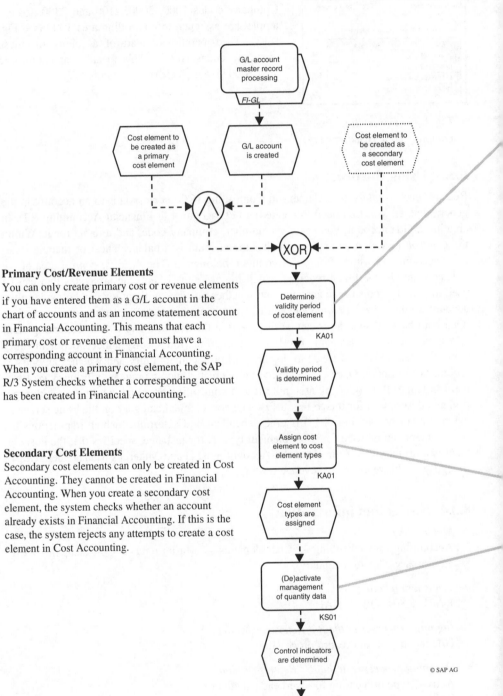

Primary Cost/Revenue Elements

You can only create primary cost or revenue elements if you have entered them as a G/L account in the chart of accounts and as an income statement account in Financial Accounting. This means that each primary cost or revenue element must have a corresponding account in Financial Accounting. When you create a primary cost element, the SAP R/3 System checks whether a corresponding account has been created in Financial Accounting.

Secondary Cost Elements

Secondary cost elements can only be created in Cost Accounting. They cannot be created in Financial Accounting. When you create a secondary cost element, the system checks whether an account already exists in Financial Accounting. If this is the case, the system rejects any attempts to create a cost element in Cost Accounting.

© SAP AG

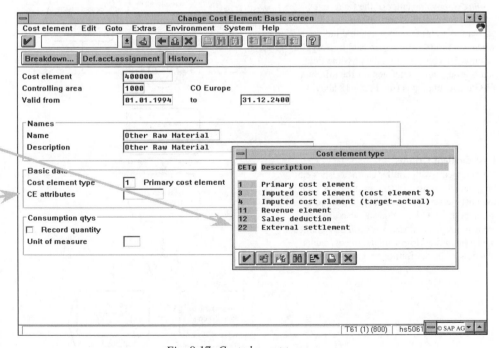

Fig. 8.16: Creation of primary cost element

Cost Element

A cost element is an item in a chart of accounts which is used within a controlling area to record the value-assigned consumption of production factors.

Controlling Area

A controlling area is an organizational unit within a conglomerate for which complete, self-contained cost accounting can be carried out. A controlling area can include one or more company codes that operate in different currencies if necessary. The associated company codes must all have the same operational chart of accounts.

Fig. 8.17: Cost element type

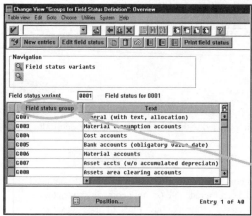

Fig. 8.18: Customizing of field status group

Field Status Group

If you assign a CO cost element to an FI-G/L account, e.g. *400000=consumption of resources,* note the entry of the field status group in the control screen of the FI-G/L account. A field status is a key that indicates whether a field on the screen is obligatory, for example. In Customizing, the possible field status groups are predefined for the different FI-G/L account types (see Fig. 8.18 above).

Cost Element Groups

Cost elements with similar characteristics can be grouped in cost element groups. You can use cost element groups to create an object analysis sheet (OAS). You can also use cost element groups to process several cost elements in one operation (for example, in cost centre planning or in distribution and assessment).

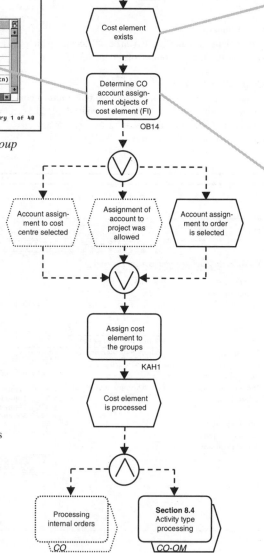

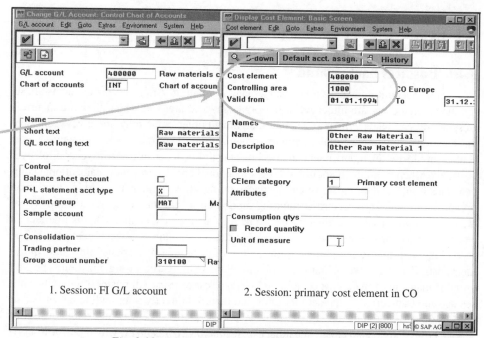

Fig. 8.19: G/L account and primary cost element

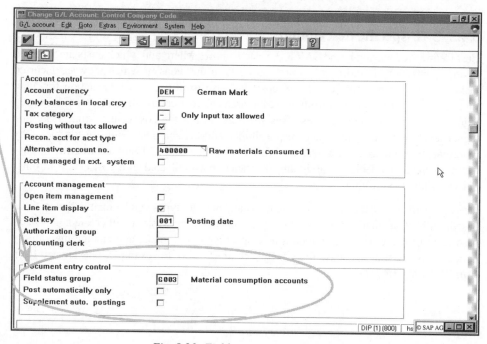

Fig. 8.20: Field status group entry

8.4 Process: Cost centre processing

8.4.1 Business background

Cost centre accounting is based on cost element accounting. After the cost elements are set up, the entered costs are allocated to the organizational areas in which they are incurred. Cost centres can be described as account assignment objects that may not always represent the locations, functional requirements or organizational hierarchy of a company. A cost centre should be an independent area of responsibility to ensure effective control over costs, and when possible, it should also be a locational area to prevent organizational competencies from overlapping. Cost element accounting shows which costs are incurred in an organization, while cost centre accounting reports on *where* the costs are incurred. There are two reasons why cost elements need to be allocated to cost centres. One is to effect an exact allocation of overhead to cost objects based on the claims of each cost centre. The second is to be able to monitor the profitability of each area of responsibility and control their costs. There are two groups that divide all cost centres in an organization. The first group is made up of main cost centres, or *primary cost centres*. All business subunits whose costs are transferred to the activity units and incurred directly after additional service or work is done on the unit for sale are primary cost elements. The second group consists of service cost centres, also called subsidiary or *secondary cost centres*, which perform services and activities supporting the production in other cost centres.

8.4.2 SAP-specific description

Cost Centre Accounting in the SAP R/3 System shows where and which costs are incurred in an organization. Entering and assigning costs to the areas in which they are incurred makes it possible not only to control costs but also to utilize this information for other functions in Cost Object Controlling. A hierarchical cost centre structure must be set up before you can create cost centres. This structure groups the cost centres you create into higher-level decision, control and responsibility areas. Each cost centre in the hierarchy represents the smallest area of responsibility in an organization. There are an array of allocation methods available for assigning overhead costs collected in a cost centre to other objects within Controlling.

Master records for cost centres, cost elements and activity types can be maintained as time-based. This means that if time-based fields are changed, the system will create a new database record for the period in which a new specification is made, and change the validity period of the existing database record. Cost centre V9400, for example, was created from 01/07/1997 to 31/12/9999.

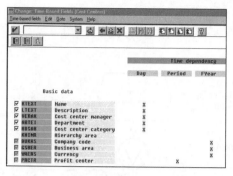

Fig. 8.21: Time-based fields for cost centres (Customizing)

A change is made to one of the specifications in the cost centre. A new cost centre manager is defined for the period from 01/01/1999 to 12/31/9999. The *Cost centre manager* field was defined in Customizing as time-based (see Fig. 8.21). You can display these two records when maintaining the master data by placing the cursor on the *Cost centre manager* field and choosing *D-down* (see Fig. 8.23).

8.4.3 Using the process

When creating a cost centre, you must assign it to a controlling area, specify a validity period for it, and give it a name and description (see Fig. 8.23). In the *Basic data* area, you enter the cost centre manager and department, specify the cost centre category, in this case, production, and then assign a hierarchy area and company code to the cost centre. By choosing the *Indicators* button, you can display the allowed allocation methods and select whether the system should record consumption quantities and lock the cost centre for certain transactions (see Fig. 8.25). For instance, if you select the *Actual revenues* lock indicator, you cannot post revenues to the cost centre.

8.4.4 Navigation information

- *Menu path*
  Accounting –> Controlling –> Cost centres –> Master data –> Cost centre –> Create

- *Transaction code*
  KS01, KSH1

- *Ingoing processes in the R/3 Reference Model*
  None

- *Outgoing processes in the R/3 Reference Model*
  Cost centre budgeting
  Cost centre planning with allocation costing
  Activity type processing
  Cost centre planning with overhead calculation
  Cost centre planning with flexible standard costing
  Cost centre planning with static standard costing

Cost centre Master Record

The fields in the cost centre master record of the SAP System are defined according to their period dependency. The following fields exist:

period-related fields (business area, allocation methods, profit centre and company code),

year-related fields (currency),

day-related fields (locking indicator, name, description, manager, address, communication data, cost centre type, record quantity indicator, department).

Standard Hierarchy

Before you can create cost centres, you must define a cost centre hierarchy. This is referred to in CCA as a standard hierarchy. The standard hierarchy is directly assigned to the controlling area when the SAP System is configured. This distinguishes it from any other (alternative) cost centre hierarchies. Every time you create a cost centre, you must assign it to a cost centre group within the standard hierarchy. This ensures that all the cost centres within a particular controlling area are grouped together.

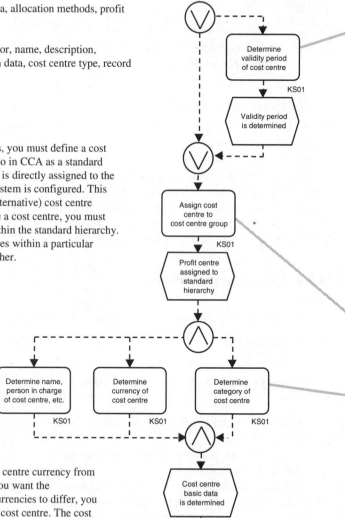

Cost centre Currency

The SAP System defaults the cost centre currency from the controlling area currency. If you want the controlling area and cost centre currencies to differ, you can overtype it when you create a cost centre. The cost centre currency is valid only for the fiscal year in which it was created. You cannot change the cost centre currency during the fiscal year.

© SAP AG

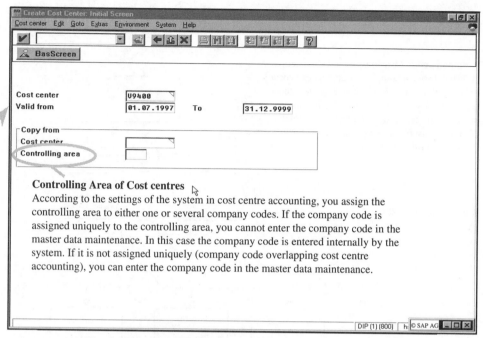

Fig. 8.22: Initial screen of cost centre creation

Controlling Area of Cost centres
According to the settings of the system in cost centre accounting, you assign the controlling area to either one or several company codes. If the company code is assigned uniquely to the controlling area, you cannot enter the company code in the master data maintenance. In this case the company code is entered internally by the system. If it is not assigned uniquely (company code overlapping cost centre accounting), you can enter the company code in the master data maintenance.

(The above text and figure 8.22 relate to the initial screen.)

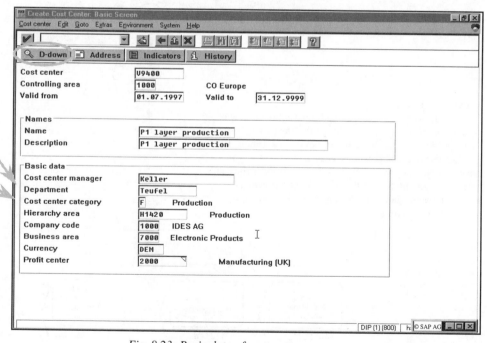

Fig. 8.23: Basic data of cost centres

Company code / Business area / Cost centre
When defining a company code, you can specify
whether the system is to create a balance sheet or a
profit and loss (P/L) statement for the business area. If
a cost centre is assigned to this type of company code,
you must ensure that you assign it to a business area in
the cost centre master as well.

Commitment Update
A lock indicator controls if an open item is
updated in the cost centre. If this indicator is
activated, you can no longer update open
items in the respective cost centre.

Cost centre Groups
You assign a cost centre to a group for the entire lifetime of
the cost centre. If you want to change the group assignment,
you must do so for the entire lifetime of the cost centre. The
SAP System does not accept the change otherwise. If you
have split the analysis period into different periods, you can
select the entire lifetime of the cost centre by selecting the
entire interval list in the *Analysis period* dialog box or by
choosing *Free records*.

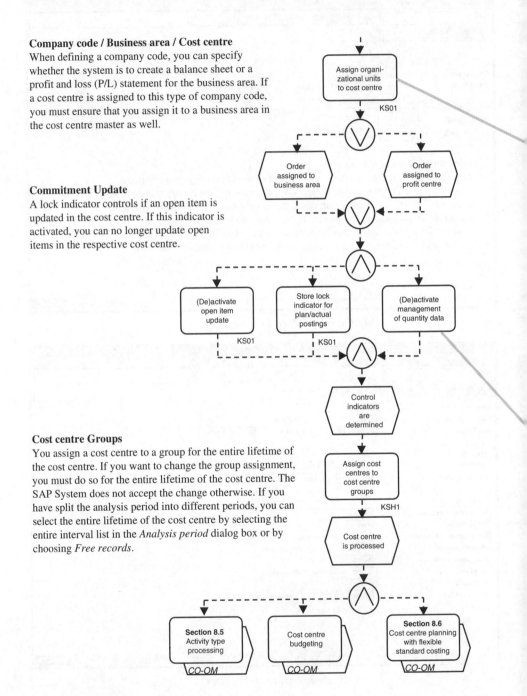

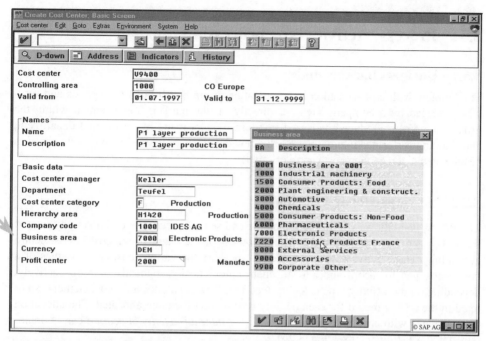

Fig. 8.24: Assigning business area to cost centre

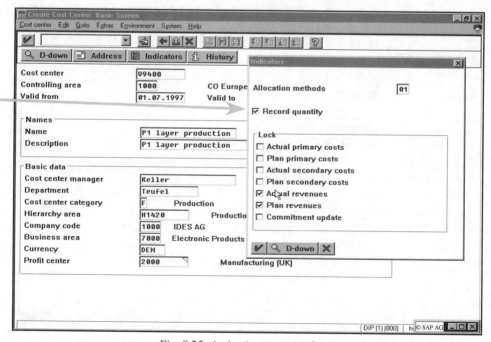

Fig. 8.25: Activating quantity data

8.5 Process: Activity type processing

8.5.1 Business background

The problem with cost allocation in an operating group is that not all the goods and services produced by a company are sold directly on the market. Some remain within the group. Equipment produced and used in-house, repairs made by an internal department, and shipping performed internally are just a few examples of internal activities that need to be allocated to a receiving cost centre or order.

8.5.2 SAP-specific description

The R/3 System allows you to plan, monitor and settle cost centres on an activity-related basis. The activity types are the allocation bases for the cause of the cost in cost centre accounting. These activity types are used to measure the various business activities of a cost centre and to record and allocate them automatically, manually or retrospectively, depending on the activity type category (see Fig. 8.28). An allocation cost element is entered in the master record for each activity type so that it can be allocated. The allocation cost elements with cost element category *43* for *internal activity allocation* can be maintained with Customizing (see Fig. 8.26).

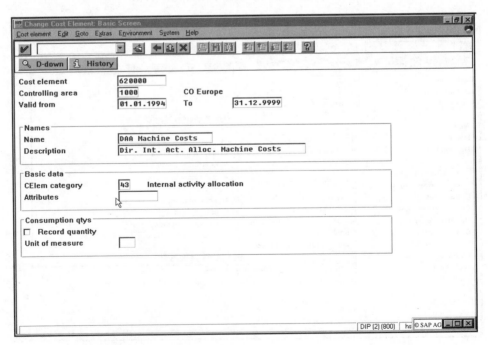

Fig. 8.26: Definition of the allocation cost element – machine costs

For activity planning purposes, the costs incurred by a cost centre are divided by the planned activities of the existing activity types to determine a plan activity price for each activity type. This price is then used for subsequent internal activity allocations. By using an allocation-by-cause principle, therefore, the activity types lead to a *reduction in costs* for the cost centre (see SAP – Overhead Cost Controlling 1996, pp. 6.1–6.12).

8.5.3   Using the process

In order to create an activity type, e.g. machine hours, in a certain validity period, a controlling area must first be defined. The activity unit *Hours* is entered as the unit in which the activity is measured in the basic data for the activity type (see Fig. 8.28). The cost centre category field can be used to define the cost centre category for which an activity type can be planned as well as the category for which an activity type can act as a sender of internal activities. If you enter an asterisk (*) here, every cost centre can access this activity type. You can also define whether the activity type is released for allocation. Activity type category *1* (manual) and the allocation cost element *Machine costs* are set as defaults.

8.5.4   Navigation information

■ *Menu path*
Accounting –> Controlling –> Cost centres –> Master data –> Activity type

■ *Transaction code*
KL01, KLH1

■ *Ingoing processes in the R/3 Reference Model*
Cost/revenue element processing

■ *Outgoing processes in the R/3 Reference Model*
Cost centre planning with static standard costing
Cost centre planning with flexible standard costing

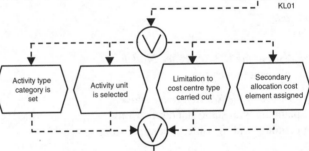
Activity Type Master Record

The data fields in the activity type master record are defined according to their period-dependency. If they are year-related, you must maintain the fields *allocation cost element*, *activity unit*, *output unit* and *factor*, as well as the activity category. If the activity type master is day-related, you must maintain the fields *name* and *cost centre type*. In the case of a period-related definition, you do not need a specific field. If you create a time-independent activity master, the cost element and the activity price indicator are predefined.

Activity Type Category

The activity type category is an indicator that controls whether and how an activity type category is allocated. Type *1* is defined as the normal activity type since the actual activity is entered and allocated directly.

Activity Type Groups

You can group together activity types assigned to specific cost centre types. Using activity type groups in this way can simplify the (activity type) planning process considerably. They can also be useful when apportioning costs using assessments (such as assessment of certain activity type groups).

Allocation Cost Element

This cost element appears in the cost element master record as the secondary cost element *internal cost allocation*.

Activity type data to be created

Section 8.3
Cost/revenue element processing
CO

Determine validity period of activity type
KL01

Cost element is processed

Validity period is determined

Process activity type parameters
KL01

Activity type category is set

Activity unit is selected

Limitation to cost centre type carried out

Secondary allocation cost element assigned

Assign activity type to activity type groups
KLH1

Section 8.
Cost center planning w/flexible standard costing
CO-OM

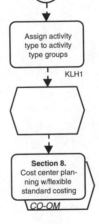

© SAP AG

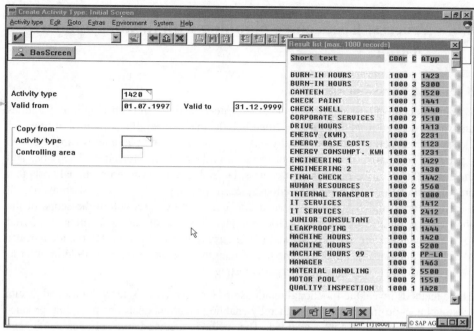

Fig. 8.27: Create activity type

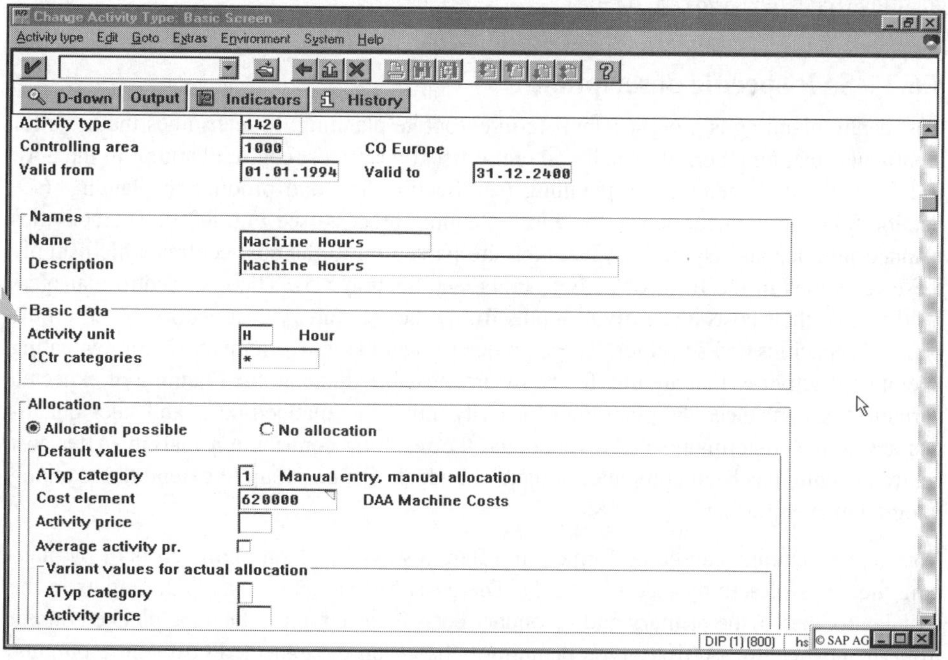

Fig. 8.28: Activity type parameter

8.6 Process: Cost centre planning with flexible standard costing

8.6.1 Business background

Within the scope of cost centre planning, the planned (activity and consumption) quantities and values derived from them are specified in a flexible manner. Planning is performed for clearly defined periods of time (usually one year). If cost centre planning is carried out on a marginal cost basis, fix costs are not included in the cost rates for internal activities and the costing rates of the primary cost centres, but rather only those proportional costs that are allocable according to the allocation-by-cause principle. The fixed costs remain with the cost centres initially and are charged off on a monthly basis within the scope of the short-term profit and loss statement, for example. This type of cost accounting is referred to as *marginal costing* in Germany and *direct costing* in the US. J. N. Harris, a controller at a chemical company, advocated the use of marginal costing as early as 1934 in order to avoid the errors associated with absorption costing.

These methods reveal the functional relationships between costs, sales volumes and profits (cost–volume–profit relationships), thereby enabling incorrect decisions regarding production and sales planning to be avoided. The methods are used not only for continuous monitoring of cost effectiveness but also for the planning tasks associated with cost accounting (see Kilger 1987, S. 65–68).

8.6.2 SAP-specific description

Cost centre planning is a part of short-term corporate planning. It determines the costs for a particular planning period, usually an entire fiscal year. Cost centre planning in the SAP R/3 System supplements sales planning (see Section 8.1) and production planning (see Section 8.2) and is integrated in the entire planning process (see Fig. 8.29). The activities planned in Sales and Operations Planning are passed on to the cost centres which supply these capacities in the form of activity units (see Section 8.5). The cost centre managers need to plan their costs and activity inputs from other secondary cost centres based on the planned capacities and activities. These predetermined values form the basis for evaluating operational activities that are unaffected by any possible fluctuations. Planning of expected variable costs enhances the planning of activity units. The planned costs and sales quantities are used to determine sales revenue and the resulting contribution margin. After cost centre planning has been completed, financial budgets can be set up to extend the planning integration even further.

Cost centre planning can be performed in different ways by planning the costs or by planning the types of activity (see Fig. 8.31). The basis for planning costs is the inputs in the cost centre, that is, the primary and secondary costs incurred to produce the planned output from the cost centre. Activity type planning is based on the expected cost centre outputs. The efficiency of the cost centre is measured by comparing the actual activities with the planned activities.

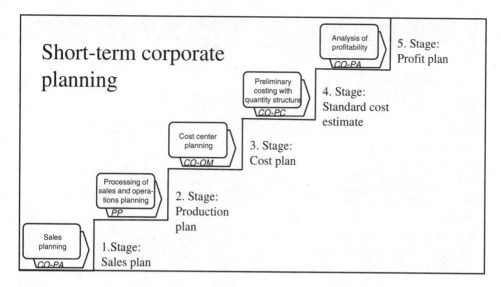

Fig. 8.29: Stages of short-term corporate planning

■ *Manual cost planning*
It is possible to plan primary and secondary costs either according to activities or independently of them. A wide range of planner profiles, tailored to specific plans and containing appropriate planning layouts (planning entry masks), are available for manual cost planning in the different planning areas. Planning layouts can be grouped together in a planner profile according to various criteria. One specific planning layout for one specific planning area is supplied for each planner profile with the standard SAP R/3 System for cost centre planning. The standard planner profile *SAP101*, for example, contains a planning layout called *1-201* (see Fig. 8.30), which can be used for both activity-dependent and activity-independent planning of primary costs.

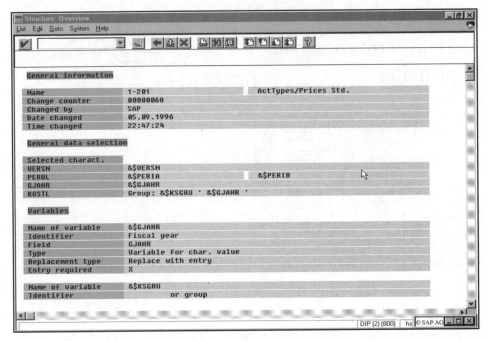

Fig. 8.30: Layout 1-201 for activity-dependent/independent cost planning

Manual planning of secondary costs enables secondary costs to be planned on a quantity basis in the form of activity inputs on receivers (cost centres or orders). An activity input is only possible in those operational areas for which unique allocation bases, i.e. activity types, can be defined. Within the framework of *activity-independent* activity input planning, the input of activities is planned for each receiver cost centre independently of the types of activity there. The plan activity quantity that is input by a receiver cost centre is multiplied by the activity price for the sender cost centre/activity type and posted under a secondary cost element for internal activity allocation. The R/3 System credits the sender cost centre with the amount corresponding to the product of the planned activity quantity and the activity price, and debits the receiver cost centre with the product of the received activity quantity and the activity price. If manual activity prices have not been set for all cost centres and the missing activity prices are to be calculated iteratively, the R/3 System evaluates the activity relationships between the cost centres within the framework of the activity price calculation using the iteratively calculated activity prices. The planned activity input is compared with the actual activity quantities at the receiver cost centres that have been posted via the internal activity allocation. By evaluating the planned activity input quantity with the plan activity price for the activity type, either manually or iteratively, the R/3 System calculates the planned secondary costs at the receiver cost centres. These planned secondary costs can be compared with the posted secondary actual costs (product of the actual activity quantity and plan activity price for the activity type), and any variance determined.

Activity-dependent activity input planning enables secondary costs to be planned according to a particular activity type of the receiver. You plan the input of activity type B at a sender cost centre for activity type A of a receiver cost centre. The purpose of activity type B is the provision of activity type A at the receiver cost centre. The R/3 System posts the planned debit at the receiver cost centre under a secondary cost type for internal activity allocation. If the activity type plan does not include any manual activity prices, the SAP System uses the iteratively calculated activity price to calculate the debit at the receiver cost centre. The R/3 System credits the sender cost centre with the amount corresponding to the product of the planned activity quantity and the activity price, split into a total amount and a fixed amount, and debits the receiver cost centre with the product of the received activity quantity and the activity price.

▓ *Automatic primary cost planning*
A *plan distribution* is available for planning primary costs automatically. This distribution is designed to permit primary-cost-related allocation of cost centres, in other words it only allocates primary costs. The sender and receiver information (which is the sending cost centre and which is the receiving one) is recorded in the controlling document (line items). The data origin required by the accounting department is no longer updated in the controlling document, as in this case the information is mainly to be forwarded from the cost plan.

▓ *Automatic secondary cost planning*
Automatic secondary cost planning entails planning secondary costs on the basis of user-defined keys. In contrast with manual secondary cost planning, the R/3 System calculates the plan values on the basis of the determining factors specified by the user.

▓ *Indirect activity allocation*
Indirect activity allocation represents a tool for automatic allocation of actual and planned activities. In contrast with manual activity input in the plan or actual activity allocation, this tool allows activities to be allocated with the aid of user-defined keys. In addition, it is possible to determine the activity quantity indirectly from the activities of the receivers if the sender's activities are extremely difficult – if not impossible – to measure. A *plan assessment* is available for planning secondary costs on a value basis. Suitable assessment rules must be defined for this purpose. The plan and actual assessment are usually identical. This means that the same sender–receiver relationships are used for a plan assessment that calculates the assessment values and the receiver base in a similar manner.

▓ *Manual activity type planning*
In the final analysis, activity types are used to control activities at the cost centres, as they also permit the operating rate and the rate of capacity utilization of these centres to be measured. When the activity types are planned, the R/3 System generates a plan credit, which is posted with a secondary cost type, on the basis of the planned activity quantity for an activity type at the cost centre concerned. This cost type is stored in the activity type master record and can be overwritten again separately for each cost centre. The plan credit ensures that the sender cost centre is credited in full irrespective of the activity inputs specified in the plan. The "plan activity" and "capacity" variables

are used for an iterative calculation of the activity prices and can also be analyzed in the information system. An equivalence number is calculated in addition for each activity type. Equivalence numbers are weighting factors which are used to break down the planned, activity-independent costs according to activity types. Once the planned, activity-independent costs have been broken down in this way, they are also taken into account in the iterative activity price calculation. Equivalence numbers can be defined separately for each period. Average values are shown on the overview screen for activity type planning (see Fig. 8.33).

■ *Automatic activity type planning*

Indirect activity allocation represents a tool for automatic allocation of actual and planned activities. In contrast with manual activity input in the plan or actual activity allocation, this tool allows activities to be allocated with the aid of user-defined keys. In addition, it is possible to determine the activity quantity indirectly from the activities of the receivers if the sender's activities are extremely difficult – if not impossible – to measure.

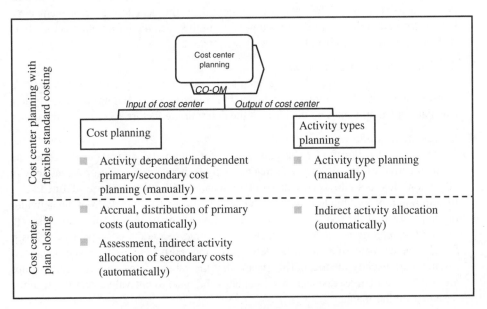

Fig. 8.31: Cost centre planning methods

8.6.3 Using the process

The initial stage in cost centre planning – after the required master data has been created and the planning preparations carried out – involves planning the activity type 1420 for cost centre V9400 (see Fig. 8.32). Within the context of activity type planning, therefore, enter a plan activity quantity of 1200 hours for the cost centre, which, with distribution key 1, corresponds to a monthly activity of 100 hours. The same periodic distribution applies to the planned 1200 hours of capacity. The activity unit hours (H) as well as the secondary allocation cost element 620000 are taken automatically from the activity type master 1420 and set in the planning mask. The rate indicator D is significant for the plan price iteration performed in the planned closing for the cost centre.

After the activity type 1420 has been planned, activity-based planning of the primary costs can be performed for cost centre V9400. In doing so, define the fixed and variable proportions of the primary costs for the cost centre based on activity type 1420. The entered annual plan values are then distributed uniformly similar to activity type planning with distribution key 1. The planned depreciation and interest from asset management as well as the planned personnel costs from HR supplement primary cost planning.

Within the course of secondary cost planning, the exchange of activities between the sender cost centre V9400 and the receiver cost centre V9410 in the model company is planned in the form of machine hours (activity type 1420). This is carried out on an activity-neutral basis in the model company, i.e. without reference to an activity type at the receiver cost centre V9410. The results are the supplied (cost centre V9400) and planned (cost centre V9410) activity quantities. These activity quantities are not valued with the planned rate for the activity type/cost centre 1420/V9400 and "converted" to planned secondary costs until plan price iteration has been carried out.

8.6.4 Navigation information

▪ *Menu path*
  Accounting –> Controlling –> Cost centres –> Planning

▪ *Transaction code*
  KP26, KP06

▪ *Ingoing processes in the R/3 Reference Model*
  Cost centre processing, Activity type processing, Planning preparations, Processing statistical key figures, Planning integration for cost centres, Personnel cost planning, Sales and operations planning, Long-term planning – overall/individual, Material requirements planning – overall/individual

▪ *Outgoing processes in the R/3 Reference Model*
  Profit centre planning integration
  Cost centre planning closing for fixed or marginal costing

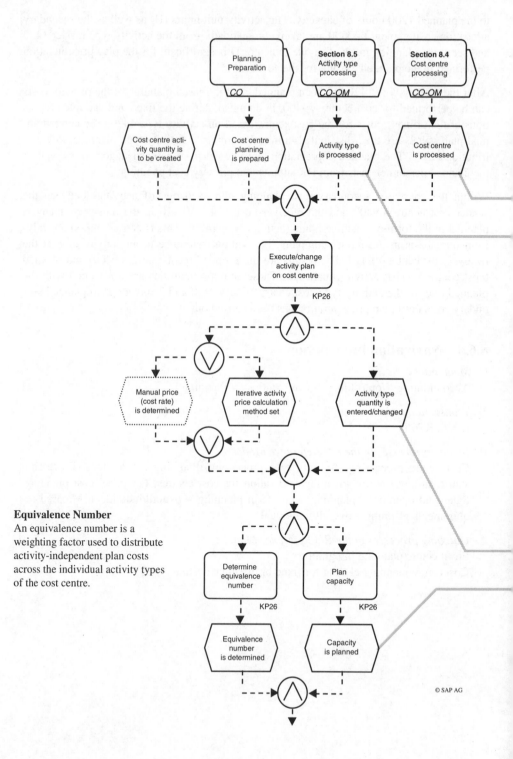

Equivalence Number
An equivalence number is a weighting factor used to distribute activity-independent plan costs across the individual activity types of the cost centre.

© SAP AG

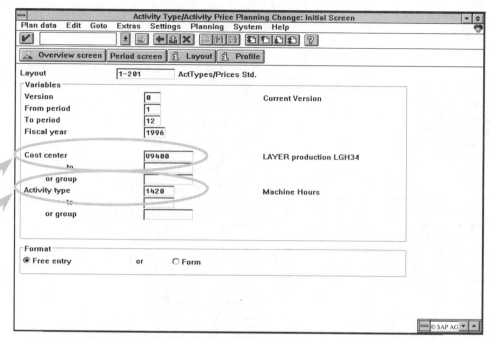

Fig. 8.32: Initial screen of cost centre planning (activity type planning)

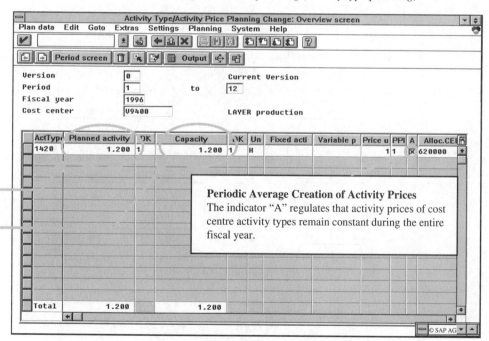

Fig. 8.33: Activity type planning

Determine Assignment of Primary Costs to Activity Type

As a rule, primary costs are planned after the activity quantity and capacity, since the activity volumes are required to plan the costs. Several methods are available for primary cost planning. The costs for activity quantities/capacities incurred due to external procurement or material issues must also be planned. Enter these costs online for each cost centre/cost element. Unit costing can be used as an aid for more detailed cost centre planning below the cost element level.

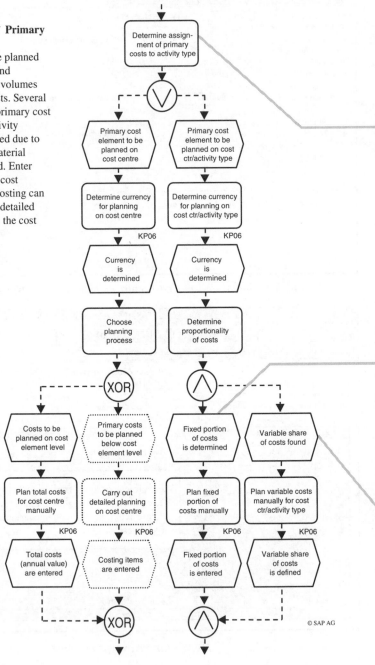

© SAP AG

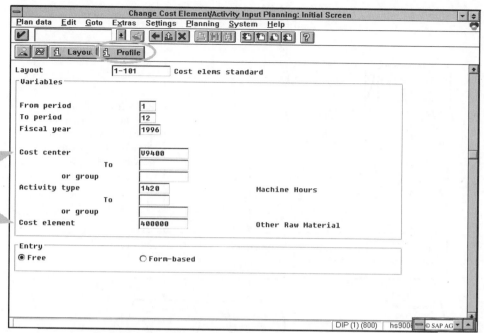

Fig. 8.34: Entering cost centre, activity type and cost element

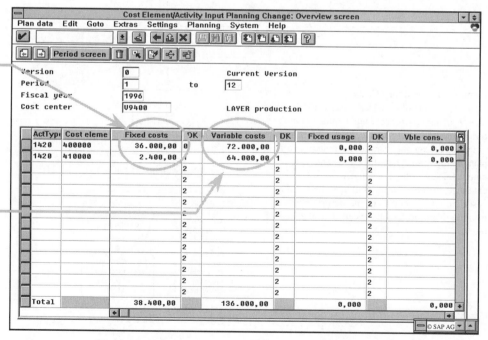

Fig. 8.35: Planning variable and fixed primary costs

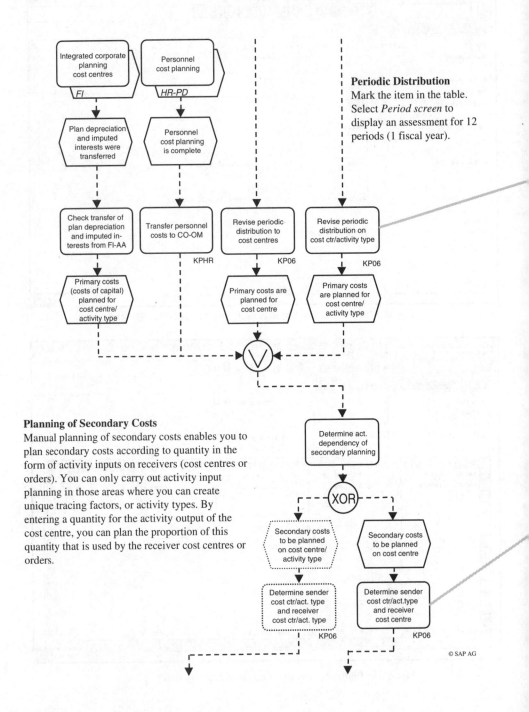

Periodic Distribution
Mark the item in the table.
Select *Period screen* to
display an assessment for 12
periods (1 fiscal year).

Planning of Secondary Costs
Manual planning of secondary costs enables you to
plan secondary costs according to quantity in the
form of activity inputs on receivers (cost centres or
orders). You can only carry out activity input
planning in those areas where you can create
unique tracing factors, or activity types. By
entering a quantity for the activity output of the
cost centre, you can plan the proportion of this
quantity that is used by the receiver cost centres or
orders.

© SAP AG

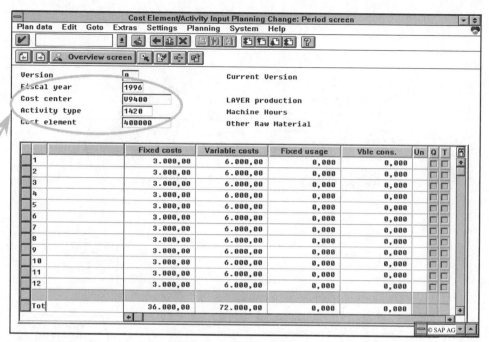

Fig. 8.36: Period screen

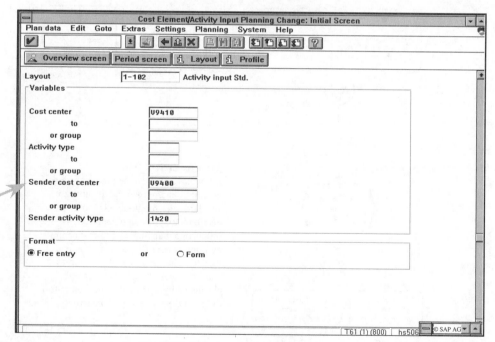

Fig. 8.37: Entering sender cost centre

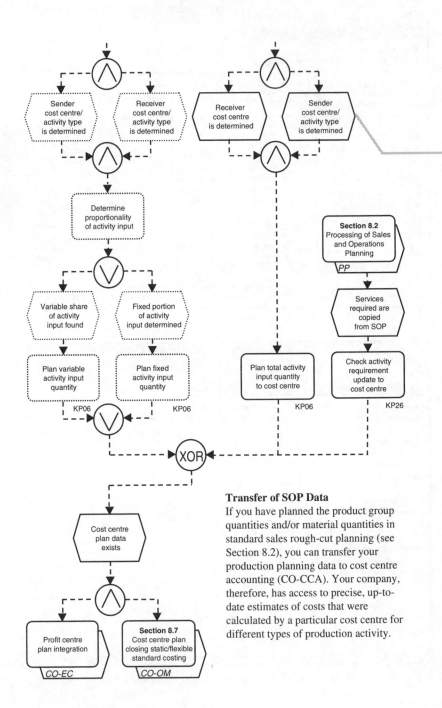

Transfer of SOP Data

If you have planned the product group quantities and/or material quantities in standard sales rough-cut planning (see Section 8.2), you can transfer your production planning data to cost centre accounting (CO-CCA). Your company, therefore, has access to precise, up-to-date estimates of costs that were calculated by a particular cost centre for different types of production activity.

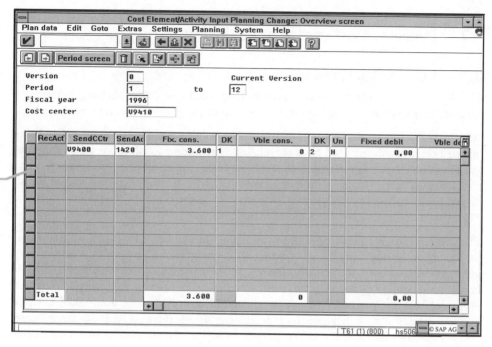

Fig. 8.38: Secondary cost planning

Results of Cost Planning

The primary and secondary costs on the cost centres are derived from the plan consumption of resources or activities required for the production process valued with the plan activity prices. The results of cost planning should be considered as temporary target values that should not be exceeded if at all possible. Using several versions you can create best-case and worst-case plan scenarios that can be compared later with the actual values incurred.

8.7   Process: Cost centre plan closing

8.7.1   Business background

The cost centre plan closing process provides important cost centre planning information for other business functions in the form of the activity prices at the cost centres.

After the necessary monthly planning data has been calculated for all the allocation bases and cost elements, the planned costs are totalled up according to allocation bases and separated into full costs, proportional costs and fixed costs. The result is the total planned costs per allocation base. The proportional, planned activity price can then be obtained for all direct allocation bases by dividing the proportional, planned costs by the planned quantity. The full activity prices can be calculated in the same way.

The cost planning is *reconciled* prior to calculating the planned activity prices. It is necessary to check, among other things, whether all the proportional costs of cost centres with indirect allocation bases are actually covered, and whether the sum of the planned, proportional transportation and energy costs coincides with the sum of the transportation and energy costs at the purchaser cost centres. Any differences that are established must be investigated and purged. The planning, which can then serve as a basis for target/actual cost comparisons and standard cost estimates, as well as for all other business considerations, is then *balanced* and complete (see also Konrad 1971, pp. 1099–1118).

8.7.2   SAP-specific description

Period-specific business transactions take place after the period-end within the framework of plan closing, that is, after the plan postings for that period have been completed. Examples of period-specific business transactions include:

■ Accrual calculation

■ Distribution

■ Assessment

■ Settlement of orders integrated in the planning

■ Indirect activity allocation

■ Reconciliation of the activity network

■ Activity price calculation

There is no fixed order that must be observed during the planning run. The plan assessment must take place subsequent to accrual calculation and distribution, however. The plan activity prices can be calculated by the system following the allocations.

8.7.3 Using the process

The *planned accrual calculation* took place following cost centre planning (see Section 8.6). This entails planning costing-based costs automatically by applying overhead percentage rates to the cost centres concerned, e.g. 4275. Results analysis parameters must be defined prior to the planned accrual calculation (see Fig. 8.39). The next step was to *distribute the plan(ned costs)* for Model Company A within the framework of primary cost planning. Distribution rules must be defined before the plan can be distributed. The allocation characteristics were defined as follows: cost centre *3140* = sender, cost centres *4275 to 4278* = receivers (see Fig. 8.40). In the next step – the *order settlement* – the costs that have accrued for an order are reposted to a cost centre. In our example, cost centre *4275* was debited with internal order *800039* (see Fig. 8.42). The activity network must be suitably reconciled (see Fig. 8.44) before planned activity prices can be calculated from the planned costs and quantities (see Fig. 8.48). It is important to ensure within the framework of the *plan reconciliation* that the activity inputs and outputs are coherent. If the planning needs to be reconciled again, the indirect activity allocation must be repeated because the tracing factors have changed. The reconciled planning can be *frozen* by blocking the activity types (see Fig 8.45).

8.7.4 Navigation information

▪ *Menu path*
   1) Accounting –> Controlling –> Cost centres –> Planning –> Allocations –> Imputed cost calc.
   2) Accounting –> Controlling –> Orders –> Planning

▪ *Transaction code*
   KO9E, KSA8, KAMN

▪ *Ingoing processes in the R/3 Reference Model*
   Cost centre planning
   Periodic reposting
   Order planning with static standard costing or marginal costing
   Indirect activity allocation

▪ *Outgoing processes in the R/3 Reference Model*
   Internal order processing
   Cost assessment
   Standard cost estimate with quantity structure
   Transfer of cost centre full costs/balances
   Profit centre planning integration

Accrual

After you have defined a costing sheet and the associated data, you can perform an accrual in the plan. This produces a log of the postings that were made. You can carry out a profit control scenario using the reporting functions (area, cost centre or line item reports). The detail lists show the values calculated for each cost centre, activity type and accrual cost element. In addition, you can go to the detail screen of overhead costing in order to analyze the values calculated in greater detail (basis cost elements, surcharge rates). For the accrual postings, you can write line items and totals records for the sender and the receiver. The posting date of the plan accrual is always the first day of a posting period.

Distribution

Distribution is a method of allocating primary costs, and primary costs only, to objects in CO. The following information is passed on to the receivers: the original (primary) cost element is retained, the sender and receiver information (which are the sender and receiver cost centres) is documented with line items in the CO document. The information tagging the origin is not updated in the CO document.

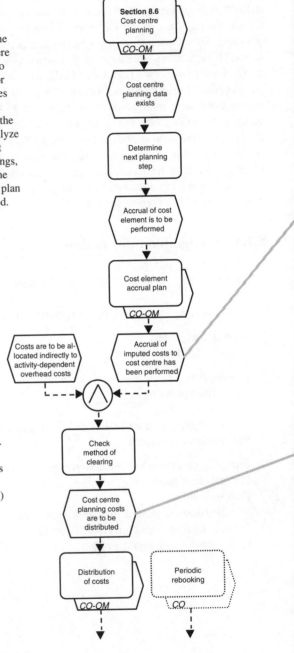

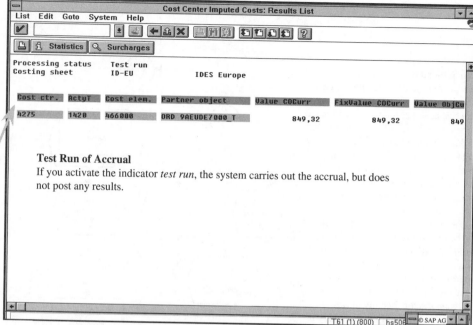

Test Run of Accrual

If you activate the indicator *test run*, the system carries out the accrual, but does not post any results.

Fig. 8.39: Cost centre accrual

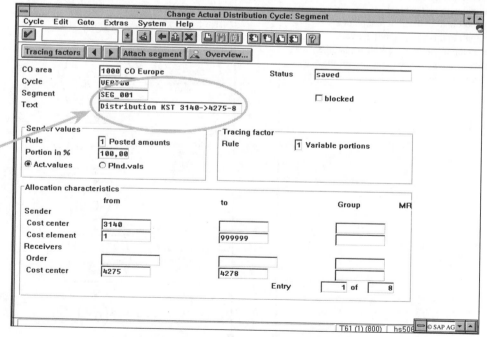

Fig. 8.40: Distribution of cost centre planning costs

Plan Settlement

You can only settle a plan for the cost centre if planning integration of orders with cost centre accounting is activated (versions). During order settlement the costs accumulated to an order are posted to a cost centre. The planning costs of an order settled to a cost centre can only be completely split into activity types, since costs are always settled to cost centres independent of their activity type. If you carry out flexible standard costing based on marginal costs and plan costs for an order in proportion to an activity type, you must also plan these costs manually for the receiving cost centre. You cannot settle them by means of planning integration. For example, you want to plan the maintenance of a production plant in an order. The costs of maintaining the plant are proportional to those of the plant's output. In this case, do not activate planning integration but rather plan the costs of maintenance manually for the receiving cost centre.

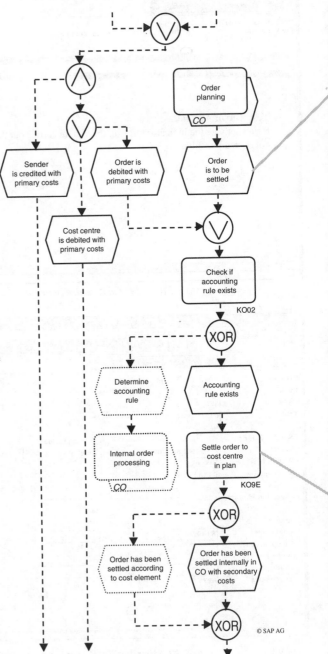

© SAP AG

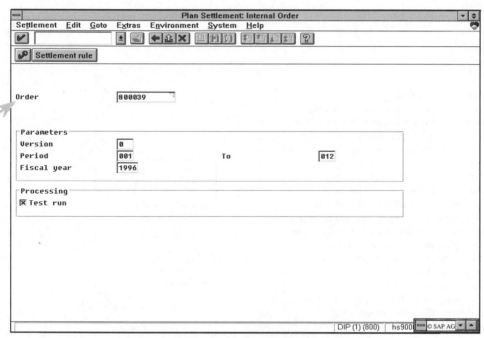

Fig. 8.41: Entering order for settlement

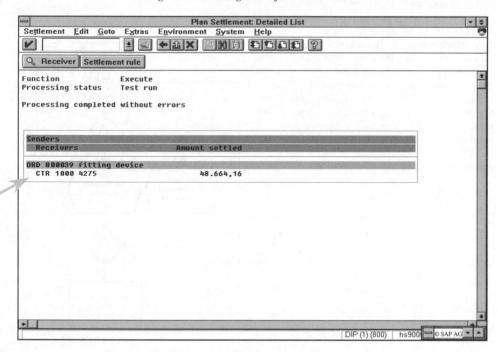

Fig. 8.42: Debiting cost centre

Plan Reconciliation

Plan reconciliation is used to check and reconcile the internal activity exchange. Cost centres can draw upon activities from other cost centres and planning-integrated orders and projects, in addition to activities in Production Planning. Reconcilation of internal activities is necessary because each cost centre plans activities and activity relationships independently. This can result in differences between sender cost centre and receiver cost centre planning. In plan reconciliation, the plan activity quantity for a cost centre is adjusted to the scheduled activity for the receiver cost centres. In this way, variable activity relationships as well as variable costs for producing the activity are corrected appropriately. The fixed portions of the activities and costs referred to are not changed by plan reconciliation. If an activity type is not scheduled, the activity quantity is not changed in the plan reconciliation framework. It is therefore unnecessary to plan scheduling for the activities produced by the end cost centres. The difference between plan activity production of a cost centre and the plan activity input of other cost centres is displayed in a list. After plan reconciliation is completed, indirect activity allocation must be repeated because the tracing factors may have changed, with the result that the indirectly allocated activity must be redistributed to the receivers.

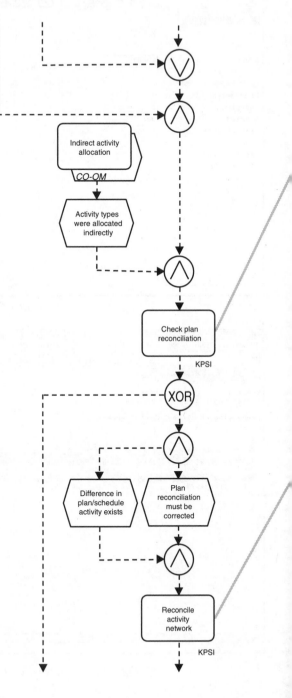

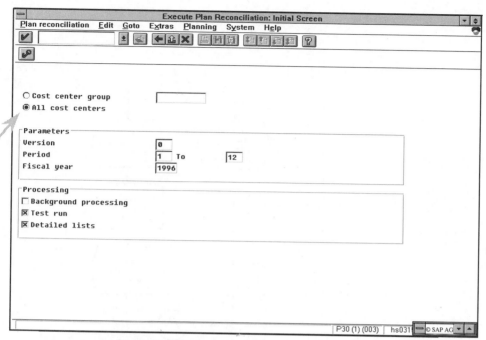

Fig. 8.43: Initial screen of plan reconciliation

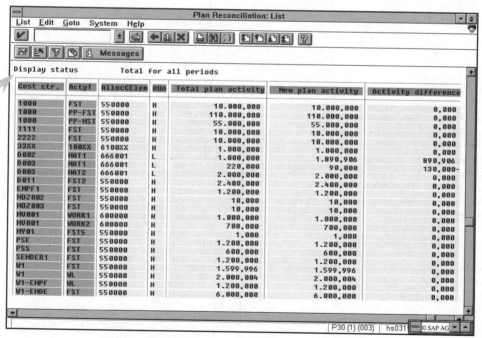

Fig. 8.44: Activity network of plan reconciliation

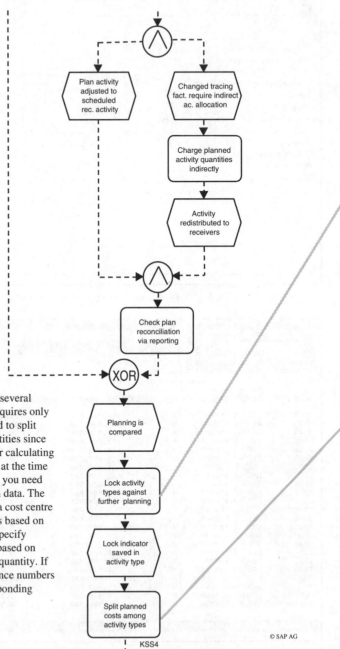

Plan Cost Splitting

While actual cost splitting requires several splitting steps, plan cost splitting requires only one. For plan costs, you do not need to split based on target costs or target quantities since there is no actual operating level for calculating the operating rate and target values at the time of planning. As a first splitting step you need only reconcile actual data with plan data. The activity-independent plan costs on a cost centre are apportioned to the activity types based on user-defined splitting rules which specify splitting methods such as splitting based on equivalence numbers or scheduled quantity. If you use splitting based on equivalence numbers or quantities, you must plan corresponding values in activity type planning.

© SAP AG

348

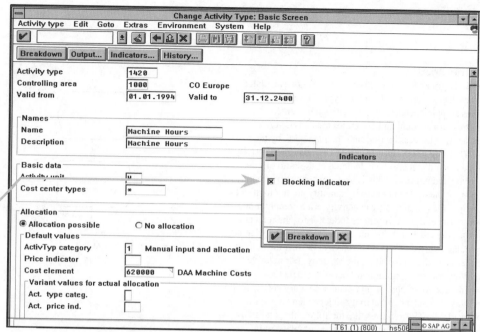

Fig. 8.45: Blocking activity types for further planning

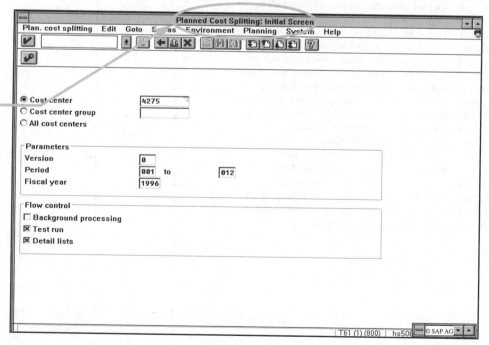

Fig. 8.46: Planned cost splitting

Activity Prices

Activity prices for plan activity types can be calculated for each cost centre and activity type. The SAP System takes all plan exchanges of activities between cost centres into account and computes the activity price in an iterative process by dividing the plan costs by the plan activity or capacity. Alternatively, the fixed activity price portion can also be calculated as the ratio of plan activity and capacity. This is useful when the provision costs for the maximum activity quantity are not to affect costing of a product. To run activity price computation, you must set the activity price indicator for the relevant cost centres to **1** or **2**. "1" means that the activity price is calculated based on the plan activity, "2" that the activity price is calculated based on the capacity. For iterative activity price computation, all necessary data (cost of all business transactions, primary and secondary costs, activity-dependent and activity-independent costs) must be available. This requires that the following conditions have been met: the planning must be complete and if orders or logistics are part of planning you must settle the orders or projects to the cost centres. You include activity-independent plan costs in your activity prices by using splitting rules which you specify as part of planned cost splitting. The SAP System apportions the activity-independent plan costs of a cost centre to activity types of the cost centre. The simplest way to do so is to apportion by equivalence numbers. The SAP System calculates the ratio of the equivalence number of one activity type to the total of all equivalence numbers for activity types on the cost centre. The activity-independent plan costs are multiplied by the weighting factor and added to the activity-dependent plan costs. Activity-independent plan costs are always fixed. Therefore, the plan fixed quotient of the activity-dependent plan costs is increased by the amount which results from the distribution of the activity-independent plan costs based on equivalence numbers.

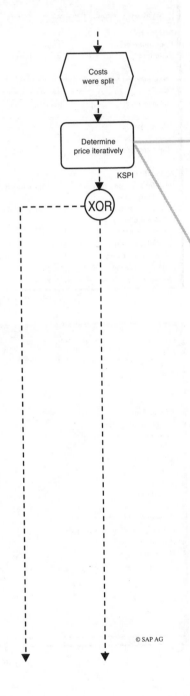

© SAP AG

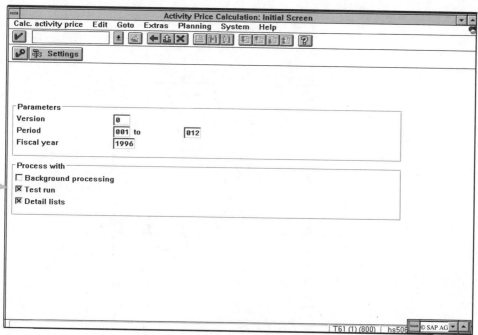

Fig. 8.47: Initial screen activity price

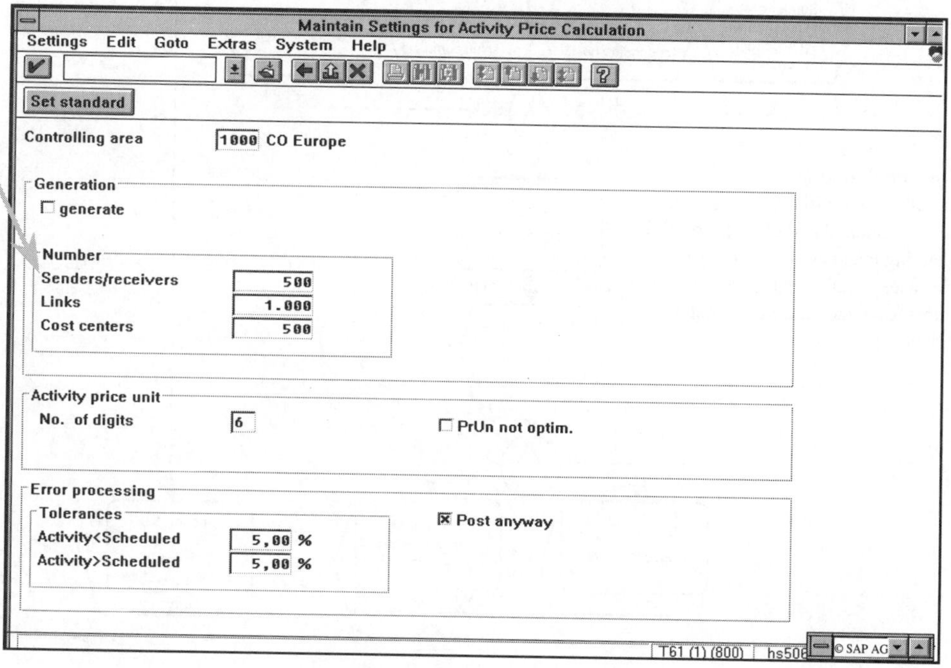

Fig. 8.48: Activity price calculation

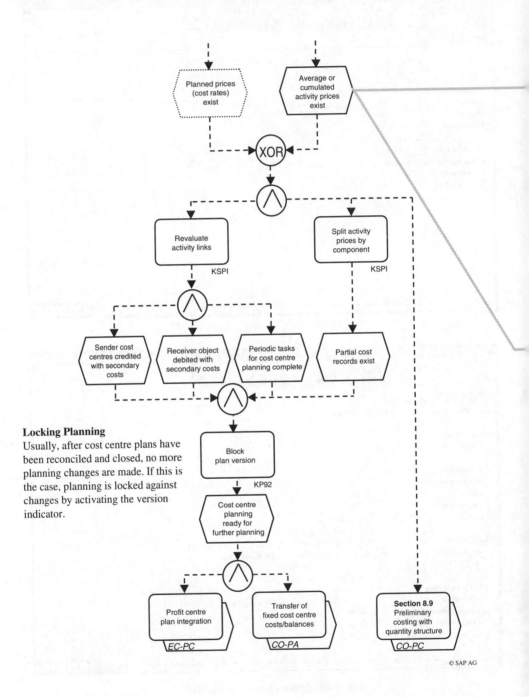

Locking Planning
Usually, after cost centre plans have been reconciled and closed, no more planning changes are made. If this is the case, planning is locked against changes by activating the version indicator.

© SAP AG

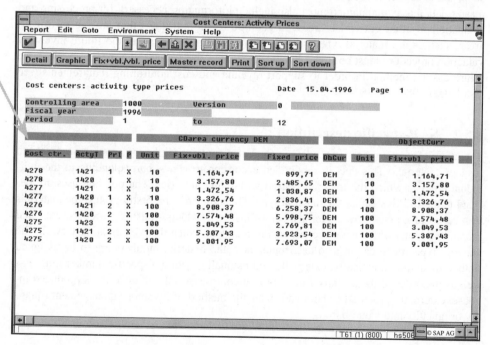

Fig. 8.49: Selection screen of activity prices

Fig. 8.50: Activity prices in report format

8.8 Process: Material master processing for costing

8.8.1 Business background

Handling and storage of materials are the subject of numerous discussions in the areas of business administration, industrial management science, information management and mechanical engineering, as well as in practice in all types of industrial plant. In the logistically oriented areas materials are initially differentiated into sold materials, production materials and purchased materials. A distinction is also made for planning purposes according to whether the material is a finished product, an assembly or an input (raw) material. It is important in accounting to know how a material should be costed and valuated. A newly defined material can have its origins in different areas. Purchasing, for example, might define a new purchased part as a result of a new component supplier, while the strategic planning department of a company could define a new sold part (article) and product development/engineering/design or production could be forced to introduce a new material on account of new developments in production engineering.

If the same material needs to be accessed by different departments with different goals and different points of view, it is essential for the structure of the material, the associated information structures and the different requirements to be coordinated by a logical, central database across all areas. As material master data in an integrated system is not simply supposed to supply the required information for production and procurement logistics, the master data that is maintained must also include information necessary for processing and evaluation in other enterprise areas. In addition to the attributes that are crucial for all areas, such as the material type, line of industry and number range, the future inventory valuation procedure must be stored in order to support the accounting aspect, as well as the future costing method in order to support revenue and cost controlling requirements (see also Kilger 1986, pp. 284–296).

8.8.2 SAP-specific description

The material master record in the R/3 System also contains all the information necessary to manage materials. This data is subdivided according to *views*, corresponding to the individual areas in which the material is used within an enterprise. The possible uses are defined in the R/3 System by the material type. The *material type* firstly groups the materials in a series of classes (raw materials, semi-finished products, finished products, etc.) and secondly defines which areas are allowed to maintain which data (by creating views). The material type specification also determines how the material numbers are to be assigned (internally and automatically, externally and manually, within a specific number range) as well as the order of the screens. In addition, it controls whether a material is produced in-house, externally procured or both and states the method of inventory management (quantity or quantity and value-based).

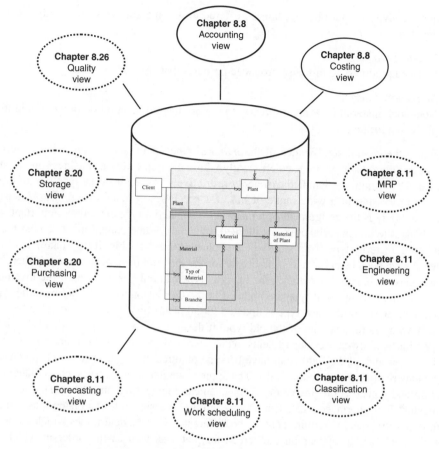

Fig. 8.51: Selected views of the material for a model enterprise

The material classes offered by the R/3 System include the following:

▪ *Raw materials*
Raw materials are procured externally and incorporated in the product that is manufactured.

▪ *Operating supplies*
Operating supplies are consumed during the manufacture of a product, but are not directly incorporated in the activity output.

▪ *Semi-finished products*
Semi-finished products correspond to in-house produced or externally procured component parts or assemblies that are incorporated in the product that is manufactured.

▪ *Trading goods*
Trading goods are externally procured materials that are not used during the subse-

quent activity output process, but are offered on the market via sales and distribution logistics.

■ *Finished products*
Finished products are in-house produced products that are sold.

■ *Non-stock material*
Non-stock material is brought directly to the production location on delivery and then processed further.

Owing to the central significance of the *material type* for uniquely identifying materials and for ensuring that they are used efficiently within the framework of business operations, all changes to it must be handled extremely restrictively. As the material type has an influence on processing of a wide range of business processes in many different user departments, not only is the assignment of a material to a material type extremely important, but also changes to this material are only allowed subject to certain conditions. It is possible to change the material type if no stocks of the material are available, if no quantities of the material have been reserved and if no orders for the material have been placed. If there are open orders, reservations or stocks, the material type can only be changed if the inventory values for the new material type are updated in the G/L account for the old material type, and if the material of the new type is updated for all plants on a quantity and value basis in the same way as the material of the old type. If the material type is changed, all the fields for previously allowed user departments, which may now be switched off, are reset to their initial values and all the fields that have become required entries as a result of the change in the material type are output in a list. The appropriate *line of industry*, such as plant engineering and construction (indicator *A*), mechanical engineering (indicator *M*), chemicals (indicator *C*) or pharmaceuticals (indicator *P*), must be assigned to the material as well, to permit industry-specific requirements to be differentiated. This determines which industry-specific fields are to appear on the screen templates as well as the order in which the screens are to be displayed. The following points are important when carrying out a cost estimate:

■ *Assigning the material to a plant*
Materials and material stocks are defined on a plant-specific basis in the R/3 System. The materials at different plants can also be planned across these plants.

■ *Choosing the costing view*
The material must be defined at plant level in order to use the costing view, as this is the level at which the valuation takes place. It is possible to specify whether the material should be included in the product costing by marking the product costing field. If not, the material can be costed using the unit costing method (without referring to bills of materials or routings).

■ *Choosing the accounting view*
The accounting view contains data that is relevant to the accounting department, such as the currency, price and valuation category and class. The valuation category determines whether the material should be valuated using a standard method or individually. A material stock derived from in-house production, for example, can be valuated dif-

ferently than one which is externally procured, or different supplier prices may necessitate different valuations.

8.8.3 Using the process

When creating material master records from the costing point of view, a company must initially determine the material type (e.g. finished product, semi-finished product or raw material), as this in turn determines the control parameters for processing the material. In order to assign the material to a particular branch of industry, this branch must be stored in the material master record. The base unit of measure that is defined in Customizing determines the unit of measure in which a material is specified in inventory management. Any quantities that are specified in other units of measure within the framework of operational processes are automatically converted to the base unit of measure by the R/3 System. The valuation class and price control are particularly important for the *accounting view* of the company. The valuation class determines (together with the account determination in Materials Management) the G/L accounts in which the costs of a valuation-relevant business activity (e.g. goods receipt) are updated (automatic account determination). The price control function determines whether the standard price (indicator *S*) or the periodic unit price (indicator *V*) is relevant for the stock valuation (see Fig. 8.54). The method used to cost the material is governed by the basic data of the *costing view*. The *Product costing* field defines whether the material is costed by means of a product costing with or without a quantity structure. The origin group is required to separate materials and their costs that are updated under the same cost element. The *Material origin* field (see Fig. 8.55) in turn controls whether or not the costs of the material number are updated at all in the controlling cost audit. The *Costing lot size* field contains a default value for the costing.

8.8.4 Navigation information

■ *Menu path*
Logistics –> Materials management –> Material master –> Material –> Create

■ *Transaction code*
MM01

■ *Ingoing processes in the R/3 Reference Model*
none

■ *Outgoing processes in the R/3 Reference Model*
Standard cost estimate without quantity structure
Preliminary costing with quantity structure

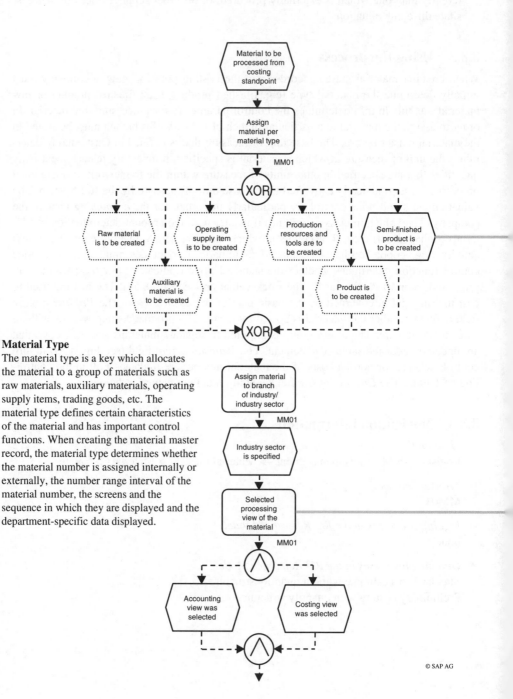

Material Type
The material type is a key which allocates the material to a group of materials such as raw materials, auxiliary materials, operating supply items, trading goods, etc. The material type defines certain characteristics of the material and has important control functions. When creating the material master record, the material type determines whether the material number is assigned internally or externally, the number range interval of the material number, the screens and the sequence in which they are displayed and the department-specific data displayed.

© SAP AG

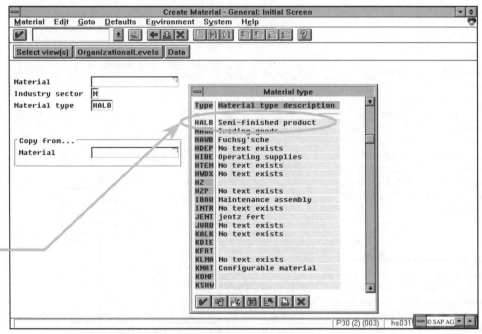

Fig. 8.52: Entering material type

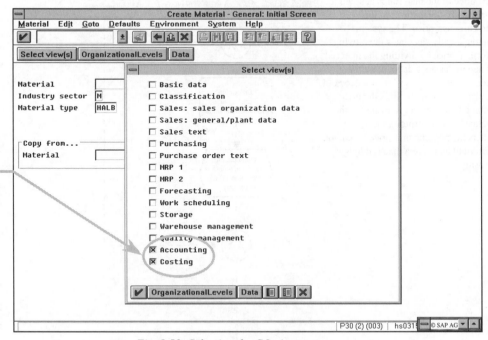

Fig. 8.53: Selecting the CO views

Standard Price (S-Price)
If material stock is valuated for a standard price, all goods movements are valuated with the same price for a certain period. If there are price variances in goods or invoice receipt (e.g. purchase price higher than standard price), the system makes postings to price difference accounts. However, this does not affect the standard price.

Moving Average Price (V-Price)
There are two types of moving prices, the moving average price and, if the material ledger for the material is activated, the periodic unit price. If the stock is valuated for the moving average price or periodic unit price, the price of the material is adapted to permanent fluctuations of the procurement price. The system automatically calculates the moving average price by dividing the material value in the stock account by the number of all storage location stock of a plant. The system alters the price after any movement relevant for the valuation. Furthermore, the system alters the periodic unit price when you carry out and save a material ledger closing.

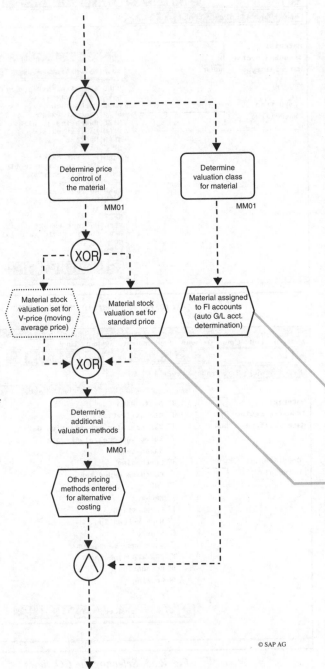

© SAP AG

Valuation Class

The valuation class allocates material to a group of G/L accounts. Indicating the valuation class allows, among other things, for automatic account assignment in material management. Moreover, it allows you to post materials of the same material type to different accounts or to post materials of different material types to the same account. Together with other factors, the valuation class defines the G/L accounts that are updated in an operation relevant for the valuation (e.g. goods movement).

Valuation Category

The valuation category determines the criteria for valuation, i.e. whether the stock of a material is valuated separately or not. In the case of split valuation, the valuation category also determines which valuation types can be selected, i.e. according to which criteria the stock can be valuated. Apart from acquisition costs, production costs and ordinary depreciation, you can distinguish in a valuation area specific valuation types, revaluation, investment support measures, special depreciation and unplanned depreciation.

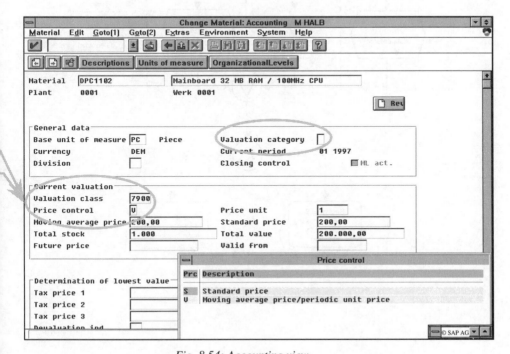

Fig. 8.54: Accounting view

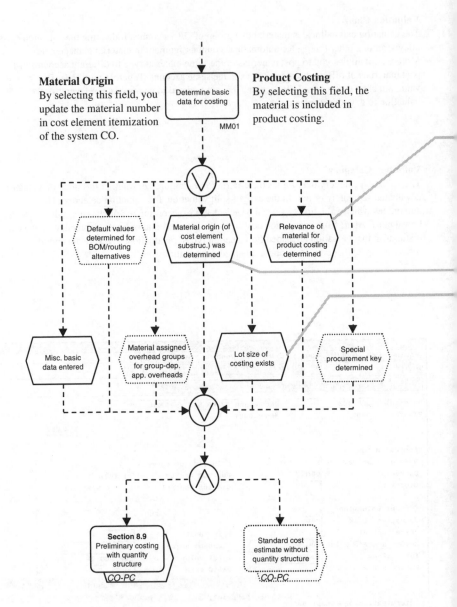

Material Origin
By selecting this field, you update the material number in cost element itemization of the system CO.

Determine basic data for costing

MM01

Product Costing
By selecting this field, the material is included in product costing.

Default values determined for BOM/routing alternatives

Material origin (of cost element substruc.) was determined

Relevance of material for product costing determined

Misc. basic data entered

Material assigned overhead groups for group-dep. app. overheads

Lot size of costing exists

Special procurement key determined

Section 8.9 Preliminary costing with quantity structure
CO-PC

Standard cost estimate without quantity structure
CO-PC

© SAP AG

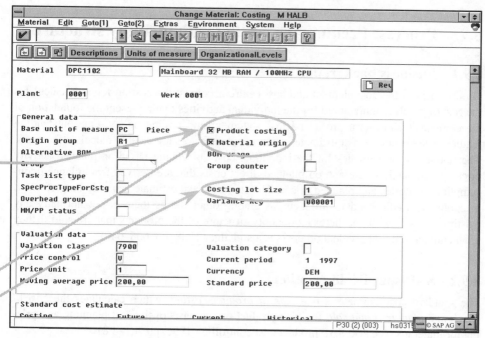

Fig. 8.55: Costing view

Costing Data

With the data displayed in the screen above you can enter further data relevant for the calculation of costs, such as costing lot size and overhead group. Enter on which alternative BOM, BOM usage and plan (planning type, planning group, group counter) the costing is based. Furthermore, you can define valuation data. This data corresponds to the data of the accounting department. Usually, it is the accounting data that is created rather than the costing data. If the valuation data displayed in the screen has already been created by the accounting department, you can no longer enter it. If the costing data is created before the accounting data, however, the valuation data serves only as default data for the accounting department.

8.9 Process: Preliminary costing with quantity structure

8.9.1 Business background

On the basis of the cost element and cost centre accounts, the costing function calculates the cost of goods manufactured for the individual activities that represent the foundation of the company's short-term profit and loss statement and pricing policy. One outstanding feature of the standard cost estimate is that planned factors are used to calculate the costs. The standard cost estimates for the individual cost objects are based on planned activity prices per allocation base and on planned direct costs that are derived from planned consumption quantities and planned prices. The standard cost estimate can only be performed in companies with standard products, as among other things there is not normally any existing know-how about the exact quantity structure of the products that are sold if they are manufactured to individual orders (see also Kilger 1988, pp. 605–640).

8.9.2 SAP-specific description

The standard cost estimate is *one type of product costing*, which calculates the *cost of goods manufactured and sold* for each product on the basis of the cost planning and pricing for materials (see also SAP product cost controlling 1996, pp. 4.1–4.8).

▪ *Cost of goods manufactured*
The cost of goods manufactured comprises those costs which arise when a material is manufactured. They are made up of direct material costs, material overhead costs, direct costs of production, production overhead costs and special production costs. The product calculation calculates the *costs of goods manufactured for each in-house produced material* in the bill-of-material structure. If the product has a multi-level structure, the costs for the lower-level materials are calculated and taken into account in the costing for the next higher material. The materials with the lowest-level code (that is, the bottommost materials in the hierarchy) are costed first, followed by the materials with the next lowest-level code, and so on. A cost component split is generated for each costed material. It subdivides all costs into material costs, costs of production, costs for external procurement, and so on (see Fig. 8.59). The cost element *direct material costs* for the finished product thus includes all the costs of usage of the lower-level materials. The structure of this cost component split is defined in Customizing for product cost controlling with the aid of a cost component structure.

▪ *Cost of goods sold*
The cost of goods sold comprises those costs which arise as a result of the operational activity process. They are made up of the cost of goods manufactured, transportation and insurance costs and administrative costs. You can assign the transportation, insurance and administrative costs to a product in the R/3 System by creating an appropriate costing sheet in Customizing.

The costing process of a product costing *with quantity structure* is performed on the basis of production planning information, such as the data in the *bill of materials* and the *routing*. If the data for costing the products is entered manually, the costing process is known as a product costing *without quantity structure*. The standard cost estimate is used specifically to *calculate standard prices* for materials with price control indicator *S* (see Fig. 8.62). Once the standard cost estimate has been released, the standard price is adopted in the master record for the material and is thus valid for the internal material valuation.

8.9.3 Using the process

First of all, a costing variant must be defined for the product costing. The costing variant determines how the costing is carried out and valuated, as it is used to calculate the selected bills of material, routings, prices and overheads. The material is then specified together with the associated plant to which the costing applies. You can enter a lot size for the costing for this material in the *Costing lot size* field (see Fig. 8.56). If no lot size is specified, the system adopts the costing lot size defined in the costing view of the material master record. The costing version serves to differentiate costings for the same material with different quantity structures. The validity period, the quantity structure date and the valuation date of the costing are specified in the control data. The quantity structure date is the date on which the bills of material and the routings are selected. The valuation date is the date on which the materials and activities are valuated in the costing. Finally, the costing is formatted on the screen and various reports can be started.

8.9.4 Navigation information

▨ *Menu path*
Accounting –> Controlling –> Product cost accounting –> Product costing –> Costing –> With quantity structure –> Create

▨ *Transaction code*
CK11, CK20, CK21, CK22, CK23

▨ *Ingoing processes in the R/3 Reference Model*
Preliminary product costing
Material master processing for costing
Cost centre plan closing with static/flexible standard costing
Cost centre planning with overhead calculation

▨ *Outgoing processes in the R/3 Reference Model*
Standard costing analysis
Profitability planning
Billing document transfer and billing valuation

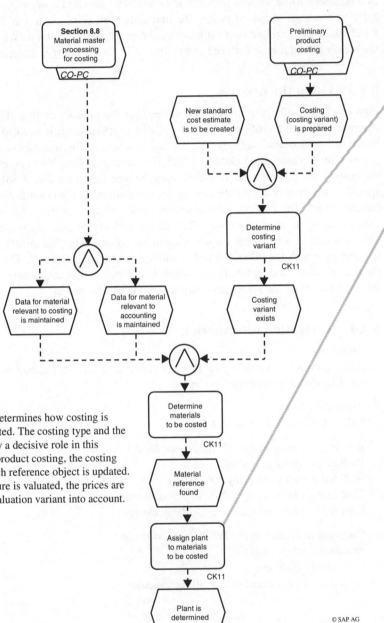

Section 8.8
Material master
processing
for costing

CO-PC

Preliminary
product
costing

CO-PC

New standard
cost estimate
is to be created

Costing
(costing variant)
is prepared

Determine
costing
variant

CK11

Data for material
relevant to costing
is maintained

Data for material
relevant to
accounting
is maintained

Costing
variant
exists

Costing Variant

The costing variant determines how costing is
carried out and valuated. The costing type and the
valuation variant play a decisive role in this
process. In unit and product costing, the costing
type determines which reference object is updated.
If the quantity structure is valuated, the prices are
selected taking the valuation variant into account.

Determine
materials
to be costed

CK11

Material
reference
found

Assign plant
to materials
to be costed

CK11

Plant is
determined

© SAP AG

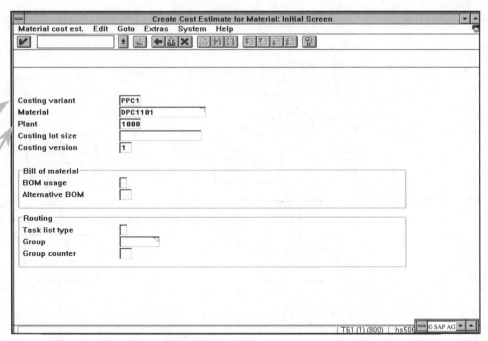

Fig. 8.56: Initial screen cost estimate for material

Unit and Production Costing

Costing can take place either in accordance with the reference object or as unit or product costing. Create a product costing if you want to determine the planning costs of the production of a material. In product costing, the costing variant determines how the bill of material (BOM) and routings are to be selected to determine the quantity structure, which prices are to be selected to valuate the quantity structure and how overhead rates are fixed. Create a unit costing if you want to determine the planning costs for material, CO production orders, internal orders, WBS elements, base objects, cost object IDs or sales documents. In unit costing, the costing variant determines which prices are to be selected in order to valuate the individual costing items and how overhead rates are fixed. Moreover, costing variants are used to determine the costs of production orders, networks, maintenance orders, make-to-stock orders and process orders.

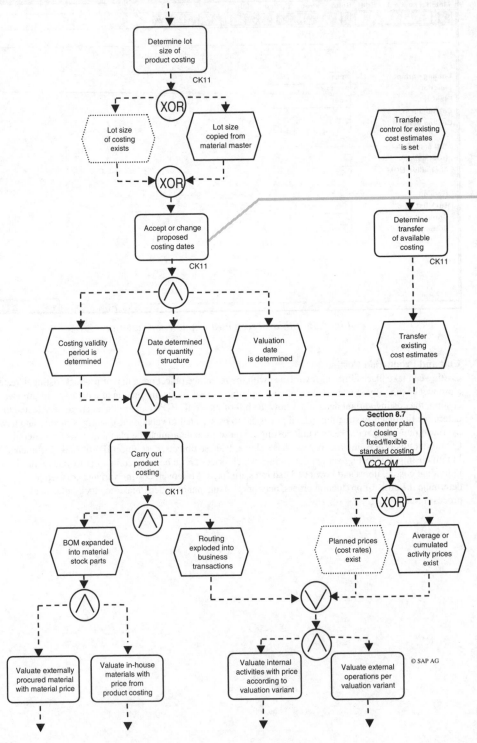

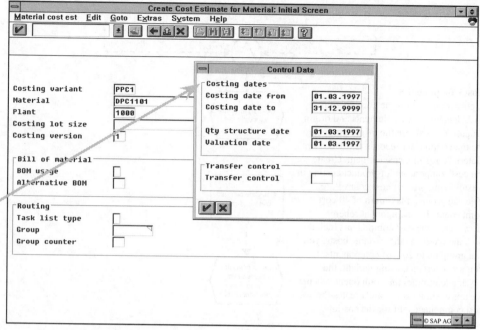

Fig. 8.57: Control data of cost estimate for material

Carrying out Product Costing

If you carry out product costing, the system creates a quantity structure by selecting and exploding exactly one BOM and one routing. The quantity structure indicates the following data:

– which operations and sub-operations are carried out in order to produce the material
– which activities are to be done in order to carry out these operations
– which material components are needed
– which operations are processed externally
– which materials are processed externally.

If various production alternatives are displayed in production planning (PP), several BOMs and routings might exist for one material in the system.

Cost Component
A cost component is the combination of cost elements or cost elements and origin groups. You can use the origin groups in the material master records to divide the material costs of a cost element. Create the cost components for product costing in Customizing product cost controlling. You can group a maximum of 40 cost components in a component scheme. However, if the cost components include both the fixed and the variable costs, you can group up to 20 cost components. If you use a certain costing variant, the system determines the component scheme for this costing variant and creates the cost component split for the costing results.

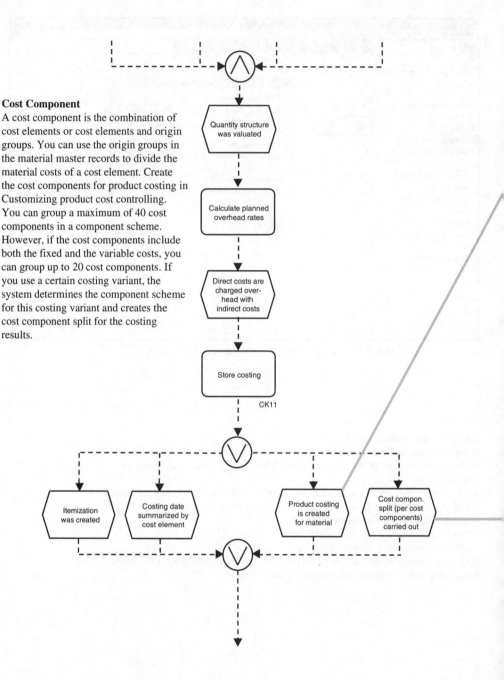

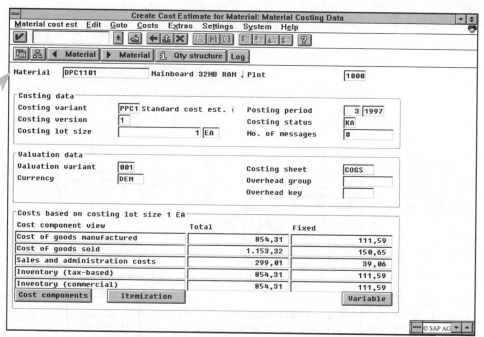

Fig. 8.58: Costing data of material "DPC1101"

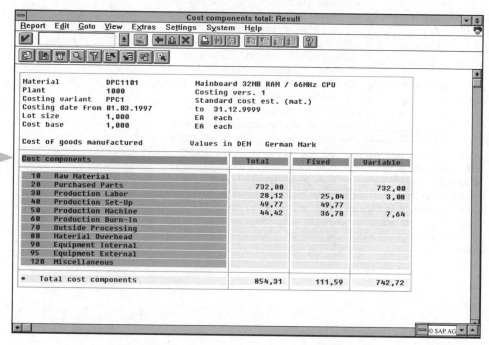

Fig. 8.59: Cost components of material "DPC1101"

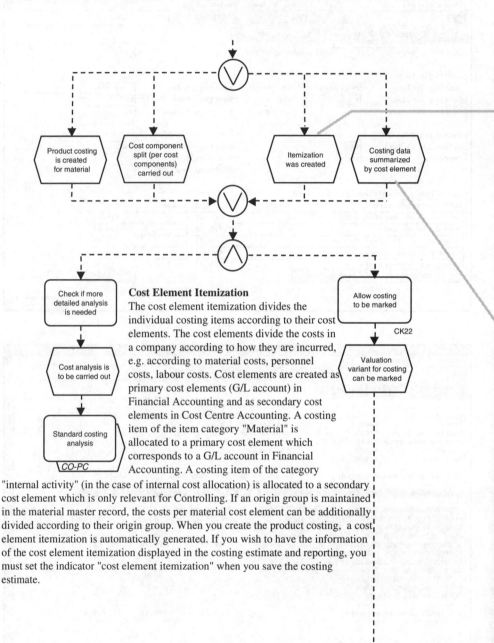

Cost Element Itemization

The cost element itemization divides the individual costing items according to their cost elements. The cost elements divide the costs in a company according to how they are incurred, e.g. according to material costs, personnel costs, labour costs. Cost elements are created as primary cost elements (G/L account) in Financial Accounting and as secondary cost elements in Cost Centre Accounting. A costing item of the item category "Material" is allocated to a primary cost element which corresponds to a G/L account in Financial Accounting. A costing item of the category "internal activity" (in the case of internal cost allocation) is allocated to a secondary cost element which is only relevant for Controlling. If an origin group is maintained in the material master record, the costs per material cost element can be additionally divided according to their origin group. When you create the product costing, a cost element itemization is automatically generated. If you wish to have the information of the cost element itemization displayed in the costing estimate and reporting, you must set the indicator "cost element itemization" when you save the costing estimate.

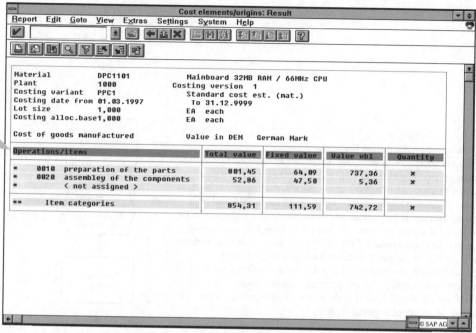

Fig. 8.60: Itemization for material "DPC1101"

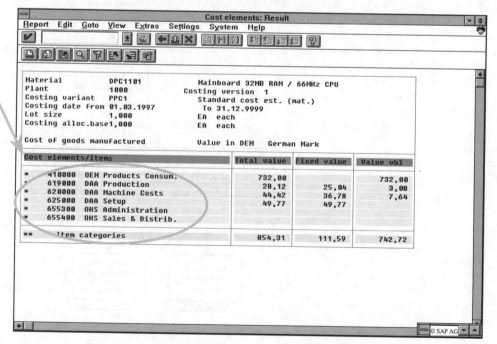

Fig. 8.61: Summary of calculation data by cost elements

Marking a Standard Cost Estimate

Allowing standard cost estimates determines the company code and posting period in which a costing estimate can be marked with a certain valuation variant. You cannot mark costing estimates with another valuation variant in this period. After having allowed for a costing estimate to be marked, you can transfer the costing results to the material master as future standard price. However, you can only transfer the costing results if the costing has been carried out with the given valuation variant. You can mark the costing estimate repeatedly until you have released it. If you have allowed for the cost estimate to be marked with an incorrect valuation variant, you can cancel the allowance as well as the results in all material master records by means of a special report.

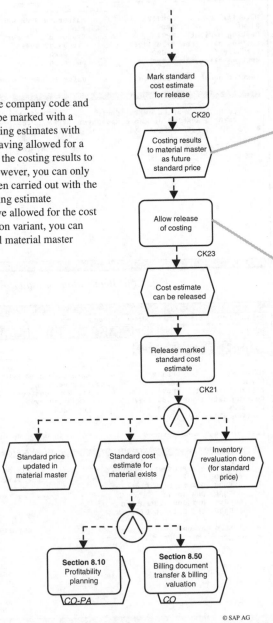

© SAP AG

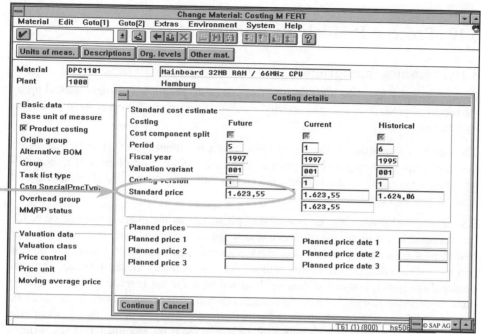

Fig. 8.62: Costing result as future standard price

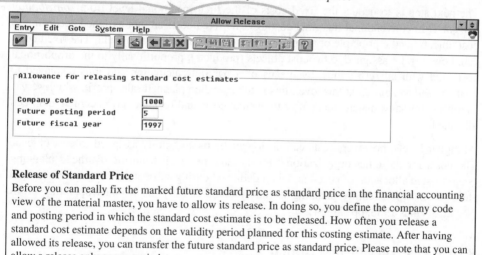

Fig. 8.63: Release of standard price

Release of Standard Price

Before you can really fix the marked future standard price as standard price in the financial accounting view of the material master, you have to allow its release. In doing so, you define the company code and posting period in which the standard cost estimate is to be released. How often you release a standard cost estimate depends on the validity period planned for this costing estimate. After having allowed its release, you can transfer the future standard price as standard price. Please note that you can allow a release only once a period.

8.10 Process: Profitability planning

8.10.1 Business background

Future-oriented goals, which are derived from strategic planning – possibly backed up by the results of production cost and activity planning – are crucial for operational profitability planning.

The aspect of responsibility for the operating profit is extremely important, which means that profitability planning must be structured primarily on the basis of areas of responsibility (profit centres, divisions, regions, and so on) and only secondarily according to cost object and production criteria.

It is an essential prerequisite of profitability planning that the planned revenue be calculated separately for each area of responsibility (market segment) and cost object. In the first step of contribution margin accounting, revenue reductions and directly assignable special costs are deducted from this planned revenue to obtain the net revenue. The proportional (marginal) costs must then be deducted from the net revenue, in order to determine contribution margin 1. The proportional, planned costs of goods manufactured can be estimated either via a so-called operating performance analysis or via the standard cost estimate. The latter method is undoubtedly the rule in industrial manufacturing enterprises.

The next step is to deduct the fixed costs of the first operational level from *contribution margin 1*. In conventional marginal costings, the fixed costs are not assigned according to cost objects, as the principle of source-related allocation cannot be upheld. The fixed costs can, however, be assigned to the cost objects (products), proportionally to the proportional costs and with all restrictions, by means of a parallel calculation and thus displayed to *contribution margin 2*. At this level, this is the so-called planned sales profit, which serves as a basis for sales management after the actual costs and revenue have accrued and been allocated.

At higher levels, however, costs can no longer be meaningfully assigned to cost objects. The costs for the other organizational levels must be taken from the overhead planning (step-by-step allocation of costs) and then deducted during subsequent contribution margin steps, so that profitability planning is finally completed by the planned operating profit (see also Vikas 1988, pp. 71–84).

8.10.2 SAP-specific description

A sales/profitability plan can be drawn up within the framework of CO-PA planning. Whereas with the actual data both types of profitability analysis (costing-based and accounting-based) are supplied in parallel, there is no common planning for the two analysis types with the planning data, in other words the user plans either

- in the form of accounts, or

- according to value fields.

Thanks to the automatic valuation of planned sales volumes in sales planning, it is possible to calculate both planned revenue and planned revenue reductions/planned costs of goods manufactured for the costing-based profitability analysis, and thus to arrive at a *planned operating profit.*

Interactive planning supports freely definable planning masks, with reference data display, formula calculations, forecasting methods and other functions. The planning can take place at any summarization level. Planning data can automatically be broken down on lower levels (top-down distribution).

The planning level for manual entry or automatic revision of planning data is freely selectable. In particular, it is not necessary to have an integrated planning level. Nevertheless, there is a consistent data set at all levels. The planning can thus be parameterized for an individual planning scenario, regardless of whether it was carried out centrally or locally, or at an aggregated or very detailed level. When a profitability segment is planned, the existing planning data for this segment and that for the segments below it are totalled according to the bottom-up principle. The planning is not linked to a specific period. Consequently, both multiple-year and rolling-year planning can be mapped. Moreover, planning values can be entered on the basis either of accounting *posting periods* or of calendar weeks.

If an annual value is entered, it is always distributed internally between *periods.* The annual values are distributed proportionally to the existing values by default. If no values exist as yet, they are distributed uniformly.

If a particular *seasonal distribution* is desired, a different distribution key can be defined in the task level menu. Each period is assigned a relative factor, according to which the entered planning values are distributed. A factor of zero is implicitly set for all periods to which no values have been assigned. The number of periods in the year is determined according to the operating concern, in other words the fiscal year variant of this concern. If the weekly planning for the operating concern is active while the system is being set, you must decide whether the distribution series should be used for period planning or for weekly planning. If a seasonal distribution that is repeated every year is mapped, the data for any year is entered and the *Cyclic* field is marked. This only applies to distribution keys based on posting periods.

8.10.3 Using the process

Valuation strategies are stored for the various plan versions within the framework of sales and profitability planning preparation. These are the controlling elements for valuating the previously planned sales volumes. It is possible to draw up several different plan versions. Different data for the same object can thus be managed in parallel.

CO-PA planning permits both *manual entry* and *automatic processing* of your profitability planning data. In particular, you can plan your revenue and revenue reductions manually, by means of an automatic valuation or retrospectively according to the relationship between the planning costs and the contribution margin. The automatic valuation can be controlled either by a costing-based valuation schema of CO-PA or by the price determination schema used for the actual evaluation (see Fig. 8.65).

The costs can also be calculated using a *valuation schema*. If a standard cost estimate is available for the product that is to be sold, it can be used to determine the cost of the goods sold. The cost elements in the standard cost estimate are entered in the value fields of the profitability analysis according to the assignments in Customizing. A detailed verification of the exact make-up of the cost of goods sold can thus be carried out in reporting.

Alternatively, the planned sales volumes can be valuated with the allocation price in the material master. Either the standard price or the average periodic unit price is taken, depending on the price control.

You can edit either a complete plan or parts of a plan automatically. It is possible, among other things, to copy between plan versions, or from actual data to planning data, or to distribute the data top-down from a higher planning level to a more detailed level. You can, for example, initially carry out planning at the product range level and then break it down into products (see Fig. 8.67). The planning data is distributed proportionally to the existing reference data. Both planning data and actual data can be used. The distribution can be either period-specific or – in order to compensate for variations – based on cumulated period values. The planning data is distributed according to a selected value field.

The *Top-Down Distribution* function permits a large number of planned profitability segments to be edited automatically and – like all the overall planning functions – can run either online or in the background. The appropriate authorization is required for these functions. The jobs for background processing can be scheduled directly in the dialog transaction. If an error occurs, it is reported in an error log. You can display the incorrect objects in this log.

Finally, you can check that the structure of the profitability plan is correct before you adopt it and block it. Unlike the online planning validation function, which simply checks whether or not a planning object is within the structure, the periodic check is very strict. All the planning data must not only be within the structure, but also at the end nodes of the plan structure. In other words, planning must be complete (including, for example, top-down distribution of planning data that was originally stored at a higher level).

The plan is normally validated against the plan structure in the background. If only a small amount of data is involved (validation of a branch), this function can also be executed online, however.

If the function is activated online, a two-part error log is generated if an error occurs. The first list contains an overview of the structure of the incorrect planning records. You can jump from this list to the graphic, in which the branch concerned is highlighted in colour and the error is described in more detail. Various profitability segments (e.g. division, XYZ, material group A and division XYZ, material group B) may be concealed behind the listed error (e.g. division XYZ does not exist in the structure). These profitability segments are displayed after an error is picked up in the first part of the log.

If background processing is selected, the error log contains both lists. Processing is terminated, however, if there are more than 100 incorrect profitability segments, because it is likely that the plan structure contains a systematic error (the complete division XYZ has not been input).

The costs planned for cost centres can be taken into account in the profitability analysis in the same way as actual cost centre costs are assessed.

8.10.4 Navigation information

▨ *Menu path*
Accounting –> Controlling –> Profit. analysis –> Planning –> Change plan data

▨ *Transaction code*
KE11, KE1G, KEPP

▨ *Ingoing processes in the R/3 Reference Model*
Profitability planning
Sales planning
Preparation for sales and profitability planning
Preliminary costing with quantity structure
Transfer of fixed cost centre costs/balances
Transfer of full cost centre costs/balances

▨ *Outgoing processes in the R/3 Reference Model*
Profitability planning

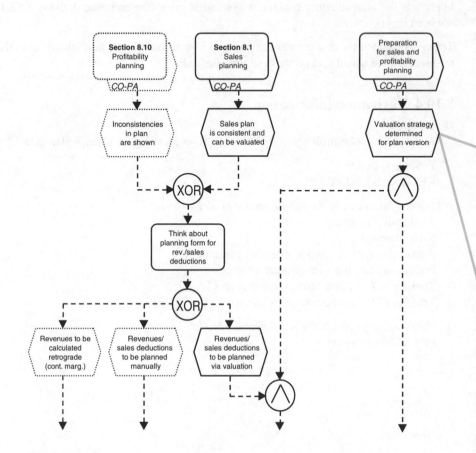

Valuation Strategy

The valuation strategy determines the methods of valuation that the system applies and the order in which they are applied. The order of the different methods is not fixed. For example, you can valuate data first using conditions, then a user exit, then a standard cost estimate followed by another user exit. You can also use the results of one valuation method as the basis for the next method. To be able to valuate actual data, you must assign a valuation strategy to a combination of a point of valuation and a record type. To valuate plan data, you must assign a valuation strategy to the point of valuation together with a record type and a plan version.

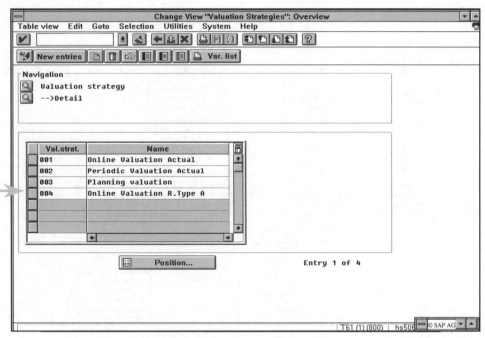

Fig. 8.64: Customizing of valuation strategy

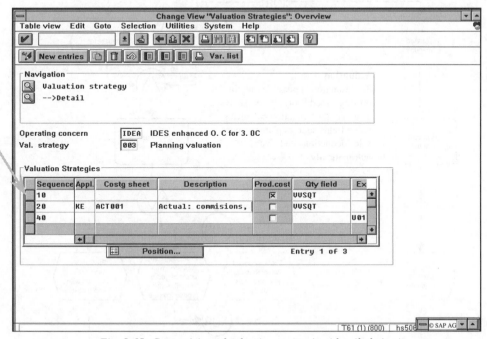

Fig. 8.65: Customizing of valuation strategies (detailed view)

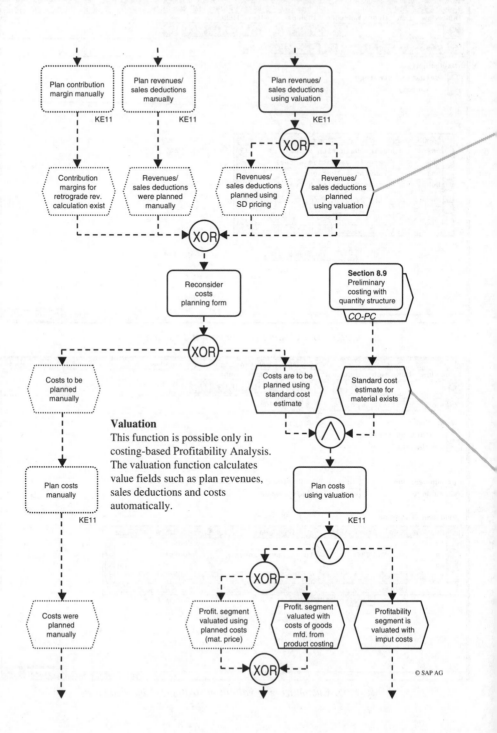

Valuation
This function is possible only in costing-based Profitability Analysis. The valuation function calculates value fields such as plan revenues, sales deductions and costs automatically.

© SAP AG

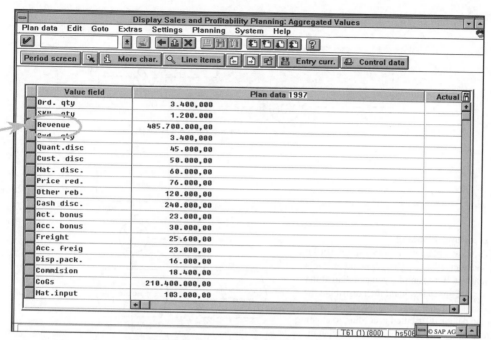

Fig. 8.66: Revenues planned using valuation

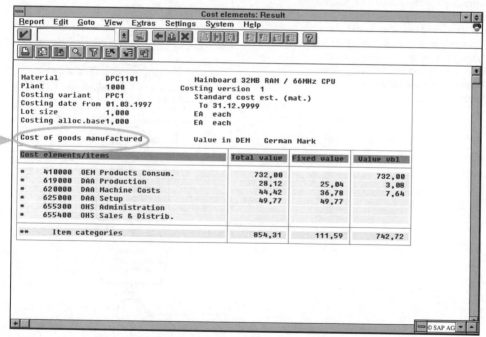

Fig. 8.67: Standard cost estimate for material DPC1101

Top-Down Planning

Top-down planning allows you to distribute data planned at a higher level to the levels below it. For example, you can plan at the product group level and then distribute the plan data to the individual products. The plan data is distributed according to existing reference data. You can use either plan or actual data as a reference. You can also distribute period by period, or aggregate the period values to smooth variances. If you enter the special character *, you can distribute a number of objects within one planning run. With respect to its user interface and detail functions, top-down planning is very similar to other functions of total planning.

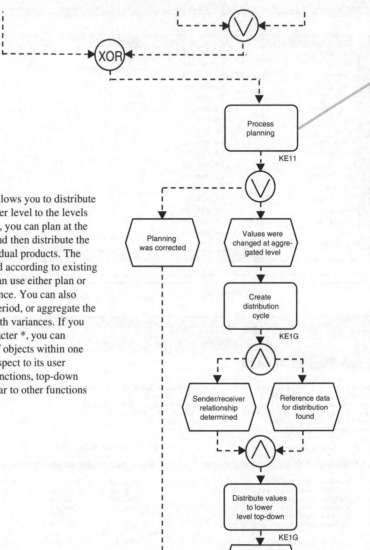

© SAP AG

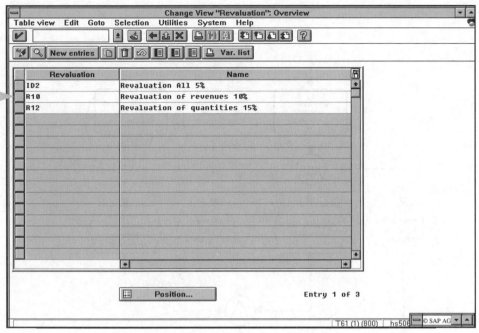

Fig. 8.68: Definition of revaluation

Revaluation

This function is only possible with costing-based Profitability Analysis. Choose the function *Revaluation* when you want to calculate surcharges or deductions for value fields. As with *Valuation*, you need to select the profitability segments you want to revaluate before you execute the function. You enter the desired revaluation factor in a dialog box. The function *Define revaluation* is an optional planning aid which can make it easier for you to enter plan data. A revaluation defines percentage surcharges or deductions for the value fields in an operating concern. To maintain the revaluation, enter a revaluation factor for each value field which you want to change. If you want to decrease the value in a particular field, you must enter a negative revaluation factor. If you want to base your 1998 plan on the 1997 actual data plus 5%, for example, choose the function *New lines* and enter the value fields for which you want to calculate a surcharge. Enter "5", for example, in each field in the *Percentage* column and then save your entries.

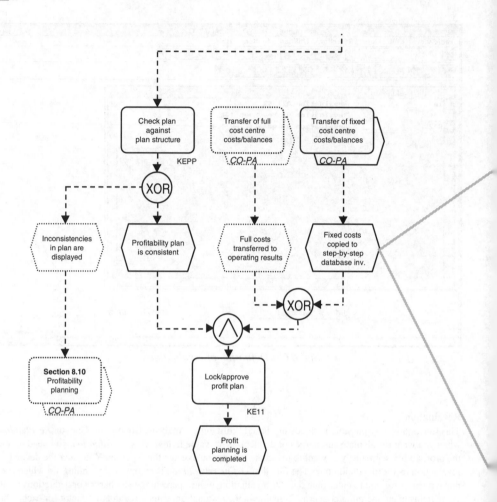

Assessment

To reflect all the actual costs from cost centre accounting in profitability analysis, you must transfer the cost centre costs which are not directly attributable to the production process. You can transfer these costs to any profitability segment and thus assign them to any level of the contribution margin hierarchies. Fixed costs from cost centres are allocated to the operating profit by means of the assessment. In the assessment costs are taken into account that are not directly involved in the value process of the product, e.g. assessment of the management board.

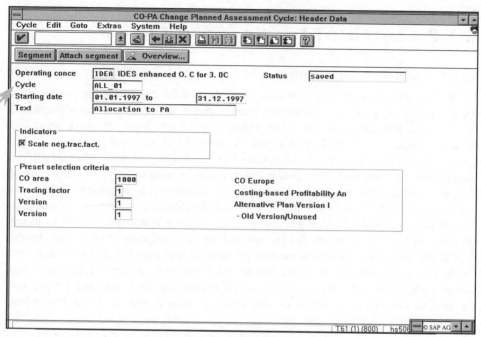

Fig. 8.69: Assessment cycle

Fig. 8.70: Cost centre management board for assessment

8.11 Process: Material master processing PP

8.11.1 Business background

The material master record is a central piece of data within the production process. It is related in many ways to other important pieces of master data important for efficient and correct production planning. The word material is used to mean all goods used and produced within an industrial organization. A material can, however, also be a trading good, for example in a retail, distribution or wholesale business. The identifying characteristic of a material is the unique material number assigned to the material. Apart from this identification number, further descriptive information is assigned to the material (see Kilger 1986, S. 284–296). Within a sales and distribution environment, for example, the product description and possible discounts are of great importance, within a costing environment the costing records for the material are more important, and the purchasing department within an organization requires information about the replenishment lead time and the purchase order quantity in order to be able to obtain the lowest purchase price and storage costs. In the following overview, we will explain the highly integrative aspects of the material master record within the logistics process and refer to the corresponding processes in which it is involved.

The structural relationships between the individual materials which are used in an assembly or final product are described in a bill of material. The bill of material describes the relationship between these materials and whether a material is higher or lower in the structure in comparison with another material or assembly. Apart from structural relationships, the bill of material describes the quantities of the material necessary for the production of a final product or assembly, and also the offset times of individual components within an assembly (see Section 8.12). The geometrical relationships of a material are represented in a drawing. In addition, further documents, such as a patent notification, can exist, relating to the material (see Glaser *et al.* 1991, S. 10–13).

The information contained in a drawing includes:

- *Geometry details*
  Sizes, shapes and views of a material

- *Technological details*
  Shape tolerances, surface details

- *Drawing-related, organizational information*
  Drawing number, responsible clerk, reference to related detailed drawings

- *Material-related, organizational information*
  Identification number, classification, description

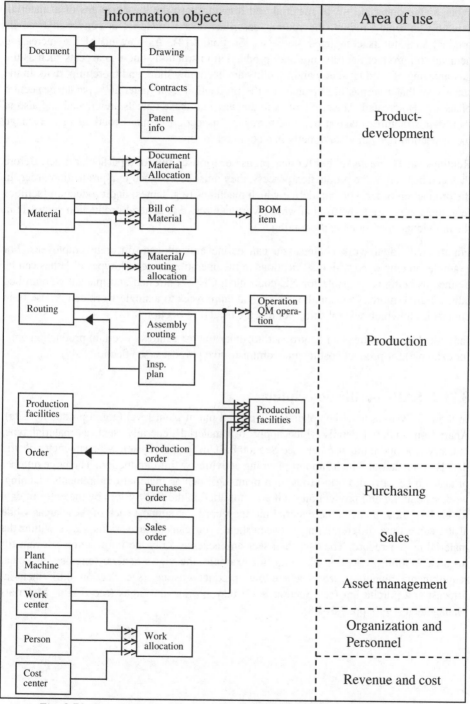

Fig. 8.71: Structural relationships between important pieces of master data

Whereas the material, bill of material and drawing describe the attributes of a material, assembly or final product, the routing describes how a material is converted from its original state to its completed state (see Section 8.14). As a result of the increasing demands on product liability, not only production instructions but also aspects such as the guaranteeing of product safety and usability are becoming more and more important. In the same way that routings are created for the production of a material, separate inspection plans are also created. The similarities in the way that these objects are created and also in their data structures make it possible to regard inspection plans as routings or to manage the inspection-relevant data directly in a common routing.

Routings can be created either for general use or for use only for a particular order. Before they can be used in the production process, they must be assigned to a production order. In the production order, you can define which machines (e.g. lathes) and production facilities (e.g. tools, jigs) are to be used at which work centres (e.g. general production centre 1) in the individual operations in the routing.

For the individual work centres you can define and allocate different employees. For example, an employee with qualifications in the operation of certain types of lathes can be defined as being responsible for NC-controlled, CNC-controlled and manually controlled lathes. Furthermore, you can allocate several employees to a single work centre, useful in companies in which several shifts per day are used (see Section 8.13).

Individual work centres can be grouped together to cost centres (a certain production area, for example) for product costing and administrative purposes (see Section 8.44).

8.11.2 SAP-specific description

In the R/3 System, materials planning is carried out at plant level (e.g. a production site). Apart from material details which apply to a material generally, such as material type, industry type and number range (see Section 8.8), in the R/3 System you can enter specific details of a material which support planning activities within production. The large number of tasks to be carried out in production planning, such as material requirements planning, work scheduling and production itself are supported in the R/3 System by the entry of data for each of these areas in the material master record. To support each of these areas while at the same time differentiating between them, you can create various views within the material master record. The user then sees and accesses only the information relevant for his area. Within production planning, for example, the views general (engineering) data, requirements planning, work scheduling, product costing (see Section 8.8), material forecast and purchasing (see Section 8.20) may be relevant areas (see SAP – Materials Management 1996, pp. 3.5–3.8).

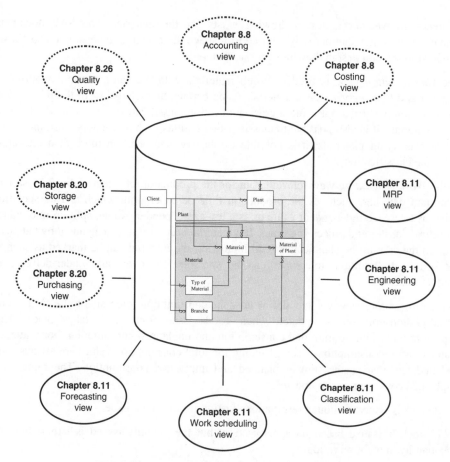

Fig. 8.72: Production planning view of a material

In the *MRP view* you define how a material is procured, planned and controlled within production. The *procurement type* specifies whether a material is to be procured externally or produced in-house, or whether both procurement sources are possible. In the *MRP controller* field, you specify who is responsible for planning the material. The *MRP procedure* determines whether consumption-based planning (stochastic planning, reorder point planning) or deterministic (plan-driven) planning is to be used for a given material (see Section 8.18). Further attributes in the MRP view of a material include the strategy group, which is used to support differing planning situations at final product level for companies needing to deal with *make-to-order, production to stock* and *lot-size production* as well as to cover planning requirements at lower assembly levels such as *preplanning with final assembly, preplanning at assembly level*. Furthermore, the expiry indicator (phase-out indicator) can be used to control the point from which the material is no longer to be used.

The *Engineering view* allows the entry of data describing the material, such as gross weight with a unit of weight, a volume (with a corresponding unit of measure) and a reference to whether a design drawing exists for the material. The SAP document management system can not only be used to manage the design drawings, but also allows you to store several design drawings for one material.

The *Classification view* is used to group materials with the same or similar attributes together and to categorize these materials using certain characteristics. In the R/3 System classification is carried out using a cross-application classification system in which, apart from materials, it is also possible to classify other entities such as vendors, customers, etc. When classifying materials, it is possible to classify a material in more than one class (multiple classification).

In the *Work scheduling view* relevant data for the production of a material can be stored. Important data here includes the production time per operation, which can be specified either as a lot-size-independent value or as a lot-size-dependent value, split up into values for setup, transfer and processing times. If a material is subject to management by batch, as is often the case in the chemical or food industries, the material can be marked as such in the screen. In addition, tolerances can be specified for over- and under-delivery in production.

In the *Forecasting view* you can define how the consumption forecast is to be carried out. Usually, consumption is updated when goods issue from stock takes place. This consumption is split up into total consumption and unplanned consumption. For materials planned using consumption-based planning, the total consumption values are always used and updated, that is, the sum of planned and unplanned consumption. The figures for unplanned consumption are updated:

- if stock is issued without a reservation existing for the stock issue

- if stock is issued based on a reservation, but the quantity issued is larger than the quantity in the reservation

The period indicator tells you in which units of time the forecast and consumption values are to be stored. Using the forecast profile, the system determines how the requirements of a material are to be forecast. The R/3 System uses the constant model, the trend model, the seasonal model and the trend/seasonal model (see Section 8.18).

8.11.3 Using the process

In the model company, materials are created for various main circuit boards. In the MRP view, the existing basic data is extended by entering the data relevant for production. When creating a material master record, the following situations may take place:

- The material master record is created if no material record already exists for the material.

- Using the *Create* function, the material master record is extended if the material master record already exists and the data for a new department (view) has to be entered; this view, however, does not yet exist for the material.

- Using the *Create* function, the material master record is extended if the data for the department already exists, but the data has to be created for a new organizational area.

- The material master record is changed if new or changed data has to be entered in an existing view of a material.

Furthermore, if a similar material exists to the one which has to be created, the similar material master record can be used as a reference. In this way, the data of the existing material master record can be used as default values for the new material by copying data from the existing one and overwriting any data that needs to be changed. Any changes to a material master record, such as the date on which the change takes place or the name of the user carrying out the change, are logged. In the MRP view of the material master record in the model company, the basic data already created is extended by the data relevant for production. In the first screen, the MRP procedure defines how planning is to be carried out for main circuit board DPC1101, the specification of the person for planning the requirements of the material is made via the field MRP controller, the lot size indicator determines the procedure used to calculate the lot size for a requirement and the strategy group is used to define the planning strategies which can be used when planning requirements for the material.

The main circuit board is planned using plan-driven planning. For this reason, MRP type PD is entered. Since the model company produces requirements to stock, „30" is entered in the strategy group in the MRP view of the material. Furthermore, some additional data from work scheduling must be entered for production. Here, the setup, processing and transfer time must be entered for the lot-size-dependent production time.

8.11.4 Navigation information

- *Menu path*
  Logistics –> Materials management –> Material master –> Material –> Create

- *Transaction code*
  MM01

- *Ingoing processes in the R/3 Reference Model*
  Production resource and tool maintenance

- *Outgoing processes in the R/3 Reference Model*
  Production version processing

Material Requirements Planning (MRP) Type
By specifying the MRP type, you can determine
how a material is to be planned (e.g. see Fig. 8.73
"MRP fixing type").

Strategy Group
The strategy group is a key that specifies and
combines the planning strategies allowed for a
material.

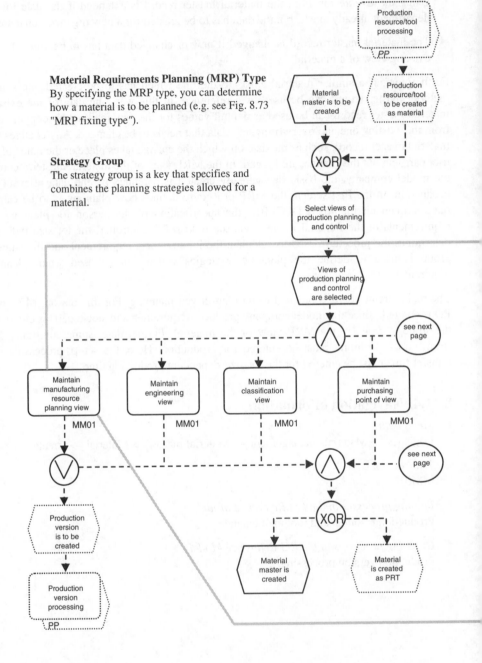

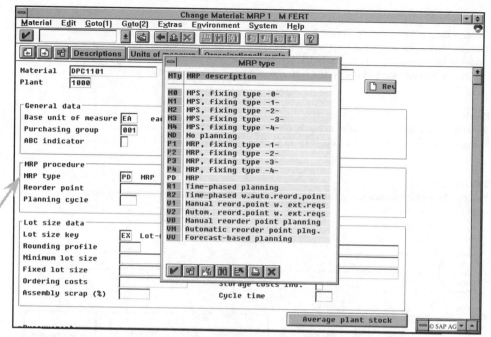

Fig. 8.73: Adjustment of MRP

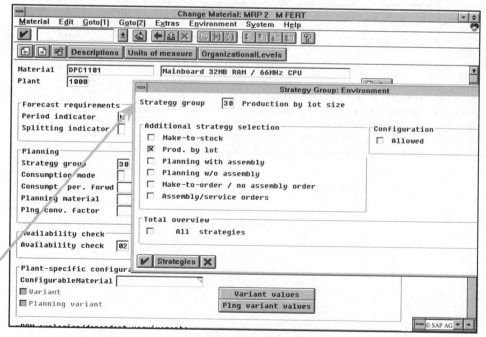

Fig. 8.74: Definition of strategy group for production by lot size

General Data of Work Scheduling
You can enter a unit of issue and a production unit that vary from the base unit of measure, a production scheduler, a production scheduler profile and an MM/PP status. Furthermore, you can specify an issue storage location and mark the material as a critical part.

Batch
If you want to manage the material in batches, you must set the indicator "batch management". You need this indicator in order to create batch master records.

Tolerance Data
You can define limit values for possible underdeliveries and overdeliveries in the shop floor area.

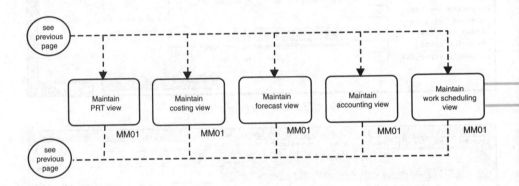

Indicating Data Relevant for Work Scheduling
You have two options. You can either enter the setup time, interoperation and processing time of the material in the field of *lot size dependent in-house production time*, as well as the base quantity to which the processing time refers, or you can enter the total production time in the field of *lot size independent in-house production time*.

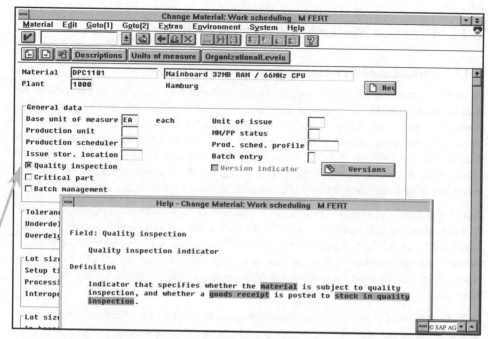

Fig. 8.75: Quality inspection indicator for goods receipt

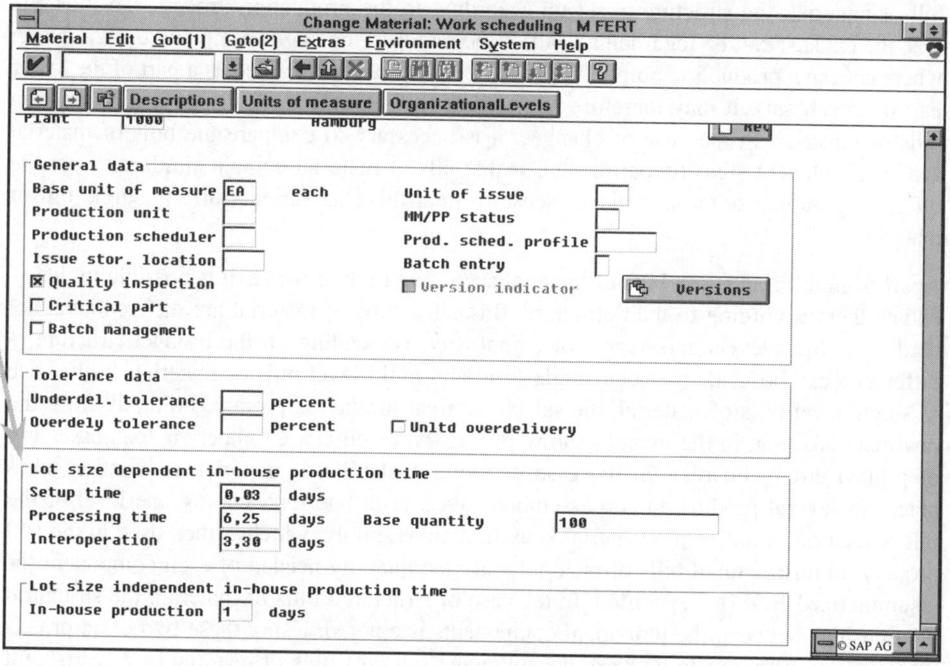

Fig. 8.76: Data relevant for work scheduling

8.12 Process: Material BOM processing

8.12.1 Business description

As with the material master record, the bill of material can also contain information for various areas. The bill of material contains the quantity of all the components such as assemblies, parts and raw materials needed in the production of a final product or an assembly. It also contains the structural relationships between the individual components (see Eversheim 1989, p. 26). The term bill of material in used in companies where the production takes place on a unit basis. In industries with process-oriented production (for example, in the food, chemical and pharmaceutical industry) the term recipe is used.

In order to carry out material requirements planning (bill of material explosion), information regarding the low-level code (BOM explosion level) quantity and offsetting lead time is required. For production scheduling, details of quantities in routings are needed, and in product costing quantity details are also necessary. The design department uses bill of material data as the basis for change management and in sales it is used in the planning of spare parts.

In many industrial companies, the administration and comparison of engineering and production bills of material plays a central role. In product development, products are structured according to functional points of view as in the drawing, whereas for the production bill of material, the structure is set up according to the production process. To illustrate this, the exhaust can be regarded as part of the motor in the engineering and design phase, whereas from a production point of view the exhaust can be regarded as a part of the lower part of the chassis. It may therefore be necessary to maintain both design and production bills of material. In the case of changes, it is necessary to compare the bills of material across all relevant areas (departments). If the bills of material contain similarities despite different grouping criteria, it makes sense to treat them as variants of one single bill of material.

Apart from differentiating bills of material according to their usage, it is possible to differentiate them according to their structure. Basically, bills of material are differentiated according to their levels and degree of complexity. Depending on the product structure, a difference can be made between single-level and multi-level bills of material. In the case of single-level bills of material, the salable or final product is produced directly from the raw materials (e.g. in the manufacturing of screws) or purchased materials (e.g. assembly of printed circuit boards). In the case of multi-level bills of material, production takes places in several production and assembly stages, each one representing one level of the bill of material. First, a raw material is used in an assembly, which is then used in the end product. In unstructured bills of material, only the quantity needed of each component (as a summarized BOM) is specified. In the case of structured bills of material, the structural relationships between the individual components is entered. Using these two basic principles, we can differentiate between the following types of bills of material (see Eversheim

1989, pp. 26–30; see Glaser *et al.* 1991, pp. 13–30; see Hackstein 1989, pp. 133–150; see Scheer 1990, pp. 79–113):

■ *Single-level bill of material*

The single-level bill of material contains assemblies and individual items assigned to the level immediately below the header material. The quantities of the items refer to the assembly defined in the BOM (bill of material) header. Due to the fact that the bill of material can be displayed using no more than two levels, it remains easy to display. The total view of a product containing assemblies on more than one level can, however, only be displayed using a multi-level BOM.

■ *Multi-level bill of material*

The multi-level bill of material displays the internal structure of a product with the logical relationships between the components in the whole multi-level bill of material. It shows all the assemblies and individual components needed in the production of the assembly or final component specified in the bill of material header, along with their required quantities on all levels of the bill of material.

■ *Summarized bill of material*

The summarized bill of material contains the quantities of all the subordinate assemblies and individual components needed in the production of the assembly or final component specified in the bill of material header, without any information regarding the structure of the bill of material.

■ *Variant bill of material*

Variant bills of material are used to illustrate similar product structures in which the differences between the individual bills of materials (variants) are limited to only a few bill of material items. The purpose of this is to avoid having to maintain a new set of information for each variant and thus to reduce the storage requirements and maintenance effort to a minimum.

Which bill of material type is to be used depends, among other factors, on the purpose of the bill of material. Multi-level bills of material are used primarily within the BOM explosion and are often used in mechanical engineering companies, especially where special machines and larger machines are produced. Summarized bills of material are often used for product costing purposes, in simple production and assembly bills of material and the creation of requirements, whereby only the quantity requirements for individual components and raw materials need to be determined. Single-level bills of material are often used in mechanical engineering companies such as in the manufacture of semi-standardized product groups, or in the case of multi-level serial parts with a high level of standardization. Variant bills of material are used in companies whose range of products is based on similar products with a high proportion of common parts. Included in this area are manufacturers of machines or products with standard variants.

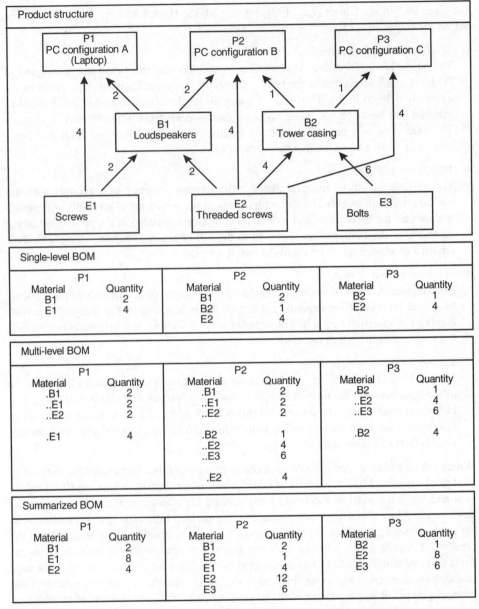

Fig. 8.77: Product structure and bill of material types

Whereas the bill of material provides information about which components are needed in the production of the material contained in the bill of material header, in some situations it is necessary to investigate in which assemblies a certain component is used. The component where-used list provides, as its name suggests, information on the assemblies in which a certain component is used. The person engaged in the design of a product, for example, needs to know this information to be able to work out what effects a change carried out on a standard part might have on other components. Additionally, in the case of problems in production, it is possible to determine which production processes are affected by a change, and preventive measures can be taken.

8.12.2 SAP-specific description

In the R/3 System bills of material are defined in the production planning area. The bill of material structure consists of a bill of material header, in which for example the allocation of the bill of material to a plant, the validity period and the status (released, blocked for production purposes) are specified, and a part containing the bill of material items. The item category divides the items into various groups. Some of the item categories are relevant for planning and production purposes, others simply have an informational character. Bills of material can be used in the SAP System to represent various objects (e.g. material, equipment, functional locations, documents). The main item categories predefined in the R/3 System are as follows:

- ■ **L for stock items**
  Stock items are components that can be stored in stock and can be seen in inventory management. Partial quantities of a BOM item can be defined. These differ in the locations in which they are used. The various locations are represented in the BOM by sub-items. Sub-items have no operative importance in the bill of material and are not taken over into the production order.

- ■ **N for non-stock items**
  Non-stock item means that the material is procured directly for the production order and does not go into stock. As a result of this, non-stock items are always integrated directly in the purchasing process. If the bill of material contains a non-stock item for which a cost element has been created, the system carries out a check. If the cost element is a primary cost element, the system checks whether the G/L account it determines exists in the corresponding company code. The system finds the appropriate company code using the plant to which the bill of material is to be assigned and the valuation area assigned to the plant. Secondary cost elements are only maintained in cost accounting.

- ■ **R for variable-sized items**
  When this item category is entered, the system can automatically determine the exact quantity of the material needed using the sizes entered by the user and a predefined formula.

- ■ **I for PM structure element**
  In a maintenance bill of material there are items relating to the engineering structure of

the equipment (PM assembly). No plant data is required for such materials. Therefore, no plant check is carried out for materials with this item category. Items with this item category should only be used in maintenance bills of material (e.g. equipment BOM, material BOMs used in maintenance, functional location BOM).

■ *T for Text item*
A text item has an informational character. Various texts can be attached to items with this item category.

■ *M for phantom material*
This item category is important in the process industry (planning recipe). Materials that only appear temporarily in the production process are entered as components with this item category.

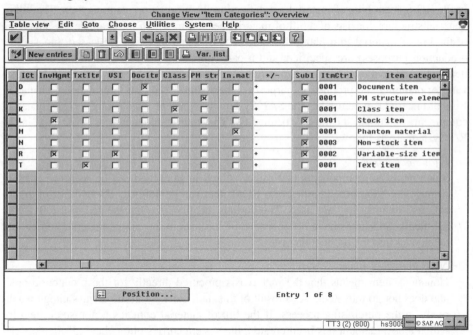

Fig. 8.78: Customizing the possible item categories in the bill of material

In the R/3 System the following bill of material types exist:

■ *Simple material BOM*
The simple bill of material describes the structure of a final product or an assembly via the bill of material items. When a bill of material is to be created for a certain plant, a series of checks takes place. A material master record with the corresponding plant data must exist for the bill of material header material. When BOM items are entered, the system checks whether each of the material components has been created in the relevant plant. For a material whose BOM is to be allocated to another plant, the material must also exist in the other plant to which the BOM is to be allocated. One impor-

tant thing to note is that only simple bills of material can be converted into variant bills of material. This means that a multiple bill of material cannot be converted into a variant bill of material.

■ *Variant bill of material*

A variant can be described as a change to a basic structure of a product, which is created by removing or adding components. The variant bill of material allows you to create several variants for each item. This makes sense when several similar products are produced, whose component parts only vary slightly. Variant bills of material are always created, as the name implies, as a variant of an existing bill of material. Variant bills of material fall into one of the following bill of material categories:

- Material BOMs

- Document BOMs

- Equipment BOMs

- Functional location BOMs

Several products, created as variants in a variant bill of material, are grouped together in a BOM group and stored in the system under one and the same internal number. All of the variants of a variant bill of material can be recognized via the BOM group (bill of material header). This means that:

- as soon as one of the bills of material in the BOM group is processed, all of the other variants are blocked for processing

- if one variant is changed with reference to a change number, all of the other variants in the BOM group must also be processed with reference to a change number

■ *Multiple bill of material*

In order to save costs, it might make sense to manufacture a product using various different production processes. Depending on the size of an order, it might make sense to process a very large order on a highly integrated and automated production line, whereas a smaller order could be produced more cost-effectively on normal machines due to the lower setup costs involved. Multiple bills of material allow the allocation of different production versions to the individual items. A multiple BOM groups several bills of material together, in order to be able to describe an object (product) in different compositions (alternatives) for the different production processes. A product can be produced in a different way with a different composition depending on the quantity to be produced (lot size). The alternatives of the bill of material usually only differ slightly, and then often in the component quantities. The R/3 System can suggest a production alternative depending on the planned lot size. Multiple bills of material are only used for material BOMs.

■ *Configurable bills of material*

A configurable bill of material is used to represent a product with a large number of variants in a so-called maximum bill of material. An example of this might be the various models of a car. The maximum bill of material contains, apart from the common components needed in all variants, all those components that might be needed in any particular variant. During configuration at the time of customer order entry, the system selects both the common and the suitable variant parts for the configurable material. The maintenance of a bill of material for a configurable product takes place in the same way as for a normal material BOM. However, there are some special features that have to be mentioned. The *configurable bill of material* is created for a *configurable material.* Whether or not a material is configurable can be defined in the customizing settings for the material type (this then applies to *all* the materials with this material type) or it can de defined for an *individual* material by making the appropriate entry in the *engineering view* of the material master record (see Section 8.11). The bill of material *usage* influences the explosion of the bill of material for a specific application area. This means that the bill of material must be meant for use in the particular application in which it is to be exploded, for example a customer order bill of material in sales. When creating a configurable bill of material, *all* of the components, that might be needed in the production of any possible variant of the bill of material, have to be entered as bill of material items (maximum BOM). The components that are only needed in certain variants have to be assigned selection conditions. For example, for stock materials a bill of material with variants only makes sense if selection criteria are entered which enable the variant parts to be selected. If no selection criteria are entered (no value assignment is made), the bill of material cannot be exploded correctly. The components with selection conditions attached to them are then not selected and the system only selects the common (non-variant) parts. Thus for a stockable material for which no value assignment has taken place in the material master record, the first step should be to create a bill of material without variant (selectable) items. Only when the variants are created should the variant parts be added to the bill of material and be assigned dependency knowledge. To help with the configuration process, so-called configuration profiles can be created in the R/3 System. A configuration profile contains characteristics which describe attributes of the material (for example, in the case of a car the characteristics *model, colour, accessories*), and describe the possible combinations of the characteristic values by means of object dependencies (dependency knowledge). Such a dependency could say that no air-conditioning (value of characteristic *accessories*) is allowed for (characteristic) *model* (value) *815.*

8.12.3 Using the process

In the model company the structure of the main circuit board *DPC1101* is represented by means of a simple bill of material. This bill of material is allocated to plant *1000* in Hamburg. Under certain circumstances you can allocate the bill of material to further plants (function *Create plant allocation*). In order to define the BOM usage, various typical usages have been defined in the customizing part of the R/3 System. In our example, the bill of material is only relevant for production. If the material for which you want to create a bill of material has a material type which is not allowed in combination with the usage you enter, an error message is issued. The bill of material is to be valid as from 11.02.1997. If you want to create the bill of material *without reference to a change number*, don't enter anything in field *Change number*. Enter the date from which the bill of material is to be valid in the system in field *Valid from*. Enter a *Change number* if the bill of material can only be changed using a change number from the moment it is created. The bill of material can then only be changed or extended when using a change number. Generally, bills of material are only processed using a change number after they have been released for production. The generally valid validity date can be replaced by another valid-from date for a special change to an object. For this, you need to create a date element and allocate the date element to one or more change objects. For the main circuit board in the example three items are to be created with item category *L* (see Fig. 8.81). This means that all three items are stockable items. In the individual items it is possible to use a different valid-from date to the one used for the whole bill of material (bill of material header). It is also possible, at any time, to enter a new item (e.g. as the result of a design change) along with its validity date in the bill of material before the validity date is reached. If several identical resistors of a circuit board are used in various places within the circuit board production, you can enter data regarding the location, exact coordinates, the type of assembly and the type of machine control as sub-items (field SIs). In Fig. 8.82 material *DPC1014* is defined as an MPS item. This is done by entering *M0* for MPS parts in the MRP type field in the MRP screen of the material master record (see Section 8.17, MPS planning). The two screen excerpts on the right show the material master record with the MRP type. The base unit *pc* is taken over automatically from the material master record.

8.12.4 Navigation information

- *Menu path*
  Logistics –> Production –> Master data –> Bills of material

- *Transaction code*
  CS00, CS01

- *Ingoing processes in the R/3 Reference Model*
  none

- *Outgoing processes in the R/3 Reference Model*

BOM Usage

Many companies have only one universally applicable BOM structure for all areas of their company. This structure usually takes the form of complete single-level BOMs, created in the design department, and is used in both material management and the assembly workshop. The standard SAP System allows you to maintain individual BOMs for any area of your company you require. These BOMs are maintained independently of each other and are assigned to different internal BOM numbers. In this way, each area only deals with the specific data it requires.

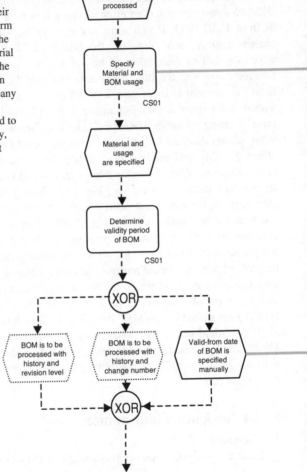

Validity of Material BOM

To enable you to define the precise conditions under which a bill of material is valid in different areas of a company, you define the area of validity and a validity period. The validity period for a BOM is restricted by the following entries in the BOM header and BOM item: *valid-from date* and *valid-to date*. For example, in a BOM, you replace component "A" with component "B" with reference to a change number with a specific valid-from date. The system stores both the status of the BOM before the change with the old component "A" and the status of the BOM after the change with the new component "B". In addition to the validity period, you can also define an area of validity by allocating the same BOM to a material in different plants.

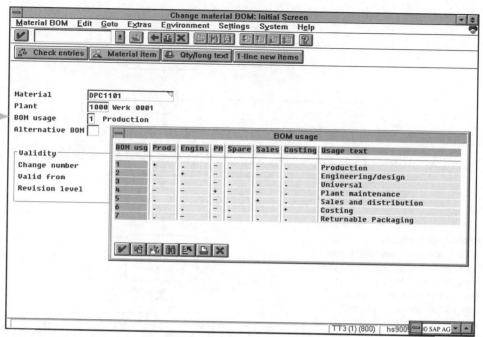

Fig. 8.79: BOM usage

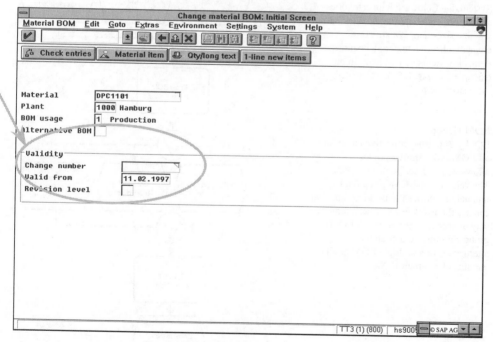

Fig. 8.80: Validity of BOM

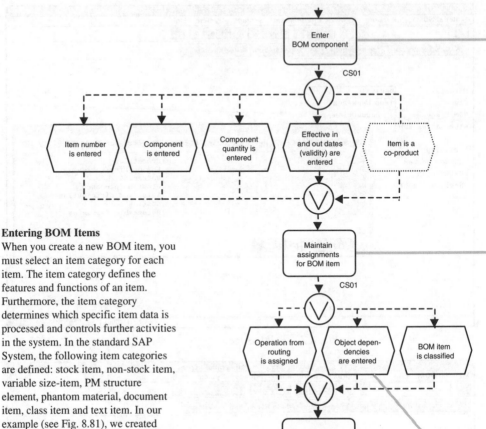

Entering BOM Items

When you create a new BOM item, you must select an item category for each item. The item category defines the features and functions of an item. Furthermore, the item category determines which specific item data is processed and controls further activities in the system. In the standard SAP System, the following item categories are defined: stock item, non-stock item, variable size-item, PM structure element, phantom material, document item, class item and text item. In our example (see Fig. 8.81), we created three stock items "L".

BOM Group

BOM group is the collective name for all BOMs with similar products. This allows you to describe them together. The value in the BOM group field uniquely identifies the BOM group. You can use the BOM group as an alternative way of accessing the BOM. A BOM group comprises either all the alternatives of a multiple BOM or all the variants of a variant BOM.

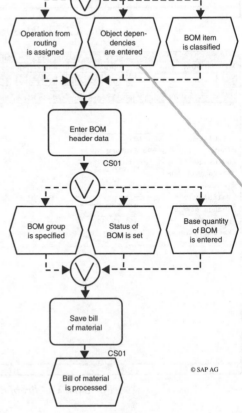

© SAP AG

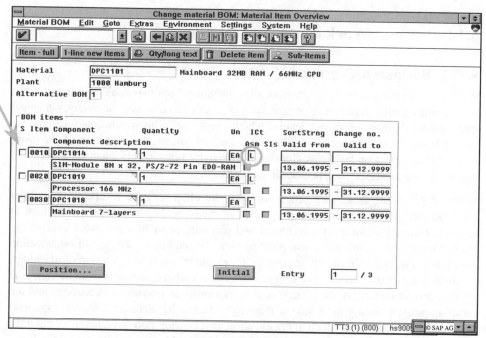

Fig. 8.81: BOM items

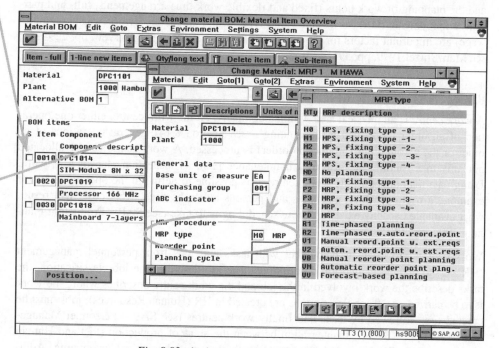

Fig. 8.82: Assignments for BOM items

8.13 Process: Work centre processing

8.13.1 Business background

Work centres play a central role in production planning from two points of view. Firstly, work centres are the main source of capacities in production planning. Secondly, personnel management (human resources) decides which employees with which qualifications can be employed at which types of work centre. Related to this, the definition of the work centre has an effect on both cost elements and activity types within financial accounting and wages and salaries within personnel management.

Within the planning area, work centre resources are often regarded as operating supplies e.g. machines, tools, jigs and NC programs. Whereas the last-mentioned points look at resource planning more from a technical and planning point of view, work centres are viewed more from an organizational point of view. Depending on the type of organization concerned, a work centre can correspond to, for example, a machine, a group of machines, a person or a group of people. Looking at work centres from a technical point of view, the most important factors are the allocation of work centres to operations in routings and the resulting product costing, lead time scheduling and capacity planning. From an organizational point of view, the production organization, that is, shop floor production, continuous flow production, the scheduling of employees with consideration of their qualifications, and the planning of work hours (fixed and flexible work time arrangements, full- and part-time employment, shift work) and wage types (time wage, piecework wage, premium wage) are important factors for the payment of employees (see Kilger 1986, pp. 229–284; see Marr/Stitzel 1979, pp. 391–423).

8.13.2 SAP-specific description

A *work centre* is an physical area within a company. At the work centre, either one operation of an order (contained in the routing – see Section 8.14), several operations of an order or the whole order (production order) is processed. A work centre can be allocated not only to a routing, but also to a maintenance plan, an inspection plan or a network. Using data maintained in the work centre, it is possible to define in the operations of, for example, a routing, which machines and persons are to be used, what costs will result, what available capacity exists and how scheduling is to take (see SAP – Production Planning 1994, pp. 3.8).

Work centres are often used together with tasks and jobs from personnel management (HR-PD) to create detailed job descriptions. The job describes the job classification, the tasks describe the work involved in the job and the work centre describes where the work is to be carried out. If job descriptions are created in HR (Human Resources), jobs must be created first, followed by tasks and finally work centres (see SAP – Personnel Management 1995, pp. 3.3–3.4). If integration between the areas of production (PP) and Human Resources (HR-PD) is wanted, an integration button must be set in Customizing. Additionally, common capacity types must be marked with the indicator *Capacity category Person* (see Fig. 8.83).

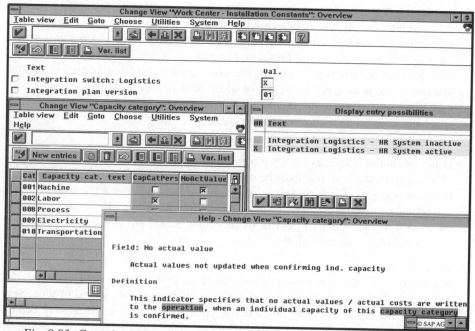

Fig. 8.83: Capacity category person and integration button in HR-PD Customizing

Work centres can be organized hierarchically. The *work centre hierarchy* is created by setting one work centre hierarchically above or below another work centre. One work centre can appear in several hierarchies. In this way, it is possible to obtain figures regarding the available capacity by aggregating the figures of the individual work centres or hierarchy levels. A difference is made between so-called statistical work centres and production work centres. Statistical work centres are only used to aggregate data. Production work centres are only used in the operations of routings, maintenance plans, inspection plans and production orders. They contain data needed in the operation for costing, scheduling and capacity planning purposes, as well as for information purposes in production.

■ *Costing*
Using product costing, the manufacturing costs for the production of goods in a company can be determined. Product costing connects the operation with cost accounting via the costs centres (see Section 8.5) and activity types (see Section 8.4) attached to the work centre. When the work centre is used for an operation, values can be entered for the activity types defined in the work centre. In product costing, the manufacturing costs use the cost rates that have been planned for these activity types. The activity types determine how the entered values are to be treated in product costing. A *cost centre* is a part of an organization split according to area of responsibility or physical area or cost point of view. The cost centre is allocated to a controlling area. Work centres belonging to different plants can be allocated to one and the same cost centre. The

plant is allocated to one company code. A work centre can only be allocated to one cost centre in a certain period of time but several work stations can be allocated to one cost centre. A cost centre contains the activity types defined in the controlling area and defines which activity types can be used in the work centre. The *activity types* are used to describe the different types of activity that can be carried out within a cost centre. They are defined in the controlling area. Per cost centre and period, a cost rate is entered for each activity type. This cost rate consists of a fixed and a variable amount. The cost rate is used to define the rate at which activities are charged (in product costing). In the work centre, only activity types that have been defined for the cost centre to which the work centre is allocated can be used.

■ *Scheduling*
Using scheduling, the dates for the processing of the operations are determined. To be able to do this, the lead time must be calculated and compared with the working times of the work centre. The basis for the calculation of the lead time is the entered values and quantities in the operations. To calculate the lead time, formulas can be defined in the system to individually calculate the operation setup, processing and conversion times within the production order.

■ *Capacity planning*
A capacity is the ability to perform a particular task. In the SAP System, capacities define the available supply of labour and machines within a certain period of time. Several capacities, split into different capacity types, can be assigned to a work centre. Possible work centre capacities with different capacity types might be, for example, machine capacities, labour capacities, reserve capacities for rush orders, and energy requirements. In capacity planning, the capacity requirements of operations are determined in the production orders and compared with the available capacity as stored in the work centres. The basis for the calculation of capacity requirements is the values and quantities entered in the operations. The required capacity is calculated via formulas in the work centres. Using work centre hierarchies, it is possible to sum both the available capacity and capacity requirements from lower levels in the work centre hierarchy to higher levels within the capacity planning functionality.

Using capacities, the available working time and the capacity available at a work centre can be stored. The definition of the available capacity can take place either for one work centre or for many work centres. The starting point when defining the required capacity is the working time at the work centre in question. This is determined on the basis of the time when work is due to start and when work stops at a work centre. Furthermore, the working time is necessary for the calculation of dates within lead time scheduling, as an operation can only be processed at a work centre during working hours. The working time cannot, however, be completely used for production purposes. Factors such as coffee breaks or technical and organizational problems reduce the actual working time. To calculate the amount of time left, during which productive work can be carried out at a work centre, the coffee breaks have to be deducted from the working time, leaving the time that could theoretically be used for productive work at the work centre. By subtracting the time for technical and organizational problems, we are left with the actual amount of time that can be used for production. This productive work time is the time that is entered in the system as the available capacity (work time). The time resulting from the technical organizational down-time is stored in the work centre/capacity in the form of a degree of utilization. Using this degree of utilization, the system can determine for each capacity what degree of the working time of the shift the capacity can be used in.

8.13.3 Using the process

In the first screen, work centre *1801*, which has already been created in the model company, is displayed. This is why the transaction is started in display mode. It is therefore not necessary to look for the work centre. In the basic data screen, *standard value key SAP2* (see Fig. 8.85) with the corresponding setup, machine and labour times with indicator *2* is used. By pressing the *Capacities* key in the upper part of the screen, the system branches to the capacity overview data screen (see Fig. 8.86). In Model Company A, the capacities for *Machine* and *Labor* are displayed. Using the scheduling key, which is also in the upper part of the screen, you can enter various scheduling methods of production (see Fig. 8.87).

8.13.4 Navigation information

- *Menu path*
  Logistics –> Production –> Master data –> Work centre

- *Transaction code*
  CR00, CR01

- *Ingoing processes in the R/3 Reference Model*
  Job description

- *Outgoing processes in the R/3 Reference Model*
  Job description

Copy Data to HR-PD

If you are changing a work centre and the interface to the Personnel Planning and Development System (PD) is active, you can locate work centres which already exist in the PD System using a search string. The system lists the work centres whose descriptions contain the search string and which were created either in PD or in both PD and Logistics. If the work centre data is already maintained in PD, you can copy it to Logistics and add to it, if necessary.

Standard Value Key

In the work centre Basic Data screen (see Fig. 8.85), you can assign a key word to a maximum of six standard values in an operation by a standard value key. When you make this assignment you have to specify a dimension (for example, time or area) for each of the standard values. In addition, you can specify an entry rule which controls whether a standard value must be maintained in the task list.

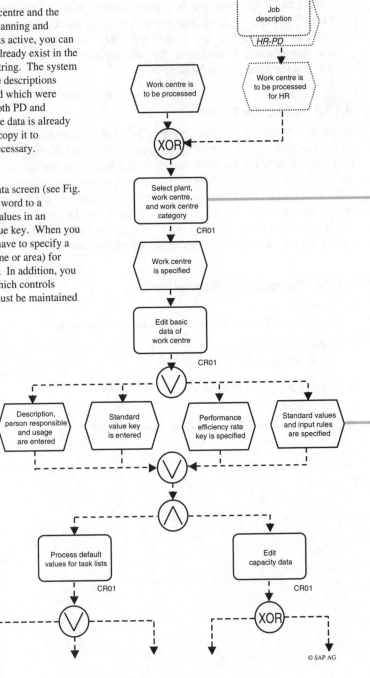

© SAP AG

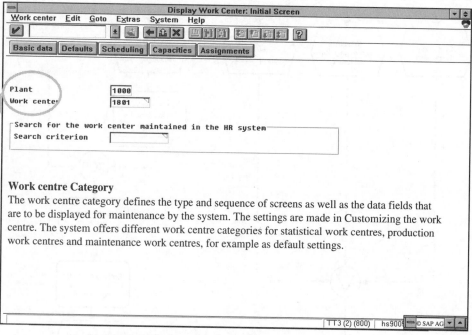

Fig. 8.84: Initial screen of work centre

Work centre Category

The work centre category defines the type and sequence of screens as well as the data fields that are to be displayed for maintenance by the system. The settings are made in Customizing the work centre. The system offers different work centre categories for statistical work centres, production work centres and maintenance work centres, for example as default settings.

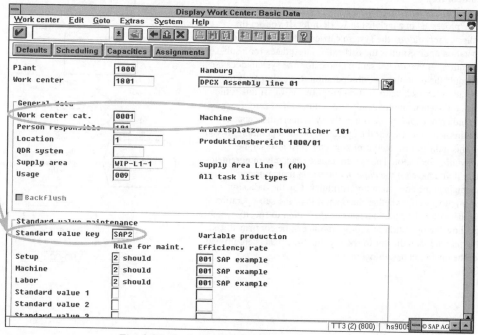

Fig. 8.85: Basic data of work centre

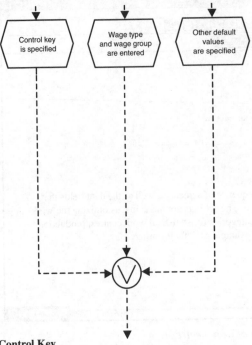

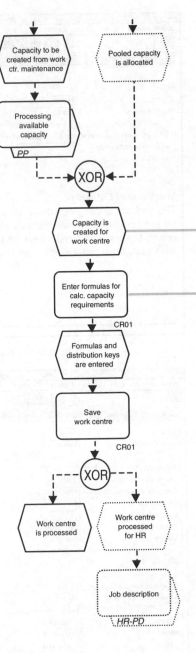

Control Key

A control key determines how an operation or a sub-operation is to be processed in a task list or work order. If you set the indicator *scheduling*, the system carries out scheduling for an operation or determines the earliest or latest dates for a sub-operation. If you do not set this indicator, the system does not schedule the operation or sub-operation (for example, if the operation serves documentation purposes only). If this is the case, the system automatically sets a duration of zero. If you set the indicator *capacity planning*, the system creates capacity requirements records for the operation or sub-operation. If you set this indicator for a control key, you must also set the *scheduling* indicator. The system creates capacity requirements only if you have set the *capacity planning* indicator and maintained the corresponding formulas. Use the indicator *costing* to specify whether the operation or the sub-operation can be costed. Use the indicator *confirmation* to specify whether and how the operation or sub-operation can be confirmed. Use the *time tickets* indicator to specify that time tickets are printed for the operation or sub-operation.

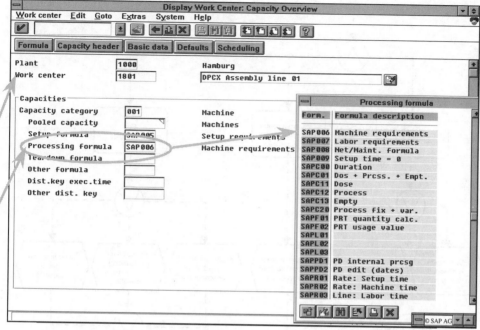

Fig. 8.86: Capacity overview

Capacity Categories

On the *Capacity Overview* screen, you can assign capacities with different categories to the work centre. Examples of capacity categories in a work centre are: machine capacity, labour capacity, reserve capacity for rush orders and energy requirements. The data that identifies the capacity is the capacity category and the pooled capacity key. If you do not enter a key for the capacity, it will be assigned only to the work centre that you are currently maintaining. If you do enter a key for the capacity, it becomes a pooled capacity which can be used by several work centres. A pooled capacity must exist before you can assign it to a work centre.

Distribution of Capacity Requirements

The distribution of capacity requirements over the length of the operation is actually dependent on the capacity category. For example, a setup crew creates a capacity requirement in the labour category at the beginning of the operation, and a machine operator who checks processing every four hours creates another capacity requirement in the same category. In contrast, for the same period of time, the capacity requirements for a different category "machine" are evenly distributed. The different ways of distributing capacity requirements are controlled using the distribution key in capacity planning.

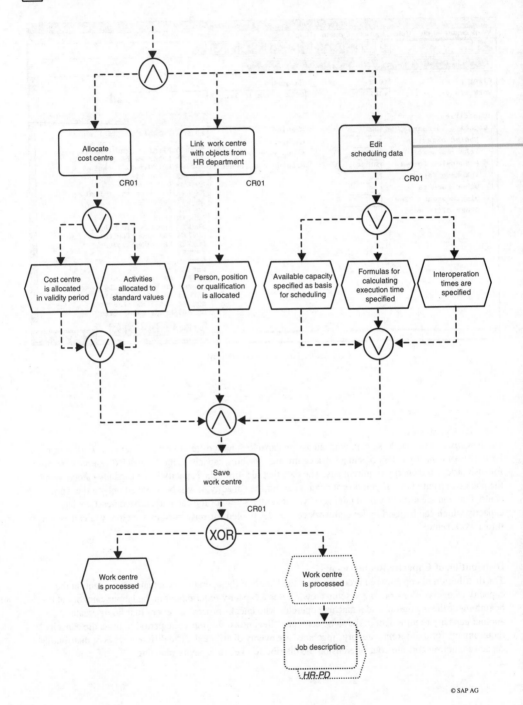

© SAP AG

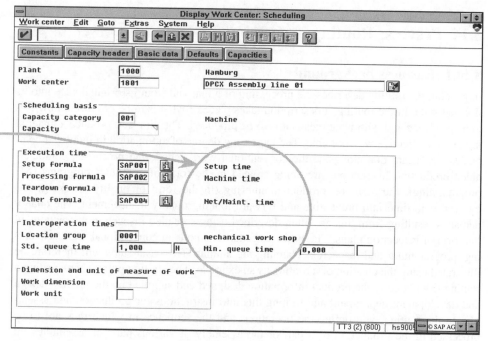

Fig. 8.87: Scheduling

Scheduling Basis

The system determines the available capacity to be used in scheduling based on the capacity category and capacity you entered when maintaining each work centre. The operating time of the capacity is used to calculate operation execution time, for example in the production order, or to calculate the time required for other types of internal processing, such as networks and maintenance orders. This capacity may not be a capacity assigned to one particular work centre (for example, a pooled capacity) as well as a work centre capacity.

Formulas for Calculating Execution Time and Other Types of Internal Processing

Operation execution time at a work centre is made up of three segments: setup, processing and teardown. If you want the formula to reflect splits, you must enter the exact number of partial lots as a parameter into the formula. If you do not enter a formula to calculate the execution time of one of the three above-mentioned operation segments, the system sets the duration of each segment to zero and, therefore, does not include it in the lead time calculation. If you do not enter a formula for calculating the duration of other types of internal processing time, the system automatically uses the duration that you entered for the activity in the network, or the operation in the maintenance order.

Interoperation Times

Interoperation time is the period of time between the point at which the workpiece leaves one work centre and the beginning of the operation at the next work centre. Interoperation time is made up of move time and queue time. Queue time is the time a workpiece waits at the work centre before being processed.

8.14 Process: Routing processing

8.14.1 Business background

In general, the routing describes the processing of a material from its original state into its finished state. In the routing, a description takes place of what is to be produced, how it is to be produced and with what means it is to be produced. The aim is to produce a material in the most effective way possible. The increasing degree of automation in industrial companies has meant that alongside the conventional work scheduling processes, computer-aided production instructions are being created in the form of computer programs (NC programming). Furthermore, product monitoring (in the form of quality checking) has evolved with time into preventive and forward-looking quality management. The quality demands resulting from this are often described using so-called inspection instructions in the form of inspection plans. The basic procedure methods in conventional work scheduling, programming and inspection planning are similar. The basic steps will therefore be illustrated using the creation of a routing as an example. The starting point when creating a routing lies in taking the product information designed and supplied by the product design and development department and turning this into instructions for production and assembly. In the routing, you define the operations and the sequence in which they are to be processed in the production of a part or the assembly of various parts or assemblies. In addition, allocation to the individual operations of production facilities, work centres and capacity requirements takes place in the routing. The creation of a routing involves the following tasks (see Eversheim 1989, pp. 30–56; see Hüllenkremer 1990, pp. 48–57):

- *Defining the starting material*
  This involves determining the type and dimensions of the starting material.

- *Determining the sequence of operations*
  This involves determining the sequence of operations needed to convert the material from its starting state to the desired final state.

- *Machine selection*
  This involves selection and allocation of required machines to the operations in which they are needed.

- *Allocation of PRTs (production resources and tools)*
  Here, the tools and devices, which are not an integral part of any machine, are selected and allocated to the operations in which they are needed.

- *Entering required times*
  The main purpose here is to determine the target times for the processing of the individual operations.

Several methods of creating routings have evolved. The amount of time and effort involved in creating the various types of routings depends mainly on the degree of standardization of the material to be processed.

If a new product is being developed, all of the above-mentioned tasks should be carried out. This is the case when a routing is created for non-standardized parts. In this type of planning, new devices have to be designed and built.

In *change planning,* changes are made to routings by adding or deleting whole operations or by replacing individual work instructions of production facilities. This process is usually accompanied by the search for similar objects supported by a classification system and assumes a range of materials based on semi-standardized parts.

In v*ariant planning,* the routing is changed by varying individual parameters. Adding or deleting individual routing operations is not allowed. A prerequisite for this type of planning is the creation of a family of parts, that is, a grouping together of parts with identical or similar geometric attributes or having the same or similar production methods. Each family of parts uses a standardized basic routing and the variants to be produced are very similar.

In *repetitive planning,* the existing planning results are used again completely. The order-independent routings are extended by adding data relevant for planning purposes, such as dates, order number and quantity. Repetitive planning involves the least amount of time and effort in planning, but it requires a standardized product range.

Despite routings being different in the amount of time and effort needed to create them, they can also be differentiated according to their usage. The term *reference operation set* is used to describe a routing that is allocated to a material to be produced and contains standard information. *Alternative routings* are used when a material can be produced using more than one routing with the same result. *Variant routings* contain all the operations that might be needed to produce a material. The operations needed to actually produce the material are then selected at a later point in time. Outline routings only contain rough information. This information is defined in more detail within production. This type of routing is used particularly in cell manufacturing where the responsible employee in the production process creates the routing using his specialist knowledge.

Routing management plays a particularly important role in helping the work scheduler to find existing or similar routings. Using a classification system, identifying information concerning groups of materials or similar production methods can be stored. This information can then be used to find the required objects quickly via a text search or the entry of the classification search criteria. Efficient routing management can only exist if data such as routing history and valid-from and -to dates of routings are correctly maintained, and if routings are changed or deleted when needed.

Historically, in conventional production methods, the production equipment has been controlled and operated by human beings. In computer-aided systems, the NC programs and robots are controlled via programs, which are created by human beings. The programs contain instructions which control movement and logic functions. The control of the tool depends on the contours and surface of the processed part. In comparison with conventional routing management, differences exist both in the way data is managed and in data transfer.

The central output information in *NC programming* is the documents created in the design and development department. Depending on the machines available, a decision must first be made as to whether the programs are to be created manually or automatically with the help of computers (see Diedenhoven 1985, S. 58–65). At the same time, a decision has to be made about the production method and which machines to use. No matter what type of programming is used, the following three main tasks have to be carried out:

■ Calculation of geometric data

■ Definition of technological data (definition of the processing sequence, which tools to use)

■ Encoding of data and setup of the control program

In *manual programming,* the data needed for the NC program is calculated, encoded and transferred in the form of lists, using the available existing documents. Thus, the geometric data of the part from the constructional drawing must be enlarged to scale to calculate the intersection points for the NC program. The data from the control program created in the form of lists is then entered into the control equipment, either manually or using an external storage medium such as a diskette or magnetic tape.

Using *computer-aided programming,* it is possible to reduce the amount of work needed to create an NC program, since the program carries out the calculation of geometric data itself and the NC control data is created automatically. The aim here is to create the program as independently of a special machine as possible.

In programming, the use of a program depends especially on the technical capabilities of the type of programming involved. For example, in manual programming, the NC programmer creates a control-independent program at his alphanumeric programming device. This program is entered directly in the command structure and the encoding of the numerically controlled machine takes place on the basis of the construction drawing. In the case of semi-automatic programming, part of the program creation process takes place via special symbol and function keys connected directly to the CNC computer. Due to the close relationship between the programming and the machine-specific characteristic data, this type of programming is limited since the programs created can only be used by other NC machines if a lot of additional changes are carried out.

The disadvantage of machine-related programming can be reduced if the programming module allows the possibility of automatic (text) programming. Here, the manufacturing process is described in individual steps from raw to finished part using the construction drawing and a part program such as APT, EXAPT or COMPACT II. Using a preprocessor, the part program is first converted into a machine-independent format. Geometric calculations, which may result from the tool movements, are then taken over by the processor. An important feature of the CLDATA (Cutter Location Data) format created by the preprocessor is that the geometric and technological data, which were separate before the preprocessor run, are joined together in the tool and switch instructions. The postprocessor transforms the control data available in a machine-independent format into control data for whichever machine is involved.

In the programming types mentioned above, the programmer always has to check the alphanumeric data he has entered at the machine to see if it is correct. In the production process itself, this alphanumeric data is not important, but the visual aspect is. This type of programming can be supported by graphically interactive programming. Here, the geometric data of the object is created. After the processing method has been decided, the tool is selected and the starting point of the tool defined in the drawing. By defining the processing start and stop point and the technological data, the processing run is calculated by the module and the machine-independent tool format created.

Inspection planning is often one of the tasks of quality management, which also involves quality checking, the evaluation of quality data and quality control (see Sections 8.26, 8.27 and 8.28). In order to be able to set up the appropriate documents for quality inspection in production and assembly, the tasks involved in inspection planning are of particular importance. When creating an inspection plan, the product specification, the drawing and the routing are required. The department defines the maximum quantity criteria for a material, the design department supplies dimensions to be checked, and work scheduling supplies the requirements on production facilities, production resources and tools and also defines the inspection operations (see DIN 1987, pp. 126–128).

First, the attributes that need to be checked have to be defined. Starting with the information and documents available, such as the functional specifications, construction drawing, bills of material, routing and purchasing documents, the required documents must be selected and checked to see whether they are correct. Quality-relevant attributes are attributes such as physical and geometric attributes, completeness, and the look and functionality of the product. When creating the inspection specifications, the necessary inspection characteristics and their specified sizes are defined, along with the inspection method to be used within the quality inspection process. In the inspection instruction, the inspection processing is described for each inspection characteristic. This involves specifying the type of inspection, the number of samples, the maximum number of faulty pieces per sample, and the amount of time between each sample-taking. Using an inspection drawing, it is possible to indicate which parts of the object are to be inspected. It is thus important, before production begins, to realize whether the quality check could be made more difficult or even impossible by the geometric attributes of the object itself. The task involved in creating the inspection sequence plan (inspection plan) is to optimize the logical sequence and scheduling of the individual inspection operations per inspection characteristic. Here, the individual inspection times are defined. The last step is to allocate the inspection to a central inspection area or a production work centre, depending on the location and type of inspection that is to take place.

Since the product specification, the drawings and the routing are prerequisites for the creation of inspection plans, the amount of work involved in order-dependent inspection plan creation can also be split up into the areas of new, change, variant and repetitive planning, depending on the degree of product standardization.

8.14.2 SAP-specific description

In the R/3 System, a routing describes the sequence of individual operations needed in the production of a material. The routing is plant-specific, meaning that it is unique within a plant. Individual operations in a routing can, however, also be allocated to another plant if the other plant belongs to the same company code. The routing is not created for a particular production order. It is used as a basis for product costing, for lead time and capacity scheduling, for capacity planning and as an instruction for the actual processes to be carried out in production (see SAP – Production Planning 1994, pp. 3.9–3.13). The main elements in the routing are:

■ *Material*
The material is described using its characteristic physical attributes. When assigning a material to routing, the following possibilities exist:

- Routings can be grouped together in groups. These contain routings that are based on similar production methods and/or are used to manufacture similar materials. Within a group, routings are uniquely identified by a counter.

- Routings that are used to produce materials using different production methods can be stored in different groups.

- A routing can be used to produce different materials (mirrored parts such as left and right closet doors). The different materials can even be allocated to different plants in the R/3 System.

■ *Operations*
The operation characterizes the work step to be carried out, the time needed to carry it out and the quantity to be produced. The lead time contains at least the specification of a setup time, a process time and a teardown time. It can be extended for scheduling purposes by a queue time, that is, the time the material has to remain at the work centre before processing can begin, a move time, that is, the period of time in which the material is transferred to the next work centre, and a wait time, which is the amount of time the material has to remain at the work centre after processing of the operation has been completed and until it is transferred to the next work centre.

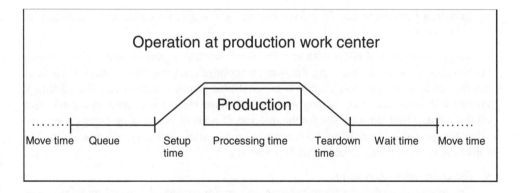

Fig. 8.88: Times involved in a production order

Queue and setup time, as well as wait and teardown time, may overlap since operations can be carried out in parallel.

■ *Production resources and tools*
Operations must be allocated to specific production resources such as manually, CNC- and DNC-controlled machines. The required PRTs such as tools, devices and NC programs, as well as measuring instruments and inspection equipment, have to be planned. Production resources and tools are movable operating supplies which can be allocated to both in-house and external operations in the routing. When allocating a production resource or tool to an operation, you can specify what quantity of the PRT is required and for how long. It is also possible to create a material master record for a production resource or tool. Production resources and tools with a material master record can be either produced in-house or procured externally. It is also possible to create a special PRT master record. However, no purchasing (external procurement) can take place for such a master record. A production resource or tool with an **NST** master record can be allocated to an operation when the PRT screen has been maintained in the material master record and the material status allows such an allocation.

■ *Inspection characteristics*
The inspection plan is closely related to the routing. An inspection plan contains the individual inspection operations, the characteristics to be inspected per inspection operation and the specification of the inspection tool to be used. An inspection plan can be used for inspections at goods receipt time, goods issue time, for first samples and general inspections within the production process. In the R/3 System, it is not necessary to create inspection plans since the inspection characteristics can be stored directly in the routing. The inspection characteristics can be allocated directly to an operation or an inspection is defined as an inspection operation. An inspection characteristic contains a characteristic description, the inspection method and the sampling method. Characteristics relevant to quality are things such as the entry of physical and geometric attributes of a product. The inspection method determines which method is to be used to carry out the inspection. The sampling procedure determines whether a 100%

sample, a percentage sample, a fixed sample or a sample according to a sampling plan is to take place.

Routings can be created either with or without reference to a material and with or without specification of a group (meaning that similar routings are grouped together). If routings are first created without reference to a material, this can take place later. If a routing is created with reference to an existing material, when the routing is created, the system lists all the routings that already exist for the material. If none of the existing groups is entered when the routing is created, the R/3 System internally allocates the system to a group. The following types of routing exist in the R/3 System:

■ *Standard (normal) routing*
The routing describes the manufacturing process for a material. Several routings can be created for a material, which differ from each other in, for example, lot size or usage (production, rework, prototyping). To reduce the time and work involved in creating a routing, reference routings can be copied into them as often as required and in any order. Since materials, routings and plants can be combined with each other in any combination, routings are highly flexible. Thus, the production of mirrored objects such as the left and right sides of a door can be dealt with in one single routing.

■ *Reference operation set*
In contrast to the routing, the reference routing is not assigned to a material. A reference routing contains a sequence of operations that can typically be used in many routings, i.e. operations that tend to be needed over and over again and that can be referred to when needed. Reference routings can be used as a reference (the operations exist in the routing but cannot be changed) or as a copy (the operations are physically copied into the routing and can be changed as required). Reference routings can be used in standard routings or production orders. This reduces the amount of data that needs to be entered when the routing is created. It also means that a change to the reference routing means an automatic change to all the standard routings in which the reference routing is used as a reference.

■ *Rate routing*
Rate routings are used in production rate-based routing maintenance and can be used, for example, in serial production. Whereas in normal routings the base unit is usually constant (e.g. piece), and the times (e.g. processing time) maintained via standard values, the opposite is the case for rate routings.Production quantities are maintained per product and the time is constant. Therefore, a rate routing describes what quantity of a product can be produced within a certain time. A rate routing contains *one* sequence of operations. Via the production quantity, the production time and the corresponding units, one production rate is defined for each operation. The production rate is the result of dividing the production time by the quantity. It is therefore possible to specify the production quantity in, for example, tonnes per shift. In all other points, the functionality and maintenence of rate routings and normal routings is identical. Work centres that are allocated to operations in rate routings should have standard value keys in which the standard values for production time, setup and teardown have been predefined.

■ *Reference rate routing*

Reference rate routings are used as a reference in rate routings. A reference rate routing consists of *one* sequence of operations. The production rate in the operation is defined via the production quantity and the reference time, as is the case with rate routing. The functionality and maintenance of reference rate routings correspond to those of reference routings.

Apart from the drawing and the bill of material, the routing is a basic piece of information needed in production and is used as instructions for the manufacturing process. Apart from describing the production process, the routing is the central instrument for planning the scheduling of the operations. Using the times entered in the routing, an order-independent forward or backward scheduling can be carried out. If the times entered lead to a finish date which is later than the allowed latest completion date, three procedures exist which enable the production lead time to be reduced:

■ Reduction of queue, wait and move times down to the minimum duration

■ Overlapping operations, that is, before an operation is fully completed, a partial quantity is transferred to the next operation

■ Splitting an operation, that is, the quantity to be produced in an operation is split among several capacities (e.g. machines) and the operation carried out at the same time on one or more machines

A development in the area of computer-aided creation of routings is the creation of programming instructions for NC-controlled machines. Here, depending on the degree of CAD/NC-integration, geometric and technological data created by the computer can be used (see Diedenhoven 1985, pp. 58–65). A second area of development is the partial automation of conventionally created routings. Here, by setting up variants for a product family and varying parameters, a variant routing can be created from a reference routing. In addition, by setting up a suitable classification system, change planning can be partially automated by using reference routings (see Hüllenkremer 1990, pp. 48–57). In the R/3 System, the demands on computer-aided planning are supported firstly by the configuration of routings (see Section 9.3) and secondly by the automatic calculation of standard values. The calculation of values for setup, machine processing, move, inspection and queue times is performed on the basis of tables and formulas stored in the R/3 System. Apart from the automation of routing creation, for integrated processing administration it makes sense to enter data for subsequent operations. This is done in the R/3 System by assigning a *control key* to an operation.

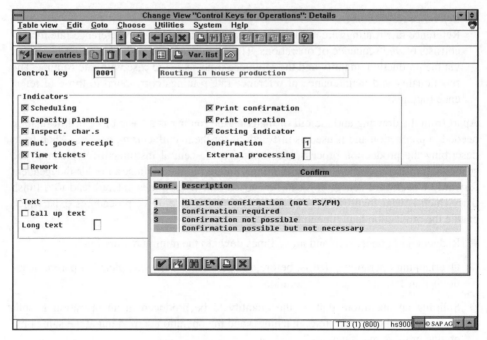

Fig.: 8.89: Parameters in the control key

The control key contains indicators which are either optional or mandatory depending on which control key is used. These control keys are maintained in Customizing.

The control key defines, for example, how an operation or sub-operation is to be treated. It defines whether costing or capacity planning is to take place for the operation or the sub-operation. Depending on the control key, various plausibility checks take place. Splitting and overlapping, for example, are only allowed if scheduling takes place for the operation. The external processing indicator causes purchase order requisitions to be created when the production order is created (see Section 8.32).

8.14.3 Using the process

In the initial screen, a material number must be entered when creating a standard routing. In our example, the group is assigned internally by the R/3 System. The routing for material *DPC1101* (main board) is to be valid for production purposes as from June 14, 1995. Because of this, usage *1* has been entered on the header detail screen (see Fig. 8.92). The screen on the right shows the entries defined in Customizing for the usage field. In this case, there are no lot-related restrictions for production. The routing is released immediately for use in production by setting release status *4*. The operations are processed using the *basic sequence*. Both operations are assigned to work centre *1801* (see Section 8.13). The first operation is processed using control key *PP04* (see Fig. 8.94). For this control key, no completion confirmation is required. The completion of the second operation with control key *PP01* must be confirmed.

In the operation detail screen (see Fig. 8.95) the times for production are entered. For the final assembly of the main board (operation 0020), a setup time of 5 minutes is needed, along with a machine processing time of 15 minutes. In addition, the corresponding activity types have been allocated to these values (see Section 8.5, activity type maintenance). Activity type *1420* has been created for machine hours.

8.14.4 Navigation information

▓ *Menu path*
Logistics –> Production –> Master data –> Routings

▓ *Transaction code*
CA00, CA01

▓ *Ingoing processes in the R/3 Reference Model*
none

▓ *Outgoing processes in the R/3 Reference Model*

Plant Material

A routing is assigned to a specific plant defined in the routing header. However, you can assign individual operations of a routing to a different plant, if one or several operations are to be carried out in another plant. The plants specified in the individual operations and the one specified in the routing header must belong to the same company code. A routing can be allocated to a material. The following options are available. You can create routings in different routing groups for a material. This is useful, for example, if the material can be produced using different production methods. You can create routings in the same routing group for a material. You can identify these routings by their group counter. You can create a routing for different materials (for example, mirror-image parts, left and right car doors). The different materials can originate from different plants. When you create a routing for a material, the system displays a list of all existing routings for this material. You can create a routing without a material and then allocate a material at a later time.

Groups

Routings are combined into groups. A group can contain routings that describe similar production processes or that are used for the production of similar materials. A group can, for example, be used to combine routings with different lot size ranges or production alternatives. If, for example, you are producing a product inside and outside the country, you can combine both routings in one group. You can also create these routings in different groups. The routings in a group are distinguished by their group counters. When you maintain a routing, the system loads all routings belonging to the same group. You are, therefore, advised to combine only small numbers of routings in a group.

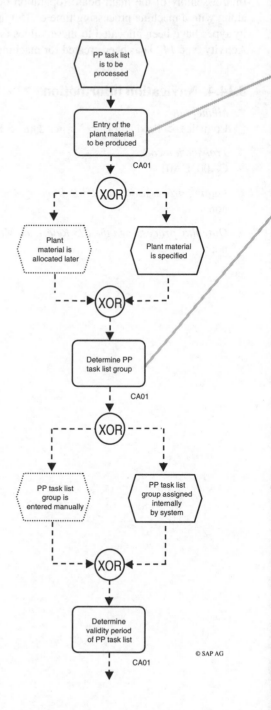

© SAP AG

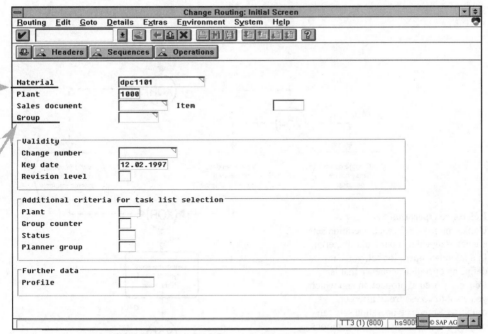

Fig. 8.90: Initial screen of routing creation

Change Number
An alphanumeric change number identifies a change master record. The change master record specifies when a change takes effect and combines all objects included in the change. The change number documents all changes and determines the point at which they become valid.

Key Date
The key date is the date from which new routing objects become valid. If you call up existing routing objects, the system accesses the data that is valid on the key date. If you change a routing using a change number, the valid-from date specified in the change number record is used as a key date. The key date for new objects is the valid-from date.

Profile
Often certain fields in routings have the same values. In this case, it can be useful to set default values for these fields to reduce the amount of data you have to enter. A profile is a collection of default values for the routing header and operations. You can create and maintain profiles in Customizing. However, you can also change default values in routing maintenance.

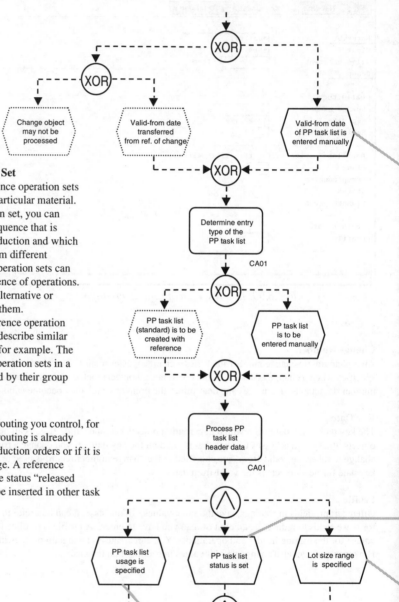

Reference Operation Set
Unlike routings, reference operation sets are not assigned to a particular material. In a reference operation set, you can define an operation sequence that is frequently used in production and which you want to access from different routings. Reference operation sets can only contain one sequence of operations. You cannot maintain alternative or parallel sequences for them.
You can combine reference operation sets in a group if they describe similar production processes, for example. The individual reference operation sets in a group are distinguished by their group counter.

Status
With the status of the routing you control, for example, whether the routing is already released for use in production orders or if it is still in the creation stage. A reference operation set must have status "released (general)" in order to be inserted in other task lists.

© SAP AG

432

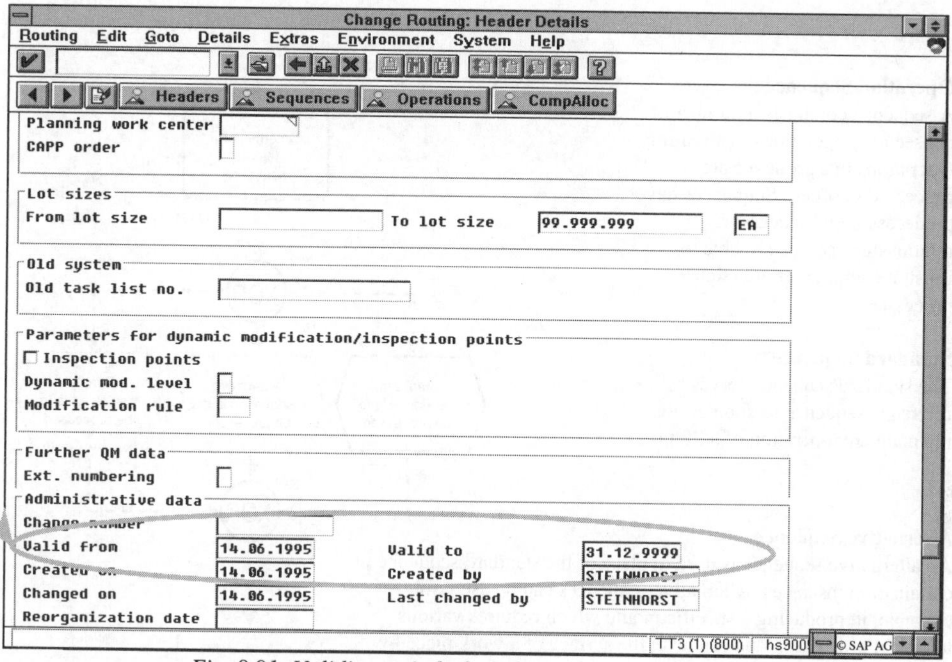

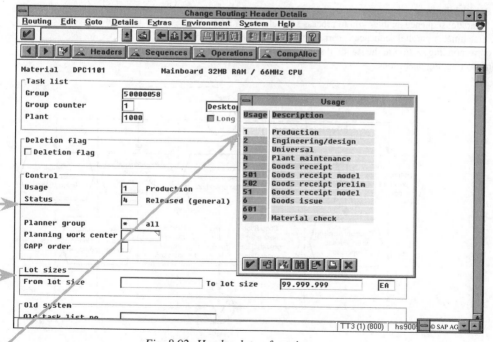

Fig. 8.91: Validity period of routing

Fig. 8.92: Header data of routing

Operation Sequence
A sequence combines a number of consecutive operations in a routing. Operations in a sequence are processed in order. Sequences have predecessor and successor relationships so you are able to illustrate complex production processes.

Standard Sequence
The standard sequence serves as reference sequence as soon as you maintain any operation of a PP task list.

Alternative Sequence
An alternative sequence is used in place of the standard sequence in certain circumstances. Alternative sequences can be used, for example, in producing a specific mould which requires various technical processes. You can level the surface of a work piece by cutting, sanding or shaving it.

Parallel Sequence
A parallel sequence enables you to process several operations at the same time. A parallel sequence is carried out at the same time as the corresponding section in the standard sequence. It is a special form of overlapping operations.

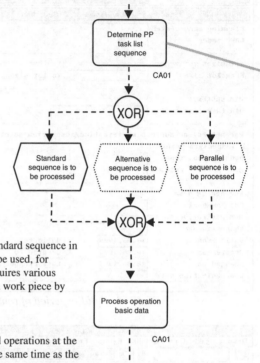

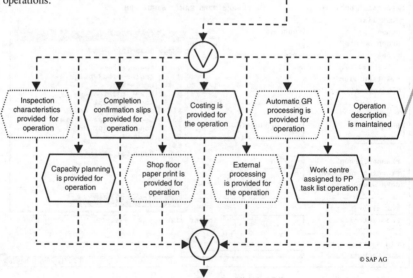

© SAP AG

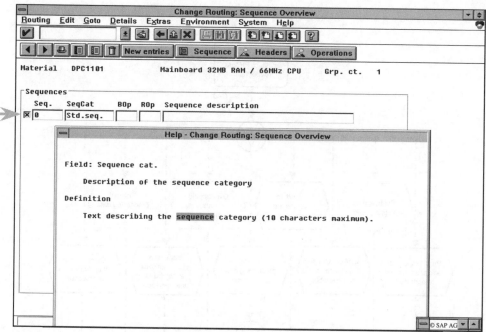

Fig. 8.93: Routing sequence

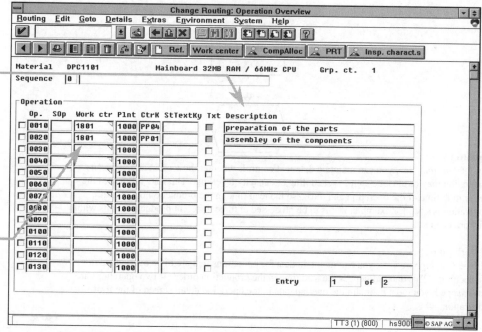

Fig. 8.94: Assignment of work centre to PP task list operation

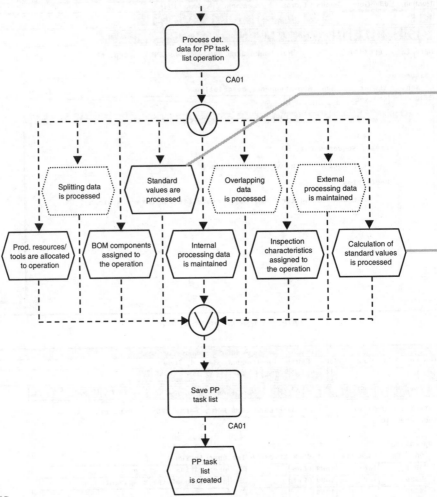

Splitting
In the *Splitting* area, you can maintain data that controls whether, how often and when an operation may or must be split in scheduling or capacity levelling. This data influences the execution time of the operation and thus also the lead time in the production order. An operation is split, for example, if it is to be processed at three different production units within a work centre.

Overlapping
In the *Overlapping* area, you can maintain data for operations that are to be overlapped in scheduling. This data influences the lead time in the production order. If two operations are overlapped, you must maintain the overlap data in the operation detail screen of the **first** operation.

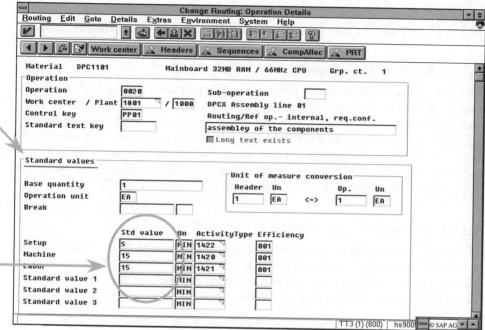

Fig. 8.95: Standard values for operation 20

Operations

The individual processing steps that make up the production process are described in the operations. An operation specifies the work centre required to carry out a processing step as well as the corresponding standard values. For each operation, you can maintain an operation text which describes how the workstep is to be carried out. The sequence in which the operations of a routing are to be carried out is specified using operation numbers. Using a control key, you can specify which functions should be carried out for an operation in a task list. This key controls e.g. the cost estimate, scheduling, capacity planning, completion confirmation or printing of the production documents. In the detail screen of an operation, you can enter specific operation data, for example data on external processing, splitting, overlapping, standard values and the calculation of standard values. Any material component, production resource/tool or inspection characteristic required in the production process can be directly allocated to the associated operation.

8.15 Process: Transfer of results to demand management

8.15.1 Business background

The independent requirements for which capacity requirements were determined in SOP (Sales and Operations Planning) must be transferred to demand management. The sales and operations plan is thus the basis for subsequent planning levels in production planning, such as demand management, MPS and MRP. It is therefore necessary to break down the requirements determined for the product groups among the individual product group members. The data is split among the product group members (disaggregation) on the basis of the distribution factors in the planning hierarchy (see Section 8.2).

8.15.2 SAP-specific description

When the data is transferred from Sales and Operations Planning (SOP) to demand management, independent requirements are generated for all the materials for which requirements are to be transferred. The R/3 System supports the following three methods of transferring the results of SOP (see SAP – Production Planning 1994, pp. 5.6–5.10):

- Transfer of the planned data of all the members of a single-level product group

- Transfer of the planned data for a single material

- Transfer of data of a material from flexible planning

Apart from the basic data involved, such as the product group, material etc. it is important to enter the transfer strategy. There are four possible ways of defining the transfer strategy, which can take place either at material or single-level product group level:

- direct transfer of the sales plan

- transfer of the sales plans of the materials concerned according to the percentage share of each material within the product group

- direct transfer of the rough production plan

- transfer of the production plans of the materials concerned according to the percentage share of each material within the product group

When data is transferred from flexible planning, the plant must have been maintained as a characteristic of the information structure and the data must be transferred in the corresponding units of measure.

The connection between SOP and production planning can be carried out in two ways in the R/3 System. The transfer can either take place automatically or the data can be used as a reference, for example within MPS. The transfer of the data can be set up in the R/3 System so that it takes place in the background without the user being aware of it.

Furthermore, it is also possible to carry out the disaggregation function mentioned above in terms of both quantity and time. In this way, requirements determined on a weekly or monthly basis can be split down into planning on a day-to-day basis.

8.15.3 Using the process

The trigger for this process is the fact that planned data is to be transferred to demand management. As mentioned, this data can result from the Sales plan generated in Controlling or from the production plan (in production management). In the model company, the data is transferred from the production plan to demand management. To do this, within the R/3 System, the menu Transfer to demand management for a material is selected within the disaggregation part of Sales and Operations Planning. In the first step, materials *DPC1101*, plant *1000* and the version are entered. In the second step, the transfer strategy is marked and the transfer period specified by entering a date. If no requirements type is entered, as in this case, it is determined using the MRP group and strategy group fields in the material master record. Since the company (Model Company A) determines the production requirements mainly by market analyses carried out by the marketing department in conjunction with the planning and production departments, produces independently of customer requirements and manufactures its products in lots, planning strategy *Lot production for customer and stock orders* has been defined in the material master record. Furthermore, it is possible to transfer a particular version of the plan, which has been defined as the active version. If the indicator *invisible transfer* has not been marked, the requirements are displayed and can be changed if necessary after the transfer (see Fig. 8.97).

8.15.4 Navigation information

■ *Menu path*
Logistics –> Production –> SOP –> Disaggregation –> Tsfr PG to Dm.Mngt

■ *Transaction code*
MC75

■ *Ingoing processes in the R/3 Reference Model*
Processing of sales and operations planning

■ *Outgoing processes in the R/3 Reference Model*
Demand management

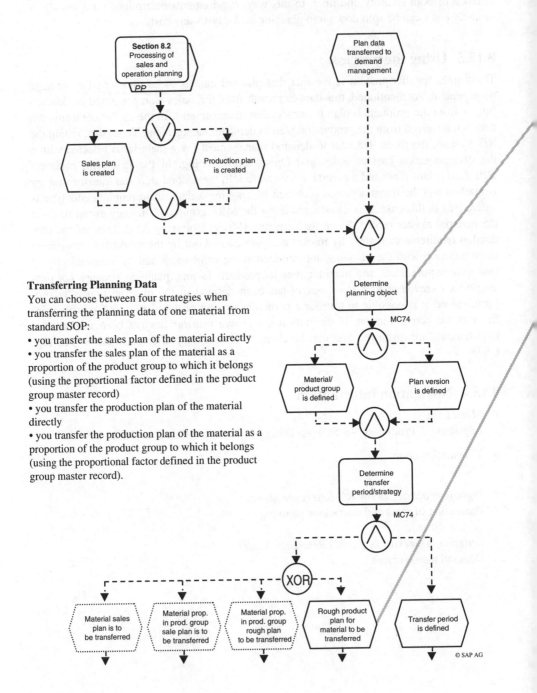

Transferring Planning Data

You can choose between four strategies when
transferring the planning data of one material from
standard SOP:
• you transfer the sales plan of the material directly
• you transfer the sales plan of the material as a
proportion of the product group to which it belongs
(using the proportional factor defined in the product
group master record)
• you transfer the production plan of the material
directly
• you transfer the production plan of the material as a
proportion of the product group to which it belongs
(using the proportional factor defined in the product
group master record).

© SAP AG

440

```
┌─────────────────────────────────────────────────────────────────────────────┐
│ ─                    Transfer Planning Data to Demand Management        ▼ ◆   │
│ Disaggregation  Edit  Goto  Extras  System  Help                          ◐   │
│ ┌──┐┌──────────┐  ┌─┐┌──┐┌───┐┌──┐ ┌──────┐┌──┐ ┌────────┐ ┌─┐             │
│ │✔ ││          │  │±││ ◄││←⬆✕││  │ │      ││  │ │        │ │?│             │
│ └──┘└──────────┘  └─┘└──┘└───┘└──┘ └──────┘└──┘ └────────┘ └─┘             │
│ ┌────────────┐                                                                │
│ │Transfer now│                                                                │
│ └────────────┘                                                                │
│                                                                               │
│   Material        DPC1101         Mainboard 32MB RAM / 66MHz CPU              │
│   Plant           1000            Hamburg                                     │
│   Version                                                                     │
│                                                                               │
│  ┌─Transfer strategy and period──────────────────────────────────┐          │
│  │ ○ Sales plan for material or PG members                        │          │
│  │ ○ Sales plan for mat. or PG members as proportion of PG        │          │
│  │ ◉ Production plan for material or PG members                   │          │
│  │ ○ Prod.plan for mat. or PG members as proportion of PG         │          │
│  │                                                               │          │
│  │ Fro 12.02.1997 To                                             │          │
│  │ ☐ Invisible transfer                                          │          │
│  └───────────────────────────────────────────────────────────────┘          │
│                                                                               │
│  ┌─Independent requirement specifications────────────────────────┐          │
│  │ Requirements type                                             │          │
│  │ Version                                                       │          │
│  │ ☒ Active                                                      │          │
│  └───────────────────────────────────────────────────────────────┘          │
│                                                                               │
│                                          TT3 (1) (800)  hs900 ═ © SAP AG ▼ ▲  │
└─────────────────────────────────────────────────────────────────────────────┘
```

Fig. 8.96: Initial screen of transferring planning data to demand management

```
┌─────────────────────────────────────────────────────────────────────────────┐
│ ─                    Plnd ind. reqmts Create: Schedule Lines           ▼ ◆   │
│ Planned indep.reqmts  Edit  Goto  Settings  Environment  System  Help     ◐   │
│ ┌──┐┌──────────┐  ┌─┐┌──┐┌───┐┌──┐ ┌──────┐┌──┐ ┌────────┐ ┌─┐             │
│ │✔ ││          │  │±││ ◄││←⬆✕││  │ │      ││  │ │        │ │?│             │
│ └──┘└──────────┘  └─┘└──┘└───┘└──┘ └──────┘└──┘ └────────┘ └─┘             │
│ ┌─┐┌─┐┌─┐┌──┐┌─┐┌──┐┌─┐┌──┐ ┌──────────┐ ┌─┐┌─┐┌─┐┌─┐                     │
│ │►││ ││ ││  ││ ││  ││ ││  │ │⚙ Forecast│ │ ││ ││ ││ │                     │
│ └─┘└─┘└─┘└──┘└─┘└──┘└─┘└──┘ └──────────┘ └─┘└─┘└─┘└─┘                     │
│                                                                               │
│  Material  DPC1101         Mainboard 32MB RAM / 66MHz CPU    Plnt   1000      │
│  Total plnnd qty  650      EA  RqType       LSF   Version/actve 00 / ☒       │
│  Desired qty      65           Cons.ind.plng                                  │
│                                                                               │
│  ┌─Schedule lines────────────────────────────────────────────────┐          │
│  │ S  Reqmts date    Plnnd qty     Splt   Value   / DEM          │          │
│  │ ☐ M  02.1997      100                  162.355,00             │          │
│  │ ☐ M  03.1997      120                  194.826,00             │          │
│  │ ☐ M  04.1997      100                  162.355,00             │          │
│  │ ☐ M  05.1997      110                  178.590,50             │          │
│  │ ☐ M  06.1997      100                  162.355,00             │          │
│  │ ☐ M  07.1997      120                  194.826,00             │          │
│  │ ☐ M  08.1997                                                  │          │
│  │ ☐ M  09.1997                                                  │          │
│  │ ☐ M  10.1997                                                  │          │
│  │ ☐ M  11.1997                                                  │          │
│  │ ☐ M  12.1997                                                  │          │
│  │ ☐ M  01.1998                                                  │          │
│  │ ☐ M  02.1998                                                  │          │
│  └───────────────────────────────────────────────────────────────┘          │
│                                          Page    1     / 1                    │
│                                                            ═ © SAP AG ▼ ▲     │
└─────────────────────────────────────────────────────────────────────────────┘
```

Fig. 8.97: Sales data of transfer

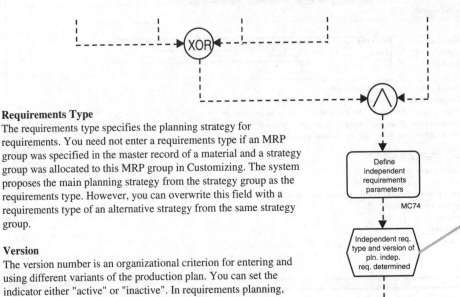

Requirements Type

The requirements type specifies the planning strategy for requirements. You need not enter a requirements type if an MRP group was specified in the master record of a material and a strategy group was allocated to this MRP group in Customizing. The system proposes the main planning strategy from the strategy group as the requirements type. However, you can overwrite this field with a requirements type of an alternative strategy from the same strategy group.

Version

The version number is an organizational criterion for entering and using different variants of the production plan. You can set the indicator either "active" or "inactive". In requirements planning, only active versions are planned. Moreover, you can compare the different versions of a production plan. Several versions are allowed, i.e. you can carry out several programme plannings and afterwards decide on one programme version.

How to Transfer Data to Demand Management with Mass Processing

You can use SOP's mass processing function to transfer the results of SOP to demand management. In this process: 1. You create a transfer profile. This procedure can be performed either online or in Customizing. 2. You create a planning activity and include this action (the transfer profile) in it. 3. You create a mass processing job for this activity. 4. You schedule this mass processing job.

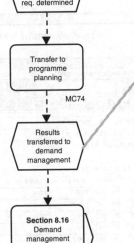

Define
independent
requirements
parameters

MC74

Independent req.
type and version of
pln. indep.
req. determined

Transfer to
programme
planning

MC74

Results
transferred to
demand
management

Section 8.16
Demand
management

PP

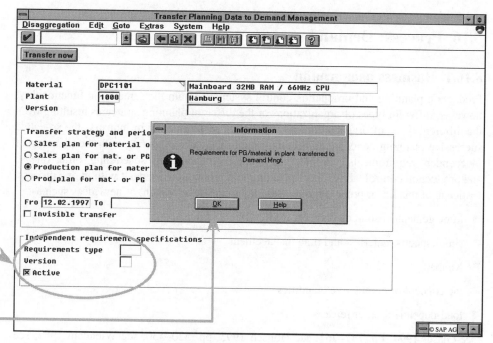

Fig. 8.98: Transfer completed

If you do not set the indicator "invisible transfer", the transfer of the SOP values to demand management will be processed in the foreground, thereby allowing you to control or even correct the planned values.

8.16 Process: Demand management

8.16.1 Business background

Production planning and production control systems contain the same basic functionality; however, different types of organizations or the different planning strategies resulting from the different types of organizations have different requirements. In industry, the so-called successive planning concept has become established, where starting with the planning of independent requirements, via materials management, capacity scheduling, order release and production control, all levels of planning and production are dealt with in one process. Criticism of this linear process has recently led to the development of new ideas such as:

- Management Resources Planning (MRP II)

- simultaneous materials and time management

- Kanban

- the concept of cumulative quantities

- load-dependent order release

(see Glaser 1994, pp. 747–761; see Hoitsch 1993, pp. 520–530; see Wiendahl 1987; see Zäpfel 1994, pp. 719–745).

One of the main developments to classical PPC systems, which usually start with MRP (Material Requirement Planning), is the MRP-II concept developed by Oliver Wight (see Wight 1983). The main feature of the MRP-II concept is the fact that the work scheduler can integrate the sales and production capacity information at an early planning stage. The aim behind this is that management obtains information at an early stage about whether the Sales and Operation plan has to be changed or whether capacities have to be increased by running additional shifts. Whereas the emphasis is put more on the internal organizational view (production) in classical PPC systems, in the MRP-II concept, the emphasis is more on a market-oriented view of things.

The production planning module of the R/3 System contains the planning functionality contained in the MRP-II concept. With the integration of the Sales Information System and the Sales and market analysis components of Controlling, SAP has developed the complete planning functionality starting with the strategic planning level (yearly planning) through to the operative production planning and scheduling level. However, whereas the MRP-II concept aims to plan costs and profit-maximizing elements within planning, SAP has developed a different approach in the R/3 System due to the large number of factors and large data volumes involved in real-life situations. As in the successive planning concept, the results are passed on from one planning level to the next, whereby interactive processing is possible between the two planning levels, for example between capacity planning and capacity levelling.

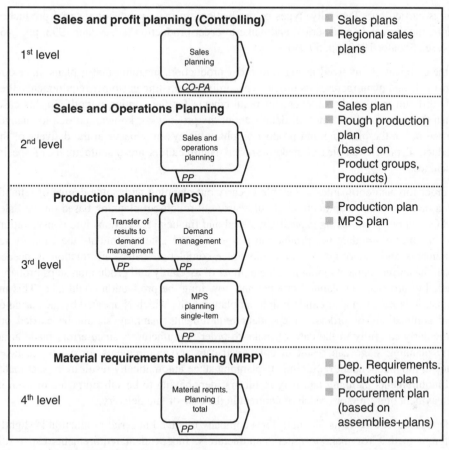

Fig. 8.99: Planning levels in MRP II – the concept of the model company

The main aim in production planning is to plan the requirement quantities of the materials to be produced in the coming periods (independent requirements) based on finished products, product groups and saleable spare parts. The basis for these requirements can be either existing customer orders or expected sales calculated using forecast values. The independent requirements should be calculated to make the maximum profit, taking capacity, material and financial restrictions into consideration. The result of the planning run is a production plan making maximum use of available resources, which is passed on to the next planning levels of the PPC system in the form of independent requirements. There, the requirements are determined for the lower-level assemblies and materials (dependent requirements).

One criterion often mentioned in literature to differentiate the different type of demands placed on a PPC system is the type of production carried out in a company (see Glaser *et al.* 1991; see Große-Oetringhaus 1974; see Schäfer 1969; see Schomburg 1980), which is taken into consideration in the planning of independent requirements. The characteristic feature in the description of the type of production is how often the same form of production is carried out. Typically, types of production are mass production, serial production (large, medium and small series) and make-to-order production (see Keller 1993, pp. 246–247; see Schäfer 1969, pp. 59-79).

If the company is involved in make-to-order production, meaning that it plans, develops, constructs and manufactures its products according to existing customer requirements, then it is difficult to plan the independent requirements for the coming periods. In this case, when the order is placed, not all details about the product are known and due to changes carried out in the planning and production phase, delays may occur in the delivery of the product. Typical examples of make-to-order manufacturers are manufacturers of special machines.

In order for such companies to be able to carry out planning with some degree of reliability, a make-to-order manufacturer should carry out rough-cut planning based on the Sales and Operations plan, taking capacity, material and financial restrictions into consideration, and be able to simulate the production process. To be able to simulate the capacity requirements and determine the probable order completion dates, information is needed about the current capacity situation, the number of assembly and production steps probably needed to produce the planned product and how long the production could take. This information is stored in a so-called rough-cut planning file which is updated by the partial or final completions of orders. Independent requirements planning should be carried out particularly carefully in the case of make-to-order manufacturers since errors made at an early planning stage can result in unlevelled capacity requirements. Errors or mistakes made at the independent requirements planning stage automatically result in inexact material requirements planning and may result in orders having to be subcontracted or even in the payment of a fine for breach of contract in the case of late delivery.

Independent requirements planning for a company involved in serial production is slightly different to that for make-to-order manufacturers. Independent requirements can result from existing customer orders and from forecast additional sales. Rough-cut planning here is more exact and forecast values can be obtained from marketing studies. However, here it is important to have reliable forecast values, as the following problems may arise if the forecast values are not reliable.

■ If too many products are manufactured, certain products may not be able to be sold and will lie in stock.

■ If too few products are manufactured, competitors may be able to take advantage of the situation.

To determine reliable forecast values, several different forecast models are used in PPC systems (see Hoitsch 1993, pp. 372–383; see Kernler 1993, pp. 114–140).

■ *Method of exponential smoothing*
   The method of first and second degree exponential smoothing makes sense in the case of trend consumption values.

■ *Method using the mean value*
   This makes sense if the consumption values are constant.

■ *Method using regression analysis*
This method makes sense in the case of trend consumption values.

As with the production type, independent requirements planning also depends on order type and the product range, that is, the degree of standardization of the products. The order type specifies what form the production and assembly is to take for the order. The product structure describes the structure of a product regarding the lower-level components. Product standardization describes to what degree the final product is standardized in its geometric, structural and production aspects. This, in connection with the order type, can have an effect on the tasks of design, costing, production and sales (see Keller 1993, pp. 239–306).

In the case of orders for *make-to-order production*, differences can occur between one period and the next. If more orders are received than are expected, this might result in capacity overloads in certain periods. If fewer orders are received than expected, either capacity loads must be reduced or the components produced to stock. In the case of *Orders based on outline agreements,* the product, delivery date and quantity may be contractually agreed upon and this leads to a more reliable planning situation. If the product has been defined but not the quantity or the date of delivery, final products or components have to be produced to stock before the expected date of delivery or material provision date, to be able to meet the delivery date. If only the product group is known, such as Recaro seats, but not the exact product, quantity and delivery date, call-offs may happen with various orders in different variants at irregular intervals. Large differences in orders can be dealt with by the preproduction of common parts, i.e. materials or assemblies needed in various variants. The order can result from *internal development orders* from the construction and design department for products that are not yet released for production for the open market. Depending on how urgent these orders are, they can be regarded as being fully available and can be moved forward or postponed in times when production capacity is available without influencing existing customer orders. If a development order is connected to a customer order, e.g. for the production of special tools, it should be treated and planned like a customer order.

8.16.2 SAP-specific description

To create the production plan, a decision must be made as to the planning strategy to be used to plan a material. The planning strategies represent sensible strategies for the planning and production or procurement of a material. You can decide whether production is to take place based on a customer order (order production) or independent of customer orders (stock production). It is also possible to use both customer and stock orders. If the production time is relatively long in comparison with the normal delivery time in the market, the final products, or at least certain components, should be manufactured in advance, before the customer orders arrive. To do this, sales quantities (for example from the Sales and Operations plan) are preplanned. The production plan is created using independent requirements. These can take the form of planned independent requirements or customer independent requirements (see SAP – Production Planning, pp. 6.1–6.6).

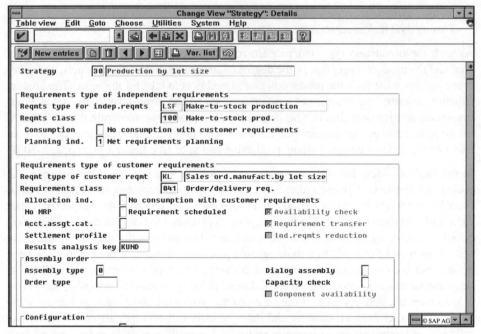

Fig. 8.100: Control parameters for the planning strategy (Customizing)

Planning strategies are defined using requirement types which contain the necessary control parameters. Requirement type *LSF* for lot production is selected for Model Company A and allocated to strategy *30* in Customizing (see Fig. 8.100). Further control parameters for preplanning are the requirements class (a group of requirement types) and the planning indicator. The planning indicator specifies whether gross or net planning is to take place. In the case of gross requirements planning, the available stock is not important and only planned receipts are taken into consideration. In the case of net requirements planning, the available stock and all goods receipts and goods issues within the planning horizon are considered. The requirement type can be either a requirement type from demand management or a requirement type from sales order management or a combination of both requirement types. In this way, you can determine which customer independent requirements are to be offset against planned independent requirements and whether an availability check is to take place according to ATP (available to promise) logic.

By allocating a planning strategy to a material, the correct requirement type (and with it all the control parameters assigned to the requirements class) is automatically determined when planned independent requirements or customer orders are created. For this to happen, the planning strategy, the strategy group and the allocation of the strategy group to the material must be maintained. The allocation of a planning strategy to a strategy group makes it possible for a material to be planned using any of several planning strategies. One main strategy and up to seven alternative strategies can be defined in the strategy group. To cover the variety of planning requirements possible, many planning strategies have been predefined in the R/3 System, referring to the final product, assembly or individual material. These planning strategies include:

■ *Make-to-stock production*

Using the planning strategy M*ake-to-stock production,* the production quantities and dates are determined using sales forecasts. These sales forecasts are passed on to the production planning department in the shape of planned independent requirements. Customer orders can be displayed for information purposes but they do not increase production requirements. The quantities produced are manufactured to stock and sales to customers also take place from stock using this strategy. Both gross and net planning are possible using this strategy. The production plan, i.e. the planned independent requirements, is reduced at the time of goods issue. The requirement closest to the goods issue date is reduced. If a customer inquires about the availability of a product, the availability check is carried out according to ATP logic using existing inventory. This type of strategy is recommended in the case of, for example, mass production.

■ *Production by lot size for sales and stock orders*

Using the planning strategy P*roduction by lot size for sales and stock orders,* several customer orders (depending on the production date) can be grouped together to form one lot. The size of the lot depends solely on production factors. To fill up the stock level, for example for sale from stock, it is possible to create additional stock orders, which increase the total quantity to be produced. Customer order requirements are not offset against stock orders. The customer order requirements are reduced when the goods are issued for the customer order. Availability checking using ATP logic is also possible. Stock orders are reduced by sales from stock. This strategy is most suitable for companies who mainly deal with orders for customers with a large order volume, but who also want the possibility to sell smaller requirements via a sale from stock.

■ *Preplanning with final assembly*

The strategy *Preplanning with final assembly* has been designed specifically for those companies who, apart from having their own production, also have an assembly department. The aim of this strategy is to start production before the customer requirements arrive with the help of planned independent requirements. In contrast to customer independent production to stock, the customer requirements are in this case offset against the planned independent requirements. Additional requirements which result from the fact that the customer requirement quantity is greater than the quantity planned for using planned independent requirements result in additional requirements being created in the system. Planned independent requirements not used by customer requirements result in an increase in stock levels of the finished products. For customer orders, an availability check can be carried out either using ATP logic with the available stock on hand or against the preplanning. In the case of the availability check against preplanning, the system checks whether, at the time of the customer order, enough planned independent requirements have been planned to cover the customer order. Preplanning with final assembly can be recommended when the quantity of final products to be manufactured can be reliably ascertained. With this strategy, the emphasis is put on long-term, constant customer-independent planning and the possibly to react quickly to customer wishes in the short term.

■ *Preplanning without final assembly*
The planning strategy *Preplanning without final assembly* is used to manufacture or procure assemblies before the customer order for the final product is received. The material is manufactured up to and including the level below final assembly and the assemblies and components needed in final assembly are kept in stock until the customer order arrives. Whereas production and procurement are started as a result of the planning of independent requirements, the final assembly is initiated as a result of the customer order. It is therefore possible to create planned orders for the final product that are only released for production when the customer order for the final product arrives. For this reason, an availability check can only take place as a check against preplanning, since at the highest production level, no planned orders that can be produced are created. Therefore, at the highest level, no ATP check against stock and planned receipts can be carried out. Additional customer requirements greater than the preplanned production quantities are covered by the production plan automatically being adapted. The planning strategy *Preplanning without final assembly* is most often used when a large part of the value added to a material occurs during the final assembly.

■ *Preplanning at assembly level*
With the strategy *Preplanning at assembly level (preplanning of assemblies)* the planning takes place via the creation of planned independent requirements for assemblies, by means of which the production of the assemblies is initiated. When customer orders arrive for the final product, the bills of material for the final products are also exploded. The dependent requirements resulting from the explosion of the BOM are offset against the planned independent requirements of the assemblies. If the dependent requirements turn out to be more than the planned independent requirements of the assemblies, the production plan is automatically adapted. The following control parameters have to be maintained for materials whose planning is to be carried out with planning strategy *planning at assembly level*:

– In the material master record (in the MRP 2 screen) the indicator *planning at assembly level* must be entered in field *mixed MRP*.

– The *cons.ind.planning* indicator in the item screen of independent requirements creation must allow the offsetting of requirements against customer requirements, reservations and dependent requirements.

Furthermore, for planning purposes, a so-called *phantom assembly* can be created in the R/3 System. This means that for planning purposes certain assemblies are grouped together logically but not physically. The planning strategy *Planning at assembly level* is especially useful for manufacturers of products with many variants when it is possible to predict requirements quite well for certain assemblies, but impossible to do this for final products due to the number of variants involved.

■ *Make-to-order production*
Make-to-order production describes the type of production where a product is manu-

factured especially for a customer order. The strategy *Make-to-order production* represents a type of production in which each product is only produced once, although over a period of time the same or similar production processes may be repeated. Each product is produced individually for one customer, which means that usually no products are stored in stock in the case of make-to-order production. The customer orders are planned as requirements for production using the customer order number. The materials produced cannot be used for other customer orders, and the quantities produced are only stored for the individual customer order. In MRP, an individual planning segment is created for make-to-order production. Starting with the customer order, the individual requirements can be passed on to any level of the BOM structure, which means that assemblies and components needed in the customer order are procured especially for the customer order and managed in the customer order stock for the material. The production and/or procurement costs of the customer order are managed in a special settlement order or project. This way, it is possible to analyze the planned and actual costs of the order. It is also possible to create a so-called assembly order for the make-to-order item (see Section 9.5). The assembly order initiates the automatic creation of a production order or planned order and provides an exact date of delivery. The date of delivery is based on the availability and the production requirements of the assemblies and components.

- *Make-to-order production with configuration*
With the strategy *Make-to-order production with configuration* the final product can be delivered in a large number of variants. The variant desired by the customer is configured individually in the customer order. Some of the components of the configurable final product are obligatory, others optional. Instead of creating a bill of material for each possible variant, all of the components are entered in one large bill of material known as a maximum bill of material. This maximum BOM contains not only all the common parts of the variants, but also all the variant parts (see Section 8.12). The specification of the variant of the configurable material to be delivered takes place in the customer order. The attributes of the product are stored in the R/3 System as characteristics and have various values. The characteristic *monitor size* can have the values 14", 15", 17" or 20" for a PC. The relationships between the individual characteristics and the characteristic values (and thus the circumstances or conditions under which a component is to be selected in BOM explosion) are defined in so-called object dependencies. Here, you can define either per BOM or in general which characteristics and characteristic values lead to the selection of the individual components. The object dependencies also determine which dependencies have to be observed during the configuration process. A dependency might be, for example, that a personal computer with a voltage of 220 volts is delivered with 50 Hertz and a personal computer with a voltage of 110 volts is delivered with 60 Hertz. With this planning strategy, no preplanning at final product level is possible (see Section 9.1).

8.16.3 Using the process

After the results from SOP have been transferred, the planned independent requirements for material *DPC1101* can be determined in demand management. The example for Model Company A shows the entry of independent requirements for a material. It is, however, also possible to carry out planning at product group level. On the initial screen (see Fig. 8.102), you can see the selection parameters with requirement type *LSF* for lot production, which were automatically taken over from the material master record for material *DPC1101*. The demand management shown works with active version *00*. Via the selection button *Requirement parameters*, you have the possibility to default the requirement parameters or to change them. For requirement type *LSF* a period split has been chosen as the display form (see Fig. 8.103). The next function *Determine origin of requirement types* in the process has already been carried out via the production plan. The whole production plan contains a monthly split of the requirements from February to July, but with different planned quantities. As a result of demand management, you can check the planned independent requirements in a separate step (see Fig. 8.106) in the stock/requirements list (in this case *MRP element IndReq*), and follow the development of the stock quantity.

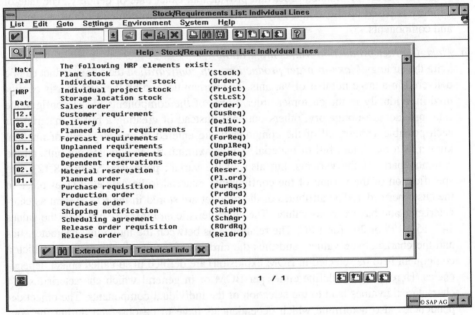

Fig. 8.101: Standardized MRP elements in the R/3 System

8.16.4 Navigation information

■ *Menu path*

for demand management: Logistics –> Production –> Master planning –> Demand management –> Planned indep. requirements –> Create

for the current stock/requirements situation: Logistics –> Production –> Master planning –> Demand management –> Environment –> Stock/reqmts. list

■ *Transaction code*
MD61 (demand management), MD04 (stock/requirements list)

■ *Ingoing processes in the R/3 Reference Model*
Transfer of results to demand management
Processing of independent requirements for long-term planning
Planning scenario activation
Forecast

■ *Outgoing processes in the R/3 Reference Model*
Processing of independent requirements for long-term planning
Total MRP
Single-item MRP
Materials planning sales order related
Total MPS
Single-item MPS
Interactive MPS
MPS sales order related
MPS project related
Planning scenario processing

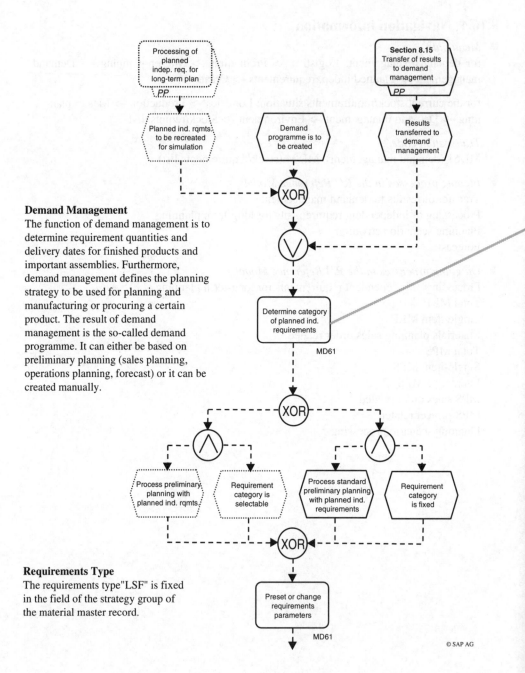

Demand Management

The function of demand management is to determine requirement quantities and delivery dates for finished products and important assemblies. Furthermore, demand management defines the planning strategy to be used for planning and manufacturing or procuring a certain product. The result of demand management is the so-called demand programme. It can either be based on preliminary planning (sales planning, operations planning, forecast) or it can be created manually.

Requirements Type

The requirements type "LSF" is fixed in the field of the strategy group of the material master record.

© SAP AG

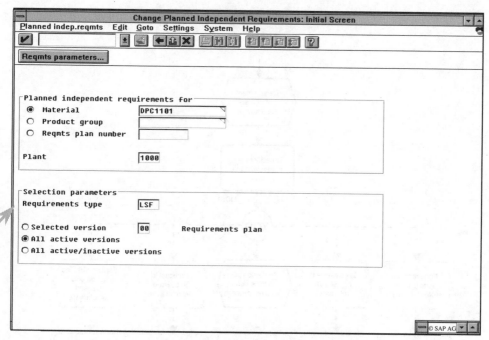

Fig. 8.102: Initial screen of demand management

Planning Strategies/Requirements Type

The planning strategies represent the business procedures for planning production quantities and dates. In the SAP System, a very broad spectrum of production planning strategies is available ranging from pure make-to-order production to make-to-stock production. Depending on the strategy selected, sales orders and/or sales forecast values are used to create the demand programme. You also have the option of moving the stocking level down to the assembly level so that final assembly is triggered by the incoming sales order. Alternatively, you can also carry out demand management specifically for the assembly. You can combine planning strategies which means, for example, that you can select the strategy *Planning with final assembly* for a finished product but still select a different strategy, such as *Planning at assembly level,* for an important assembly in the BOM of this finished product. The planning strategies available for a material are listed in Customizing and are assigned to the material in the material master record via the strategy group. Requirement types containing important control parameters are defined for each of the strategies. In the SAP standard system, a whole range of strategies are available, such as make-to-stock production or production by lot size for sales and stock orders, planning with final assembly, planning without final assembly, planning with planning material, planning at assembly level, planning at phantom assembly level, make-to-order production, make-to-order production with configuration, make-to-order production for material variants, planning material variants without final assembly, planning material variants using planning materials, planning variants and standard product planning.

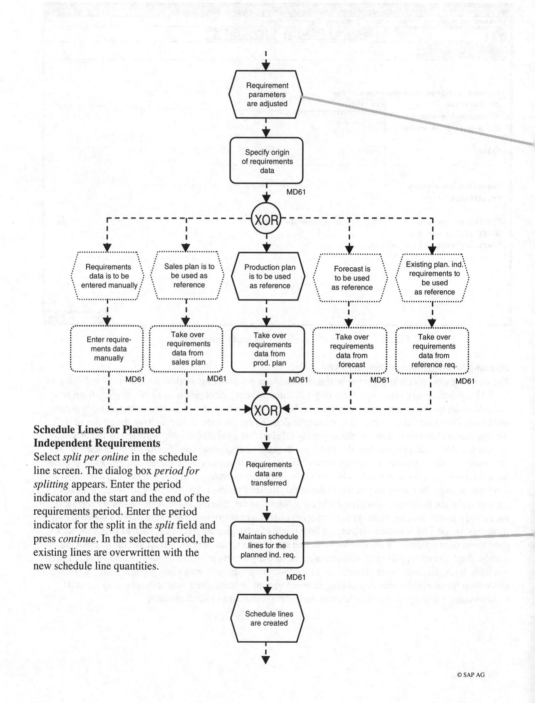

Requirement
parameters
are adjusted

Specify origin
of requirements
data

MD61

XOR

Requirements
data is to be
entered manually

Sales plan is to
be used as
reference

Production plan
is to be used
as reference

Forecast is
to be used
as reference

Existing plan. ind.
requirements to
be used
as reference

Enter require-
ments data
manually

Take over
requirements
data from
sales plan

Take over
requirements
data from
prod. plan

Take over
requirements
data from
forecast

Take over
requirements
data from
reference req.

MD61   MD61   MD61   MD61   MD61

XOR

**Schedule Lines for Planned
Independent Requirements**

Select *split per online* in the schedule
line screen. The dialog box *period for
splitting* appears. Enter the period
indicator and the start and the end of the
requirements period. Enter the period
indicator for the split in the *split* field and
press *continue*. In the selected period, the
existing lines are overwritten with the
new schedule line quantities.

Requirements
data are
transferred

Maintain schedule
lines for the
planned ind. req.

MD61

Schedule lines
are created

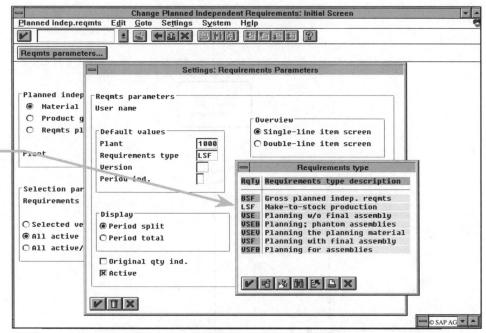

Fig. 8.103: Requirements parameters of demand management

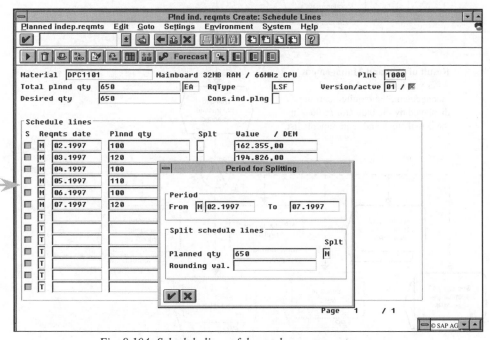

Fig. 8.104: Schedule lines of demand management

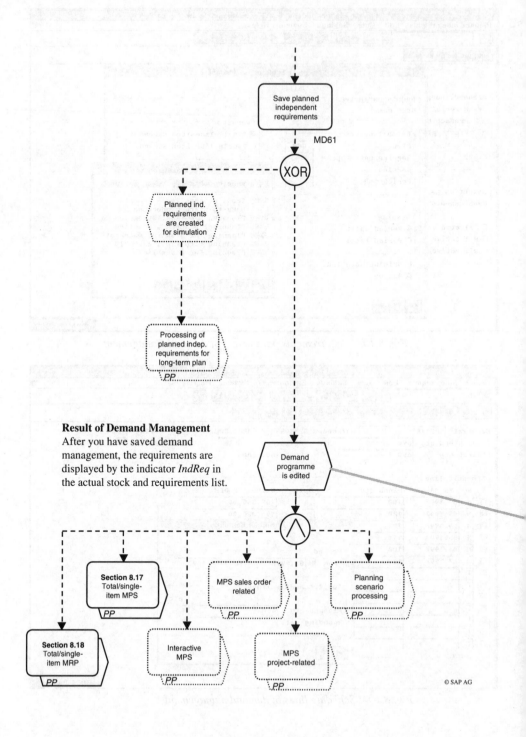

Save planned
independent
requirements

MD61

XOR

Planned ind.
requirements
are created
for simulation

Processing of
planned indep.
requirements for
long-term plan
PP

Result of Demand Management
After you have saved demand
management, the requirements are
displayed by the indicator *IndReq* in
the actual stock and requirements list.

Demand
programme
is edited

∧

Section 8.17
Total/single-
item MPS
PP

MPS sales order
related
PP

Planning
scenario
processing
PP

Section 8.18
Total/single-
item MRP
PP

Interactive
MPS
PP

MPS
project-related
PP

© SAP AG

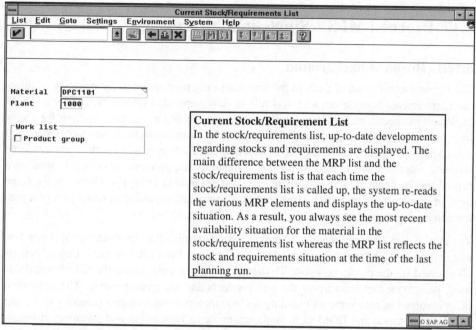

Fig. 8.105: Initial screen of current stock/requirements list

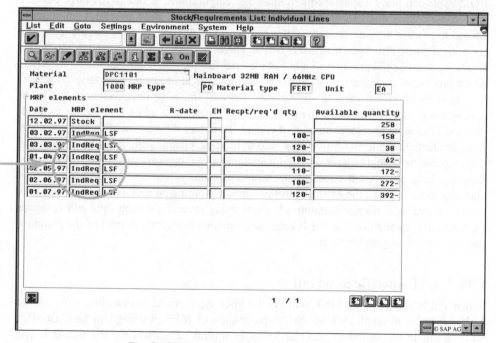

Fig. 8.106: Current stock/requirements list

8.17 Process: MPS – Single-item processing

8.17.1 Business background

The importance of material costs in the manufacturing process led to the planning of material requirements being given a central role in EDP-supported information systems. BOM explosion has been a central element of production planning and control systems for a very long time. The processing of the BOM explosion within material requirements planning and responsibility for the process have been treated in different ways both in the available business literature and indeed in practice. Materials requirements planning is seen as a central task of a materials management system (see Grochla 1978, pp. 33–68); at the same time, at least parts of materials requirements planning are regarded as being part of a production management system (see Schneeweiß 1993, pp. 157–185).

The aim of material requirements planning is to determine the requirements of dependent materials generated from the independent requirements from sales or marketing of materials planned via the production plan. To determine these requirements, the bill of material is used, describing the structure of the end products and their components. The individual tasks involved in requirements planning include material requirements planning involving BOM maintenance and BOM explosion, requirements monitoring and inventory management with the management of inventory quantities and values (see Section 8.18). The BOM explosion plays a special role in industrial corporations, as due to the large number of possible components, a very large data volume is involved and a powerful computer is needed to process the data. To reduce this problem, it is possible to carry out planning just for critical parts, also known as MPS items. These are raw materials, assemblies (semi-finished goods) or end products of a bill of material that play an important role in the value added process of a company („A" parts) or take up critical production resources. The aim is to plan these critical parts in such a way that cost-intensive resources are used in an optimum way and production bottlenecks avoided. These parts add a lot of value to products and as such tie up a large amount of capital. To reduce the amount of capital tied up in these products in the form of inventory, and to increase planning stability, the planning of certain products should be given special attention, since the master production schedule of these products has a great effect on the whole production process. By the restriction of planning to these parts, the MRP controller can carry out planning more quickly and thus create alternative master production schedules using several planning runs and compare the schedules. In addition, the MRP controller can also change the results of the planning run interactively in graphic form.

8.17.2 SAP-specific description

A material is marked as an MPS item via the MRP type. For MPS planning, a number of MRP types are available, via which the processing of MPS planning can be defined in more detail. In Customizing, you can maintain several parameters for the material type (see Fig. 8.107). For items to take part in MPS planning, the value M must be set as the

MRP procedure. Furthermore, it is possible to change the fixing type, i.e. it determines the way in which, and when, order proposals are fixed planned in the planning time fence during the planning run (no automatic changes to planned orders in this period). In the example, MRP procedure *MO* with fixing type *0* has been selected. Fixing type *0* for MPS planning means that order proposals are not automatically fixed (see SAP – Production Planning 1994, pp. 6.9–6.10).

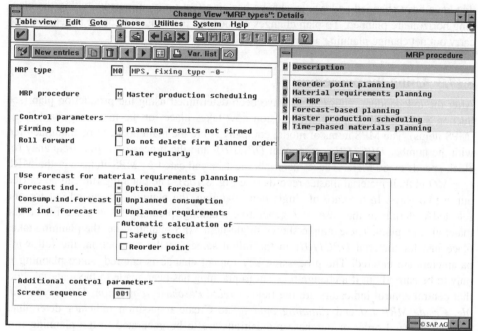

Fig. 8.107: Settings for the MRP procedure (Customizing)

A further control parameter in the MRP type is the *Roll-Forward* indicator. In order to be able to change the fixed master production schedule to adapt to a changed requirements situation, the indicator can be used to delete planned orders no longer needed. The indicator results in fixed order proposals that lie before the so-called roll-forward horizon being deleted in the planning run and new planned orders with the correct dates being created. In roll-forward planning you can define that the master production schedule is updated in a defined period. The MPS planning run, as well as the MRP run after it, can be carried out in different ways (see Section 8.18). The ways in which the planning is carried out is controlled via the processing key. In *regenerative planning* all of the materials in a plant are planned. This makes sense the first time a planning run is carried out and when due to technical errors the consistency of the data cannot be guaranteed. The disadvantage of regenerative planning is the high demands placed on the computer since every material is planned, even those for which no planning-relevant change has been made. To minimize this disadvantage, it makes sense in a productive system to carry out *net change planning*. With this type of planning, only materials for which a change has been carried out that is relevant for planning purposes are planned. Such changes are goods issues, customer orders, changes to the bill of material structure, etc. Net change planning allows the planning run to be carried out at short intervals, for example daily. The advantage of this is that you can always work with an up-to-date planning situation. With *Net change planning in the planning horizon,* the processing time of the planning run is reduced even further. With this type of planning, only changes in the planning horizon are considered in the planning run. Changes outside the planning horizon are ignored. This also means that only materials that have been changed and whose change has an effect on requirements within the planning horizon are planned. To plan changes outside the planning horizon, it is necessary to carry out net change planning at larger intervals.

8.17.3 Using the process

After the independent requirements have been determined using the production plan (see Section 8.16), a bill of material explosion now takes place for the most important items (MPS items). The MPS items of model company A are the main board to be manufactured with the number *DPC1101,* component *DPC1019* and the processor with a frequency (or clock speed) of 66 MHz. These materials must be indicated as MPS items via the MRP type *MO* in their material master records (see Fig. 8.108). The planning run can be carried out in two ways. In the case of single-item planning, the planning is carried out for one selected material; in the case of regenerative planning, planning takes place for all the materials in a plant. The example shows single-item MPS planning, i.e. the planning takes place just for material *DPC1101.* In the initial screen of the transaction, the following parameters are entered. The processing key for net change is entered, since planning is only to be carried out if a change relevant to planning has been made to the material. Further central control indicators are the fields *Create Purchase requisition, Delivery schedule, Create MRP list* and *Planning mode.* The Create requisition indicator determines whether planned order or purchase requisitions are to be generated in the planning run. The *Delivery schedule* indicator controls whether delivery schedules are to be created, no delivery schedules or delivery schedules only in the opening horizon and purchase requisitions outside the opening horizon. Delivery schedules can only be created automatically by requirements planning if a scheduling agreement exists for the material to be purchased with a valid planning indicator in the source list. The *Create MRP list* indicator determines whether an MRP list is to be created for each material after the planning run or whether no MRP list is to be created. The planning run adapts the production plan to date or quantity changes. If the requirement quantity is increased, for example, this can lead to a correction to the quantity of the order proposal generated in the planning run. MPS item *DPC1019* is marked as a material to be procured externally. Via the entry of the appropriate indicator 2 for Create purchase requisitions, purchase requisitions are created automatically. If the material already exists in stock, the system first accesses and reserves these. Once all the parameters have been set for MPS planning, the planning run can be started. It is also possible to run the planning run in the background or display the results of the planning run. The results of the planning run can be displayed in the MRP list. No purchase requisitions were generated for MPS item *DPC1019* since existing stock is available (MRP element *AR-RES).*

8.17.4 Navigation information

■ *Menu path*
for MPS item planning: Logistics –> Production –> Master planning –> MPS –>
MPS –> sng. item, sng. level
for the current stock/requirements situation: Evaluations –> Stock/reqmts list
for the MRP list: Evaluations –> MRP list – material

■ *Transaction code*
MD01, MD02, MD04 (current stock/reqmts situation), MD05 (MRP list), MD40,
MD41, MD42 (MPS planning)

■ *Ingoing processes in the R/3 Reference Model*
Customer contract release order processing
Consignment fill-up processing
Rush order processing
Free delivery processing
Customer schedule line processing
Processing subsequent delivery free-of-charge
Sales order processing with project system
Demand management
Standard order processing
Customer delivery schedule processing for scheduling agreements

■ *Outgoing processes in the R/3 Reference Model*
Planned order conversion
Total MRP
Purchase requisition assignment
Single-item MRP
Materials planning – interactive
Materials planning sales order related
Results processing – MPS

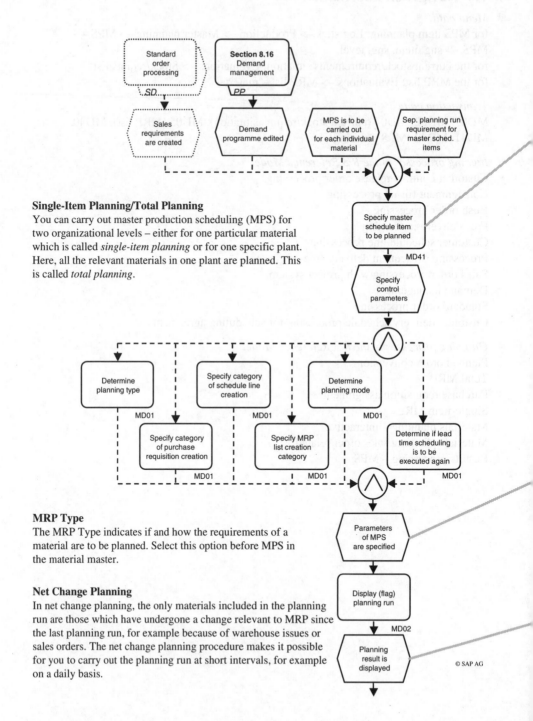

Single-Item Planning/Total Planning
You can carry out master production scheduling (MPS) for two organizational levels – either for one particular material which is called *single-item planning* or for one specific plant. Here, all the relevant materials in one plant are planned. This is called *total planning*.

MRP Type
The MRP Type indicates if and how the requirements of a material are to be planned. Select this option before MPS in the material master.

Net Change Planning
In net change planning, the only materials included in the planning run are those which have undergone a change relevant to MRP since the last planning run, for example because of warehouse issues or sales orders. The net change planning procedure makes it possible for you to carry out the planning run at short intervals, for example on a daily basis.

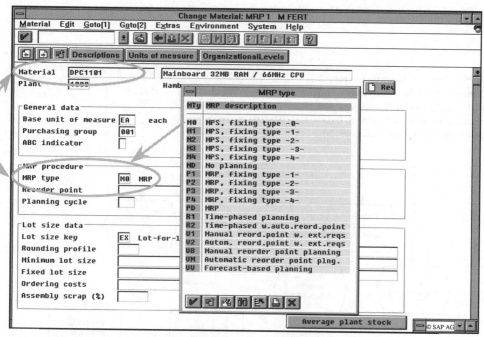

Fig. 8.108: Definition of MRP type in the material master

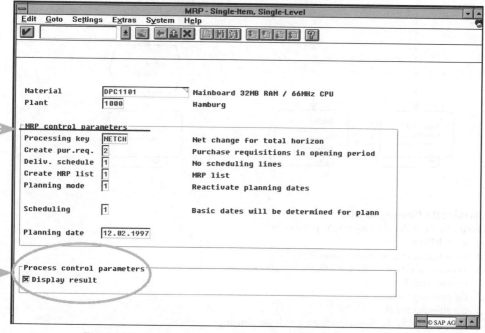

Fig. 8.109: Initial screen: specify parameters of MPS

MPS in Several Planning Levels
If there is more than one master schedule item in the BOM (as in Figure 8.111 DPC1101), you carry out planning at several planning levels. (MRP element: *IndReq* for a later planned order conversion, *PlOrd* for a reservation.)

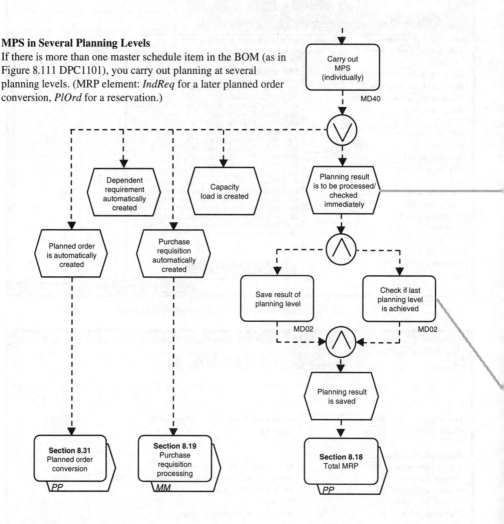

Checking the Planning Results
In order to check the planning results you require:
❑ the MRP list
❑ the actual stock and requirements list
❑ a comparison of the MRP list with the actual stock and requirements list
❑ the planning situation
❑ the planning result
❑ a comparison of the planning situation with the planning result
❑ the pegging
❑ the customer order status report.

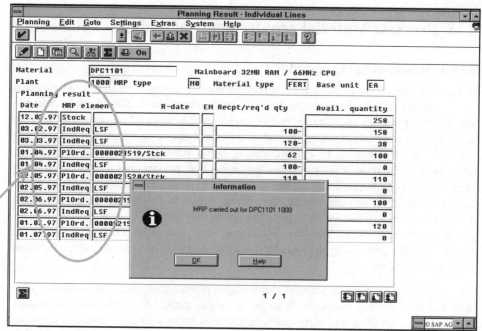

Fig. 8.110: Planning result of master schedule item

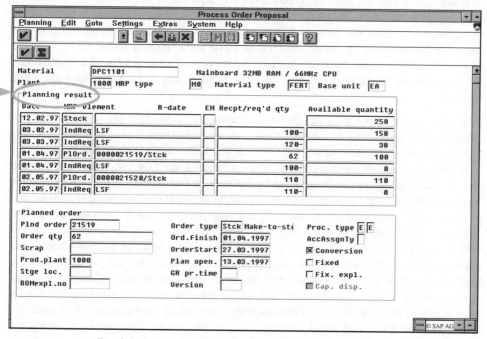

Fig. 8.111: Planning result of the last planning level

8.18 Process: Material requirements planning – Total

8.18.1 Business background

In *Material requirements planning* the requirements of assemblies, individual parts and raw materials needed to fulfil the production plan are determined. This involves determining both the quantities and dates of the requirements. The planned requirements are compared with the materials available in stock and planned stocks (materials that are not available now but are planned to be available on the date at which they are required). A prerequisite for this is that the MRP controller has access both to data regarding material movements and to both planned and current order data. If the calculated requirements do not correspond to an economical lot size, the optimal lot size is determined for the production orders of materials produced in-house. The production orders are then passed on to the production department, whereas the requirements for parts to be procured externally are passed on to the purchasing department (see Grochla 1978, pp. 33–141; see Schneeweiß 1993, pp. 157–185).

The main processes used in material requirements planning are *consumption-driven planning* and *deterministic planning*. Whereas in consumption-driven planning the requirements of the assemblies and parts can be determined using a forecast based on consumption in previous periods, in deterministic planning requirements (which is mainly used for „A" and „B" parts) the basis for determining the requirements is the bill of material. To express this more simply, it could be said that consumption-driven planning is based on the past, since it is based on consumption values in the past. Deterministic planning, on the other hand, is based on the future since it is based on real requirements for a material in the future. Factors that may have an effect on which procedure is used to determine future requirements are the product structure, the type of order entry and value of the goods to be planned.

Consumption-based planning or *stochastic planning*, as it is often known, tries to determine future requirements of a material using mathematical and statistical methods. Using various statistical methods, future requirements can be determined. In economic literature, it is often recommended to use consumption – driven planning for low-value materials and for materials not immediately affected by changes in production. A distinction is often made between material supplies, such as nails and lime, operating supplies, such as oil and office material, and production material such as metal rods, sheets, screws, springs and gaskets (see Grochla 1978, pp. 58–69). The large number of low-value materials needed in industrial organizations makes exact planning necessary in spite of the low value of the individual materials involved. For this reason, it is necessary to find the most accurate method of planning future requirements based on past consumption. *Constant material consumption* is supported by forecast methods using mean value calculation and first order exponential smoothing. For *trend consumption,* linear trend determination, first order exponential smoothing with trend correction and second order exponential smoothing are used. *Seasonal consumption* uses first order exponential smoothing with trend correction and second order exponential smoothing (see Arnolds *et al.* 1996, pp. 95–116; see Hoitsch 1993, pp. 372–383).

Plan-driven or *deterministic planning* uses existing *independent* requirements to determine the *dependent* requirements of materials. Using gross or net planning, bill of material explosion takes place starting with the end product and going down to the individual material in the bill of material to determine the dependent requirements from the independent requirements generated in the sales or cost accounting areas. The dependent requirements take spare parts and scrap quantities into consideration and determine the *gross requirements* of a material. Then, the available storage location, plant and order stocks are subtracted from the gross requirements to determine the *net requirements* (see Arnolds *et al.* 1996, pp. 81–93; see Hackstein 1989, pp. 132–154; see Grochla 1978, pp. 37–58; see Hoitsch 1993, pp. 360–372; see Scheer 1990, pp. 79–130). It must be possible to determine the optimum order quantity for materials to be procured externally as well as the optimum lot size for materials to be produced in-house. Furthermore, it must be possible for both the bill of material to be exploded automatically and for the MRP controller to check or review the explosion at every level of the BOM. An important factor in the bill of material explosion is the offset lead time. This guarantees that the subordinate material is available before the order production date of the material to be produced. This offset lead time can be entered in the basic data of the material master, the bill of material or the routing. For this reason, this data has to be accessed in requirements explosion. The offset lead time is maintained in the material master record of the part if the lead time is independent of the material, in which the part is used. If this time depends on the material for which the part is used, the offset lead time is maintained in the bill of material of this material. If several operations are needed in the production of a material, the total processing time is determined by adding the lead time of the individual operations stored in the routing and thus the offset lead time is allocated to the part.

When the independent requirements are planned, the link between the customer order and the period-related dependent requirements relevant for production is lost if several customer orders are grouped together in one planning period. Via lot sizing and the transfer of dependent requirements into other periods, the relationship between requirements and order is also lost in requirements planning (requirements explosion). In this way, it is no longer possible to track the origins of individual requirements. This information, however, is important if the company is involved in make-to-order production. Only if requirements tracking can be carried out can the company inform the customer about the progress of their order. Additionally, if a production lot is delayed, it must be possible to find out which orders might be affected by the delay. Via the *pegging* of requirements, it is possible, at any point in time, to provide information about the progress of an order or how any delays might affect the production of an order. Depending on the type of pegging used (single-level or multi-level), it is possible to track the link between the final product and the material on the layer below it in the bill of material or to the lowest level in the bill of material (see Scheer 1990, pp. 138–153).

To be able to carry out material requirements planning reliably, it is necessary to have an exact overview of existing stocks. Apart from the stocks physically available in the company, it must be possible to obtain information on stocks in order or in production and to use this information in requirements planning. Requirements planning must also take into consideration stocks that are physically present in the warehouse but are reserved for other orders, as well as purchase orders and production orders reserved for other purposes. When determining the available stock, stock in quality inspection in the goods receipt and goods issue areas plays an important role. This covers all the stock which, at the time of material requirements planning, cannot be used due to, for example, missing quality information. Apart from quantity-based inventory management, value-based inventory management must also be possible as this information is needed for tax and accounting purposes.

8.18.2 SAP-specific description

The central task of material requirements planning is to guarantee material availability, i.e. to provide the materials needed both internally and for sales purposes at the required time. This involves monitoring stock levels and the creation of order proposals for purchasing and production. The activities involved in material requirements planning are all the tasks needed to determine the type, quantity and time of requirements and the quantity and dates of materials needed to meet these requirements. To determine the quantities needed, the stocks, reservations and quantity on order must be taken into consideration; to determine the dates, the delivery and lead times must be considered. To determine the order proposal for a material, the MRP controller defines per material a suitable MRP type and lot sizing procedure. Using the methods recommended in economic literature, both *deterministic* and *consumption-based* planning methods are available in the R/3 System (see SAP – Production Planning 1994, pp. 7.1–7.12; Materials Management 1996, pp. 4.1–4.10).

In *deterministic planning*, it is possible to decide whether and how materials are to be planned. The aim of *MPS planning* is to plan materials which are very important for production purposes very carefully. This typically involves materials which make up a large part of sales (see Section 8.17). In the case of *deterministic planning without BOM explosion,* customer orders and material reservations are directly used in planning. It is thus regarded as being part of the plan-driven methods as existing requirements are referred to in planning. The system checks whether existing stocks suffice to cover the requirements. If not, an order proposal is generated.

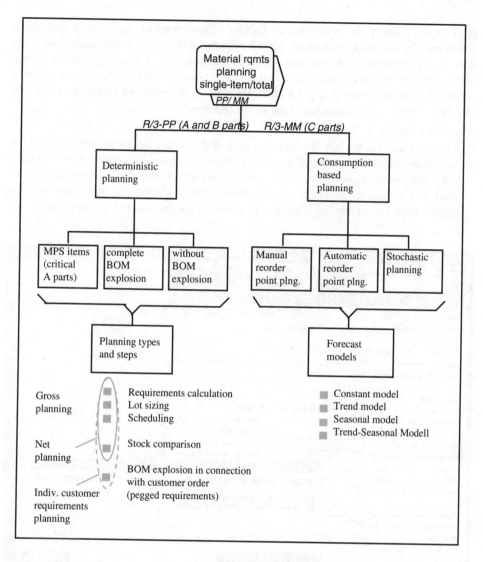

Fig. 8.112: Material requirements planning overview

In *deterministic planning with complete BOM explosion*, the R/3 System carries out requirements calculation for all the requirements to be planned. Afterwards, the lot sizes are determined and via scheduling the material provision dates for the needed assemblies and components. For each new order proposal of an assembly, the BOM is exploded in the planning run. For existing order proposals, the bill of material is only exploded again if the quantity or requirement date of the order proposal or the bill of material structure has changed. However, the bill of material can be exploded again if required in the initial screen via the *planning mode*. The quantity and the date of all the assemblies needed to produce the product are influenced as follows. The dependent requirement quantity is determined by the quantity factor of the bill of material item. The requirement date of the dependent requirement is determined via the production time of the component to be produced. This means that the planned start date of the planned order for the component to be produced is the requirement date for the BOM item. In deterministic planning in R/3, you can choose between the following planning procedures:

■ *Gross planning*
In gross planning, the bill of material is exploded, the lot size determined and scheduling carried out *without* taking the available stock situation into account. In the planning run, only expected goods receipts, planned orders and purchase requisitions are considered. For materials, for which gross planning is to be carried out, you must enter the indicator for gross planning in the mixed MRP field in the material master record.

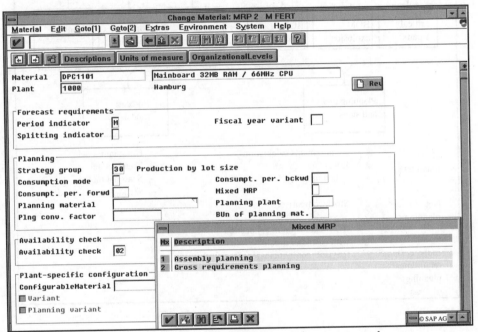

Fig. 8.113: MRP entries in the material master record

■ *Net planning*

In net planning, BOM explosion is carried out with lot sizing and scheduling taking available stock into consideration. For all storage locations belonging to the plant and which are not excluded from planning or planned separately, the following stocks are grouped together to form the plant stocks:

– valued, unrestricted stock

– quality inspection stock

– unrestricted use consignment stock

– consignment stock in quality inspection

Additionally, you can define in Customizing whether the transit stock and blocked stock should be considered as part of the plant stock. Net requirements planning means that, for each requirements date, the system checks whether the requirement is covered by the plant stock or planned receipts. If not, the system calculates the missing quantity. The quantity to be ordered is determined in lot sizing. The available stock in net requirements planning is determined as follows:

Plant stock
– *Safety stock*
+ *Planned receipts (purchase orders, fixed planned orders, production orders)*
– *Requirement quantity (e.g. planned independent requirements, customer independent requirements, material reservations, forecast requirements for unplanned consumption)*

= *available stock*

■ *Individual customer order planning*

A special individual customer order planning run is available for the requirements planning of customer orders. In this way, it is possible to track a customer order over several production levels, to store material for a special customer order and to collect costs for one customer order. An order proposal is generated for each customer order without previous lot sizing. Existing production orders and purchase orders for these customer orders are considered, as are already delivered partial quantities that are managed as special stock. In addition, it is possible to get an overview of the production status of the complete BOM structure starting with the customer order number in a special report.

In deterministic planning, it is possible to peg requirements. Single-level planning is shown in the planning result, the *MRP list* and the *stock/requirements list*. For each dependent requirement, the material number and the planned order number leading to the dependent requirements are specified. Via the *Pegged requirements* function, which is available as an additional function in the planning result, MRP list and the stock/ requirements list, it is possible to track the requirements back to the origin and to see which requirements led to which order proposals and which independent requirements (especially customer orders) would be endangered if an order proposal were changed with respect to date or quantity, or did not exist at all.

Within the *BOM structure,* a differentiation must be made between the production structure and planning structure. Whereas the production structure provides answers to the question when and in which quantity a material or an assembly must exist within the production process (allocation of the material or assembly to production level), the low-level code is to provide the material at the right time for the whole production process. The *assignment of low-level codes* takes into account the fact that materials can be used in several products or several levels of one product. The low-level code is the lowest level in which a material is used in all product structures. Using the low-level code, the system groups the total requirements for a material at the lowest level at which it occurs.

The sequence in which materials are planned according to the assignment of the low-level code is stored in the R/3 System in the *planning file*. Using the planning file, the MRP controller can see the structure of the planning levels at any time. It is possible to display the planning file for all the materials in one plant, for one material (by entering the material number), to reduce the display to certain planning levels or just to see the planning entries for MPS items. When the planning run is carried out, it is possible to define whether all materials are to be planned or only certain materials and how planning is to take place. In regenerative planning, all the materials for which planning can take place are planned for a plant. In single-item planning, planning takes place for the selected material. Single-level single-item planning only plans the bill of material item of the material selected. Multi-level single-item planning plans all levels of the selected material. The planning file contains all materials which are relevant for a planning run. This means that as soon as a material master record has been created with MRP screens and a valid MRP type, an entry for the material is automatically created in the planning file.

The type of planning in the R/3 System is split into three types, which can be chosen when carrying out the planning run:

■ *Regenerative planning*
In regenerative planning, all materials which can be planned are planned. All order proposals generated in a previous planning run are deleted and new order proposals generated.

■ *Net-change planning*
In net-change planning, the only order proposals to be replanned are those which no longer apply as a result of changes which have taken place since the last planning run. In order for net change planning to take place, materials receive an extra indicator, the total change indicator, when changes are made to the material that are relevant from a planning point of view. Usually, this indicator is set automatically by the system as soon as such a change occurs. Such changes could be:

  – material stock changes resulting in a change to the stock/requirement situation of the material

- the creation of purchase requisitions, purchase orders, planned orders, sales orders, forecast requirements, dependent requirements or reservations

- changing of the fields relevant to planning in receipts, issues or the material master record

- deletion of planned goods receipts and goods issues

■ *Net-change planning in the planning horizon*
In net-change planning in the planning horizon, the only materials to be planned in the planning run are those for which a change relevant to planning has taken place within a period defined as the planning horizon. Once the planning horizon has been defined, all materials undergoing such a change receive a further indicator, the short-term net-change planning indicator, in the planning file. If the planning run cannot be completed correctly, this indicator remains in the planning file, so that the material is planned again in the next planning run carried out with net-change planning. Via Customizing it is possible to define whether the entries are to be deleted in the case of a termination in the planning run (for example, if a certain material does not exist in the plant for which planning is to take place).

Consumption-based planning is based on a series of consumption values and is used together with the forecast to plan future consumption. The procedures used in consumption-based planning have no reference to the master production schedule, i.e. net requirements planning is not initiated via independent or dependent requirements. The determination of requirements is initiated either by the stock level falling short of a predetermined reorder level or via forecast requirements calculated from past consumption values. For consumption-based planning to work correctly, it requires a well-functioning and up-to-date inventory management system.

The MRP types used in consumption-based planning are used mainly in companies or areas without their own production facilities or in production companies to plan requirements of „B" and „C" parts and operating supplies. The type of order proposal generated automatically by material requirements planning depends on the procurement type of the material involved. In the case of materials produced in-house, a planned order is generated. In the case of externally procured materials, the MRP controller can decide whether a planned order or a purchase requisition is to be generated. If he chooses a planned order, he must then convert the planned order into a purchase requisition in a separate step and pass this on to purchasing. The advantage of this is that this method involves an additional check of the order proposal by the MRP controller before it is processed by the purchasing department. This means that the purchasing department can only order the material when the MRP controller has checked the order proposal and converted it into a purchase requisition. Without this extra step, a purchase requisition is created immediately and the purchasing department accepts responsibility for the material availability and inventory situation. The MRP types used in consumption-based planning are *reorder point planning*, *stochastic planning* and *rhythmic planning*.

- *Reorder point planning*

  In reorder point planning, the available plant stock is compared with the reorder point. The reorder point consists of the safety stock and the expected average material requirements during the replenishment lead time. Therefore, to calculate the reorder point (reorder level), the safety stock, past or future consumption and the replenishment lead time must all be taken into consideration. The safety stock is used to cover additional requirements during the replenishment lead time caused by both additional consumption and delays in delivery. Thus, when calculating the safety stock, both the past or future consumption values of the material and the vendor's adherence to delivery dates (or internal production dates) must be taken into consideration.

  The reorder level (point) and the safety stock are thus central control parameters in reorder point planning and can be calculated by the system as well as manually by the MRP controller. For this reason, a distinction is made in reorder point planning between *manual* and *automatic reorder point planning*. In manual reorder point planning, the user must define the reorder point and safety stock himself and enter them in the material master record of the corresponding material. In automatic reorder point planning, the reorder point and the safety stock are determined using the integrated forecast program. Using past consumption values, the system forecasts future consumption values for the material. Using these forecast values and depending on the service level calculated by the MRP controller and the replenishment lead time of the material, the system calculates both the safety stock and the reorder point for the material and enters these in the material's master record. Since the forecast program is run regularly, the safety stock and the reorder point are adapted to fit the existing consumption and delivery situation and are an important factor in reducing stock levels.

  If the available stock level falls below the reorder level, the system automatically generates an order proposal. However, if a purchase order or production order that could cover the required quantity has already been created in the purchasing or production departments, no additional order proposal is created. The quantity of an order proposal generated depends on the lot-sizing procedure used for the material. Each material is assigned a separate lot-sizing procedure. The order proposal is also scheduled, i.e. the system calculates the date on which the vendor or the production department has to deliver the material.

  The monitoring of the plant stock availability in reorder point planning is taken care of by the inventory management program. Each time a goods issue takes place, the system checks to see whether the stock level falls below the reorder level. If so, an entry in the planning file is created for the next planning run. In the same way, when a material is returned to stock, the system checks to see whether the available stock exceeds the reorder point. If so, a planning entry is also created so that the planning run can remove unnecessary order proposals. If fixed planned receipts become unnecessary due to materials being returned or other goods receipts, these planned goods receipts are proposed for deletion by the planning run. In this case, the MRP controller must get together with the purchasing department to decide whether the purchase order or the production order involved can be stopped or cancelled.

In reorder point planning, net requirements planning is only initiated when the stock level falls below the reorder point. Planned goods receipts such as customer requirements, planned independent requirements or reservations are only displayed in reorder point planning and are not taken into consideration in net requirements planning. The available stock is calculated as follows:

Plant stock
+   *order stock (purchase orders, firm planned orders, firm purchase requisitions)*

=   *available stock*

If the available stock is less than the reorder point (level), the shortage quantity is the difference between the reorder level and the available stock. The requirement date is determined by the system as the date of the planning run. When calculating the shortage quantity, the system does not consider the safety stock. However, if the stock level falls below the safety stock, the MRP controller receives an exception message.

■ *Stochastic planning*
Stochastic planning is also based on the consumption of a material, as is consumption-based planning, and forecast values are calculated for future consumption by the integrated forecast program as in consumption-based planning. However, in contrast to consumption-based planning, the forecast values are used as the basis for the planning run. The forecast program is run at regular intervals, using past consumption values to determine future requirements. This provides the advantage that the requirements calculated automatically are adapted to fit the current consumption situation. If material has already been consumed in the current period, the forecast requirements are reduced by the amount of these issues, so that the part of the forecast requirements already consumed is not planned again. The period for the forecast (day, week, month or accounting period) and the number of forecast periods can be determined individually for each material. Sometimes, the period for the forecast is not fine enough. Therefore, it is possible to define that forecast requirement values for a material can be split into smaller periods.

The requirement quantities forecast by the system are taken over into material requirements planning and net requirements planning is carried out. In net requirements planning, the system checks for each period whether the forecast requirements for the period are covered by available stock or firm planned receipts from either purchasing or production. In the case of shortage, an order proposal is generated. The quantity of the order proposal is determined according to the lot-sizing procedure used for the material. If necessary according to the lot-sizing procedure, several requirement quantities are grouped together to form one lot. For each order proposal, the system calculates the date on which the order proposal has to be converted into a purchase order or production order, so that the purchase order can be sent to the vendor in time or the production order can be started. This is because the material can only be delivered on time if the vendor receives the purchase order on time or the production department can start producing the production order on time.

In stochastic planning, the total forecast requirements are the basis of the net requirements calculation. The system only regards the forecast requirements as goods issues. Other planned issues such as customer requirements, planned independent requirements or reservations are only displayed and are not considered in net requirements calculation. For each forecast requirement, the system checks whether the requirement is covered by available stock or other goods receipts (purchase orders, firm order proposals). The available stock per requirement date is calculated as follows:

Plant stock
– *Safety stock*
+ *Receipts (purchase orders, firm order proposals)*
– *requirements quantity (forecast requirements)*

= *available stock*

A shortage exists when the available stock becomes negative, i.e. when the requirements quantities are larger than goods receipts. The shortage quantity is stored by the system. The requirement date is calculated by the system as being the date of the forecast requirements. In this calculation, the system assumes that the requirements occur at the beginning of the period. This means that the requirements date is the first working day in the period.

■ *Rhythmic planning*
If a vendor always delivers goods on a particular day of the week, it makes sense to plan the material in the same rhythm, delayed by the delivery time of the material. This can be carried out using rhythmic planning. For rhythmic planning to be carried out for a material, the material master record of the material must contain the MRP type for rhythmic planning and the planning rhythm.

Rhythmically planned materials are assigned a planning date in the planning file. This date is set when the material is created and then set again each time the material is planned. It corresponds to the day on which the material is next to be planned. It is calculated using the planning rhythm in the material master record. Using this procedure, a material can be planned only on certain days specified by the user. If, for example, all the materials supplied by a vendor are assigned to the same planning rhythm, they are all always planned on the same days. The purchase requisitions generated in the case of shortage can be processed by the MRP controller per vendor in the R/3 purchasing module. Additionally, it is possible to enter a planning date when starting the planning run. This has the advantage of being able to pull the planning run forward to an earlier date. If the planning run is supposed to be carried out on Monday, for example, it is possible to carry out the planning run for Monday on the previous Saturday.

Based on the different consumption patterns available, various forecast models can be used in the R/3 System.

■ *Constant model (constant consumption pattern)*
A constant consumption pattern exists if the consumption statistically varies around an average value. In such a case, you can use the forecast models *Constant model* and *Constant model with correction of the smoothing factors.* Forecasting using both of these models is carried out using first order exponential smoothing. Here, different combinations of parameters are tried out when smoothing the factors to obtain the combination of parameters resulting in the lowest mean absolute deviation.

■ *Trend model or (trend consumption pattern)*
In the case of a trend consumption pattern, the consumption increases or decreases over a long period of time, possibly with occasional fluctuations. In this case, it makes sense to choose the trend model or a model using second order exponential smoothing. With the trend model, the system calculates the forecast values using first order exponential smoothing. When using a model with second order exponential smoothing, you can choose between a model with or without parameter optimization.

■ *Seasonal model (seasonal consumption pattern)*
With a seasonal consumption pattern, fluctuations from a base value occur at regular intervals. With such a consumption pattern, it makes sense to use the seasonal model. Using the seasonal model, the system calculates the forecast values using first order exponential smoothing.

■ *Seasonal trend model (seasonal trend consumption pattern)*
In the case of a seasonal trend consumption pattern, seasonal fluctuations occur around a constantly increasing or decreasing average value. In the case of such a consumption pattern, it makes sense to use the seasonal trend forecast model. Here, the system calculates the forecast values using first order exponential smoothing.

Before a forecast can be carried out for a material, the forecast parameters must have been entered in the material master record of the material concerned. You can carry out model selection manually by analyzing a time series of consumption and assigning a forecast model. The model selection can also be carried out automatically by having the R/3 System analyze the consumption and then selecting the appropriate forecast model. If no model can be selected, the system defaults the constant model.

Independent of the MRP type used, i.e. deterministic or consumption-based planning, lot-sizing and scheduling can be carried out after the determination of requirements. The aim of lot-sizing is to find the economically optimum combination between production and storage costs. In the R/3 System, three different types of methods of calculating the optimum lot size can be used. Which type of method is to be used is defined in the material master record of the material. Furthermore, in the material master record, you can specify minimum or maximum lot sizes.

■ *Static lot-sizing procedures*
With static lot-sizing procedures, only factors specified by the MRP controller are used to determine the lot size. The procedures available are:

– *lot-for-lot*
When a shortage occurs for a material with lot-sizing procedure lot-for-lot, the system sets exactly the shortage quantity (requirements minus available stock) as the lot size. For the corresponding requirements date, the planned warehouse stock is 0. Planning takes place on a daily basis. This means that if several requirements exist for one day, they are grouped together to form one order proposal and not one order proposal per requirement.

– *fixed lot size*
It makes sense to choose a fixed lot size for a material when technical situations, such as pallet size or tank contents, make this necessary. When a shortage occurs for a material with a fixed lot size, the system takes the fixed lot size defined in the material master record as the lot size for the requirement. If this quantity is not large enough to satisfy the requirement, the system creates several lots each with the fixed lot size under the same date until the requirement quantity is met. If the fixed lot size is used, it is possible to define a threshold value. This threshold value is used to terminate the planning of a material if the system creates more order proposals for the material on one date than the value of the threshold value.

– *fixed lot size with splitting and overlapping*
In the case of fixed lot size with splitting, the fixed lot size is split into several partial quantities which are not produced at the same time but instead are overlapped. The partial quantities into which the system divides the total quantity has to be entered in field *Rounding value*. The fixed lot size must be a multiple of the rounding value. The time by which the partial quantities should overlap is entered in field *Cycle time*. Using this lot-sizing procedure, the system creates order proposals the size of the rounding value until the quantity of the fixed lot size is reached. The end dates are offset by the cycle time. In the MRP Customizing functionality in menu point *Lot size calculation, you* can define whether the order proposals are to overlap backwards or forwards. In forward overlapping, the planned orders are scheduled into the future starting with the requirement date. The planned start date of the individual planned orders is offset by the cycle time. In backward overlapping, the planned orders are scheduled into the past starting with the requirement date. The planned start date of the individual planned orders is offset by the cycle time.

- *replenish to maximum stock level*

  When a shortage occurs for a material for which *replenishment up to maximum stock level* is to take place, the lot size, that the system uses is the difference between the available stock and the maximum stock level defined in the material master record. Replenishment up to maximum stock level is only used in reorder point planning.

■ *Periodic lot-sizing procedures*

Using periodic lot-sizing procedures, the system groups several requirement quantities for a period together in one lot. The period concerned may be a day, week, month or a period with a flexible length such as an accounting period. In the case of a daily lot size, all the requirements falling on one day or a certain number of days are grouped together to form one lot. In the case of a period with a flexible length, all the requirements within one or a freely definable number of periods are grouped together to form a lot. The periods are defined in the same way as accounting periods. The lot size created is also known as a periodic lot size.

- *optimizing lot-sizing procedures*

  In the case of static and periodic lot-sizing procedures the costs that occur as a result of storage, setup and purchasing are not taken into account when calculating the lot size. The aim of optimizing lot-sizing procedures is to choose the lot size in such a way as to minimize the total costs. These total costs are made up of costs independent of the lot size (setup or purchasing costs) and storage costs. If purchase orders are placed frequently, the storage costs are kept to a minimum. However, the large number of purchasing activities result in high purchasing costs. If goods are not purchased frequently, the purchasing costs are reduced. However, the storage costs are a lot higher since the available stock must cover the requirements over a much longer period of time. The various optimizing lot-sizing procedures only differ in the way in which costs are minimized. The procedures that exist are the part-period balancing procedure, least-unit cost procedure or Groff lot-sizing procedure.

Once the lot sizes needed to cover the requirements exist, the last step is to determine the dates for the materials to be produced or procured. Two factors are necessary to do this; firstly, the scheduling type, i.e. whether forward or backward scheduling is to take place, and secondly the procurement type, i.e. whether the material is to be produced in-house or procured externally. Additionally, certain interdependencies exist with the MRP types.

■ In the case of *deterministically planned* materials and with *stochastic planning*, the requirement dates in the future are known. This is the date on which the material must be available. The calculation of the start and end dates for in-house production and the release date for purchasing for these two procedures thus always takes place using *backward scheduling*. Only if the start or release date determined in scheduling lies in the past does the system automatically switch to forward scheduling starting with the planning date.

■ In *reorder point planning* the dates are determined using *forward scheduling*. Once the stock level falls below the reorder level it means that procurement activities have to be initiated. Starting with the date of shortage the availability date of the material in the future is determined.

In the case of in-house production, a difference is made in the planning run between the planned start and end dates. The planned end date is the latest end date and the planned start date the earliest start date of production. These dates take into consideration the goods receipt processing time or the in-house processing time in the material master record. The in-house production time can be stored as a lot-size dependent or independent value. In the case of external procurement, the planned end date corresponds to the delivery date, the planned start date corresponds to the release date. The processing time for purchasing and the goods receipt processing time are entered in working days, and the planned delivery time of the material is entered in calendar days. In the case of in-house production, the system always creates *planned orders*. These planned orders are used to plan the quantities needed in production. Once planning has been carried out, the planned orders are converted into production orders. For external procurement, the system either creates a *planned order* or creates a *purchase requisition* directly. Order proposals for external procurement are used to plan the quantity to be procured externally. Once planning has taken place, the planned order is converted into a purchase requisition and the purchase requisition into a purchase order. Whether purchase requisitions are created in the planning run or planned orders are created first can be defined in the initial screen of the planning run via the creation indicator for purchase requisitions. If a scheduling agreement exists for a material and an entry relevant for planning has been created in the source list, the planning run can automatically create scheduling line items. This is achieved by entering the creation indicator for schedule line items in the initial screen of the planning run.

8.18.3 Using the process

Once the independent requirements from demand management have been created (Section 8.16) and single-item MPS planning has been carried out for MPS items (see Section 8.17), total *material requirements planning* is carried out. This planning run is carried out for all the materials of the plant, in the case of the model company plant 1000 in Hamburg, and takes place in batch. It is possible to display certain stop points in the planning run (see Fig. 8.114). The example shows a stop point for material *DPC1014* on low-level code *003*. The other control data (see Fig. 8.115) are the same as the parameters described in the initial screen of MPS planning (see Section 8.17). Whereas in MPS planning the BOM explosion only takes place for critical items, in MRP the BOM explosion takes place for all levels of the bill of material. The planning run took place for the four components *DPC1101*, *DPC1014*, *DPC1018* and *DPC1019*. The material with material number DPC1101 is the final product of Model Company A, the other three components are assemblies. These assemblies are partially procured externally. The result of planning displays the number of purchase requisitions created and the number of purchase requisitions deleted (which existed as a result of a previous planning run) in the statistics (see Fig. 8.116). Exceptions can occur in the planning run. In this case, the situation is marked with an exception message. The MRP controller can display the reasons for the exceptions in a log (by pressing the button Exception in the upper header line). After the planning run, the components of the bill of material can be seen in the MRP list. For each dependent requirement (DepReq) you can see whether they are to be produced in-house or procured externally and what quantity is required for each component (see Fig. 8.117).

8.18.4 Navigation information

▪ *Menu path*
Logistics –> Production –> MRP –> MRP –> Sng-item multi-lvl

▪ *Transaction code*
MD02, MD03

▪ *Ingoing processes in the R/3 Reference Model*
MPS – project related, Standard order processing, Consignment fill-up processing, Customer delivery schedule processing for scheduling agreement, Rush order processing, Customer contract release order processing, Free-delivery processing, Customer schedule line processing, Processing subsequent delivery free-of-charge, Sales order processing with project system, Demand management, Single-item MPS, Interactive MPS, MPS sales order related, Planning file entry

▪ *Outgoing processes in the R/3 Reference Model*
Planned order conversion, Purchase requisition processing
Results processing – MRP, Cost centre planning with static standard costing, Cost centre planning with flexible standard costing

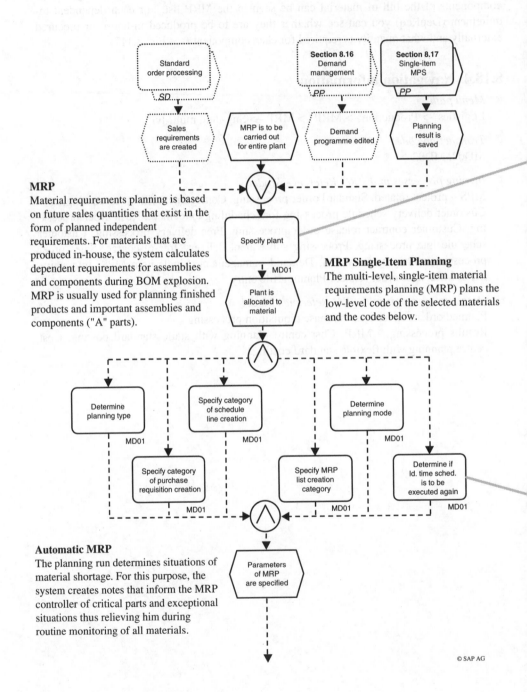

MRP

Material requirements planning is based on future sales quantities that exist in the form of planned independent requirements. For materials that are produced in-house, the system calculates dependent requirements for assemblies and components during BOM explosion. MRP is usually used for planning finished products and important assemblies and components ("A" parts).

MRP Single-Item Planning

The multi-level, single-item material requirements planning (MRP) plans the low-level code of the selected materials and the codes below.

Automatic MRP

The planning run determines situations of material shortage. For this purpose, the system creates notes that inform the MRP controller of critical parts and exceptional situations thus relieving him during routine monitoring of all materials.

© SAP AG

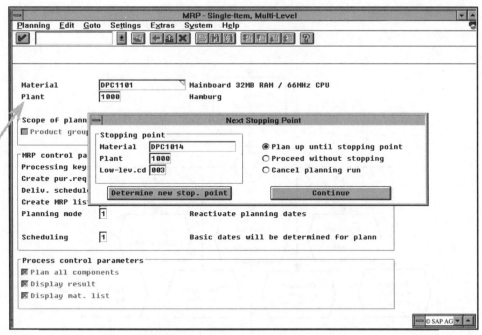

Fig. 8.114: Initial screen – Determine planning run

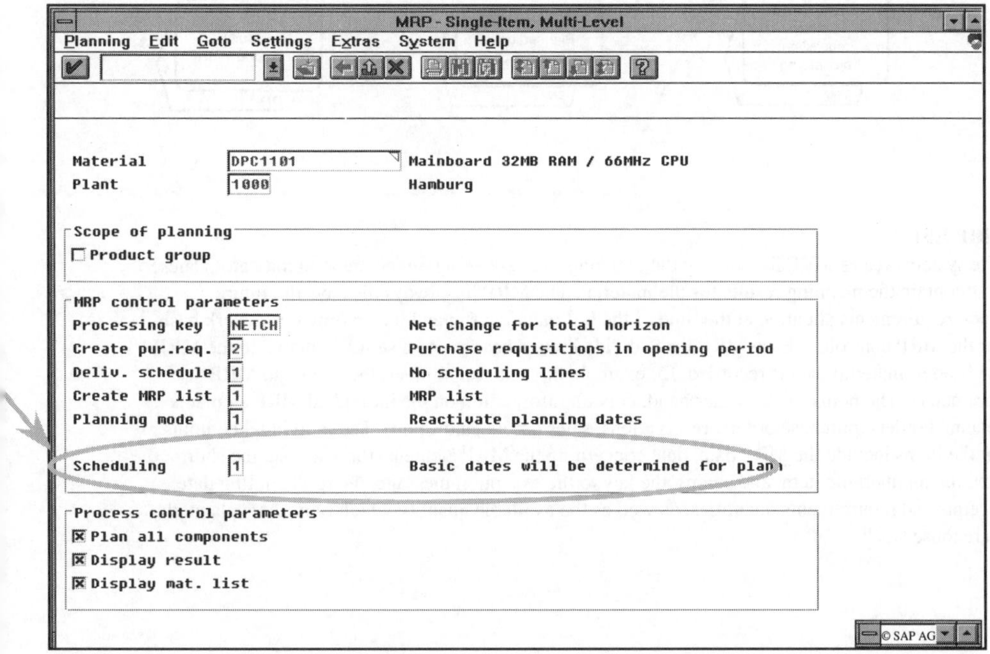

Fig. 8.115: Initial screen – Determine planning run

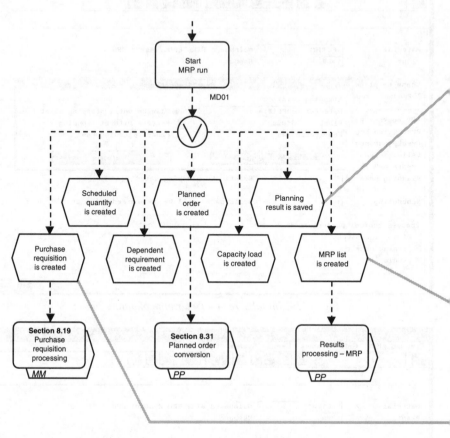

MRP Lists

The system creates MRP lists during the planning run depending on the creation indicator. These lists contain the planning results for the material. The MRP list always displays the future stock/requirements situation at the time of the last planning run and it also provides a work basis for the MRP controller. Each MRP list is divided into a header and a series of items. In the MRP list header, material data is recorded, for example the material number, the plant and MRP parameters. The items, on the other hand, contain information on the individual MRP elements (planned orders, purchase orders, reservations, sales orders, and so on). The individual columns for the items include the MRP date, data concerning the MRP element (for example, the short text, the number, the item, and so on), the key to the exception message, the rescheduling date, receipts and requirements quantities, as well as the available quantity which represents planned warehouse stock.

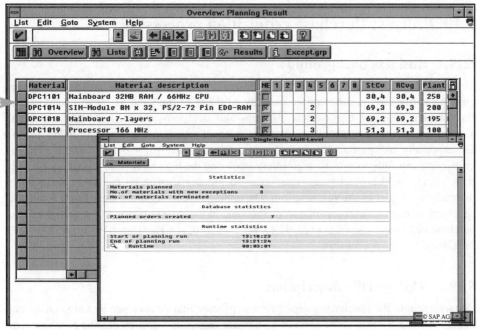

Fig. 8.116: Planning result

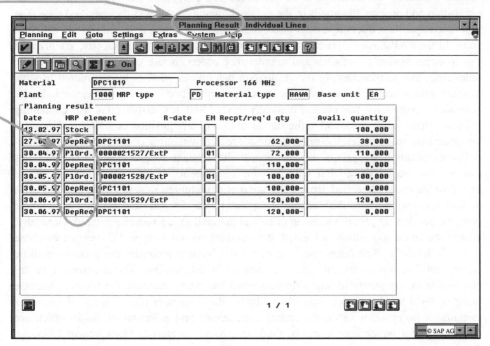

Fig. 8.117: MRP list

8.19 Process: Purchase requisition processing

8.19.1 Business background

The task of procurement is to purchase the materials needed as a result of material requirements planning in the required quantity, at the right time and as cheaply as possible. Procurement planning thus affects all areas and decisions involved in the purchasing, storing and issuing of materials to cover the material requirements. For high-value materials (especially „A" parts), with irregular consumption patterns, it is necessary to plan requirements carefully to avoid a high safety stock and the high storage costs connected with it. A request to the purchasing department to procure a material can take place either manually or as part of the planning run. Depending on the organizational form, it may be necessary to have several separate steps involved in the release process of requisitions and purchase orders (see Arnolds *et al.* 1996, pp. 225–230; see Hartmann 1993, pp. 409–427; see Grochla 1978, pp. 69–79).

8.19.2 SAP-specific description

Requests sent to the purchasing department to procure materials or services are carried out in the SAP R/3 System in the form of a purchase requisition document. The purchase requisition identifies the materials to be procured. The purchaser can release the purchase requisition and procure the goods in the required quantity for use at the specified date. The purchase requisition document is an internal document, which is not used outside the company. In the SAP System, purchase requisitions are either created indirectly, via material requirements planning, network and maintenance orders, or are entered manually. In the latter case, the person entering the requisition determines what is to be ordered in what quantity and when it is needed. The purchase requisition creation indicator indicates whether the requisition was created manually or via MRP. It is displayed in lists containing information on requisitions and in the statistical data of a requisition item. Requisitions can be created for stock materials (material master record without account assignment), materials for consumption (material master record with account assignment) or expense items (no material master record but with account assignment). If no material master record exists for the material needed, the specification of the required material must take place via a short text. In addition, the account assignment category with the account assignment data, the purchasing group, valuation price and material group must be entered. Generally, when a purchase requisition is created, the standard document type *NB* (normal purchase order) is defaulted. The document type in the R/3 System identifies the processing to be carried out. Various document types are allowed for requisitions. The document type decides whether the purchase requisition involved has been created for a normal purchase order or for a stock transfer order. In addition, the document type controls the number assignment (internal or external number assignment) and selection of fields which are displayed or for which entries can be made (see SAP – Materials Management 1996, pp. 5.1–5.4).

The *purchase requisition* document can contain requirements for several materials. These materials are each entered in the purchase requisition as a requisition item (see Fig. 8.120). Purchase requisitions are processed item for item, i.e. each item in a purchase requisition represents an individual requirement. Important fields of a purchasing document item are the item category and the account assignment category. The item category controls how a material or service is to be procured, the field selection and whether, and if so which, additional screens need to be displayed. In addition, it determines whether goods and/or invoice receipt is to take place for the item (see Sections 8.24 and 8.25). In the R/3 Customizing functionality, the possible item categories must be defined for each document type, e.g. for document type *NB* the item categories *normal, consignment, subcontracting, third-party, stock transfer* and *service* have been defined (see Fig. 8.118). Each item has a detail screen with additional control possibilities. For item category *normal*, for example, goods receipt and invoice receipt are both expected in the standard settings; for *consignment*, however, no invoice receipt is expected. For the item category *subcontracting* an additional screen appears, in which the components provided for the vendor can be displayed, changed or entered if necessary. The item category *third-party* also presents the user with an additional screen, in which he can enter the address to which the goods are to be delivered. This address appears on all documents apart from the purchase requisition. For documents with item category *service*, extra screens appear in which the services to be provided can be entered in more detail. The account assignment controls whether an item is to be charged to an auxiliary account assignment. It defines which account assignment data (e.g. cost centre, account number, etc.) are necessary for the item (see Fig. 8.118).

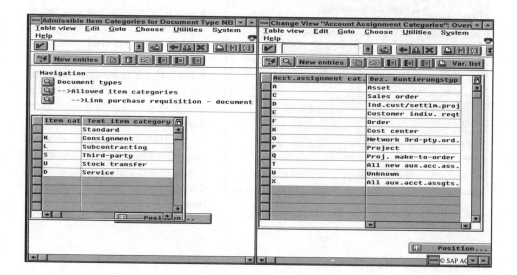

Fig. 8.118: Document type – Item category – Acct. assignment category (Customizing)

If purchase requisitions exist in the system, either because they have been entered manually or created by a planning run in MRP, the next step is to release the requisitions. This is because a purchase order can only be created from a released purchase requisition (see Section 8.22). In purchasing it is possible to release requisitions with or without using the classification system. The release procedure without classification can only be used to release requisitions and is used as a correction and authorization procedure for requisitions. The aim of this procedure is to check the material number, quantity and dates in the purchase requisition as well as the account assignment and source of supply to make sure they are correct. The requisition is released item for item. The procedure using the classification system replaces the manual signature process. The person responsible for the purchasing document processes it in the system and thus marks it as having been seen by the responsible person. A difference between this procedure and the procedure without classification is that the whole document is released and not the individual item.

If a purchase requisition is released using the release procedure without classification, the items possibly need to be approved before they can be ordered. In this case, the system takes the *release conditions* (shows which release strategy has been allocated to a requisition item), the *release strategy* (shows which persons in which sequence have to release the item) and the *release indicator* (indicates whether an item can be ordered after it has been released by a certain person or department) into consideration. Release conditions, strategies and indicators are all defined in the Customizing functions.

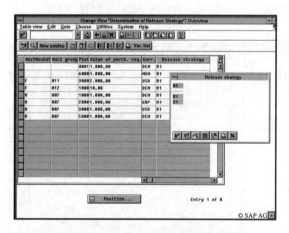

Fig. 8.119: Customizing the release strategy

The conditions according to which a purchase requisition can be released are the account assignment category, the material group, the plant and the total value (see Fig. 8.119). If the requisition item fulfils one of the defined release conditions (e.g. requisition value more than 10 DM, material group 012, plant 1000), the requisition is automatically assigned to a release strategy when it is created. If it does not meet any of the conditions, it is automatically released.

8.19.3 Using the process

Materials requirements planning has automatically generated a purchase requisition with the number *10004389*. The purchase requisition has been created with document type NB, item category normal and no account assignment (see Fig. 8.120). The requisition for the main board is to be converted into a normal purchase order and delivered to plant 1000 on February 19. The requisition has been changed by the person who requested the material.

He has selected a vendor from the Foster City area and entered the vendor number 2 as a fixed source of supply in the requisition. The purchase requisition is passed on to the responsible buyer in the R/3 System. The buyer checks the requisition and releases it if necessary. To release it, the person releasing the items must mark the items to be released (see Fig. 8.122) and enter his release code (see Fig. 8.123). This way, it is possible for auditing purposes to check at a later date who was responsible for the purchase order. This release step can be carried out automatically if the appropriate entries are made in Customizing (see Fig. 8.119).

8.19.4 Navigation information

■ *Menu path*
Logistics –> Materials management –> Purchasing –> Requisition –> Create

■ *Transaction code*
ME51, ME52, ME54

■ *Ingoing processes in the R/3 Reference Model*
Conversion of planned orders, Processing the results of material requirements planning, Processing the results of MPS, Total MRP / Single-item MRP, Total MPS / Single-Item MPS, Third-party order processing, Production order creation, Network maintenance, Maintenance order creation and processing, Planned order conversion, Results processing MRP, Results processing MPS, MRP individual, MRP entire, Material planning – interactive, Order creation and processing, Service order creation and processing, Service order release, Planned order processing, Requisition processing, MPS sales order related, MPS project related, Creation of production order, Requisition processing for stock material, Requisition processing for consumable material, Subcontract requisition processing, Consignment requisition processing, Requisition processing for stock transfer, Third-party requisition processing, Purchase requisition processing for service

■ *Outgoing processes in the R/3 Reference Model*
Delivery schedule, Release order for service, Contract release order for stock material, Contract release order for consumable material, Contract release order for consignment material, Contract release order for subcontracting, Budget execution/ verification, Purchase order processing for fixed asset, Purchase order processing for stock transfer, Subcontractor delivery schedule, Consignment order processing, Purchase order processing for subcontracting, Processing third-party purchase order, Purchase order processing for service, Processing of RFQ issued to vendor, Processing of RFQ issued to subcontractor, Processing of RFQ issued to vendor for service, Processing third-party order.

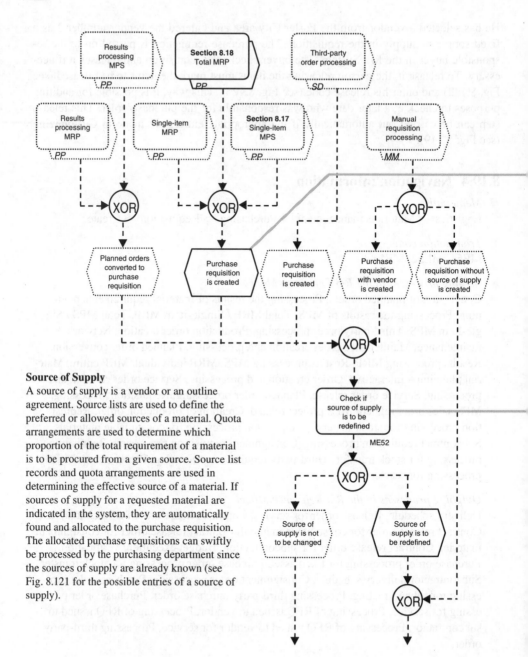

Source of Supply

A source of supply is a vendor or an outline agreement. Source lists are used to define the preferred or allowed sources of a material. Quota arrangements are used to determine which proportion of the total requirement of a material is to be procured from a given source. Source list records and quota arrangements are used in determining the effective source of a material. If sources of supply for a requested material are indicated in the system, they are automatically found and allocated to the purchase requisition. The allocated purchase requisitions can swiftly be processed by the purchasing department since the sources of supply are already known (see Fig. 8.121 for the possible entries of a source of supply).

© SAP AG

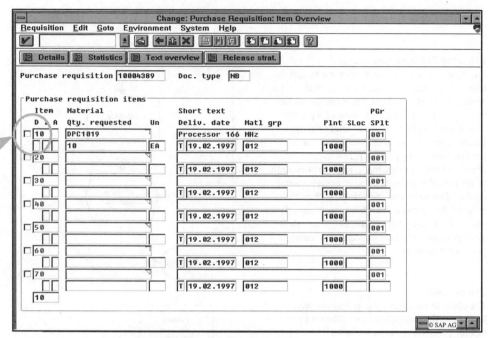

Fig. 8.120: Purchase requisition items

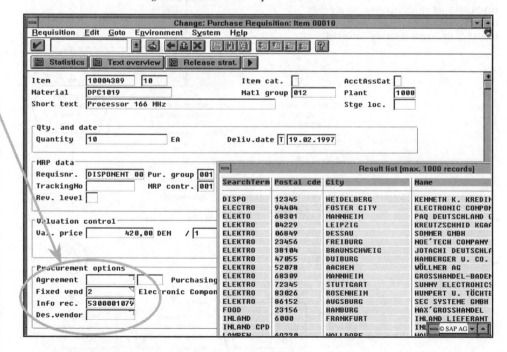

Fig. 8.121: Entering source of supply – Selection of vendor by matchcode Frankfurt

Releasing Purchase Requisitions

Purchase requisitions can be released by certain release strategies assigned to an approval procedure. First, you must determine by whom and in which sequence the release of a purchase requisition is to be processed. After this, the purchase requisition can be converted into a purchase order (see process path Section 8.22 "Purchase order processing"). Release points can be persons, departments or other organizational entities. Due to certain conditions, such as the value of the purchase requisition, the material group of the requested materials etc., the release strategy is automatically allocated in creating a purchase requisition.

Release Codes

The codes of all release points that still have to approve the requisition have to be set so that the purchase requisition can be converted into a purchase order.
If you have set up alternative release points, the various options available for the final release of this requisition are displayed.

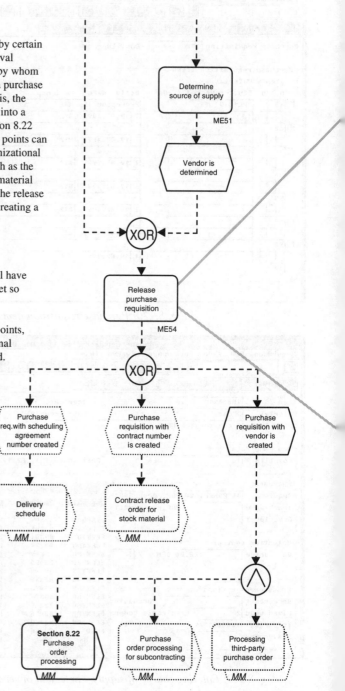

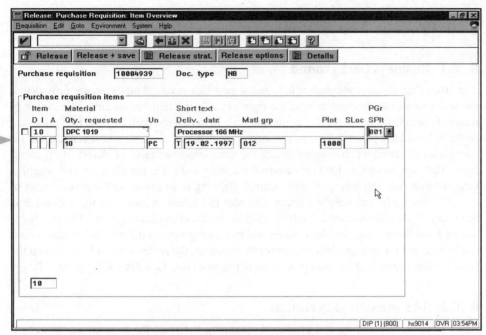

Fig. 8.122: Selecting items for release

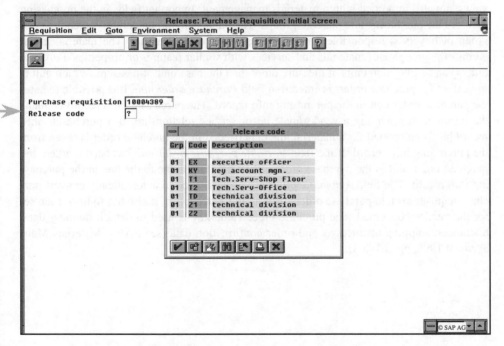

Fig. 8.123: Release of purchase requisition

8.20 Process: Material master processing MM

8.20.1 Business background

The task of materials management is to make sure that required materials are provided at the best cost and at the right time at the right place in the required quantity. The value of materials in industrial and trading companies can be measured partly by the role they play in the value added process. Due to the large role material costs play in revenues, the rational use of materials is becoming one of the most important tasks of industrial organizations. This task can be divided into internal planning tasks, i.e. the planning and administering of materials requirements, and external planning tasks involving the procurement of materials from external supply sources. In order to be able to carry out these tasks, it is necessary to store all the needed information in the material master record. The specification of a low-level code, lead time offset and processing time in the material master record can be relevant for deterministic requirements planning; the replenishment lead time on the other hand is needed for external procurement purposes (see Grochla 1978, pp. 13–32).

8.20.2 SAP-specific description

Apart from the accounting and production planning views of the material master record described in Sections 8.8 and 8.11, further views, such as the purchasing and storage views, are also important within materials management. Important fields in the purchasing view are the purchasing and material groups. The purchasing group defines which buyer or group of buyers is responsible for the procurement of the material. The material group permits the grouping of materials and services with similar features or properties. Purchase orders can be placed in units of measure other than the base unit of measure. Which unit is to be used for purchase orders is entered in field *Purchase order unit*. It is possible to enter the purchase order unit in the purchasing info record. The purchasing info record contains the information regarding a vendor/material or service relationship. If a purchasing info record has been created for a material, the data needed in the purchase order is taken from the purchasing info record. If the field *Variable purchase order unit* has been marked, the purchase order unit in the purchase order can be a different one to the one in the purchasing info record. The field *Automatic purchase order* is used to automatically convert purchase requisitions into purchase orders. Before this can happen, it also has to have been set for the vendor concerned. The purchase order value key is used to default dunning data, tolerances, shipping instructions and order confirmation data (see SAP – Materials Management 1996, pp. 3.5–3.8).

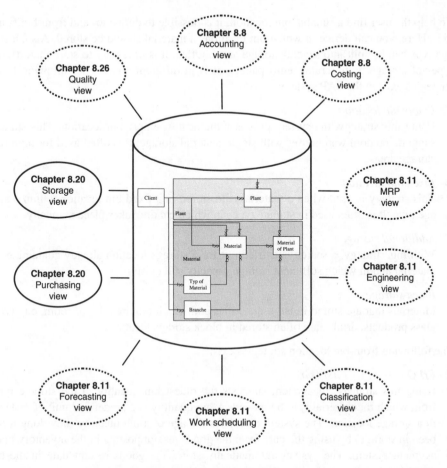

Fig. 8.124: Material management views of the material

The storage-relevant material master data can be looked at in the R/3 System from the point of view of the plant and storage location data or from the point of view of the warehouse management system. If the warehouse management system (WM) is in use, stocks can be traced down to bin location level. The warehouse number describes the type of warehouse, e.g. central warehouse, high rack storage area, block store or picking warehouse. Generally, the base unit of measure of the material is also used in the storage view. However, if the material is managed in another unit in the warehouse, or if materials are issued in another unit of measure, this can be specified in the fields *WM unit of measure* or I*ssue unit of measure*. Chemicals may be subject to certain legal requirements or safety regulations. These can be identified by the dangerous goods number. This number helps to describe which hazardous substances are contained in the material. Within a storage type, materials can be assigned to a fixed bin location. The maximum bin location quantity defines the maximum quantity of a material that can be stored in the bin location. The minimum bin location defines the minimum quantity that must exist in a bin location.

To help the user find a suitable bin location, it is possible to define to- and from-bin strategies. Here, you can define in which bin locations a material should be stored. Also, a storage type can be split into several storage areas. Often, it is necessary to store the different types of storage units (crates, euro pallets, etc.) in different areas. The following to-bin strategies exist in the SAP system:

- *Empty bin location*
  Using this strategy, the system proposes the nearest empty bin location. This strategy supports random warehouses with single material storage. It is often used for high rack storage areas.

- *Fixed bin location*
  This strategy is used when a material is to stored in a fixed bin location within a storage type. It is often used in storage types in which picking takes place manually.

- *Additional storage*
  With this strategy, a search is carried out for a storage location already containing the material and in which sufficient storage capacity still exists.

- *Block storage*
  Materials that are stored in large quantities and which require a lot of room, e.g. tyres, glass products, drinks, are often stored in block storage locations.

The following from-bin location strategies exist:

- *FIFO (First In – First Out)*
  Using this strategy, the system suggests the oldest bin quantity in the storage type, from which the material is to be moved. A bin quantity is a predefined unit of material in a storage location. The system calculates the age of a bin quantity (how long it has been in storage) by using the date from the goods receipt posting in the inventory management system. The system automatically stores the goods receipt date in the bin quantity when the goods receipt posting takes place.

- *LIFO (Last In – First Out)*
  In the construction industry, newly received material is often stored on top of existing material (e.g. gravel, sand). Using the FIFO strategy, the goods received last would have to be moved out of the way to get to the material with the oldest goods receipt date. For such cases, the LIFO strategy offers a more suitable solution. When searching for a suitable bin quantity, the system always proposes the bin quantity last posted into storage.

If you mark the storage view (without using the warehouse management system), you can maintain storage-relevant data at storage location level. You can enter storage conditions, such as room and temperature conditions for the material, and special dangerous goods information. If you set the batch requirement indicator, you can make sure that the material is managed in batches. Apart from specifying the weight and volume dimensions of the material, you can also enter a storage unit of measure.

8.20.3 Using the process

The products to be manufactured, the main boards *DPC1102* and *DPC1101*, are described from a costing and production point of view in Sections 8.8 and 8.11. This section describes the creation of material *DPC1014*, the 32 MB RAM storage memory, which is to be used in the production of the main board. When creating the material master record, the material number *DPC1014* in the model company is entered by the clerk. When entering the material type, you can choose from a list of possible material types (the definition of the material types takes place in Customizing). The material type selected controls the material number assignment. In this case, the external number *DPC1014* is allowed. In the example, material *DPC1014* has been assigned to the mechanical engineering line of industry. So that the tasks of materials management can be carried out, the views are marked for accounting, purchasing, classification and storage (see Fig. 8.127). In the purchasing screen, a reminder of 5 days and a goods receipt (GR) processing time of 1 day have been defined. For INTRASTAT processing, the foreign trade data with the commodity code have been entered.

8.20.4 Navigation information

■ *Menu path*
Logistics –> Materials management –> Material master –> Material –> Create

■ *Transaction code*
MM01

■ *Ingoing processes in the R/3 Reference Model*
none

■ *Outgoing processes in the R/3 Reference Model*

Industry Sector

The industry sector is a branch of industry which groups companies according to their activities, for example plant engineering and construction, mechanical engineering, chemical industry or pharmaceutical industry. By specifying the industry sector, a table-based program control is carried out which determines e.g. the selection of data fields on the screens, the sequence of screens or the allocation of a material type. If there are materials that are repeatedly allocated to the same industry sector, it is advisable to predefine their allocation in the system respectively, i.e. to define the value for the industry sector. This value then automatically appears in the respective field every time you create a material master record.

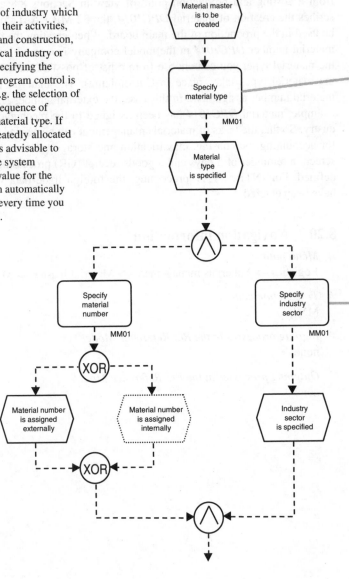

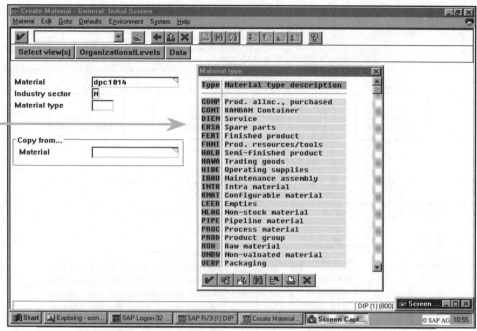

Fig. 8.125: Selecting material type from proposal list

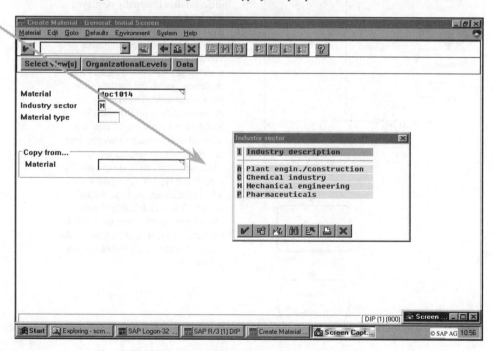

Fig. 8.126: Selecting industry sector from proposal list

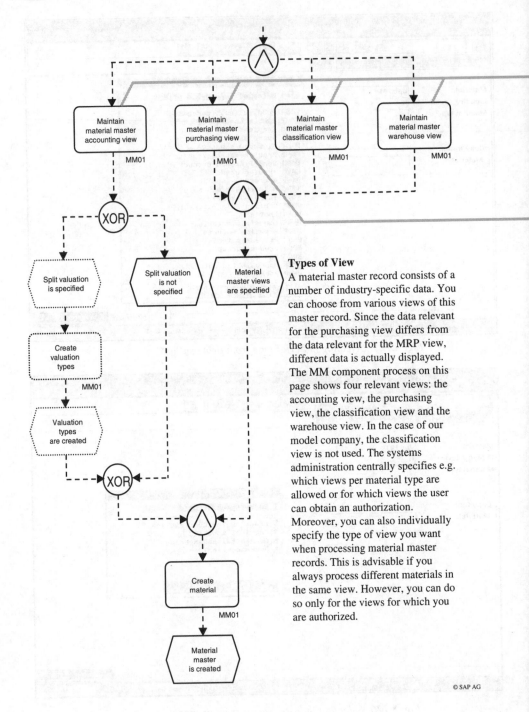

Types of View

A material master record consists of a number of industry-specific data. You can choose from various views of this master record. Since the data relevant for the purchasing view differs from the data relevant for the MRP view, different data is actually displayed. The MM component process on this page shows four relevant views: the accounting view, the purchasing view, the classification view and the warehouse view. In the case of our model company, the classification view is not used. The systems administration centrally specifies e.g. which views per material type are allowed or for which views the user can obtain an authorization. Moreover, you can also individually specify the type of view you want when processing material master records. This is advisable if you always process different materials in the same view. However, you can do so only for the views for which you are authorized.

© SAP AG

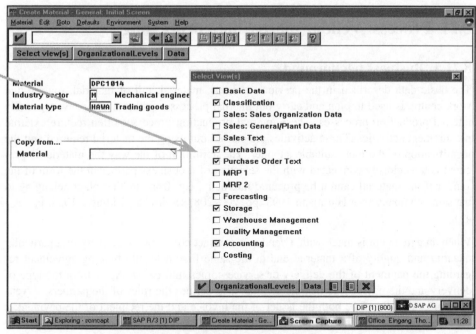

Fig. 8.127: Selecting relevant views of MM

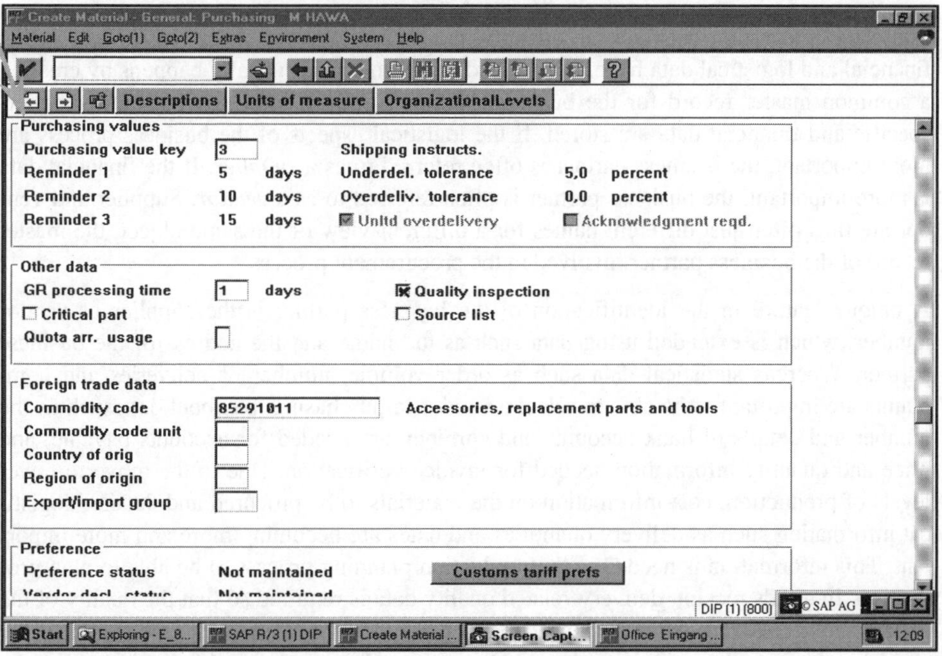

Fig. 8.128: Data relevant for purchasing

8.21 Process: Vendor master data processing

8.21.1 Business background

The basic data described in the previous sections: material, bill of material, routing and work centre, is used to plan and carry out internal processes within a company, especially internal production processes. These internal production processes often require external procurement activities. These activities are carried out using the material required and the identification of the most suitable supplier. The definition of the way the material is procured is thus closely connected with the selection of a business partner in the form of the vendor if the material cannot be procured internally, e.g. from another plant belonging to the same company (see Hartmann 1993, pp. 200–208; see Melzer-Ridinger 1994, pp. 29–43).

When an agreement is made with a vendor, a contract covering the delivery of a particular quantity and quality of a material and at the same time a legally binding agreement regarding the payment of the delivery or service comes into being. Apart from the type of delivery and the payment terms, the contract also defines the roles of the partners. A vendor, for example, can be both the issuer of the invoice and the recipient of the payment; a supplier of goods, on the other hand, can be the issuer of the invoice, but not however recipient of the payment. Another possibility is that the goods are supplied by a decentralized plant, but the invoice received from and payment made to a central subsidiary.

The close integration between the quantity and values involved in deliveries means that financial and logistical data have to be regarded together. This usually happens by creating a common master record for the business partner (vendor), in which both the supplier-specific and financial data are stored. If the logistical aspects of the business process are more important, the business partner is often referred to as a *supplier*. If the financial data is more important, the business partner is often referred to as a *vendor*. Supplier and vendor are thus often just different names for a different view of the same object, the master record of the business partner involved in the procurement process.

A unique feature in the identification of the business partner is the supplier or vendor number, which is extended using data such as the name and the address of the business partner. Whereas statistical data such as order volume, number of deliveries and complaints are important to be able to select a vendor in purchasing, payment data such as the number and details of bank accounts and currency are needed for accounts payable, and price and quantity information needed for invoice verification. Due to the move to fewer levels of production, cost information on the materials to be procured and detailed logistical information such as delivery quantities and dates are becoming more and more important. This information is needed in the production planning process to be able to plan production. In goods receipt, delivery-related quality data is required so that the quality of the goods can be checked. After the inspection of the goods has taken place, the results of the check can be passed on to the vendor evaluation area. The vendor evaluation in turn can be considered when planning future business activities (purchasing operations).

8.21.2 SAP-specific description

The vendor master record contains information about a company's vendors. Apart from the name and the address of a vendor, the vendor master record contains data regarding the currency and payment terms, as well as names of important contact persons in the company (sales people, for example). The vendor master record is maintained from both the accounting department (see Section 8.23) and the purchasing department. For this reason, a vendor master record consists of three areas of data: *general data, company code data* and *purchasing organization data*. The general data part contains data which applies to all company codes within a company group. Purchasing data is maintained per purchasing organization and includes data which is important for the purchasing department of a company, such as contact person, delivery terms, etc. (see Fig. 8.130). In addition to the data that applies for a purchasing organization, data can be maintained which applies to a certain plant or vendor sub-range (important in the retail business), for example terms of payment or incoterms, which differ from those applying to the purchasing organization (see SAP – Materials Management 1996, pp. 3.2–3.4).

Terms of payment are agreements made concerning the time of payment of invoices to be paid and possible cash discounts (for example, the term *payable within 30 days net* or *2% cash discount for payment within 10 days*). This means a certain percentage discount is granted on the invoice amount if the invoice is paid within a certain period, according to the terms in the invoice. The terms of payment agreed upon with a vendor can be stored in the vendor master record. When a purchase order is created (see Section 8.22), the terms of payment entered in the vendor master record are defaulted in the purchase order item but can be overwritten.

For suppliers, from whom goods are only purchased once or only very occasionally, special vendor master records called one-time vendor master records can be created. This makes sense when, for example, the usual vendor cannot supply the required goods for one reason or another and the goods have to be purchased from another vendor. The difference between one-time vendor master records and other vendor master records is that a one-time vendor master record can be used for several different vendors. In this way, it saves having to create one vendor master record for each vendor. For this reason, a one-time vendor master record may not contain any vendor-specific data. When a purchasing document is created using a one-time vendor, the system automatically branches to a master data screen. Here, you have to enter the vendor-specific data such as the name, address and bank details of the vendor. This data is stored separately in the purchasing document. One-time vendors can be displayed, blocked or deleted just like any other master records. When a one-time vendor master record is created, it has to be assigned to a one-time vendor account group. The account group results in the vendor-specific data fields in the vendor master record being suppressed. The relevant data is entered when a purchasing document is created.

The business partner „vendor" can assume many *roles* in its business dealings with a company. The first role a vendor or supplier can assume during the procurement process is that of the recipient of the purchase order. This can be followed by the role of the supplier of the goods, the issuer of the invoice and finally the recipient of the payment. One or more of these roles in the procurement process may be taken over by other vendors. For this reason, it is possible to assign *partner roles* to vendors. The vendors assuming these other roles are then used in the subsequent logistics and accounting processes. When creating a vendor master record, the partner roles defined as required partner roles in the partner scheme of the account group are defaulted on the *partner roles* screen. In the standard system the partner roles vendor, purchase order recipient, supplier, invoice issuer and payment recipient have been defined. In customizing, you define which of the partner roles are optional and which required. Apart from the role vendor, all of the partner roles are optional. If no other roles have been maintained, the data of the role vendor applies automatically to all other partner roles.

In certain cases, you might want to prevent goods being procured from a vendor, for example when the vendor has delivered inferior quality (see Section 8.28). In the vendor master record, you can set an indicator to block the vendor. Once this indicator has been set, it is not possible to create purchase orders for the vendor. The block applies until the indicator is removed again. If you would like to block a vendor just for a particular material, it is possible to do this in the source list (list of possible sources for a material in a certain period of time).

8.21.3 Using the process

When you create a vendor master record, you have to enter an account group for the vendor. The vendor group controls among other things the possible number range for a vendor master record. The example shows vendor *DE-001*. In this case, the company data has been created for the vendor and thus it is not necessary to enter the account group. In the initial screen, the selection window for the purchasing organization is shown and purchasing organization *0001* selected.

The selection fields for the general data address, control data and payment data have not been marked. This means that in this case the only data to be maintained is the purchasing data and the partner roles.

When a vendor master record is newly created, you enter a reference vendor master record on the initial screen, from which data can be copied.

Once you have pressed Enter, you come to the purchasing data screen (see Fig. 8.130) with the name and address of the vendor and the purchasing organization you entered displayed. You can make entries in the vendor conditions, sales and control data blocks.

Terms of payment are defined in Customizing in the form of codes. The term of payment ZB01 (3% discount for payment within 14 days) has been entered for Model Company A. These terms of payment are defaulted in purchasing documents and are fixed in the invoice. The incoterms, representing international standards, are defaulted for the terms of delivery. If you enter a minimum order quantity, the R/3 System issues a message if you enter a purchase order (see Section 8.22) with a quantity less than the minimum order quantity. Via Customizing and user parameters, you can define whether the message issued is a warning or an error. The field *Control Pricing date* in the conditions entry block is an optional entry and controls whether the purchase order date or the date of delivery is used as the date to be used in determining the prices. For the daily work of the buyer, it might be useful to store the name and telephone number of the salesman. The other control data are used as default data for subsequent purchasing documents except for the ABC indicator, which is used to classify the vendor. In this way, it is possible to specify in the vendor master record the way in which the processing of the goods receipt and invoice receipt is to take place. In this way, you can define that goods-receipt-based invoice verification is to take place (see Section 8.22).

On a further screen, it is possible to define the vendors for the various partner roles. Quite a familiar situation is where the ordering address is different from the delivering address or the issuer of the invoice.

8.21.4 Navigation information

- *Menu path*
  Logistics –> Materials management –> Purchasing -> Master data –> Vendor –> Purchasing –> Create

- *Transaction code*
  MK01

- *Ingoing processes in the R/3 Reference Model*
  Complaints against the vendor

- *Outgoing processes in the R/3 Reference Model*

Account Group

When you create a vendor master record, you must enter an account group. The account group determines the type of number assignment, the number range from which the account number used by the system to identify the vendor is assigned, whether or not a one-time vendor is involved, which fields screens contain and whether entries in these fields are mandatory or optional, which data retention levels below the purchasing organization are allowed (for example, vendor sub-range) or which partner schemas (partner determination procedures) are valid. Once a vendor master record is created, you cannot change the account group.

Incoterms

The acronym *Incoterm* stands for International Commercial Terms. They define international regulations for the interpretation of certain positions in a contract that are common in international trade. They regulate e.g. the distribution of costs to the buyer and vendor and the transfer of risks (see Fig. 8.130).

Vendor Number

Each vendor master record is assigned a unique number (the vendor's account number used by Financial Accounting – see Section 8.23). You require this number to call up the master record or to enter purchase orders. Numbers can be assigned on an internal or external basis. Internal number assignment means that the system assigns the numbers. External number assignment means that you enter a number when you create the master records. For external number assignment, alphanumeric numbers are also allowed.

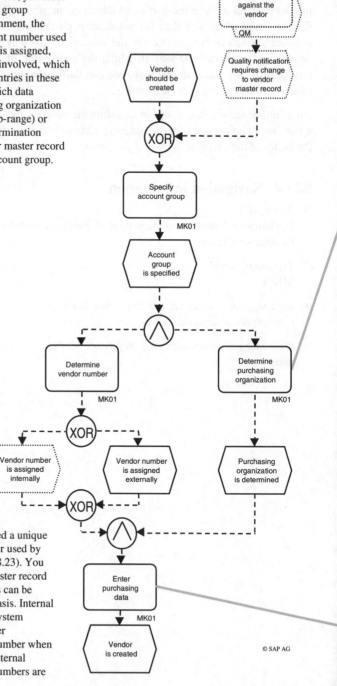

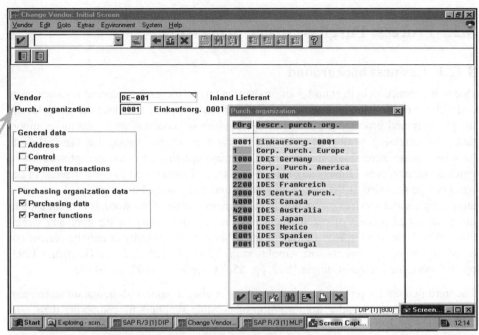

Fig. 8.129: Initial screen vendor master record

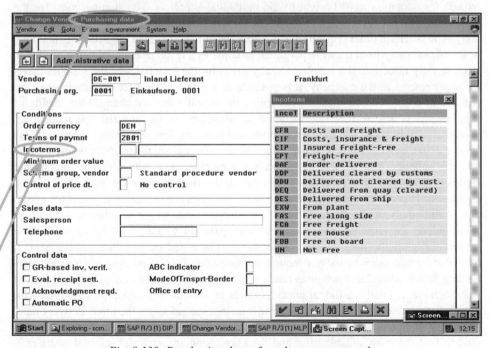

Fig. 8.130: Purchasing data of vendor master record

8.22 Process: Purchase order processing

8.22.1 Business background

Due to the reduction in the number of production levels, increasing material resource costs and a closer relationship between companies and their suppliers to reduce inventory levels, the planning and processing of purchasing activities is becoming more and more important. The increasing number of externally procured goods has meant that material costs have become an increasingly important part of manufacturing costs and the optimization of purchase quantities and times one of the central tasks. Procurement in a wider sense of the word can be regarded as the task of procuring materials, assemblies, final products, operating supplies and services externally. In the narrower sense of the word, it is often used to mean the actual process of purchasing goods, which, depending on the company's relationship with the vendor, may be carried out as a once-only activity or may be carried out based on outline agreements (see Arnolds *et al.* 1996, pp. 225–261; see Hartmann 1993, pp. 460–484; see Melzer-Ridinger 1993, pp. 55–74; see Rauh 1992, pp. 61–72).

The starting point for procurement or processing is often a request for quotation whose aim is to choose the best vendor from a group of possible suppliers by comparing their *reliability, availability to deliver, quality* and *price*. Generally, companies tend to require quotations from the possible suppliers before placing an order. Before this can happen, a request for quotation must be sent to the individual suppliers. The starting point for the purchasing process is usually a requirement for a material that has to be purchased externally. The purchase order requisition can either result from material requirements planning or by manual entry from a user department, or come as a result of material being needed in stock or for production. If a supplier already exists for the material, and the supplier meets the requirements of the company, it is possible to create a request for quotation when the requisition is entered and checked. Assuming the supplier has not changed the quality of supplies and is able to meet the technical requirements of the material, the request for quotation mainly applies to the factors price, delivery date and deliverable quantity. If no vendor exists, a check must be made to see which potential suppliers could be used. Once potential suppliers have been discovered among the companies with which the purchasing company works, the most reliable supplier can be determined using the function of vendor evaluation. This can be used to determine which vendors are to receive requests for quotation. Additionally, a check should of course also be made to see whether new suppliers could deliver the required material. To do this, external sources must be found. Such a request for quotation does not, of course, have to be based on an actual requirement. It may also be necessary to issue a request for quotation for the purpose of updating purchasing information. The quotations received from the suppliers are entered and compared with each other. Firstly, a formal check is made to see how the quotation compares with the request for quotation and how complete it is. In a second stage, the price, delivery date, quality payment terms, etc. are then also compared. The comparison of all the quotations is used to find the most suitable offer and the corresponding vendor(s) selected and a purchase order issued. When the vendor sends the order acknowledgement, the contract becomes a legal document and the delivery terms and conditions stipulated in the purchase order are contractually binding for both parties (see Hartmann 1988, pp. 384–412).

When the contract is completed, a decision is usually made as to whether the purchasing activity is planned as a one-time purchase or whether both parties are interested in establishing a longer-term agreement. Whereas a one-time purchase of materials or services normally takes place either with new suppliers or irregular requirements, in the case of regular purchasing activities with selected vendors, an *outline agreement* is usually agreed upon. A purchasing outline agreement is a contract covering a certain period agreed upon with a certain vendor (see Section 9.6). The purchasing company agrees to purchase a particular quantity or value of goods in a certain period of time with certain price and payment conditions. The vendor agrees to deliver the agreed quality and quantity of goods at the dates agreed upon at the same conditions. Outline agreements are often used in the case of *Just in Time* delivery (see Günther 1992, pp. 16–24; see Wildemann 1990; see Schulte 1994, pp. 189–205). For this to work properly, a prerequisite is a well-planned product range and production schedules. This is why outline agreements are often used in companies with standardized products produced using mass or serial production.

Since unforeseen circumstances in the procurement cycle, i.e. from the request for quotation, via the purchase order to the delivery of the goods, can lead to a delay in the whole purchasing process, it is necessary to monitor purchase orders to make sure that the purchasing conditions defined in the purchase order are met. The monitoring of purchase orders involves the monitoring of delivery dates, the purchase order history and possibly sending reminders to the vendor. Monitoring the delivery dates means making sure the agreed delivery date can be met by sending a request to the vendor asking him to confirm the production status of the goods at certain, predefined points in time. If the delivery is not made at the time or date agreed upon, a reminder can be sent or, in the case of existing outline agreements, a fine for breach of contract is due. The purchase order history, the buyer can see various information about purchase orders, such as order confirmations, delays in delivery announced by the vendor, open purchase orders, cancelled purchase orders or deliveries for which reminders have been sent.

8.22.2 SAP-specific description

The purchase order consists of a purchase order header and purchase order items. If data is entered at purchase order header level, this data applies to the whole purchase order. Payment and delivery terms are examples of data entered at purchase order header level. Purchase order items contain data regarding the material or service purchased, such as item category, account assignment category, material number, material short text, quantity, material group, date of delivery, price and requesting plant. The item category controls whether the material in the purchase order item requires a material number, the possible or required account assignment of the item, whether the material is managed in stock, and whether goods receipt (GR) and/or invoice receipt (IR) is to take place for the item. It is possible to charge the costs purchase order to a cost centre or a customer order. The account assignment category specifies the type of object to be charged with the costs, e.g. cost centre or customer order, which accounts are to be charged at goods receipt and invoice receipt time and which account assignment data must be entered. Additionally, it is possible to enter additional data per item such as the exact required time of delivery and item-specific texts (see SAP – Materials Management 1996, pp. 5.6–5.9).

When the purchase order is being created, the purchasing clerk can refer to an existing purchase requisition. He can select purchase requisitions from a list and generate purchase orders for these requisitions. The aim of purchasing is to create and process purchase orders with as little time and effort as possible (see Fig. 8.131).

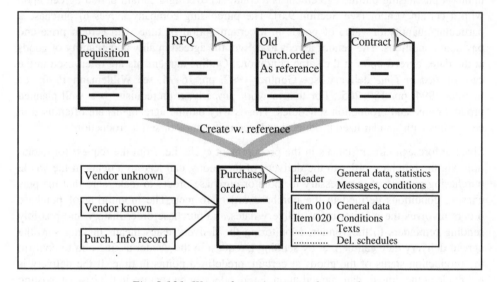

Fig. 8.131: Ways of creating a purchase order

When you create a purchase order, you have the following three possibilities:

■ *Vendor known*
   The buyer chooses this way if he knows which vendor the goods are to be purchased from.

■ *Vendor unknown*
   When the items to be purchased have been entered, possible sources of supply are suggested for the individual items. Such sources of supply can be vendors, outline agreements or purchasing info records. Purchasing info records can be an important source of information for the purchasing department. They contain information on a vendor–material relationship and contain the prices and conditions of a vendor for a particular material.

■ *Assigned requisition exists*
   With this method, requisitions that have been assigned to a vendor or outline agreements are listed per purchasing group.

8.22.3 Using the process

On the initial screen you enter a reference to the existing purchase requisition *0010004389*. Vendor *2* is automatically selected by the system. In the example for the model company, document type NB (normal purchase order), which is defaulted by the system, is used. The two organizational element fields *Purchasing organization* with the value *1000* and the *Purchasing group* with the value *100* are also defaulted by the system via parameters in the user's master record. Confirm that the data on the initial screen is correct. You then come to the purchase order item overview screen. Item 10 with the material *DPC1019* is a stock material (the item category does not contain any entry). The purchase order quantity and the net price taken over automatically from the requisition are not changed. The purchase order is to update data in a purchasing info record. For this reason, *A* has been entered in field *InfoUpdate*. Important fields on the item screen are the fields *GR*, *GR non val*, *IR* and *GR-based IV*. The first field controls whether a goods receipt is to take place for the purchase order item. In combination with the second field, the goods receipt can be carried out without having been valued. The field *IR* controls whether an invoice can be received with reference to the purchase order item. The fourth field determines whether the invoice receipt is to take place with reference to goods receipts. The menu buttons *Deliv. Schedule* and *Conditions* in the upper half of the screen allow you to enter delivery schedules and to extend the pricing using pricing conditions for things such as planned delivery costs, for example *freight costs* and *customs duty (see Fig.* 8.134).

8.22.4 Navigation information

- *Menu path*
  Logistics –> Materials management –> Purchasing –> Purchase order –> Create –> Vendor known

- *Transaction code*
  ME21, ME23, ME25, ME51, ME90

- *Ingoing processes in the R/3 Reference Model*
  Vendor quotation processing
  Purchase requisition assignment

- *Outgoing processes in the R/3 Reference Model*
  Delivery and confirmation expediter
  Info recording processing
  Status analysis
  Budget execution/verification

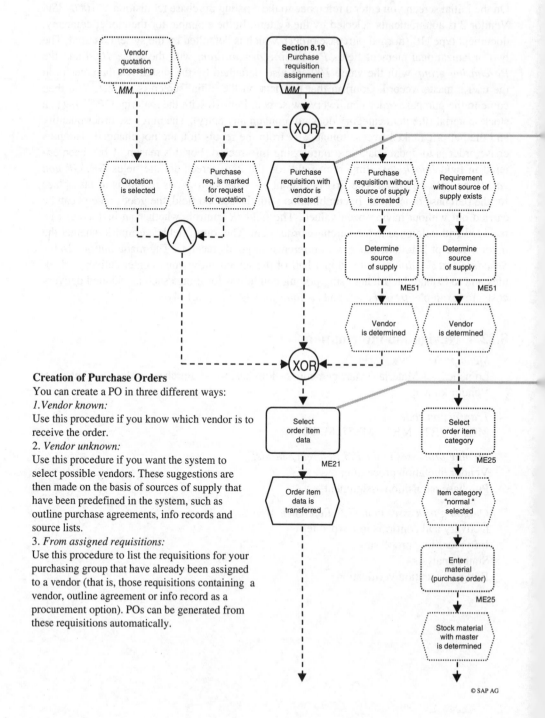

Creation of Purchase Orders

You can create a PO in three different ways:

1.Vendor known:

Use this procedure if you know which vendor is to receive the order.

2. Vendor unknown:

Use this procedure if you want the system to select possible vendors. These suggestions are then made on the basis of sources of supply that have been predefined in the system, such as outline purchase agreements, info records and source lists.

3. From assigned requisitions:

Use this procedure to list the requisitions for your purchasing group that have already been assigned to a vendor (that is, those requisitions containing a vendor, outline agreement or info record as a procurement option). POs can be generated from these requisitions automatically.

514

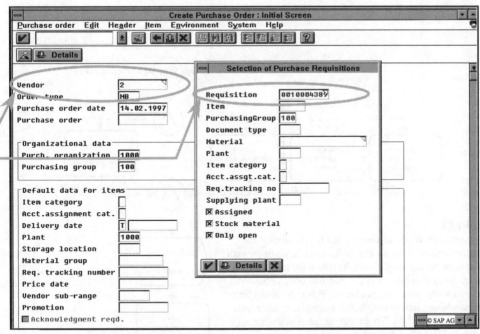

Fig. 8.132: Purchase order with purchase order requisition

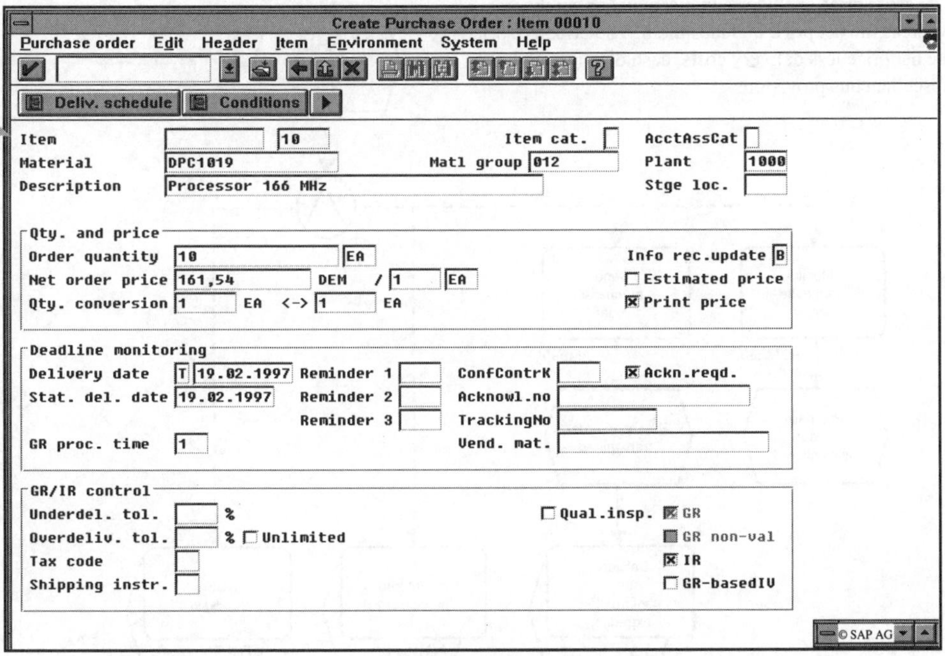

Fig. 8.133: Purchase order items

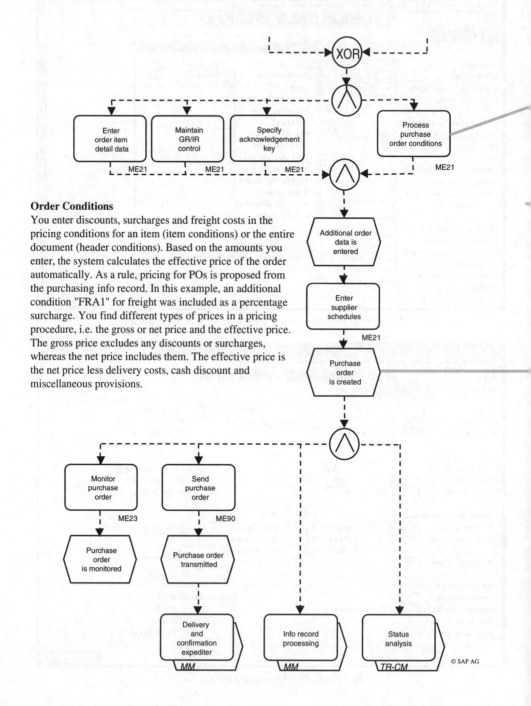

Order Conditions

You enter discounts, surcharges and freight costs in the pricing conditions for an item (item conditions) or the entire document (header conditions). Based on the amounts you enter, the system calculates the effective price of the order automatically. As a rule, pricing for POs is proposed from the purchasing info record. In this example, an additional condition "FRA1" for freight was included as a percentage surcharge. You find different types of prices in a pricing procedure, i.e. the gross or net price and the effective price. The gross price excludes any discounts or surcharges, whereas the net price includes them. The effective price is the net price less delivery costs, cash discount and miscellaneous provisions.

© SAP AG

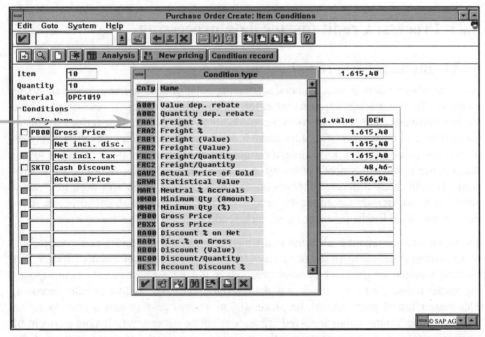

Fig. 8.134: Purchase order conditions

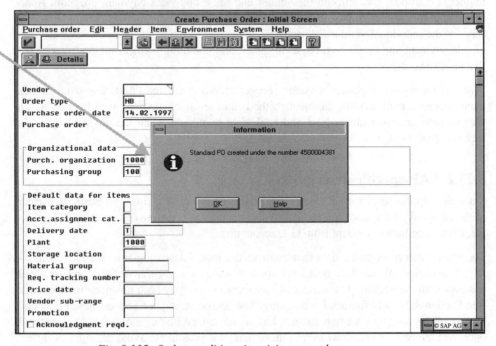

Fig. 8.135: Order conditions in pricing procedure

8.23 Process: Credit master data processing

8.23.1 Business background

A company's suppliers from a financial accounting point of view are known as vendors or creditors. The increasing internationalization of companies makes it necessary to take various monetary and fiscal aspects into consideration; at the same time various organizational types and business relationships make it necessary to deal with many different types of payment processes. If, for example, a company commissions a plant, it often has to pay the supplier a down payment before the supplier starts production. If a company buys products from many different suppliers on an irregular basis, it doesn't need to create a vendor (creditor) master record for the vendor, but instead creates a so-called general one-time account used for the payment for all such vendors.

The vendor master record is a central tool which supports the processing and management of accounting transactions in financial accounting. Since legal requirements stipulate that business transactions have to be posted to accounts, it is necessary to create a corresponding master record for each account, e.g. debitor (customer) and creditor (vendor) account. This master record must control the processing of various posting data according to the various business transactions involved. Thus, it might be necessary to initiate payment of an invoice from delivery processing after the goods receipt check or the receipt of the invoice, i.e. to post a liability to the vendor and settle this via a payment program. Apart from supporting different posting transactions, different payment methods might be necessary for the individual vendors. Apart from the common payment methods, such as point of sale payment and credit card payment, other, less common payment methods may exist that have to be supported.

Whereas for regular suppliers a vendor master record is created containing data such as name, address, bank details, payment methods and terms of payment (see Section 8.21), for one-time accounts the address and bank data is entered when the payment or credit memo is processed.

8.23.2 SAP-specific description

Since the supplier is also managed in financial accounting as a financial business partner of the company, the vendor master record also contains accounting data such as, for example, the reconciliation account from G/L accounting.

The master record contains data that controls the material posting transaction. Additionally, it contains all the data necessary to deal with business transactions and financial postings with the vendor. The vendor master record is used by both materials management (see Section 8.21) and financial accounting. The central storage of vendor master data and the use of this data by both departments has the advantage that data only has to be entered once. Via the *central maintenance* of master data, it is possible to avoid the entry of different data for the same supplier in different areas. If the vendor's address changes, for example, this changed data only has to be entered once and both the materials management and the accounting departments can immediately work with the new, changed data. The vendor master record contains, for example, the name, address, language (for communications purposes) and telephone number of the vendor as well as his tax data, bank data and the number of the reconciliation account in G/L accounting.

No matter what type of vendor is involved, for balance sheet purposes a reconciliation account is necessary, to which postings are made when a transaction is carried out. This guarantees that a corresponding posting, made to a sub-ledger account, such as accounts payable, is posted consistently in G/L accounting. In this way, liabilities from deliveries and services can be seen as cumulated values at any time. Reconciliation accounts are G/L accounts, whose balance always reflects the sum of the balances of sub-ledger accounts. They thus support integration and consistency of data in sub-ledger and general ledger accounting. Examples for reconciliation accounts are domestic liabilities, foreign liabilities or liabilities to affiliated companies. You must enter a reconciliation account in each vendor master record (see Section 8.23.7). The reconciliation is also used to specify additional data, such as the layout and structure of screens (see Fig. 8.136).

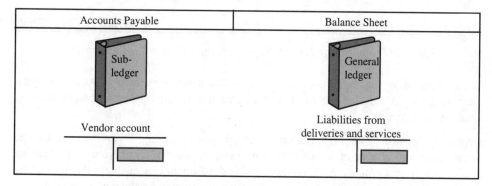

Fig. 8.136: Tasks of the reconciliation account

The screens for entering and maintaining vendor master data can be changed to meet your requirements in Customizing depending on the type of data you want to store in the vendor master record (see Fig. 8.137). However, the reconciliation account must always be entered. The status of fields in a screen is determined by the system administrator. A field can have one of the following statuses:

- ready for input (optional field)

- required entry

- field only displayed

- field suppressed

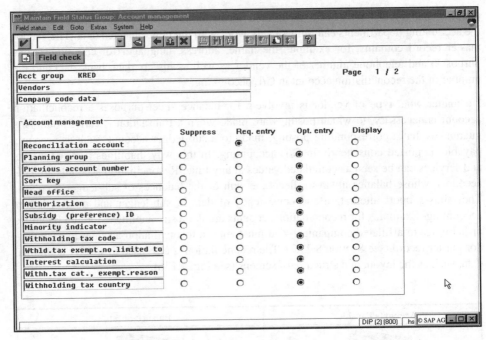

Fig. 8.137: Status of fields in the customer master record – Customizing

The account group, e.g. *0001* as shown in Fig. 8.136, determines the field status for all the fields in the vendor master record. You must enter the account group when you create a vendor master record.

Depending on how your organization is set up, you can assign authorizations for the maintenance and display of master data. For example, you can set up your authorizations in such a way that employees in the accounting department can maintain the accounting data for a supplier but possibly only have display authorization for the purchasing data.

8.23.3 Using the process

If master data is created by both the purchasing and the accounting departments, before maintaining data you should search using the matchcode to see if the general part of the vendor master data already exists. This avoids data being entered redundantly. In the initial screen of vendor master data processing, you enter the number of the vendor (if external number assignment applies to the vendor). The example in Model Company A refers to vendor *1000* in company code *1000*. If all the selection fields are marked, all of the entry screens for the vendor master record are displayed one after the other (see Fig. 8.138).

If a business partner is to be managed in the system as both a vendor and a customer, you can offset the open items against each other in the payment and dunning programs. You can choose the customer line items when you display the vendor line items of an account.

Offsetting is, however, only possible if you enter the customer number of the vendor to be also managed as a vendor on the *Control data* screen. On the *Payment transactions* screen, you can enter several bank accounts. The field *Alternative payee* may also be important in payment processing. Payments are then made to the address or the bank details of the vendor entered (see Fig. 8.140).

General data includes the address of the vendor and data for telecommunication, such as telephone and telefax (see Fig. 8.141).

Company code data includes company-specific information such as payment methods, dunning procedures (see Fig. 8.143) and correspondence. Payment methods might be cheque or bank transfer, etc. By specifying the reconciliation account 160000, a connection is made to general ledger accounting.

8.23.4 Navigation information

▪ *Menu path*
Logistics –> Materials management –> Purchasing –> Master data –> Vendor –> Central –> Create

▪ *Transaction code*
XK01

▪ *Ingoing processes in the R/3 Reference Model*
Vendor invoice processing
Preliminary posting of vendor invoices

▪ *Outgoing processes in the R/3 Reference Model*
Preliminary posting of vendor invoice
Vendor invoice processing

Account Group

When you create a master record, you must specify an account group, which determines, for example, how the account is numbered, a number interval for assigning the account numbers or which fields are displayed on the screens when you enter or change vendor master data, and whether these fields are optional or required entries. After creating the master record, you cannot change the account group. However, your system administrator can change the above-mentioned account group specifications. This may be necessary, if you want to add fields to the vendor master record that were previously suppressed from display. If you use internal number assignment, the system assigns a number when you save the vendor master record. Until then, the word "INTERNAL" appears on the screen in place of the account number. If you use external number assignment, enter the vendor's account number.

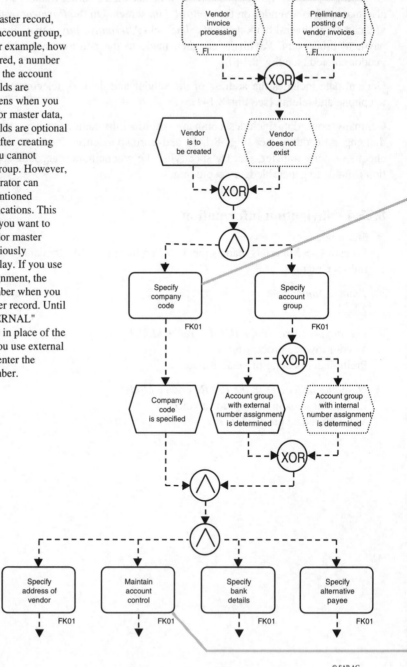

© SAP AG

522

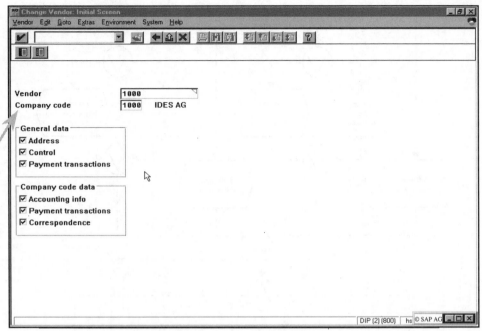

Fig. 8.138: Initial screen of vendor master record

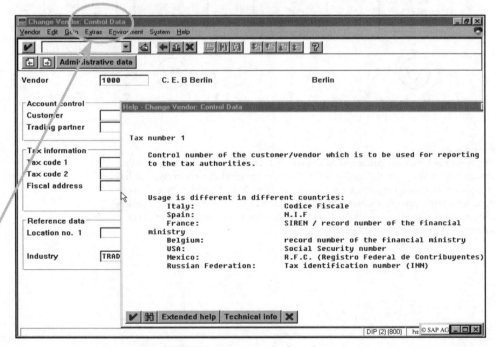

Fig. 8.139: Account control of vendor

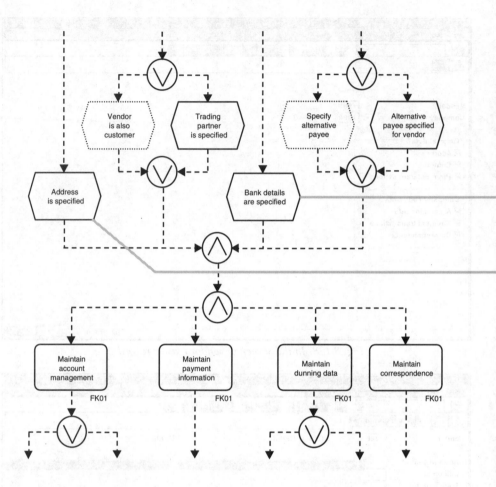

Business Partners

The vendor is a business partner who can assume different roles. For example, in the procurement transaction, the vendor is first the order recipient of a company, then he is the supplier of goods, the invoice party and finally the payee. One or even several of these roles might refer to alternative vendor master records. Therefore, several partner roles can be assigned to the vendor. The alternative data is used during the relevant subsequent functions in logistics and accounting.

Fig. 8.140: Payment transactions of vendor

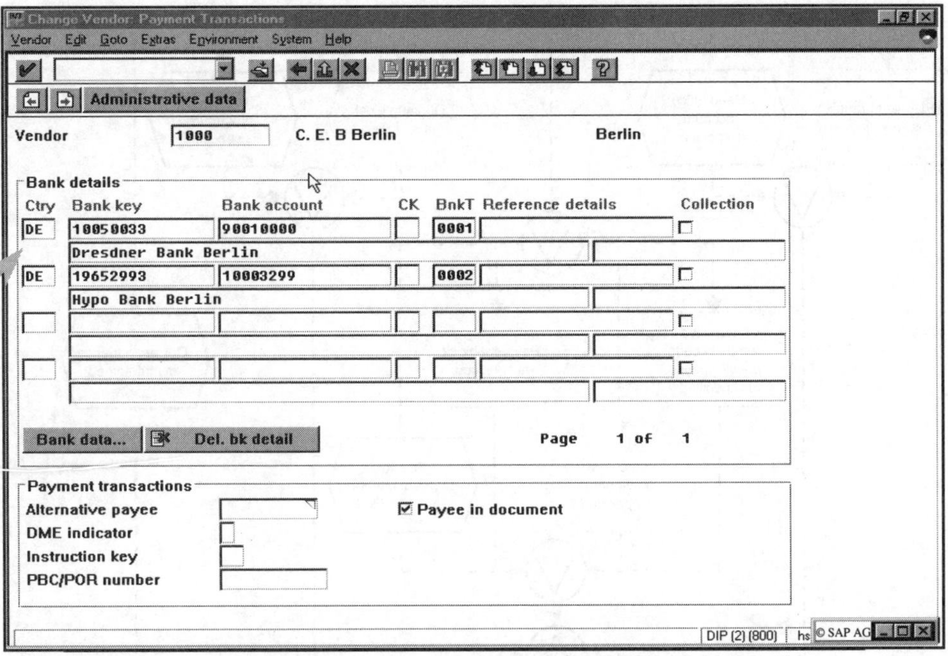

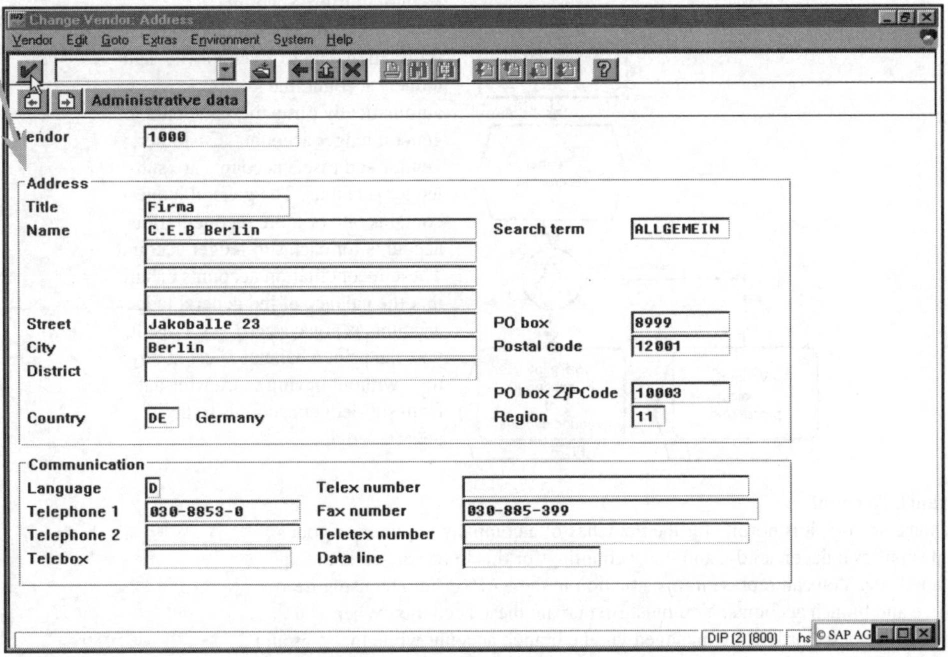

Fig. 8.141: Address of vendor

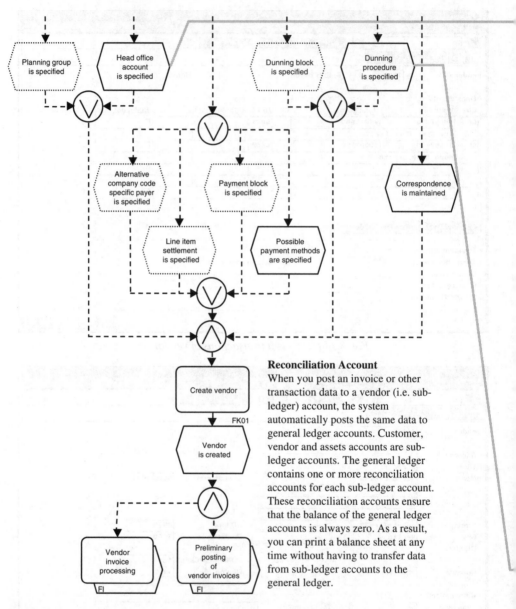

Reconciliation Account

When you post an invoice or other transaction data to a vendor (i.e. sub-ledger) account, the system automatically posts the same data to general ledger accounts. Customer, vendor and assets accounts are sub-ledger accounts. The general ledger contains one or more reconciliation accounts for each sub-ledger account. These reconciliation accounts ensure that the balance of the general ledger accounts is always zero. As a result, you can print a balance sheet at any time without having to transfer data from sub-ledger accounts to the general ledger.

© SAP AG

Branch Account

In some sectors, it is normal for the branches of a company to purchase goods and supplies independently, and the accounting for this to be carried out at the head office. You can represent this situation in the SAP System by using head office and branch accounts. You must first create these accounts. When you have done so, the orders are managed via the branch account while the sales and transaction figures are not posted to this account but rather automatically to the head office account. The payments are also cleared centrally (i.e. via the head office account) which means that payments can be made for several branches via the head office account in one step.

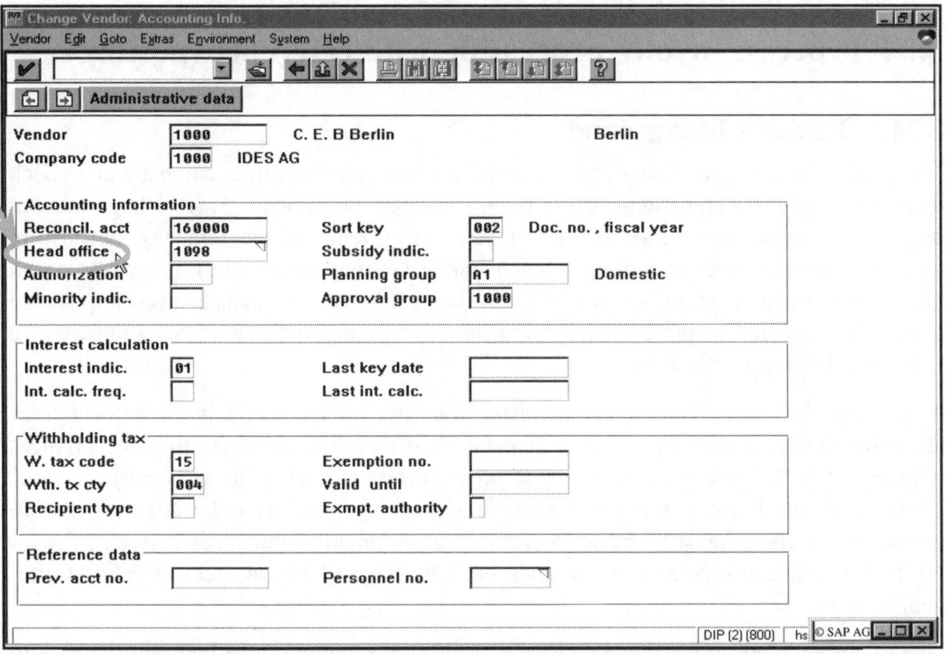

Fig. 8.142: Account management of vendor

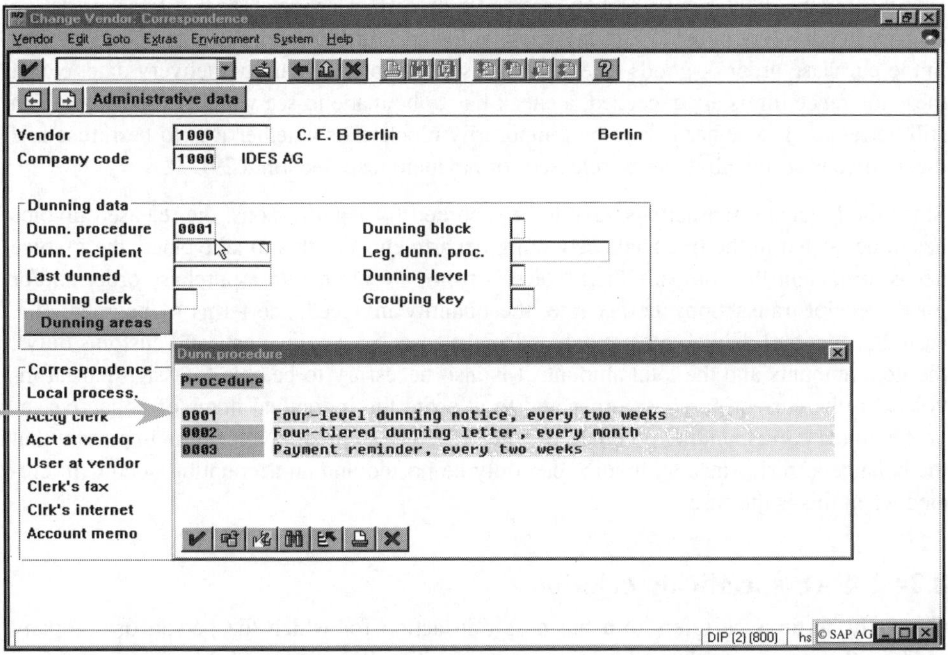

Fig. 8.143: Dunning data of vendor

8.24 Process: Invoice processing with reference (posting)

8.24.1 Business background

The goal of invoice processing is to enter the invoices received by a company and check them for correctness and completeness before payment takes place. Since a large number of invoices nowadays are received not only in the currency of the company, but also in foreign currencies (pounds sterling, French francs, German marks, etc.), it must be possible not only to enter invoices in various currencies but also for balance sheet purposes to convert the various foreign currencies into the appropriate currency of the company (see Hartmann 1993, pp. 491–493).

Invoices can be received based on a purchase order or a goods receipt, in exceptional cases also without reference to a previous document. It is therefore necessary to check invoices with regard to the criteria *quantity, price, payment terms, packaging and transport costs*. The invoices must also be compared with the appropriate purchase order or goods receipt. In addition, a check must be made to ensure that the invoice amount is correct. In cases where the data is not correct, the invoice must be blocked for payment or refused altogether.

Due to currency and price fluctuations, price differences might arise between the data in the purchase order and data in the invoice. It is therefore necessary to maintain tolerance amounts for the delivery of a certain material by a certain vendor. These tolerances define by how much the item data in an invoice is allowed to differ from the corresponding data in the purchase order or goods receipt with respect to price, quantity, delivery date, etc. If these tolerance limits are exceeded, a check has to be made to see whether the invoice can still be released, whether it is to be temporarily blocked or whether it is to be refused. If the invoice is accepted, it can be released for payment (see Section 8.29).

Since the financial transactions have to be recorded for legal reasons, the released invoice has to be posted in the financial accounting department. For this to take place, the invoice needs to contain the company the invoice is from, a reference to a purchase order and/or goods receipt transaction, the tax rate, the quantity invoiced, the terms of payment (i.e. cash discount and delivery costs such as freight costs, packaging costs and customs duty), the item amounts and the total amount. It is also necessary to be able to assign partial invoices to the correct purchase order and to allocate the individual items of collective invoices to the corresponding purchase orders. When posting an invoice, it is important that the balance is zero, since an invoice can only be posted and an accounting document created when this is the case.

8.24.2 SAP-specific description

Generally, an invoice refers to a business transaction for which the person or company sending the invoice wishes to receive payment. The R/3 System differentiates between invoices based on the type of transaction (see SAP – Materials Management 1996, pp. 8.1–8.11):

- *Purchase-order-based invoices*
  In the case of invoices based on a purchase order, payment can be made for all the items in the purchase order, whether or not an item was received in several partial deliveries. All of the deliveries of one item are summed up in one invoice.

- *Goods-receipt-based invoices*
  In the case of invoices based on a goods receipt, an invoice is normally received for each separate goods receipt.

- *Invoices without any reference*
  In the case of invoices received without any reference to a purchasing transaction, the purchasing transaction can be charged directly to a material, a G/L account or an asset account.

If an invoice based on a purchase order is received, the system can refer to data stored in the system in the purchase order and propose values from the purchase order, such as the terms of payment, the quantity to be invoiced, the amount to be invoiced per item, etc. when checking the invoice. These default values can be overwritten if other values have been specified by the vendor in the invoice. The system checks whether your entries are allowed and, if necessary, issues a warning or an error message (see warning in Fig. 8.149).

When posting the invoice, the system determines the accounts to which postings have to be made. The *account determination* is based partly on the entries you make when entering the invoice and partly on information already stored in the system. The following questions have to be answered during invoice verification:

- *Questions regarding the posting of the invoice*
  Is the invoice to be posted gross or net?
  Which creditor account has to be credited?
  To which G/L accounts do postings have to be made?
  Which amounts have to be posted?

- *Questions regarding the material in the invoice*
  To which valuation class does the material belong?
  Which price control method is used for the material?
  To which accounts do postings for the material have to be made?
  Is the current stock quantity less than the invoice quantity?
  What is the purchase order price?
  Has a goods receipt posting already taken place for the purchase order?

In order for the correct postings to be made based on this information, the accounts have to be defined for the chart of accounts and the correct postings set up in Customizing when the R/3 System is first set up (see Fig. 8.144).

| Chart of accounts | ☐ Chart of accounts - international | Chart of accounts | ☐ International CH of Actgs |
| Process | ☐ Inventory posting | Process | ☐ Offsetting entry for inventory posting |

Account assignment

Val. gp. cde	Val. class	Account
0001	3000	300000
0001	3001	300010
0001	3030	303000
0001	3040	304000
0001	3050	305000
0001	3100	310000
0001	7900	790000
0001	7920	792000

Account assignment

Val. gp. cde	Acct modif	Val. class	Debit	Credit
0001	BSA	3049	399999	399999
0001	BSA	3050	399999	399999
0001	BSA	3100	400000	400000
0001	BSA	7900	799999	799999
0001	BSA	7901	799999	799999
0001	BSA	7907	399995	399995
0001	BSA	7920	799999	799999
0001	BSA	BTZ1	231000	231000
0001	BSA	ROH	799999	799999
0001	BSA	SLF1	231000	231000
0001	HDM	3000	191300	191300
0001	HDM	3001	191300	191300
0001	INV	3000	233000	283000
0001	INV	3001	233000	283000

© SAP AG

Fig. 8.144: Customizing of automatic account determination

For automatic account determination to be carried out correctly, the accounts for the debit and credit postings for the individual posting transactions, such as, for example, inventory posting, offsetting entry for inventory posting, minor price differences, freight clearing account postings, have to be entered into the system (see Fig 8.144). Here is a definition of some of the terms used in automatic account determination:

■ *Process*
The process posting key is used to determine the accounts or posting keys for automatic account determination.

■ *Valuation grouping code (Val.gr.cde)*
A group of valuation areas. Using a minimum number of entries, postings for valuation areas with the same postings can be carried out in a similar way using this code. It determines, in conjunction with other factors, the G/L accounts to which goods movements are posted.

■ *Account modification key (Acct modif)*
Key used to differentiate account postings for one posting key

■ *Valuation class (Val.class)*
Allocation of a material to a group of G/L accounts. The valuation class makes it possible on the one hand to make postings for materials belonging to the same material type to different accounts and on the other hand for materials with different material

types to be posted to the same G/L accounts. Examples of valuation classes could be 7900 for semi-finished goods, 7920 for manufactured goods, etc.

When posting a goods receipt, the system makes the following postings: the inventory account is debited with the value of the delivery (purchase order net price * goods receipt quantity), and the GR/IR clearing account is credited with the same amount. When the invoice is posted, the GR/IR clearing account is debited with the amount and the vendor account credited (see Fig. 8.145).

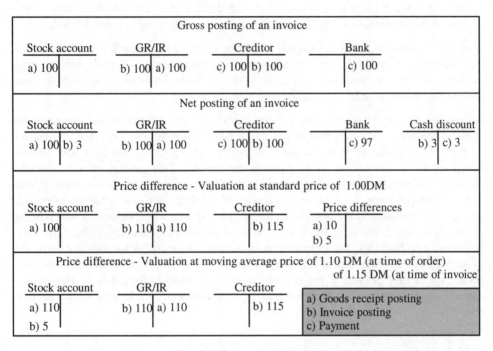

Fig. 8.145: Account postings

Cash discounts are usually agreed upon at the time of purchase. When an invoice is entered, these terms of payment are displayed as default values in the creditor screen and can be overwritten if they have changed since the time of ordering. The cash discount amount can be posted in one of two ways. Either the cash discount is posted to a neutral operating profit account or it is credited to the cost object (i.e. stock account, cost centre, etc.). The way in which the cash discount amount is posted depends on the *document type* used to post the invoice. In the standard system, the document types *RE* for *gross posting* and *RN* for *net posting are used*. When entering the invoice, the document type to be used to post the invoice is entered on the initial screen.

■ *Gross posting*
    When gross posting is carried out for the invoice, the cash discount amount is not taken into consideration when the invoice is posted. It is only considered when the payment

run for the invoice takes place in financial accounting. The neutral profit account is credited and the creditor account debited. In addition, the tax account is also debited.

■ *Net posting*
The cash discount amount to be expected is taken into consideration when posting the invoice. The cash discount amount is posted to a cash discount clearing account. For postings to a stock account, the offsetting entry made depends on the price control of the material involved. In the case of a material with moving average price control, the cash discount amount is credited to the stock account and the cash discount clearing account debited. In the case of a material with standard price control, the account *profit from price differences* is credited and the cash discount clearing account debited.

If an invoice contains cash discount and tax, when the invoice is posted, it is posted with a tax amount that is too high, since the tax does not include the cash discount. This happens no matter whether the invoice is posted gross or net. In the financial accounting payment transaction, the tax posting is corrected automatically.

An invoice can only be posted if the balance is zero. If minor differences exist between the totals of the debit and credit amounts, it might take too much time and effort to find out what the cause of the difference is and then to correct the posting. Instead, a new posting line is created in the invoice which balances this amount. This can happen automatically for minor differences. Via the Customizing entries for invoice verification, it is possible to enter a tolerance amount for minor differences. If the difference lies *inside* the tolerance, the system automatically creates this additional posting line when simulating and posting the invoice. This difference is posted to a neutral profit or loss account. If the difference lies outside the tolerance, the system issues a warning. If the entries are then not corrected in such a way that either a zero balance or a minor difference within the defined tolerance results, the invoice can still be posted, but the invoice is blocked for payment. The invoice can only be paid once it has been released in a separate step (see Section 8.29 – Invoice release).

8.24.3 Using the process

The process described here refers to the invoice verification of the logistics application. On the initial screen, the connection between the invoice and the purchase order is made by entering purchase order number *450004381*. The document type indicator *RE* is defaulted automatically by the system and results in the invoice being posted net (see Fig. 8.146). On the next screen (creditor screen), the invoice amount of (gross) *15669,38 DEM* is entered. Two possibilities exist to enter the tax amount. You can enter the tax amount manually or you can enter the correct tax indicator, e.g. *V0,* and by marking an additional field, the tax is calculated automatically by the system. The payment term *ZB03* (14 days 3% cash discount), taken from the purchase order referenced when entering the invoice, is defaulted and accepted (see Fig. 8.147). The next screen is the purchase order item selection screen. The required items are selected and if necessary, the quantity or amount corrected if these are different from the values in the invoice. With the *Simulate* button, the system checks the invoice to see whether the balance is zero. If unforeseeable delivery costs are only charged at the time of the invoice, these can be entered via the menu Process->delivery costs and also checked in the invoice. If the balance of the invoice document is not zero, the figures can be changed after pressing the *Correction on/off* button. When the invoice balance is zero, the invoice can be posted. In the example shown, invoice *5100004280* was posted but not yet released for payment (blocking reason: date difference).

8.24.4 Navigation information

■ *Menu path*
Logistics –> Materials management –> Invoice verification –> Invoice verification –> Document entry –> Enter invoice

■ *Transaction code*
MRHR

■ *Ingoing processes in the R/3 Reference Model*
Preliminary posting of invoices
Entry of services performed
GR processing with order reference for fixed asset

■ *Outgoing processes in the R/3 Reference Model*
Preliminary posting of invoices
Transfer of primary costs
Project update
Third-party order processing
Down payment release
Vendor down payment clearing
Automatic payment
Availability check (capital investment)
Direct assignment of special direct costs
Budget execution/verification

Invoice Verification with Reference

Each invoice contains various items of information.
To post an invoice, you must enter this information
into the system. If an invoice refers to an existing
transaction, certain items of information will already
be available in the system. The system proposes this
information as default data so that you only need to
compare it and, if necessary, correct any possible
variances. If an invoice refers to a purchase order,
for example, you only need to enter the number of
the purchase order (see number 4500000315 in this
example). The system selects the right transaction
and proposes data from the purchase order, including
the vendor, material, quantity ordered, terms of
delivery, terms of payment. You can, of course,
overwrite this default data if there are variances. You
can display the purchase order history to see, for
example, which quantities have been delivered and
how much has already been invoiced

Posting Date

The date you enter must be within the allowed
posting period defined in Financial Accounting.

Document Number

Only make an entry in this field if the invoice
document number is not to be assigned by the
system. Your system administrator has defined
whether the document number should be assigned by
the user or by the system.

Document Type

The entry in this field controls the appearance of the
document. There are two standard document types in
the standard system: RE (the invoice is posted gross)
and RN (the invoice is posted net).

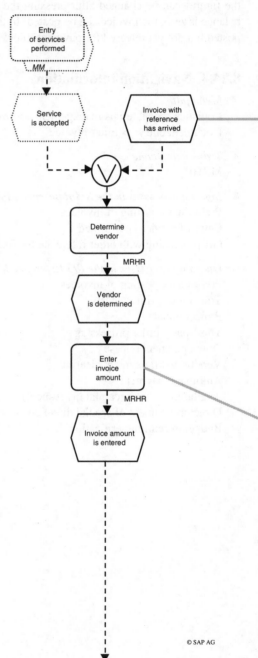

© SAP AG

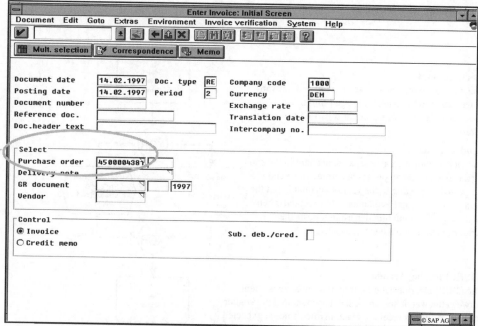

Fig. 8.146: Entering invoice with reference to purchase order

---

Enter Invoice: Vendor Items

Document Edit Goto Extras Environment Invoice verification System Help

Detail...

Vendor	2	Electronic Components Distributor	Item	001
		Foster City		

Posting

Amount	15.669,38	DEM	Business area	
Tax amount		DEM	Tax code	V0
Tax amount		DEM	Tax code	

☐ Calculate tax

Payment control

Baseline dte	14.02.1997		Payment terms	ZB03	14	Days	3,000	%
Discnt base		DEM			30	Days	1,000	%
Discnt amnt		DEM			60	Days net		

Pmnt block
Pmnt method   Invoice reference

Allocation/text

Allocation
Text

© SAP AG

Fig. 8.147: Entering invoiced amount

Stock Account

The stock account manages the inward and outward movement of a material. At the end of the fiscal year, the balance of this account is carried forward to itself.

Vendor Account

For each vendor there is a separate account in the sub-ledger to which all amounts concerning this vendor are posted. A posting to the vendor account is not the same as a payment. Payment is only executed when the Financial Accounting department posts the vendor's payment to a bank account.

GR/IR Clearing Account

The GR/IR clearing account is an intermediate account between the warehouse stock sheet account and the vendor account. At goods receipt, the net invoice amount expected is posted from the stock account to the GR/IR clearing account. This posting is then cleared by an offsetting entry on the vendor account at invoice receipt.

Small Differences

An invoice can only be posted if the balance is zero. It is very time-consuming to determine the reasons and change the individual items if the balance is not zero. So if there is only a slight difference between the debit and credit amounts, you can enter a new item to clear the difference. This can occur automatically for small differences. In Customizing for Invoice Verification, you can maintain a tolerance limit for small differences; if the difference is within the tolerance limits, the system automatically generates a posting line that posts the difference to a non-operating expense or income account.

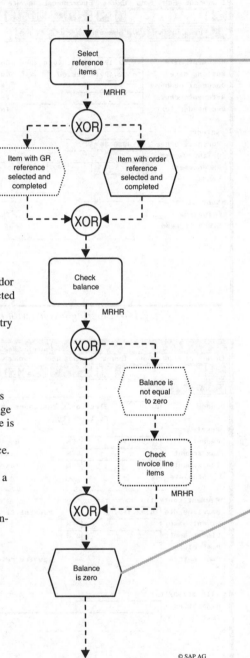

© SAP AG

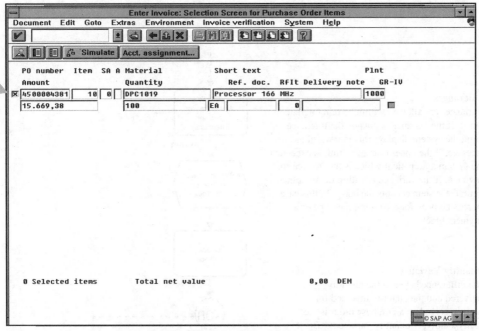

Fig. 8.148: Selection of purchase order item

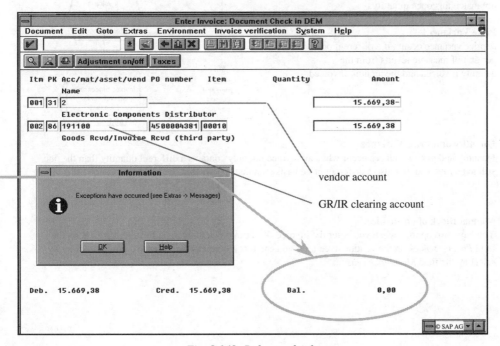

Fig. 8.149: Balance check

Tolerances

Variances are allowed within certain tolerance limits. If the variance is outside the tolerance limit, the system displays this in a warning message. If the upper tolerance limit is exceeded, the system automatically blocks the invoice for payment. If the variance is within the tolerance limit, the system accepts the entry. In this case, there is no need for a warning message or a payment block.

Quantity Variance

The difference between the quantity delivered and the quantity invoiced for goods received on a purchase order is the open quantity. A quantity variance exists if the quantity you enter from the invoice does not match this open quantity.

Price Variance

A price variance occurs if a different price per unit of measure results from the quantity invoiced and the amount invoiced.

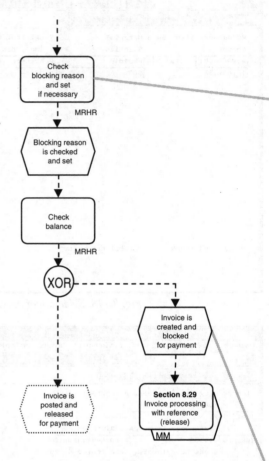

Quantity and Price Variance

Quantity and price variances occur when an invoice not only contains a different quantity than the one still to be invoiced, but also a different price basis than that specified in the purchase order.

Manual Block of an Invoice

You have two options when you enter the invoice. You can block an invoice by entering an **R** on the field *Payment block* on the vendor screen. Or you can block invoices that refer to a purchase order by selecting the field *Man.block.reasn.*

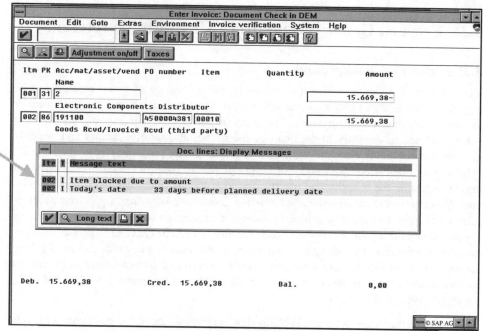

Fig. 8.150: Reasons for blocking an invoice

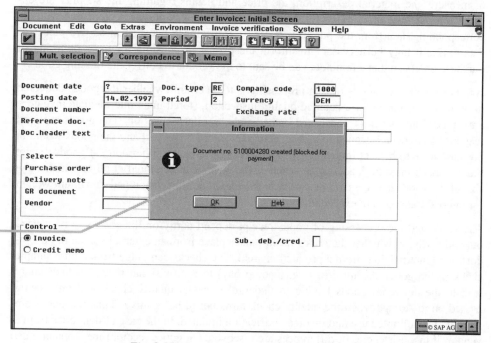

Fig. 8.151: Invoice is created and blocked

8.25 Process: Goods receipt processing with PO reference

8.25.1 Business background

Depending on the way in which it is looked at, the processing of goods receipts can be regarded either as a part of the purchasing process, a task within inventory management or as part of warehouse management. The tasks of goods receipt processing are also not solely confined to the entry of the quantity receipt but also involve quality and possibly also price checks. However, the basic task of goods receipt processing is to enter the receipt of goods delivered by a vendor or freight carrier, to confirm the receipt, to carry out checks regarding the quantity and quality, and to enter any other data that might be relevant. Whereas in the case of so-called *planned goods receipts* either a purchase order or release order (in the case of purchased goods) or a production order exists, (in the case of goods produced in-house, *unplanned goods receipts* have to be checked in greater detail as no reference document exists against which the correctness of the goods can be checked. Unplanned goods receipts can also take place as a result of free-of-charge deliveries or return deliveries (see Arnolds *et al.* 1996, pp. 363–365; see Hartmann 1993, pp. 488–490; see Pfohl 1996, pp. 121–127).

No matter whether a goods receipt is planned or unplanned, one of the main tasks of goods receipt processing is to enter the receipt of the goods. Here, the delivered quantity and unit of measure, the material description, the price and details regarding the supplier are entered. If a purchase order exists for the goods, the goods receipt data is compared with the corresponding data from the purchase order. If a difference between these two pieces of data exists, it may be necessary to inform the people responsible for the monitoring of purchase orders so that a reminder can be sent to the vendor to deliver the missing goods.

Another function of goods receipt processing is to determine whether the goods delivered have to be transferred for a detailed quality inspection, stored in an intermediate inventory area, placed into stock or consumed immediately, e.g. in production. The goods received may also have been assigned to a cost centre, an order or a project and the goods would in this case have to be sent immediately to the area concerned. Furthermore, at goods receipt time, a check must be made to see whether the goods can be stored at all or whether the size of the goods is excessive, i.e. whether the maximum dimension and maximum weight for internal transport are exceeded.

The scope and the processing of goods receipt depend partly on the checks to be carried out and partly on whether the goods receipt takes place from an external source (by a vendor) or an internal one (from a production area). The checks can range from a pure sample check in the goods receipt area (e.g. loading bay) to a provisional receipt, which might lead to the delivered goods having to undergo a special quality check and only being passed on to storage when the quality check turns out to be positive. Then the goods are released for unlimited use and invoice verification initiated. In the case of deliveries from a vendor, if inconsistencies or differences are discovered at goods receipt time, contact must be made with the purchasing or invoice verification area and the goods possibly refused or the invoice blocked for payment. In such a case involving internal supply (from production), contact must be made with the production department and possibly a new order initiated for the missing pieces. In both cases, the results of the goods receipt process are stored in a document called a *goods receipt slip*. The person receiving the goods signs the goods receipt slip to confirm delivery of the goods and the correctness of the data contained in the goods receipt slip. In addition, due to the large number of different situations that can arise at goods receipt time, a goods receipt status has to be entered. Examples of such statuses are:

- Goods accepted and freely available (unrestricted use)

- Goods accepted and blocked until checked by quality inspection

- Goods in quality inspection

- Goods are being transported

- Goods damaged

- Goods posted into stock

8.25.2 SAP-specific description

When goods receipt (GR) is posted for a purchase order, the system proposes the *open order quantity* of an item as the item quantity in goods receipt. When the goods receipt is entered, the delivered quantity of an item is compared with the open order quantity. In this way, the system can recognize *under- and over-deliveries* immediately. The open order quantity is changed automatically each time goods are received for a purchase order item or each time the purchase order item quantity is changed (see SAP – Materials Management 1996, pp. 6.4–6.5).

- *Underdeliveries*
Underdeliveries are generally allowed in the SAP standard system. In the purchase order item, it is possible to define an underdelivery tolerance as a percentage. Any goods receipt which lies within this tolerance is regarded as a partial delivery and accepted. The system does not issue a warning. If the delivered quantity lies outside the tolerance defined for underdeliveries, the system issues a warning. If the underdelivery does not represent a partial delivery but instead a final delivery, the final delivery indicator must be set. In Customizing you can define that the final delivery indicator is set *automatically* in the case of an underdelivery where the quantity lies within the underdelivery tolerance. In this case, an underdelivery within the tolerance is interpreted as a final delivery.

- *Overdeliveries*
In the standard system, no overdeliveries are allowed. The system automatically issues an error in the case of overdelivery. If you want to allow overdeliveries, you can set the *unlimited* indicator in the purchase order. In this case, any quantity delivered will be accepted. The system does not issue any message. You can also enter a percentage amount, by which a delivery can be overdelivered. A goods receipt with a quantity

larger than the order quantity plus percentage overdelivery is not accepted by the system.

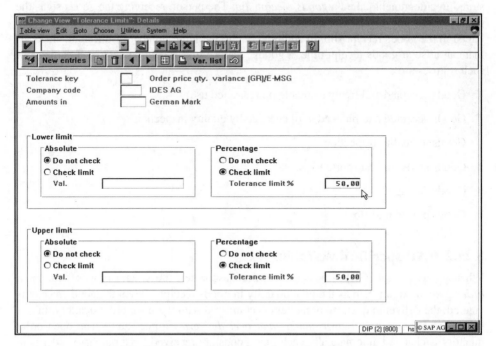

Fig. 8.152: Customizing goods receipt tolerances

In inventory management customizing, you can define two tolerances for difference regarding the purchase order price unit.

■ *Error tolerance*
   If the difference is larger than this tolerance, the system issues an error message, meaning that the goods receipt cannot be posted.

■ *Warning tolerance*
   If the difference is larger than this tolerance but smaller than the error tolerance, a warning is issued in goods receipt processing. It is, however, possible to post the goods receipt. Purchasing receives a message informing the responsible person about the difference.

When the total quantity has been delivered, the final delivery indicator is set automatically in the purchase order at goods receipt time. In the case of an underdelivery or overdelivery, the final delivery indicator is set *automatically* if this has been set up in Customizing. In the case of an underdelivery outside the underdelivery tolerances, you can set the final delivery indicator *manually* at goods receipt time or in the purchase order item, so that the item is regarded as having been fully delivered. If you enter a return delivery for an item that has been marked as completely delivered, and as a result of this the underdelivery tolerance is exceeded, the final (complete) delivery indicator is automatically removed. A purchase order item is also regarded as completely delivered when the total order quantity of the item has been delivered, even if the complete delivery indicator has not been marked. In this case, it is not necessary to set the indicator.

Material valuation for a material is automatically carried out when the goods receipt is posted. The value at which a material is posted depends on the order in which goods receipt and invoice receipt is posted.

- *Goods receipt before invoice receipt*
  The goods are posted based on the price in the purchase order.

- *Invoice receipt before goods receipt*
  The goods are posted based on the price in the invoice.

The main task of material valuation is to record the stock (inventory) value of a material. The stock value of a material is determined using the formula: stock value = stock quantity * material valuation price. The stock value of a material thus changes when either the stock quantity or the material valuation price changes.

For most goods movements in inventory management, the movement leads to a change in the stock quantity and thus also the stock value. In the case of materials valued using the *moving average price,* a goods receipt with reference to a purchase order can also lead to a change in the material valuation price. This is the case when the purchase order price differs from the material valuation price. Planned delivery costs entered in the purchase order also affect the valuation of a material at goods receipt time. When the goods receipt is posted, accruals are created for planned delivery costs. In this way, the expected material costs are immediately charged to the material. A subsequent charge to the material at invoice receipt time then only has to take place if a difference occurs between the purchase order price (including planned delivery costs) and the invoice price. It is also possible to post goods receipts net. This means that cash discount amounts are considered in the valuation of a material at goods receipt time. A material valued using the moving average price is then valued at goods receipt time with the purchase order price minus cash discount amount.

Automatic account assignment takes place at goods receipt time. This means that when a goods receipt is posted, the system automatically determines the accounts in financial posting to which postings have to be made, without the user having to make any additional entries. If the movement results in postings being made to G/L accounts in financial accounting, in addition to the *material document*, which records the movement from an inventory (quantity) point of view, one or *more accounting documents* are created by the system. The combinations of the parameters *movement type, value string, posting (transaction) key* and possibly *account modification* are the factors the system uses to determine the correct account automatically in Customizing (see Fig. 8.153).

- *Movement type*
  Key for a goods movement, e.g. *101* (goods receipt to stock).

- *Value string*
  Key for a certain business transaction, e.g. goods receipt, always using the same account assignment attributes. The posting key is always needed for automatic postings.

- *Posting key*
  Used to determine the G/L account to which a posting line is posted. This means that at least two posting keys result from one posting (one per posting line).

- *Account modification*
  Key, which depending on the business transaction involved, is used to modify and differentiate account determination.

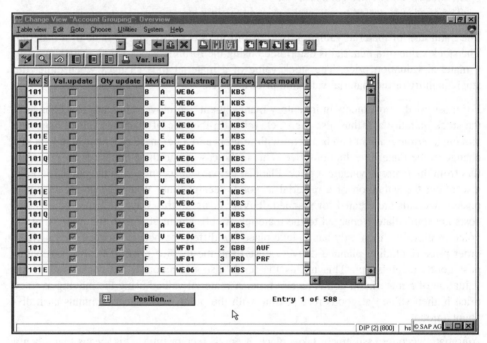

Mv	S	Val.update	Qty update	Mv	Cns	Val.strng	Cr	TEKey	Acct modif	
101		☐	☐	B	A	WE 06	1	KBS		☑
101		☐	☐	B	E	WE 06	1	KBS		☑
101		☐	☐	B	P	WE 06	1	KBS		☑
101		☐	☐	B	U	WE 06	1	KBS		☑
101	E	☐	☐	B	E	WE 06	1	KBS		☑
101	E	☐	☐	B	P	WE 06	1	KBS		☑
101	Q	☐	☐	B	P	WE 06	1	KBS		☑
101		☐	☑	B	A	WE 06	1	KBS		☑
101		☐	☑	B	U	WE 06	1	KBS		☑
101	E	☐	☑	B	E	WE 06	1	KBS		☑
101	E	☐	☑	B	P	WE 06	1	KBS		☑
101	Q	☐	☑	B	P	WE 06	1	KBS		☑
101		☑	☑	B	A	WE 06	1	KBS		☑
101		☑	☑	B	U	WE 06	1	KBS		☑
101		☑	☑	F		WF 01	2	GBB	AUF	☑
101		☑	☑	F		WF 01	3	PRD	PRF	☑
101	E	☑	☑	B	E	WE 06	1	KBS		☑

Position...   Entry 1 of 588

Fig. 8.153: Customizing movement type/value string (automatic account determination)

8.25.3 Using the process

Once you have received the delivery note from the supplier and discovered that the delivery refers to a purchase order, you can enter the goods receipt in the R/3 System. On the initial screen, movement type *101* (goods receipt to stock) is entered if the system does not propose this automatically (see Fig. 8.155). It is important to enter the number of the purchase order to which the delivery applies, in this case *4500004381*, and the number of the plant, here *1000*. If you don't know the number of the purchase order, you can follow the menu path to enter a goods receipt for an unknown purchase order number and enter search criteria to help you find the correct number.

The other fields on the initial screen can be filled out if required. For example, here you can specify that a goods receipt slip is to be printed, you can enter a text at document header level, a reference to a delivery note, etc. The fields *Document date* and *Posting date* are always filled with the date on which you enter the goods receipt but can be over-written.

If the item data are correct and complete on the next screen, the goods receipt can be posted. If you change the item data, the system branches to the item detail screen (see Fig. 8.156). Here, you can compare the quantity storage location, etc.

When you post the goods receipt, the stock quantity, the stock value and, as a result of the automatic account determination, the corresponding G/L accounts, e.g. stock account, GR/IR clearing account, are updated. To document the postings, a material document and accounting document(s) (if relevant) are created automatically (see Fig. 8.157). The structure of the display screen of the material document is more or less identical to the selection screen for a goods receipt with reference to a purchase order. If goods receipts have been entered incorrectly, they have to be cancelled and then re-entered correctly. If you analyze the material document, you can check the posted quantity, the purchase order number to which the movement applies and the movement itself (+ receipt, – for issue). In the background, the system automatically updates the purchase order history and data for the vendor evaluation.

8.25.4 Navigation information

■ *Menu path*
Logistics –> Materials management –> Inventory management –> Goods movement –> Goods receipt –> For purchase order –> PO number known

■ *Transaction code*
MB01, MB1C

■ *Ingoing processes in the R/3 Reference Model*
Delivery and confirmation expediter

■ *Outgoing processes in the R/3 Reference Model*
Inspection lot creation for goods receipt from purchase order
Budget execution/verification
Placement in storage processing
Automatic creation of transport orders for material document

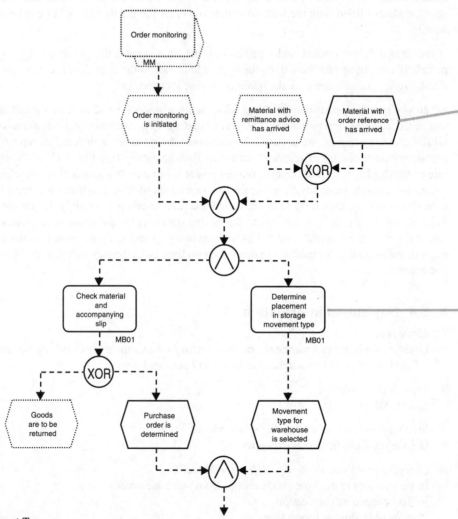

Movement Type

The movement type has important control functions in Inventory Management. For example, the movement type plays an important role in updating quantity fields, in updating stock and consumption accounts and in determining which fields are displayed during entry of a document in the system. When you enter a goods movement in the system, you must enter a movement type to differentiate between the various goods movements. A movement type is a three-digit identification key for a goods movement. The identification key "101" means goods receipt for purchase order, the key "201" means goods issue for a cost centre and "321" means release from quality inspection stock.

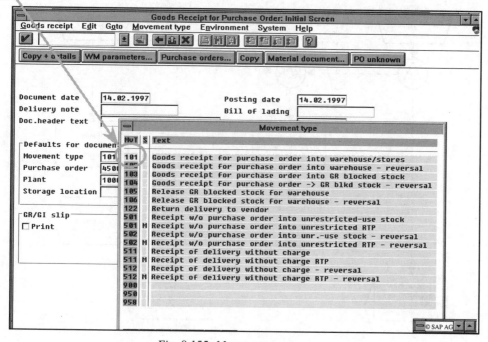

Fig. 8.154: Goods receipt with reference to purchase order

Fig. 8.155: Movement types

Material Document

A material document is generated as proof of the movement and as a source of information for any other applications involved.

Stock Account

In the SAP System, there is no separate account for each material. Instead, different materials with similar features are grouped together in a common account (for example, raw materials, acids). The account relevant for a material is defined in the system when the material master record is created.

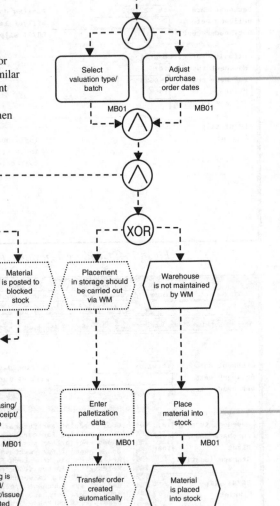

© SAP AG

548

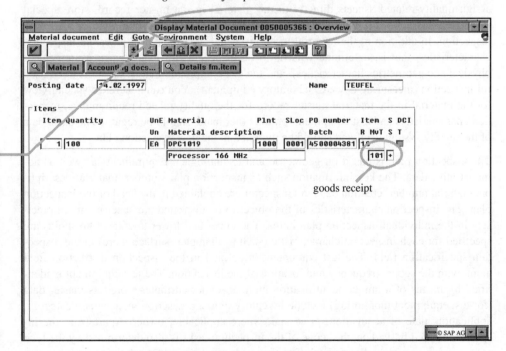

Fig. 8.156: *Adjust purchase order dates*

Fig. 8.157: *Material document after placement into storage*

8.26 Process: Material master processing QM

8.26.1 Business background

Companies are increasingly extending the scope of quality systems from merely inspecting products after manufacture to turning them into planning and predictive quality assurance systems within the product creation process. Both the technical safety of the product and its usability for the client must be guaranteed here. The functions of the quality system can be divided into quality planning, quality control and quality inspection. *Quality planning* covers all actions associated with the selection, classification and weighting of quality characteristics and the derivation of the corresponding inspection characteristics, with a view to correctly assessing the extent to which customer or product demands are being met. Using the results of the quality inspection, *quality control* is responsible for ensuring that the specified quality parameters are observed and, if necessary, intervening with corrective action. The aim of *quality inspection* is to make the planning and implementation of inspection during the manufacture of the product as cost – effective as possible, to store all results and to analyze these in the light of the specified requirements. Quality inspection itself can be divided into inspection planning, inspection implementation and inspection data analysis (see Melzer-Ridinger 1995, pp. 1–34).

The point of departure for carrying out quality inspection is the material itself. You can assign quality-related aspects directly to the material in the master record, store special inspection instructions in the routing or create a customized inspection plan for a specific inspection. In addition to the material to be inspected, you must also enter the inspection characteristics, that is, determine what is to be inspected (for example, measurement of physical and geometric characteristics), and the test equipment, that is, the tools to be used for inspection (measuring devices, laboratory equipment). You can generate a special view for the material in the material master record for the quality-related requirements; inspection characteristics and test equipment, on the other hand, should be regarded as basic data of the quality system itself and should be included in the new inspection plan.

The inspection plan is based on geometric and technological requirements as well as administrative data. The key information such as inspection plan number, material description, material number, creation date and inspector are contained in the head of the inspection plan. The inspection characteristics of the object to be inspected are specified more precisely in the individual inspection plan items. The upper and lower tolerance thresholds are specified for each inspection characteristic (such as diameter, surface, bore) in the inspection specification field. The test equipment is defined in the inspection instruction field along with the scope, frequency and location of the inspection. The test equipment is identified by means of a unique identification number. Other attributes stored as master data (for test equipment monitoring) include inventory number, description, accuracy category, application, date of acquisition, price and, where applicable, owner. Apart from the inspection-related basic data, the scope of the inspection tasks is also determined by the type of inspection and inspection trigger. The type of inspection can be subdivided, for example, into experiment type as well as first sampling, pilot lot and continuous series-type inspections. The origin can be distinguished after the inspection on the basis of a goods receipt (from a vendor or production area or within a production process) or in goods issue and delivery to the customer.

8.26.2 SAP-specific description

You can enter quality-related master data in the R/3 System both in the material master and in the inspection plan by defining the test equipment, inspection characteristics and inspection method. Additionally, the Quality Management module uses other material master information as well as vendor and customer master data to carry out a wide range of different inspections in Procurement, Production as well as Sales and Distribution. The material master contains basic data for quality management which also influences the inspection process. To create quality-specific data for a particular material, you must first choose *Quality management* in the view selection. In the material master record, you can, for example, specify whether quality management is *active* for procurement and whether a particular material is to be posted as quality inspection stock before the inspection is performed. It is, however, not possible to post the material as inspection stock for purchase orders allocated to an account or goods issue postings (see SAP – Quality Management 1996, pp. 4.1–4.2).

An important indicator in the Quality Management view is *Inspection type*. The inspection type determines how the inspection is carried out for a particular material (see Fig. 8.159). In the R/3 Customizing system, you can define common inspection types with corresponding default values. These values are displayed to the member of staff while the business transaction is being processed, providing him or her with information for the material inspection to be carried out. You can, therefore, specify whether the inspection is to be based on an inspection plan or material specification, or whether it is to be carried out without an inspection plan. On the basis of this, the system automatically attempts to select an inspection specification (inspection plan or material specification) and to assign this to the inspection lot, that is, to the material and the quantity to be inspected. A sample can be specified for each inspection by setting the appropriate indicator. You can specify the following types of sample:

❑ *Specify manual sample*
When creating an inspection lot you have to enter the sample size manually.

❑ *Initiate sample calculation manually*
The process for determining the sample size is initiated manually. The system then calculates the sample size on the basis of the percentage in the inspection percentage field. If there is no entry here, you must set the 100% inspection indicator.

❑ *100% inspection*
The sample size corresponds to the lot size.

❑ *Inspection percentage*
The system calculates the sample size on the basis of the entered percentage. If, for example, a goods delivery of 10000 pieces has been received and the percentage is 2%,

the sample should consist of 200 pieces.

■ *Skips allowed*
   Skip means that an inspection is not necessary for this particular material.

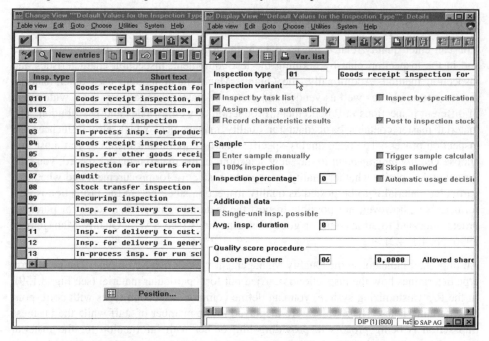

Fig. 8.158: Inspection type for goods receipt for order-customizing

You also determine here whether or not an automatic usage decision is to be used. The *usage decision* determines what happens to a material after inspection. Information which is used for material inventory management purposes can be stored in the system, for example whether a particular material is to be posted as unrestricted-use stock, blocked stock or scrap. If the indicator for the automatic usage decision is set and the goods in an inspection lot have been found to be free of defects in the operative inspection, the system can then carry out the steps for completing the inspection automatically (see Section 8.28). At the same time, the inventory postings are made and the goods released from the inspection stock. Automatic implementation of these activities assumes that no characteristic in the inspection lot has been rejected, all of the required characteristics have been confirmed, and no defect records have been generated. In order to use the QM module in Procurement, you also have to maintain special data in the material master record. You must, therefore, at least set the QM indicator in Procurement and enter a control key. The *control key* determines whether an agreement is necessary regarding technical terms of delivery, quality assurance agreements, vendor releases, quality certificates, obligation to provide documentation ("documentation required") and the activation of invoice blocks. By entering the certificate category defined in Customizing, you can specify that a certificate is to be requested from the vendor for each purchase order item. In addition to this, you can stipulate whether a certificate is to be provided for a particular purchase order item for each goods receipt, whether the receipt of a certificate is to be checked for each purchase order item in goods receipt, and which type of message is to be generated if the required certificate does not exist.

8.26.3 Using the process

Extending the *DPC1101* material master record to include the QM master data and the data from Sections 8.08, 8.11 and 8.20 does not represent a new transaction but simply involves adding a new view to the material master. This is why the material master record is called with the *Create* command and is not accessed via the change mode. The *Quality Management* input mask is accessed directly if you have chosen the appropriate view. Use the *QM inspection data* pushbutton to access the parameter list for the inspection types. Inspection type *01* (incoming inspection) was selected for Model Company A (see Fig. 8.159). In the general QM view (see Fig. 8.160) you can maintain other basic data such as the *goods receipt time* and the *documentation required* fields. The *QM inspection data* checkbox is set automatically as the inspection type was set in the previous step. If a quality inspection is performed for procurement, as planned for Model Company A, you must activate the *QM procurement* parameter before you save the material master record.

8.26.4 Navigation information

■ *Menu path*
Logistics –> Materials management –> Material master –> Material –> Create

■ *Transaction code*
MM01

■ *Ingoing processes in the R/3 Reference Model*
none

■ *Outgoing processes in the R/3 Reference Model*
Master inspection charac. Processing
Master inspection charac. Processing in production
Inspection plan processing
Material specification
Sample processing
Appraisal cost entry (QM order)

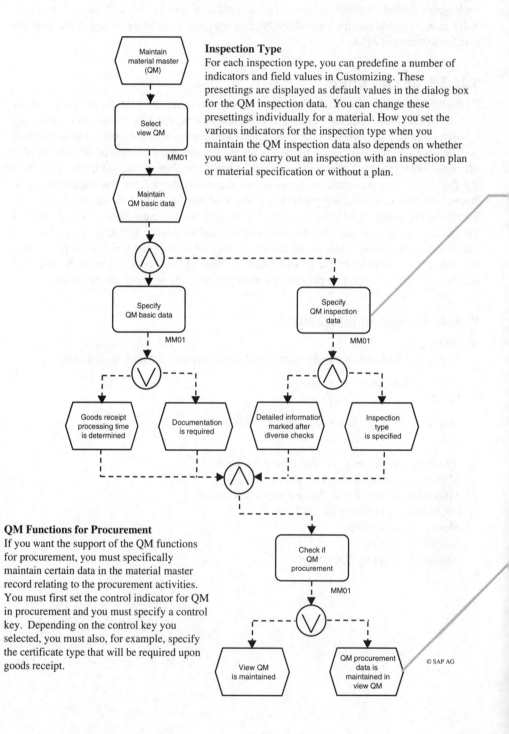

Inspection Type

For each inspection type, you can predefine a number of indicators and field values in Customizing. These presettings are displayed as default values in the dialog box for the QM inspection data. You can change these presettings individually for a material. How you set the various indicators for the inspection type when you maintain the QM inspection data also depends on whether you want to carry out an inspection with an inspection plan or material specification or without a plan.

QM Functions for Procurement

If you want the support of the QM functions for procurement, you must specifically maintain certain data in the material master record relating to the procurement activities. You must first set the control indicator for QM in procurement and you must specify a control key. Depending on the control key you selected, you must also, for example, specify the certificate type that will be required upon goods receipt.

© SAP AG

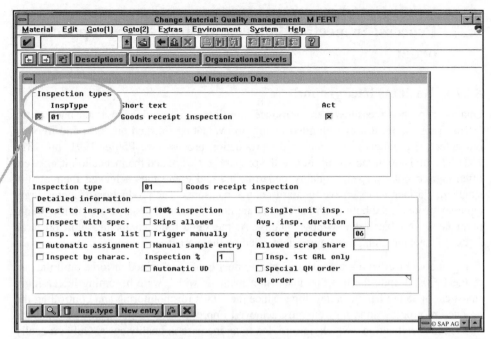

Fig. 8.159: Inspection type

Fig. 8.160: QM general and procurement data

8.27 Process: Inspection lot creation for GR from purchase order

8.27.1 Business background

Quality inspection measures were introduced into industrial production as far back as the 1920s. These were, however, limited mainly to evaluating finished products and filtering out defective products at the end of the production process (see Pfeifer 1991, pp. 131–153). The division of labour meant that the preparatory work and the inspection itself were often carried out by special quality departments, and companies achieved their quality standards through an extensive range of control measures. The production of increasingly complex products led both to an increase in appraisal costs and to surplus quantities being permanently produced due to poor quality. At the same time, companies built up large stocks to meet the high sales figures demanded by the market.

The primary objective of guaranteeing end product quality remained in force until the end of the 1970s, despite the fact that inspection methods which were becoming increasingly statistical in nature had been developed since the 1930s for monitoring and controlling the production process. Industry generally achieved improvements in quality by refining the inspection specifications, which, in turn, led to an increase in quality costs. Only gradually did companies move away from controls at the end of the production process (source inspection) towards inspections during production (production monitoring). Initially, the focus here was on checking for defects; since the late 1970s/early 1980s, however, the tendency has been increasingly towards defect prevention. This is based on the realization that *inspecting quality* within the production process – especially with increasingly complex products and closely related product parts – cannot guarantee the necessary quality. The main focus within quality assurance has, therefore, shifted from *inspection* to *predictive planning,* with the aim of avoiding defects. The objective is to discover possible areas of potential defects prior to production and to incorporate appropriate measures for avoiding them as early as the planning stage. This approach was soon consolidated by the emergence of an increasing number of new methods such as Failure Mode and Effect Analysis (FMEA), defect-tree analysis and the Shainin and Taguchi method.

In addition to traditional CAQ systems, which are basically designed to support inspection planning, test equipment planning, test equipment administration, inspection order administration/execution and inspection data evaluation, CAE/CAD systems have, within the framework of IT integration, been designed with a view to introducing quality assurance measures within product planning and development. This is because errors which the designer makes during the drafting phase of a product generally lead to disproportionately high costs at the manufacturing stage. Over and above the quality assurance developments in the product creation chain, increasing demands (stemming from environmental and producer liability factors) led to quality assurance measures being extended to cover the entire incoming/outgoing material and product flows. Goods-specific inspections at goods receipt from a vendor or at goods issue to a customer, therefore, became increasingly important for the companies concerned (see Arnolds *et al.* 1996, pp. 377–392; see Dillinger 1994, pp. 997–1015; see Herzog 1992, pp. 50–60; see Melzer-Ridinger 1994, pp. 29–43).

Since a company can be both the vendor and the customer, outgoing inspections at the vendor and incoming inspections at the customer double the appraisal costs. Moreover, measuring equipment for performing the inspection must be provided by both the customer and the vendor, leading to unnecessarily high capital outlay for both partners. Since the vendor cannot dispense with an outgoing inspection due to the laws governing producer liability, forgoing an incoming inspection is more likely to be an option for the goods recipient. An incoming inspection is, however, also necessary to ensure that warranties retain their validity. For this reason, a binding agreement must be made between the vendor and customer if such an incoming inspection is to be dispensed with. To cover all possible eventualities, a quality management system must support inspection processing which consists of pre-production measures, prototype and pilot run monitoring as well as measures for regular delivery.

In the case of procuring technically sophisticated standard parts, most of the technical quality and delivery data is already available. Apart from the price and the delivery date for maintaining the business relationship, variables include the observance of standard quality criteria. Depending on the maturity of the business relationship, the quality assurance measures can include the following:

- Choice of vendor
- Clarification of technical product specifications
- Definition of quality agreements and warranty measures
- Inspection of the production process and production audit of safety-critical parts
- Provision of a statistical process control certificate
- Provision of first samples and pilot lots

Once the initial obstacles for the vendor and customer have been overcome and if the product meets the relevant quality requirements, the long-term objective is to maintain the standard attained and, following further developments, to improve it. This is why, even after a contract has been concluded, it is important to carry out a sampling inspection. For the vendor, this serves above all to guarantee the quality standard, and for the customer, to update the vendor evaluation data.

Quality inspection in goods receipt is necessary if the delivered parts have a decisive influence on the quality of the end product and if there is no contractual agreement stating that the vendor accepts all liability and fully guarantees adherence to the quality agreements. In this case, a quality inspection must be carried out, with the results being logged and used as the basis for the vendor evaluation (see Budde 1992, pp. 88–96) and other follow-up actions. The quality of the purchased parts is inspected on the basis of quality characteristics which are specified in the quality agreements as target values and tolerance specifications. The quality inspection can either be carried out as a full or as a sampling inspection. The former is mainly for highly safety-critical parts or if a sampling inspection has yielded a failure rate above the permissible level and if the usable parts are to be filtered out before returning the batch. To save time and costs, sampling inspections are often used when large production lots are delivered from single-unit production. "The AQL system has proved most successful amongst the attributive sample systems. This is based on the AQL value (Acceptable Quality Level) which expresses the maximum permissible proportion of defective units as a percentage of the inspection lot" (Arnolds *et al.* 1996, p. 389).

The quantity of a product which has been delivered and is to be inspected is referred to as the *inspection lot* (the population upon which a full or sampling inspection is to be carried out). In order to yield consistent inspection results, the inspection lot should, where possible, consist of units of the same type which have been produced under identical manufacturing conditions. The conditions surrounding the raw material, tools, the machinery used and the production process should all be identical.

8.27.2 SAP-specific description

The R/3 System takes account of the changed requirements vis-à-vis quality management by anchoring QM in the appropriate applications, such as Procurement, Warehouse Management, Production and Sales and Distribution. Quality Management also features a link to Controlling where, for example, the appraisal and nonconformity costs are taken into account. The trigger for an inspection can be goods receipts, goods issues, deliveries, returns, stock transfers, and so on. The quality inspection is one of the most important parts of quality management. It is based on the quality planning specifications which are laid down, for example, in the inspection plan, and it also yields essential results as basic data for quality control, in other words the defect analysis and derivation of follow-up actions for improving quality. In general, quality management in the R/3 System helps you meet quality demands in the areas of Procurement, Production as well as Sales and Distribution (see SAP – Quality Management 1996, pp. 3.1–3.7).

■ *Fulfilling quality requirements in procurement*

   – *release of supply relationships*
     The quality department releases a vendor for a particular material. It can place a time restriction on the release or limit it to a specified quantity. If a vendor has serious quality problems, the quality system can protect itself by blocking inquiries, purchase orders or goods receipts for particular materials from this vendor.

   – *inquiry*
     The vendor can obtain the technical terms of delivery laid down for a particular material automatically from the quality system in the form of an appendix. If the material has to be released by the quality department, this is communicated to the buyer.

   – *vendor selection*
     In the vendor evaluation, the Materials Management module provides the buyer with information on the vendor's delivery reliability and prices. The buyer can obtain data from the QM module on the quality of the goods already delivered and the

quality management system of the vendor. The system administers aggregated quality scores for this purpose and automatically updates them for the vendor evaluation. In certain industries, vendors must adhere to a quality management system whose effectiveness must be demonstrated, for example in accordance with ISO-9003, and attested by approved authorities in the form of certificates. For this reason the QM module offers the possibility of stipulating quality management systems, of noting and evaluating those vendor systems which are already in operation, and of making comparisons in the vendor selection.

– *purchase orders*
When the purchase order is issued, the quality department must release the vendor for the delivery of a given material (providing that this has been stipulated). The release of this supply relationship can be restricted to a fixed period and a specified maximum quantity. Along with the purchase order, the vendor automatically receives information on the latest technical terms of delivery, the current quality assurance agreement and, where applicable, on the obligation of including a certificate when the goods are delivered.

– *source inspection*
Occasionally a vendor may replace an incoming inspection with a source inspection. In such cases the system enables target delivery dates to be monitored and inspection lots to be created in time for the acceptance date.

– *goods receipt*
If a particular material requires certification, the existence of the certificate must, at the very latest, be acknowledged at the point of receipt of goods. Submission of the certificate can be required per purchase order item, per batch or goods receipt. The quantity of goods received is usually posted to the quality inspection stock for the duration of the incoming inspection. This stock is them deemed unavailable. You can only make changes in inspection lot processing; manual entry using Materials Management tools is not possible. The scheduled duration of the incoming inspection is taken into account in Planning. In goods receipt, inspection lot processing is triggered automatically. The system generates an inspection lot record in addition to the goods receipt document. It also selects a suitable inspection plan and determines the sample sizes in accordance with the quality level. Following this, the inspection can begin immediately. The required work documentation, such as sample drawing and inspection instructions, is available for immediate printing. The usage decision represents the end of subsequent inspection lot processing in the QM module once the inspection is complete. In exceptional situations, you can release the lot from the quality inspection stock prematurely providing that you have the appropriate authorization to do so. This does not usually take place until after the end of the inspection in conjunction with the usage decision.

■ *Fulfilling quality criteria in production*

- *integrated planning*
  Work and inspection operations within the production process are becoming increasingly integrated or even amalgamated. Strict separation is no longer possible due to operator inspections and process characteristic control which have an impact on the quality of the products. This is why teams from the production and quality management departments elaborate the routings jointly.

- *inspection operations*
  For this reason, the inspection characteristics of the QM module are integrated in the work scheduling and production processing components of the PP module (Production Planning and Control). The characteristics – be they inspection characteristics or process characteristics – are created for a particular operation. Test equipment is assigned as production resources/tools. Production and inspection activities must not be mixed within an operation, otherwise the operation will be treated as a production operation.

- *inspection lots*
  When you create a production order, the system generates a special inspection lot data record for administering the inspection specifications and inspection results of all operations.

- *confirmations*
  Inspection result confirmation to the QM module can be linked to operation confirmation to the PP module.

- *inspection frequency*
  Routings can dictate inspection frequencies; time or quantity-related inspection grids are possible during ongoing production. Using the inspection grid in the QM module, you can monitor the production process on a continuous basis with regard to the process and inspection characteristics.

- *partial lots*
  You can divide the total quantity of the production order into partial lots if partial quantities with different characteristics exist. If the end product consists of batches, the partial lots can be assigned to individual batches either during or after the production order. The inspection results are incorporated in the batch characteristic values here.

- *quality control charts*
  The grid-controlled inspection serves as the basis for statistical process control with the aid of quality control charts, a graphic tool for documenting the quality-related progress of a production process. The QM module supports the following types of control chart for inspection characteristics with normal distribution: average chart with tolerance (acceptance chart), average chart without tolerance (Shewhart chart) and a standard deviation chart. Control charts are updated and displayed during results recording. The system calculates the action and warning limits, if required, from the current inspection results or from the results of an initial run. A control chart may encompass a number of inspection lots or production orders. The control

charts are principally intended for quality management in production. In special cases, however, they may be useful for inspection lots of different origins, for example in goods receipt.

■ *Fulfilling quality requirements in Sales and Distribution*

- *goods inspection*
  As part of sales and distribution processing, the system enables you to inspect goods on the basis of the delivery data record. For this purpose, it creates and releases an inspection lot when the delivery record is created. Picking and inspection can thereby be coordinated flexibly; the system does not stipulate any particular procedures.

- *batch specification*
  If the stock of a particular material is managed in batches, the QM module incorporates the inspection results in the specifications, thereby indirectly enabling suitable batches to be selected.

- *quality certificates*
  In some industries it is normal practice to enclose quality certificates with the delivery, documenting the specifications of the material and/or the inspection results of a batch. Certificate printing is triggered via the central SAP message control system when the shipping documents are generated. To use the certificate processing facility, the user needs to draft layout forms for the certificates, create templates for determining the characteristics to be included in the certificates, assign master data such as materials, specify how the certificates are to be distributed (recipients, language, distribution form) and define the language settings. Following this, the system automatically generates quality certificates and can output these via a printer, fax or EDI interface. The system can then store these quality certificates in the optical archive using SAP ArchiveLink. To generate the quality certificates, the system makes use of information available within its environment. This includes data from Quality Management (inspection lot, usage decision, inspection results), from Materials Management (material master, batch master) and from Sales and Distribution (delivery, sales order, customer master).

Inspection processing covers the steps from the point at which the inspection is triggered, through lot-based or continuous inspection with inspection result logging to generation of the usage decision, that is, the initiation of follow-up actions on the basis of the inspection results. These actions can be releasing or blocking a lot, for example. Inspection processing can be based on an inspection plan or material specification, or it can be carried out without a plan. It is essential that you create an inspection lot in the R/3 System in order to be able to inspect a material.

An *inspection lot* is the quantity of a material which is to be subjected to a quality inspection. In the R/3 System an inspection lot is stored as an *inspection lot record;* this documents the inspection request and describes the origin and scope of the inspection as well as the inspection status. The inspection lot also serves as the basis for administering inspection requirements, inspection results, appraisal costs and the usage decision. The individual steps are specified for each inspection type in the material master at the plant level and can, for the most part, be executed automatically. You can create inspection lots either *manually* or *automatically* for goods movements in the Materials Management system (goods receipt, goods issue, stock transfer) and when you create deliveries in the Sales and Distribution system. You can also create an inspection lot manually for a released production order. Furthermore, the system can create an inspection lot record with special attributes for a particular production order.

In the case of *inspection types with an inspection plan*, the system selects the appropriate inspection plan for the material and the inspection lot origin. If a material specification exists, the system can make use of this and thereby determine the inspection requirements independently of the inspection plan. The inspection specifications form the basis for printing the shop floor papers and, later on, for recording the inspection results. Once the shop floor papers have been printed, the inspection staff must select the samples required for the inspection in accordance with the sample drawing instructions and make these available to the work centres defined for each operation. The inspection can then begin with the inspectors following the inspection instructions. The inspection instructions stipulate the test equipment and the inspection characteristics for each inspection operation as well as the methods, standard values and sample sizes for each inspection characteristic. The inspector can also make a note of the inspection results on the same sheet of paper if the form has been created in accordance with the inspection instructions. The system then waits for the inspection results to be confirmed.

Inspection results are recorded with reference to a specific inspection lot. The QM module recognizes two types of inspection result: the inspector can confirm results for planned or unplanned inspection characteristics or simply enter the defects detected. After the inspection result have been recorded, the characteristics are valuated by means of an acceptance or rejection decision. The system compares the entered characteristic values with the quantitative or qualitative specifications and with the sample instructions. It then issues either a positive (acceptance) or negative (rejection) decision. Once the results have been recorded or if the inspection is aborted, the inspector or other authorized member of staff makes the usage decision for the inspection lot. The inspection results can then no longer be changed. Providing that no inspection characteristics have been rejected, the system can also make the usage decision automatically (see Section 8.28).

8.27.3 Using the process

Since the QM indicator in Procurement is stored in the *DPC1014* material master, the system posts the stock to the quality store (see Fig. 8.161) after the goods receipt (see Section 8.25). An inspection lot with the number *2262* is created *automatically*. The inspection lot quantity of *111* is displayed in the inspection lot detail screen with the base unit of measure *Pieces* (in this case, 100% inspection). The status *CHCR* indicates the sample calculation, and inspection type *01* a goods receipt inspection for order (see Fig. 8.163).

8.27.4 Navigation information

■ *Menu path*
Logistics –> Quality management –> Quality inspection –> Insp. lot processing –> Inspection lot –> Display

■ *Transaction code*
QA01, QA03

■ *Ingoing processes in the R/3 Reference Model*
GR processing with reference to subcontract order
Processing goods receipt
GR processing with PO reference for stock material
Quality info record
Inspection plan processing
Material specification

■ *Outgoing processes in the R/3 Reference Model*
Results recording for goods receipt
Processing defects

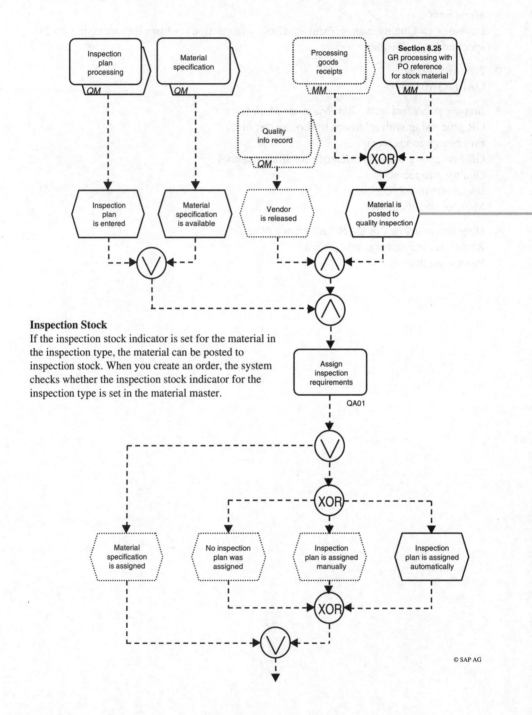

Inspection Stock

If the inspection stock indicator is set for the material in the inspection type, the material can be posted to inspection stock. When you create an order, the system checks whether the inspection stock indicator for the inspection type is set in the material master.

© SAP AG

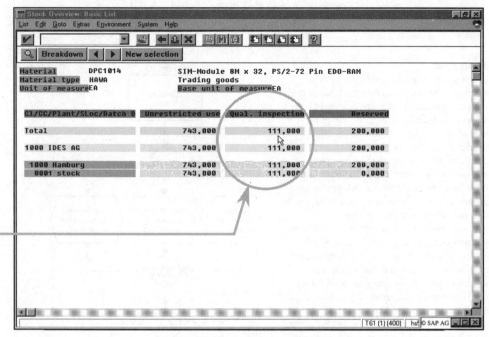

Fig. 8.161: Quality inspection

Material, Inspection Plan, Inspection Lot

The inspection plan defines what is to be checked and how this is to be carried out. Once the inspection lot has been created, the system automatically tries to assign an inspection plan according to the data in the material master. If this is not possible, the inspection planner must decide which inspection plan is to be used for inspection. Before you assign an inspection plan to an inspection lot, you must activate the relevant inspection type in the material master and set in the activated inspection type the indicator which specifies that an inspection plan is required and assigned automatically. Note that the material must already be assigned to the inspection plan.

Material Specification

In the Quality Management module, quality inspections can be carried out not only by means of inspection plans, but also by means of material specifications that are valid throughout the company. The material specification represents, like the inspection plan but in less detail, instructions for the quality inspection. The standard values in the material specification serve as inspection specifications. Consequently, you have an inspection specification that can be used as a replacement for or a supplement to an inspection plan used at plant level.

Sample Size

If you use an inspection plan, the system calculates the sample size on the basis of the sampling procedures that are assigned to the inspection characteristics. If no sampling procedure is assigned to any inspection characteristic, the sample size for this characteristic depends on the base unit of measure in the material master. For example, if the base unit of measure is kilograms, the sample size is one base unit, i.e. 1 kilogram. If the base unit measure is e.g. unit, box, package or bottle, the sample size is 100% of the inspection lot. If you are not using an inspection plan, the sample size is calculated on the basis of the value entered for the inspection percentage (percentage of the lot size) in the material master. If you have not entered any value, the sample size is 100% of the inspection lot. If the appropriate indicator is set in the material master record, you must trigger the calculation manually.

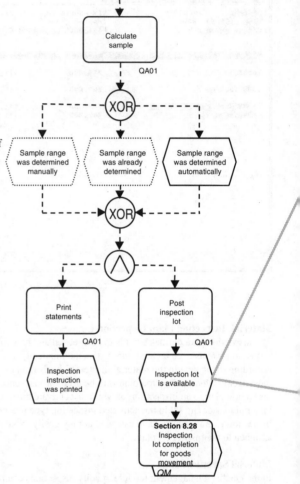

Inspection Lot

An inspection lot is created automatically when a material is received from an external source (from a vendor with a purchase order) or an internal source (within production with a production order). In order to create an inspection lot, QM must be active for the material. This indicator must be set for the inspection type you activate in the material master. Moreover, an inspection lot origin must be maintained for the movement type (Customizing). When you carry out a goods movement in inventory management, the system determines whether an inspection lot should be created for the movement type. It does this by checking whether a lot origin exists for the movement type. If an origin exists, the system checks if the inspection type defined for the inspection origin is activated in the material. If a lot origin exists and the corresponding inspection type is activated, an inspection lot is automatically created.

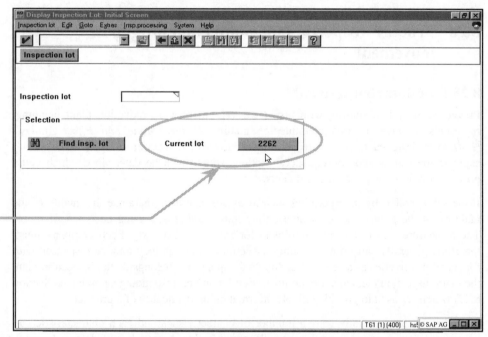

Fig. 8.162: Selection of inspection lot

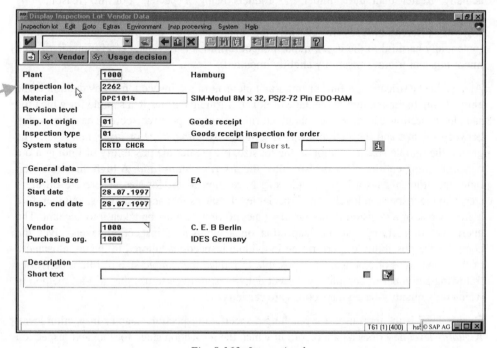

Fig. 8.163: Inspection lot

8.28 Process: Inspection lot completion for goods movement

8.28.1 Business background

Preventive planning, starting with product development and production plant planning, represents a move towards guaranteeing quality. *Failure Mode and Effect Analysis (FMEA)* is designed to recognize potential sources of defects at an early stage and to estimate the causes and consequences. Actions should then be determined which could prevent or reduce the incidence of defects.

If the sub-supplier, by incorporating such measures, can also guarantee the quality of the majority of the goods, the associated outlay must be assessed using cost–benefit ratios. These measures are often only employed for safety-critical parts. Each company must, therefore, generally carry out incoming inspections, although they may be dispensed with for specific deliveries as a result of contractual stipulations. Alongside the inspection plan, the main inspection elements are the inspection lot and corresponding sample (see Section 8.27) which are used to provide reliable information on the quality of a product.

Since the system generally tests a number of characteristics and each characteristic can trigger an error message, it is theoretically possible that the number of defects found is actually greater than the number of products being inspected. For this reason, it is advisable to *classify* the characteristics to highlight trends in the evaluation. One possible way of differentiating is to classify the characteristics as critical nonconformities (potentially harmful to the user), major nonconformities (function severely impaired), and minor nonconformities (usability slightly impaired).

Alongside classification, a further important element in the inspection lot evaluation is the entry stating the maximum percentage of nonconforming entities in a sample for which the sample inspection can give the manufacturing quality a positive score. The relationship between lot size and inspection scope is termed *inspection stage* or *inspection level*. The greater the sample size in relation to the lot size, the greater the possibility of finding more nonconforming entities. This is also called the *discrimination ratio*. A high discrimination ratio, therefore, means a high sample size in relation to the lot size. There are different stages in the inspection levels. The "special level" means that small samples, and therefore a greater risk of a decision in favour of "nonconformity", must be taken into account. The alternative of carrying out the inspection on a number of inspection levels gives the company the possibility of performing individual inspections tailored to the circumstances of the company. For example, it is possible to reduce the sample size in future deliveries following a number of completely correct deliveries, or even to use the skip-lot method in which only quantity-based inspections are carried out.

Quality level is the term used for reaching a specified inspection stage or inspection level. A *quality level* describes a data record in which the inspection stage for the next inspection is stored. The time at which a quality level is to be changed is referred to as *dynamic modification.* The dynamic modification rule determines when and which characteristics of a quality level are to be updated. This can be when the lot is created or after the usage decision, for example.

If the inspection is based on the inspection lot, the sample or even the inspection plan, the system stores the results and updates the quality level, as described. Afterwards, depending on the quality result, you must specify what is to happen to the inspected goods. The possible follow-up actions can be planned in advance and stored in usage decisions. For example, you can cancel lots, release them for use or send specific messages. Most important is that the appraisal and possible nonconformity costs be reported to Controlling for future calculations (see Arnolds *et al.* 1996, pp. 385–392; see Melzer-Ridinger 1995, pp. 127–169).

8.28.2 SAP-specific description

To complete the inspection, the inspector first valuates the inspection results of the inspection characteristics in the Quality Management module. All the results are compared against the predefined limits and the valuation catalogue. Using preselected values, such as sample size and acceptance number, the system determines whether an inspection characteristic is to be accepted or rejected. The usage decision for the inspection lot can be made when all the required characteristics and optional characteristics have been valuated and completed (see SAP – Quality management 1996, pp. 5.1–5.7).

When the inspection is complete, you can make the usage decision for an inspection lot providing that all the necessary inspection lot data is available:

■ the lot must be released

■ results must be recorded for each of the inspection characteristics

■ no status should be active which causes the usage decision to be blocked

The system uses the inspection lot status to document which activities still need to be carried out for a lot, which have already been completed and whether the usage decision can be made. If you have the appropriate authorization, you can also make a usage decision if no, or only incomplete, results have been recorded for a particular lot. If the *Documentation required* indicator is set for a material (see Section 8.26) and if a usage decision has been made for a lot with this material, the system automatically branches to the long text editor. The usage decision is regarded as divergent if the lot is rejected although none of the characteristics has been rejected, or if the lot is accepted despite at least one characteristic being rejected. The system cancels an inspection if open characteristics still exist once the inspection is complete. You can initiate an inspection for which a usage decision is to be made by directly entering the inspection lot, by using the matchcode search function (for example, material, plant or other short texts) or by carrying out a specific inspection lot search using various criteria. A code exists for the individual usage decisions; this is stored in a catalogue and lists possible follow-up actions.

The results for a particular characteristic can be displayed in summary form. Depending on how the processing mode is set, the system displays only the characteristics which are relevant for the usage decision, or all the characteristics in the inspection plan. The system displays information on the characteristic weighting, defect class, a short text on the inspection characteristic, number of nonconforming sample units, estimated share of nonconforming sample units, the processing status of the results record and the characteristic valuation for each characteristic.

If an inspection lot is relevant for stock, the usage decision functions can be used to maintain the inspection lot inventories manually. Using the specific entries made, the system performs the appropriate inventory postings for Materials Management. If quantities that are still open need to be posted, you can update the inventories at any time when processing the usage decision, *before* the usage decision is made, *when* the usage decision is made or *after* the usage decision has already been made and the inspection is complete. You can also post specified quantities of an inspection lot to *unrestricted-use stock, scrap, sample, new material, reserves* and *return to vendor*. If a *usage decision* is also to be made, the number of entities to be rejected can be entered. This quantity, also known as *defective quantity*, refers to the sample quantity (quantity actually inspected). You can include it in a complaints against the vendor list; it is updated in the QM information system and is used for analysis purposes (for example, totals of defective quantities and reject-to-sample-quantity ratio).

If a usage decision is to be made for an incoming inspection lot, the *quality score* must also be calculated for the inspection lot. The quality score is a value which describes the quality of the inspected lot. You can enter the quality score directly or with the help of special procedures. Procedures for calculating the quality scores can be defined for inspection types in the material master. You activate the inspection type with the quality score procedure when creating or changing a material master record. The quality score can be determined via the usage decision, the share of defects in the lot, the characteristic defect share and the quality scores of the characteristics. In the first case, the material is assigned an inspection type which takes the quality score from the usage decision in the inspection catalogue. In the other cases, the inspection type contains a procedure for calculating the quality score. In order to use a quality score procedure which is based on the weighted share of defects in the lot or on the quality score of the characteristics, you must carry out the inspection using a plan. In the first case, you must also maintain the data for the weighting of the characteristics; in the second case you should assign a defect class to the characteristic in the event of a rejection during results recording.

The Quality Management system features a procedure for tracing the *appraisal costs* for a particular work centre. In the results recording and usage decision functions, values can be confirmed for the different activity types defined for a particular operation (for example, setup time, machine time or labour time). The system sends these confirmation values to Controlling (CO) to calculate the costs. In order to make this possible, you first need to create a QM order in the QM module. If quality-related defects are confirmed, specific corrective measures need to be taken to deal with the cause of the problem. These measures include modifications to the production process, changes to the composition of a product or new procurement procedures. Furthermore, the inspected goods are sometimes not released until certain measures such as follow-up inspection, rework, repairs or special laboratory tests have been carried out.

8.28.3 Using the process

First of all, record the following results for inspection lot *2264*: *109* pieces – good and *2* pieces – scrap (see Fig. 8.164). After this, activate the *defect overview* switch and select the *code* for the usage decision using the selection list in the next screen. For Model Company A, a usage decision code *A10* has been selected for conditional acceptance (see Fig. 8.165). Once the usage decision has been made, the system, following a procedure specified in the material master (see Fig. 8.165), calculates a quality score (see Fig. 8.166) for the inspection lot. To complete the inspection lot, a manual follow-up action is triggered.

8.28.4 Navigation information

▨ *Menu path*
Logistics –> Quality management –> Quality inspection –> Insp. lot processing –> Usage decision –> Record

▨ *Transaction code*
QA11

▨ *Ingoing processes in the R/3 Reference Model*
Processing defects
Results recording for goods receipt

▨ *Outgoing processes in the R/3 Reference Model*
Goods issue processing for stock material
Consignment goods issue processing
Quality info record
Appraisal costs recording (QM order)
Direct activity allocation
Processing defects

Making a Usage Decision

You can make the usage decision for an inspection lot after the inspection is finished, as long as all the required inspection lot data is available. To be able to make a usage decision, the following conditions must be met: the inspection lot must be released, results must have been recorded for the inspection characteristics and no active status exists that blocks the usage decision. After you have called up the function for recording the usage decision, but before you make the usage decision, you can also record defects for the current inspection lot and then activate a quality notification for one or more defect records.

Usage Decision Code

To enter the usage decision code for an inspection lot, make sure the characteristics overview or defects overview screen is displayed and select the possible entries help for *UD code* field. The system displays a dialog box containing the contents of the usage decision catalogue (catalogue type 3) in a hierarchical tree structure. If your system administrator has defined default selected sets in Customizing for specific inspection types, the dialog box will only contain the code groups and codes predefined in the selected set. Otherwise, all code groups and codes that are available in the usage decision catalogue will be displayed. Copy the desired code into a code group. The system copies the code and all relevant information into the fields for the usage decision code.

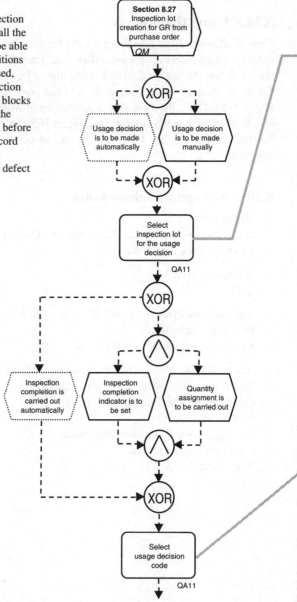

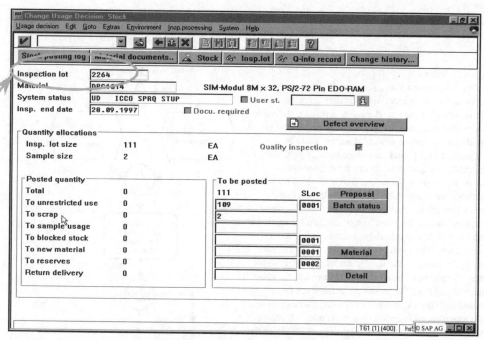

Fig. 8.164: Inspection lot with results recording

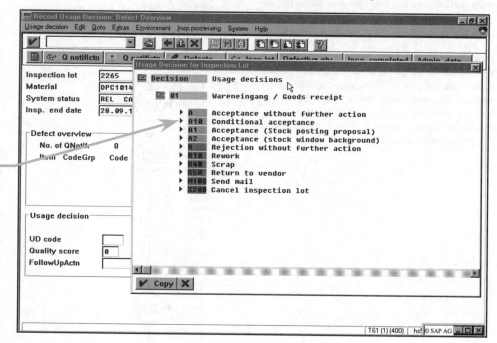

Fig. 8.165: Usage decision

Quality Score

When you make a usage decision for an inspection lot created for goods receipt, the quality score must also be determined for the lot. A quality score is a statistical value that describes the quality of an inspection lot. A quality score can be entered directly or can be calculated by a predefined procedure. A procedure for calculating a quality score can be defined for an inspection type in the material master. You then activate the inspection type that contains a quality score procedure when you create or change a material master. The quality score can be defined for each usage decision code and calculated by the quality score procedure. When you access the screen for entering the usage decision for the inspection lot, the quality score may already be calculated and displayed, if the score is determined from the procedure defined for the material. This value is not overwritten when you select the usage decision code group and code. Therefore you could end up with a quality score of 100 from the usage decision although the inspection lot has been rejected. The upper and lower limiting values for the quality score are defined at the client level in Customizing.

Follow-up Actions

When quality-related defects are confirmed, you often must initiate specific corrective actions (tasks) to eliminate the source of a problem. For example, these tasks could involve modifications to the production process, changes to the composition of the product or new procurement procedures.

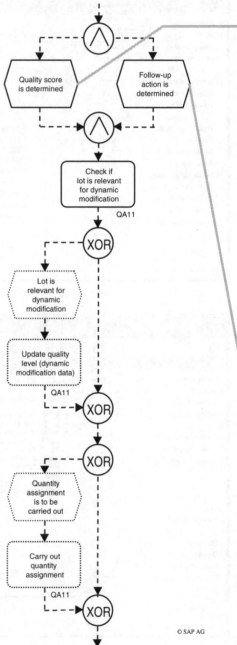

© SAP AG

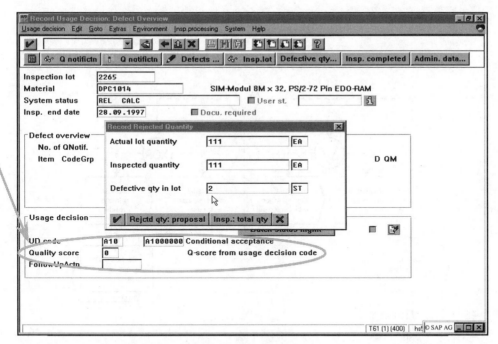

Fig. 8.166: Quality score

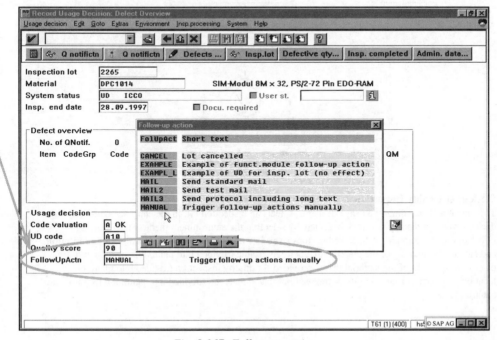

Fig. 8.167: Follow-up action

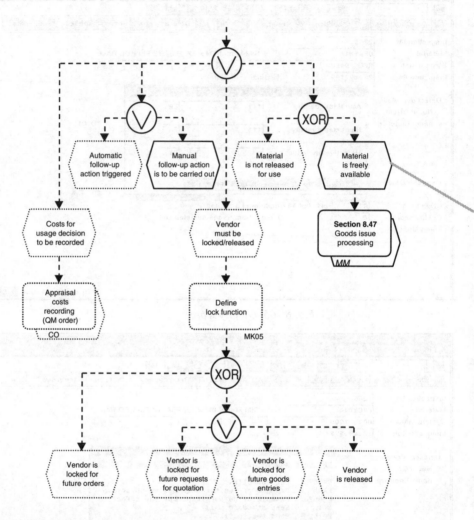

Stock after Quality Inspection

The function "Recording of a usage decision" selects an inspection lot. In the entry screen of the usage decision you can display the stock overview by selecting the environment menu. The following information, for example, is displayed: a stock overview of a material (divided into plant, bin location and batch), the quantity of the material that is freely usable (divided into plant, bin location and batch), the quantity of the material that is provided for quality inspection (divided into plant, bin location and batch) or the quantity of the material that is reserved (divided into plant, bin location and batch).

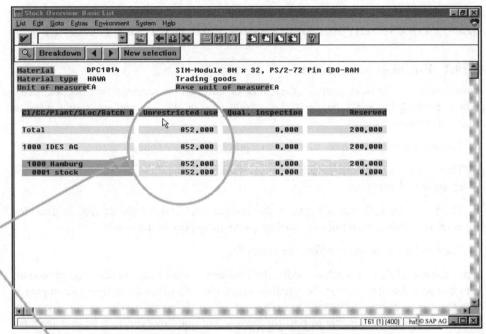

Fig. 8.168: Stock overview – unrestricted use

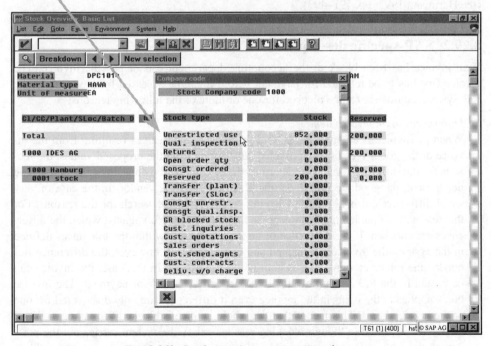

Fig. 8.169: Stock overview – company code

8.29 Process: Invoice processing with reference (release)

8.29.1 Business background

Before incoming invoices are paid, they must be checked for accuracy (see Section 8.24). When checking invoices, there may be several reasons why a company might want to block an invoice.

■ The invoice might have no reference to a purchase order or goods receipt.

■ There may be large differences between the invoice data and the purchase order, for example different prices.

■ There may be differences between the invoice data and the goods receipt data, for example different quantities or problems with the quality of the goods.

■ The invoice might arrive before the goods do.

If the invoice refers to a purchase order, the first step in the invoice verification procedure is to compare the item data of the purchase order with the invoice and then to compare it with the goods receipt. If blocking reasons exist, e.g. differences in price, quality, delivery quantity, it should be possible to post the invoice but not, however, to release it for payment in order to get the supplier to carry out the activities defined in the purchase order (see Hartmann 1993, pp. 491–493).

8.29.2 SAP-specific description

If an invoice has been blocked, the accounting department cannot pay the invoice. The invoice first has to be released for payment before it can be accessed for payment. In the R/3 System, an invoice can be blocked for one or more of the following reasons:

■ *Differences in an invoice item*
When an invoice is entered, the system proposes certain values resulting from the invoice or the goods receipt. If an invoice item differs from the proposed values, the reasons for the differences must be determined, for example by consulting the purchasing department, the goods receipt department and possibly the vendor. In the case of very small differences, it is not worth carrying out an extensive search for the reasons. For this reason, the system contains tolerance limits (see Fig. 152) against which the differences are checked. If the difference of an invoice item is within the tolerances defined in the system, the invoice is accepted and can be paid. If, however, the difference lies outside the tolerance range, the system issues a message. In this case, the invoice can be posted in the R/3 System but it is automatically blocked for payment. The invoice block applies to the items in the invoice even if differences are only discovered for one of the invoice items. This means that the whole invoice is blocked for payment. When an invoice is posted (although blocking reasons exist), the system carries out the postings to the accounts; at the same time, R is entered in the „blocking reason" field so that the financial accounting department is unable to pay the invoice (see Fig. 8.170).

The following blocking reasons exist for *differences to invoice items* (the blocking indictor is shown in brackets):

- *quantity variance (M)*
  A quantity variance exists when the invoice quantity is larger than the difference between the quantity of goods received and the quantity already invoiced. In the R/3 System, a quantity variance is always seen together with the value of the variance. The product of order price and variance quantity is used as the basis to determine whether the invoice is blocked. This means that for cheaper items relatively large quantity variances are allowed; more expensive items on the other hand are only allowed a smaller variance.

- *price variance (P)*
  A price variance exists when the invoice price (invoice amount divided by invoice quantity) is not the same as the net order price.

- *purchase order price unit variance (G)*
  A purchase order price unit variance occurs when the relationship between purchase order price unit quantity and purchase order quantity in the invoice is not the same as that at goods receipt time. If no goods receipt has taken place so far, the invoice is compared with the purchase order.

- *date variance (D)*
  A date variance occurs when the date of the invoice is earlier than the delivery date entered in the purchase order. In the SAP System, the date variance depends on the amount of the invoice item; the product of the item amount and the number of days' variance is used as a basis to see whether the invoice is blocked. In this way, relatively large date variances are allowed for items with a low amount but only very small date variances for invoice items with a high amount. In the case of items entered with reference to a scheduling agreement, no date variance check takes place as no unique delivery date exists in the scheduling agreement.

- *quality check (I)*
  If the material has been marked as relevant for quality inspection, the material is posted to quality inspection stock at goods receipt time. The invoice is blocked until the quality inspection check has been successfully completed. In the case of several goods receipts for one purchase order item, quality inspection is carried out for each goods receipt. The invoice is blocked if any of the quality inspection checks is not completed successfully. However, if the invoice is posted before goods receipt takes place, the invoice cannot be blocked for quality reasons.

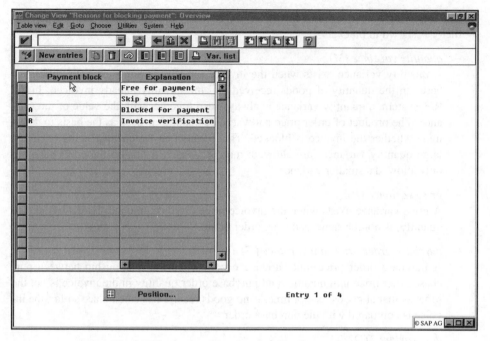

Fig 8.170: Customizing invoice blocking indicators

- *Invoice item amount*

  If an invoice with a high amount is entered, it might make sense to block the invoice so that it can first be checked. This especially makes sense for invoices entered without reference to a purchase order. Items blocked due a high invoice amount are given the blocking reason *Other variances (S)*. In the customizing of invoice verification functionality, you can define whether the check of the invoice item amount is always to take place, or whether it is only to take place for purchase order items with certain item categories or goods receipt indicators. The tolerance ranges define the amount above which an item is to be blocked. The tolerance can be defined separately for invoices items entered with reference to a purchase order and those entered without reference to a purchase order.

- *Stochastic block*

  Apart from the automatic blocking of invoices due to variances or the value of the invoice item, it is also possible to block invoices at random. Stochastic blocking is used for this purpose. If stochastic blocking is active, when an invoice is entered for which no other blocking reason exists, the system decides whether the invoice is to be blocked according to a certain percentage amount defined in Customizing. You can also define in Customizing whether stochastic blocking is active or not.

- *Manual block*

  Apart from blocking reasons set automatically by the system, you can also block an invoice manually. You block an invoice manually by entering *R* in the creditor screen in the field *Payment block* or, in the case of invoices entered with reference to a purchase order, by marking the field *BlRsn* for an item in the item screen. When the invoice is posted, *R* is the set automatically in the field *Payment block* on the vendor screen. Items blocked manually are assigned blocking reason *Manual block (Q)*.

8.29.3 Using the process

Before you get to the basic list of invoice items (see Fig. 8.171), you first have to select blocked invoices. You can carry out selection according to company code, business year, vendor, purchasing group and blocking reason. You can carry out selection according to these criteria so that not too many invoice items appear in the basic list. If you have marked the field *Automatic release* on the initial screen, the invoices containing blocking reasons that no longer apply are released automatically. If you want to carry out *manual release* as shown in this example, you first see the number of the invoice and the invoice item in the basic list. Additionally, the blocking reasons are marked with an *X* in the relevant column. The most important columns are *Q* for quantity variance, *P* for price variance and *D* for date variance. In the example, the blocking reasons for invoice *5100004280* are removed. Once the last blocking reason has been removed for an invoice, it is possible to release the invoice.

8.29.4 Navigation information

■ *Menu path*
Logistics –> Materials management –> Invoice verification –> Invoice verification –>
Further processing –> Release invoices

■ *Transaction code*
MR02, MRHR,

■ *Ingoing processes in the R/3 Reference Model*
Preliminary posting of invoice
Entry of services performed
GR processing with order reference for static asset

■ *Outgoing processes in the R/3 Reference Model*
Preliminary posting of invoice
Transfer of primary costs
Project update
Third-party order processing
Down payment release
Automatic payment
Vendor down payment clearing
Availability check (capital investiment)
Direct assignment of special direct costs
Budget execution/verification

Cancelling Individual Blocking Reasons

When you process a blocked invoice item, it is possible to cancel individual blocking reasons. This could be useful in the following cases:

1. An invoice contains several blocking reasons. The time required to investigate each reason can differ. If a particular blocking reason is no longer valid, you can cancel it, without this affecting the other blocking reasons.

2. In your company, different employees may be responsible for processing individual blocking reasons. Your system administrator can authorize different employees to process different blocking reasons. Each employee can, therefore, cancel the blocking reasons for which he or she has authorization.

When you cancel the last blocking reason in an invoice, the system automatically releases the invoice.

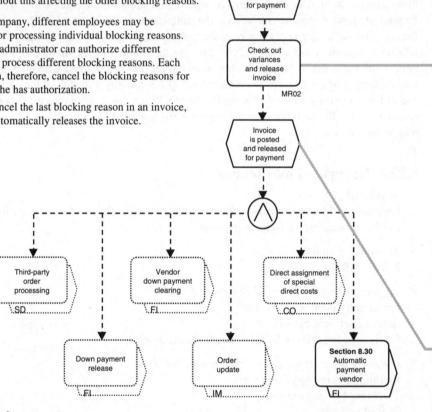

Automatic Release

It is only possible to release invoices blocked due to quantity, price or schedule variance automatically if their blocking reasons are no longer valid. These types of invoice do not usually require further processing and can be released automatically. Select the field "Release automatically" in the initial screen for releasing invoices.

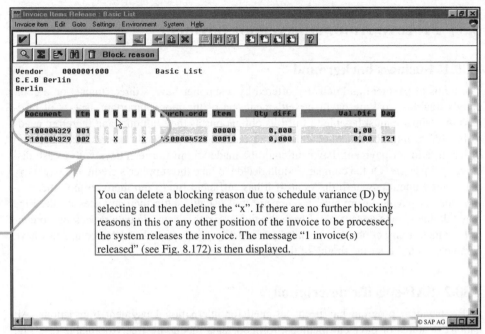

Fig. 8.171: Checking and deleting blocking reasons

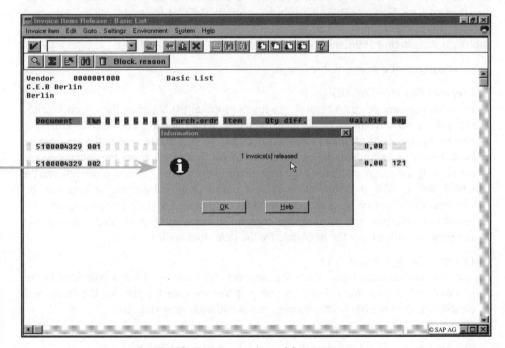

Fig. 8.172: Invoice is released for payment

8.30 Process: Automatic vendor payment

8.30.1 Business background

The terms of payment and delivery offered by a supplier have a direct impact on a company's liquidity, making payment settlement one of the more important aspects of business. A company must be able to fulfil its obligations as they fall due, and therefore needs to be able to monitor its collections and disbursements. It usually has a choice between different terms of payment. Payment could be made within fourteen days with a cash discount of 3 percent. Or the company could decide to take the supplier's credit and pay thirty days later without any cash discount. If it has sufficient funds and there are no other reasons for not paying an invoice, a company will usually settle their invoices by the time they fall due to take advantage of cash discounts. Using electronic data processing to control payment transactions is especially useful in accounts payable where companies have complete control over the timing of the payments they make.

8.30.2 SAP-specific description

SAP's payment program has been designed for international payment transactions. All national features of payment methods, forms or data media are freely definable (see Fig. 8.173). The most common methods of payment and the forms for them are delivered with the standard SAP System. These have been specially defined for each country. Standard methods of payment include checks, wire transfers and bills of exchange (see SAP Subledger Accounting 1996, p. 4.1–4.26).

Automatic payment consists of three steps:

■ *Proposal Run (see Fig. 8.177)*
First, the payment program creates a payment proposal list based on the selection criteria and the specifications made in documents, master record, and special tables. It checks the due dates of open items, proposes payment methods, selects the appropriate bank details, and simulates the payment documents. It also generates the data necessary for printing the forms or creating the data media. This list of proposed payments can be edited online. The payment methods and banks proposed by the system can be changed. Items can be blocked from payment or allocated to a different payment. The amount of cash discount can even be changed in items to be paid. You can skip this first step and still trigger the payments for the items that are due.

■ *Payment Run (see Fig. 8.181)*
The payment program then creates the payments for those open items contained in the proposal list. It posts the documents and prepares the data for printing the forms and creating the data media, payment advice notes and accompanying lists.

■ *Payment Media*
The print programs finally print the forms and generate the data carriers.

Payment methods, house banks, and *forms* that the company uses have to be set up or modified in Customizing (see Fig. 8.173).

A sequence can be set up for how the payment program chooses among different accounts if there are several house banks available for making payments. House banks are banks at which the company (company code) has its bank accounts. They are defined in the system using a key (bank ID), and each account kept at these banks is stored under an account ID. A general ledger account has to be created for each bank account.

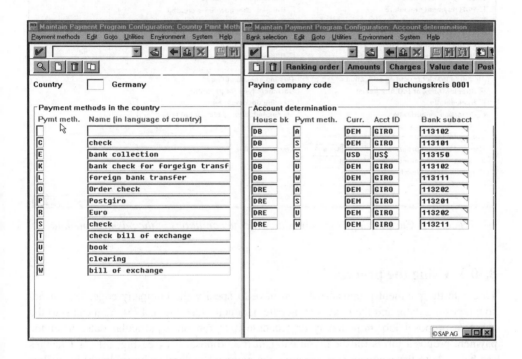

Fig. 8.173: Customizing the payment methods - house banks - bank sub-account

For each payment method for a company code, you have to specify where payments can be made and under what criteria the payment method is selected. Minimum and maximum amounts can be specified as criteria for using a particular method of payment. For instance, items less than 500 USD are paid by check while items over 500 USD are paid by bank transfer. A maximum amount must always be specified. Otherwise the system will not use the method. These amounts, however, do not apply if a user specifically enters a method of payment for a particular open item. Moreover, you need to specify which payment methods are used for foreign payment transactions. Instead of generating one payment for all open items regardless of their due date, you can have the system create a different payment for each group of items with the same due date by selecting the *Payment per due day* parameter (see Fig. 8.174).

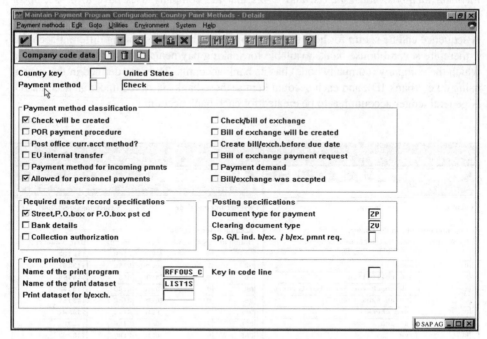

Fig. 8.174: Customizing company code with the conditions of the payment method

8.30.3 Using the process

To create the payment proposal list, you have to specify the company code, vendor account, posting date, and the next posting date parameter (see Fig. 8.176). You can start the payment proposal job immediately or schedule it to run on a particular date. After the payment proposal job is finished, you can edit the proposal list (see Fig. 8.177). Changes can be made to the payment (for example, the payment method or house bank) as well as to the items to be paid (for instance, block indicators, cash discount). The method of payment may already be specified in the item, in the master record of the business partner (see Fig. 8.179, *S* for checks and *U* for bank transfers), or may have to be determined by the payment program using the predefined criteria. The house bank is specified or determined in the same manner as the payment method.

Once the payment proposal list is completed, you can schedule the payment run. The payment run job will consist of either only one step, the payment program, or as many steps as are required for each payment medium program (print program). The print programs can, however, be executed as a separate job at a later date.

8.30.4 Navigation information

■ *Menu path*
Accounting –> Financial accounting –> Accounts payable –> Periodic processing –> Payments

■ *Transaction code*
F110, MRHR

■ *Ingoing processes in the R/3 Reference Model*
Travel request processing
Travel expense accounting
Invoice processing without reference
Consignment invoice processing
Vendor invoice processing
Processing of asset acquisition
Customer down payment request
Vendor down payment request
Down payment release
Customer invoice processing
One-time customer invoice processing
Leasing payment
Customer request for payment
Cash planning
Subsequent condition settlement
Vendor request for payment

■ *Outgoing processes in the R/3 Reference Model*
Bill of exchange presentation
Availability check (capital investment)
Down payment release
Budget execution/verification
Project update

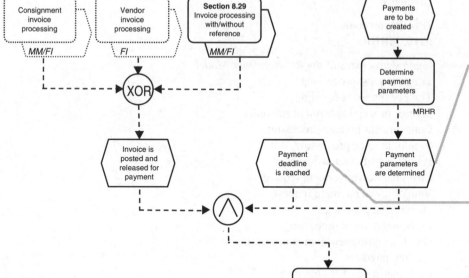

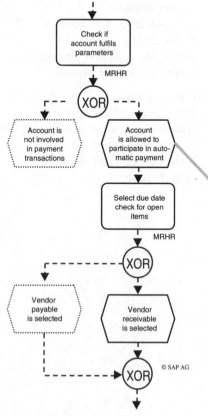

Open Items

The due date of the items is determined on the basis of the baseline date and the terms of payment in the open items. The payment program calculates the cash discount periods and the due date for net payment. Company code-specific grace periods for payables can be specified. The grace period is added to the due date calculated. Consequently, the payment can be made at a later date. A minimum cash discount percentage rate can be specified for outgoing payments per company code. If you cannot achieve the specified minimum percentage rate, you pay on the due date for net payment. You use the minimum cash discount percentage rate if the net term is more favourable than a possible cash discount. If a minimum rate has not been specified, the program pays with the highest possible cash discount. Before each payment run, you specify the date of the next payment run. The program then determines whether an item is to be taken into consideration in the current or the next payment run.

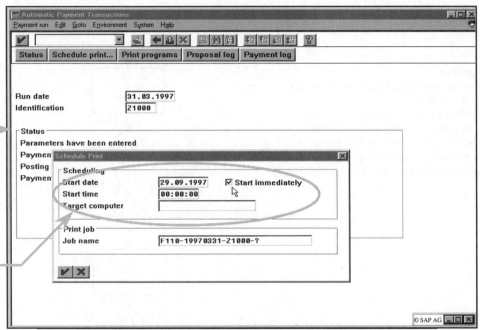

Fig. 8.175: Initial screen of automatic payment

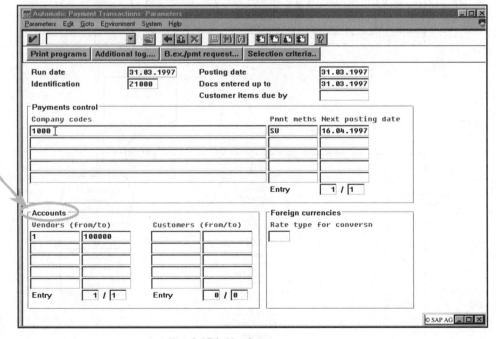

Fig. 8.176: Vendor account

Due Date

The time at which an item is paid depends on several factors:

1. Whether it is a payable or a receivable.
2. The strategy where you decide between cash discount payments and net payments.
3. Whether you make bill of exchange payments before the due date.

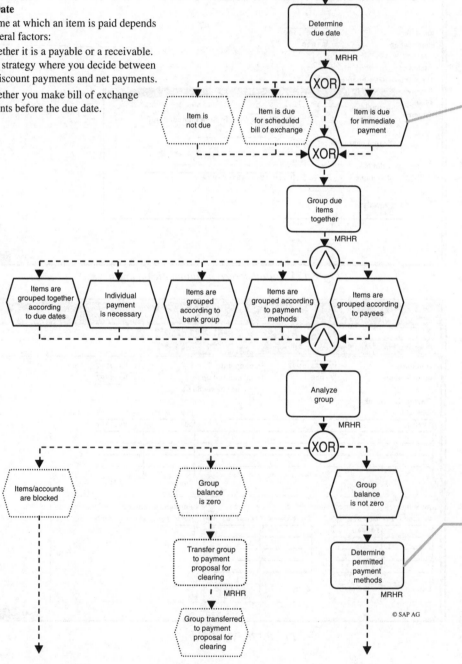

Determine
due date

MRHR

XOR

Item is
not due

Item is due
for scheduled
bill of exchange

Item is due
for immediate
payment

XOR

Group due
items
together

MRHR

∧

Items are
grouped together
according
to due dates

Individual
payment
is necessary

Items are
grouped
according to
bank group

Items are
grouped according
to payment
methods

Items are
grouped according
to payees

∧

Analyze
group

MRHR

XOR

Items/accounts
are blocked

Group
balance
is zero

Group
balance
is not zero

Transfer group
to payment
proposal for
clearing

MRHR

Determine
permitted
payment
methods

MRHR

Group transferred
to payment
proposal for
clearing

© SAP AG

590

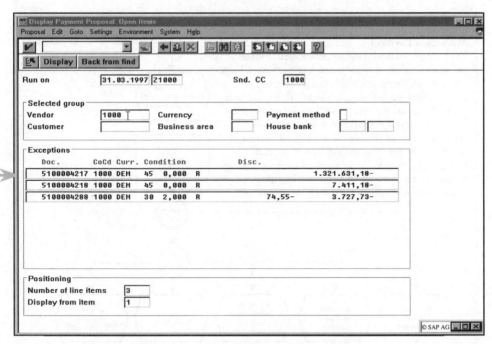

Fig. 8.177: Payment proposal – open items

Fig. 8.178: No payment block/item due for payment

Methods of Payment

The payment method is the procedure used to make payments (e.g. check transfer or bill of exchange). First, you make all the specifications that are required for each payment method in each country. This is necessary for all the payment methods used by your organization in each country. If you have companies (company codes) in Germany, France and the US, for example, you define the payment method "check" for each country. You then define the payment methods you use for each company code. With this configuration function you also specify the conditions of their use.

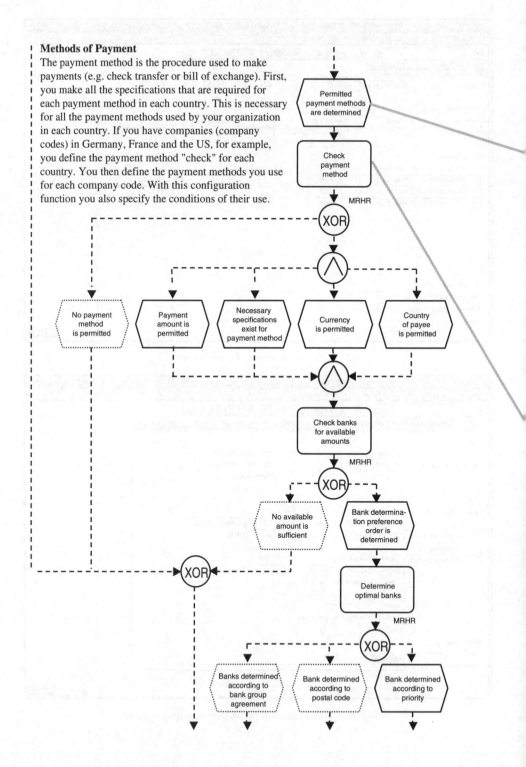

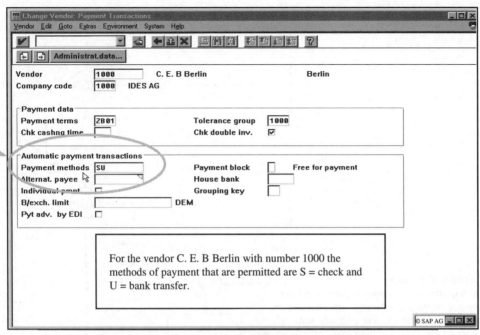

Fig. 8.179: Payment methods in vendor master record

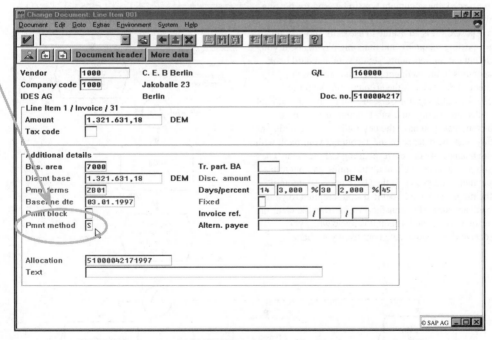

Fig. 8.180: Invoice 5100000161 is being paid with payment method S

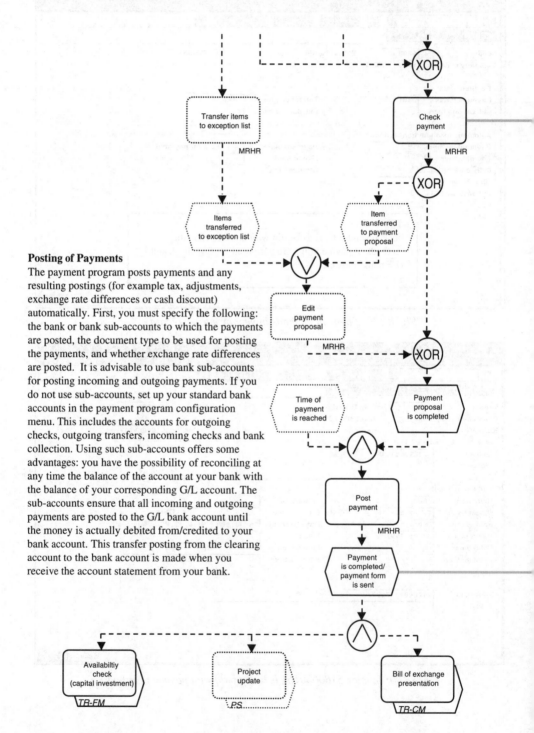

Posting of Payments

The payment program posts payments and any resulting postings (for example tax, adjustments, exchange rate differences or cash discount) automatically. First, you must specify the following: the bank or bank sub-accounts to which the payments are posted, the document type to be used for posting the payments, and whether exchange rate differences are posted. It is advisable to use bank sub-accounts for posting incoming and outgoing payments. If you do not use sub-accounts, set up your standard bank accounts in the payment program configuration menu. This includes the accounts for outgoing checks, outgoing transfers, incoming checks and bank collection. Using such sub-accounts offers some advantages: you have the possibility of reconciling at any time the balance of the account at your bank with the balance of your corresponding G/L account. The sub-accounts ensure that all incoming and outgoing payments are posted to the G/L bank account until the money is actually debited from/credited to your bank account. This transfer posting from the clearing account to the bank account is made when you receive the account statement from your bank.

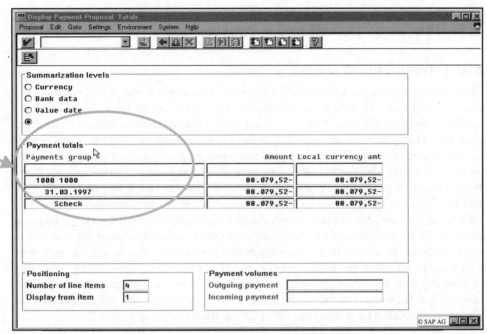

Fig. 8.181: Posting of incoming payment

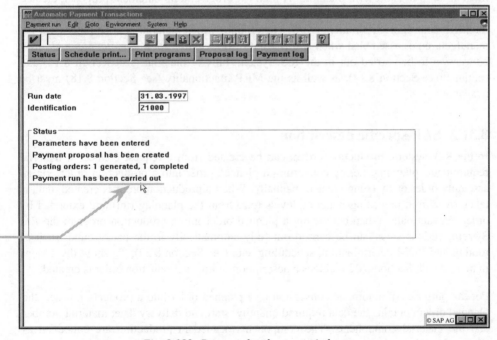

Fig. 8.182: Payment has been carried out

8.31 Process: Planned order conversion

8.31.1 Business background

Once the long-term tasks of Sales and Operations Planning, i.e. the processes from Sections 8.1, 8.2 and 8.16, as well as the medium-term processes of MPS and MRP as described in Sections 8.17 and 8.18, have been carried out, production with its medium- to short-term tasks gets more and more important. These medium- to short-term tasks include the conversion of planned orders into production orders, the creation of production orders, preliminary costing for production orders, production order release, production itself and the settlement of production orders. These processes can vary according to the task itself and the type of company involved. A plant manufacturer or manufacturer of special machines, for example, has to make an offer with preliminary costing before the production planning phase. A manufacturer who produces in series, on the other hand, may be able to carry out order release two to three months before production is due to start due to a more stable and homogenous production plan. A manufacturer of small series using production or assembly lines in production releases complete orders in rough planning for the production line and the workers in the production/assembly lines release the orders operation for operation (see Keller/Kern 1991, pp. 105–125; see Ruffing 1991, pp. 97–172).

At the very latest, planned orders are converted into production orders when going from medium-term to short-term planning. A *planned order* is a procurement proposal, created either automatically by material requirements planning (see Section 8.18) or manually by the MRP controller. A *production order* determines which material is to be processed, i.e. manufactured or assembled when and at which work centre. For *automatic planned order conversion* to be carried out in the R/3 System, bills of material (see Section 8.12) and routings (see Section 8.14), as well as the MRP functionality (see Section 8.18) must be available.

8.31.2 SAP-specific description

In the R/3 System, production orders can be created from a request created in material requirements planning, i.e. by converting a planned order into a production order, via an assembly order or by being created manually. When a production order is created, data is taken over from preceding planning levels (e.g. from the planning run) and extended by order-relevant data. When converting a planned order into a production order in the R/3 System, various steps can be carried out fully automatically in the background, such as routing and BOM determination, scheduling, etc. (see Section 8.32). To show these steps in more detail, Section 8.32 includes a description of how a production order is created.

For the purposes of automatic conversion of a planned order into a production order, the planned order contains the data required quantity, start and delivery date, material number and the material components. The components needed in production are contained as items in the planned order and are taken over into the production order directly when the planned order is converted. No new explosion of the bill of material takes place. When the planned order is converted into a production order, the dependent requirements for the components are turned into reservations. The operation and production resource data is taken as usual from the routing of the material to be produced. If the quantity is changed when converting the planned order into a production order, or if the end date is changed, a planning entry is generated, which results in the material and its components being planned again when the next material planning run takes place. Conversion of planned orders into production orders can take place either for an individual planned order or as a collective conversion (see SAP – Production Planning 1994, pp. 9.1–9.5).

8.31.3 Using the process

In Model Company A, collective conversion of planned orders is to be carried out. To do this, the plant, the MRP controller, and the order type of the production order have to be entered. The example refers to production orders with internal number assignment. For this type of production orders the order type is *PP01*. If the order is to be converted within a predefined planning horizon, this horizon can be defined by entering the corresponding data (see Fig. 8.183). After this, the planned orders to be converted are shown in a list. The MRP controller marks the planned orders to be converted and the conversion takes place when he presses the Save button. You can see the production orders created in the stock/requirements list under *PrdOrd* (see Fig. 8.185).

8.31.4 Navigation information

■ *Menu path*
Logistics –> Production –> MRP –> Planned order –> Convert –> Prod. order –>
Collect. conversion

■ *Transaction code*
CMRP, CO40, CO41

■ *Ingoing processes in the R/3 Reference Model*
Planned order processing
Material requirements planning
Single-item MRP
Material planning – interactive
Material planning sales order related
Total MPS, Single-item MPS, Interactive MPS
MPS – sales order related, MPS – project related

■ *Outgoing processes in the R/3 Reference Model*
Creation production order
Purchase requisition processing
Creation of process order, Process order processing

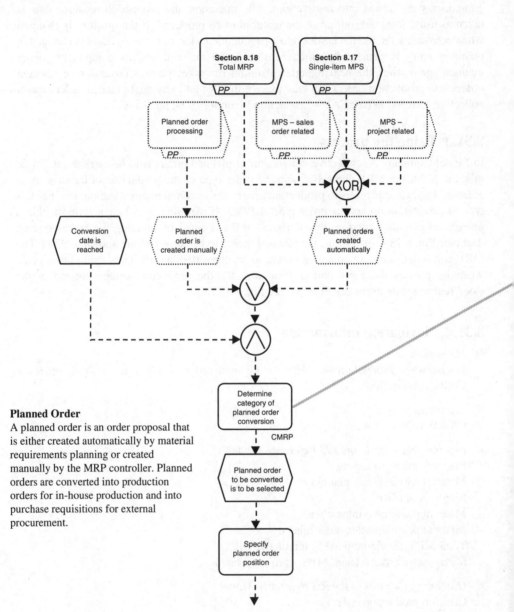

Planned Order

A planned order is an order proposal that is either created automatically by material requirements planning or created manually by the MRP controller. Planned orders are converted into production orders for in-house production and into purchase requisitions for external procurement.

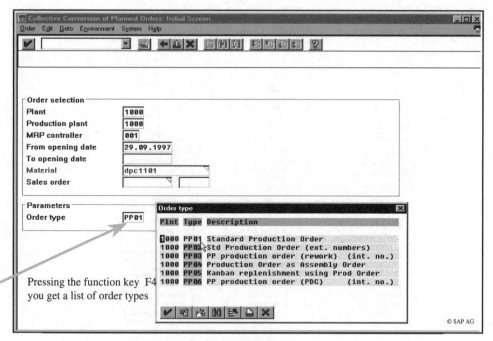

Fig. 8.183: Initial screen of planned order conversion

You have two options to convert planned orders into production orders:

Converting Single
You can convert only one single planned order into a production order. The system automatically searches for a routing and a BOM. If a fixed lot size is given in the material master record of the material to be produced (see Fig. 8.73), this lot size is proposed as the total volume of the planned order.

Converting Multiple
Via a collective conversion you can simultaneously convert several planned orders that are assigned to the same material requirements planning group within a plant into production orders. You can select the planned orders you want to convert collectively according to their opening dates.

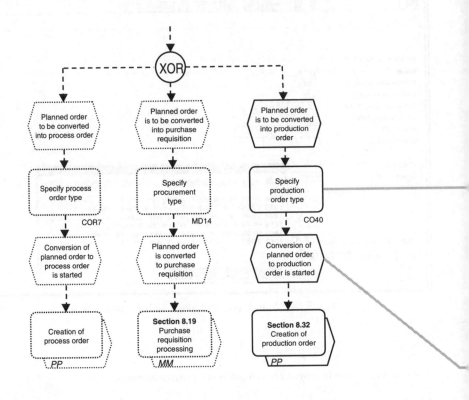

Result of Conversion

In this example, planned order *12723* has been converted into production order *60001008* and the production order can now be created. The components required for production have been taken from the positions of the planned order and have been inserted directly into the production order during the conversion. The components' dependent requirements have been converted into reservations (MRP element AR-RES) (see Figure 8.185). The operation and production resource type (PRT) data were taken from the routing of the material to be produced.

If you change the required quantity or one of the order dates when you convert the planned order, an entry is made in the MRP file. During the next material requirements planning run, this entry triggers a new planning run for the material and its components.

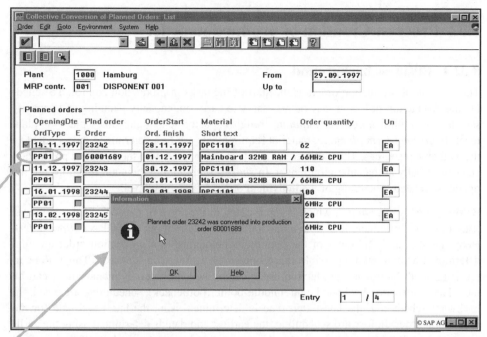

Fig. 8.184: Selection of planned order for conversion

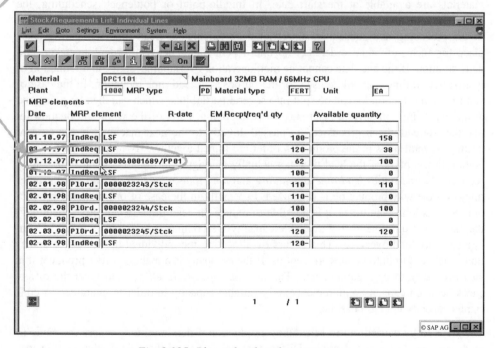

Fig. 8.185: Planned order after conversion

8.32 Process: Creation of production order

8.32.1 Business background

The creation of production orders is the start of the tasks in production control. To schedule the production orders, it may be necessary to carry out capacity planning and capacity scheduling. Within *long-term planning*, rough capacity scheduling takes place at plant level. In *medium-term planning*, material requirements are first determined independent of the available resources. Then, the requirements are compared with the available production capacity usually at machine group level. In *short-term planning* the main functions are the operation-related scheduling of the individual orders at machine level.

Before *capacity scheduling*, which is represented in the form of capacity load overviews, lead time scheduling and lead time reduction must be carried out (see Glaser 1986, p. 69). Here, the start and end dates of the operations belonging to a production order are first determined without taking possible capacity restrictions into consideration. This is done to see if the end date of the production order determined in materials management can be met. Here, forward, backward and middle-point (bottleneck) scheduling are used. In backward scheduling, the latest start date is determined using the latest end date for the production order. In forward scheduling, the earliest end date is determined using the earliest start date for the production order. However, this is only realistic if all the required materials are available at the start date. In middle-point or bottleneck scheduling, the starting point is the bottleneck operation in the production process. Starting here, the times of the preceding and subsequent operations are calculated. Lead time scheduling takes place for each individual order, i.e. no interdependencies between orders are taken into consideration. If the end date cannot be met, operation overlapping, splits, and reduction of interoperation times can all be used for the purposes of lead time reduction. In the case of splitting, a production lot can be split into several partial lots, which can then be processed at the same time on several machines. In overlapping, parts of the whole production lot that have already been processed are passed directly to the next machine. In the case of nesting, several parts in the production order are joined together. By reducing the interoperation times, parts of the lead time not actually belonging to the processing time can be reduced. The activities *lead time scheduling* and *lead time reduction* depend among other things on the way production is organized. Especially in the case of order-related production with its long wait times, it is possible to reduce the lead time. In capacity scheduling, the capacity requirements and available capacity are compared in graphical or table form in a capacity load overview. This occurs by allocating the individual operations or operation sequences to individual work centres. If the company is a make-to-order producer it is also necessary to peg requirements. The task of *capacity levelling* is to level the differences between capacity requirements and available capacity in order to guarantee as constant a capacity load as possible.

The steps to be carried out in scheduling production orders are more or less the same in medium- and short-term planning. Differences only occur in the objects involved. In medium-term planning, the object to be planned is the order, the planning horizon is months or weeks and the capacities to be planned are the groups of machines or resources. In short-term planning, the object to be planned is the operation, the planning horizon days or minutes and the capacity to be planned the resources or individual machines. The reason for carrying out medium- or short-term planning is that due to unforeseen events between the planning dates, delays in production can take place caused by, for example, machine breakdown, labour illness or injury, or broken tools, or even urgent orders received that have to be processed with a higher priority. The way in which the individual tasks are carried out depends on the type of production and the way in which production is organized. A make-to-order manufacturer, for example, has to be able to carry out lead-time scheduling both on the basis of lead times and using routing data (see Section 8.14). This is necessary because when planning starts, no complete bills of material or routings exist but the manufacturer still has to be able to give some sort of rough completion date when making an offer. Only in the various stages of the order do bill of material and routing data become successively available. The data used for planning purposes must then be checked, especially with regard to the completion date, and the dates must then be corrected using existing routing data. A manufacturer who produces materials in large series, on the other hand, has all the planning data already available when production begins. Scheduling can thus take place completely using routing data. If flow production with tight time limits exist, middle-point scheduling is unnecessary, as the production resources are linked together and therefore no individual machine can represent a bottleneck. However, in shop floor production, all three scheduling processes may make sense.

8.32.2 SAP-specific description

There are three ways to create a production order in the R/3 System:

- *With reference to a material*

  In this case, the production order refers to a material to be produced in a particular plant. An important control field for the production order is the *order type* on the initial screen. This field controls not only whether internal or external number assignment is to take place, but also the areas of classification, commitments management or status management for the various stages of production (see Fig. 8.187). On the operation overview screen, all of the *operations* taken over from the routing and scheduled for the order are listed.

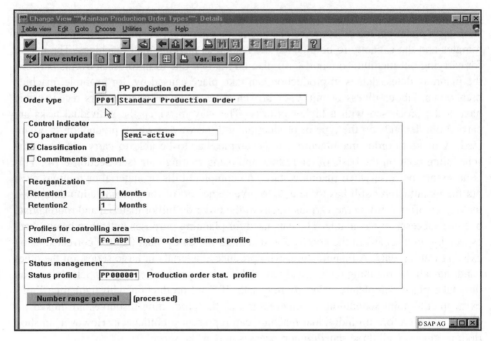

Fig. 8.186: Customizing the order category

■ *Without reference to a material*

On the header screen of the production order, you have to enter a short text as a re-placement for the material number. You then have to decide whether the processing is to take place using a reference operation set. If no reference operation set is to be used, the system automatically generates a master sequence containing one operation. If the selected routing contains alternative sequences, these can only be taken over in the production order if alternative sequences have been allowed for the order type in Cus-tomizing. The system looks for a valid routing and a valid bill of material. If several bills of material exist, the system tries to find a suitable one using the criteria validity date, lot size, status and usage. If it is not possible to select one bill of material, the production controller has to choose one manually. Additionally, the desired settlement receiver is determined for the settlement rule.

■ *With reference to a planned order*

If the components MRP, routings and bills of material are all in use, it is possible to create planned orders containing nearly all the information needed in the creation of a production order. A planned order contains the required quantity, the start and end date, the material number and the material components. The components needed for the production are included in the planned order as items and when the planned order is converted into a production order they are also taken over into the production order. No new BOM explosion takes place. During the conversion of a planned order into a production order, the dependent requirements for the components are turned into reservations. The operation data and the production resource data are taken as usual from the routing of the material to be produced.

One of the most important screens in the production order is the *operation overview screen*. This screen contains the operations taken from the routing and scheduled for the production order (see Fig. 8.189). Each *operation* has an *operation number*, possibly a *sub-operation number*, the number of a *work centre*, the *control key*, which determines what is to happen to the operation (for example, whether completion confirmation must take place, whether scheduling can take place, whether the operation is to be printed, etc.), the *status* of the operation, whether it has already been released, the *start and end date* of the operation, the *short description* and the *allocation indicator* to material components, production resources and trigger points. If *components* exist in the routing, they must always be allocated to an operation in the production order. Components which have not been allocated to an operation in the routing are automatically allocated to the first operation in the production order when the production order is created. However, you can switch the allocation of a component from one operation to another at any time. Components that are to be procured specifically for an order can be marked in the bill of material with such an indicator. When the order is created, purchase requisitions are created automatically for these components. In the purchasing functionality of materials management, the components are purchased specifically for the order and provided for the production order. For operations to be carried out by another company (external processing), purchase requisitions are also created for the purchasing department. This close integration between production and purchasing functionality guarantees smooth operation processing (see SAP – Production Planning 1994, pp. 9.1–9.5). From the operation overview screen, depending on the application and need, it is possible to branch to individual detail screens. The most important detail screens are:

▪ *General data*
This screen contains general data about the operation, such as percentage of scrap, number of shop floor papers to be printed, wage group and setup key. It also contains the costing relevance indicator, which defines whether the operation is to be included in product costing.

▪ *Default values*
This screen contains the default values, i.e. planned values for the processing of an operation and the corresponding units of measure. Using the default values, the costs, times and capacity requirements for an operation are determined.

▪ *Interoperation times*
On the interoperation times screen, you can maintain scheduling data relating to the times outside the processing time. This screen is only relevant for operations for which scheduling has been defined in the control key.

▪ *External processing*
This screen contains data for operations to be processed externally, i.e. operations that are to be carried out by a supplier. The screen is only relevant for operations for which external processing has been allowed in the control key.

■ *Calculation of standard values*
Apart from the possibility of entering standard values manually, you can also let the system calaculate standard values. On this screen, you can enter values which determine how the standard values are to be calculated (e.g. via CAP or by guesswork), in which year the standard values were determined, which information was used to determine standard values and using which standard value code the standard values were calculated.

■ *Splitting*
On the splitting detail screen, you can maintain data controlling whether, how and when an operation can or must be split for scheduling purposes. This data has an effect on the processing time of the operation and thus on the lead time of the production order. This screen is only relevant for operations whose control key allows scheduling.

■ *Overlapping*
On the overlapping detail screen, data can be maintained for operations for which overlapping is to take place. This data has an effect on the lead time of the production order. The screen is only relevant for operations whose control key allows scheduling.

■ *Operation dates*
This screen contains the results of lead time scheduling for the operation. It is only relevant for operations whose control key allows scheduling. Scheduling determines dates for the setup time, processing time, teardown time and wait time. For each of these times, the system works out the duration and the earliest/latest date and time. When the system calculates the earliest dates, it assumes that only the minimum queue time is used. When the system calculates the latest dates, it assumes that the normal queue time will be used.

■ *Allocation of capacity requirements*
On this screen, you can split the total requirements for the operation into partial requirements. Either the quantity or the times can be split.

8.32.3 Using the process

A production order has been created for Model Company A based on a planned order. On the initial screen, the reference number of the planned order, *23243*, has been entered. Order type *PP01* (see Fig. 8.187) was proposed by the system (internal document number assignment). On the production order header screen, the scheduling data has been taken over from the planned order. In Model Company A, backward scheduling takes place. A total quantity of 110 pcs is to be produced (see Fig. 8.188).

On the operation overview screen you can see the operations required to manufacture material *DPC1101*. For operation *0010* the *COMP* indicator has been marked (see Fig. 8.189). This indicator indicates that material components exist which are necessary for this operation. You can see a list of the components by marking operation *0010* and pressing the *Components* button (see Fig. 8.190). Additionally, you can see columns PRT and TPt on the operation overview screen. If column PRT is marked, it means that production resources and tools have been allocated to the operation. If column *TPt* is marked, it means that trigger points have been allocated to the operation. When the production order is created, *scheduling* is carried out. You can see the results in the operation times screen. To see the scheduling data for the operation, press the button *Stnd.val*. Ten minutes setup time have been calculated for operation *0010* (see Fig. 8.191). After saving the production order, reservations are created for the required components. You can see the newly created production order with the document number *60001690* in the stock/requirement list.

8.32.4 Navigation information

■ *Menu path*
Logistics –> Production –> Production control –> Order –> Create –> With a planned order

■ *Transaction code*
CO01, CO40

■ *Ingoing processes in the R/3 Reference Model*
Planned order conversion
Results processing MRP
Results processing MPS
Standard order processing
Customer contract release order processing

■ *Outgoing processes in the R/3 Reference Model*
Missing parts processing
Production order preliminary costing
Release of production order
Standard order processing
Customer contract release order processing
Purchase requisition assignment

Scheduling

In order processing and monitoring, the scheduling function calculates the production dates and capacity requirements for all the operations within an order. Starting with the basic order dates, the system schedules the start and the finish of an order. The basic order dates are either taken from the planned order, or entered manually on the header screen of the production order (see Fig. 8.188).

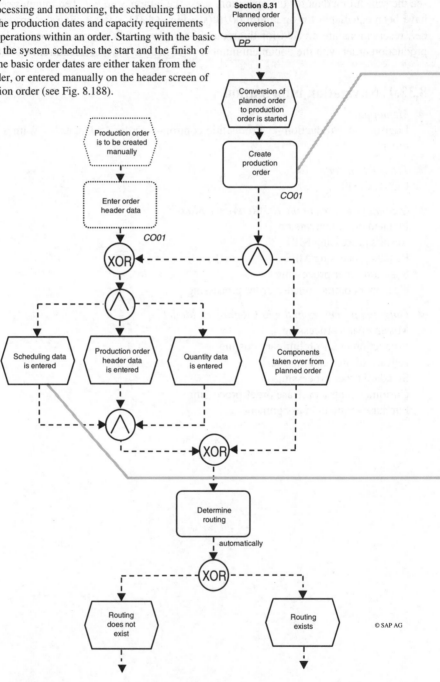

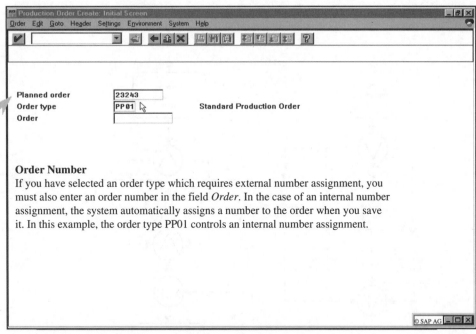

Fig. 8.187: Initial screen of production order creation

Order Number

If you have selected an order type which requires external number assignment, you must also enter an order number in the field *Order*. In the case of an internal number assignment, the system automatically assigns a number to the order when you save it. In this example, the order type PP01 controls an internal number assignment.

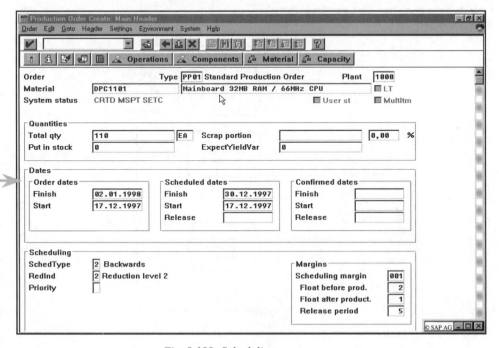

Fig. 8.188: Scheduling

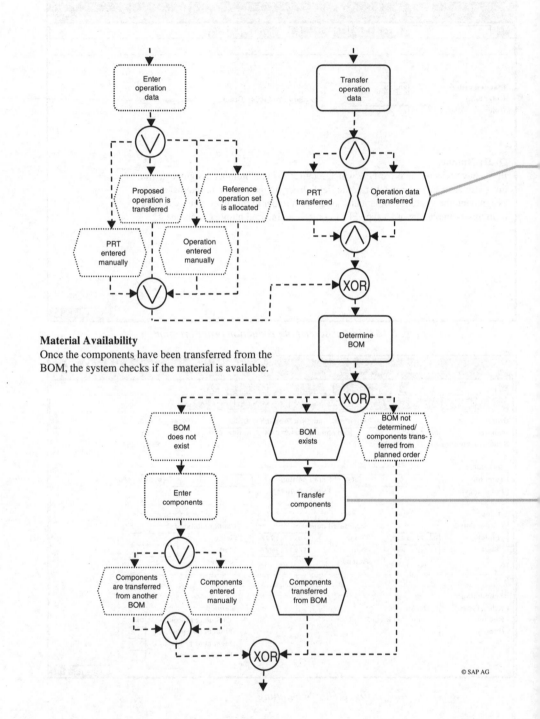

Material Availability

Once the components have been transferred from the BOM, the system checks if the material is available.

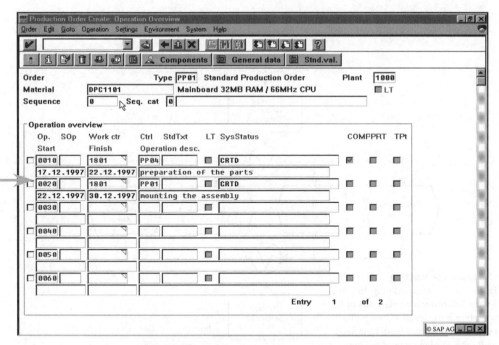

Fig. 8.189: Operation data

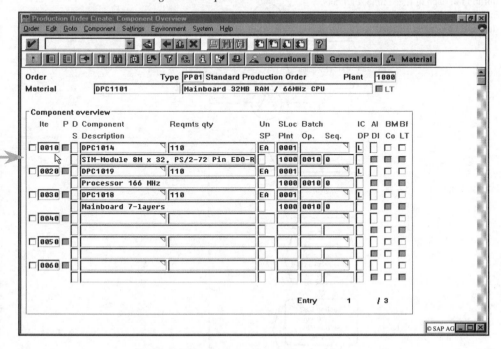

Fig. 8.190: Component overview

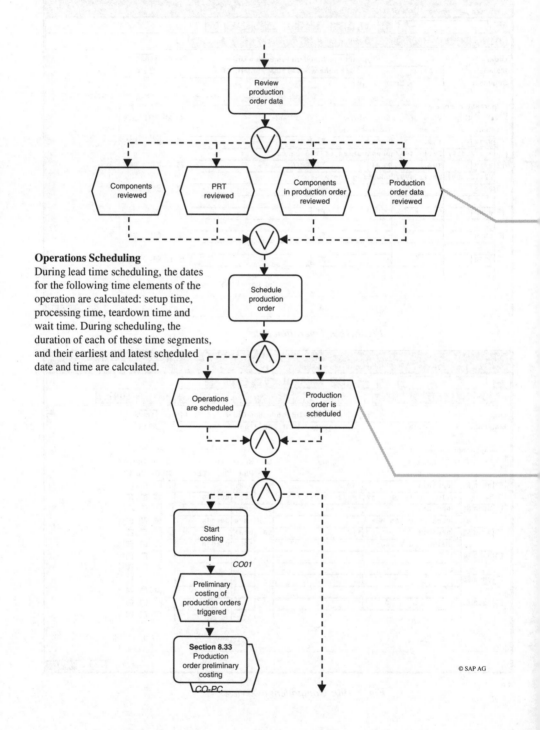

Operations Scheduling
During lead time scheduling, the dates
for the following time elements of the
operation are calculated: setup time,
processing time, teardown time and
wait time. During scheduling, the
duration of each of these time segments,
and their earliest and latest scheduled
date and time are calculated.

© SAP AG

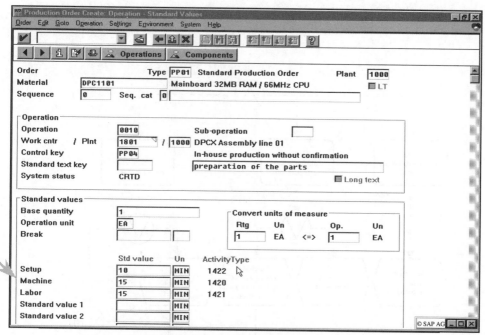

Fig. 8.191: Change machine standard value

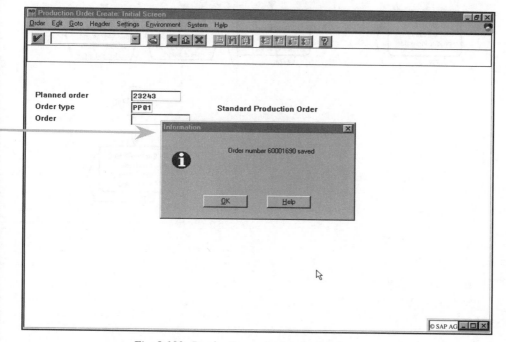

Fig. 8.192: Production order is scheduled

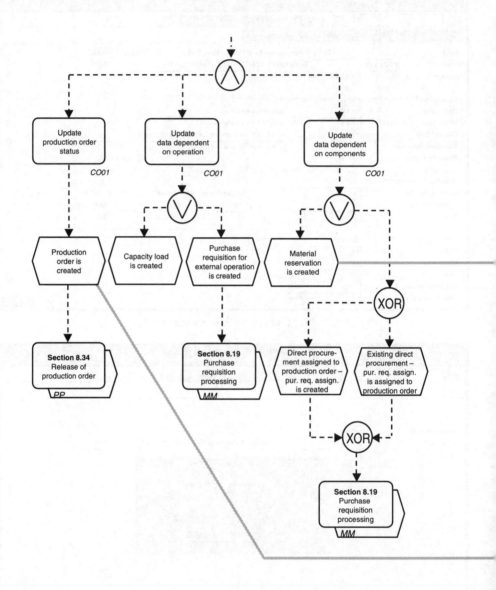

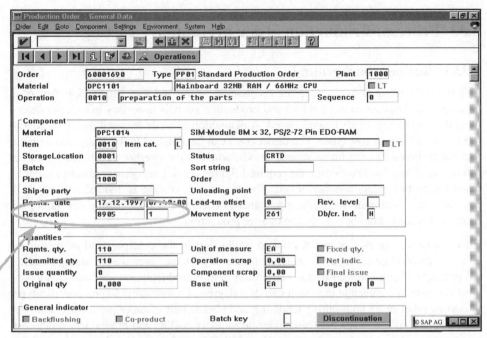

Fig. 8.193: Material reservation

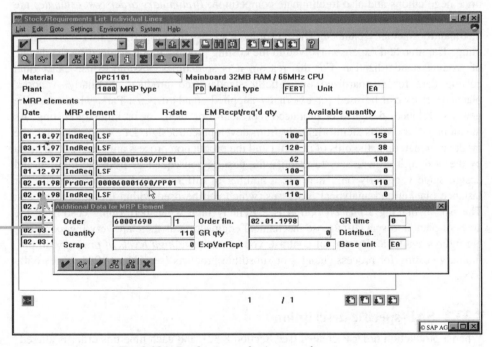

Fig. 8.194: Production order is created

8.33 Process: Production order preliminary costing

8.33.1 Business background

This type of costing is used to prepare the manufacturing and total production costs of a given product. Access to the material and production costs is necessary in order to determine the cost of the goods manufactured. A distinction is made between direct and overhead costs with both cost types. The direct costs can be assigned individually and without settlement directly to the manufactured goods, whereas the overhead costs are based on surcharges. Even for direct costs, the required figures are not necessarily always available when the cost calculation is performed. For this reason, costing is divided into standard cost estimates, preliminary costing, simultaneous costing and final costing depending on whether it is carried out before, during or after production.

Preliminary costing is carried out prior to production in the company and is, therefore, based on planned costs. It covers concrete orders or customer inquiries regarding individual products. Preliminary costing is carried out before production on the basis of incomplete data which means that the result carries a degree of uncertainty. In practice, this type of costing takes place both during tendering and also as part of order processing. For this reason Kilger differentiates between tender preliminary costing and preliminary order cost estimates. *Tender preliminary costing* takes place before placing an order and is used for price negotiations and also to eliminate competition. *Preliminary order cost estimates* are carried out after the order has been placed and yields more precise planning data based on the quantities actually planned. These estimates are usually carried out after work scheduling. The time and expense involved in the costing process are determined by the degree of product standardization. For this reason, it is sometimes possible to use exact final costing data for standardized or partially standardized products. Similarly, vendors' planned prices can be used for externally supplied standard parts. Parts which must be newly developed, designed or produced represent a problem for preliminary costing. As mentioned, these parts stem originally from development/design. Due to the fact that the production materials, the bills of material and the production process are greatly influenced by the design, it is necessary to identify the costing consequences from the drafting and design stage very early on. There are a number of different quick costing methods, for instance blanket and analytical processes, which can be used within the design process. The risk of making a *miscalculation* is extremely high when performing costing in the areas of plant and special-purpose mechanical engineering as there are very few comparable figures available. By way of contrast, you can achieve *high levels of precision* in preliminary costing for process changes or substitute products (see Kilger 1988, pages 650–655).

8.33.2 SAP-specific description

When a production order is created (see Section 8.32), and each time this order is altered, the system calculates the planned costs which are expected to be incurred during production. These planned costs are assigned to the production order via primary and secondary cost types. The material costs and costs for external procurement (primary cost elements) are assigned to the order via primary postings such as material withdrawals or the purchase of external parts, for example. Costs such as production costs, material overheads and production overheads (secondary cost elements) are assigned to the order via an internal cost allocation. The cost elements are stored in cost segments which are maintained per fiscal year. In order to determine in which period of which fiscal year the planned costs for an order will be incurred, the system uses the latest start date or the date on which the materials are required. Both the planned and the actual costs are maintained in the cost segments. The system updates actual costs upon each withdrawal, confirmation, and other postings relating to the order, for example goods receipt for external procurement. This means that you can make a planned/actual cost comparison at any time (see SAP – Production Planning 1994, pp. 12.1–12.8).

8.33.3 Using the process

Triggered by the *production order creation* process, the system automatically pre-costs the appropriate production order. *Production order preliminary costing* causes the operations in the routing to be valuated based on the dissolved quantity structure using costing records from Overheads Controlling and the BOM items with the material prices from Materials Management (see Fig. 8.196). On the basis of the planned costs of the pre-costed production order (see Fig. 8.198), you can now decide whether or not the production order is to be executed. If the pre-calculated costs of a production order point to profitability, the *production order release* logistics process can be started, which in turn triggers the *production order execution* logistics process.

8.33.4 Navigation information

■ *Menu path*
Accounting –> Controlling –> Product cost acctg –> Order-related prod. –> Planning
–> CO production order –> Create/ change plan

■ *Transaction code*
KKF4, KKE2, VA02

■ *Ingoing processes in the R/3 Reference model*
Production order processing (without quantity structure)
Preparation of preliminary costing
Creation of production order

■ *Outgoing processes in the R/3 Reference model*
Unit/base planning costing
Product cost analysis in order-related manufacturing
Execution of production order
Production order – simultaneous costing

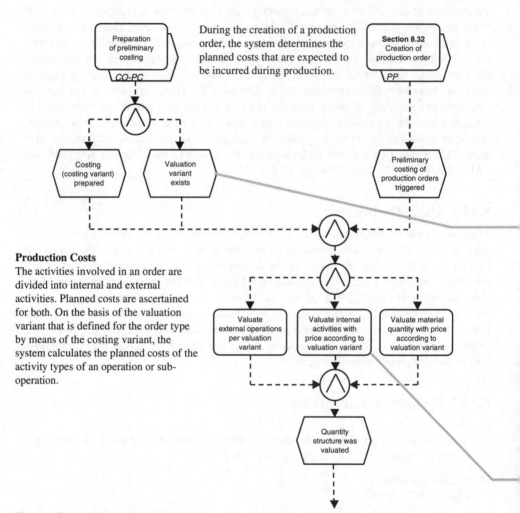

Production Costs
The activities involved in an order are divided into internal and external activities. Planned costs are ascertained for both. On the basis of the valuation variant that is defined for the order type by means of the costing variant, the system calculates the planned costs of the activity types of an operation or sub-operation.

Planned Costs of Internal Activities
In order to ascertain the planned costs of executing an operation, the system creates a quantity structure for the activities that have been completed. This quantity structure is then valuated with a price. The most important data needed to create a quantity structure for an activity (i.e. the activity types and formulas) are found in the work centre. Any activity that is calculated is assigned to an activity type, which, in turn, is assigned to a formula in the work centre. Using this formula and the standard time of an operation you can calculate how many activities to expect for a specific activity type of a specific operation. Once the system has calculated this, you can valuate the activity to be performed for each activity type.

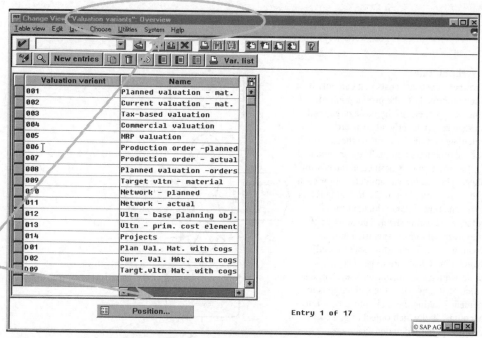

Fig. 8.195: Valuation variants overview

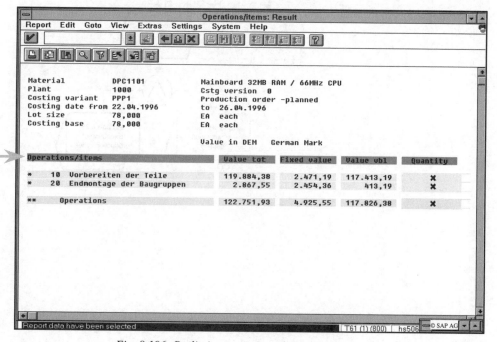

Fig. 8.196: Preliminary costing of operations

Overhead Rates

Overhead costs are costs that can only be added indirectly to the production order, (for example, electricity costs or general storage costs). Overhead costs are calculated on the basis of overhead rates for the production order. They are updated to the cost elements defined in the costing sheet. The costing variant defined for each order type and plant in Customizing refers to a valuation variant which, in turn, refers to a costing sheet. The amount of the overhead rates is specified in the costing sheet. The costing sheet specifies which direct costs are to be charged, under which circumstances a surcharge is calculated, how large the surcharge is in percent – taking these circumstances into account – and which object (e.g. a cost centre) is credited under which cost element in the case of actual postings.

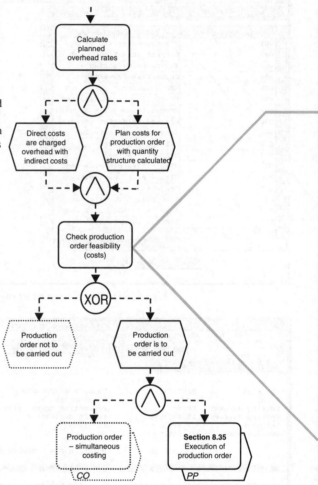

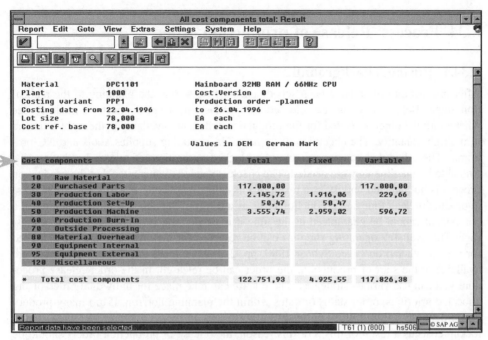

Fig. 8.197: Cost components

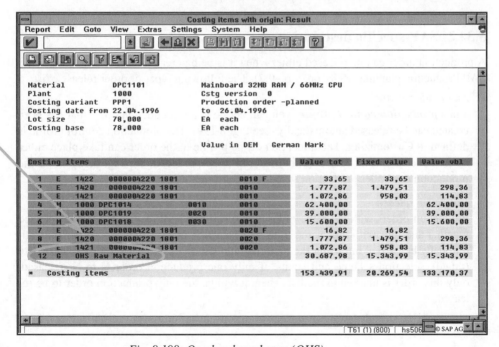

Fig. 8.198: Overhead surcharge (OHS)

8.34 Process: Release of production order

8.34.1 Business background

After production orders have been scheduled, they pass from the planning to the realization stage. Before they can be released for production, a check must be made to see whether all the objects needed for the production orders are available at the right time and in the right quantity. The check involves materials, operating supplies, tools and NC programs. The scheduled components may be blocked at the time of release but have to be available by the time they are needed. The check is needed to guarantee that the production process is not delayed unduly as a result of missing components, and to avoid an increase in production lead time and production costs as a result of the delay. If the availability of a component cannot be guaranteed at the time it is needed the system issues an error message. The available operating supplies can be reserved for the order and are thus blocked for use by other orders (see Scheer 1990, pp. 203–215). If all the required resources are available at the start of production, the order can be released. In the order release procedure you can use various strategies. The release can take place for individual orders using allocated priorities, order status or dates within the planning horizon. If too many production orders are released, this can lead to a bottleneck in production and increased capital lockup costs as a result of this. For this reason, the release of production orders should be based on the capacity situation in the production department.

8.34.2 SAP-specific description

A production order can be released either when it is being created or in change mode (see SAP Production planning 1996, pp. 9.6.–9.7). The following types of order release exist:

■ *Automatic release*
Via a **production control profile**, you can define that a production order that has been created can be released automatically (see Fig. 8.199). The production control profile is defined in Customizing. The allocation of the profile to the order can take place either in the material master record of the material to be produced (see Fig. 8.75) or via the production controller production scheduler (Customizing).

■ *Collective release*
Production orders with the same order type, plant and MRP controller can be selected together and released at the same time. The selection of the production orders can additionally be carried out using the material number, order number (range), release date (range), selection scheme and status. If only one production order is to be released, only this order is marked in the list. Then, it will be the only production order to be released.

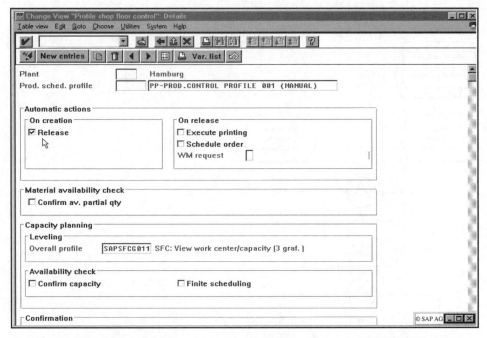

Fig. 8.199: Customizing the automatic release at order creation

8.34.3 Using the process

The initial screen is used to select production orders that you want to release. In the example for Model Company A, order *60001497* has been specified. The order list (see Fig. 8.201) proposes the orders to be released. By marking the order concerned, and pressing the „Release" button in the upper part of the screen, the order is released. Unfortunately, the production order could not be released in the first run because material was not available (see Fig. 8.202).

8.34.4 Navigation information

■ *Menu path*
Logistics –> Production –> Production control –> Order –> Release

■ *Transaction code*
CO01, CO02, CO05

■ *Ingoing processes in the R/3 Reference Model*
Creation of production order

■ *Outgoing processes in the R/3 Reference Model*
Capacity leveling; Missing parts processing; Execution of production order; Printout of production order; Inspection lot creation for production

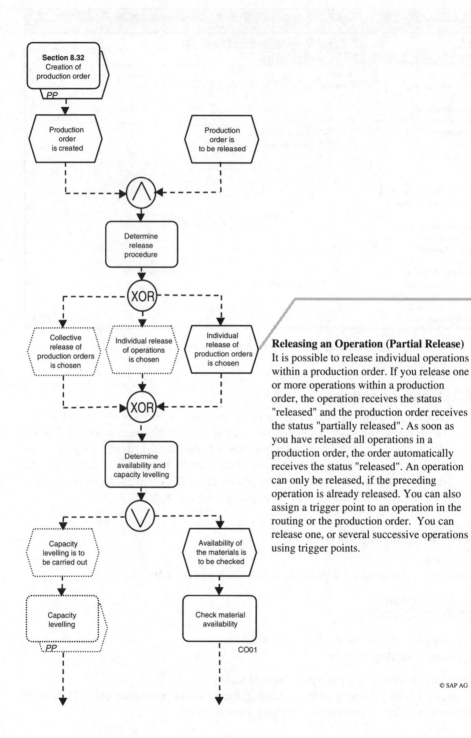

Releasing an Operation (Partial Release)
It is possible to release individual operations
within a production order. If you release one
or more operations within a production
order, the operation receives the status
"released" and the production order receives
the status "partially released". As soon as
you have released all operations in a
production order, the order automatically
receives the status "released". An operation
can only be released, if the preceding
operation is already released. You can also
assign a trigger point to an operation in the
routing or the production order. You can
release one, or several successive operations
using trigger points.

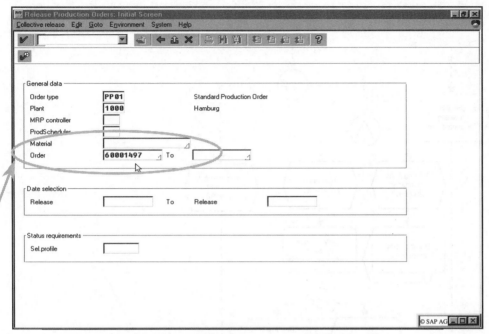

Fig. 8.200: Individual release of production order

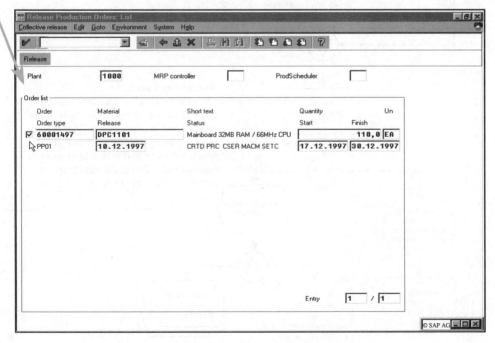

Fig. 8.201: Order list for release of production order

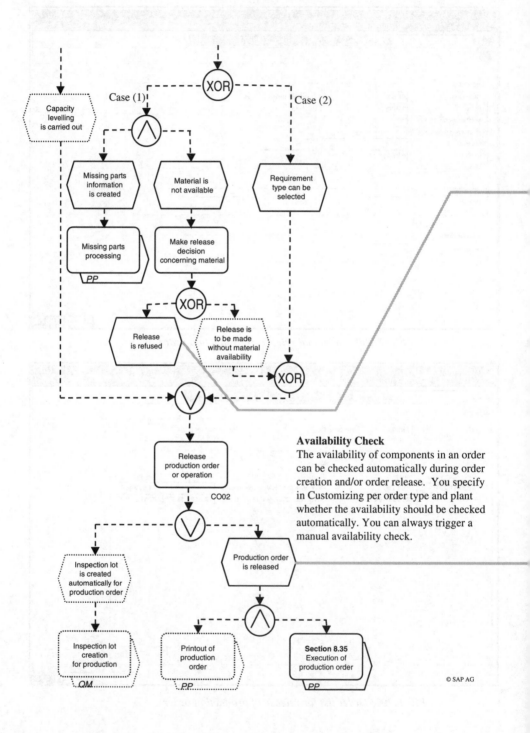

Availability Check

The availability of components in an order can be checked automatically during order creation and/or order release. You specify in Customizing per order type and plant whether the availability should be checked automatically. You can always trigger a manual availability check.

© SAP AG

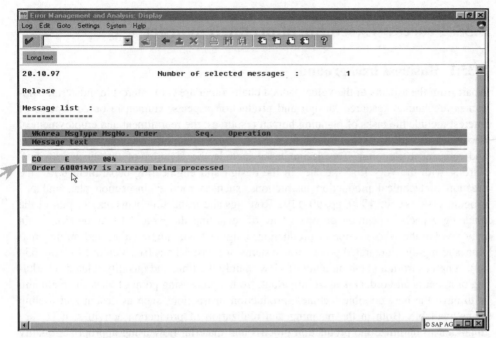

Fig. 8.202: Material availability negative (Case 1) – Release is refused

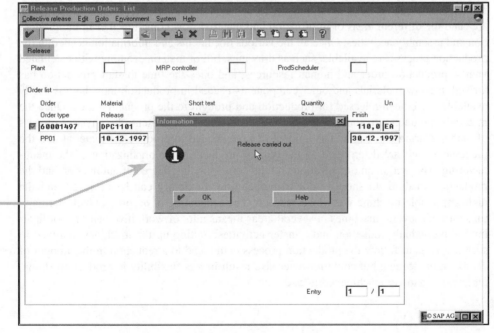

Fig. 8.203: Production order is released

8.35 Process: Execution of production order

8.35.1 Business background

Apart from the aspects of the value - added chain, other areas of interest in industrial companies are human resource, design and production aspects. Human resource aspects of interest include the tasks of planning human resources, the recruitment and employment of personnel, as well as payroll accounting, and accompanying tasks such as career planning and retirement planning. The design tasks include the creation of technical drawings, starting with the very first sketches in the design and engineering department up to the creation of technical production instructions, such as routing, inspection plan and NC programs (see Venitz 1990, pp. 90–119). Routings and inspection plans may be part of the planning aspects depending on one's way of regarding the issue. The production chain may involve the whole scope of production, ranging from simple lathes and milling machines to highly - integrated production systems or transfer lines (see Venitz 1990, pp. 65–89). Whereas from a planning point of view mainly the time and quantity-related scheduling of material and orders is most important, from a processing point of view the main aim is to have the best possible technical production instructions such as design and tooling plans available. Both in the planning and realization of production activities, it is very important to optimize the production process and material flow using appropriate quality assurance measures.

The various areas all meet up within the actual manufacturing process in the production area and the different areas of information and material flow come together in the production and assembly activities. Once all the various documents and information needed in the production process are available, such as drawings, bill of material, routing with calculated values, production order and human resources, and once the time to start production has arrived, the raw materials and other components needed in production must be physically available, have been released for production and brought to the production area. Once the materials, production resources, needed tools and labour are present, the physical process of manufacturing can begin. The amount of time needed to produce the material and the processing itself are determined by the type of production, the organization of the manufacturing tasks within an organization and the corresponding degree of automation and the production method. In shop - floor manufacturing, flexibility can be achieved and the highest possible machine work-load reached. The scheduling of an order which normally runs through several machines in several areas means a lot of work involved in coordinating the individual production and transfer activities. Setting up the machines involved in such a way as to follow the production process could lead to a reduction in the amount of coordination needed, but could however also result in less flexibility in production (transfer lines) or a lower machine work-load.

8.35.2 SAP-specific description

Once an order has been released (see Section 8.34), the materials needed in production must be issued so that production can start. The order status maintained in the order gives the production controller information about the current status of an order at all times. Depending on the activities being carried out on an object (for example, a production order, an operation or a component), the object status is changed. Once a status has been set, it in turn affects which further activities can be carried out on the object. In the R/3 System, a differentiation is made between the system status and the user status.

■ *System status*

A system status is a status set by the system, informing the user that a certain activity or process has been carried out on an object. A system status cannot be influenced in any way by the user, i.e. it can be neither directly deleted nor changed. Once a production order has been released, the system automatically sets the system status *released*. This status can only be changed by carrying out a subsequent activity which itself changes the status.

■ *User status*

A user status is a status that can be created as an extension of an existing system status. It is possible to create and activate as many system statuses as required. Before a user status can be defined, a *status scheme* must exist. A status profile can be defined in Customizing for an order type (see Fig. 8.204). A production order can contain as many statuses as required, for example the statuses *released, preliminary costing, printed* and *confirmed* can all be set at the same time. The status profile defines the possible user statuses. Their function can be documented using a descriptive text. In addition, in the status profile each user status is assigned a sequence number specifying the expected sequence of user statuses in the production order; an initial status can be defined, which is automatically set when the object is created. Also, it is possible to define that when a particular activity is carried out, a certain user status is set automatically.

Status changes that take place during the processing of an order can be documented and seen in the form of status change documents. A status change document documents which status was changed, who changed the status of an object, when the status was changed, whether the status was activated or deactivated and in which transaction the status change took place. For performance reasons, it is advisable only to activate status change documents at order header level.

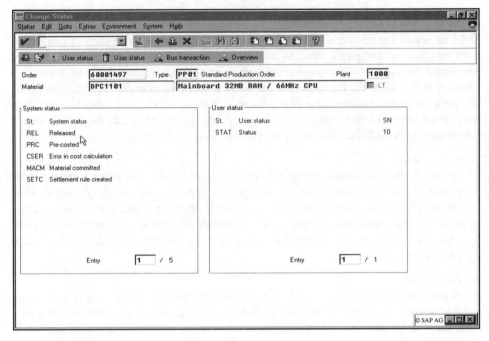

Fig. 8.204: status profile

■ *Working time*

An important factor for order processing is the determination of the working time. The work time defines *when* work can take place. The factory calendar for the plant defines on which days work takes place and which days are holidays. You define the working time in the system by specifying the work start and finish times and the breaks. The working time defined in the work centre and the operation or work centre calendar (see Fig. 8.208) are used when determining the wait, setup, processing and teardown times. For the calculation of the daily working time, the system uses the rate of utilization of the work centre in addition to the start, finish and break times. This defines the relationship between actually productive working time and theoretically possible working time as a percentage. It is used to represent the effects of technical and organizational interruptions. This value, which is needed for scheduling purposes, is defined for the capacity type, which is the basis for scheduling. The working time of the work centre is defined for the capacity type, which is in the scheduling screen of the work centre. The work centre calendar has the highest priority. If no calendar has been specified in the work centre, the system uses the operation calendar. If no calendar has been maintained in the operation either, the Gregorian calendar is used. The *wait time* is calculated independent of the factory calendar from 0.00 to 24.00 hours. The *transport time* is determined via the parameters in the transport time matrix. The *working time per work day* is defined in the transport time matrix by specifying the work start and finish times. Externally processed operations are scheduled using the delivery time in days using the Gregorian calendar.

8.35.3 Using the process

In Model Company A, production order *60001497* is displayed. The header screen (see Fig. 8.205) shows the start and finish dates and the scheduling of the production order. Using the planned finish date and the horizon key confirmed a release date of 20.10.1997, a planned start date of 17.12.1997 and a planned order finish date of 30.12.1997. The status PRC indicates that preliminary costing has already taken place for the production order (see Section 8.33). Fig. 8.206 shows the availability check (according to the ATP method – available to promise) available for components in production order processing.

During production, you can see an overview of dates for operations with the exact wait, setup, processing, teardown and idle times In a Gantt diagram, you can display the production processing data in graphical form (see Fig. 8.207). On the operation overview screen of the production order, you can follow the status of the individual operations and their finish dates (field *Finish*). The planned end date of operation 0010 is 23.12.1997 and for operation 0020 30.12.1997 (see Fig. 8.208).

8.35.4 Navigation information

■ *Menu path*
Logistics –> Production –> Production control –>
Goto –> Operation overview
Goto –> Graphic –> Gantt chart

■ *Transaction code*
CO02

■ *Ingoing processes in the R/3 Reference Model*
Release production order
Kanban replenishment
Capacity leveling
Printout production order
Production order preliminary costing

■ *Outgoing processes in the R/3 Reference Model*
Goods issue for production orders
Kanban event
Goods receipt processing from production
Kanban goods receipt for in-house production
Completion confirmation of production order

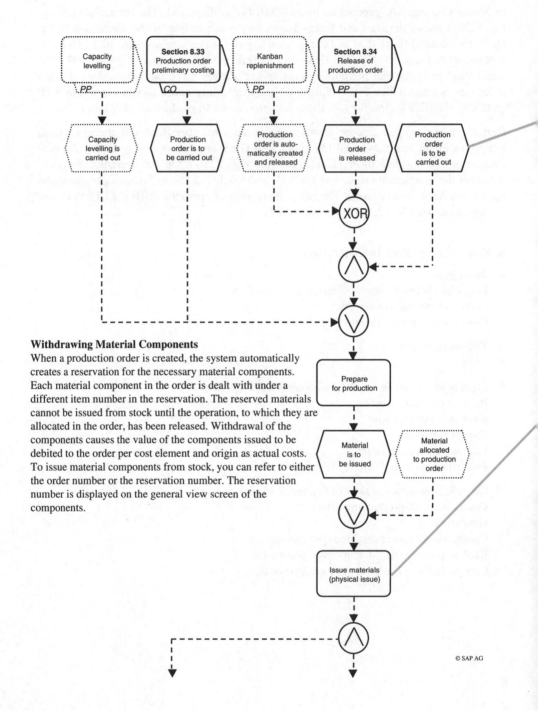

Withdrawing Material Components

When a production order is created, the system automatically creates a reservation for the necessary material components. Each material component in the order is dealt with under a different item number in the reservation. The reserved materials cannot be issued from stock until the operation, to which they are allocated in the order, has been released. Withdrawal of the components causes the value of the components issued to be debited to the order per cost element and origin as actual costs. To issue material components from stock, you can refer to either the order number or the reservation number. The reservation number is displayed on the general view screen of the components.

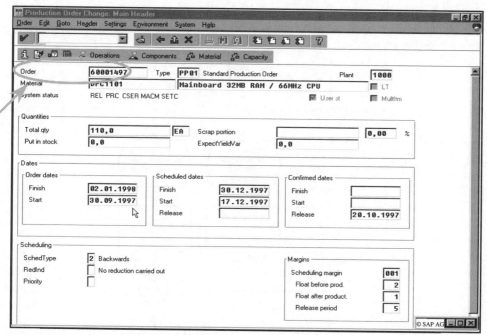

Fig. 8.205: Production order – header data

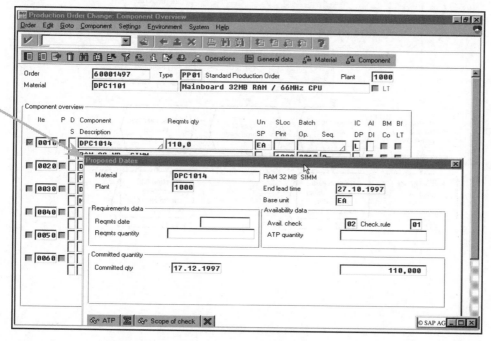

Fig. 8.206:Production order – proposed dates

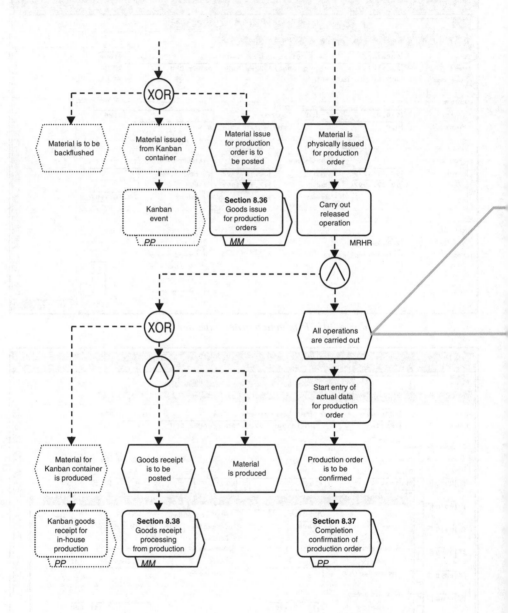

© SAP AG

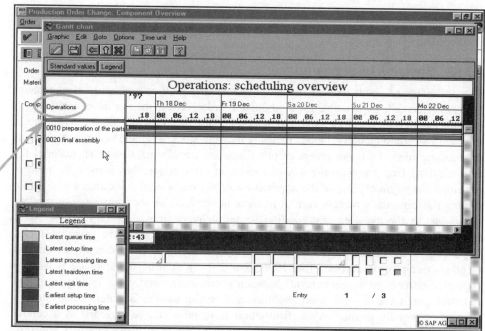

Fig. 8.207: Production order – operations scheduling overview

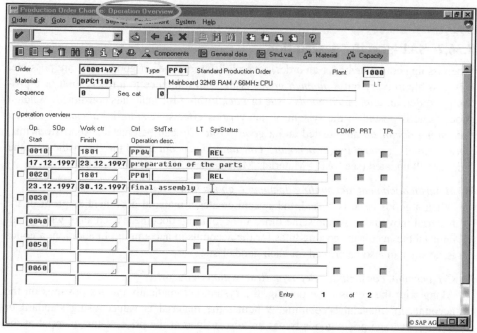

Fig. 8.208: Production order – operation overview

8.36 Process: Goods issue for production order

8.36.1 Business background

The processing of goods issues is a central task in inventory or warehouse management. Materials reserved, for example for a production order, reduce the available stock. A *reservation* can thus be seen as a request to make a certain material available at a certain point in time in a certain quantity. Goods issues reduce the stock level and occur as a result of production orders, customer orders or other requests (replacement material, material for consumption). Depending on the way of looking at reservations, they involve the following steps: *the physical issue* of the required material from a storage location and possible *picking* (i.e. physically placing various material at one location for a customer or production order), or the *planning of a goods issue* and delivery from a central location. Apart from the change to quantities, goods issues also lead to a change in the value of stocks. Depending on the different tasks involved, the goods may be stored differently at the time of goods receipt or issue (see Pfohl 1996, pp. 92–140). A storage warehouse is used to cope with differences in requirements between goods receipt and goods issue processing. A buffer warehouse is a short-term solution and is also used as an intermediate storage solution, especially production. A distribution warehouse can be regarded as a central storage warehouse, in which various goods and materials from many suppliers and production plants are delivered, maybe reassembled and sent out to sales or further production plants.

8.36.2 SAP-specific description

When issuing components for an order, several different types of goods issue are possible. It is possible to carry out a *planned goods issue* with reference to a reservation or a production order, an *unplanned goods issue* or *backflushing* for materials consumed. When a goods issue is posted in the system, it has various effects. A *material document* and an *accounting document* are created and a *goods issue slip* can be created. Apart from this, *stock accounts*, *general ledger accounts*, *consumption accounts* and the *reservations* in the order are all updated (see SAP – Materials Management 1996, pp. 6.7 and 6.9).

■ *Material document, accounting document, goods issue slip*
When a goods issue is posted, the system creates a material document as proof of the material movement. At the same time, an accounting document is created, which contains all the necessary posting lines for the accounts in accounting. In addition, a goods issue slip can also be printed for each goods issue.

■ *G/L account, consumption account. Reservation in the order*
Along with the goods issue posting, the system automatically creates postings on the accounts in financial accounting. Whether the material is valued using standard or moving average price, goods issues are also valued at the price of the material at the time at which the goods issue takes place. A goods issue thus reduces the total value and the total quantity of stocks proportional to the price. In this way, the price of the

material remains unchanged. Apart from the updating of the inventory figures in the material master record, the consumption figures are also updated when a goods issue takes place if planning takes place for the material. The consumption figures of a material are used for the creation of forecasts in requirements planning. If the goods issue takes place with reference to a reservation or a production order, the issued quantity is updated in the reservation item. The reservation item is marked as completed when the total reservation quantity is issued or when the final delivery indicator is set manually in the goods issue. A *reservation* is a request to the warehouse to keep materials ready for issue for a specific purpose at a later point in time.

8.36.3 Using the process

In Model Company A, a *planned* goods issue is to be carried out for a production order. On the initial screen, you do not have to enter movement type *261* (this is taken from the menu path). If you press *Enter*, you immediately come to the screen for the goods issue and make the connection *for order*. A pop-up window appears, in which you enter the number of the production order, in this case *60001497* (see Fig. 8.209). If you don't know the number of the production order, you can look for the reservations belonging to the production order according to various criteria. On the next screen, you mark the materials for which you want to carry out the goods issue (see Fig. 8.210). The data is checked once more on the overview screen (see Fig. 8.211) and the material document *49003706 is* then posted.

8.36.4 Navigation information

■ *Menu path*
Logistics –> Materials Management –> Inventory Management –> Goods movement
–> Goods issue

■ *Transaction code*
MB1A

■ *Ingoing processes in the R/3 Reference Model*
Execution of production order

■ *Outgoing processes in the R/3 Reference Model*
Removal from stage processing
Automatic creation of TO for material document

Goods Issue with Reference to Order

The system automatically creates a reservation for the components planned in the order. When you enter the goods issue, you can refer to the order or the reservation. The system determines all components to be withdrawn. You need not enter the movement type or the plant, as these are automatically copied from the reservation. If you know the order number, enter it directly. If you do not know the order number, you can search for the corresponding reservation using various selection criteria (e.g. material, works, etc.).

Unplanned Goods Issue

Unplanned goods issue means that an additional material or a further quantity of a component already withdrawn is required in the production process. This goods issue is unplanned since it does not refer to any reservation. You post this as goods issue without reference.

Backflush

In the case of this kind of withdrawal, the components are already available in the plant. They are physically being consumed in the production process. The consumption, however, is not reported until the quantity that has been consumed is known, i.e. until the order is being confirmed. You need not enter any goods movement in inventory management for these components.

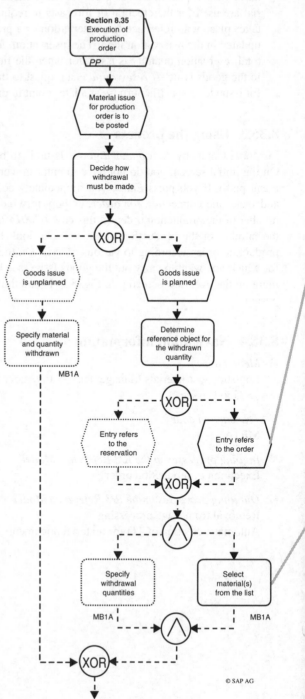

© SAP AG

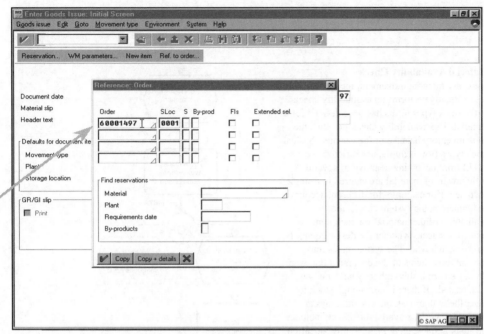

Fig. 8.209: *Goods issue with reference to order*

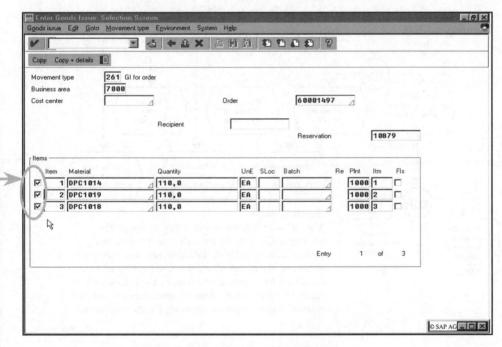

Fig. 8.210: *Selecting the material for goods issue*

Material Availability Check

For every material movement, the system automatically performs an availability check of the stock types if this has been defined for a material. The availability check prevents the book inventory balance of the various physical stock types (for example, unrestricted-use stock) from becoming negative. If several withdrawals of material are entered in a single document (for example, for different account assignments), the system checks the availability of the material for each item entered. It checks whether the desired quantity can be withdrawn. The system takes into account those items of the document that were already entered, although they have not yet been posted. If there is not enough stock to cover the withdrawal, the system issues an error message. The availability check includes the stock in question at plant, storage-location and special-stocks level.

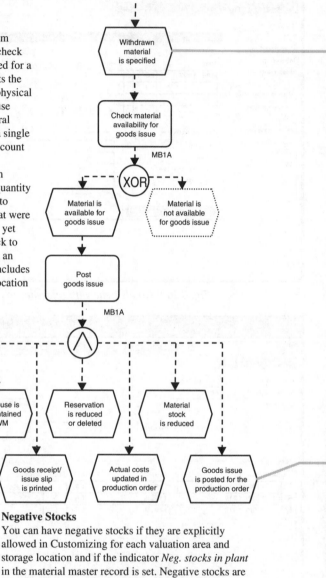

Negative Stocks

You can have negative stocks if they are explicitly allowed in Customizing for each valuation area and storage location and if the indicator *Neg. stocks in plant* in the material master record is set. Negative stocks are required if for organizational reasons goods issues are entered before the corresponding goods receipts and the material is already physically located in the warehouse.

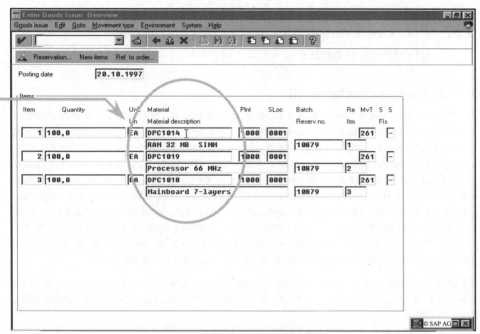

Fig. 8.211: List of withdrawn material with indication of reservation no.

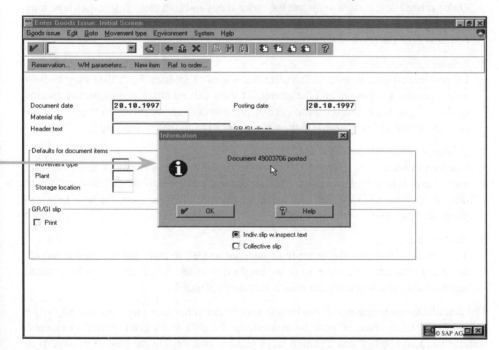

Fig. 8.212: Goods issue is posted for the production order

8.37 Process: Completion and confirmation of production order

8.37.1 Business background

In order to plan future production processes it is necessary not only to have planned or customer orders, but also to enter data regarding the time and cost of production from past orders. How up - to- date machine and production data is and the analysis of this data, for example the comparison of planned and actual data, affect the way in which future orders are carried out. Completion confirmation data may be needed in cost accounting to calculate the costs of future orders, in personnel management to be able to carry out wage calculation and the determination of payment for overtime, in plant maintenance to plan maintenance of machines, in sales to provide the customer with information regarding the current status of the order, in inventory management to update the current stock situation and in quality management to determine necessary quality control measures.

To deal with the various requirements, the completion confirmation data can be split up into the following categories (see Kraemer/Wiechmann 1990, pp. 10–21; see Scheer 1990, pp. 235–240):

- *Order-related data*
  Order-related data is used to update the order status and statistics. It specifies how long the machine was in use, how long an operation took, how many units were produced and how high the level of scrap was.

- *Labour-related data*
  Labour-related data is used to calculate the wages or salaries. Such data may be how long a person was present and the amount of work carried out, e.g. the quantity and the quality of goods produced (in the case of piecework wage or premium wage) and the amount of material consumed (in the case of, for example, premium wage).

- *Resource-related data*
  Resource-related data refers to the machine times and the amount of time tools are used. Here, it is important to note the number and cause of problems (machine downtime, broken tools). Tool data also refers to where tools were used, for how long and planned expiry and maintenance data.

- *Material data*
  Material data describes the quantity of material needed to carry out the production order. Using the quantities entered in the production order, future orders can be planned more reliably and necessary material reservations planned.

The completion confirmation of production orders can either take place periodically or be event-driven. In the case of periodic processing, the data for a given period is entered, collected and completion confirmation takes place in one step. In the case of event-driven completion confirmation, the data is confirmed as soon as the event takes place. The entry of the completion confirmation data can take place either manually by the user filling out a settlement form or entering times, quantities and scrap at an entry terminal or it can take place automatically by noting the machine data in production and then passing this data on to the PPC and other evaluation systems involved.

8.37.2 SAP-specific description

A completion confirmation documents the processing status of orders, operations, sub-operations and individual capacities. It therefore helps in the monitoring of orders. A completion confirmation records which quantity of a material is produced in an operation and which quantity cannot be used and is thus to be regarded as scrap. It also records which resources were actually needed, the work centre at which the operation was carried out and who carried out the operation. It is possible to carry out a completion confirmation for an order, an operation, a sub-operation, an individual capacity of an operation or an individual capacity of a sub-operation. Operations and sub-operations are treated in the same way when carrying out a completion confirmation. In the R/3 System, completion confirmation can be carried out for the following data (see SAP – Production Planning 1994, p. 9.8):

■ *Quantities*
  Completion confirmation can be carried out for the yield and the scrap produced in an operation (this function is not available for sub-operations).

■ *Performance data*
  Completion confirmation data can be entered for data such as how long it took to setup a machine or how long the machine was in operation. In addition, you can enter rough data to adapt the default data used in scheduling and capacity planning.

■ *Times*
  In completion confirmation, you can say when set up processing, and teardown for an operation started and was completed.

■ *Labour data*
  You can enter, for example, the personnel number of the employee who carried out the operation or the number of employees who carried it out.

■ *Work centre*
  You can enter the work centre at which the operation was carried out.

■ *Posting date*
  For each completion confirmation, you enter a posting date. The system proposes the date on which you enter the completion confirmation. However, you can overwrite this with another date.

■ *Goods movements*
  For each completion confirmation you can enter planned and unplanned goods movements.

■ *Reason for differences*
If the completion confirmation differs from the planned data as a result of an event such as damage to machinery, you can enter a key documenting the reason for this deviation in the field *Reason*.

In Customizing (see Fig. 8.213) you can define whether, in confirmations, partial completion or final completion confirmation is defaulted, or whether the type of confirmation to be entered depends on the underdelivery tolerance entered. In the latter case, if the quantity to be confirmed (yield + rework quantity + scrap) is below the underdelivery tolerance, the system automatically sets the indicator for partial completion confirmation. If the confirmation quantity is equal to or larger than the underdelivery tolerance, the indicator for final completion confirmation is set.

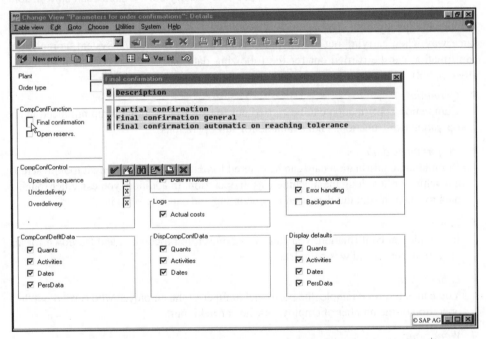

Fig. 8.213: Customizing the confirmation function per order type

A completion confirmation can take place for either an *operation* or an *order*.

■ *Completion confirmation for an operation*

  – *wage-completion slip*
  To confirm quantities, duration activities or labour data, completion confirmation is carried out for the wage-completion slip.

  – *event*
  To carry out completion confirmation for a particular time (e.g. start of setup or end

of processing), completion confirmation is carried out for the time event. When you carry out completion confirmation for an event, the system calculates the time automatically (e.g. the time between the time when setup starts and the time when setup ends is the confirmed setup time). Each confirmed event is allocated to a record type group. Setup events are allocated to record type group *1*, processing events to record type group *2* and teardown events to record type group *3* (see Fig. 8.217).

■ *Completion confirmations for an order*
If you enter a completion confirmation at *order header level*, the system confirms all the operations as completed, if their control key either allows or requires completion confirmation. The operations are confirmed in relation to the quantity confirmed in the order header.

8.37.3 Using the process

In Model Company *A*, completion confirmations are carried out at operation level. On the initial screen, the *Selection* button has been pressed, and all production orders selected for material *DPC1101* (see Fig. 8.215). After selecting the required production order, and selecting *Goto–>Quants/Activities* via the menu, you come to the entry screen for the operation (see Fig. 8.216). Alternatively, or in addition to this, you could carry out confirmation for dates or labour. If the operation has only been partially processed, you can still enter confirmation data to document the current status of the operation. In this case, set the *partial confirmation* indicator. If the operation is fully processed, set the *completion confirmation* indicator. In the example of Model Company A, partial confirmation has been carried out for a quantity of *50* pcs and the document saved.

8.37.4 Navigation information

■ *Menu path*
Logistics –> Production –> Production control –> Confirmation –> Enter –> For order

■ *Transaction code*
CO11, CO15

■ *Ingoing processes in the R/3 Reference Model*
Execution of production order
Inspection point valuation
Plant data collection

■ *Outgoing processes in the R/3 Reference Model*
Incentive wage entry and management
Inspection point valuation
Reprocessing backflushed items

Confirming Individual Capacities

You can also enter confirmations for *individual capacities*. An individual capacity is a subdivision of the capacity requirement of an operation (over several machines or persons). A split number is assigned to each individual capacity that you create (see Fig. 8.214). You can confirm individual capacities in the following two ways. If you enter the capacity category and the split number, you can confirm quantities and activities for an individual capacity or, by entering a summary confirmation, you can enter a degree of processing for all individual capacities. This means that all planned activities are confirmed in proportion to the degree of processing. Sub-operations that have already been confirmed manually are only affected by a summary confirmation if you set the *final confirmation* indicator. This causes the status *final confirmation* to be set in the individual capacity and the capacity requirements to be deleted.

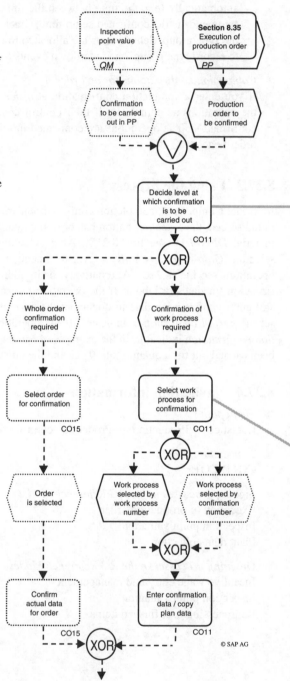

© SAP AG

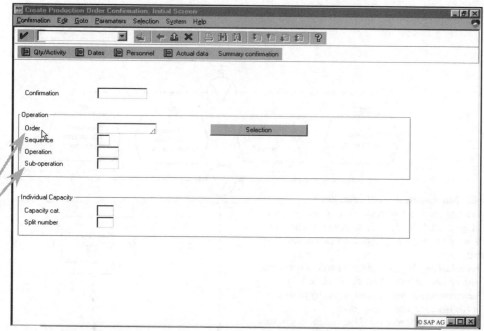

Fig. 8.214: Initial screen of production order confirmation

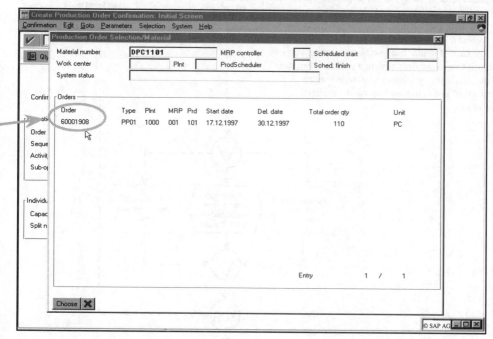

Fig. 8.215: Selecting work process for confirmation

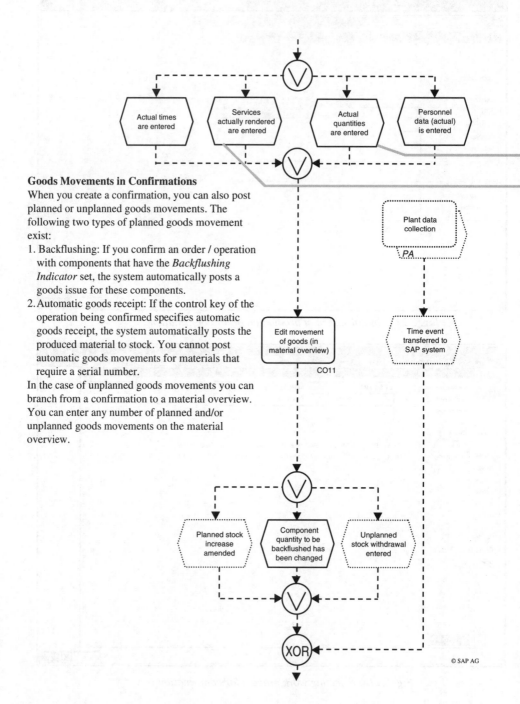

Goods Movements in Confirmations

When you create a confirmation, you can also post planned or unplanned goods movements. The following two types of planned goods movement exist:

1. Backflushing: If you confirm an order / operation with components that have the *Backflushing Indicator* set, the system automatically posts a goods issue for these components.

2. Automatic goods receipt: If the control key of the operation being confirmed specifies automatic goods receipt, the system automatically posts the produced material to stock. You cannot post automatic goods movements for materials that require a serial number.

In the case of unplanned goods movements you can branch from a confirmation to a material overview. You can enter any number of planned and/or unplanned goods movements on the material overview.

© SAP AG

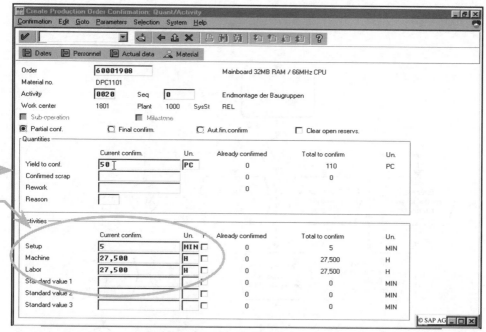

Fig. 8.216: Actual confirmation

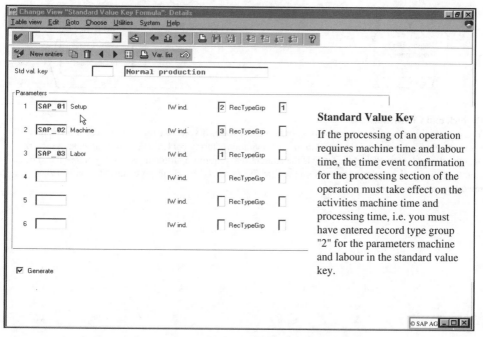

Standard Value Key

If the processing of an operation requires machine time and labour time, the time event confirmation for the processing section of the operation must take effect on the activities machine time and processing time, i.e. you must have entered record type group "2" for the parameters machine and labour in the standard value key.

Fig. 8.217: Customizing of standard value key

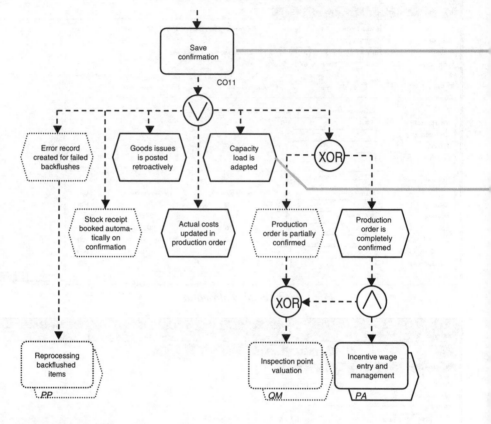

Rework and Confirmations

You can confirm rework at operation or at order header level. If you confirm at order header level, it is assumed that the rework was incurred in the last operation. During confirmation, you can enter a rework quantity directly. The rework quantity is the amount that requires additional processing before it can be counted as yield. When the system determines the *Expected yield variance,* it counts the confirmed rework quantity as yield.

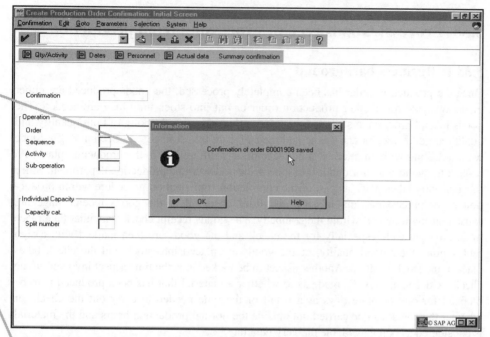

Fig. 8.218: Confirmation of order is saved

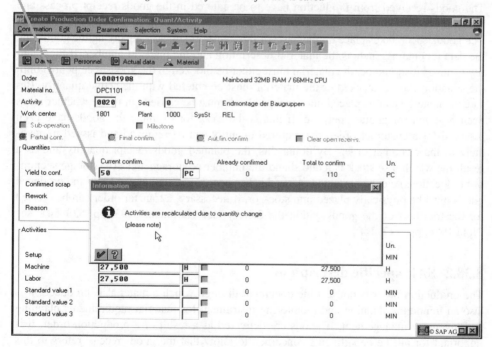

Fig. 8.219: Capacity loads are adapted

8.38 Process: Goods receipt processing from production

8.38.1 Business background

Once the production order has been completely processed, the goods produced are either made available for another production order or put into stock until they are needed. The goods receipt processing steps to be carried out involve the checking of both quantity and quality at goods receipt entry time and their placing into storage (see Section 8.25). Since we are dealing with an internal goods receipt, any differences to the production plan with respect to quantity and/or quality must be discussed with the production department. Since this normally takes place as part of the completion confirmation procedure within production order processing, any missing quantities observed at the goods receipt stage are caused during transport within the company. The goods receipt check can either take place in an area set aside especially for the check and the goods are then marked with a sign representing their good quality, or the goods are placed into stock and the check takes place at the stock location. Another aspect to be looked at is the time aspect involved in the check. A decision must be made as to whether a material that has been produced is to be blocked for one or more days as a result of the time needed to carry out the check, or whether the check can be carried out outside the normal production hours and the material is considered as being available the very next day.

The goods received from production have to be entered in the goods receipt process and the goods receipt slip has to be signed as proof that the goods have indeed been received. The goods check takes place on the basis of the transport slip accompanying the goods and the data it contains, such as the material description and the material number. If the quantity is not as it should be, the material must either be blocked in the goods receipt area until the situation can be checked or the material must be entered with the actual quantity. Before the material can be placed into stock, a check must be carried out to see whether it has been reserved for another purpose. If this is the case, for example the goods have been reserved for a customer order, the required quantity can be removed and issued immediately to the customer order. By doing this, the planned goods receipt quantity and as a result the warehouse stock is reduced and the number of storage areas (or storage sections or bin locations) can be corrected. After this has been done, the remainder of the produced goods must be physically placed into stock or, if necessary, a transfer order can be created for the transport of the goods within the factory (see Hartmann 1993, pp. 528–541; see Pfohl 1996, pp. 117–140).

8.38.2 SAP-specific description

The production order is not just the document through which a material is produced, it is also an important planning and monitoring instrument for material requirements planning and inventory management. If goods are delivered as a result of a production order, it is important for all the departments concerned to know that the goods receipt refers to this production order, as then the goods receipt department can check whether the goods delivered really correspond to the goods planned. When the goods receipt is entered, the system can propose data from the production order (material produced, quantity). This is useful since it facilitates both the entry of the goods receipt and checking (under- and over-delivery). The delivered quantity and the date of delivery are updated in the production order. If the goods are to be placed into stock, a storage location can be defined in the production order. The storage location is proposed by the system when the goods receipt is being entered and can either be accepted or overwritten. If no storage location has been defined in the production order, it must be entered at goods receipt entry time. The goods receipt can be posted into one of three stock types: unrestricted use stock, quality inspection stock or blocked stock. In the production order, it is possible to define whether the material is to be posted into quality inspection stock, but the final decision regarding to which stock the goods issue is to be posted is made at goods receipt time (see SAP – Materials management 1996, S. 6.9).

8.38.3 Using the process

For material *DPC1101* a production order with the number *60001908* has been created. The main boards for Model Company A have been produced, three of which cannot be used (see Fig. 8.220). On the initial screen of the transaction *Goods receipt for order* you enter the document number of the production order. For this example goods receipt document movement type *101* (receipt to stock) has been chosen (see Fig. 8.221). In the next step, you see a selection screen with the items from the production order, for which goods receipt from production can take place. The example shows one item with a quantity of 110 pcs which are accepted and the goods receipt. A material document *50005999* is created and the goods receipt slip printed.

8.38.4 Navigation information

■ *Menu path*
Logistics –> Materials management –> Inventory management –> Goods movement –> Goods receipt –> For order

■ *Transaction code*
MB01, MB1C, MB31

■ *Ingoing processes in the R/3 Reference Model*
Valuation control during inward stock movement
Process management monitoring
Execution of production order

■ *Outgoing processes in the R/3 Reference Model*
Settlement of production order, Inspection lot creation for GR from production
Placement in storage processing, Automatic creation of TO for material document
Settlement of process order, Process record archiving

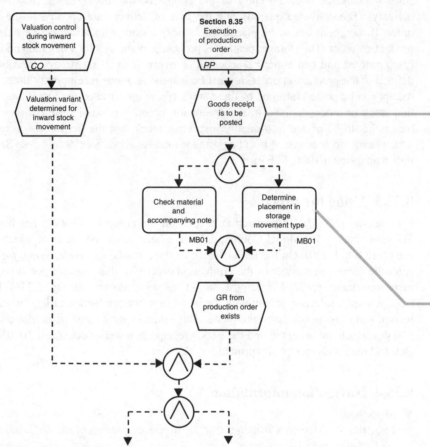

Goods Receipt/Issue Slip (GR/GI Slip)

When you enter the goods receipt, you can print the goods receipt/issue slip (such as a goods receipt slip or a pallet note). There are three versions available for printing a goods receipt/issue slip. When you select the version "individual slip", one GR/GI slip is printed per material document item. When you select the version "individual slip with inspection text", one slip is printed per material document item. In addition, however, the printout includes any quality inspection text if contained in the material master record. In the third version, a "collective slip" is printed containing all of the items of the material document. You can select the desired version when you enter a goods movement.

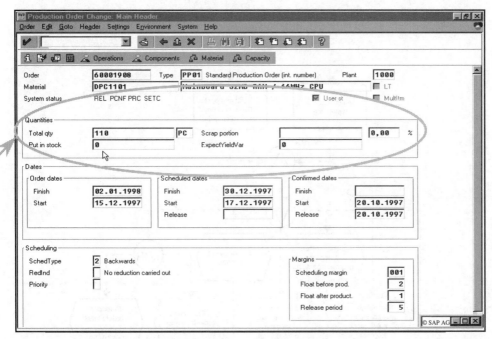

Fig. 8.220: Goods receipt quantities

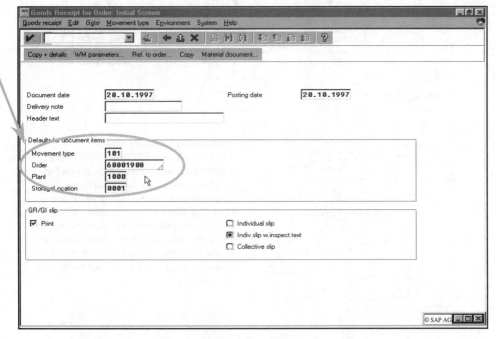

Fig. 8.221: Initial screen goods receipt for order

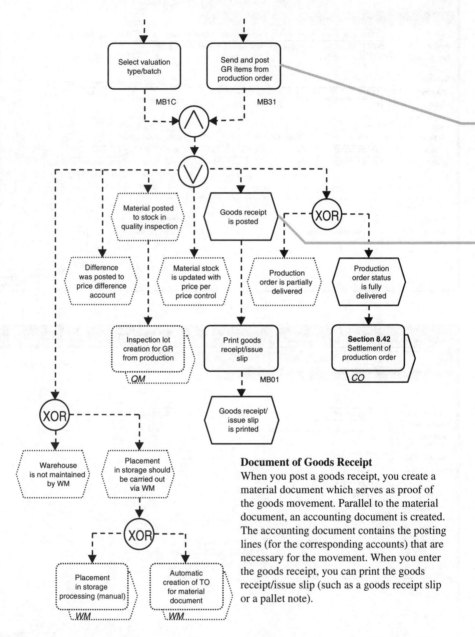

Document of Goods Receipt

When you post a goods receipt, you create a material document which serves as proof of the goods movement. Parallel to the material document, an accounting document is created. The accounting document contains the posting lines (for the corresponding accounts) that are necessary for the movement. When you enter the goods receipt, you can print the goods receipt/issue slip (such as a goods receipt slip or a pallet note).

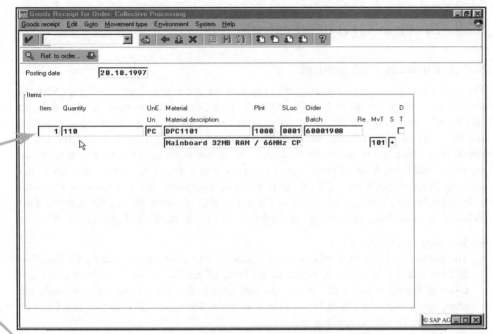

Fig. 8.222: GR – Collective processing

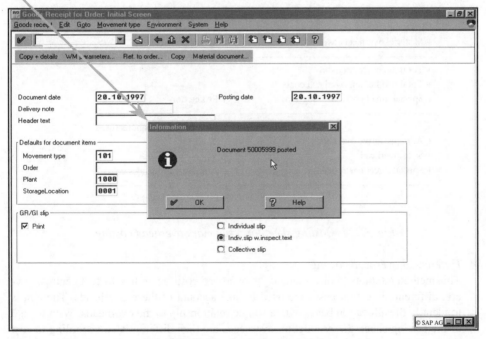

Fig. 8.223: Goods receipt is posted

8.39 Process: Overhead calculation

8.39.1 Business background

The purpose of the overhead costing is to separate the costs into direct costs and overhead costs. Overheads are costs such as those for electricity or general storage costs, which can only be allocated to the product indirectly. The direct costs are allocated directly to activities on a source-related basis, whereas the overhead costs are allocated with the aid of costing rates. The use of an overhead costing is advisable for companies whose activities are performed in multi-level production processes with heterogeneous cost allocation and ongoing product alterations. The majority of these companies are repetitive or make-to-order manufacturers, as it is the series or the order that represents the source element. Two different types of overhead costing are used (see also Haberstock 1987, pp. 177–186):

- *Summary overhead costing*
  The entire overhead costs of a plant are calculated as a single, summary overhead. Either the direct material costs or the direct costs of production (direct labour costs) are taken as the allocation base. It is important to note that the production overheads are charged *without* being split between cost centres. They are added to the direct labour costs as *one* overhead (see Fig. 8.224).

Direct materials costs
+ Material overhead costs   = Material costs

+ Total direct labor costs
+ Total production overhead costs
+ Special direct costs (production)   + Production

                                                            = Cost of goods manufactured
+ Administrative overheads
+ Sales overheads
+ Special direct costs (sales)   + Administration/sales costs
----

                                                            = Cost of goods sold

Fig. 8.224: Costing sheet for a summary overhead costing

- *Differential overhead costing*
  This method attempts to differentiate the overhead costs according to cost centres. Several different allocation bases are used to take account of these overheads. The aim is to identify the allocation bases with a source relationship to the overheads. With the aid of the costing sheet, the production overheads are then differentiated according to cost centres and charged to the associated, direct production wages. The differential overhead costing method is therefore also referred to as wage overhead costing.

8.39.2 SAP-specific description

In order to calculate overheads, control data must be defined in the SAP R/3 System and linked to a *costing sheet*. A costing sheet links all the elements of the overhead costing together. It is defined in Customizing for product cost controlling and contains the following lines (see Fig. 8.225):

■ *Base lines*
These lines are assigned to a calculation base. A calculation base designates a group of cost elements, to which an overhead is to be applied according to identical conditions. The calculation bases are assigned individual cost elements or cost element intervals for each controlling area (see Fig. 8.226). All the material costs or all the costs of production are grouped together, for example, by assigning the relevant cost elements to two calculation bases. From Release 3.0 onwards, different overheads can be applied to all the fixed and variable cost portions of the same base cost element. The overhead amount can depend both on the direct costs (e.g. costs for the materials used, costs for the activities performed) and on the material itself. It is possible to define material-related calculation bases by entering the origin groups in the material master records for the materials used and then specifying these groups in the calculation bases.

■ *Overhead*
When defining an overhead, it is necessary to specify the conditions under which it is to be applied, the amount either in per cent or the per unit of measure and the period for which it is to be applied. A distinction is made in the R/3 System between percentage and quantity-related overheads. If a percentage overhead is defined, a fixed *percentage rate* is charged under certain conditions on top of the base costs concerned. This method enables a percentage overhead of 10%, for example, to be charged on all material costs. If a *quantity-related* overhead is defined, on the other hand, a *fixed amount* is charged under certain conditions on top of the base costs concerned. This method enables $10 per unit of measure, for example, of a material that is withdrawn from stock to be charged on all material costs. In order to be able to calculate with a quantity-related overhead, the *Origin Material* indicator must be set in the material master record of the material that is used. This indicator specifies that the material costs are updated in Controlling with reference to the material number. This ensures that the unit of measure of the material is known to the system.

■ *Totals rows*
These rows are used for subtotals. They can also serve as a reference for an overhead row. In this case, a credit code is used.

Overhead costs are charged to the product in the form of overheads. The R/3 System makes a distinction between overhead costs in the *product costing* and overhead costs in the *base object costing*.

In order to be able to calculate overheads in a *product costing* (with or without a quantity structure), the key for the costing sheet must be entered in the valuation variant in Customizing for product cost controlling, together with a costing variant containing this valuation variant in the initial costing screen. Overheads are calculated *automatically* within the framework of a product costing or a costing run on the basis of the costing sheet that has been entered. The overheads are calculated on the basis of the information contained in the itemization for the costed material. As the system updates an itemization for every element view, the overheads can be calculated for specific element views. A calculation base for the costing element is entered for this purpose in Customizing for product cost controlling, in order to define the element view that is to be used as a basis for calculating overheads. The maximum level of detail when overheads are analyzed in a product costing without a quantity structure is the cost element. It is not possible to analyze the costs at the origin group level.

In order to be able to calculate overheads in a *base object costing*, the key for the costing sheet must be entered in the master record for the base object. If user-defined overhead criteria are to be specified for certain base objects, a costing sheet containing this overhead key must be selected. Overheads are only calculated for those costing items that are assigned to a cost element. The maximum level of detail when overheads are analyzed in a base object costing is likewise the cost element.

The *time* at which the overhead costing takes place depends on the quantity structure. In a *product costing with a quantity structure*, overheads are calculated at the same time as the costing. In a *product costing without a quantity structure* or in a *base object costing*, overheads are calculated at the time the costing is saved, providing it contains a costing item of the *G* type. The overheads are updated under the cost elements defined in the costing sheet. In addition to the two applications described here, overhead costings referred to any cost object are possible (production order, run schedule header, process order, sales order, project, etc.).

8.39.3 Using the process

A number of parameters must be set before the overhead costing can be started (see Fig. 8.229). The costing sheet (see Fig. 8.225) contains the freely selectable parameters that can be defined flexibly. This sheet consists of several rows, which are processed from top to bottom when the overhead is calculated. The calculation bases must be updated first of all. The base rates for cost elements *400000* to *419999* have been set for Model Company A (see Fig. 8.226). The associated overhead types, for example *C000* for material overheads, have been specified in the costing sheet. The overhead rows contain percentage overhead rates. These are entered on a separate detail screen. A percentage rate of *20%* has been entered for Model Company A for the *C000* overhead for each of controlling areas *1000* and *2000* (see Fig. 8.227). A credit code must be entered in the overhead rows. This code contains the credit rules (credit cost element, credit object = *cost centre* or *order* and validity period). A credit cost element *655110* has been specified for Model Company A with the relevant cost centre *4130*. You can perform a test run if you wish before finally running the overhead costing (see Fig. 8.229).

8.39.4 Navigation information

■ *Menu path*

1) Tools –> Business Engineering –> Customizing –> Controlling –> Product Cost Controlling –> Product Cost Planning –> Basic Settings for Product Costing –> Overhead

2) Accounting –> Controlling –> Product Cost Accounting –> Order-related production –> Period-end closing –> Overhead –> Individ. processing

■ *Transaction code*
KZS2, KZE2, KGP2, KGI2

■ *Ingoing processes in the R/3 Reference Model*
Transfer of primary costs
Simultaneous costing of cost object
Simultaneous cost object costing with allocation costing
Simultaneous costing in process manufacturing
Production order – simultaneous costing
Simultaneous costing in sales-order-related production
Simultaneous costing in engineer-to-order production
Order release (investment)
Project release (investment)
Order planning with cost assessment an overhead cost
Order planning with static and flexible standard costing
Project cost planning and revenue planning

■ *Outgoing processes in the R/3 Reference model*
Order budgeting
Project cost and revenue planning, project results analysis
Internal order settlement
Periodic settlement
Period-end closing when creating non material goods
Period-end closing in process manufacturing
Period-end closing in repetitive manufacturing
Period-end closing in production order processing
Simultaneous costing in sales-order-related production
Period-end closing in sales-order-related production
Project results analysis

Overhead Calculation

The overhead calculation functions allow you to apply indirect costs to your orders using predefined overhead rates. The calculation is based on the individual primary cost elements which most significantly influence the different types of overhead. In a manufacturing company, for example, these are normally labour and material costs. In order to make an overhead calculation, you must first define the calculation base, overhead and credit. This control data must then be linked in a costing sheet. To apply overhead to an order, you must enter the key of the costing sheet you want to use for your overhead rates in the field of the object (i.e. order, project, object of the calculation etc.).

Costing Sheet

The costing sheet combines all the different components of an overhead calculation (i. e. base, overhead and credit). It comprises multiple lines that are processed top to bottom during the overhead calculation. Base lines are defined by the assignment of a calculation base and determine the cost element base to which overhead is applied. Overhead lines are defined by the assignment of an overhead and can refer to a base line or a totals line. Totals lines are used to generate subtotals, and have no calculation bases or overhead assigned to them.

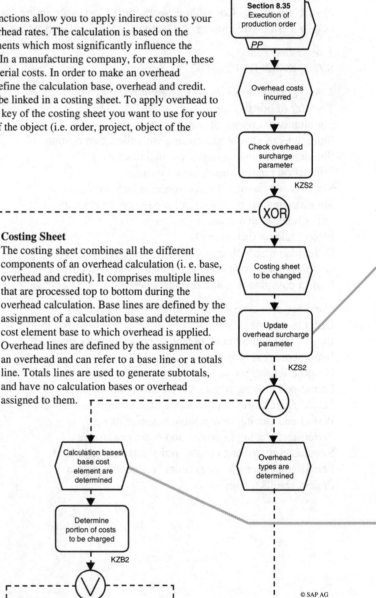

© SAP AG

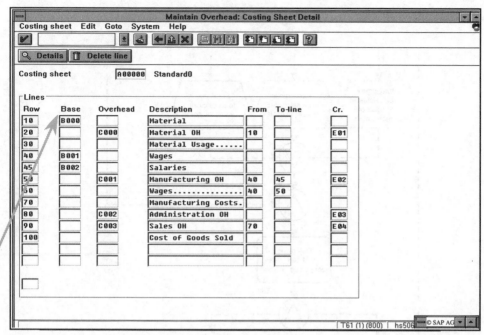

Fig. 8.225: Stucture of costing sheet

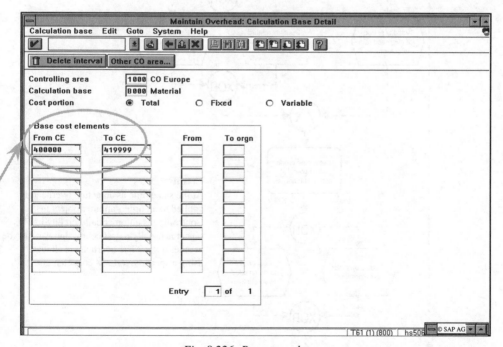

Fig. 8.226: Base cost elements

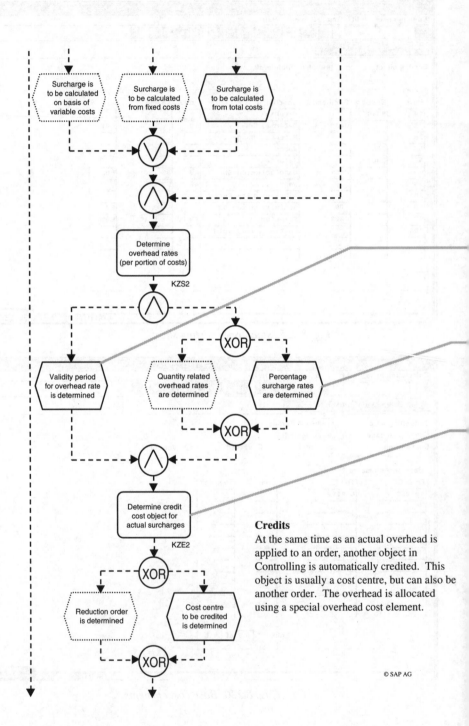

Credits

At the same time as an actual overhead is applied to an order, another object in Controlling is automatically credited. This object is usually a cost centre, but can also be another order. The overhead is allocated using a special overhead cost element.

© SAP AG

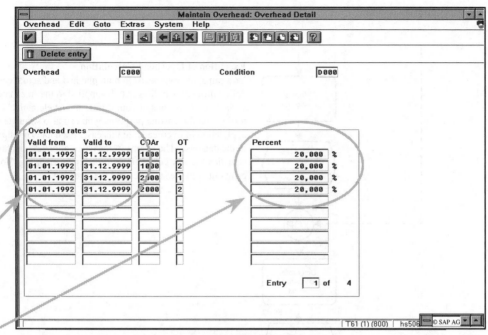

Fig. 8.227: Validity period for overhead rates

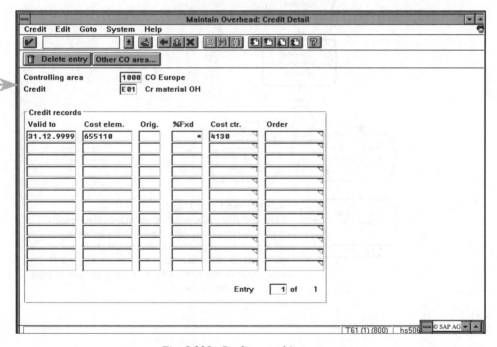

Fig. 8.228: Credit cost object

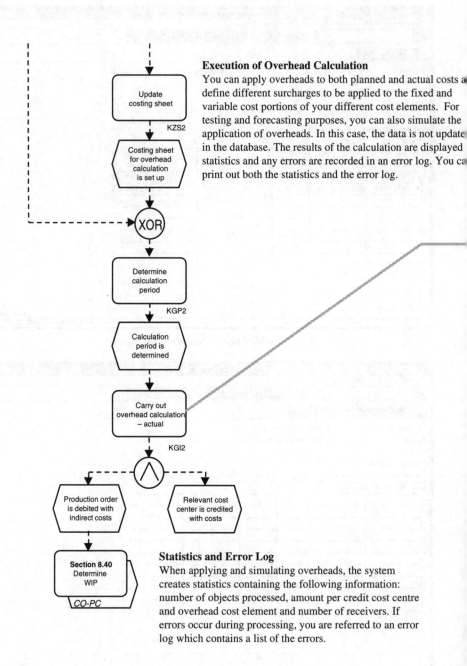

Execution of Overhead Calculation

You can apply overheads to both planned and actual costs a define different surcharges to be applied to the fixed and variable cost portions of your different cost elements. For testing and forecasting purposes, you can also simulate the application of overheads. In this case, the data is not update in the database. The results of the calculation are displayed statistics and any errors are recorded in an error log. You ca print out both the statistics and the error log.

Statistics and Error Log

When applying and simulating overheads, the system creates statistics containing the following information: number of objects processed, amount per credit cost centre and overhead cost element and number of receivers. If errors occur during processing, you are referred to an error log which contains a list of the errors.

© SAP AG

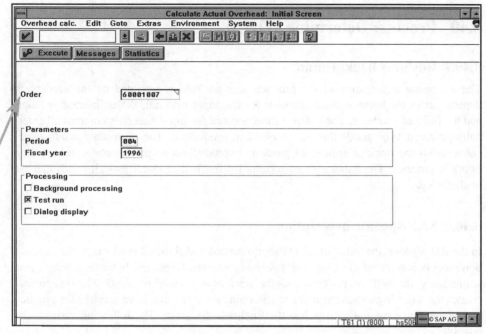

Fig. 8.229: Initial screen of actual overhead calculation

Note

You can repeat the overhead calculation for any period as often as you like. If the values
on the order or in the overhead definition have changed, the system only applies the
difference. This may be a positive or a negative value.

8.40 Process: Determine WIP

8.40.1 Business background

The increasing aggregation of the products that are sold is recorded by the accounting department in the balance sheet accounts for the input material, the unfinished products and the finished products. The balance sheet account for input materials contains all externally procured WIP goods that are received in production. The *unfinished products* account shows the stock of unfinished products in production on the balance sheet key date (work in process). The balance sheet account for finished products lists all goods that are ready for sale.

8.40.2 SAP-specific description

In the R/3 System, the value of all the semi-finished and finished products in the production process is referred to as the *WIP (work in process)*. In general business management terminology, the WIP is also known as the *stock of unfinished products*. The system calculates the work in process, in order to determine the *costs* that have accrued for production orders that have not yet reached the final delivery stage. The following variants are possible:

■ *Calculation of work in process for each order*
  This function is supported within the framework of the period-end closing for the cost object costing in conjunction with order-related production.

■ *Calculation of work in process for all production orders*
  This function is implemented via the reconciliation ledger for all orders belonging to the *Production* object class.

The *work in process* that is determined is periodically forwarded to financial accounting. You can define a posting rule, which links the work in process for which activation is mandatory with two G/L accounts, such as *stock of unfinished products* (balance sheet) and *changes involving stocks* (profit and loss statement), in Customizing for product cost controlling.

A results analysis key is also defined in Customizing for product cost controlling (see Fig. 8.230). This key integrates the control parameters for calculating the WIP. A link is then formed between the results analysis key and the system status of the order (this step is known as the *valuation method*).

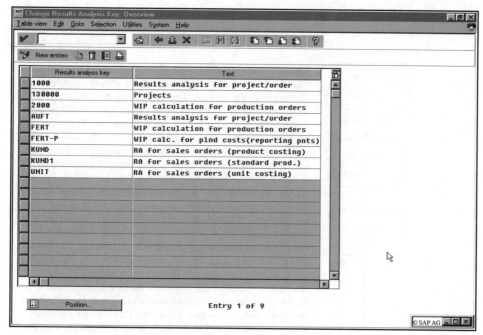

Fig. 8.230 Customizing the results analysis key

8.40.3 Using the process

Before the system can start calculating the work in process, you must specify the controlling area and the order to which the calculation is to apply. You must also specify the period and the fiscal year, that is, the month up to and including which the WIP is to be calculated. The specified results analysis version determines, for example, whether the calculated data is to be forwarded to financial accounting, a cross-company valuation can be carried out or a valuation simulated.

8.40.4 Navigation information

■ *Menu path*
Accounting –> Controlling –> Product cost accounting –> Order-related production –> Period-end closing –> Work in process –> Individ. Processing –> Calculate

■ *Transaction code*
KKAX

■ *Ingoing processes in the R/3 Reference Model*
Overhead calculation

■ *Outgoing processes in the R/3 Reference Model*
Variance calculation,   Settlement production order,
Product cost analysis in order-related manufacturing

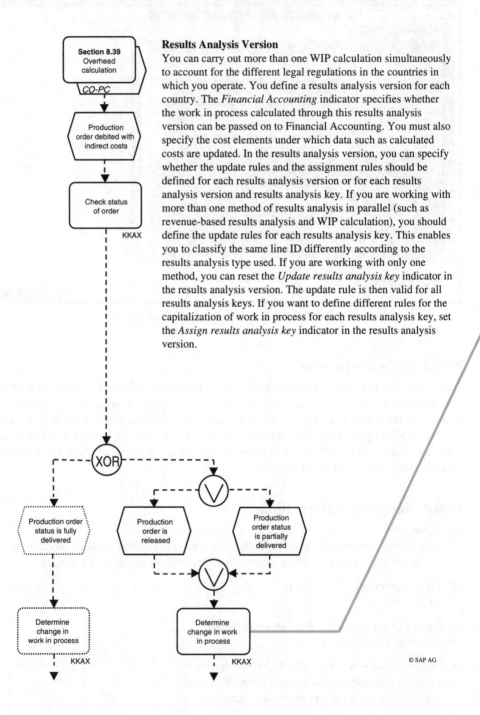

Section 8.39
Overhead
calculation

CO-PC

Production
order debited with
indirect costs

Check status
of order

KKAX

XOR

Production order
status is fully
delivered

Production
order is
released

Production
order status
is partially
delivered

Determine
change in
work in process

Determine
change in work
in process

KKAX

KKAX

© SAP AG

Results Analysis Version

You can carry out more than one WIP calculation simultaneously to account for the different legal regulations in the countries in which you operate. You define a results analysis version for each country. The *Financial Accounting* indicator specifies whether the work in process calculated through this results analysis version can be passed on to Financial Accounting. You must also specify the cost elements under which data such as calculated costs are updated. In the results analysis version, you can specify whether the update rules and the assignment rules should be defined for each results analysis version or for each results analysis version and results analysis key. If you are working with more than one method of results analysis in parallel (such as revenue-based results analysis and WIP calculation), you should define the update rules for each results analysis key. This enables you to classify the same line ID differently according to the results analysis type used. If you are working with only one method, you can reset the *Update results analysis key* indicator in the results analysis version. The update rule is then valid for all results analysis keys. If you want to define different rules for the capitalization of work in process for each results analysis key, set the *Assign results analysis key* indicator in the results analysis version.

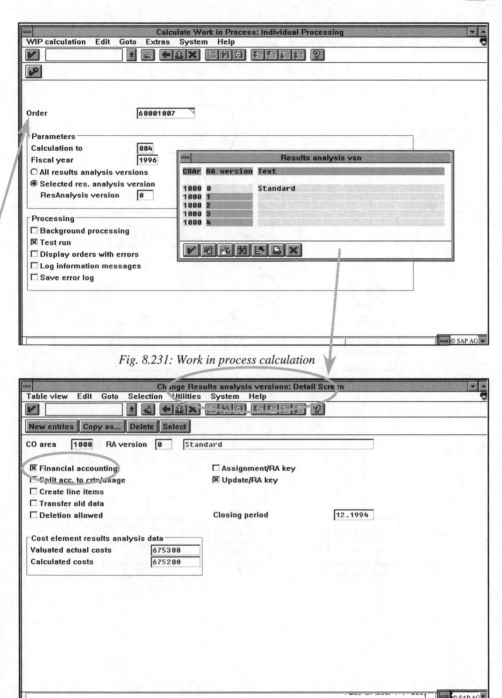

Fig. 8.231: Work in process calculation

Fig. 8.232: Customizing of results analysis versions

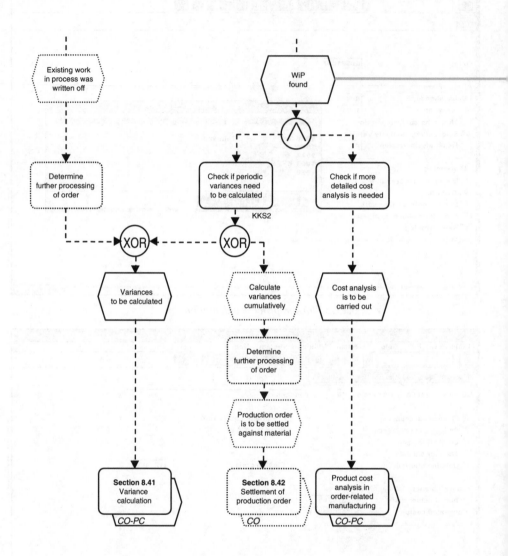

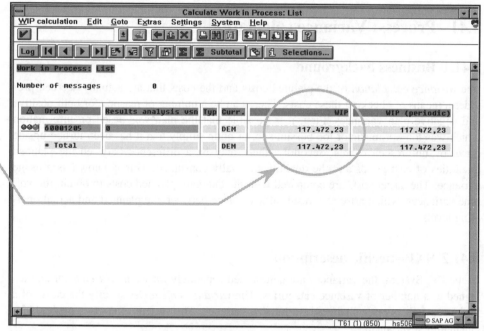

Fig. 8.233: List of work in process

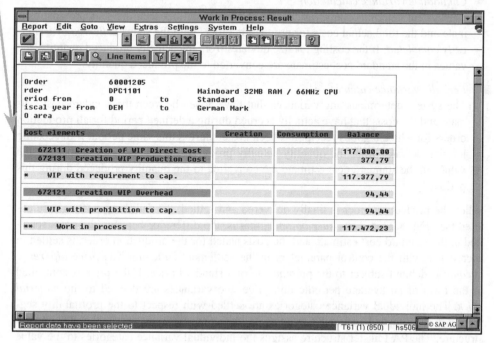

Fig. 8.234: Standard report from the info system of cost elements/orders/WIP

8.41 Process: Variance calculation

8.41.1 Business background

The *variance calculation* of the planned costs and the costs that are actually accrued provides a means of checking these costs. There can be a number of reasons for both positive and negative plan variances. First, it is possible that the plan was based on information which was too optimistic or too pessimistic, or quite simply that it has been turned upside down by unforeseen events. Secondly, there may be a difference between the planned quantities of cost goods and the quantities actually consumed. This is known as a usage variance. The target costs are compared with the charged, planned costs to obtain the volume variances, which arise as a result of a variance between the planned and actual operating levels.

8.41.2 SAP-specific description

In the R/3 System, the variances are determined separately *for each cost element* and assigned to a number of variance categories. The *variance categories* specify the cause of a variance, such as price changes or a lot-size variance. The system offers two methods for calculating a variance:

■ *Cumulative variance calculation*
The system determines any variances that have arisen between the standard cost estimate and the total actual costs for production orders with the status *delivered* or *technically completed*. If the costing lot size deviates from the actually produced quantity, the values in the standard cost estimate are converted to the produced quantity.

■ *Periodic variance calculation*
The system determines any variances that have arisen between the standard cost estimate and the costs that have actually accrued during a defined period for all production orders for which a goods receipt has been posted during this same period. If the costing lot size deviates from the quantity actually produced during the relevant period, the values in the standard cost estimate are converted to the quantity produced during this period.

When the production order is finally delivered and settled, the following postings are entered (see Fig. 8.235). The *order balance*, that is, the difference between the costs specified in the standard cost estimate and the costs stated for the production order, is settled in accordance with the control parameters in the settlement structure. The *price difference account* is debited subject to the prerequisite of a standard price. If the price is controlled in the form of an average periodic unit price, the variances are debited to the *material stock*. The individual variance categories are settled with respect to the profitability segment for the finished material according to the control parameters in the PA transfer structure. The PA transfer structure assigns the individual variance categories to the value fields of an operating concern.

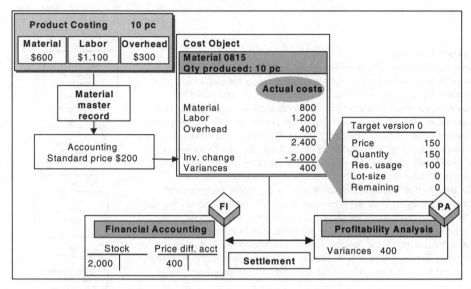

*Fig. 8.235: Relationships relevant to a variance calculation
(taken from: SAP product cost controlling 1996, pp. 5–10)*

8.41.3 Using the process

Before a variance can be calculated in the R/3 System, the order, the period and fiscal year to which the calculation is to apply must be entered. If the *All Target Cost Versions* option is selected, the variances are calculated for all the target cost versions in the controlling area. The target cost versions determine which values are compared in order to determine the variance, which variance categories are calculated and how the actual costs are distributed within a cost object hierarchy.

8.41.4 Navigation information

■ *Menu path*
Accounting –> Controlling –> Product cost accounting –> Order-related production –>
Period-end closing –> Variances –> Individual processing

■ *Transaction code*
KKS2

■ *Ingoing processes in the R/3 Reference Model*
Period-end closing in process manufacturing, Period-end closing in production order processing

■ *Outgoing processes in the R/3 Reference Model*
Controlling in process manufacturing, Controlling in order-related production
Settlement of production order, Settlement of process order

Variance Calculation

The system does the following during variance calculation. It selects the objects to be processed and calculates the target costs for each object. It calculates the target costs, so that the same reference basis is used for calculating variances between the actual costs and the planned costs. The planned costs are adjusted to the actual costs in relation to the actual quantity and the planned quantity. Then the system calculates scrap for each object and the costs for scrap are deducted from the total actual costs. This ensures that the actual costs relating to the yield quantity are taken into account. The system calculates the costs to be controlled for each object. They are calculated so that variance calculation only finds genuine variances and ignores the costs for work in process and scrap. The system deducts the value of the work in process and the scrap from the actual costs. It compares the target costs for each cost element or cost element and origin group with the costs to be controlled, and puts the variances then calculated into variance categories. Finally, the system updates an amount for each variance category calculated for each cost element or cost element and origin group.

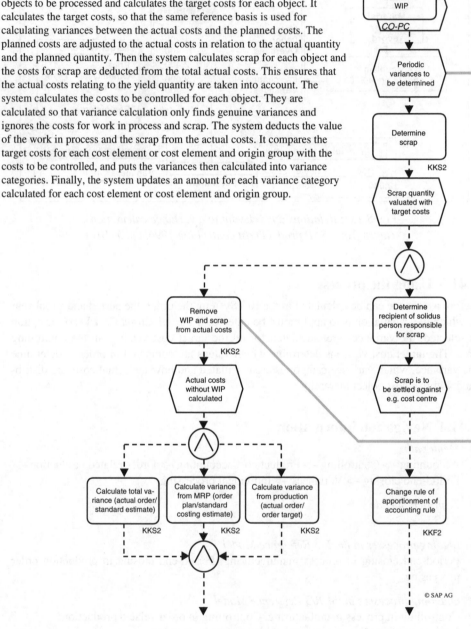

676

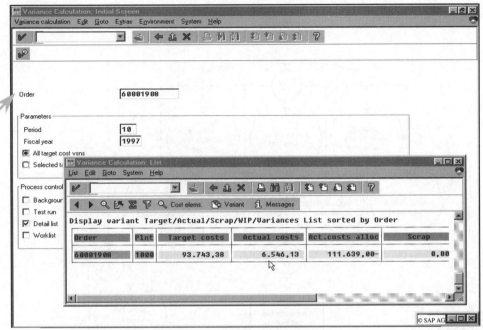

Fig. 8.236: Initial screen of variance calculation

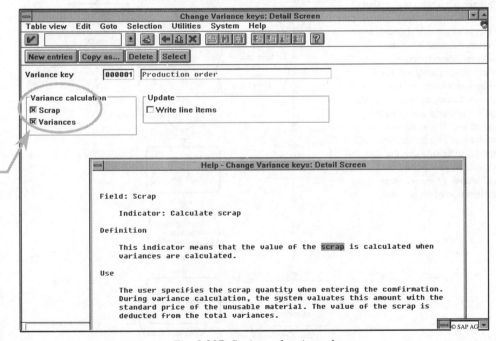

Fig. 8.237: Settings of variance key

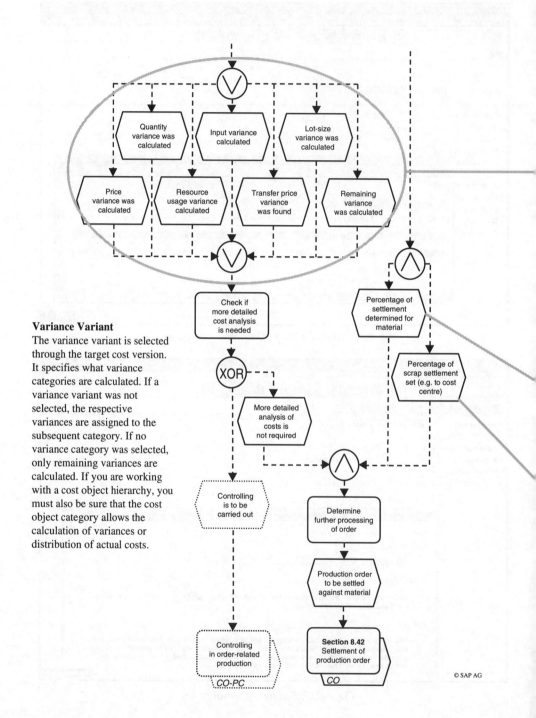

Variance Variant
The variance variant is selected through the target cost version. It specifies what variance categories are calculated. If a variance variant was not selected, the respective variances are assigned to the subsequent category. If no variance category was selected, only remaining variances are calculated. If you are working with a cost object hierarchy, you must also be sure that the cost object category allows the calculation of variances or distribution of actual costs.

© SAP AG

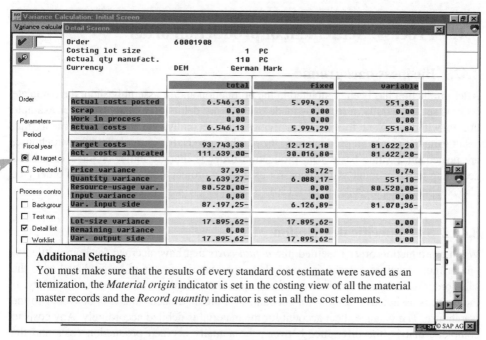

Fig. 8.238: Settings of variance calculation

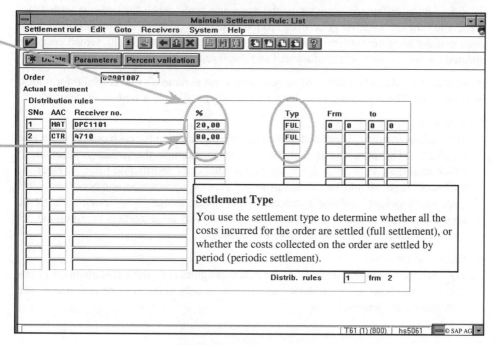

Fig. 8.239: Settlement rule

8.42 Process: Settlement of production order

8.42.1 Business background

After production has been completed in the production and/or assembly shop, the complete order is settled. Firstly, a record is made of the order debits on a value basis, for example due to withdrawals or to external activities, and secondly, the inward movements that result from the receipt in production of the finished goods, for example into the warehouse, are posted on a value basis. The production order is thereby either credited or debited according to the account assignment, for example a project, cost centre or sales order (see also Nuppeney/Raps 1993, pp. 110–120).

8.42.2 SAP-specific description

When a production order is settled, the *actual costs* that have accrued for it are settled to one or more receiver objects, for example to the material that is to be produced or to the sales order. Offsetting entries that credit the production order are created automatically. If the order is assigned to a *material* account, it is credited each time it is delivered to the warehouse. The balance sheet account for the material is debited accordingly. Any costs to complete, that is, the difference between the actually accrued production costs and the costs credited to the order as a result of the movement into the warehouse, are posted into the stock, price difference accounts or the operating profit when the order is settled, according to how the material price is controlled. The debit postings also remain in the production order after the settlement and can be displayed at any time. The settled costs are updated for the receiver object concerned and displayed in reporting.

In order for a production order to be settled, settlement parameters that are valid for it must be maintained. These parameters include a *settlement profile* and a *settlement structure*.

- *Settlement profile*
  The settlement profile is defined in the customizing function for each type of order (see Fig. 8.240). This profile is used to specify data, for example the settlement receivers to which an order can be settled, the maximum number of distribution rules, whether the settlement share should be calculated in per cent or equivalence numbers (*settlement rule*) and a default settlement structure. The system assigns a *settlement rule* to the production order automatically when it is opened. This assignment is based on the default rule defined in Customizing (see Fig. 8.240).

- *Settlement structure*
  The settlement structure determines the actual assignment of debit cost elements to settlement cost elements. Each debit cost element is only allowed to be assigned to one settlement cost element.

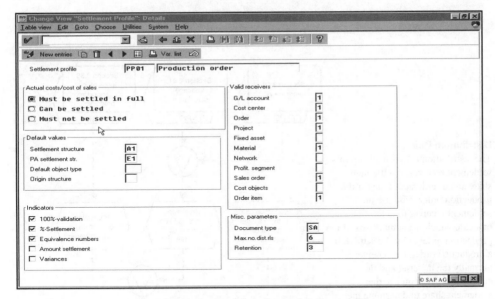

Fig. 8.240: Customizing the settlement profile

8.42.3 Using the process

The purpose of settling an order is to transfer the costs of this order to target objects affecting stocks or net income. Order *60001908* is settled to material *DPC1101* in Model Company *A* (see Fig. 8.241). The settlement type *FUL* for full settlement has been changed over in this model Company to *PER* for periodic settlement. Enter the period and the order number on the initial screen (see Fig. 8.242). The operating profit and the credit to the order are shown apportioned to the various cost elements (see Fig. 8.243). The actual operating profit deviates from the planned figures, because the manufactured quantities are less. The new status in the production order documents the settlement after implementation.

8.42.4 Navigation information

■ *Menu path*
Logistics –> Production –> Production control –> Period-end closing –> Settlement

■ *Transaction code*
KO88

■ *Ingoing processes in the R/3 Reference Model*
Variance calculation; Period-end closing in production order processing; Goods receipt processing from production

■ *Outgoing processes in the R/3 Reference Model*
Reorganization of production order; Transfer of production variances, production order reorganization

Distribution Rule

The distribution rule is made up of a settlement receiver, a settlement share and a settlement type for the production order. You use the settlement receiver to determine the object to which the actual costs of the production order are to be settled. In a production order, the receiver is normally the material and the customer order. You use the settlement share to determine the percentage rate or the equivalence number with which the costs are apportioned to the individual settlement receivers. You use the settlement type to determine how the costs that were incurred for the order are to be settled (full settlement).

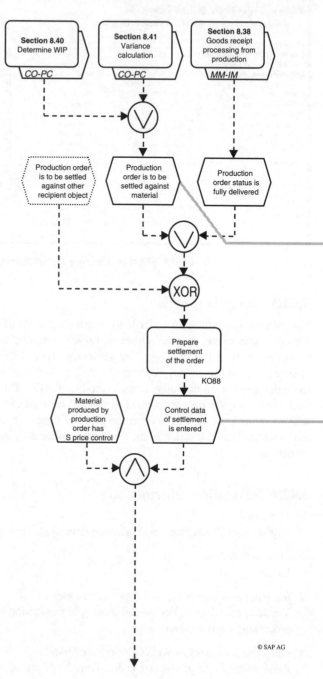

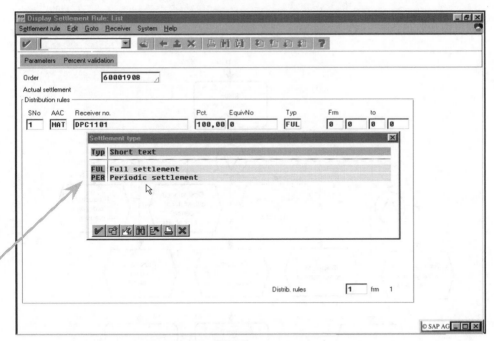

Fig. 8.241: Settlement rule

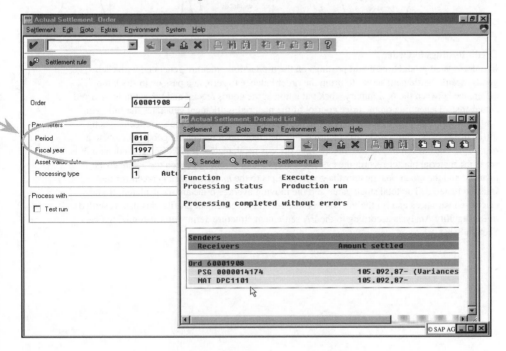

Fig. 8.242: Production order settlement

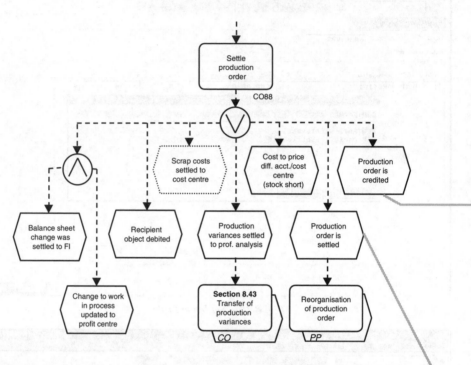

Credit Postings to Order

In order-related production, credit postings on the production order are generated with each goods receipt. Settlement serves to bring the order balance to zero, and pass on to stock the difference between the preliminary stock valuation at the goods receipt and the actually incurred actual costs. Depending on the price control of the material, settlement generates the following posting. If price control indicator **S** is set in the material master record, the system charges the difference between the actual costs incurred and the credit postings for the goods receipts to a *price difference account*. The moving average price is recalculated. If price control indicator **V** is set in the material master record, the system charges the difference between the actual costs incurred and the credit postings for the goods receipts to the *material stock account* for the finished material. The total stock value and the moving average price are recalculated. If you calculated variances and set the *Variances* indicator in the settlement profile, this data is settled to Profitability Analysis according to the PA settlement structure defined in Customizing (see Section 8.43).

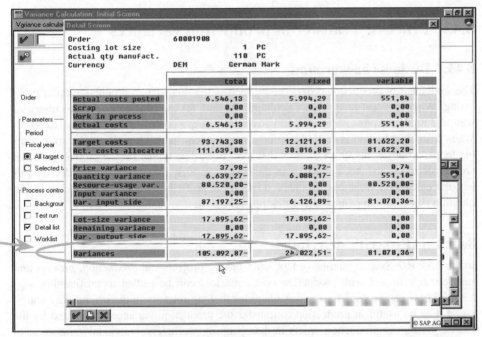

Fig. 8.243: Production order is credited

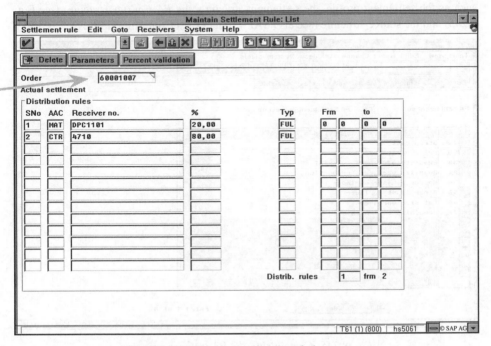

Fig. 8.244: Production order is settled

8.43 Process: Transfer of production variances

8.43.1 Business background

The settlement of production orders can be seen as the final step in production order processing. When the cost factors are calculated, the data for the final costing is calculated as well, the final costing is performed and any variances are posted in the financial accounts. When a stock valuation is carried out for average prices, which are differentiated according to cost components, the variances that have been determined for the production order are transferred to the stock analysis. In the case of a stock valuation for fixed/default values, the calculated variances are charged off in the profitability analysis for the period in question (see also Nuppeney/Raps 1993, pp. 110–120).

8.43.2 SAP-specific description

In the SAP R/3 System internal orders, sales orders, projects and *production, process and run schedule orders* with production cost collectors can be settled to profitability segments. These can be used for various functions that are relevant to the *profitability analysis*. It may be useful in production to transfer the production variances calculated by the CO-PC System to production orders in the operating profit. The individual variance categories can be transferred separately. The settlement is controlled by various parameters, such as the settlement profile, the settlement structure, the *PA transfer structure* (see Fig. 8.245) and the source structure (see also SAP-Product Cost Controlling 1996, S. 5.7–5.9).

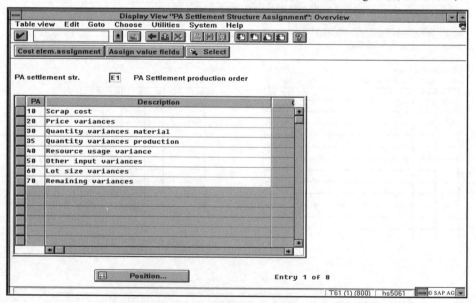

Fig. 8.245: Customizing the PA transfer structure

8.43.3 Using the process

When a production order is settled, the CO-PA System creates a line item for every item in the settlement rule that is assigned to a profitability segment account and updates the segment level concerned. The posted amount is assigned to the value field defined in the PA transfer structure for the system setting (see Fig. 8.245). This step assigns the variance categories (possibly still related to cost elements) to the value fields of an operating concern (see Fig. 8.246). In Model Company *A* the value field *VV300* (material variances) has been assigned to PA transfer structure *E1* with the profitability analysis assignment *30* (material quantity deviation). You can assign more than one variance category to a value field if you wish.

You can settle the orders either in a dialog or in the background in the individual applications. The result of the settlement is formatted in a log (see Fig. 8.247).

8.43.4 Navigation information

- *Menu path*
  Accounting –> Controlling –> Product cost accounting –> Order-related production
  –> Period-end closing –> Settlement –> Individ. processing

- *Transaction code*
  KO88

- *Ingoing processes in the R/3 Reference Model*
  Settlement of process order
  Settlement of run schedule header
  Value control with overhead costing
  Value control with static standard costing
  Value control with flexible standard costing

- *Outgoing processes in the R/3 Reference Model*

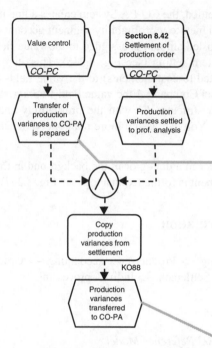

Production Variances

In the R/3 System, you can settle production orders and run schedules with production cost collectors to profitability segments. If the products are controlled by a standard price (S), it may be useful to transfer the production variances calculated in CO-PC for final production orders as well as run schedule headers (settled periodically) to CO-PA. The individual variance categories can be transferred separately.

PA (Profitability Analysis) Settlement Structure

The PA settlement structure is required to settle the production variances to CO-PA. The fixed and variable costs incurred in a cost element can be assigned to different value fields of the operating concern. You assign this settlement structure to a settlement profile. The individual variance categories, such as price variance, quantity variance, etc., are assigned to cost element-related PA settlement assignments. You assign these PA settlement assignments to the value fields of an operating concern in this PA settlement structure.

Value Fields

The production variances which you have settled are saved in the value fields. When you open the contribution margin report (see Section 8.54) this data is displayed in the respective lines of the multi-level cost absorption. The operating concern comprises one or more items, or "PA settlement assignments". There, you assign a cost element group and a variance category to one value field in the operating concern.

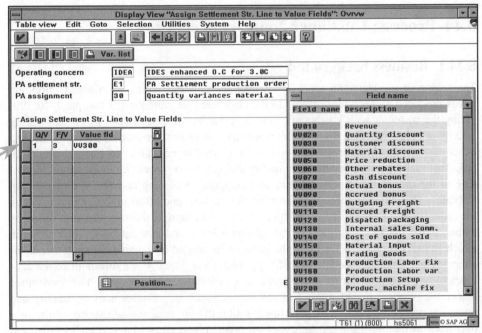

Fig. 8.246: Assign settlement str. line to value fields

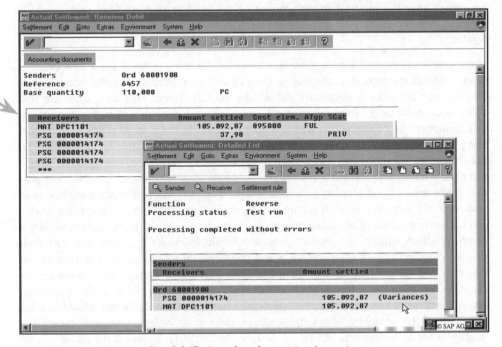

Fig. 8.247: Actual settlement (variances)

8.44 Process: Customer contract processing

8.44.1 Business background

The selling of products and services involves all activities which contribute to bringing goods produced and services offered to the customer (see Gutenberg 1984, pp. 1–6). Providing the customer with goods created in an organization can be seen as the key selling activity in industrial concerns. For an organization to offer a product means that a demand either exists or has been created. Therefore, in general terms, sales processing includes all tasks from sales prospecting through inquiry and quotation processing to the actual processing of the order, right up to delivery and shipping processing and the resulting billing activities. The initiating force for the order and the time and effort involved in processing the order depend very much on the type of service offered in the target market – for example, is the market consumer- or manufacturer-led – and consequently, on the way in which an order is placed – for example, is the order created for a particular customer or for an anonymous market (see Riebel 1965, pp. 663–685). Equally, we differentiate the activities to be performed during order processing as follows: activities which are performed before the physical manufacturing of the product such as pre-sales activity, inquiry and quotation processing; activities performed during the physical manufacturing of the product such as monitoring the progress of an order in special mechanical engineering and plant engineering or controlling the planned costs in the building industry; and activities performed after the physical manufacturing of the product such as final settlement for projects, delivery processing and billing (see VDI 1991, pp. 10–90; pp. Pfohl 1996, pp. 69–170).

If the product is created for an anonymous market, the driving force for a new order is usually market research. If a company produces goods as a result of an order from a specific customer, the order is frequently initiated by the sales force. Therefore, there are also differences in the tasks of the sales force for consumer goods with a short life expectancy and consumer and capital goods with a longer lifespan. In the case of goods with a short lifespan, the sales force's main task is to sell the product to a middleman who passes on the product to the actual consumer. Longer-life consumer goods are, among other things, technically more complex and therefore the consumer requires information about the product in the form of consultation with a sales representative. More in-depth consultation in particular of a technical nature is required in the capital goods industry as goods are produced for use in processing or manufacturing products. The customer in this case is usually a company which expects the product to meet specific functional requirements. The high degree of complexity of these products and the technical requirements require both the customer and the manufacturer to have extensive specialized knowledge. Therefore, for capital goods companies, technical consultation plays a signicant role in order processing. As well as general customer care, the following tasks can primarily be considered as sales activities. If the company offers its products using sales orders, quotation processing usually needs to be performed first of all (see Section 9.4). Before a quotation can be created, a customer inquiry has usually come in. Depending on how often inquiries come in, inquiries are often evaluated for selection. How quotations are created depends on the type of company and can include the following activities (see Backhaus 1984, pp. 113–152; cf. VDI 1983, pp. 3–43):

- Checking the technical feasibility of customer requirements
- Pricing (determining the manufacturing costs and the sales price)
- Determining the delivery date
- Checking availability and reserving stock

As the activities listed above show, data in other areas needs to be accessed at the quotation creation stage. Equally, extensive activities in other areas of the company are initiated at this stage. In the case of customer-oriented production, cost information must be determined during quotation creation. During preliminary costing, basic production data such as bills of materials, routings, and means of production need to be accessed. The scope of quotation processing, which can result in the placing and processing of an order, depends on the degree of standardization of the product, the influence the customer has and the product structure. Therefore, in the case of customer-specific development and production, for example, when non-standard or partially standard products are to be produced, the sales data in the order needs to be forwarded to development/construction. Here the required construction papers are created on the basis of the technical specification. The costs are based on the type of construction (new, modification, variant construction or construction according to a fixed concept).

If a company produces for an anonymous market, planning for the sales programme is not initiated by concrete sales orders. Therefore, when launching new products onto the market, the company must base its prognoses on market analyses. If the company produces standard products which have already been sold for some time, prognoses can be made using past data but taking into account expected future influences on demand. Due to the midterm to long-term nature of planning, demand can be planned on the basis of product group.

When an order is placed, the type of order processing must be defined. If the company produces for an anonymous market, order processing is limited to shipping processing from stock, delivery note creation and billing. If the company produces for specific customers, the internal procedures for production and adminstration must be defined and monitored.

Orders can be one-time in the same way as purchase orders and they can be recurring orders. These recurring orders are often set up in practice as long-term contracts. They can be divided up into the following phases: the contract negotiating phase, in which delivery and payment terms are often agreed on for a specified period; the contract implementation phase, in which the goods are delivered and settled several times over a specified period. This type of agreement, in which the customer agrees to accept a specified quantity of a particular product over a given period, is known as an outline agreement. Outline agreements can be either contracts or scheduling agreements. In a *contract,* a sales quantity (quantity contract) or a sales value (value contract) is defined. However, the delivery dates and quantities remain open when the contract is finalized. As with the contract, the scheduling agreement is also seen as a special form of order processing. However, whereas the contract simply contains a quantity or value and a time period, the *scheduling agreement* also contains binding delivery dates and quantities.

It makes sense to use outline agreements when the sales quantities are relatively easy to foresee and when the product spectrum is made up of the same or similar products or product groups to make planning easier. Therefore, outline agreements are often used in component supplier firms in the automotive industry in which the same or similar parts are installed in various categories of product (for example, seats, radios, wheel rims).

8.44.2 SAP-specific description

In the R/3 System scheduling agreements, you can process quantity contracts and value contracts. The quantity contract in the R/3 System contains basic quantity and price information. However, the delivery dates and quantities are not specified. The customer fulfils a contract by placing orders on the basis of the contract. These orders are known are release orders (see Section 8.45).

To create a quantity contract, you must first of all enter a sales document type and, if necessary, maintain the relevant organizational data. The values for the sales organization, distribution channel and the product division are usually proposed from user-specific parameters. You have the option of entering a sales office and a sales group. You then maintain the contract-specific data such as the customer number of the sold-to party, the customer purchase order and the target quantities (see SAP – Sales and Distribution 1994, pp. 6.8–6.9).

You change a quantity contract by entering the document number in the *Contract* field or by searching for it using a matchcode. If release orders have already been created for a contract, the R/3 System issues a message which informs you that subsequent documents should be taken into account and gives you the option of displaying the subsequent documents. You can also display the following information for each release order item:

■ Delivery overview in which the ordered, confirmed, delivered and billed quantities are displayed

■ Status overview which lists the various status characteristics of the document items

■ Release overview in which the release orders are displayed with the individual release quantities and the overall release quantity

At any time, you can display one or more contracts and perform activities such as accessing information from an existing contract to answer a customer query, obtaining an overview of incomplete contracts, or evaluating all contracts for a particular business partner or material. A quantity contract is completed when it no longer contains any deliverable items. If, however, a contract still contains open items, you can still assign the "completed" status to the contract by assigning a reason for rejection to the open items. The system sets the contract status to "completed".

8.44.3 Using the process

To create a quantity contract, a sales employee for Model Company *A* has selected the order type *CO* for outline agreements. She still needs to maintain organizational data for sales and distribution such as the sales organization (that is, the code for the organizational unit which is responsible for selling specific products or services), distribution channel (that is, the code for the channel through which the goods or services reach the customer) and the product division (that is, the code for the grouping of materials, products and services) for the contract type (see Fig. 8.248). Then she needs to maintain the business data on the header screen of the contract. This includes the sold-to party, who ordered the goods or service, in this case the customer number for Model Company *B,* the validity period (Valid-from and Valid-to dates). The business partners sold-to party, ship-to party and payer can be different people; however, they are the same legal person in the example shown (Henderson Inc., Chicago).

The sales employee then enters material (*DPC1101 main board*), target quantity und quantity unit in the contract item. She enters the material as an alphanumeric key. This key uniquely identifies the material. The target quantity is the total quantity which the customer wants to purchase over the validity period defined above. The quantity unit specifies the units for the target quantity. The units could be pieces, litres, kilograms (see Fig. 8. 50).

8.44.4 Navigation information

■ *Menu path*
Logistics –> Sales/distribution –> Sales –> Outline agreement –> Contract –> Create

■ *Transaction code*
VA41

■ *Incoming Process Link in the R/3 Reference Model*
Customer quotation processing

■ *Outgoing Process Link in the R/3 Reference Model*
Customer contract release order processing
Status analysis

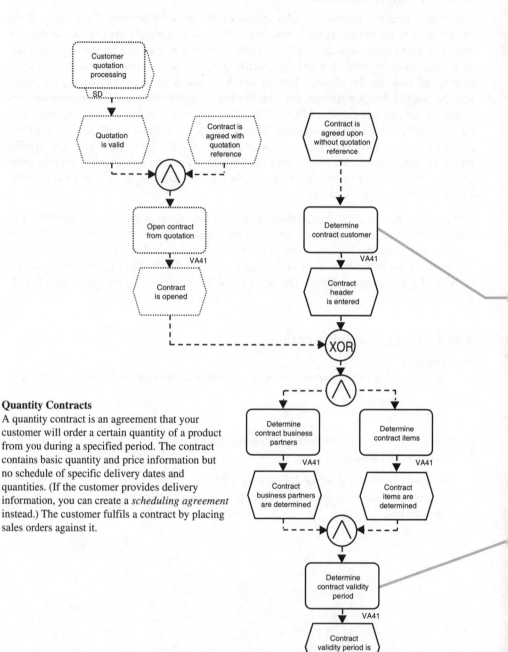

Quantity Contracts

A quantity contract is an agreement that your customer will order a certain quantity of a product from you during a specified period. The contract contains basic quantity and price information but no schedule of specific delivery dates and quantities. (If the customer provides delivery information, you can create a *scheduling agreement* instead.) The customer fulfils a contract by placing sales orders against it.

© SAP AG

694

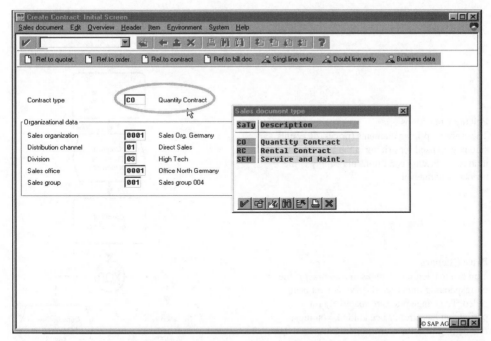

Fig. 8.248: Initial screen of customer contract processing

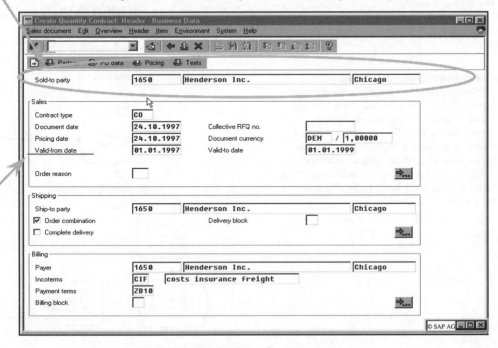

Fig. 8.249: Header data of customer contract

Pricing Conditions

These are all pricing elements (prices, discounts, surcharges) used for pricing at the header and item level. Pricing conditions may apply at the header or item level.

Price Changes

You can make price changes to a contract if the corresponding time periods have not yet been billed. To change prices retroactively for a period that has already been billed, you must manually cancel the corresponding invoices. The price changes can then be made effective with a newly created invoice.

Completion of Quantity Contracts

A quantity contract is complete when there are no more items to be delivered. If there are still outstanding items in the contract but you nevertheless want to close it, you can assign a reason for rejection to these items. The system then sets the status of the contract as complete. The procedure for rejecting items in a contract is identical to the procedure for rejecting items in a sales order.

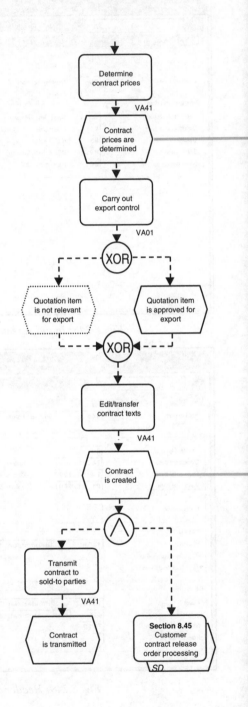

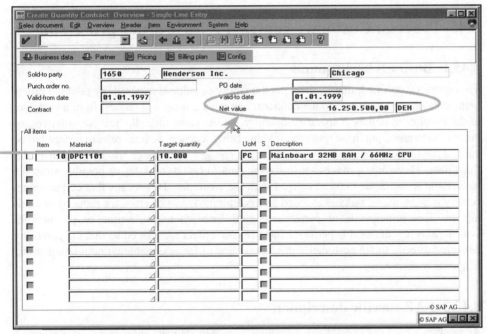

Fig. 8.250: Line item screen of customer contract

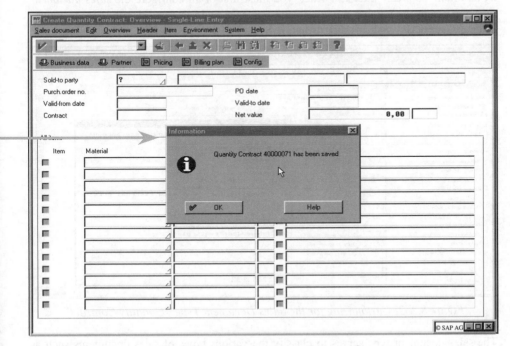

Fig. 8.251: Customer contract is created

8.45 Process: Customer contract release order processing

8.45.1 Business background

The contract is fulfilled, that is, the agreed quantity or value is released, by released orders being created with reference to the contract. The release order is a request from a customer to the supplier to deliver a specified quantity. At the same time, the release order contributes to the agreed purchase quantity or value being reached. Several release orders can be created for one contract item. A release order can generally make use of previously defined data. Therefore, it makes sense for the data to be taken as far as possible from the header and items in the contract agreed with the customer. This means that certain unnecessary duplication of tasks is avoided and potential sources of error are reduced to a minimum. This principle is of particular significance when just-in-time or production-synchronous procurement is performed and release orders are created so that the goods are delivered directly to the customer's production line as far as possible without being stored temporarily elsewhere.

8.45.2 SAP-specific description

As a contract does not contain any schedules lines with delivery information, it is released by an order. To create a release order, you must first of all configure the *sales document type* and assign the number ranges, screen sequence and sales and distribution document category (see SAP – Sales and Distribution System 1994, pp. 6.8–6.9).

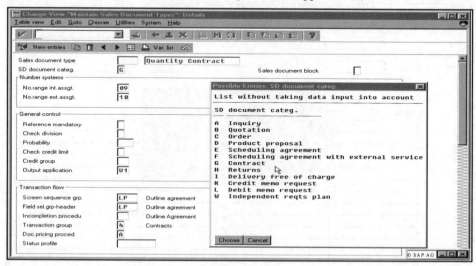

Figure 8.252: Customizing for the Sales Document Type "Quantity Contract"

The sales document type serves to classify the various types of sales documents such as the quotation and the order. In Customizing, you define the order types which are to be used for release orders. The subsequent steps in the release order such as pricing, credit control, delivery scheduling and route determination are performed in the same way as in order processing for a standard order (see Section 9.1).

8.45.3 Using the process

The sales employee in Model Company *A* creates the customer release order which has been agreed on in the outline agreement, in this case, the quantity contract (CO) using the order type *OR* (standard order). The release order can only be created if the contract is still valid. The organizational data (sales organization, distribution channel, product division) is the same as the data used to create the outline agreement. The sales employee must then specify the number of the outline agreement to which the release order is to refer. Using the function keys *Copy* and *selection list*, she can either copy all items or only selected items from the outline agreement into the release order (see Fig. 8.253). If the sales employee chooses the item selection option, the quantities not yet released for the contract items are displayed. She must then enter the quantity to be released for each item. In the pricing overview screen, the sales employee can change existing prices and taxes as well as define new ones (see Fig. 8.254). She can branch to a separate screen by selecting *Schedule line items* where she can split the order quantity over several periods (see Fig. 8.255). On the business data screen, the sales employee can then define shipping deadlines, the shipping point and the route. The possible routes are displayed for selection in a dialog box (see Fig. 8.256). The *Delivery block* field also appears on the business data screen. This field can be filled with an indicator for one of several permitted blocking reasons (see Fig. 8.258). For example, the order may need to be blocked after a credit limit. The sales employee can view the credit limit for a customer on the credit management screen in the customer master record and initiate a credit limit check (see Fig. 8.257).

8.45.4 Navigation information

- *Menu path*
  Logistics –> Sales/distribution –> Sales –> Order –> Create –> Sales document –> Create w/reference –> To contract

- *Transaction code*
  VA01

- *Incoming Process Link in the R/3 Reference Model*
  Customer contract processing

- *Outgoing Process Link in the R/3 Reference Model*
  Creation of production order
  Planned order processing
  Credit control
  Delivery processing

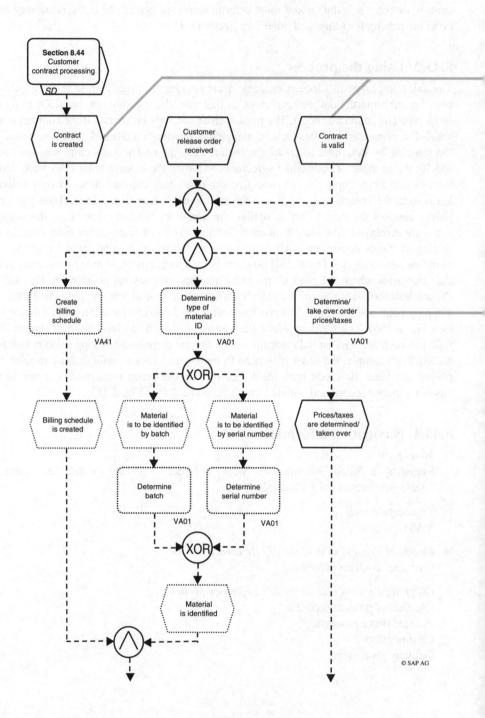

© SAP AG

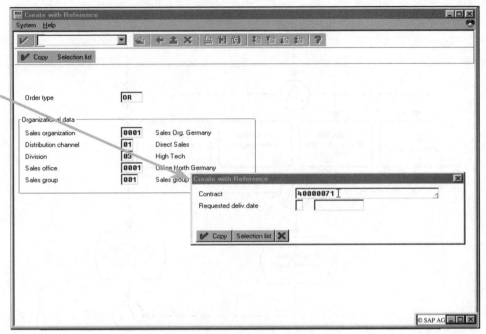

Fig. 8.253: Create order with reference

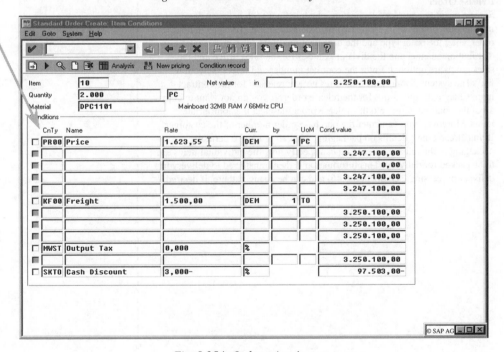

Fig. 8.254: Order prices/taxes

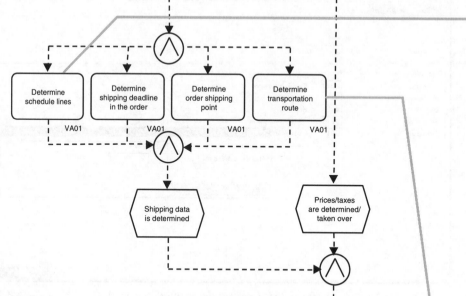

Release Order

Since a quantity contract contains no schedule lines with delivery date information, you have to create release orders against it. To create a release order, enter the order type and the organizational data sales organization, distribution channel and the division. Entries for the sales office and the sales group are optional. Enter the contract number and select "selection list". The system displays the quantities not yet released for the contract item. Change the quantities for the release order. If you do not want to copy all of the contract items into this release order, deselect the appropriate items. Moreover, you can enter the purchase order number of the customer. If you already have details on packaging, you can propose a certain packaging in the release order. You can specify how the individual items are to be packed for delivery. This information is then transferred to delivery in delivery processing (see Section 8.46) and can be changed there, if desired.

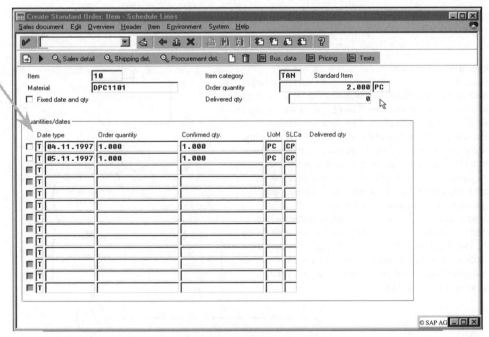

Fig. 8.255: Schedule lines

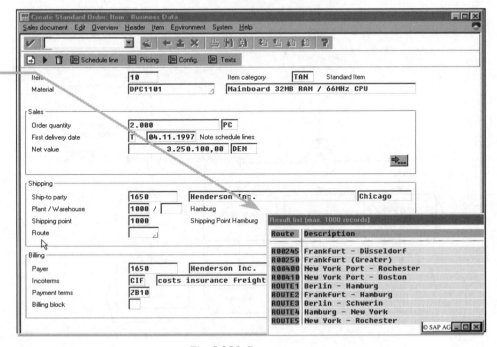

Fig. 8.256: Route

Credit Management

Since the credit standing of customers varies, you might wish to decide on the acceptance of an order according to your own credit assessment. The FI system allows you to arrange an individual credit limit for every customer. This credit limit is then checked in financial accounting and sales and distribution before any postings are made. If the limit is exceeded, the system creates a warning message. You specify the credit limits at different levels but always related to a customer. A total credit limit specifies the credit limit of a customer in all credit control areas. The total of credit limits granted within a control area must not exceed this total credit limit. With the individual credit limit, you can specify the actual credit limit of a customer in a control area. The individual credit limit you grant must not exceed the maximum individual credit limit.

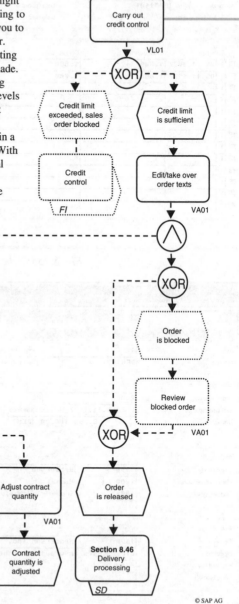

© SAP AG

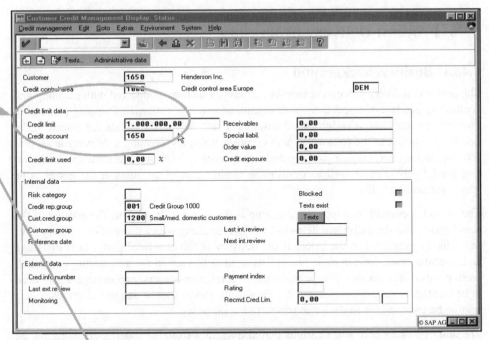

Fig. 8.257: Credit limit control

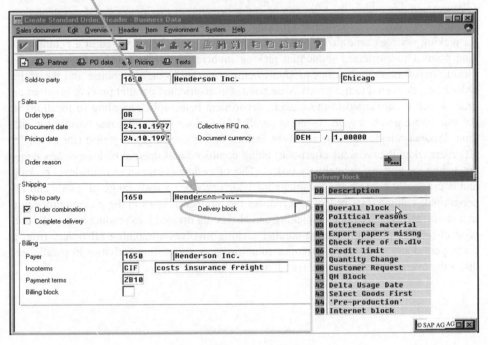

Fig. 8.258: Delivery block

8.46 Process: Delivery processing

8.46.1 Business background

Shipping and delivery processing involves all tasks which are connected with planning and controlling goods movement from your organization to the customer. Shipping processing ranges from the most straightforward case, cash sale, where the goods are issued at the goods issue point, to the following more complex activities: creating a delivery note, performing picking, organizing packing and transportation, planning the route, and monitoring partial deliveries as well as performing quality control activities at the goods issue stage (see Section 8.47).

The central document in shipping processing is the *delivery*. It contains the address of the ship-to party and the individual items to be delivered along with a description of the goods, the delivery quantity and the price. If the delivery involves a third party, bills of lading and, in some cases, foreign trade report lists need to be created for transferring goods between plants. If the goods are to be delivered to foreign customers, export papers also need to be created. In certain cases involving dangerous goods, special dangerous goods papers need to be enclosed for loading and tranportation purposes.

The aim of *picking* is to stage various partial quantities from the order. Depending on the type of staging, picking can either be centralized or decentralized. Depending on the type of object and procedures, picking can be order-oriented or product-oriented, sequential or parallel. In the case of decentralized picking, goods are collected by the person responsible for picking whereas centralized picking involves the goods being staged at a central picking point. Order-oriented sequential picking involves the order being forwarded to the picking department, the various products being collected in the warehouse and the entire order being delivered to the goods issue point. Order-oriented parallel picking involves an order which is forwarded to the picking department being split according to locations in the warehouse and being processed in parallel by various employees responsible for picking. Product-oriented picking involves various orders over a given period (for example, all orders taken the previous afternoon) being combined and internal picking orders being created on the basis of the delivery orders. This procedure is known as multi-level picking and is especially suitable for organizations which produce a wide range of goods and receive small-volume sales orders as it reduces the number of steps in the picking procedure to a minimum. Product-oriented picking can also being divided into product-sequential and product-parallel picking. Product-parallel picking involves combining all orders from a given period and is designed to reduce route times as performing activities in parallel reduces the overall processing time (see Jansen/Grünberg 1992, pp. 4–15).

Certain materials such as machines or critical parts need to be packed and sent in special containers, crates, pallets, wire boxes or containers. The *packing* process serves to assign each item to the appropriate packing materials so that the goods are not damaged during transportation and to ensure that the respective transportation and, where relevant, export regulations are taken into account.

The aim of *Transportation and route planning* is to ensure that the requested goods reach the customer in time and using the best route from a time and cost point of view. For example, in the case of transportation by truck, this can involve planning each delivery destination. When goods are transported by a truck then transferred to a train and then back to a truck at the destination, this involves determining delivery and pick-up times. In practice, insufficient stock or limited transportation capacity often means that the customer receives several partial deliveries. In these cases, it is essential that the link to the order remains and that open items can be determined.

8.46.2 SAP-specific description

You perform shipping processing in the R/3 System using the *delivery* and *goods issue* documents (see Section 8.47). The central document in shipping is the delivery. When you create a delivery, the shipping activities for the orders due for delivery are initiated. If you create a delivery with reference to an order, the data relevant for shipping is copied from the order or an outline agreement. If you create a delivery without reference to an order, you must maintain the delivery data manually. Data for the ship-to party comes from the customer master record, the data for the delivery items from the material master record (see SAP – Sales and Distribution System 1994, pp. 7.1–7.7).

Deliveries form the basis for the follow-up functions such as issuing the goods, printing the shipping papers and billing. Goods issue completes the shipping process and the transaction is then ready for billing. The delivery is made up of a document header and any number of delivery items. The document header contains general shipping data which is valid for the entire document. This includes the shipping point, dates for delivery and transportation scheduling (for example, the goods issue date or the date the goods are to arrive at the ship-to party location), weight and volume data for the entire document as well as the number of the sold-to party and the ship-to party. The document items contain information such as the material number, the delivery quantity, plant and storage location data, the picking date, weight and volume data for the individual items as well as tolerance levels for overdelivery or underdelivery.

Delivery types and item categories enable you to meet your organization's specific requirements for shipping in the R/3 System. The standard R/3 System contains the following delivery types:

- Delivery   (LF)

- Delivery without reference   (LO)

- Returns delivery   (LR)

- Replenishment delivery   (NL)

When you create a delivery with reference to an order, the system proposes the delivery document type. The delivery without reference is not based on an order and is designed for use in decentralized shipping. When you create this kind of delivery, you must specifically enter the delivery document type. Control elements which are defined in tables enable you to configure each delivery document type so that it has its own range of functions. The document types can be modified to suit your organization's requirements. You can also define new document types. The delivery document types can serve, for example, to define the following:

- From which number range is the document number taken for internal and external number assignment?

- Which partner functions are allowed and which have to be created?

- Do you have to base the delivery on an order or can you also create it without reference to an order?

- Which requirements must items which do not come from an order fulfil in order to be included in the delivery?

- Is route determination to be performed and, if so, should the validity of the route be checked?

- According to which rule is the storage location for an item to be determined if no storage location is specified?

- Which types of output are allowed for the transaction and according to which determination procedure are they proposed?

The definition of item categories makes it possible to control processing of the individual products in the delivery (see Fig. 8.259). The item category is copied from the order item. A standard item in a standard order becomes a standard item in the delivery. If you create a delivery without reference to an order, the system proposes the item category on the basis of the delivery document type and the item category group assigned to the material.

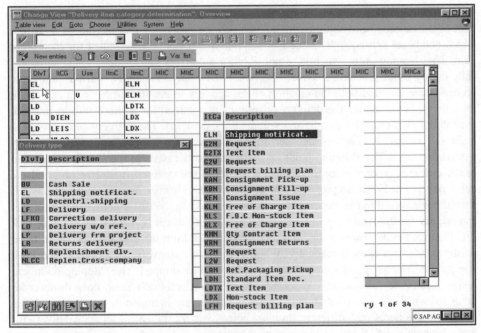

Figure 8.259: Customizing for Delivery Item Category Determination

Just as with the delivery document type, you can modify the existing item categories and, via Customizing, create new ones. The definition of item categories enables you to answer the following questions:

- Do I have to enter a material number for an item?

- Is the delivery quantity 0 allowed?

- Should a check be performed to determine whether the delivery quantity exceeds the minimum quantity defined for the material?

- Should a check be performed to determine whether the actual delivery quantity exceeds the requested delivery quantity and whether this overdelivery is allowed?

- Is the item relevant for picking?

- Does a storage location need to be specified for the item?

- Does a storage location need to be determined automatically?

When a delivery is created, the system updates the underlying order automatically. You can record agreements regarding complete and partial deliveries. You can also combine various orders in one delivery. As soon as the material availability date or transportation planning date for a schedule line in the order is reached, the schedule line becomes due for delivery. The creation of the delivery initiates the shipping activities such as picking and transportation planning.

One shipping point is responsible for processing a delivery. *Shipping points* are independent organizational units within which deliveries are processed and monitored and from which goods are subsequently issued. A shipping point can be determined for each order item. The shipping point which is responsible for a delivery can be determined automatically during order processing. Otherwise, you must enter it manually. Various automatic processes are initiated with the creation of the delivery to acquire further data and check its validity. For example, the delivery quantity is determined for an item and the material availability checked. The weight and volume are calculated. The delivery situation in the order is checked. A check is also performed to determine whether any partial delivery agreements exist. The shipping point is determined on the basis of the shipping condition in the customer master record, the loading group in the material master record, and the delivering plant. For example, you can define in the customer master record that goods should be delivered to the customer as soon as possible. In the material master record, you can specify for the loading group that the goods must always be loaded by crane or fork lift. The plant is determined for each order item either from the customer or the material master or you can enter it manually. When you create a delivery for an order, you must specify the shipping point from which the order is to be shipped. The shipping point you define cannot be subsequently changed. When an order is delivered, only those order items for which the specified shipping point is defined are included in the delivery. If the order contains items with different shipping points, you must create a separate delivery for each shipping point. If the customer requests complete deliveries, it does not make sense to define different shipping points for items in the order as this would lead to the order being split into several deliveries.

If the shipping situation changes or the picked quantity is confirmed, you can subsequently change the delivery. Order items or shcedule lines which have the same shipping criteria are combined in one delivery. If the items have different data, for example two items have different ship-to parties, two deliveries need to be created for the order. Order items from different orders can be combined in one delivery if they have the same shipping criteria and the sold-to party is in agreement. The entire order as well as the order items and schedule lines must fulfil certain prerequisites before a delivery can be created. The order may not be blocked at header level and the order must contain at least one deliverable item due for delivery. A delivery block is set automatically or you can set it manually when, for example, the credit limit is exceeded. However, the delivery block only takes effect if it has been assigned to the appropriate delivery type in Customizing. The schedule line must be due for delivery on the selection date and may not be blocked for delivery. A schedule line is due for delivery as soon as the material availability date or transportation planning date is reached. In contrast to the delivery block at header level, the delivery block at schedule line level does not require any Customizing settings to make it effective. The quantity to be delivered must be greater than 0, the order item data must be complete, the status of the material must allow delivery and the goods must be available, if availability is checked. When you create a delivery, the order is updated and the delivery status at header and item level is adjusted accordingly.

The *route* specifies the mode and means of transport and plays a role in transportation scheduling. For example, in the route you can specify that the goods must be sent by rail to Chicago. This means that transportation scheduling must take into account the time required to reserve loading space in a freight train. A route can be determined for each order item. Route determination in the order depends on the country, point of departure in the shipping point, the shipping conditions in the order, the transportation zone in the material master record as well as the country and transportation zone of the ship-to party. If you change the ship-to party in the order, the route is redetermined for each item. The delivery type specifies whether the route should be redetermined in the delivery. It is advisable to redetermine the route in the delivery as it is only at this point in time that the exact weight of the delivery is known. For example, if, in the case of an overdelivery, goods are too heavy to be sent by air, you will have to transport them by rail. It is also possible that an order is delivered in partial deliveries which means that the total weight of a delivery can be less than the weight recorded in the order. Therefore, a smaller truck than planned can be used to transport the delivery. For this reason, in addition to the previously mentioned criteria, a weight group is used to redetermine the route in the delivery. The weight group is determined on the basis of the total weight of the delivery. You can overwrite the route determined by the system in the delivery. In contrast to the order in which a route can be defined for each order item, the route in the delivery applies to all delivery items. When the system redetermines the route in the delivery, it can check whether the route determined for the order item and the route found for the delivery are still consistent. You can define a consistency check for each delivery document type in Customizing.

When you enter an order, you can specify a requested delivery date for each schedule line for an item. During order processing the system can schedule automatically when the required shipping activities such as picking, loading and transporting need to be started so that the requested delivery date can be met. You distinguish between *times* which are required to perform particular activities and *deadlines* which are used to calculate these times. The system requires values for past experience from the shipping department to be able to calculate the shipping deadlines. The values are stored as transit time, loading time, pick/pack time and transportation lead time.

- The *transit time* is the time required to transport the goods to the customer. It is defined for a route. When you define the transit time, you can also specify the forwarding agent's factory calendar for the route. This factory calendar can differ from the company's factory calendar. For example, you can define that the 6-day week calendar applies for the forwarding agent.

- The *loading time* is the time required to load the goods. It is determined using the shipping point, the route and the loading group for the material.

- The *pick/pack time* covers the time required to assign the goods to a delivery, and to pick and pack them. It is calculated on the basis of the shipping point, the route, and the weight group of the order item.

- The transportation lead time is the time required to organize transport. This can include chartering a ship or booking a truck with a forwarding agent. It is defined for a route.

Important deadlines for ensuring goods are sent in time are the material availability date, the transportation planning date, the loading date, the goods issue date, and the delivery date.

■ On the *material availability date,* you must start the activities which are performed during the pick/pack time.

■ On the *transportation planning date,* you must start to organize transportation of the goods.

■ The *loading date* is the date on which the goods must be ready for loading and the vehicles required to transport the goods must be available.

■ The *goods issue date* is the date on which the goods must leave your organization to ensure that they arrive on time at the customer location.

■ The *delivery date* is the date on which the goods should arrive at the customer location. The difference between the goods issue date and the delivery date is calculated on the basis of the transit time between the delivering plant and the customer location for the selected route. The delivery date can be either the requested or the confirmed delivery date.

8.46.3 Using the process

You can create a delivery with or without reference to a sales order. Order *5325* for Model Company *A* is released for delivery and is entered as a reference on the inital delivery screen. The entire delivery or a part of it is due for delivery, that is, the material availability date (point in time when you must start picking and packing the goods) or the transportation planning date (point in time when you must start organizing the transportation of the goods) has been reached for the item. You can enter a shipping point manually or it can be copied automatically from the order data (see Fig. 8.259).

The system displays the delivery items it creates on the quantity screen (for example, one item for Model Company *A*). You can display any errors which occur during delivery creation using the log button. In the previous example for Model Company *A,* the next step is creating a picking list. You can save the data entered up to this point at this stage and complete processing after goods issue has been performed. In our case, the delivery is completed after picking is performed (see Fig. 8.261) and you branch directly into goods issue processing. An important field on the picking screen is the *pick quantity.* If the picked quantity matches the proposed delivery quantity (Model Company *A* with a delivery and picking quantity of *2000* pieces), the delivery item is assigned the status *Completely picked.* You are now able to post goods issue.

Monitoring the delivery is completed when you post goods issue in shipping and the transaction has been billed. Material stock is reduced by the issued quantity (see Section 8.47) and at the same time, the relevant value changes are made (see Section 8.49).

8.46.4 Navigation information

■ *Menu path*
Logistics –> Sales/distribution –> Shipping –> Delivery –> Create

■ *Transaction code*
VL01

■ *Incoming Process Link in the R/3 Reference Model*
Standard order processing
Free delivery processing
Processing subsequent delivery free-of-charge
Consignment fill-up processing
Customer contract release order processing
Customer schedule line processing
Customer delivery schedule processing for scheduling agreement
Purchase order processing for stock transfer

■ *Outgoing Process Links in the R/3 Reference Model*
Inspection lot creation in the delivery/sales order in sales and distribution
Credit control
Picking
Billing
Transportation planning
Goods issue processing for stock material
Consignment goods issue processing

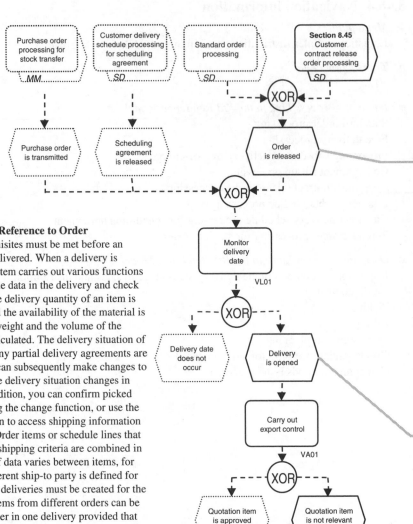

Delivery with Reference to Order

Certain prerequisites must be met before an order can be delivered. When a delivery is created, the system carries out various functions which add to the data in the delivery and check its validity. The delivery quantity of an item is determined and the availability of the material is checked. The weight and the volume of the delivery are calculated. The delivery situation of the order and any partial delivery agreements are checked. You can subsequently make changes to a delivery if the delivery situation changes in any way. In addition, you can confirm picked quantities using the change function, or use the display function to access shipping information in a delivery. Order items or schedule lines that have identical shipping criteria are combined in one delivery. If data varies between items, for example a different ship-to party is defined for each item, two deliveries must be created for the order. Order items from different orders can be grouped together in one delivery provided that they have identical shipping criteria and that the sold-to party allows this.

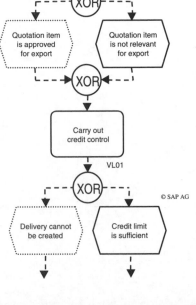

© SAP AG

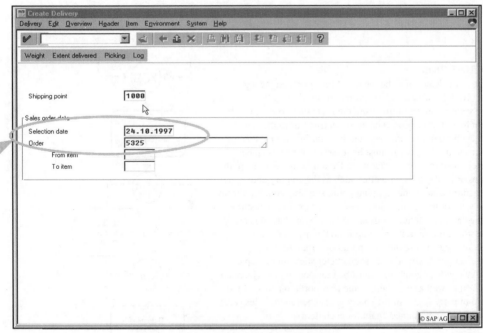

Fig. 8.260: Create delivery

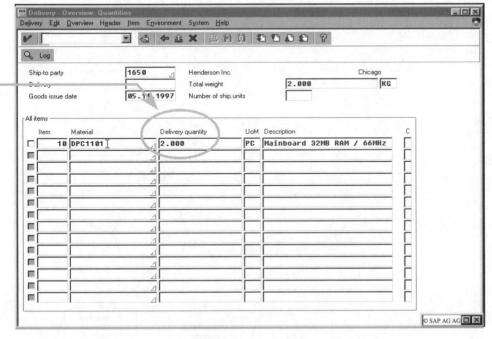

Fig. 8.261: Delivery quantity

Delivery Route

The route determines the means of transport and the legs involved. It influences transportation scheduling. For example, the system can determine from the route that goods are to be sent by rail to London. Therefore, during transportation scheduling, it takes into account how far in advance loading space in the freight car must be reserved. A route can be determined for every order item. Determining the route in the sales order depends on factors such as the country and departure zone of the shipping point, shipping condition from the sales order (it might have been agreed with the customer, for example, that the goods are to be delivered as soon as possible), transportation group from the material master record (you can use the transportation group to group together goods with the same characteristics, for example bulky goods or goods that must be transported in refrigerated trucks) as well as the country and transportation zone of the ship-to party. If the ship-to party is changed in the sales order, the route is determined again for each item.

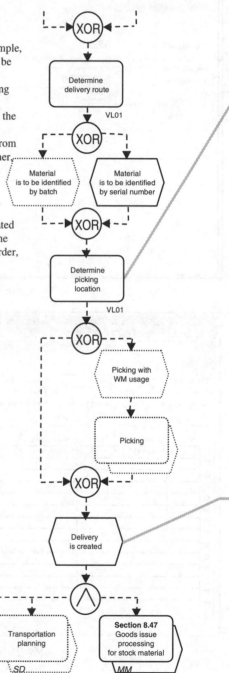

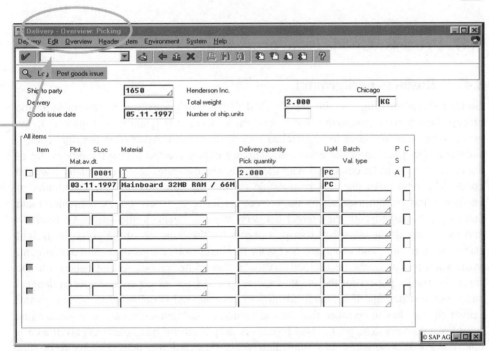

Fig. 8.262: Picking

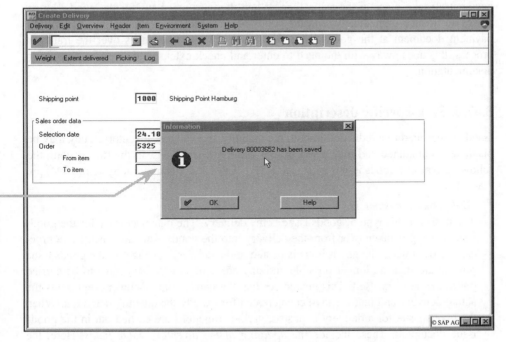

Fig. 8.263: Delivery is created

8.47 Process: Goods issue processing

8.47.1 Business background

Goods issue processing contains the physical delivery of goods to a customer. As in the process *Goods issue processing for a production order,* the quantity and quality of the goods to be delivered have to be checked (see Section 8.36). Apart from the final control and the proper packing of the goods, the delivery papers created during the processing of the delivery have to be compared with the goods and measures taken to actually load the goods. The final order check is responsible for making sure that the correct quantity of goods ordered are put together on the correct carrier (e.g. pallets, crates, containers) and that they are marked with the correct delivery address. A check also has to be made to make sure that all the necessary transport papers for the transport of the goods by freight carrier, train or ship, and which are necessary for the customer's goods receipt department, exist. Such papers might be the delivery note, the printed goods receipt papers for the customer, freight papers for the freight carrier, special customs papers and special dangerous goods instructions. If the total quantity to be delivered is delivered in several partial deliveries, care has to be taken that the individual, partial deliveries can be recognized as part of one delivery. The goods issue process is simplified if it takes place as part of a cash sale. The goods issue takes place immediately since the customer does not have to be sent the goods and the goods issue entry, the transfer of the goods, the invoice creation and payment all take place at the same time. When the customer pays for the goods, he receives an invoice immediately with the goods or must pick up the goods by showing the payment document at the goods issue site. Since the customer takes over the transport process, this does away with the need to enter and check extensive delivery and transport documentation.

8.47.2 SAP-specific description

Goods issues lead to a reduction in both the quantity and value of inventory. They may be planned or unplanned and may result from a variety of situations. In the R/3 System, the following types of goods issues exist (see SAP – Sales and Distribution System, 1994, pp. 7.8–7.10):

■ *Deliveries to customers*
   The basis for this type of goods issue is the delivery. The data necessary for the goods issue posting is taken over from the delivery into the goods issue document. The process is closed when the goods issue is posted in the delivery. Changes to the goods issue posting are then no longer possible and any corrections necessary have to be carried out in the delivery itself. This guarantees that the goods issue document represents the actual delivery and that the invoice is created for exactly the quantity delivered. When the goods issue for a delivery is posted, various functions are carried out in the goods issue document. These include the *updating of the inventory value fields.* Here, the warehouse stock of the material is reduced by the amount of the delivered quantity,

Furthermore, values are determined and the relevant stock accounts are updated. When the goods issue is posted, the value changes to the corresponding stock and stock change accounts in financial accounting are updated automatically. The *sales requirements* which resulted from the sales order are reduced, *previous documents* in the sales process are updated, as are the processes to be invoiced. The goods issue for a delivery can only be posted when all the data in the delivery is complete. For example, all the data concerning the storage location from which the goods are to be issued, the batch and the movement type must be available in the delivery. Furthermore, the picking status of all the items to be delivered must be fulfilled, meaning that goods issue can only take place for items that have been picked and if an item was picked in the warehouse management system, the picking status in the warehouse management system must also have been fulfilled (for example, all the transfer orders for a delivery must have been confirmed). The goods issue document is not a sales document, rather it belongs to the materials management (MM) and financial accounting (FI) modules. The document, and thus an overview of the quantity and value update postings, can be displayed from within the sales processing transactions. If a company is not using the sales component (SD module), the movement types *consumption to customer order* and *consumption to sales* in the MM inventory management system can be used to post a goods issue for a customer.

■ *Goods issues for production orders*
When goods are issued to production, this is done with reference to the production order(s) for which the components are needed. Such goods issues can be either a planned goods issue with reference to the production order or reservation, an unplanned goods issue or backflushing. In the first case, all of the components to be issued are determined by the R/3 System via the production order or the reservation, and are issued with reference to the document concerned. If an additional, unplanned goods issue for a material is necessary, this goods issue posting is carried out without reference. In the case of backflushing, the components are already at the production site. They are physically removed and consumed during the production process, but the consumption is only posted when the quantity consumed is known, i.e. when the completion confirmation takes place for the order. In this case, it is not necessary to create a material consumption posting manually in the system for the components as this takes place automatically with the completion confirmation.

■ *Other internal goods issues*
Goods issues can take place not only for production but also for other usages (e.g. cost centres, CO orders, maintenance orders, projects, assets) and the components reserved for these objects. In this case, certain data, such as the movement type, the plant and the object to which the costs are to be assigned, are taken from the reservation at goods issue posting time. The goods issue is posted with reference to the reservation. The reservation, which is entered before the goods are issued, can take place at either plant or storage location level within the R/3 System. As a result of the reservation, the available quantity in MRP is reduced by the reserved quantity.

■ *Returns to supplier*

If goods supplied to a customer have to be returned to the vendor for any particular reason (e.g. poor quality or incorrect goods), this can be carried out in the R/3 System, even if the goods receipt posting has already taken place. When a return posting is made, the posting should refer to the *purchase order*, which was referred to in the goods receipt document, or the *material document*, with which the goods receipt posting took place. In this way, the system can default data (such as the storage location) from the original document, carry out plausibility checks (the quantity to be returned must not exceed the delivered quantity), reduce the delivered quantity in previous documents (purchase order history) and reverse other postings which take place (e.g. a goods receipt to consumption). To enter a return delivery, the first thing that should be checked is whether the goods were posted into stock, to consumption or to the goods receipt blocked stock. If the material document created for the goods receipt is used as a reference when posting the return delivery, only the items from this document are defaulted. Items posted into the GR blocked stock are not defaulted. If the purchase order is used as a reference for the return delivery, all of the items for which a goods receipt has been posted are defaulted. The return delivery is posted like a normal goods receipt for a purchase order except that movement type 122 (return to vendor) is used instead of movement type 101 (purchase order to stock). A material document is created for a return delivery from stock or consumption. This material document can be printed as a return delivery note. The material document also creates an accounting document since the delivery is valued. In addition, in the case of a return delivery, all of the update postings to the inventory and general ledger accounts that took place at goods receipt time are reversed. The open purchase order quantity is also increased by the quantity of goods returned. If the goods are in the GR blocked stock, and not in the company's own stock, the return delivery simply results in the quantity marked as being in GR blocked stock in the purchase order history being reduced. As proof of the return delivery only a material document is created.

■ *Scrapping*

If a material can no longer be used, the material has to be scrapped. Scrapping can be made necessary if a material cannot be used any more because, for example, it has been stored too long and as a result of this the quality is no longer sufficient, the goods are no longer up - to - date or because parts, such as glass, have been broken. Scrapping in the R/3 System is posted as a goods issue without reference to a document. Scrapping can take place when the material is in unrestricted use stock, in quality inspection stock or in blocked stock. The posting results in the quantity of the corresponding stock type being reduced, the value of the scrapped material being posted from the inventory account to a scrapping account and the corresponding cost centre being charged with the costs of the material. The value postings are based on the value of the goods taken from the material master record at the time the scrapping posting takes place.

In the case of planned goods issues, a reference document or reference data from the R/3 System such as reservations or production orders should always be used in the posting. When the goods issue posting is carried out, the system can then take data from the reference document (account assignment, material number, quantity), which facilitates both the entry and the checking of data (under- and over-deliveries). Furthermore, the issued quantity is updated in the reference document and the reserved quantity reduced after each goods issue. In this way, the inventory management department can follow the issue procedure and the stock/requirement situation can be correctly updated. If you do not know the number of the reference document, it can be found via the material number or the account assignment in the R/3 System. For each goods movement, the system automatically carries out an *availability check* for the stocks, if this has been set for the material. The availability check avoids negative stocks for stock types (e.g. unrestricted use stock). If several goods issues are posted in one document (with different account assignments, for example), the system checks the availability *when entering each item*. The system checks whether the required quantity can be issued. The items that have already been entered in the document but not yet posted are also taken into consideration in this availability check. If not enough stock is available, the system issues an error. The availability check takes place on the stock level involved (plant, storage location and special stock levels) for the current month and also the past month if necessary. Depending on the movement type involved in the goods issue process, different stocks are checked.

- For goods issue postings to consumption, the unrestricted use stock is checked.

- For a stock release from quality inspection stock, the quality inspection stock is checked.

- For consumption of materials in consignment stock, the unrestricted use consignment stock is checked.

In addition to the physical stock types, a check of the available stock can also be carried out from a planning point of view. Using this check, you can prevent, for example, a quantity of a material, that has already been reserved, from being used for another purpose. The availability check of the stock types takes place automatically and cannot be changed in the system. Non-availability leads to an error message by the system. The check of the available stock in MRP is activated in the material master record and can be set up in Customizing. Your system administrator can define whether an availability check is to take place and whether non-availability is to result in a warning or an error. Using a goods issue posting in the R/3 System as an example, it is easy to see how a simple goods issue can lead to extensive business activities. Starting with a goods issue posting, and depending on the purpose of the goods issue and the modules being used, such as warehouse management system or quality management, the following, integrative steps take place:

- *Creation of a material document*
  The material document is documentary evidence of the goods movement.

- *Creation of a financial accounting document*
  The financial accounting document is created at the same time as the material document and contains all the posting lines with posting to the accounts necessary for the movement.

- *Creation of a goods issue slip*
  A goods issue slip can be printed when a goods issue is posted.

■ *Inventory update*
When the goods issue is posted, the total valued stock, the unrestricted use stock and/or the reserved stock (if the goods issue is posted with reference to a reservation or production order) is reduced by the quantity issued.

■ *G/L accounts update*
When the goods issue is posted, the system automatically creates posting lines for the general ledger accounts in financial accounting.

■ *Update of consumption values*
Apart from the stock fields in the material master record being updated, an update is also carried out to the consumption statistics of the material when a goods issue takes place for a material which takes part in the planning process. The consumption of a material is used in material requirements planning for the creation of a consumption forecast. MRP recognizes both planned and unplanned consumption. If the consumption was planned using a reservation or order, the total consumption figures are updated. If the consumption was not planned, both the total consumption and the unplanned consumption are updated.

■ *Update of the reservation*
When a goods issue is created with reference to a reservation or an order, the issued quantity is updated in the reservation item. The reservation item is marked as being completed when the total reservation quantity has been issued or when the delivery completion indicator is set manually during goods issue posting.

■ *Update of the production order*
In the case of a goods issue with reference to a production order, the issued quantity of the components in the production order is updated.

■ *Update in subsequent applications*
Further updates can take place in subsequent applications. In the case of a goods issue for internal consumption, for example, costs are assigned to the object causing the consumption (e.g. cost centre, order, asset).

■ *Creation of a transfer request when MM-WM is in use*
If the storage location is managed using the warehouse management system, a transfer request is created along with the goods issue posting.

■ *Creation of an inspection lot if QM is in use*
If quality inspection in the QM system is in use, an inspection lot is created at goods issue time, using which quality management carries out a quality check.

8.47.3 Using the process

The physical issue of goods is started with the end of the delivery process and a previous credit limit check. After the credit limit check has been successfully completed, goods issue can take place and the material physically removed from stock. For this to take place, you have to select the appropriate movement type on the initial screen. In the model company, you would like to issue the goods for an order. Therefore, movement type *261* is entered. In the initial screen, the user can also enter a short note in the field document header text, such as *Careful – fragile goods*. The organizational fields plant and storage locations are required entries, whereas the marking field in which you mark whether or not goods issue notes are to be printed is an optional field. The document date and the posting date have both been set automatically to the date on which the transaction is called, and in this example neither date has been overwritten (see Fig. 8.264). The material goods issue note number is assigned internally (by the system) and therefore no entry has been made in this field. Before coming to the next screen, you have to enter the plant and the storage location from which the material is to be issued. For Model Company *A*, the main board *DPC1101* with a quantity of *2000 pcs* has been entered to be issued to the order (see Fig. 8.265). If the company has to use batch management for the materials, it would be necessary to additionally enter the number of a batch from which the material is to be issued before the goods issue can be posted. The goods issue document is then posted and the goods issue note automatically printed.

8.47.4 Navigation information

▪ *Menu path*
Logistics –> Materials management –> Inventory management –> Goods movement –> Goods issue

▪ *Transaction code*
MB1A, MB01, VL01

▪ *Ingoing processes in the R/3 Reference Model*
Transportation processing; Delivery processing; Decentralized shipping processing; Rush order processing; Cash sales processing; Processing returnable packaging issue; Project implementation; Maintenance order execution, Service order execution, Network confirmation; Project release (investment); Order release (investment); Reservation processing; Inspection lot completion for goods movement; Inspection lot completion in SD

▪ *Outgoing processes in the R/3 Reference Model*
Credit control; Transfer of primary costs, Service order execution, Availability checking (investment); Project update; Removal from storage processing; Automatic creation of TO for material document

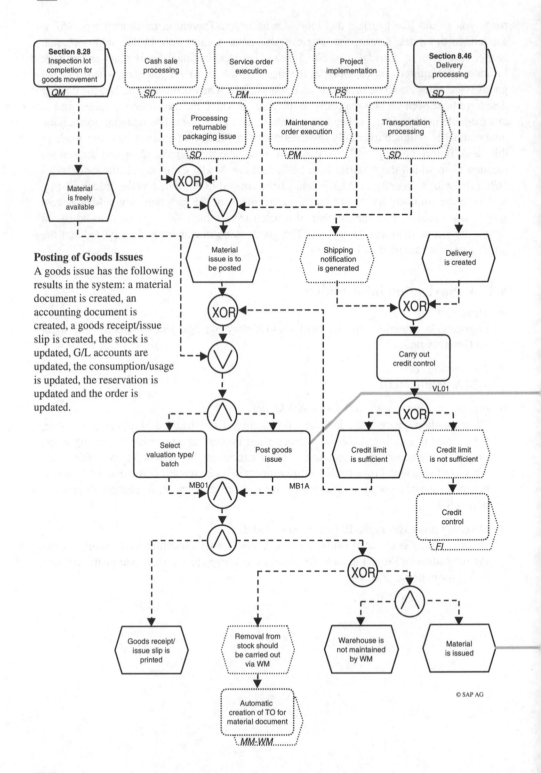

Posting of Goods Issues
A goods issue has the following results in the system: a material document is created, an accounting document is created, a goods receipt/issue slip is created, the stock is updated, G/L accounts are updated, the consumption/usage is updated, the reservation is updated and the order is updated.

© SAP AG

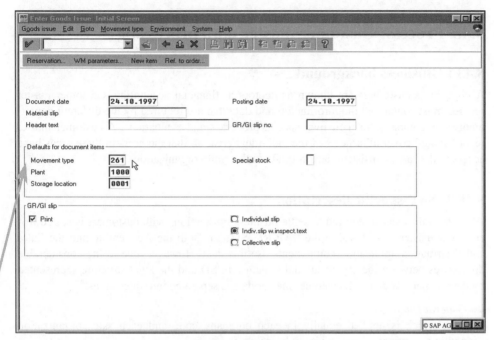

Fig. 8.264: Movement type "261"

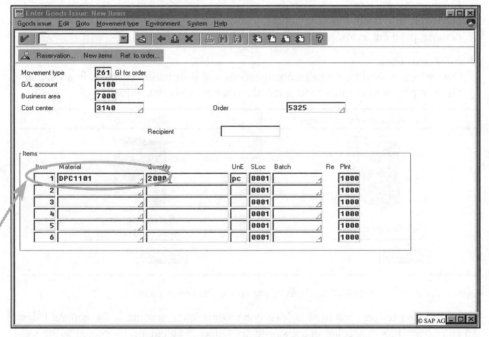

Fig. 8.265: Issue material "DPC1101"

8.48 Process: Customer master data processing

8.48.1 Business background

A company's customers are known as debtors in financial accounting. Customer master records must contain all the information and data that are required by the different departments of a company for their own special processes and evaluations. A customer master record should cover all aspects of the individual areas so that the users in these areas have access to the same consistent data throughout the entire organization.

8.48.2 SAP-specific description

All of the information required to settle business transactions with customers is stored in a customer master record within the SAP R/3 System. Both the Accounting and the Sales and Distribution application components use this data. However, due to the considerable differences between the organizational structure in SD and the legal structure represented by the company code in FI, customer master data is separated into three areas:

- *General Data*
  Data which is applied equally in each company code and each sales organization within a company (name, address, language and so on).

- *Company Code Data*
  Data which is specific to each company code, for example, the reconciliation account number, payment terms, and dunning procedures.

- *Sales Area Data*
  Data which is used by the sales organizations and distribution channels in a company, for example for sales order processing, distribution, and invoicing.

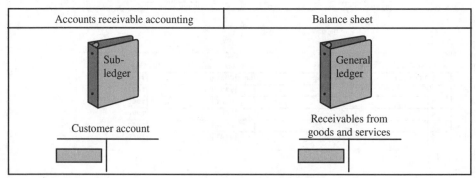

Fig. 8.266: Tasks of the reconciliation account

Each subsidiary ledger must have at least one reconciliation account in the general ledger. An entry posted to an account in the subsidiary ledger is automatically posted at the same time to the appropriate reconciliation account.

8.48.3 Using the process

First the customer must be assigned to an account group. The account group determines how the customer account is numbered (either internally by the system or externally by the user), the number range used to assign the number, and the fields that are to be displayed on the entry screens (see Fig. 8.267). The general data is entered next. This includes the customer address (see Fig. 8.268), account control, and information about payment transactions. In the account control group box on the control data screen, you can specify that the customer is also a vendor so that the payment and dunning programs can offset open items between these two accounts. If the customer is a trading partner, you can also specify the company ID to eliminate interunit payables and receivables. The customer's bank details and the payer/payee are stored in the payment transactions screen. The screens for accounting info, payment information, dunning data, and correspondence and insurance data make up the company code data. Accounting info consists of the customer's reconciliation account in the general ledger as well as reference data such as the old account number and the buying group (see Fig. 8.269). Terms of payment, tolerance groups for cash discounts and price differences, as well as payment methods for automatic payment, are set on the payment information screen. In the correspondence screen, you can store information such as dunning procedures, a dunning notice recipient, a dunning block indicator, your account number at the customer, and the clerk responsible for the account at your company as well as the clerk at the customer's company (see Fig. 8.270).

8.48.4 Navigation information

■ *Menu path*
Accounting -> Financial accounting -> Accounts receivable -> Master records -> Create

■ *Transaction code*
FD01

■ *Ingoing processes in the R/3 Reference Model*
none

■ *Outgoing processes in the R/3 Reference Model*

Account Group
You can define account groups for the customer
as a contractor, goods recipient, payer, invoice
recipient. If you define a one-time customer
(CPD), all partner functions are combined. It
might become necessary to change the function
of a customer, i.e. to assign a new function to
him, e.g. because so far he has acted only as
payer and is now the main contractor. This is
only possible by changing the account group
since the screen and field selection in the
customer master record is controlled by the
account group and the master record of a
contractor, for example, consists of different
screens than that of the payer. You can change
an account group with its partner function only
from a lower to a higher level, i.e. you cannot
assign the partner function of the payer to a
contractor since you would have to suppress the
fields already maintained for the contractor
from display. However, a payer can become a
contractor.

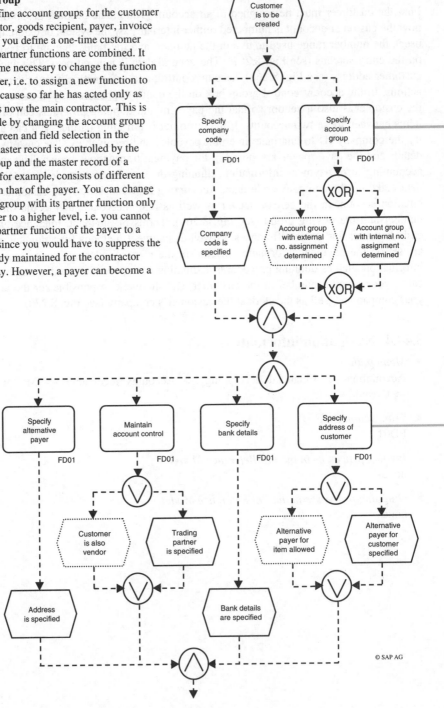

© SAP AG

728

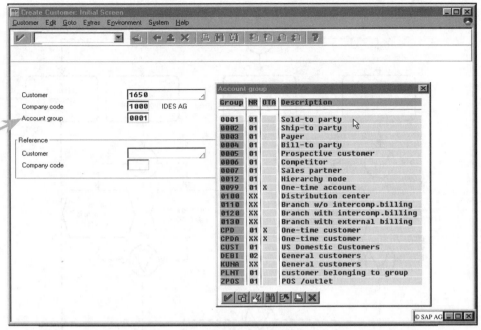

Fig. 8.267: Create account group of customer

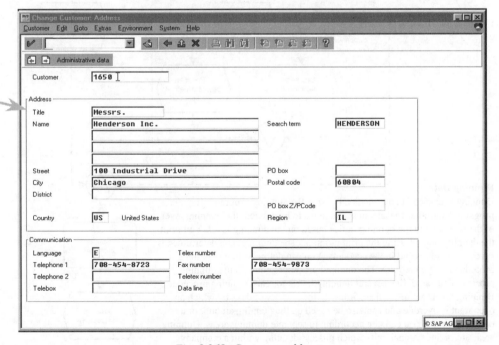

Fig. 8.268: Customer address

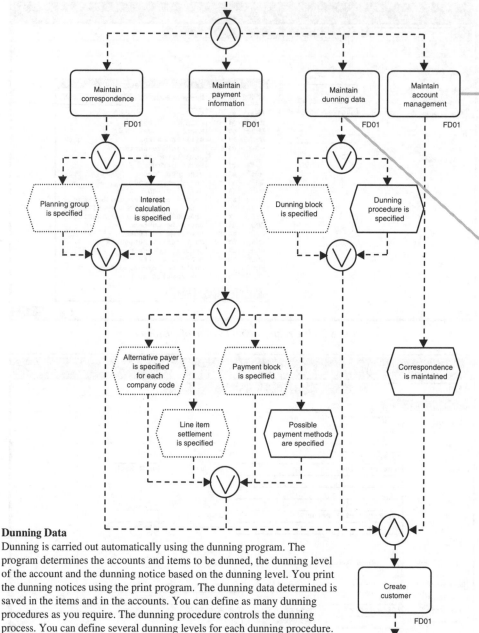

Dunning Data

Dunning is carried out automatically using the dunning program. The program determines the accounts and items to be dunned, the dunning level of the account and the dunning notice based on the dunning level. You print the dunning notices using the print program. The dunning data determined is saved in the items and in the accounts. You can define as many dunning procedures as you require. The dunning procedure controls the dunning process. You can define several dunning levels for each dunning procedure. Dunning levels are defined according to the number of days by which an open item is overdue and can also be based on the dunning amount or a percentage rate. You can dun according to separate dunning areas. Dunning areas are organizational units which process dunning within a company code. The dunning area can correspond to a division or to a sales organization.

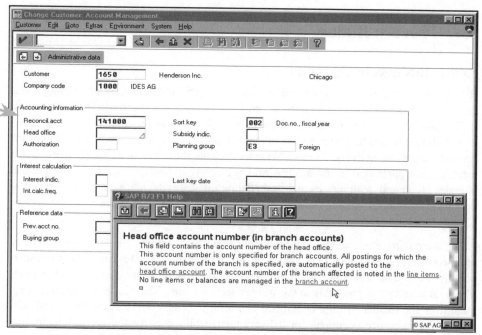

Fig. 8.269: Account management – customer

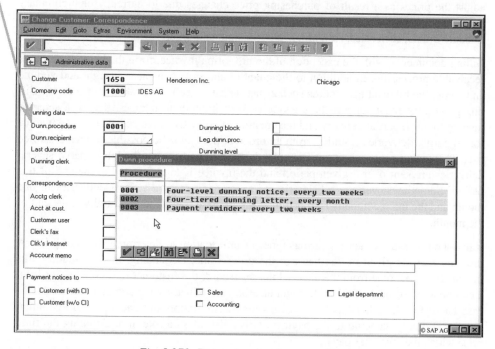

Fig. 8.270: Determine dunning procedure

8.49 Process: Billing

8.49.1 Business background

Billing processing is often described as the last step in order processing, although this process is not actually complete until the customer payment is received. The main task in billing processing is the *creation of an invoice* on the basis of an order or delivery. However, billing can also be performed in advance. For example, milestone billing can be performed before the delivery. Down payments such as these are often made when larger machines are purchased in the mechanical engineering industry. The billing process also includes *credit* and *debit memos* and *cancellation invoices* which are created as a result of complaints and *pro forma invoices* which are created so that export licences can be applied for.

Credit memos are required when, for example, a customer returns goods or when invoices are incorrect. A debit memo is needed if, for example, during a sales call, a field salesperson gives a retailer a product which the retailer normally purchases from his wholesaler. The field salesperson posts this to the wholesaler's account. The wholesaler requests payment from the retailer. Billing documents can refer to orders, services rendered, and deliveries. The reference document for delivery-related billing is the delivery. Quantity and price information is taken directly from the delivery. It may be necessary to change or adjust the prices as a result of purchasing price changes due to currency or preliminary price discrepancies. Order-related billing is performed for various types of order such as standard orders, cash sales, rush orders and consignment orders.

Billing documents, with the exception of the pro forma invoice, form the basis of accounts receivable processing. In addition to the quantity and price per piece, weight and volume and so on, the relevant tax records such as tax on sales need to be taken into account. Billing processing must support the creation of both individual invoices, that is, a separate invoice for each partial delivery and the creation of collective invoices, that is, one invoice for all partial deliveries resulting from an order. It must also be possible to create invoice lists. This makes sense when, for example, the ship-to party is not the bill-to party, several deliveries are sent over a given period and the invoice is to be created at the end of this period. Sometimes, various subsidiaries of a company receive several deliveries in one month and the main company is to be billed for all these transactions centrally at the end of the month.

It may be necessary to access various types of information to determine the sales price. A discount may be given on the basis of the order value. Depending on the situation, this information can come from the material master record, the customer master record or from a combination of both of these. It might also be determined by the company on a case-to-case basis. On the other hand, surcharges for transportation and packaging are common practice. Equally, keeping to the payment target also plays a role in determining the final price which the customer pays.

8.49.2 SAP-specific description

Billing is the last step in a business transaction in Sales and Distribution. At the billing stage, the system accesses data from sales and shipping and automatically copies the data relevant for billing such as quantities and prices into the billing documents. Billing forwards data to Financial Accounting and Controlling. As billing is part of Sales and Distribution and is also closely connected to Financial Accounting, both the organizational data in Sales and Distribution (for example, sales organization, distribution channel, product division) and the organizational data in Financial Accounting (for example, company code and the assignment of the sales organization to a company code) play an important role in the billing documents (see SAP – Sales and Distribution System 1994, pp. 8.1–8.8).

In the R/3 System, billing documents include invoices, credit and debit memos, pro forma invoices and cancellation documents. You can create separate invoices for one or more deliveries directly. Using a work list, you can create multiple invoices collectively. You can combine several billing documents in a collective invoice and bill one sales document or delivery in several billing documents (invoice split). As a rule, you create billing documents on the basis of a reference document. For example, invoices are created on the basis of a sales order or deliveries, debit and credit memos on the basis of a debit and credit memo request, returns credit memos on the basis of a returns credit memo request, pro forma invoices on the basis of a sales order or a delivery, cancellation documents with reference to an invoice and invoice lists on the basis of a billing document.

Billing documents are controlled by *billing document types*. All billing documents have the same structure which consists of a document header and any number of document items. The document header contains general data which apply for the entire document. This includes the number of the payer, the billing date, the net value for the entire document, the document currency, the document number and the number of the accounting document in the FI (Financial Accounting) module, the payment terms and incoterms. The document items include the material number, the billing quantity, the net value for the individual items, the weight and volume, the number of the reference document (for example, the underlying delivery), the pricing elements for the individual items and the numbers of the preceding and subsequent documents with the respective item numbers for the individual items. There are various billing types to enable you to process the different business transactions in Sales and Distribution.

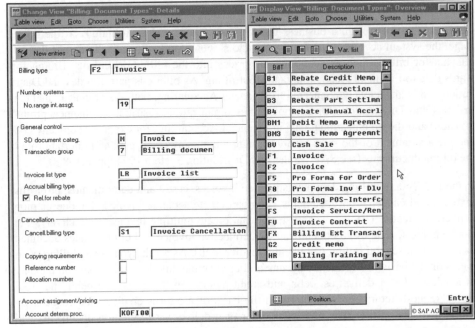

Figure 8.271: Billing types

Control elements, which are defined in tables, enable you to configure each billing document type so that it has its own range of functions. You can define new billing document types in Customizing. The definition of billing document types helps you answer the following questions:

■ From which number range should the document number come?

■ Which partner functions are allowed at header level?

■ Which partner functions are allowed at item level?

■ Which billing document type can I use to cancel a billing document?

■ Should the billing document be forwarded directly to Financial Accounting, be blocked for forwarding or not forwarded at all?

■ According to which determination procedure should account determination for Financial Accounting be performed?

■ Which output types are allowed for the transaction and according to which determination procedure are they proposed?

Pricing, which includes taxes, discounts and surcharges, rebates and so on, plays an important role in the billing process. At the billing stage in the R/3 System all pricing elements can be copied and updated according to the scale, new pricing can be performed, manual pricing elements can be copied and new pricing performed for the remaining pricing elements, pricing elements can be copied and taxes redetermined, and pricing elements can be copied and the freight redetermined.

Invoice lists enable you to send the payer (that is, the person settling the invoice) at regular intervals or on specified days a list containing several billing documents (invoices, debit and credit memos). The billing documents in the invoice list can be individual or collective documents. (Collective invoices contain items from more than one delivery.) In the standard R/3 System, there are two different types of invoice list for invoices and debit memos and for credit memos. However, if necessary, invoices and debit and credit memos can be processed at the same time. The system then automatically creates a separate invoice list for credit memos. For example, the payer may be the headquarters of a purchasing group which is to settle all invoices for goods which are delivered to the various members of the group. The payer for the group pays for the invoice lists and then invoices the amounts to the individual members. He receives a discount, known as a del credere, for this service. Depending on the tax structure in the country of the payer, the payer may have to pay tax for the del credere. In Germany, for example, a tax rate of 15% applies for del credere commission. During invoice list processing, you can pay this tax amount to the payer in advance by creating special condition records for this purpose.

In addition to discounts and surcharges such as cash discount and processing debit and credit memos, the R/3 System also supports rebate processing. A rebate is a special type of discount which is granted to the customer on the basis of his sales volume over a specified period. You record the rebate terms in a rebate agreement. In the agreement, you specify the recipient of the rebate payment and the criteria which form the basis for the rebate (customer, customer and material, material and so on). As rebate payments are always paid after the validity period for the rebate agreement has elapsed, the system must trace all billing documents which are relevant for rebate processing. The system posts accruals automatically to give the accounting department an overview of the cumulative rebate value. The rebate agreement is completely settled when the customer receives a credit memo for the entire value of the rebate.

You can use payment plans to process payment in instalments in the R/3 System. An invoice is created for each instalment in a payment plan. This billing document enables you to print out an invoice which lists the individual payment dates and the exact amounts. The system calculates the corresponding percentage of the billing value for each payment date. On the last payment date, the system takes the rounding differences into account. An accounts receivable line item is created in FI for each instalment. You use payment terms to define the instalments. The payment terms are controlled by a payment term key. In Customizing, you can specify the number of instalments, the payment dates and the percentage of the billing value for the key.

The invoice can be processed in different ways for each customer (separate invoice, collective invoice, invoice split and using a billing due list). If the data and the partners for all items in the delivery are the same and no split criteria have been defined, the system creates one invoice for this delivery. If the header data and header partner for several specified deliveries or orders are the same and if no split criteria apply, *one* invoice is created for all the deliveries or orders.

If deliveries are to be billed in several invoices according to specific criteria, you can use the invoice split function. For example, if you want the different product groups to be calculated separately, the split is performed according to product division. The system always attempts to combine deliveries for one customer in a collective invoice. You can, however, define split criteria in the R/3 System which prevent the system from combining delviries or sales orders in a collective invoice. If orders or deliveries cannot be combined because of these criteria, the system performs an invoice split. If and how deliveries are combined or split depends on how you define the criteria for the billing type, the reference document type (for example, the order, delivery or billing document to which the billing document refers) and the item category in the reference document.

When you process the billing due list, you do not need to explicitly enter the individual documents to be billed. The system selects the documents due for billing on the basis of selection criteria such as sold-to party, date, document type and number. In this case, the system can also combine several deliveries in one invoice. You can also simulate the billing due list. The system takes all documents which are due for billing into account and creates a list of billing documents that it would create. Incorrect billing documents are displayed with the appropriate processing status. It is also possible to display information regarding the billing items and foreign trade. If you process the billing due list and actually create billing documents for the list, you can also display this information in a log.

The system forwards billing data in invoices and credit and debit memos to Financial Accounting and posts this data to the appropriate accounts. Costs and revenue can be posted to the following accounts: *accounts receivable*, *general ledger* (such as the petty cash account), *revenues, sales deductions and accruals* (for rebate agreements). The system uses account determination to find automatically the appropriate accounts in a business area to post the amounts to. This business area can represent a sales area (if the accounts are to be posted with regard to sales), or a plant or product division (if the goods are to be posted with regard to the product). This is defined in Customizing. Account determination can depend on the chart of accounts for the company code, on the sales organization, the account assignment group of the customer (from the customer master record), the account assignment group of the material (from the material master record) and the account key (in the pricing procedure). The system uses the condition technique to perform account determination. The aim of account determination is to find the revenue accounts to which the price conditions are to be posted and the sales deduction accounts to which the surcharges and discounts are to be posted.

In the standard R/3 System, all billing document types are configured so that the offsetting entry is made to the accounts receivable account. If the offsetting entry is to be made to a G/L account (for example, a cash clearing account), you must create a billing document which contains the cash clearing account key EVV. The key controls that the invoice amount is posted to the relevant G/L account.

8.49.3 Using the process

In Model Company *A*, there is a delivery which is relevant for billing. You release the delivery for billing and enter the document number *80003652* on the billing document overview screen. You mark the items which are to be billed and reach the pricing screen by choosing the *Pricing* key (see Fig. 8.273). Using the condition types, the system selects and displays all pricing elements such as gross prices, discounts and surcharges, freight and taxes. In the example, you accept the net price and add no new conditions (see Fig. 8.274). You save the billing document. It is stored under the number *90004585*.

8.49.4 Navigation information

■ *Menu path*
Logistics –> Sales/distribution –> Billing –> Billing document –> Create

■ *Transaction code*
VF01

■ *Ingoing processes in the R/3 Reference Model*
Delivery processing; Returns processing; Rebate settlement processing; Third-party order processing; Processing credit/debit memo request; Rush order processing; Cash sale processing, Processing returnable packaging issue; Consignment issue processing; Business event execution; Rental contract processing; Network confirmation; Completion an processing of service contract; Expenses-related service order billing

■ *Outgoing processes in the R/3 Reference Model*
Billing document transfer and evaluation
Customer invoice processing
Status analysis
Project conclusion and update

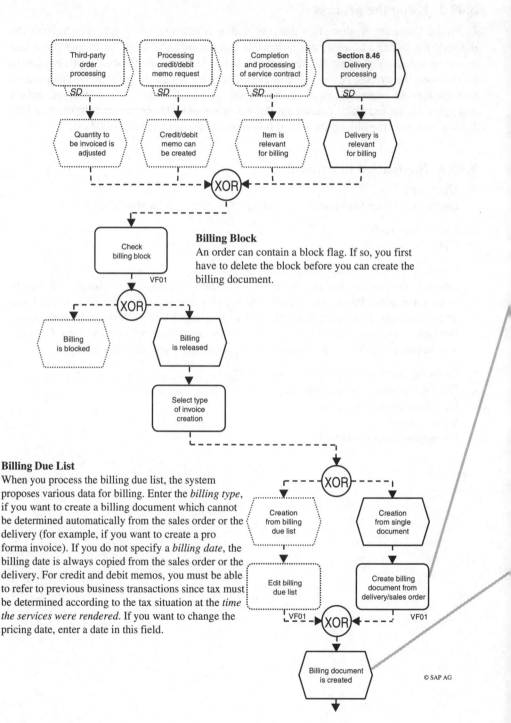

Billing Block

An order can contain a block flag. If so, you first have to delete the block before you can create the billing document.

Billing Due List

When you process the billing due list, the system proposes various data for billing. Enter the *billing type*, if you want to create a billing document which cannot be determined automatically from the sales order or the delivery (for example, if you want to create a pro forma invoice). If you do not specify a *billing date*, the billing date is always copied from the sales order or the delivery. For credit and debit memos, you must be able to refer to previous business transactions since tax must be determined according to the tax situation at the *time the services were rendered*. If you want to change the pricing date, enter a date in this field.

© SAP AG

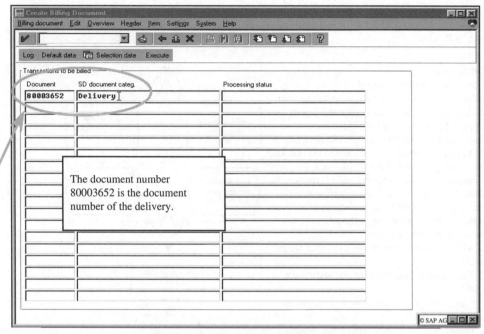

Fig. 8.272: Create billing document

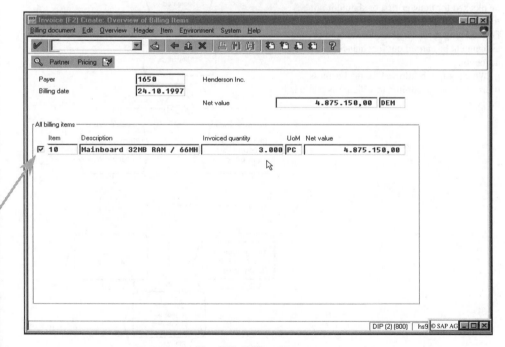

Fig. 273: Billing items

Billing type

Billing documents are controlled by the billing document type. Each billing document type can be set using control elements so that it has its own scope of functions. The billing document types can be adapted to meet your specific demands. If the billing document types defined in the standard version of the SAP R/3 System do not fulfil your company's requirements, new billing types can be defined. The following elements can be controlled by the billing document type:

a) From which number range should the document number be taken?

b) Which partner functions are allowed at header level?

c) Which partner functions are allowed at item level?

d) Which billing type can be used to cancel the billing document?

e) Should the billing document be transferred immediately to financial accounting or should it be blocked for transfer first or should it not be transferred at all?

f) According to which procedure should account assignment be carried out for financial accounting?

g) Which output is allowed for the business transaction and according to which procedure is it proposed?

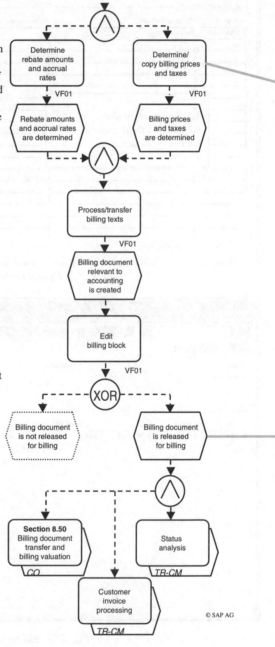

© SAP AG

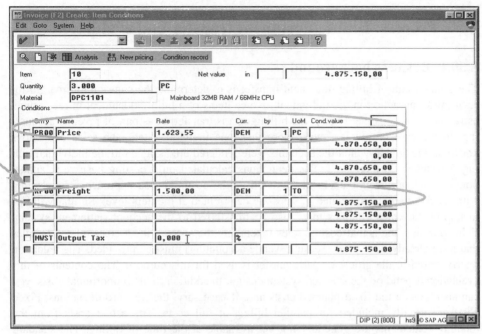

Fig. 8.274: Billing prices

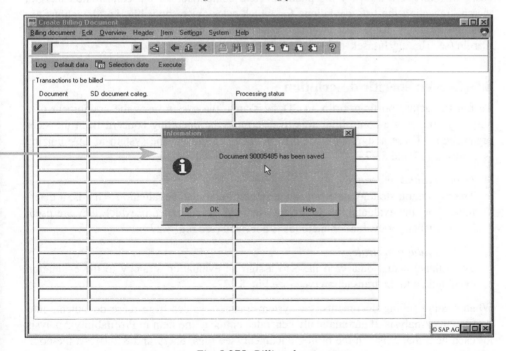

Fig. 8.275: Billing document

8.50 Process: Billing document transfer and evaluation

8.50.1 Business background

The primary aim of billing document transfer is to determine the contribution margin for each sales transaction in the individual invoice items of a billing document in real - time, as far as this is possible. Firstly, the billing data is transferred as part of revenue accounting. In the case of invoices with more than one individual item, the sales deductions known at the time at which the accounts were rendered are assigned to the individual billing line items. Furthermore, sales deductions calculated on a costing basis, e.g. annual bonuses and sales reimbursements, as well as the costing-based approaches for dealing with special direct costs related to sales are determined at the item level. Similarly, information on the sales volumes must also be transferred to the account settlement system. Following this, the actual cost of sales (excluding the special direct costs related to sales that have already been processed in revenue accounting) must be provided. The valuation matrix stored in the article or parts master is used for this purpose. The contents of this evaluation depend on the selected system design. In addition to the proportional costs, you can also include the fixed planned costs and, if necessary, the standard deviations. Fixed costs are usually included for parallel billing at full costs. The actual costs from the monthly settlements are generally not yet available at the time of billing. The standard costs, therefore, are used for the planned/actual comparison of the contribution margin, thereby revealing the true deviations for which sales are responsible, i.e. deviations excluding deviations in the cost of goods manufactured and differences in the contribution margin (see Herzog/Jurasek 1993, S. 131–136).

8.50.2 SAP-specific description

To transfer actual postings from an SD sales area, the system uses the assignment of a company code and a controlling area to determine the operating concern from the sales organization. These assignments are set up when configuring the system in Customizing (see Figs. 8.277 and 8.278).

- *Define evaluation strategy*
  The evaluation strategy determines the setup of automatic evaluation. That is, it determines how the evaluation methods are used and the sequence in which they are used. The sequence for evaluation methods is not fixed (see Fig. 8.278).

- *Assign evaluation strategy*
  To evaluate actual data, you have to assign an evaluation strategy to the evaluation event linked to the transaction type (see Fig. 8.277).

When posting billing documents, the system transfers values from these documents into Profitability Analysis. It automatically generates online a line item in Profitability Analysis for each item that exists in the billing document (see Figs. 8.279 and 8.280). At the point of billing, the operative logistics system uses the price determination function to calculate the sales revenue and enter it into the billing document. If there are any sales deductions such as rebates or cash discounts that may be taken, it enters these into the document as well. The stock value (the delivery price for merchandise or the total of the cost of goods manufactured) can also be determined and transferred. In addition to the customer and material number, the system transfers all the characteristics that are defined in Profitability Analysis and contained in the billing document to the line item it generates. A derivation may also be made to supply information to those characteristics for which derivation rules are defined. You can run product costing (that is, determine the cost of goods sold) to analyze the sales revenues and deductions which were calculated in the sales system and transferred to Profitability Analysis.

8.50.3 Using the process

In transferring billing documents, you are able to obtain the figures for sales revenue, sales deductions, and even the costs of sales (see Fig. 8.279). Model Company A has sales revenue of 2.700,00 (see Fig. 8.280). By including the sales deductions and costs of goods sold, you can see the profit margin for this product. When billing documents are released to finance, the system records sales, sales deductions and cost of sales (based on standard costing) in Profitability Analysis. The sales and product results used for Profitability Analysis are then always up to date. This data is stored in value fields (see Fig. 8.276) which are structured in the profit margin table for reporting purposes.

8.50.4 Navigation information

■ *Menu path*
1) Logistics –> Sales and distribution –> Billing –> Billing document –> Create –> Release for bookkeeping (if necessary)
2) Accounting –> Controlling –> Profitability analysis –> Information system –> Display line items –> Actual

■ *Transaction code*
VF01, KE24

■ *Ingoing processes in the R/3 Reference Model*
Value control with allocation costing
Value control with overhead costing
Value control with static standard costing
Value control with flexible standard costing
Billing
Preliminary costing with quantity structure

■ *Outgoing processes in the R/3 Reference Model*

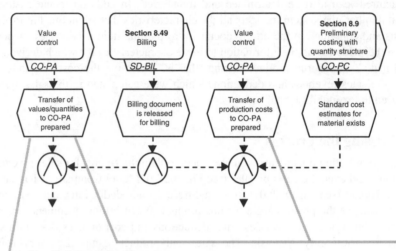

Standard Operating Concern

In the SAP standard system, the operating concern "S001" is provided as an example.
You can use it as reference for your own operating concern. However, do not use it for
productive operations.

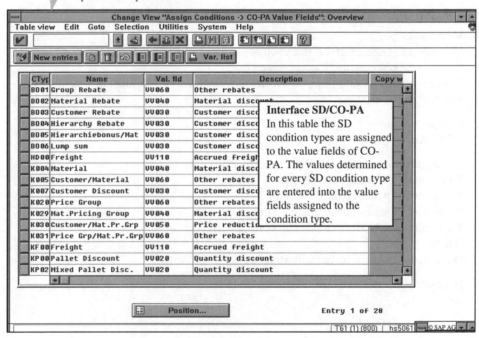

Fig. 8.276: Assign conditions to CO-PA value fields

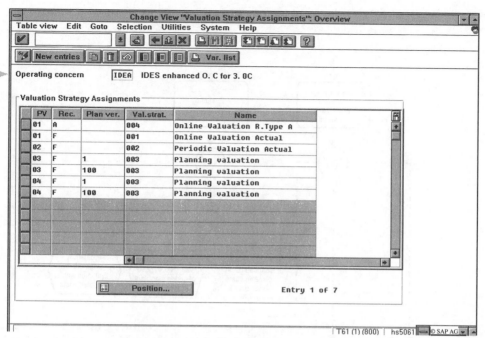

Fig. 8.277: Customizing of valuation strategy

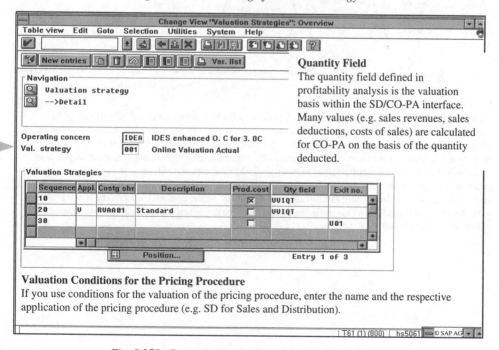

Quantity Field
The quantity field defined in profitability analysis is the valuation basis within the SD/CO-PA interface. Many values (e.g. sales revenues, sales deductions, costs of sales) are calculated for CO-PA on the basis of the quantity deducted.

Valuation Conditions for the Pricing Procedure
If you use conditions for the valuation of the pricing procedure, enter the name and the respective application of the pricing procedure (e.g. SD for Sales and Distribution).

Fig. 8.278: Customizing of valuation strategy in detail

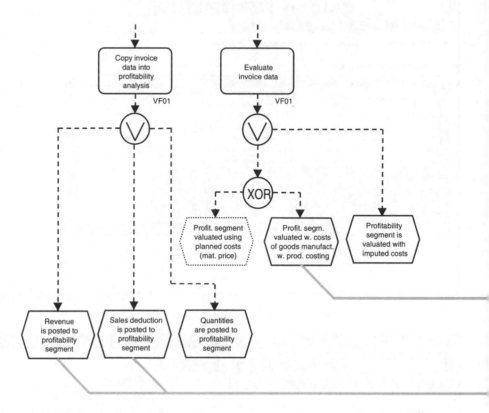

Operating Concern

An operating concern represents a part of an organization for which the sales market is structured in a uniform manner. For individual segments that are defined by classifying characteristics such as product group, customer group, country and distribution channel, an operating concern is calculated by setting off the costs against the revenues. These segments are referred to as "profitability segments". By means of a combination of characteristic values (e.g. customer Müller, article 4711, etc.), the system creates one profitability segment for each invoice item during posting. An operating concern can contain one or more controlling areas. The user of profitability analysis should define the operating concern he is working with as user parameter (ERB). Otherwise the system asks for the operating concern but saves this setting only until the next logoff.

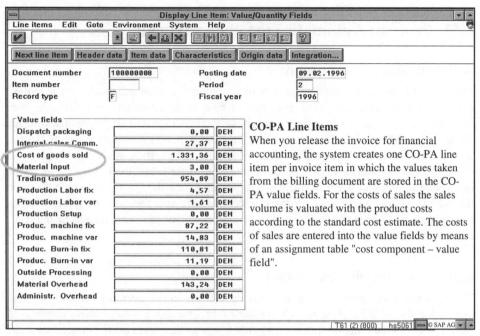

CO-PA Line Items

When you release the invoice for financial accounting, the system creates one CO-PA line item per invoice item in which the values taken from the billing document are stored in the CO-PA value fields. For the costs of sales the sales volume is valuated with the product costs according to the standard cost estimate. The costs of sales are entered into the value fields by means of an assignment table "cost component – value field".

Fig. 8.279: CO-PA line items (1/2)

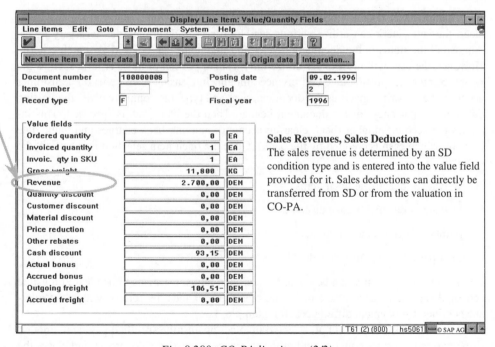

Sales Revenues, Sales Deduction

The sales revenue is determined by an SD condition type and is entered into the value field provided for it. Sales deductions can directly be transferred from SD or from the valuation in CO-PA.

Fig. 8.280: CO-PA line items (2/2)

8.51 Process: Automatic customer payment

8.51.1 Business background

Terms of delivery and payment are part of a company's sales and marketing activities. Companies frequently offer cash discounts to their credit customers. For example, they may offer a 3% reduction from an invoice price to encourage prompt payment within say 10 days. A buyer who does not pay within the 10-day period would have to pay the full invoice amount within 30 days after the invoice date, and in effect would be engaging in a deferred payment transaction. Most companies that offer credit terms such as these are never able to pinpoint when payment will be made unless they have some type of direct debiting agreement with their customers, which is rarely ever the case. Therefore, manual payment processing functions are used in posting customer payments instead of the automatic transactions in accounts payable.

8.51.2 SAP-specific description

Posting a payment receipt and clearing the open items in the customer account occur in one step in the SAP R/3 System. A remittance form containing the document numbers of the invoices or credit memos that the customer wants to clear from his or her account is the simplest example of posting an incoming payment document.

If a customer has not provided enough information about which invoices she wants to clear, the entry clerk can utilize various search criteria to determine the necessary items. Almost all the fields in the document header and line items can be used as search criteria. However, the user will most likely utilize only a small portion of those criteria such as the reference number, posting date and invoice amount. In clearing open items on a customer account, the user first specifies the document date and type, the company code, the posting date and the currency for the document header. Then the bank data is specified. This includes the account number (bank clearing account), amount, bank charges and value date (date on which cash is credited by the bank). Once the open item selection is specified, the user can:

- Activate or deactivate open items

- Activate or deactivate cash discount

- Maintain cash discount amounts

- Enter partial payments or residual items

Before any clearing entry can be made for the open items, the items to be cleared must be activated and the balance of the debit and credit entries must be zero or within the tolerance defined for payment differences, for example, 1%.

The system checks the total of all selected invoices against the specified payment amount. If the two amounts are equal or within the tolerance, it posts the document and clears the invoices with the payment. Each cleared item is assigned the number of the clearing document (for example, the number of the payment document) and the clearing date.

8.51.3 Using the process

In the status group box on the initial screen for automatic payment transactions, you can see that no parameters have been maintained (see Fig. 8.281). To set up the payment run, you need to specify the payment methods and customer account. The payment method for our model company is a check (C). However, there are other methods of payment (see Fig. 8.284). Account number *1650* is specified for our customer, Model Company B (see Fig. 8.282). The system then lists the open items that are due for payment, and the user double checks some payment specifications, for example the house bank, payment method, and so on (see Fig. 8.285). Finally, the payment run is executed. The status group box shows that the payment run was executed and that one posting order was generated and completed.

8.51.4 Navigation information

■ *Menu path*
Accounting –> Financial accounting –> Accounts receivable –> Document entry –> Incoming payment

■ *Transaction code*
F-28

■ *Ingoing processes in the R/3 Reference Model*
Trip application processing; Travel expense accounting; Invoice processing without reference; Invoice processing with reference; Consignment invoice processing; Vendor invoice processing; Processing of asset acquisition; Customer down payment request; Vendor down payment request; Down payment release; Customer invoice processing; One-time customer invoice processing; Leasing payment; Customer request for payment; Cash planning; Subsequent condition settlement; Vendor request for payment

■ *Outgoing processes in the R/3 Reference Model*
Budget execution/verification
Bill of exchange presentation
Availability check
Down payment release
Project update

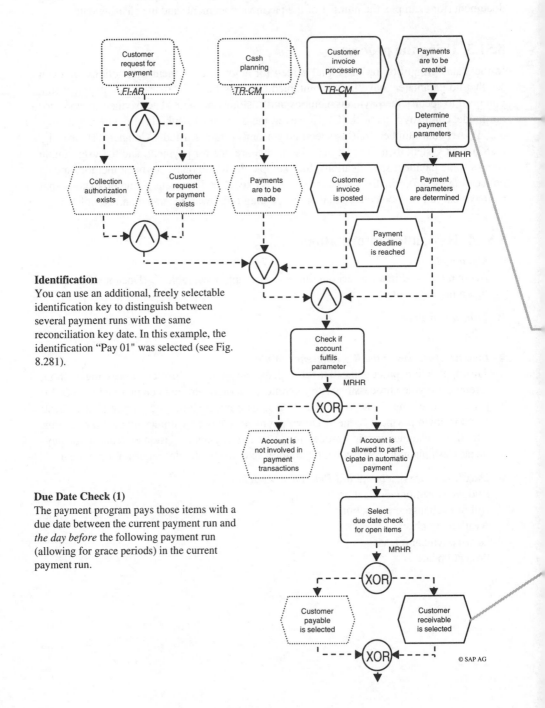

Identification

You can use an additional, freely selectable identification key to distinguish between several payment runs with the same reconciliation key date. In this example, the identification "Pay 01" was selected (see Fig. 8.281).

Due Date Check (1)

The payment program pays those items with a due date between the current payment run and *the day before* the following payment run (allowing for grace periods) in the current payment run.

© SAP AG

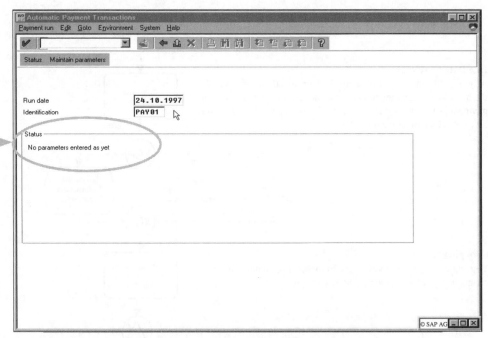

Fig. 8.281: Initial screen of automatic payment

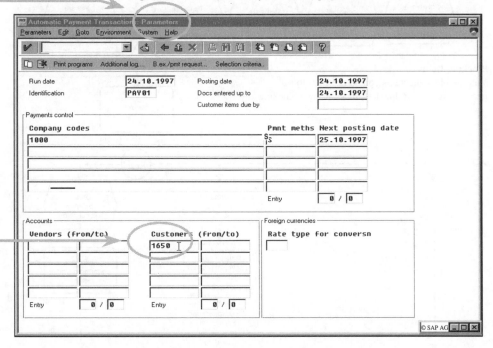

Fig. 8.282: Parameters – automatic payment

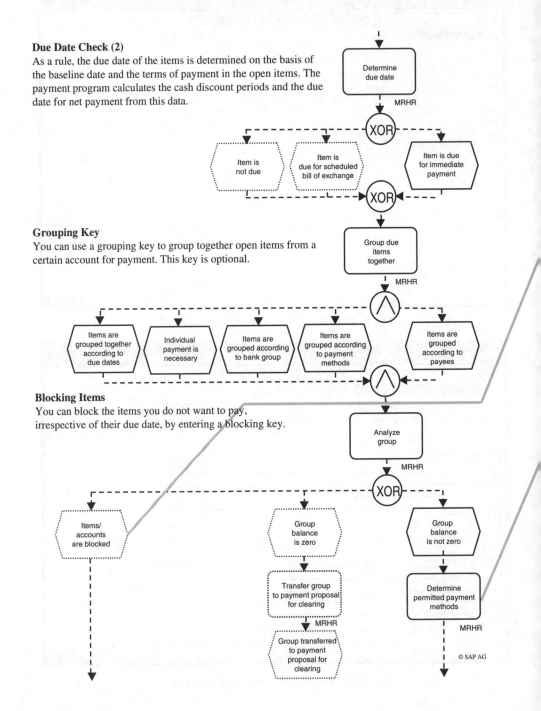

Due Date Check (2)
As a rule, the due date of the items is determined on the basis of the baseline date and the terms of payment in the open items. The payment program calculates the cash discount periods and the due date for net payment from this data.

Grouping Key
You can use a grouping key to group together open items from a certain account for payment. This key is optional.

Blocking Items
You can block the items you do not want to pay, irrespective of their due date, by entering a blocking key.

Determine
due date

MRHR

XOR

Item is
not due

Item is
due for scheduled
bill of exchange

Item is due
for immediate
payment

XOR

Group due
items
together

MRHR

Items are
grouped together
according to
due dates

Individual
payment is
necessary

Items are
grouped according
to bank group

Items are
grouped according
to payment
methods

Items are
grouped
according to
payees

Analyze
group

MRHR

XOR

Items/
accounts
are blocked

Group
balance
is zero

Group
balance
is not zero

Transfer group
to payment proposal
for clearing

MRHR

Group transferred
to payment
proposal for
clearing

Determine
permitted payment
methods

MRHR

© SAP AG

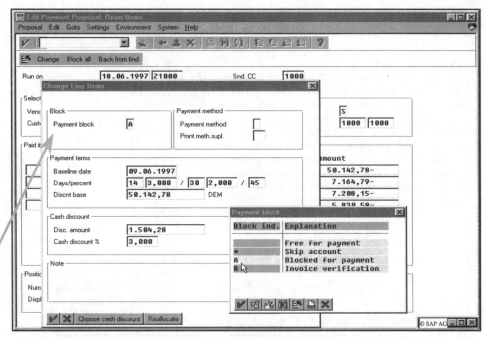

Fig. 8.283: Payment block

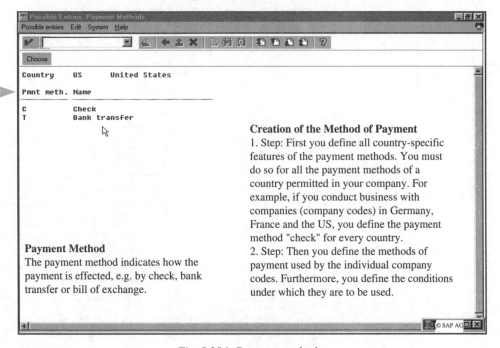

Payment Method

The payment method indicates how the payment is effected, e.g. by check, bank transfer or bill of exchange.

Creation of the Method of Payment

1. Step: First you define all country-specific features of the payment methods. You must do so for all the payment methods of a country permitted in your company. For example, if you conduct business with companies (company codes) in Germany, France and the US, you define the payment method "check" for every country.
2. Step: Then you define the methods of payment used by the individual company codes. Furthermore, you define the conditions under which they are to be used.

Fig. 8.284: Payment methods

Payment by Check

For the payment method "check" (see Fig. 8.284), you do not specify any minimum amount limits since this payment method is used if other payment methods cannot be used. You must, however, specify a maximum amount as otherwise this payment method cannot be used. The customer or vendor may be located abroad. The customer/vendor's bank is irrelevant for check payments. Foreign payment transactions are therefore possible. Payments in foreign currencies are permitted.

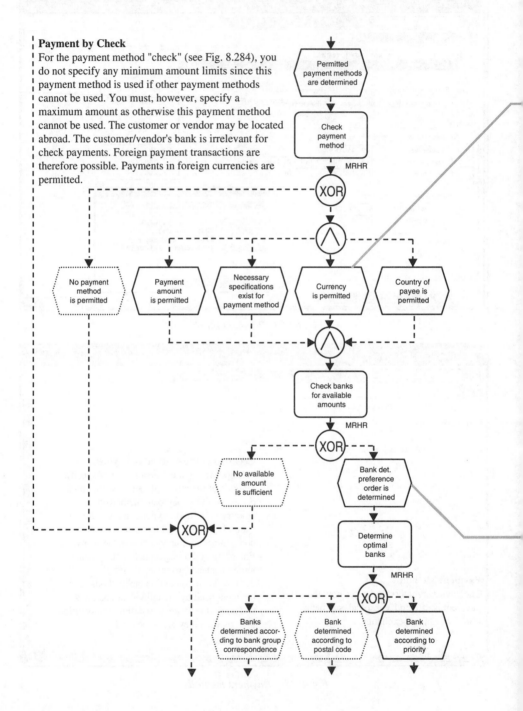

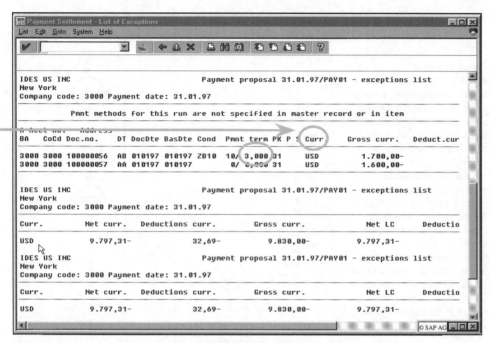

Fig. 8.285: List of exceptions

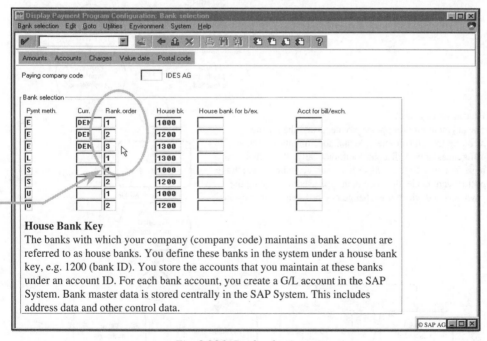

House Bank Key

The banks with which your company (company code) maintains a bank account are referred to as house banks. You define these banks in the system under a house bank key, e.g. 1200 (bank ID). You store the accounts that you maintain at these banks under an account ID. For each bank account, you create a G/L account in the SAP System. Bank master data is stored centrally in the SAP System. This includes address data and other control data.

Fig. 8.286: Bank selection

Check Payment

A check is performed to ensure that the corresponding invoice is not to be cleared through that same payment run, and also, that it has not already been paid. If a payment request cannot be paid because of one of those two reasons, the request will appear on the payment proposal exception list. In this case, the request should be cancelled, since it cannot be carried out. You can also make partial payments for invoices that have already been posted. The invoice is blocked for payment and a payment request in the required partial amount is entered.

Posting of Payments

The payment program posts payments and the postings resulting from it (for example tax, adjustments, exchange rate differences or cash discount) automatically. To do this, you must first specify the bank or bank sub-accounts to which the postings are made, the document type used for posting the payments and whether exchange rate differences are posted.

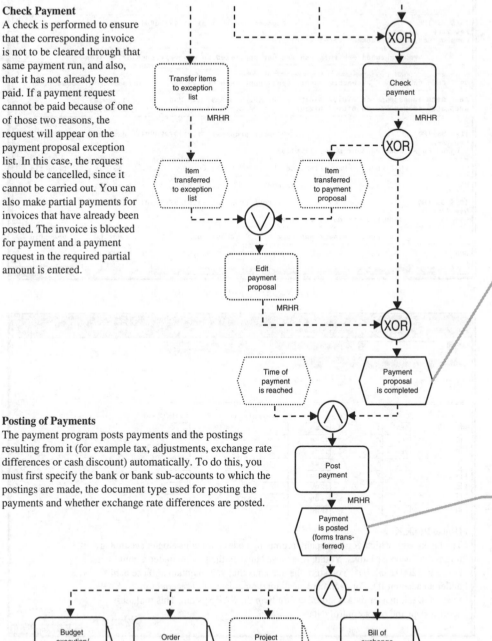

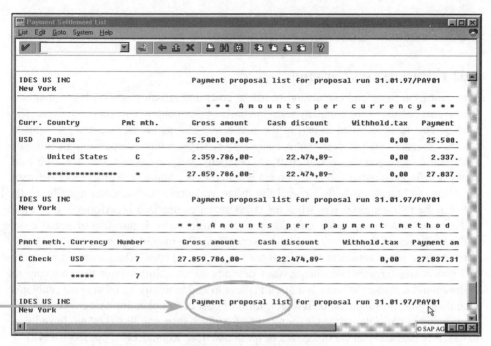

Fig. 8.287: Payment proposal

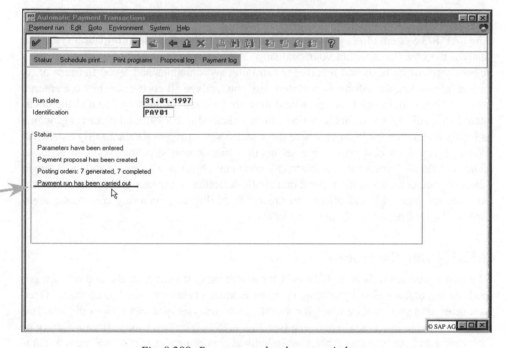

Fig. 8.288: Payment run has been carried out

8.52 Process: Cost centre analysis

8.52.1 Business background

Cost centre planning and calculation of actual costs and actual allocation base quantities for the cost centres of the company form the basis of the monthly cost centre analysis. The planned cost rates recorded as part of the cost centre closing are an essential prerequisite for the "essence" of the cost centre analysis, i.e. target/actual comparison. In this target/actual comparison, the actual costs are compared with the target costs for each cost centre and for each individual cost element within the cost centre. The differences between the actual and target costs then reveal the usage variances. A distinction must be made between the following subareas when the target/actual comparison is performed: recording of the actual assessment bases, calculation of the target costs, itemization of actual costs and compilation of the target/actual cost comparison. The monthly target/actual cost comparison alone is not sufficient to bring about a reduction in costs. The success of planning and continuous target/actual comparisons depends on an ability within the company to understand the matters at hand and a willingness to tackle jointly all of the cost problems identified. This presupposes, therefore, a form of cost centre planning that is accepted by the persons responsible for the cost centre and for which responsibility is taken. In addition to this, it is essential that the objectives be *attainable* (see Konrad 1971, pp. 1099–1118).

8.52.2 SAP-specific description

The SAP R/3 System offers you a comprehensive as well as flexible information system to analyze the cost flows within your company. You can execute standard evaluations on a regularly recurring basis and reports for extraordinary situations and tasks. Because of its online integration, the information system lets you analyze all costs once they are entered into the system and track how and where they are incurred all the way down to the document level. All reports available online can be executed in background processing, which is highly recommended in cases where the selected sets of report data are fairly extensive. When objects such cost centres are set up in a hierarchical structure, you can generate either individual reports for each hierarchy node and object or all these reports in a single selection run. Generating the reports in a single selection run means you can interactively navigate the hierarchy and offers you greater flexibility in monitoring cost centre areas (see SAP – Overhead Cost Controlling 1996).

8.52.3 Using the process

The cost centre analysis process is used for analyzing cost centres at the end of each period, during organizational planning, or when random evaluations need to be made. Once you determine your requirements for a cost centre analysis, you can turn to the standard reports available in the R/3 report tree (see Fig. 8.289). You can choose from a variety of cost centre and cost element reports for individual cost centres or cost centre areas to compare planned or target costs with actual costs. These reports can compare actual costs to planned or target costs for any cost centres you choose. In practice, they are used for monthly comparisons of target values and actual values at period-end. For more detailed analyses of cost flows, the system contains reports that let you trace the source of costs and view the partner objects, for example orders or other cost centres, which were part of the original transaction. Other reports monitor line items both actual and planned. You can execute line item reports directly or using the report-to-report interface from within other reports. You can navigate from line item reports to document display. Since the variance calculation function in CO is integrated into the online system, you can determine the cause of any variances you might find between actual and planned costs with the help of the standard SAP reports. The standard SAP reports also allow you to monitor commitments and budget management, calculate future costs using costs planned or incurred in prior periods, and effect cost controlling in a rolling year. If these standard reports do not meet your company's requirements, you can use Report Painter to create and define your own. The target/actual comparison report was selected for Model Company A in the report tree. Cost centre 1000 and period 1 to 12 for fiscal year 1996 were entered on the initial screen (see Fig. 8.290). By clicking the Execute button, you reach the report screen where actual costs are compared with target costs broken down into cost elements (see Fig. 8.291). Variances are displayed in both absolute and percentages. You can navigate to a line item and then display the document. In this example, the line item for cost element *430000* was displayed (see Fig. 8.292) in addition to its document (see Fig. 8.293).

8.52.4 Navigation information

- *Menu path*
  Accounting –> Controlling –> Cost centres –> Information system –> Choose report

- *Transaction code*
  SART

- *Ingoing processes in the R/3 Reference Model*
  Period-end closing with cost assessment an overhead cost
  Period-end closing with static standard costing / flexible standard costing
  Profit centre analysis

- *Outgoing processes in the R/3 Reference Model*

Report Painter

For customer-specific evaluations, Release 3.0 of the SAP system features the Report Painter – a tool for quick and easy creation of user-defined reports. It is based on the concept "what you see is what you get", meaning the user sees the structure of the report during report definition as it is being defined and changed into its final form. You can structure the report into sections and column blocks.

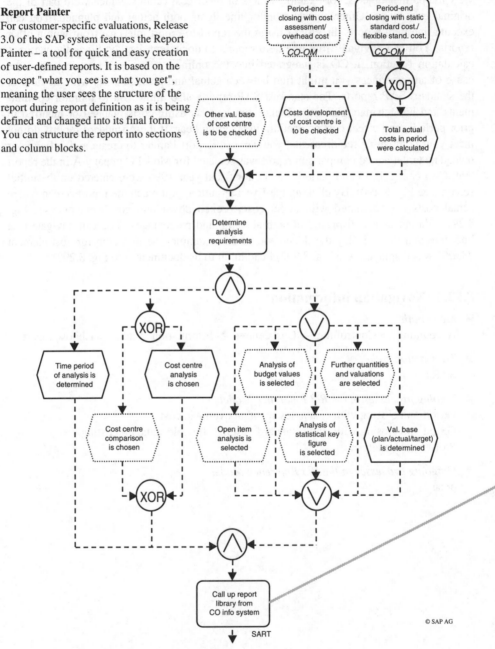

Information System Cost centre Accounting

With the interactive information system, you can analyze all transactions both individually and in summarized form, such as by cost centre or cost element. You can choose from either a line item report or reports defined with Report Painter. The line item report can analyze individual entries according to criteria entered by the user. Each business event is documented in an individual line item and saved in a CO line item file. Data is managed separately in these files by budgeted and actual events. The plan and actual line item entries are differentiated into primary and secondary postings. Primary postings are taken from external accounting to Controlling, while secondary postings are entries exclusively in internal accounting. The individual transactions in actual and commitment accounts can be analyzed with the line item report. Each individual transaction is automatically summarized in a totals record. This summarization takes place in the SAP System using the criteria established for cost centre/cost element or cost centre/cost element/activity type. The summarized data is saved in the CO totals record data and can be analyzed with Report Painter reports (e.g. Cost centre: actual/target /variance).

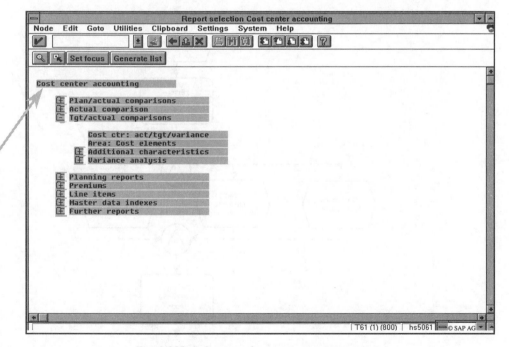

Fig. 8.289: Infosystem for cost centre accounting

Cost centre Reports
The reports for cost elements are used to analyze postings made to a cost element according to cost centres. For the designated cost centre or cost centre group, an overview is generated according to the cost element of actual and plan or actual and target values with the absolute and percentage variance. The marginal costs report includes the fixed and variable components of the actual and target costs. Furthermore, both reports show the actual and the plan quantities. The report cost centres: actual/target/variance is located in the standard report tree by way of the node target/actual comparison. This report is used in CCA based on marginal costs. It generates a company settlement document. The summation within a report takes place for each cost element or cost element group.

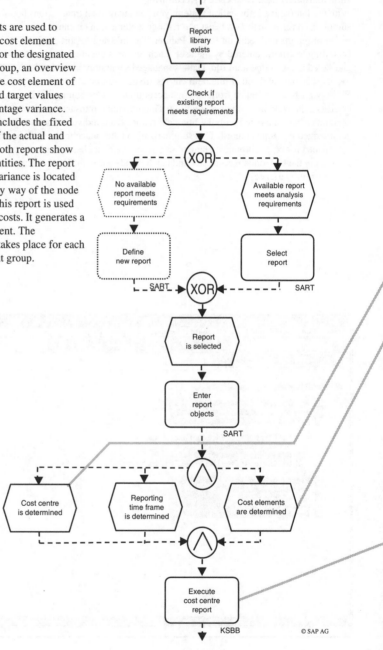

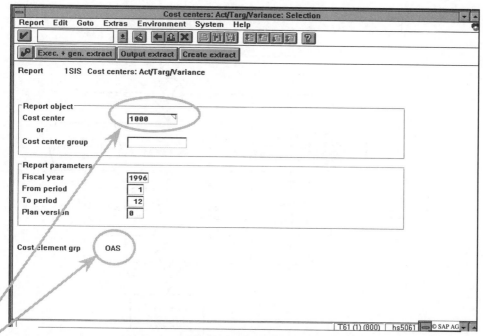

Fig. 8.290: Initial screen of cost centre analysis

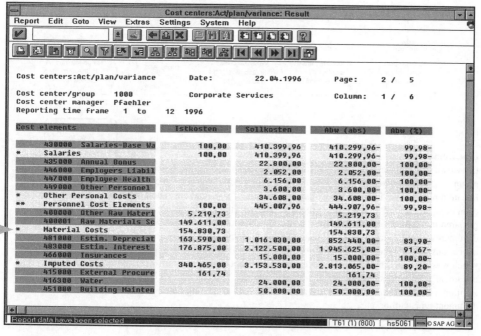

Fig. 8.291: Result of cost centre analysis

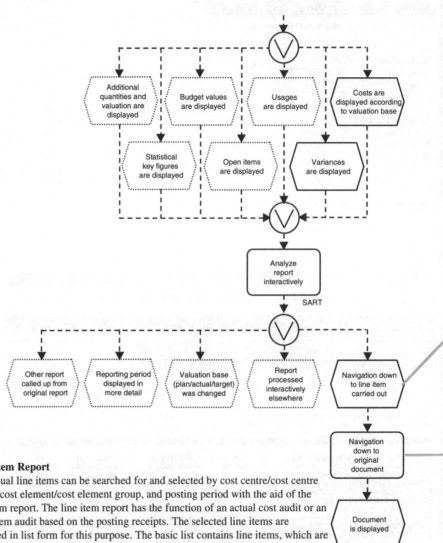

Line Item Report

Individual line items can be searched for and selected by cost centre/cost centre group, cost element/cost element group, and posting period with the aid of the line item report. The line item report has the function of an actual cost audit or an open item audit based on the posting receipts. The selected line items are prepared in list form for this purpose. The basic list contains line items, which are documents from Controlling (CO) created through internal transfer postings, allocations, and postings to Financial Accounting (FI). If you click on a line item which was generated by a posting process in FI and choose the function "Sender document", the original FI document will be displayed. You can also view additional information relevant to cost accounting, such as posting date, document type, author, etc.

© SAP AG

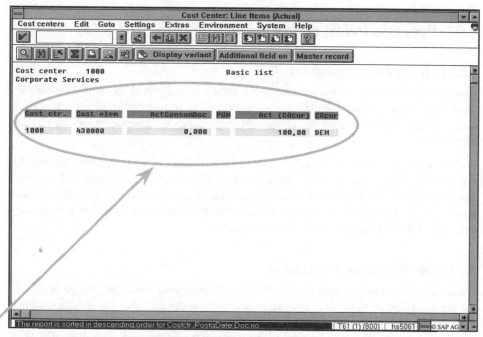

Fig. 8.292: Line items (actual)

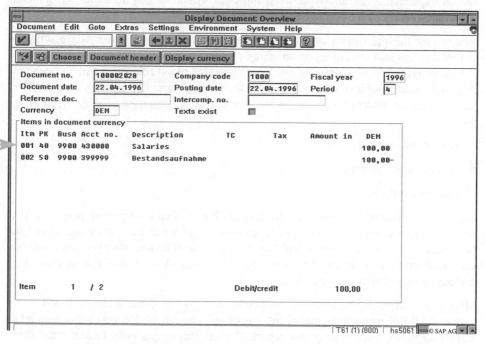

Fig. 8.293: Document for line item

8.53 Process: Profit centre reporting

8.53.1 Business background

Profit centre reporting is used to control the results of individual areas of responsibility (profit centres) within an organization. As a controlling instrument, it differs from profitability analysis in that profitability analysis mainly focuses on external factors for controlling sales.

Profit centres are usually analyzed on a periodic basis. These analyses show the internal results of each profit centre by comparing costs against revenues. The costs and revenues of a profit centre could be actual data, planned data, or a combination of both planned and actual data. Variances determined during the routine comparison of actual and planned data help in monitoring each individual profit centre.

8.53.2 SAP-specific description

Profit centre accounting using the EC-PCA application component helps you determine the operating results of profit centres and thus evaluate the performance of organizational units and sub-units. You can set up profit centres in your organization for the products, regions or functions that make up the base components of enterprise controlling. EC-PCA can be implemented by any type of organization within various industries. Operational results are evaluated on a periodic basis.

You can use the information system to analyze, individually or in summary form, all types of postings that have an impact on operating profits. The main component of the information system is the FI-SL Report Writer. You can use the reports delivered with the standard system or create your own reports to analyze the postings stored in summary record tables. The information system for Profit Centre Accounting is comprised of three types of reports:

- Report Writer reports
- Report Painter reports
- Line item reports

Report Writer reports are best suited for creating lists of data for reporting purposes. You can execute these reports in background processing. You will have to define special reports only if the reports delivered with the standard system do not cover your own individual requirements or reporting structures. All standard reports are available in client 000 and can be imported to other clients as needed.

Most of your reporting requirements will be covered by the standard reports found in the various SAP R/3 application components. However, you can use Report Painter to quickly and easily define your own special reports. Report Painter performs basically the same functions as Report Writer. Report Painter uses a graphical report structure as the basis for defining reports. The columns and rows you define for a report are exactly how they will appear once you output the report. The advantages of using Report Painter are the simple and flexible functions it offers for defining reports.

For a more detailed analysis of entries that flow to Profit Centre Accounting, you can use line item reports. These reports are separated into planned postings and actual postings, and they are based on the PCA documents that are updated in Profit Centre Accounting. Updating these documents is optional. You can navigate to the original FI, CO or SD document in line item reports that are comprised of actual postings.

8.53.3 Using the process

You can choose from a number of reports for profit centres in the standard system. A plan/actual comparison report was selected for Model Company A (see Fig. 8.294). This report lists the planned and actual postings from the cost and revenue elements of the profit centre group *Axel 1* (see Fig. 8.295). You can navigate to a detailed display of the actual line items for a cost or revenue element. The actual line items are displayed for revenue element *140000* (see Fig. 8.296). You can then display the FI document for a particular line item, for example, item *115401* (see Fig. 8.297).

8.53.4 Navigation information

- *Menu path*
  Accounting –> Controlling –> Profit centre accounting –>
  Information system –> Choose report

- *Transaction code*
  SART

- *Ingoing processes in the R/3 Reference Model*
  Profit centre planning closing
  Period closing in profit centre accounting

- *Outgoing processes in the R/3 Reference Model*
  Cost centre analysis

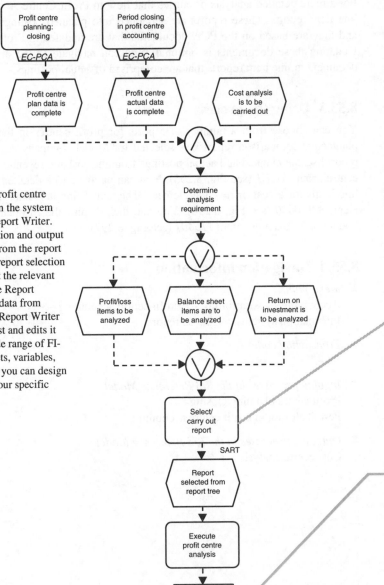

Report Selection

The standard reports for profit centre accounting implemented in the system were designed with the Report Writer. For the direct report selection and output of these standard reports from the report tree or report list, use the report selection screen in which you select the relevant entry parameters. With the Report Writer, you can report on data from various applications. The Report Writer selects the data you request and edits it as required. Using the wide range of FI-SL components such as sets, variables, formulas, cells and ratios, you can design the reports according to your specific demands.

© SAP AG

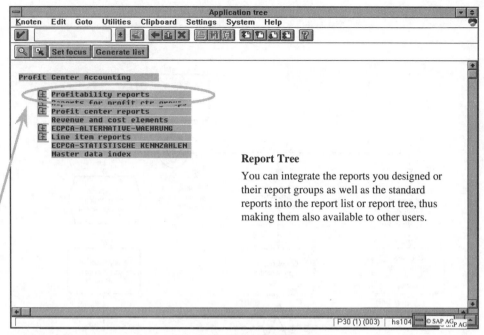

Report Tree

You can integrate the reports you designed or their report groups as well as the standard reports into the report list or report tree, thus making them also available to other users.

Fig. 8.294: Report selection

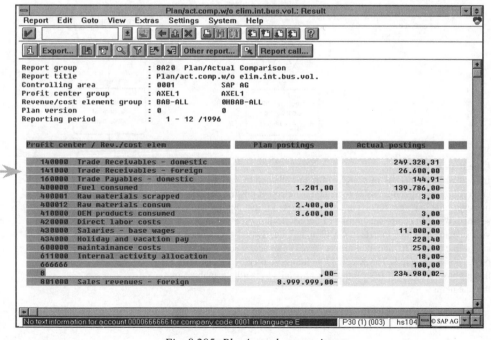

Fig. 8.295: Plan/actual comparison

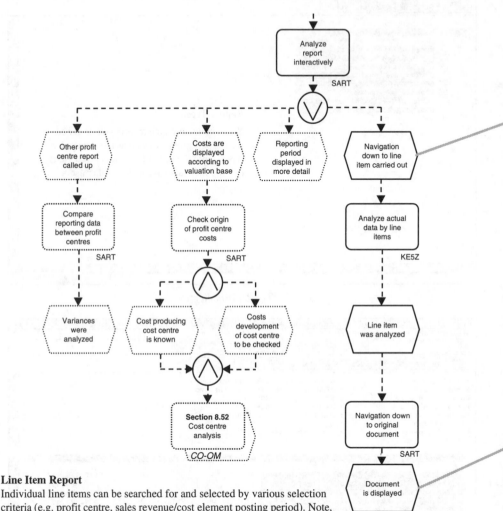

Line Item Report

Individual line items can be searched for and selected by various selection criteria (e.g. profit centre, sales revenue/cost element posting period). Note, however, that line item reports are only generated if the appropriate settings for profit centre accounting in the controlling area and the fiscal year selected have been made in Customizing, i.e. if you have defined actual line items. The line item report serves as an actual cost audit based on the posting receipts. The selected line items are prepared in list form for this purpose. You can display a number of details to facilitate analysis of the line items.

© SAP AG

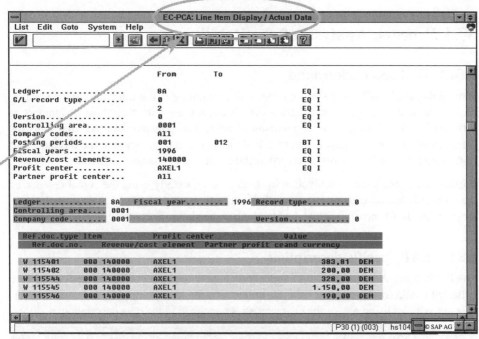

Fig. 8.296: Actual line item

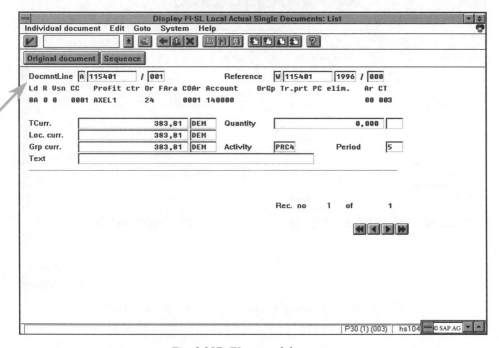

Fig. 8.297: FI – actual document

8.54 Process: Analysis of profitability

8.54.1 Business background

Profitability analysis is set up in a modern cost accounting system, for example one capable of marginal costing, as contribution margin accounting with fixed cost assignment at different levels and concurrent comparison of actual and planned data. As vital tools for the analysis of profits, comparisons of actual and planned data facilitate the measurement of the financial results of individual responsibility areas and business segments.

Profitability is analyzed monthly and, in some cases, quarterly using the actual revenue or the costing-based revenue and revenue deductions that are determined in estimated calculation methods. Comparing actual data to planned data helps in controlling profitability.

8.54.2 SAP-specific description

The Profitability Analysis (CO-PA) application component lets you easily analyze all data collected within the component using its online information system. It enables you to analyze any data set using any of the characteristics contained in the data description.

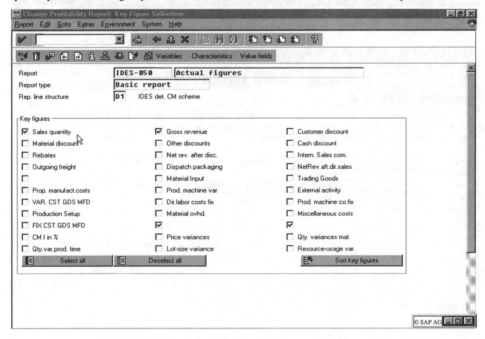

Fig. 8.298: Selection of key figures for profitability report

There are a variety of key figures to choose from for evaluation, including simple field values and values calculated from a line structure. A line structure combines related key figures into a collection of formulas for calculating a key figure. The CO-PA report tree contains sample reports for both costing-based and account-based analyses, which you can use as models in defining your own reports. When you define your reports, the system offers you all the characteristics of the operating concern you are evaluating (see Fig. 8.298). You can choose the ones that you require for your evaluation. The functions for defining reports can be accessed in Customizing as well as in the CO-PA application menu.

Report	Costing-based profitability analysis	Report	Accounts-based profitability analysis
0-SAP01	Target/actual comparison	0-SAP01	Cost element report
0-SAP02	Division comparison	0-SAP02	Target/actual comparison – controlling area currency
0-SAP03	Hit list acc. to customer group	0-SAP03	Target/actual comparison – company code currency
0-SAP04	DB I:districts/plants/material group	0-SAP04	Profit centre report
0-SAP05	Percentages	0-SAP05	Automatic currency translation
0-SAP06	Comparison: current/previous year		

Fig. 8.299: SAP sample reports

8.54.3 Using the process

To make it easier for users to execute various reports for profitability analysis, most of the settings are already made in the report definition. The user simply enters the name of the report he or she requires (see Fig. 8.300) and then can choose from a variety of options to analyze the report data even further. For example, the drill-down function lets users navigate to another analysis of characteristics, hit lists allow users to sort the report characteristics according to various criteria, and another function enables them to change the hierarchy for navigation. The profitability analysis for Model Company A is broken down into divisions and then drilled down to division *07* HiTech (see Figs. 8.301 and 8.302).

8.54.4 Navigation information

■ *Menu path*
Accounting –> Controlling –> Profitability analysis –> Information system –> Choose report

■ *Transaction code*
KE30

■ *Ingoing processes in the R/3 Reference Model*
Preparation for analysis

■ *Outgoing processes in the R/3 Reference Model*

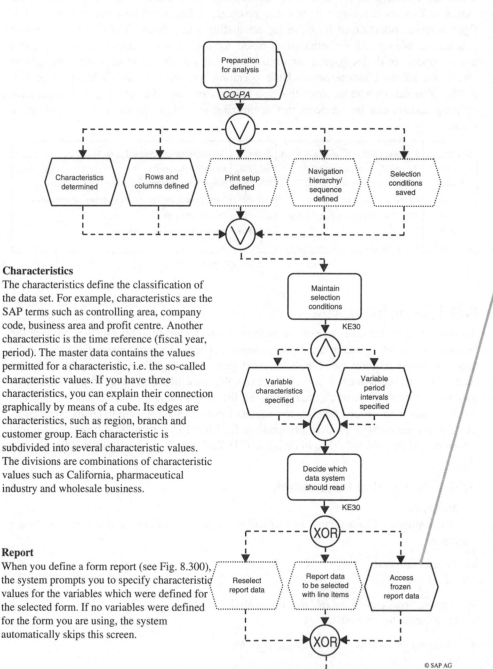

Characteristics

The characteristics define the classification of the data set. For example, characteristics are the SAP terms such as controlling area, company code, business area and profit centre. Another characteristic is the time reference (fiscal year, period). The master data contains the values permitted for a characteristic, i.e. the so-called characteristic values. If you have three characteristics, you can explain their connection graphically by means of a cube. Its edges are characteristics, such as region, branch and customer group. Each characteristic is subdivided into several characteristic values. The divisions are combinations of characteristic values such as California, pharmaceutical industry and wholesale business.

Report

When you define a form report (see Fig. 8.300), the system prompts you to specify characteristic values for the variables which were defined for the selected form. If no variables were defined for the form you are using, the system automatically skips this screen.

© SAP AG

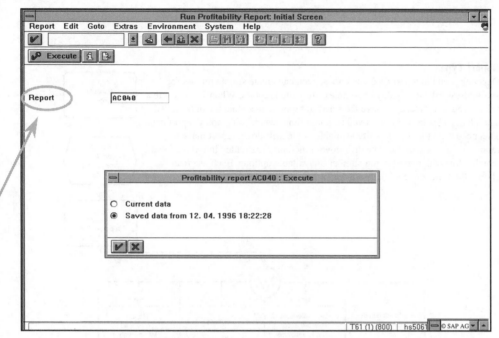

Fig. 8.300: Initial screen of profitability analysis

Drill-down Reporting Architecture

Report definitions can include characteristics, scores and forms. The result of a report is a number of lists and diagrams on the screen that can be selected interactively. Report lists can be printed and sent (e.g. as facsimile or telex), they can be prepared for the Internet or imported in MS-Word and MS-Excel as a file.

Scores

The system features a large number of scores that can be relevant for evaluations. Scores can be values and quantities as well as calculations based on user-defined formulas. For example:
• Value: costs, sales, sales deduction
• Quantity: Number of employees, sales volume
• Calculation: sales volume per employee, contribution margin.

Report Type

Depending on the report type you choose, you can create simple reports for straightforward data display or complex, formatted reports. When you execute a report, you can "freeze" or save the selected report data so that it can be called up again later. This leads to improved response times when you display report data. The menus and the functionality available in the drill-down report make the reporting tool easy to use. The drill-down functions are divided into three levels, which differ with regard to the number of available options. Each user can choose the function level that suits his or her requirements.

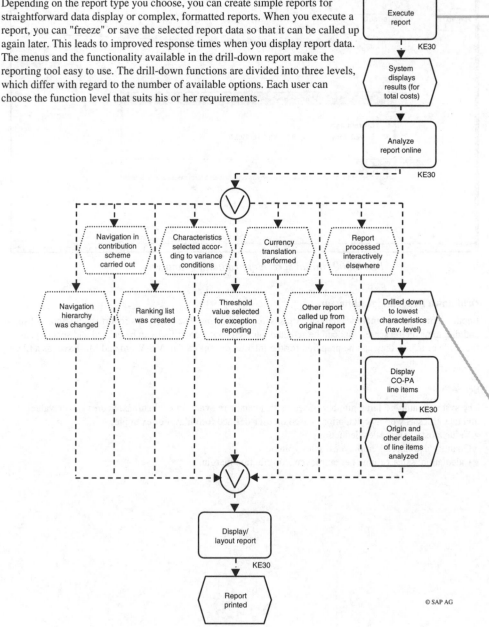

© SAP AG

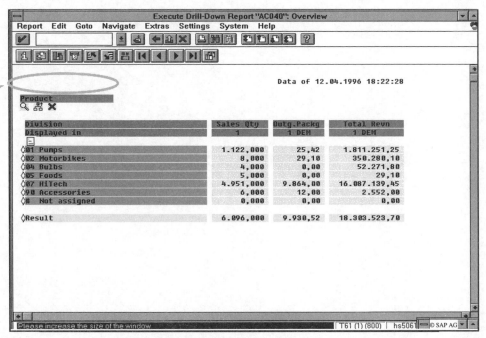

Fig. 8.301: Drill-down report

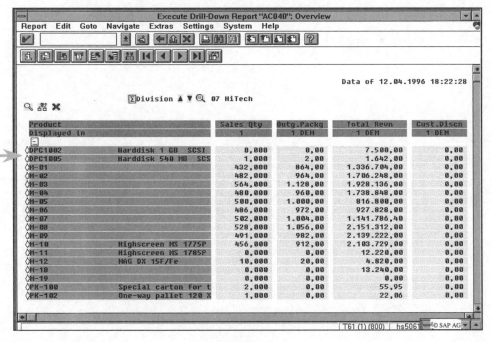

Fig. 8.302: Overview

9 Value Chain of an Order-Related Assembly Manufacturer

In the Model Company described in chapter 8, the sales support activities and the planning, production and procurement activities took place at different times. Planning, production and procurement are controlled in-house, and the customer's influence is merely apparent in the order processing process, starting with the sales order and delivery from the warehouse. In addition, outline agreements permit relatively stable planning with foresight. A large number of other enterprises belong to a market segment in which the customer's influence has direct consequences for production activities. Depending on the product and market constellation, these consequences may affect the company's assembly, manufacturing and – in extreme cases – possibly even development activities.

Thus, prior to carrying out an order, a customer-related order manufacturer will often initially obtain a quotation from the sales and distribution department. The starting point is an inquiry from the customer, which is recorded in sales and distribution. The product requirements, the quantity, the quality criteria and a fixed maximum price are the essential information that must be entered. The customer sends a letter of inquiry and possibly a drawing for this purpose. The drawing does not contain all the data necessary to submit a concrete quotation, however. Consequently, additional information must be acquired within the company before the quotation can be drawn up. The sales and distribution department therefore forwards the inquiry entered on the order form together with the drawing to the engineering/design department, whose task is to examine the technical feasibility of the requirements stated by the customer. The product requirements formulated in the drawing, the number of units and documentation relating to similar, already implemented orders form the basis for this valuation. The first step is to define the original materials. The extent to which the customer's stated requirements can be met using the available materials is analyzed. Once the original material has been established, the next step is for the purchasing department to submit a material inquiry. This inquiry lays down the technical specifications for the material. The task of the purchasing department is to determine the commercial purchase price of the materials that must be procured externally as well as the potential suppliers. Parallel to this, the information is passed on to work scheduling when the specification of the original material is completed. The work scheduling department checks whether the inquiry can be satisfied from a production point of view and defines the most important work steps. Consultation with quality assurance and production is often necessary. When the work schedules have been elaborated with sufficient precision, the documents are passed on to operating resources construction. The task of the operating resources construction department is to specify the production resources and tools and calculate the costs that are entailed. Depending on the nature of the production resources and tools, additional information may once again be required either from purchasing regarding materials that must be procured externally or from production in connection with those resources and tools that are to be produced in-house. The material price, the work schedule data and the costs for production resources and tools are then made available for the preliminary costing. The preliminary costing department calculates the

unit cost price on the basis of all the available data. After the costs of the goods manufactured have been determined, taking account of any uncertainties owing to in some cases
incomplete data, the information is passed on to sales and distribution, which fixes the
quotation price and formulates the quotation to the customer.

In the case of Model Company *B*, the customer's influence has no consequences for development activities, in other words when the order is received, no new drawings, bills of
materials or work schedules need to be prepared. It is primarily the logistic activities of the
assembly planning and purchase orders departments that are affected. Firstly, an assembly
order is created in accordance with the received and accepted order and secondly, the
motherboard requested by the customer is released on the basis of the outline agreement
with Model Company *A*. The value chain of Model Company *B* is represented below from
the specification of the master data through the complete implementation of order processing to sales controlling. It is evident that – in contrast with Model Company *A* – the
entire processing process is controlled primarily by the activities of sales and distribution.
It can however also be seen that certain processes, such as *goods receipt processing from
production*, are carried out in both companies. As the maximum processes have already
been described in detail for Model Company *A*, only the processes to the customer (see
Section 9) and to the supplier, in other words to Model Company *A* (see Section 9.1.), are
shown here for Model Company *B*.

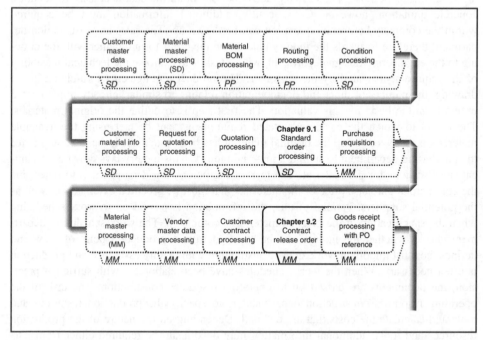

Fig. 9.1: The DNA of model enterprise B – part 1

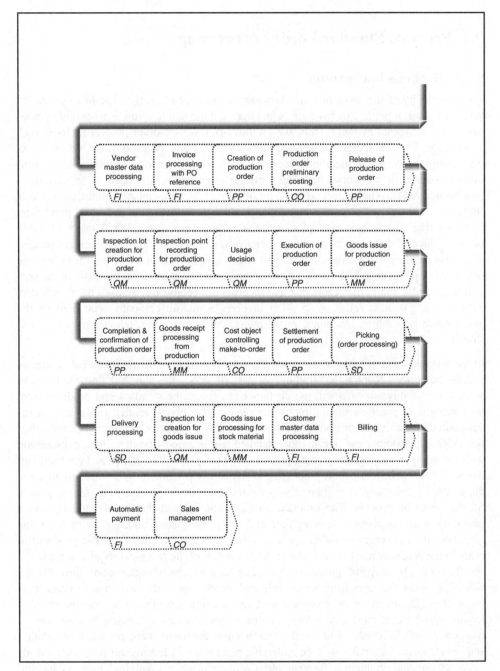

Fig. 9.1: The DNA of Model Company B – part 2

9.1 Process: Standard order processing

9.1.1 Business background

The complexity of the tasks in *order processing* can depend on the type of organization (make-to-order, repetitive or mass manufacturer) and the nature of the market (anonymous or customer-oriented market). Thus, the preliminary tasks for order processing itself such as direct mailing campaigns, sales activities, inquiries and quotations, as well as tasks which are integrated with neighbouring areas such as revenue and cost controlling (preliminary costing) or production logistics (transfer of requirements) need to be performed (see Section 8.44). Wholesalers who sell products such as semi-finished industrial products (Polymere, Tenside) or industrial electronic products (conductors) to industrial purchasers process orders with reference to quotations and outline agreements. Wholesalers who ship products directly do not perform comprehensive quotation and outline agreement processing. Instead, they use measures to initiate sales such as mail order selling to inform the consumer of their range of services. The consumer places an order on the basis of the specifications in the mail order catalogue and receives the goods directly from the warehouse. This type of business relationship often involves a trading company who delivers the goods (such as washing machines, refrigerators, coffee machines, televisions) to the customer.

In the *consumer market,* quotation processing is performed using quotation catalogues as well as authorized (contracted) trading partners. If goods are simply being produced to stock for an anonymous market, the customer can select the standard end products from the catalogue or purchase them directly from the retailer or wholesaler. In the case of order-related assembly, the customer is offered products made up of predefined components, for which the customer can define more detailed specifications through direct consultation with the salesperson from the trading partner (for example, in the kitchen and car trade). In the *producer market,* quotation processing is frequently performed by a sales employee in the producing company. A written inquiry from the customer is usually the initiating force for the quotation process. The producer to stock can convert the inquiry directly into a quotation which contains a delivery date and price information and, on the basis of this quotation, the customer can either place an order or reject the quotation. The producer to order in the producer market must check the feasibility of the technical requirements in the specification. The scope of quotation processing for the types of organization shown in the following figure increases from left to right and, in the case of the two types of organization on the right, involves development and construction activities. Component suppliers require construction papers primarily for prototypes (such as a drawing to show how a component part is installed) or for the model construction of work pieces. Construction and development can make up a considerable percentage of the overall time required for customer-oriented production, for example in tool engineering involving customer-specific variants, in special mechanical engineering and in particular plant engineering (see Gutenberg 1984, pp. 109–181; cf. VDI 1991, pp. 91–154; cf. Pfohl 1996, pp. 69–92).

Type of organization / Activities	ACM	APM	OCM	OPM	CSU	COP
Quotation	Via Catalog	yes	Via Catalog	yes	yes	yes
Processing Preliminary costing	–	–	–	–	yes	yes
Standard cost estimate	yes	yes	yes	yes	–	–
Technical feasibility	–	–	–	(yes)	yes	yes
Construction plan creation	–	–	–	–	(yes)	yes
Pricing	(Already performed)	(Already performed)	(Already performed)	yes	yes	yes
Availibility check	–	From warehouse	In some cases	yes, at assembly level	yes	yes
Reservation	–	From warehouse	In some cases	yes, at assembly level	yes	yes
Credit worthines/ Credit limit control	–	In some case	In some cases	yes	yes	yes
Contract/scheduling agreement processing	–	(yes)	–	–	(yes)	–

Key:
ACM= Anonymous manufacturer to stock in the consumer market
APM = Anonymous manufacturer to stock in the producer market
OCM= Order-related assembler manufacturer in the consumer market
OPM= Order-related assembler manufacturer in the producer market
CSU = Component Supplier
COP = Customer-oriented production

Figure 9.2: Tasks in order processing in various companies

Whereas inquiry, quotation and sales activity processing simply serve to prepare for the order, the order is a legally binding agreement between the organization and the customer. Depending on the nature of the organization, certain tasks (such as preliminary costing, checking availability, reserving goods) can be performed during quotation processing and the results copied partially into the order. Regardless of when the individual tasks are performed, tasks such as costing, pricing, the availability check, the credit limit check and delivery date determination must have been performed before order processing is completed.

Costing, for example, determines the manufacturing costs for a product. It is performed on the basis of bills of material and routings (see Sections 8.12 and 8.14) and the default times and machine hour records contained in them and, where information is not available, an estimate is required for the material consumption costs for manufacturing the product.

Pricing in the case of non-standard and partially standard products is performed on the basis of the costing data for the material. In the case of standard products, it can be determined from the pricing elements for the material as well as from the condition records for the customer (see Sections 8.8 and 8.9). Within the pricing framework, it must be possible to calculate a net and gross value. Discounts and surcharges are substracted from and added to the gross price for the material to give you the net price. Tax records are then added to give you the total price.

The *availability check* is primarily based on the parts in the warehouse. However, externally procured parts which are due to arrive within the planning period can also be taken into account during the availability check. For materials with long lead times, the availability check can also be performed during quotation processing, even although an order might not be placed. For production to stock, the availability check is performed at end product level, for production to order at assembly level. The subsequent reservation ensures that the required quantity is available at the required point in time.

The type of *credit limit check* depends on the order volume, the customer standing and the type of financing. A comprehensive credit limit check is not usually performed for products in the consumer market. In the case of expensive consumer goods (such as cars), a finance plan is often set up with the house bank. In the production market, a credit limit is often defined for customers. If the credit limit check determines that this upper limit has been exceeded, the order or delivery is blocked until the payment problems have been resolved.

The aim of *delivery date determination* is to confirm a realistic date for delivering the requested goods to the customer. In the simplest case, the delivery times from the warehouse are taken into account. In the most complex case, the production times for specific components need to be planned (see Section 8.46). On the completion of order processing, an order confirmation is usually sent to the customer and order monitoring is performed. In the case of production to stock, this involves monitoring the shipping and billing processes. For customer-related assembly in the production market, the component supplier industry, and in customer-related make-to-order production, the production status (for example, planned, released, completed) is monitored.

Processes / Function	Inquiry processing	Order processing	Delivery processing	Goods issue processing	Billig processing
Determine business partners	yes	yes or Already performed	Existing Function definition	Performed in delivery	Performed in order
Determine items	yes	yes or already performed	yes	Already performed	yes
Perform costing	yes	yes	–	–	–
Pricing	yes	yes	–	–	yes
Availability check	(yes)	yes	yes	(yes)	–
Credit limit	–	yes	yes	yes	–
Perform export control	yes	yes	yes	–	–
Determine delivery date	(yes)	yes	yes or Already performed	Already performed	–
Delivery /Transportation scheduling	–	yes	yes	Already performed	–
Picking	–	–	yes	–	–
Edit texts	yes	yes	yes	–	yes

Figure 9.3: Options for assigning sales and distribution functions

9.1.2 SAP-specific description

In the R/3 System, you can process business transactions in sales using sales documents. In terms of the data structure, these documents are related to each other and enable you to perform integrated information processing throughout Sales and Distribution, as there is a link to the shipping and billing documents. There are four groups of sales documents (see SAP – Sales and Distribution System 1994, pp. 6.1–6.17):

- Inquiries and quotations

- Orders

- Outline agreements such as contracts and scheduling agreements

- Complaints such as free of charge deliveries and returns

All sales documents have the same structure. They consist of a document header and any number of document items. The document items can be divided into any number of schedule lines. Data which applies to the entire document is stored in the document header. This includes the number of the sold-to party, the ship-to party and the payer, the document currency and the currency rate, the pricing elements for the entire document, the delivery date and the shipping point. Whereas data in the document header applies for all the items in the documents, some data is only valid for specific items. This data is stored at item level and includes the material number, the target quantity for outline agreements, the number of the ship-to party and the payer (you can define an alternative ship-to party or payer at item level), specifications for the plant and storage location as well as pricing elements for the individual items. An item can consist of one or more schedule lines. The schedule lines contain data such as the schedule line quantity, delivery date and confirmed quantity, which is required for the delivery. For example, a customer places an order for 20 pieces of a material. You enter the quantity as an item in the order. As only 10 pieces can be delivered at present and the remaining 10 pieces cannot be delivered until next month, two deliveries must be scheduled. The data for the deliveries (date and confirmed quantity) are stored in two separate schedule lines. The system does not create schedule lines for sales documents such as contracts or credit and debit memo requests, for which delivery data is not relevant.

When you initiate sales processing by creating a sales document *without reference to a preceding document*, the system copies data from the master records. The R/3 System copies data for the sold-to party and his partners (for example, ship-to party or payer) from the customer master records, data for a document item from the material master record and the relevant customer-material information records. Sometimes, the customer master specifies different partners for the various partner functions. For example, you can define several ship-to parties for one sold-to party and various partners for receiving and paying invoices. Each partner has its own customer master record and, during order processing, the system automatically copies the data from the customer master record of the relevant partner into the order. For example, the corresponding delivery data for the ship-to party is copied into the document from the customer master record. Data such as weight, delivery priorities and underdelivery and overdelivery rules are copied from the material master record into the individual items. You can change this data for each transaction. You can specify the delivering plant in the customer master record and in the material master record. You can record customer-specific data for materials in a customer-material information record. For example, you can define the material number and the description of the material at the customer as well as certain shipping data such as the delivery priority and partial delivery information.

Some data in the sales document depends on a combination of various factors (for example, customer, material and so on) and cannot be copied directly from the customer and material master records into the document. Therefore, the system has to determine the data according to the various factors at specific points in time. For example, during the configuration of the Sales and Distribution System, you record, independently of the master data, data on the various routes which depend on the location of the delivering plant and the ship-to party. If the necessary data has been maintained, the system can then determine the route automatically during order processing. Similarly, you define data for prices, surcharges and discounts for delivery scheduling and for the shipping point in advance and it is accessed during processing. If you enter a *sales document with reference* to a preceding document, for example an order with reference to a quotation, the system copies almost all the data from the preceding document.

The type of processing for the various sales documents is defined by the *sales document types, item categories* and *schedule line categories.* At sales document level, you can, for example, specify whether a credit limit check is performed for a specific document. You can also specify whether a document is blocked automatically and must be checked before you can process it further (for example, a credit memo request). At item category level, you can specify whether an item category is relevant for delivery or billing. For example, the item categories which are used in quotations are not relevant for delivery or billing. You can also define transfer of requirements and the availability check using schedule line categories. There are various sales document types in the standard R/3 System which can be modified to meet customer-specific requirements.

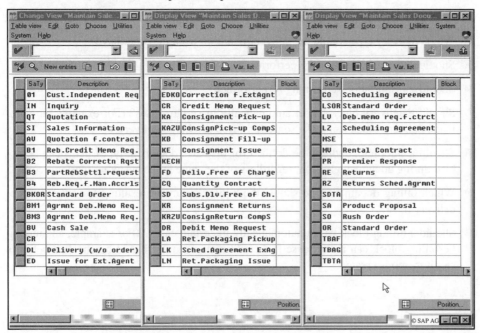

Figure 9.4: Customizing for sales document types

The configuration of the sales document types answers a multitude of questions in Sales and Distribution:

- Can the document only be created with reference to a preceding document?

- Should customer-material information records be taken into account?

- Should the delivery date be proposed?

- What value is defined for the order probability?

- Should the product division for each item be copied from the material master record or should an alternative value in the header override the value in the item?

- How should the system react if the value for the division in the header is different from the values in the items?

- Should a credit limit be performed?

- From which number range should the document number for internal or external number assignment be taken?

- Which fields are relevant for the incompletion log? (For example, the validity period is important for contracts and must therefore be specified in the document.)

- Can an incomplete document be saved or does the data have to be complete?

- Which partner functions are allowed and which have to be entered?

- Which delivery type should the delivery resulting from the order have?

- Should delivery scheduling be performed?

- Should transportation scheduling be performed?

- Should a delivery block be set automatically in certain cases? (For example, an automatic delivery block can make sense for a free-of-charge delivery.)

- Should a shipping condition be defined for the sales document type? (This can be copied during document creation, regardless of the value in the customer master record.)

- Which billing document type should the billing document resulting from the order or delivery have?

- Should a billing block be set automatically in certain cases? (For example, an automatic billing block can make sense if a credit memo request has to be checked before a credit memo is created.)

You can define additional control data at item level. Using the item category, you can specify that a material is processed differently in each sales document. Thus, in an *inquiry,* a *standard item (TAN)* is relevant for pricing but not for delivery and in an *order,* the standard item is relevant for pricing and delivery. You can also specify control indicators for a standard item in an order regarding functions such as billing, returns, pricing, automatic batch determination and export licences. You can set an indicator for billing which specifies whether the item is to be billed or is free of charge (free-of-charge delivery). If you activate the pricing function, the system performs pricing automatically (this is not relevant for text items, for example). If you set the indicator for automatic batch determination, the R/3 System attempts to find batches according to customer requirements. The export licence indicator defines whether and how export control is performed (for example, exports within or outside Europe, embargo countries).

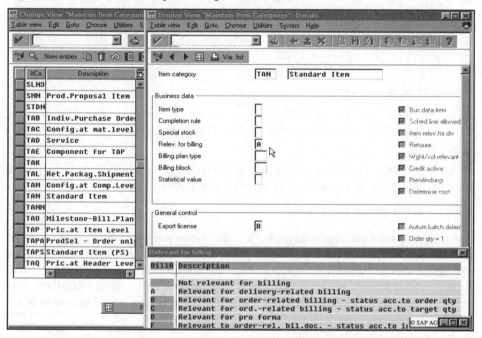

Figure 9.5: Customizing for the Sales Document Item TAN in Detail

Different item categories are allowed for each sales document type. Control elements can be used to modify existing item categories or create new ones to suit your requirements. The system administrator is responsible for maintaining the control elements. In the definition of the item category, the following questions are answered:

■ Should pricing be performed for the item?

■ When is an item considered to be completed? (A quotation item might only be considered to be completed when the entire quantity has been copied into orders.)

- Does an item refer to a material or is it simply a text item?

- Are schedule lines allowed for an item?

- Can the business data such as the payment terms at item level differ from the data at header level?

- Should the customer be contacted when the delivery is not complete?

- Which fields are relevant for the incompletion log?

- Which partner functions are allowed at item level and which are mandatory?

- Which output documents are allowed for the transaction and according to which determination procedure are they proposed?

- Is the item relevant for delivery?

- Should the weight and volume for an ítem be determined?

- Is the item relevant for billing?

- Should the cost be determined?

- Is the item a statistical item? Pricing is performed for statistical items. However, the value is not included in the total order value. Therefore, the item is not invoiced to the customer.

- Should a billing block be set automatically for an item? For example, this is important if the price for an item needs to be checked before further processing is possible.

- Is the item a returns item?

The items in a sales document can be divided into one or more schedule lines. Each schedule for an item contains a different delivery date and quantity. In the R/3 System, you can also define control elements for schedule lines. For some schedule lines, planning is performed, while others do not require inventory management. Different schedule lines categories are allowed for each sales document type and item category. In the definition of the schedule line category, the following questions are answered:

- Which fields are relevant for the incompletion log?

- Should a sales requirement be forwarded to Purchasing or Production?

- Should an availability check be performed?

- Does the schedule line involve a return?

- Is the schedule line relevant for delivery?

- Should a delivery block be set automatically for the schedule line? An automatic delivery block makes sense for free-of-charge deliveries.

The schedule line category depends on the MRP indicator which is defined for the material in the material master record (see Section 8.11). The system proposes the schedule line category automatically on the basis of table settings. You can change it manually in the sales document. The system checks any manually entered schedule line categories to determine whether they are valid.

There are various kinds of orders in the R/3 System: for example, standard orders, cash sales, rush orders and third-party orders. A *standard order* is used to send goods to a customer on an agreed date. In the simplest case, you create an order for one or more items and the system copies the data from the relevant master records. Sales, shipping, pricing and billing data is proposed from the customer master record for the sold-to party. The system also copies customer-specific master data on texts, partners and contact people. The system automatically proposes data from the relevant material master record for each material in the order. This includes data on pricing, delivery scheduling, weight and volume determination. The data which the system proposes forms the basis of the order. It can be changed and expanded. For example, your company's pricing policy may allow a sales employee to define a price manually in the order. All the usual functions in order processing such as business partner determination, item determination, pricing, the availability check, delivery scheduling, shipping point and route determination, the credit limit check and order monitoring are supported by the R/3 System. Equally, depending on the customer, you can make use of the integrated functionality such as the costing in accounting and the transfer of requirements and reservation in production and procurement logistics.

Cash sale is used when the customer picks up the goods and pays for them when the order is placed. When you create a cash sale, the system automatically proposes the current date for the delivery and billing. When you save the order, the system automatically creates a delivery and prints a cash sale invoice in the background. If the customer has already received the goods, the delivery should not be relevant for picking. If the customer picks the goods up from the warehouse, the delivery should be relevant for picking. You can use standard delivery processing to send goods. As soon as the customer receives and is satisfied with the goods, the transaction can be considered to be completed. You can only bill the cash sale if the order quantity matches the goods issue quantity. Otherwise, the cash sale must be adjusted so that the order quantity matches the quantity to be billed. The cash sale is subsequently processed as an order-related billing transaction. However, no invoice is issued. The order number serves as the reference for the accounting document which is created in Financial Accounting. If problems occur during processing, manual intervention is required. If, for example, there is an insufficient quantity of the goods in the warehouse, you need to change the order quantity. If the customer subsequently requests a price discount, because, for example, the goods are scratched, you can change the price in the cash sale document. In an extreme case, the entire transaction can be deleted, starting with the delivery. If the goods are damaged before they are collected and after they have been paid for and there is no replacement in the warehouse, you can initiate a subsequent delivery. If you change the cash sale document, you can reprint the cash sale invoice.

A *rush order* is used when the customer collects the goods immediately or on the same day on which the order is placed. The invoice is created at a later point in time.

In the case of *third-party processing,* the goods requested by the customer are not delivered by your organization but by an external supplier. The supplier sends the goods directly to the customer and sends your organization an invoice. A sales order can consist entirely or partially of third-party items. The *material type* controls third-party processing. The material type specifies whether a material is only produced internally, only procured externally or whether both types of procurement are possible. For example, a material which is created as a trading good can be only externally procured. You can define in the material master record that the material is always processed in sales as a third-party item. The R/3 System then determines the corresponding item category *TAS* automatically. If, in exceptional circumstances, a internally produced material has to be procured externally and delivered to the customer, you can overwrite the item category in the sales order. When a sales order contains several third-party items, a purchase requisition is created automatically in purchasing when you save the sales order. During the creation of the purchase order, the R/3 System can determine a supplier automatically for each requisition item. If the third party has more than one schedule line, the system creates a purchase requisition for each schedule line.

9.1.3 Using the process

In Model Company *B,* the sales employee selects sales document type *OR* (standard order) on the initial order screen as the customer requests a configured PC on a specified date. The organizational fields *sales organization, distribution channel* and *product division* are mandatory fields and cannot be subsequently changed. In the example, the sales employee references the previously entered quotation *20000010.* Using the return key, she branches to the items overview screen. The order type determines which type of overview is displayed. The items can be divided into schedule lines which contain the quantity and date (see Fig. 9.7). There is a component overview for product *DPC6.* It defines the product to be configured. The component overview shows the individual item categories for the PC *DPC6* (see Fig. 9.8). When the sales employee saves the sales document, the system automatically creates a purchase requisition in purchasing for the materials which have to be procured externally (see Fig. 9.9) and an assembly order for production in the sales order. During order processing, the sales employee can already display the individual components and the corresponding routings for the assembly. She can use the planning, component and routings keys to do this (see Fig. 9.10). Scheduling is performed for each item as it is created. The sales employee can determine which quantity has to be available on which shipping date. In the example, Model Company *B* must make a complete delivery on *14.02.1997* (see Fig. 9.11). If all steps including export and credit control functions are performed and the order text created, the system creates document number *6733* when the sales employee saves the standard order (see Fig. 9.12). The integration of the sales and production order in the R/3 System enables you to view the production order for the components to be produced in the *current requirements/stock list* at the time of order entry. In this example, document number *6733* is displayed for the sales order with the MRP element *ORDER* and document number 60001012 is created for the production order with the MRP element PrdOrd. The screen shows the creation of the assembly order in the sales order (see Fig. 9.13).

9.1.4 Navigation information

■ *Menu path*
Logistics –> Sales/distribution –> Sales –> Order –> Create –> Sales document –> Create w/reference –> To quotation

■ *Transaction code*
VA01

■ *Ingoing processes in the R/3 Reference Model*
Sales activity processing
Service notification processing
Customer quotation processing

■ *Outgoing pocesses in the R/3 Reference Model*
Preliminary costing in sales-order-related production
Creation of production order
Planned order processing
Total MRP
Single-item MRP
Material requirements planning customer order related
Total MPS
Single MPS
Interactive MPS
MPS – sales order related
MPS – project - related
Credit control
Delivery processing
Status analysis
Transfer and valuation of incoming orders
Budget execution/verification

Sales Order with Reference

You can also create a new sales order with reference to an existing document. For example, if a customer accepts a quotation you sent, the system can copy all the relevant master data from the quotation when you create the sales order. When you create a sales order with reference to another document, a dialog box appears. Enter the document number here. Order item data as well as header data is copied from the quotation to the order. Deselect the items you do not want to copy to the new document. If necessary, change the quantities of the items to be copied.

Partners

Sometimes the customer master record contains several partners for the partner functions. For example, you can enter several goods recipients for one ordering party and different partners as receiving and paying parties of the invoice. Every partner has one customer master record. In order processing, the system copies the respective data of the partner to the order. For example, for every goods recipient, the system copies the respective delivery dates of the customer master record to the delivery document.

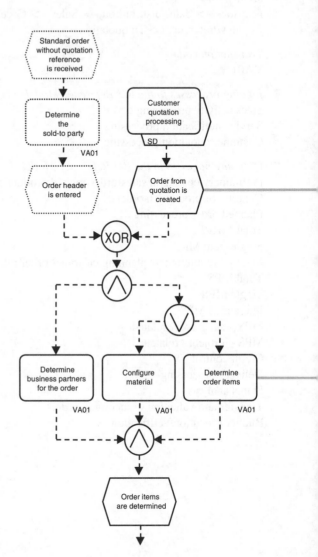

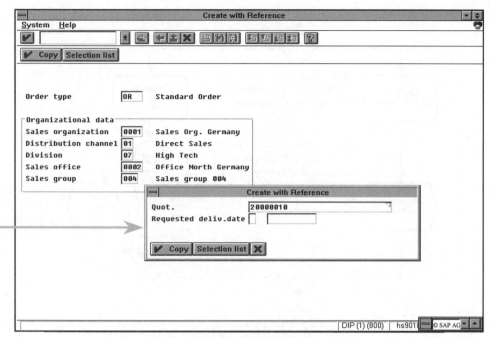

Fig. 9.6: Initial screen of order

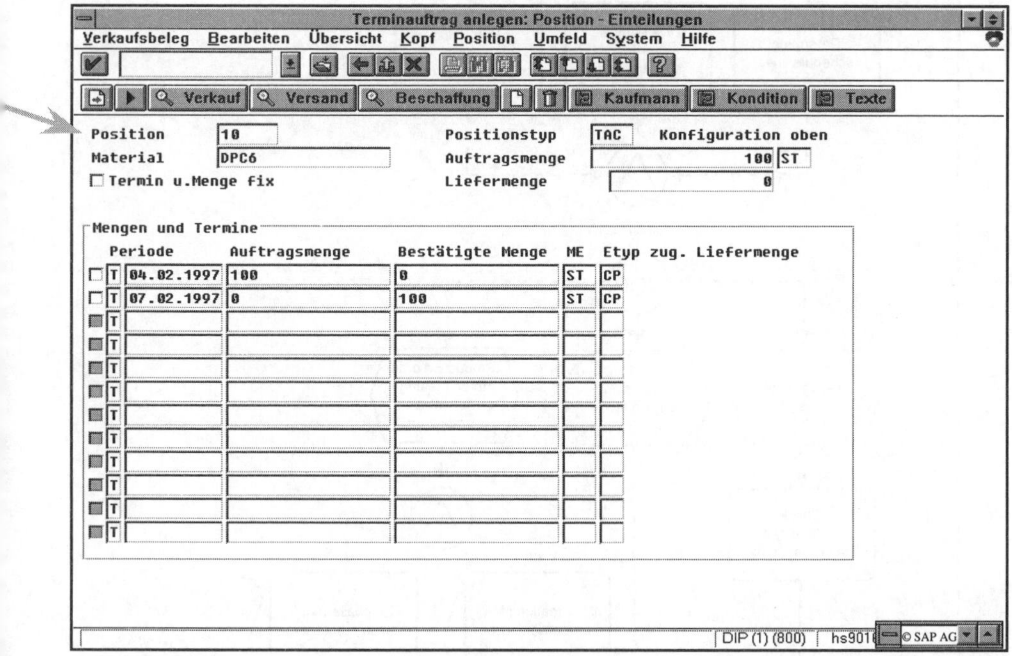

Fig. 9.7: Item 10/material DPC6

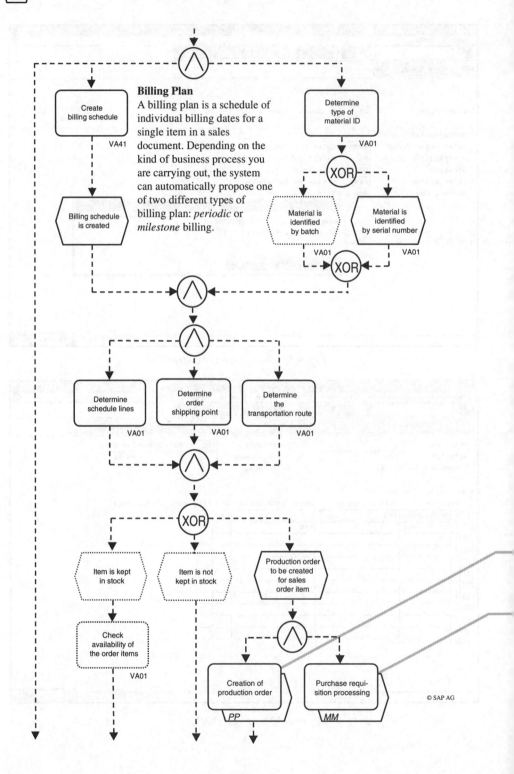

Billing Plan
A billing plan is a schedule of individual billing dates for a single item in a sales document. Depending on the kind of business process you are carrying out, the system can automatically propose one of two different types of billing plan: *periodic* or *milestone* billing.

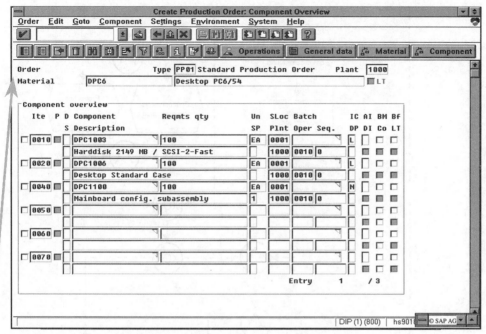

Fig. 9.8: Component overview of material DPC6

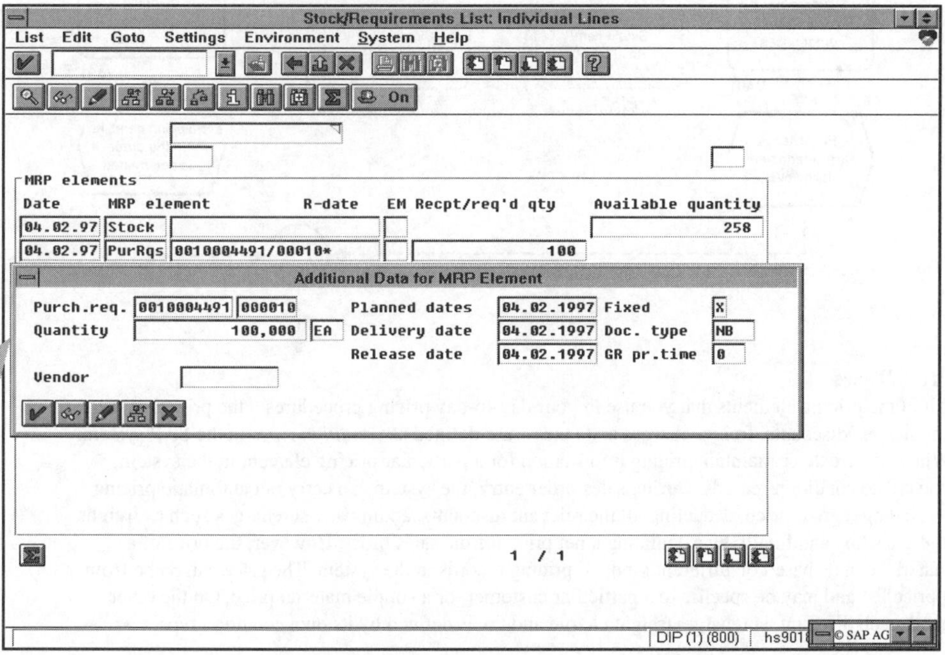

Fig. 9.9: Purchase requisition is created

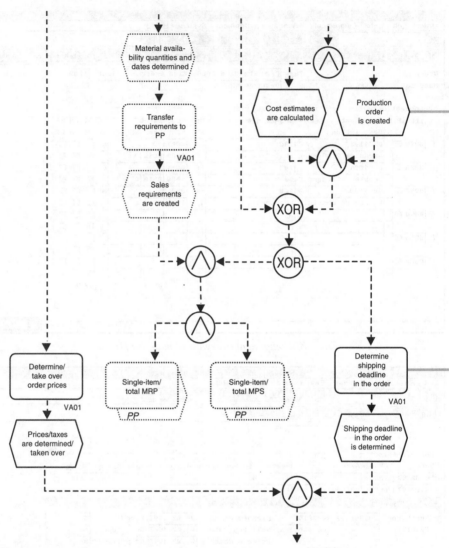

Prices/Taxes

All of the pricing elements that you use in your day-to-day pricing procedures – the prices, surcharges, discounts, freight charges and taxes – are defined as *condition types* in the SAP system. When you create or maintain pricing information for a particular pricing element in the system, you create condition records. During sales order entry, the system can carry out automatic pricing by finding a gross price, deducting all the relevant discounts, adding any surcharges such as freight and sales tax, and finally by calculating a net price for the sales order. However, the price of a material can be based on different kinds of pricing records in the system. The price can come from a price list and may be specific to a particular customer, or a simple material price. On the other hand, each discount, surcharge, freight charge and tax is defined by its own condition type.

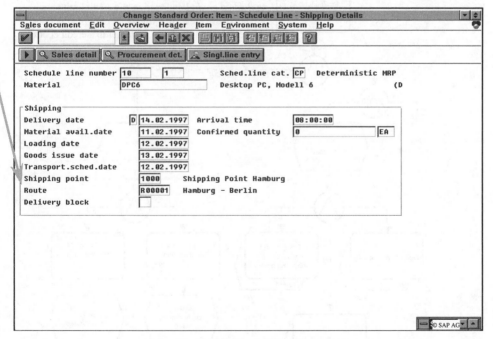

Fig. 9.10: Production order is created

Fig. 9.11: Shipping details

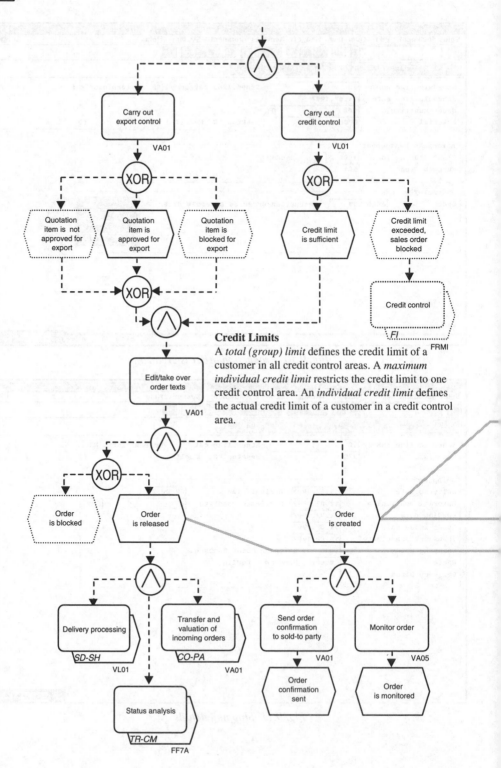

Credit Limits

A *total (group) limit* defines the credit limit of a customer in all credit control areas. A *maximum individual credit limit* restricts the credit limit to one credit control area. An *individual credit limit* defines the actual credit limit of a customer in a credit control area.

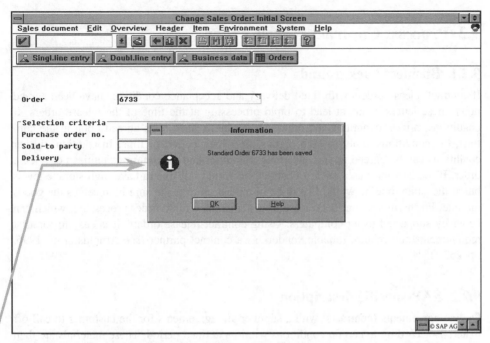

Fig. 9.12: Standard order is created

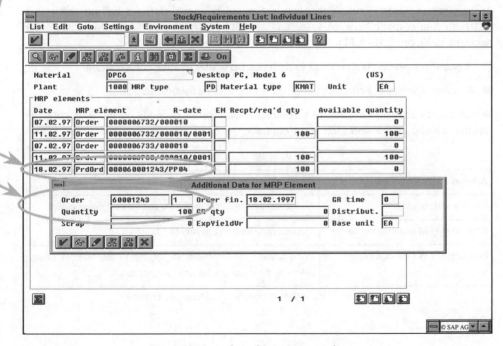

Fig. 9.13: Actual stock/requirements list

9.2 Process: Contract release order

9.2.1 Business background

If contract release orders with fixed delivery and acceptance conditions have been agreed upon, these letters of intent lead to rapid processing at the time of the release orders. If conditions, prices, quantities and other specifications have been agreed upon in the contract, the conditions apply to both parties for a long period of time. In addition, further conditions can be agreed upon concerning minimum and maximum quantities per release order. If the customer uses such a contract, he would not like to have high storage levels but at the same time he would like to be in a position to make sure he receives the goods on time. Furthermore, contract release orders guarantee rapid order processing, which can be easily supported using computers. Using contract release orders, it is easy to forecast requirements and require reliable vendors as a contract partner (see Arnolds *et al.* 1996, pp. 253–254).

9.2.2 SAP-specific description

Outline agreements (contracts) with a supplier are agreements for the customer to call-off materials according to certain conditions within a defined period. These materials are then to be delivered by the supplier. The contract is fulfilled using orders created with reference to the contract. Orders created this way are called *release orders* (or call-off orders). A differentiation is made between value and quantity contracts (see SAP – Materials Management 1996, pp. 5.10–5.11).

■ A *quantity contract* is a contract to deliver a particular quantity of a material.

■ A *value contract* is a contract to deliver goods up to a total value.

Which entries have to be made in a contract release order depends on the *item category* and the *account assignment* used in the contract:

Account assignment/Item category	Required entries in the contract release order
Account assignment **U**	An account assignment other than *U* and the assignment object
Item category **M** (material unknown)	The *material*. Set item category to " ".
Item category **W** (Material group)	*Price*, *quantity* and *material* (belonging to the material group entered in the contract). Set item category to " ".

Fig. 9.14: Data entry at contract release order time

The release documentation lists all the activities that have taken place for a contract. Before a contract release order is issued, the following information is needed: *Number of the contract, the release order quantity, the date of delivery, price, vendor data, delivery conditions, delivery costs* as well as the *instructions for the vendor*, which are taken over from the contract. In addition, additional items that are not a part of the original contract can be included in the contract release order.

9.2.3 Using the process

A quantity contract has been arranged between the two model companies covering the main board used in the personal computers. In Model Company A, an SD quantity contract exists with customer *1650 Henderson Inc.*, which stands for Model Company *B* (see Fig. 8.248). In Model Company B an *MM*-quantity contract exists for the same material. The contract number is *4600000022* and the vendor description is *1000 C.E:B. Berlin* for Model Company *A* (see Fig. 9.16). The purchase order requisition, which was created automatically from the previous process (sales order processing), is taken over in the contract release order item. The account assignment for the release order is production order *60001243*. The release order goes straight into production at goods receipt time (see Fig. 9.17). Additional control indicators must also be specified on the item detail screen. In the item data screen, the fields *GR* and *IR* have been marked. This means that the stock is to be valued. Field *GR-basedIV* (goods receipt-based invoice verification) is not marked, meaning that invoice verification is to take place based on the release order quantity. When the release order is created, the purchasing information in the purchasing info record is updated if the indicator *InfoUpdate* is set (see Fig. 9.18).

9.2.4 Navigation information

■ *Menu path*
Logistics –> Materials management –> Purchasing –> Purchase order –> Create –> Vendor known –> Purchase order –> Create w. reference –> To contract

■ *Transaction code*
ME21, ME25, ME58, ME59

■ *Ingoing processes in the R/3 Reference Model*
Purchase requisition assignment

■ *Outgoing processes in the R/3 Reference Model*
Delivery and confirmation expediter
Info record processing

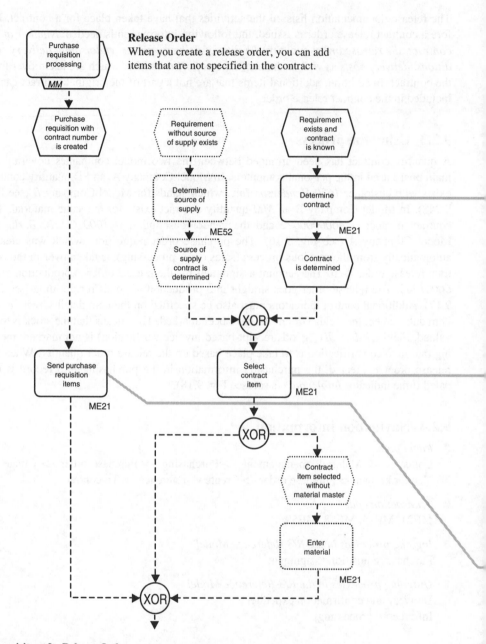

Release Order

When you create a release order, you can add items that are not specified in the contract.

Prerequisites of a Release Order

Before creating a contract release order, you require the number of the contract, the quantity to be released, the delivery date, price, vendor data, terms of payment and delivery costs. Any instructions to the vendor are adopted from the contract automatically.

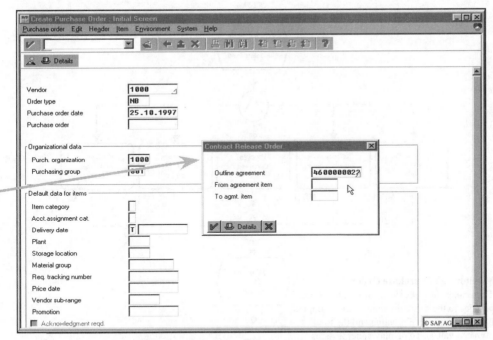

Fig. 9.15: Initial screen of purchase order

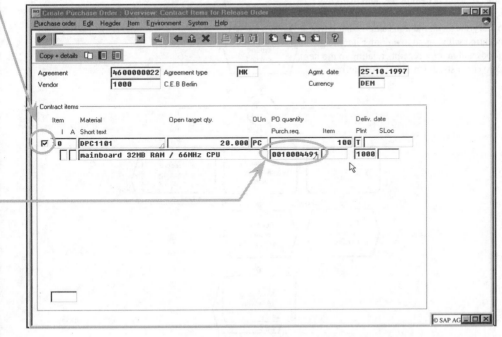

Fig. 9.16: Contract items with purchase requisition number

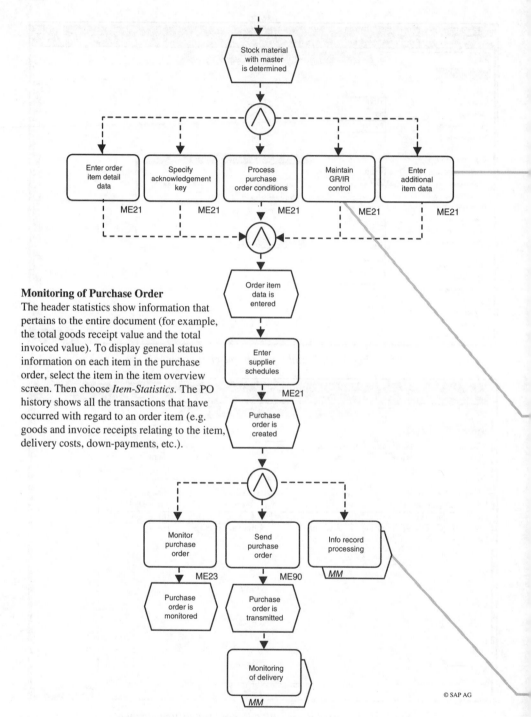

Monitoring of Purchase Order
The header statistics show information that pertains to the entire document (for example, the total goods receipt value and the total invoiced value). To display general status information on each item in the purchase order, select the item in the item overview screen. Then choose *Item-Statistics*. The PO history shows all the transactions that have occurred with regard to an order item (e.g. goods and invoice receipts relating to the item, delivery costs, down-payments, etc.).

© SAP AG

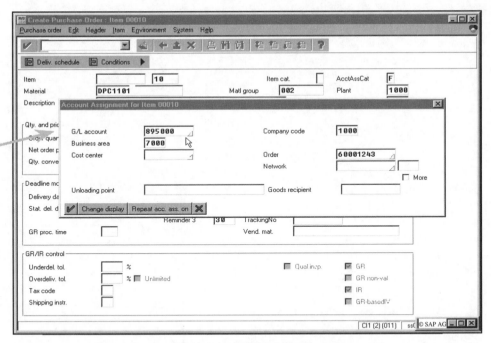

Fig. 9.17: Account assignment for item 00010

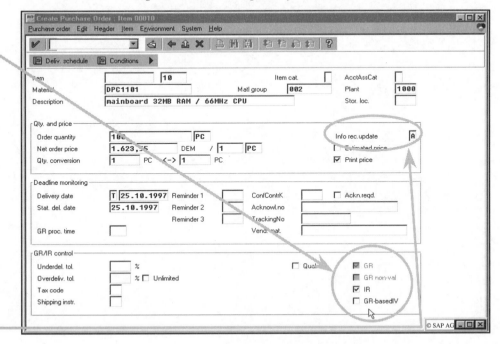

Fig. 9.18: Detailed data for item 00010

Part E
The Future

"In the future we'll be processing business transactions via the Internet. The future is already here."

10 T-Oriented Consultancy and Hypermedia-Based Training

Integrated information systems, such as the R/3 System, which operate within a defined framework permit both centralized and distributed organization of a company's structure. The company can thus handle its customer and vendor-related processes either in a centralized accounting department or locally in Purchasing or Sales and Distribution. The extent to which these flexible configuration options can be used, however, has been deliberately restricted. This is because flexibility, which is often linked to workflow concepts and tools, carries the risk of permitting such extensive use of these options that each employee organizes his or her own work processes so that they are *optimally* geared to meet his or her own *individual* needs, yet neglects "non-variable" parts, thereby encouraging *unrestricted* freedom and chaotic process organization in the company.

Such approaches are now even a subject of discussion in the field of *chaos research* (see Briggs/Peat 1995). Nevertheless, it is debatable whether it is economically and ecologically possible or desirable for companies to put all of these ideas into action. In any case, both the *chaos* and, to a certain extent, the *complexity theory* (see Lewin 1993) are tending to move away from the analytical thinking prevalent in industrialized countries towards a method of observation oriented more towards interaction and towards qualifying causal relations. This does not, however, mean that existing knowledge and experience is simply ignored. R/3 incorporates the knowledge and experience of a large number of successful companies, visualizing this in the R/3 Reference Model. The most important feature is that other companies can profit from the business ideas gleaned from companies ranging from globally - operating multinationals right down to small and medium-sized operations, using this to mould their own corporate structure. It is, therefore, possible to regard the reference models of application software providers as navigation aids or as a *map*. This navigation aid shows potential customers a range of possible paths, and helps them select an appropriate business solution, that is, determine a target-oriented business process.

An interested customer can thus be compared with a seafarer on a journey of business discovery. The main object is not simply to find the new route, you must also be able to retrace your steps. In this respect you can compare it to the outstanding achievement of the *great explorers* such as Christopher Columbus, which was to find their way back home. Only by getting back could others follow in their footsteps. Reproducibility is the all-important criterion in the organization of business processes, as they run perpendicular to company divisions and can be highly complex. The difficult thing is to ensure that, when companies describe their business processes, they are both reproducible and set up in such a way that they can respond flexibly to a variety of possible situations.

The information which describes the business situation must, therefore, be constructed and implemented dynamically. A range of processes and views determines how to enter the information environment. It is vitally important to distinguish between value-added crea-tion and administrative processes to obtain clear *decision-making and control structures*. Furthermore, processing areas defined within processes or process stations should support more flexible organization of the control views. The functional separation seen today in many companies will become less significant and total company control as a means of increasing success will become the goal.

What are these views or observations, and why are they being mentioned again with regard to hypermedia-based processing (see Sections 1.2.3 and 1.2.4)? Processes, components, functions, organizational structures and other analytical features can form solid bases for decision-making views. Each new view requires information to be processed and made available to help the staff member execute or implement the task at hand. These character-istics are based essentially on the processes and then, by extension, on the actual view structure of the observer. This new view structure requires information which is gathered as closely as possible to the time at which it is needed and whose composition is limited to the data relevant for this particular structure. Note that each company, each information user and all related details can differ. This is why new methods for providing, incorporat-ing and adapting information have become necessary.

Flexibility in the provision of information is only possible if the information units can be distinguished consistently in terms of content and organization. The smallest, intrinsically stable information unit is easy to maintain and can be used flexibly. If information con-cerning a particular topic or point changes, this need only be changed in this unit, and only once. All other sub-sections cross-referencing this unit will also be brought up to date directly.

Information units thus consist only of basic data relevant to a particular subject at the low-est level, or of a number of information units. In the latter case the information units could best be described as a composite, or a structure which contains other components and serves these up flexibly in response to the required demands. They are only called up where they are needed and only contain the information relevant for a particular process station or to a sub-section.

Not all background information is supplied to all sections; instead, it can be provided se-lectively. At this point it is not necessarily the information unit itself which physically contains all the data, rather the required data may need to be compiled from other sections or sources. Technological methods such as "intelligent agents" can be used for this, carry-ing out research for given criteria or parameters and assembling the data. The information unit and research assistance offer the user access to the required information at the relevant point. T-oriented consulting in this context means that we need a consultant who has an overview of different business areas and a detailed knowledge in one or two applications.

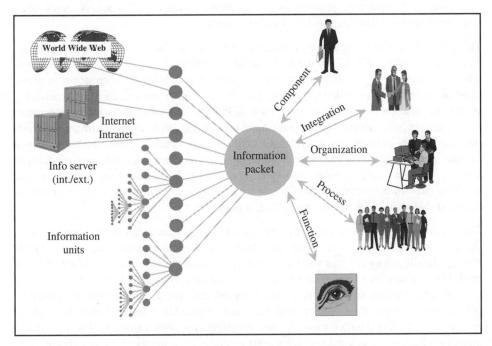

Fig. 10.1: Types and origin of information packets

Up to now we have only mentioned information support, which is supplied at the time of need, or synchronous aid. Asynchronous information provision is also of value if up-to-date information is often required on the same subject. An example of a question could be: *What new information has appeared today regarding invoicing in the profitability analysis in our company or in our branch?* Methods must be elaborated here to ensure that this information is supplied as close as possible to the time at which it was created. An *electronic inbox* or *virtual room* for new information is created for this purpose. A room is a type of information superstructure containing individual information structures. Every morning a user *visits* this room and looks to see which new information has come in on a particular subject. SAP is currently developing new document management systems such as Info Database, Workbench and CyberCity which offer these capabilities.

New technological possibilities in the fields of multimedia and networking mean that you can now meet the challenge of organizing your information flexibly, based on defined views, information units and structures. The time delay between provision of the information and the time of requirement is also being reduced thanks to new accessing and processing techniques. Multimedia is often regarded as the use of a range of different media, with text files being interactively integrated with graphic or video modules, for example. However, more important is the possibility of bringing together new options for structuring and compressing a wide range of information carriers. For this reason, a major task facing multimedia technology is creating information packets which can be organized in a variety of ways and which can be processed in a range of views but whose contents remain intrinsically stable. It should be possible to talk to partners online and to access stored data, newsgroups in the Internet and other interactive media.

This information should be available both internally within the company's own data structures and also externally. Given the multimedia technology, it is essential to establish networks, creating a *hypermedia information environment*. Internal information sources, external information providers, business partners and other information users requiring similar information communicate interactively. Partners exchange experiences and information on specific subjects within these networks. Irrespective of the industry in which two information partners are active, both could require similar information regarding a particular sub-process, for example: *How does your company solve this cost calculation problem? Has anyone created an information packet for this? Is there anyone I could talk to about this?* In combination with *intelligent agents*, a large number of these questions can be answered and information processed in advance.

The World Wide Web together with Internet and intranet solutions in combination with standard software form an environment which can determine information requirements directly. Intelligent agents provide the necessary information close in time to the point of need. High value information packets can form more quickly in the networked information environments, thereby creating a new market for information. Those administering the best information on a particular subject will be asked to provide it more frequently, thereby providing the fastest possible means of accumulating new information. In this way, information exchanges are created and are shared centrally by a number of users. These units also form parts of other information packets which regularly refer back to these units.

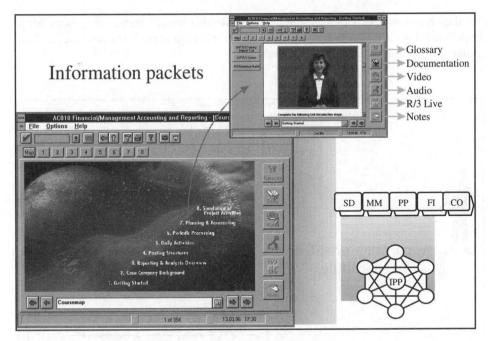

Fig. 10.2: Multimedia information packets

The increase in transparency, separation and granularity in the R/3 System serves to strengthen the openness of the information environment and the structures mentioned above. Where application functions are accessed directly via Internet interfaces (for example, using Java script), these can be used simultaneously as information interfaces. The application server is connected not only to application and presentation servers but also to information servers which compile the relevant information packets directly. Separating the application components in R/3 also has the benefit of providing better-targeted descriptions of the components which are also more closely linked to the product unit. This means that the information remains discrete in its smallest unit and represents a series of modules for other information packets which are based on these.

A wide range of defined information packets and units permits new types of information transmission methods. The distinction between training, consultancy and documentation is less sharply defined which means that they can be integrated in new structures. Consultancy and training are based on existing information sources and units, and will, in future, be used as navigation aids through information environments, showing how these link in with the R/3 applications.

In today's training courses, target group definition is one of the most complicated challenges. *Are standard training courses aimed at end users, project members, administrators or consultants?* A certain degree of suboptimization takes place generally when conventional training is offered for a highly complex application. However, if the training course is structured using the multimedia information packets, a wide range of trainees will be supplied with targeted information. SAP AG has already launched a series of new level-based training courses on various subject areas, aimed at specific participant groups. More flexible training definition becomes possible if the information environments discussed are available.

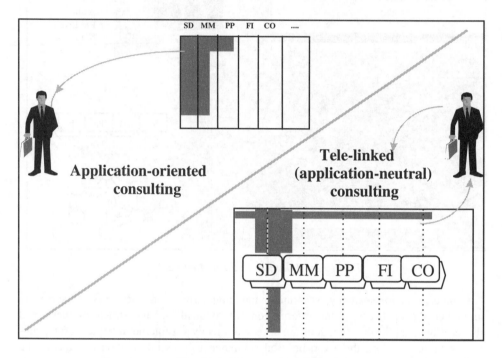

Fig. 10.3: Process consultant

It will be possible to offer customized training with different emphases based on these new information units. These relate to the selected process orientation views and permit new training structures. Courses are also information packets which simultaneously link other information units. For this reason, it is possible, just as with multimedia processing, to define new training *views* and to adopt a training programme matrix which can distinguish between target groups, project phases, company views, and so on. An administrator in the implementation phase needs a workshop explaining how to handle asset management within the new process orientation and how to use it in connection with Purchasing. In standard courses, too, information packets and flexible control of the courses will enable trainees to be issued the necessary information directly.

New processing areas and observation methods for individuals to monitor their own work will develop in this dynamic information environment; these will play an explanatory role but also serve to enhance process administration and interaction. The provision and creation of information will become a part of the value-added creation chain.

Consultancy will correspondingly move away from purely function-oriented analysis to a more process-oriented, supra-departmental view. Knowledge of the structuring possibilities within the value-added chain is implemented in the EDP system, it exists in the minds of employees and is visualized in the R/3 reference processes as it relates to the R/3 System. The aim now is to adapt the necessary knowledge so that it can meet the company's own demands.

List of R/3 Abbreviations

Abbreviation	Description
CA	**Cross-Application Components**
CA-CL	Document Management System
CA-CL	Classification
CA-CAD	CAD Integration
CA-GTF	General Task Functions
CA-DOC	Documentation Tools
CA-ALE	ALE
CA-EDI	Eletronic Data Interchange
CA-CAT	CATT
FI	**Financial Accounting**
FI-GL	General Ledger Accounting
FL-LC	Legal Consolidation
FI-AP	Accounts Payable
FI-AR	Accounts Receivable
FI-AA	Asset Accounting
FI-SL	Special Purpose Ledger
TR	**Treasury**
TR-CM	Cash Management
TR-FM	Commitment Accounting
CO	**Controlling**
CO-OM	Overhead Cost Controlling
CO-PC	Product Cost Controlling

CO-PA	Profitability Analysis

Abbreviation	**Description**
IM	Investment Management
IM-FA	Capital Investments
EC	Enterprise Controlling
EC-PCA	Profit Centre Accounting
EC-BP	Business Planning
EC-CS	Legal Consolidation
EC-EIS	Executive Information System
LO	Logistics - General
LO-MD	Logistics Basic Data
LO-EHS	Environment Data
LO-LIS	Logistics Information System
SD	Sales and Distribution
SD-MD	Master Data
SD-BF	Basic Functions
SD-SLS	Sales
SD-SHP	Shipping
SD-TRA	Transportation
SD-FTT	Foreign Trade
SD-BIL	Billing
SD-CAS	Sales Support
SD-IS	Information System
SD-EDI	Electronic Data Interchange

Abbreviation	Description
MM	**Materials Management**
MM-CBP	Consumption-Based Planning
MM-PUR	Purchasing
MM-IM	Inventory Management
MM-WM	Warehouse Management
MM-IV	Invoice Verification
MM-IS	Information System
MM-EDI	Electronic Data Interchange
QM	**Quality Management**
QM-PT	Quality Planning
QM-IM	Quality Inspection
QM-QC	Quality Control
QM-CA	Quality Certificates
QM-QN	Quality Notifications
PM	**Plant Maintenance**
PM-EQM	Equipment and Tech. Objects
PM-PRM	Preventive Maintenance
PM-WOC	Maintenance Order Management
PM-PRO	Maintenance Projects
PM-SMA	Service Management
PM-IS	Information System

Abbreviation	Description
PP	**Production Planning and Control**

PP-BD	Basic Data
PP-SOP	Sales & Operations Planning
PP-MP	Master Planning
PP-CRP	Capacity Planning
PP-MRP	Material Requirements Planning
PP-SFC	Production Orders
PP-KAB	KANBAN
PP-REM	Repetitive Manufacturing
PP-ATO	Assembly Processing
PP-PI	Production Planning for Process Industries
PP-PDC	Plant Data Collection
PP-IS	Information System
PS	**Project System**
PS-BD	Basic Data
PS-OPS	Operative Structures
PS-PLN	Project Planning
PS-APP	Project Budgeting
PS-EXE	Project Execution/Integration
PS-IS	Information System
PD	**Personnel Planning and Development**
PD-OM	Organizational Management
PD-PD	Personnel Development
PD-WFP	Workforce Planning
PD-SCM	Training and Event Management
PD-RPL	Room Reservations Planning

Abbreviation	**Description**

PA		Personnel Administration and Payroll Accounting
	PA-PAD	Personnel Administration
	PA-BEN	Benefits
	PA-SAD	Compensation Administration
	PA-APP	Recruitment
	PA-TIM	Time Management
	PA-INW	Incentive Wages
	PA-TRV	Travel
	PA-PAY	Payroll
IN		International Development
	IN-APA	Asian and Pacific Area
	IN-EUR	Europe
	IN-NAM	North America
	IN-AFM	Africa/Middle East
	IN-SAM	South America
BC		Basis Components
	BC-KRN	Kernel Components
	BC-SRV	Basis Services
	BC-ADM	System Administration
	BC-OP	Operating System Platforms
	BC-DB	Database Interface and Platform
	BC-FES	Frontend Services
	BC-FEP	Frontend Platforms
	BC-DWB	ABAP/4 Development Workbench
	BC-BEW	Business Engineering Workbench

References

Achtert, W.: Objektorientierte Software-Entwicklung. München 1995.

Adam, S.: Optimierung der Anlagenwirtschaft. Berlin 1989.

ANSI (Hrsg.): (ANSI X3.138-1988) American National Standard for Information Systems – information resource dictionary system (IRDS). Chapter (Module) 1-7 – approved version (October 19, 1988). New York 1989.

Arnolds, H.; Heege, F.; Tussing, W.: Materialwirtschaft und Einkauf. 9. Auflage. Wiesbaden 1996.

AWF – Ausschuß für wirtschaftliche Fertigung e. V. (Hrsg.): AWF-Empfehlung – Integrierter EDV-Einsatz in der Produktion – CIM (Computer Integrated Manufacturing). Eschborn 1985.

Babbage, C.: On the Economy of Machinery and Manufactures. London 1832. (4. Auflage. London 1835)

Bäck, H.: Erfolgsstrategie Logistik. München 1984.

Backhaus, K.: Investitionsgütermark   eting. 2. Auflage. München 1990.

Barengo, L.; Breu, M.; Leonardi, G.; Meyer-Wachsmuth, H.; Percie du Sert, B.; Richter, H.; Pfeiffer, M.; Utter, J.-C.: Definition of the BOS Engineering Method – A Method for the Development of Trans-European Information Systems, Version 1 (13/04/94), European Methodology & Systems Centre Methodology Group. Ohne Ortsangabe 1994.

Bartels, H.-G.: Logistik. In: Albers, W. (Hrsg.): Handwörterbuch der Wirtschaftswissenschaft. Stuttgart et al. 1980, S. 54-73.

Baumgartner, R.: Objektorientierte Vorgehensmodelle – Anforderungen und Möglichkeiten für das Software Engineering. In: EDV in den 90er Jahren: Jahrzehnt der Anwender – Jahrzehnt der Integration. Wien 1990, S. 184-198.

Bellinzona, R. et al.: Reusing Specifications in OO Applications. In: IEEE Software, March 1995, S. 65-75.

Bernus, P.; Nemes, L.: Enterprise integration – engineering tools for designing enterprises. In: Bernus, P.; Nemes, L. (Hrsg.): Modelling and Methodologies for Enterprise Integration. London et al. 1996, S. 3-11.

Berthel, J.: Personalmanagement – Grundzüge für Konzeptionen betrieblicher Personalarbeit. 3. Auflage. Stuttgart 1991.

Bleicher, K.: Organisation – Formen und Modelle. Wiesbaden 1981.

Bleicher, K.: Paradigmenwechsel im Management? In: Königswieser, R.; Lutz, C. (Hrsg.): Das systemisch evolutionäre Management. 2. Auflage. Wien 1992, S. 122-134.

Bloech, J.: Problembereiche der Logistik. In: Schriften zur Unternehmensführung. Heft 32. Wiesbaden 1984, S. 5-30.

Böcker, F.: Marketing. 3. Auflage. Stuttgart et al. 1990.

Boehm, B. W.: A Spiral Model of Software Development and Enhancement. In: IEEE Computer. 21 (1988) 5, S. 61-72.

Boehm, B. W.: Software Engineering Economics. Englewood Cliffs 1981.

Boll, M.: Prozeßorientierte Implementation des SAP-Softwarepaketes. In: Wirtschaftsinformatik. 35 (1993) 5, S. 418-423.

Booch, G.: Object Oriented Design With Applications. Redwood 1991.

Bösenberg, D.; Metzen, H.: Lean Management - Vorsprung durch schlanke Konzepte. 3. Auflage. Landsberg am Lech 1993.

Bowersox, D.-J.: Logistical Management. New York, London 1974.

Brandstetter, H.: Wertschöpfung und Werteverzehr als Maßstab zur Produktionsbewertung. St. Gallen 1993.

Brenner, W.; Hamm, V.: Prinzipien des Business Reengineering. In: Brenner, W.; Keller, G. (Hrsg.): Business Reengineering mit Standardsoftware. Frankfurt/Main, New York 1995, S. 17-43.

Brenner, W.; Keller, G. (Hrsg.): Business Reengineering mit Standardsoftware. Frankfurt/Main, New York 1995.

Brockhoff, K.: Forschung und Entwicklung. München, Wien 1988.

Briggs, J.; Peat, D. F.: Die Entdeckung des Chaos. 4. Auflage. München 1995.

Buck-Emden, R.; Galimow, J.: Die Client/Server-Technologie des SAP-Systems R/3. 3. Auflage. Bonn et al. 1996.

Budde, R.: Rechnergestützte Lieferantenbewertung. In: Handbuch der modernen Datenverarbeitung. 29 (1992) 168, S. 88-96.

Buford, J. F. K.: Uses of Multimedia Information. In: Buford, J. F. K. (Hrsg.): Multimedia systems. Reading 1994, S. 1-25.

Bühner, R.: Betriebswirtschaftliche Organisationslehre. 4. Auflage. München, Wien 1989.

Bullinger, H.-J.; Niemeyer, J.; Huber, H.: Computer Integrated Business (CIB)-Systeme. In: CIM Management. 2 (1987) 3, S. 12-19.

Bullinger, H.-J.; Wasserloos, G.: Reduzierung der Produktentwicklungszeiten durch Simultaneous Engineering. In: CIM Management. 6 (1990) 6, S. 4-12.

Bünz, D.: Die GRAI-Methode (Teil1). In: CIM Management. 3 (1987) 4, S. 56-59.

Bünz, D.: Die GRAI-Methode (Teil 2). In: CIM Management. 4 (1988) 2, S. 43-47.

Burghardt, M.: Projektmanagement – Leitfaden für die Planung, Überwachung und Steuerung von Entwicklungsprojekten. Berlin, München 1988.

Burisch, W.: Industrie- und Betriebssoziologie. 7. Auflage. Berlin, New York 1973.

Busch, R.: Entwurf eines Systems zur integrierten Fertigung (CIM) mit Petri-Netzen. In: Zeitschrift für Betriebswirtschaft. 59 (1989) 8, S. 822-838.

Bush, V.: As we may think. In: Atlantic Monthly. 176 (1945), S. 101-108.

Capra, F.: Systemisches Denken – das neue Paradigma. In: Königswieser, R.; Lutz, C. (Hrsg.): Das systemisch evolutionäre Management. 2. Auflage. Wien 1992, S. 307-309.

Chen, P. P.: The Entity-Relationship Model – Towards a Unified View of Data. In: ACM Transactions on Database Systems. 1 (1976) 1, S. 9-36.

Chroust, G.: Modelle der Software-Entwicklung. München, Wien 1992.

Cleaveland, J. C. et al.: Dividing the software pie. In: AT&T Technical Journal. (1996) 2, S. 8-19.

Coad, P.; Yourdon, E.: OOA – Objektorientierte Analyse. 2. Auflage. New York 1996.

Conklin, J.: Hypertext: An Introduction and Survey. In: IEEE Computer. 20 (1987) 9, S. 17-41.

Convent, B.; Wernecke, W.: Bausteinverwaltung und Suchunterstützung – Basis für die Softwarewiederverwendung. In: Handbuch der modernen Datenverarbeitung. 31 (1994) 180, S. 61-70.

Corsten, H.: Produktionswirtschaft. München, Wien 1990.

Corzilius, R. (Hrsg.): AD/Cycle – Ziele, Konzepte und Funktionen. München, Wien 1992.

Daenzer, W. F.; Huber, F. (Hrsg.): Systems Engineering – Methodik und Praxis. Zürich 1992.

Davenport, T. H.; Short, J. E.: The New Industrial Engineering – Information Technology and Business Process Redesign. In: Sloan Management Review. 31 (1990) 4, S. 11-27.

Davenport, T.: Process Innovation – Reengineering work through Information Technology. Boston 1993.

Davidow, W. H.; Malone, M. S.: The Virtual Corporation – Structuring and Revitalizing the Corporation for the 21st Century. New York 1992.

Davidson, W. H.: Beyond Re-Engineering: The Three Phases of Business Transformation. EMR Summer 1995, S. 17-26. (also in: IBM Systems Journal. 32 (1993) 1)

De Marco, T.: Structured Analysis and Systems Specifications. New York 1978.

Denert, E.: Software-Engineering. Berlin et al. 1991.

Detering, S.; Kienle, W.: Strategisches Unternehmensziel. In: SAPInfo – Continuous Business Engineering. Walldorf 1996, S. 38-41.

Diedenhoven, H.: Für die NC-Programmierung nutzbarer Gehalt von CAD-Daten. In: CAE-Journal. (1985) 5, S. 58-65.

Dillinger, A.: Computer Aided Quality Assurance (CAQ). In: Corsten, H. (Hrsg.): Handbuch Produktionsmanagement. Wiesbaden 1994, S. 997-1015.

DIN – Deutsches Institut für Normung (Hrsg.): Normung von Schnittstellen für die rechnerintegrierte Produktion (CIM). Fachbericht 15. Berlin, Köln 1987.

Dittrich, R. D.; Geppert, A.: Objektorientierte Datenbanksysteme – Stand der Technik. In: Handbuch der modernen Datenverarbeitung. 32 (1995) 183, S. 8-23.

Doppler, K.; Lauterburg, C.: Change Management – Den Unternehmenswandel gestalten. Frankfurt 1994.

Doumeingts, G.: Methodology to design Computer Integrated Manufacturing and control of manufacturing unit. In: Rembold, U.; Dillmann, R. (Hrsg.): Methods and Tools for Computer Integrated Manufacturing. Berlin et al. 1983, S. 194-256.

Eichhorn, W.: Die Begriffe Modell und Theorie in der Wirtschaftswissenschaft. In: Raffée, H.; Abel, B.: Wissenschaftstheoretische Grundlagen der Wirtschaftswis-senschaften. München 1979, S. 60-104.

Engelbart, D. C.: Toward Augmenting The Human Intellect. In: Communications of the ACM. 38 (1995) 8, S. 30-33.

ESPRIT Consortium AMICE (Hrsg): CIM-OSA – Open System Architecture for CIM. 2. Auflage. Berlin et al. 1993.

Eversheim, W.: Organisation in der Produktionstechnik – Arbeitsvorbereitung. 2. Auflage. Düsseldorf 1989.

Eversheim, W.: Simultaneous Engineering - Eine organisatorische Chance. In: Verein Deutscher Ingenieure (Hrsg.): Simultaneous Engineering – Neue Wege des Projektmanagement. Düsseldorf 1989.

Fahrwinkel, U.: Methode zur Modellierung und Analyse von Geschäftsprozessen zur Unterstützung des Business Process Reengineering. Paderborn 1995.

Fayol, H.: Administration Industrielle et Génerale. Paris 1916. (Allgemeine und industrielle Verwaltung. München 1929)

Fernström, C.: The EUREKA Software Factory – Concepts and Accomplishments. In: Lamsweerde, A. v.; Fugetta, A. (Hrsg.): Proceedings of the 3rd European Software Engineering Conference. ESEC´91 (21.-24. October, Mailand). Berlin et al. 1991, S. 23-36.

Ferstl, O. K.; Sinz, E. J.: Der Ansatz des Semantischen Objektmodells (SOM) zur Modellierung von Geschäftsprozessen. In: Wirtschaftsinformatik. 37 (1995) 3, S. 209-220.

Ferstl, O. K.; Sinz, E. J.: Ein Vorgehensmodell zur Objektmodellierung betrieblicher Informationssysteme im Semantischen Objektmodell (SOM). In: Wirtschaftsinformatik. 33 (1991) 6, S. 477-491.

Ferstl, O. K.; Sinz, E. J.: Ein Vorgehensmodell zur Objektmodellierung betrieblicher Informationssysteme im Semantischen Objektmodell (SOM). In: Wirtschaftsinformatik. 33 (1991) 6, S. 477-491.

Ferstl, O. K.; Sinz, E. J.: Geschäftsprozeßmodellierung. In: Wirtschaftsinformatik. 35 (1993) 6, S. 589-592.

Ferstl, O. K.; Sinz, E. J.: Grundlagen der Wirtschaftsinformatik. Band 1. München, Wien 1993.

Ferstl, O. K.; Sinz, E.: Objektmodellierung betrieblicher Informationssysteme im Semantischen Objektmodell (SOM). In: Wirtschaftsinformatik 32 (1990) 6, S. 567-581.

Frese, E.: Grundlagen der Organisation – Die Organisationsstruktur der Unternehmung. 4. Auflage. Wiesbaden 1988.

Frese, E.: Organisationstheorien – Historische Entwicklung, Ansätze, Perspektiven. 2. Auflage. Wiesbaden 1992.

Fritz, F.-J.: Business Workflow Management und Standardanwendungssysteme. In: Management und Computer. 4 (1994) 4, S. 277-286.

Gaitanides, M.: Prozeßorganisation – Entwicklung, Ansätze und Programme prozeßorientierter Organisationsgestaltung. München 1983.

Gälweiler, A.: Strategische Unternehmensführung. 2. Auflage. Frankfurt/Main, New York 1990.

Ganzhorn, K.-E.: 75 Jahre IBM Deutschland in der Informatik. In: Proebster, W. E. (Hrsg.): Datentechnik im Wandel. Berlin et al. 1986.

Gibbs, S. J.; Tsichritzis, D. C.: Multimedia Programming: objects, environments and frameworks. Wokingham 1995.

Ginige, A.; Lowe, D. B.; Robertson, J.: Hypermedia Authoring. In: IEEE MultiMedia. 2 (1995) 4, S. 24-35.

Glaser, H.: Material- und Produktionswirtschaft. Düsseldorf 1986.

Glaser, H.: Steuerungskonzepte von PPS-Systemen. In: Corsten, H. (Hrsg.): Handbuch Produktionsmanagement. Wiesbaden 1994, S. 747-761.

Glaser, H.; Geiger, W.; Rohde, V.: PPS – Produktionsplanung und -steuerung. Wiesbaden 1991.

Goldberg, A.; Rubin, K. S.: Succeeding with objects - Decision Frameworks for Project Management. Reading 1995.

Görk, M.: R/3-Einführung schneller und einfacher gemacht. In: SAPInfo – Continuous Business Engineering. Walldorf 1996, S. 28-29.

Gouillart, F. J.; Kelly J. N.: Business Transformation. Wien 1995.

Grabowski, H.: CAD/CAM-Grundlagen und Stand der Technik. In: Fortschrittliche Betriebsführung und Industrial Engineering. 32 (1983) 4, S. 224-233.

Grabowski, H.; Rude, S.; Schmidt, M.: Entwerfen in Konstruktionsräumen zur Unterstützung der Teamarbeit. In: Scheer, A.-W. (Hrsg.): Simultane Produktentwicklung. München 1992, S. 123-159.

Grabowski, H.; Schäfer, H.: Methode zur Planung von CAD/CAM-Gesamtkonzeptionen. In: Zahn, E. (Hrsg.): Organisationsstrategie und Produktion. München 1990, S. 237-273.

Grochla, E. et al.: Integrierte Gesamtmodelle der Datenverarbeitung - Entwicklung und Anwendung des Kölner Integrationsmodells (KIM). München, Wien 1974.

Grochla, E.: Einführung in die Organisationstheorie. Stuttgart 1978.

Grochla, E.: Grundlagen der Materialwirtschaft. 3. Auflage. Wiesbaden 1978.

Grochla, E.: Grundlagen der organisatorischen Gestaltung. Stuttgart 1982.

Günter, B.: Kundenanalyse und Kundenzufriedenheit als Grundlage der Customer Integration. In: Kleinaltenkamp, M.; Fließ, S.; Jacob, F. (Hrsg.): Customer Integration – Von der Kundenorientierung zur Kundenintegration. Wiesbaden 1996, S. 57-71.

Günther, H.-O.: Liefermengenplanung unter logistischen Aspekten. In: Handbuch der modernen Datenverarbeitung. 29 (1992) 168, S. 16-24.

Gutenberg, E.: Grundlagen der Betriebswirtschaftslehre. Band 1: Die Produktion. 24. Auflage. Berlin et al. 1983.

Gutenberg, E.: Grundlagen der Betriebswirtschaftslehre. Band 2: Der Absatz. 16. Auflage. Berlin et al. 1979.

Gutzwiller, T. A.: Das CC-RIM-Referenzmodell für den Entwurf von betrieblichen, transaktionsorientierten Informationssystemen. Heidelberg 1994.

Habermann, H.-J.; Leymann, F.: Repository – Eine Einführung. München, Wien 1993.

Haberstock, L.: Kostenrechnung. Band 1. 8. Auflage. Hamburg 1987.

Hackstein, R.: Produktionsplanung und -steuerung (PPS). 2. Auflage. Düsseldorf 1989.

Hahn, D.; Schramm, M.: Computerunterstütztes Qualitätsinformationssystem. In: Scheer, A.-W. (Hrsg.): Simultane Produktentwicklung. München 1992, S. 161-189.

Hammer, M.; Champy, J.: Business Reengineering – Die Radikalkur für das Unternehmen. Frankfurt/Main, New York 1995.

Hansen, H.-R.: Wirtschaftsinformatik I. 6. Auflage. Stuttgart 1992.

Harrington, J.: Computer Integrated Manufacturing. New York 1973.

Hars, A.: Referenzdatenmodelle. Wiesbaden 1994.

Hartmann, H.: Materialwirtschaft. 6. Auflage. Gernsbach 1993.

Hasenkamp, U.; Syring, M.: CSCW in Organisationen – Grundlagen und Probleme. In: CSCW: Informationssysteme für dezentralisierte Unternehmensstrukturen. Bonn et al. 1994.

Hauser, C.: Marktorientierte Bewertung von Unternehmensprozessen. Bergisch Gladbach, Köln 1996.

Heilmann, H.: Workflow Management: Integration von Organisation und Informations-verarbeitung. In: Handbuch der modernen Datenverarbeitung. 34 (1994) 176, S. 9-21.

Heinrich, L. J.; Burgholzer, P.: Systemplanung I. 5. Auflage. München 1991.

Heinrich, J.; Burgholzer, P.: Systemplanung II. 4. Auflage. München, Wien 1990.

Henderson-Sellers, B.; Edwards, J. M.: The Object-Oriented Systems Life Cycle. In: Communications of the ACM. 33 (1990) 9, S. 142-159.

Hentze, J.: Personalwirtschaftslehre. Band 1/2. 5. Auflage. Bern, Stuttgart 1991.

Herzog, R.: QS-Komponenten in Materialwirtschaft und Einkauf. In: Handbuch der mo-dernen Datenverarbeitung. 29 (1992) 168, S. 9-21.

Herzog, E.; Jurasek, W.: Vertriebscontrolling im System der Grenzplankostenrechnung. In: Männel, W.; Müller, H. (Hrsg.): Modernes Kostenmanagement. Wiesbaden 1995, S. 131-136.

Hickman, F. R.; Killin, J. L.; Land, L.; Mulhall, T.; Porter, D.; Taylor, R. M.: Analysis for Knowledge-based Systems – A Practical Guide to the KADS Methodology. New York et al. 1989.

Hill, W.; Fehlbaum, R.; Ulrich, P.: Organisationslehre I. 4. Auflage. Bern, Stuttgart 1989.

Hinterhuber, H.: Strategische Unternehmenführung. Berlin, New York 1989.

Hoffmann, W.; Hanebeck, C.; Scheer, A.-W.: Kooperationsbörse – Der Weg zum virtuel-len Unternehmen. In: Management und Computer. 4 (1996) 1, S. 35-41.

Hoitsch, H. J.: Produktionswirtschaft – Grundlagen einer industriellen Betriebswirt-schaftslehre. München 1985.

Hopp, D.: Standardsoftware – CIM-Einstieg für den Mittelstand? In: CIM Management. 6 (1990) 1, S. 30-31.

Horváth, P.: Controlling. 3. Auflage. München 1990.

Hufgard, A.: Betriebswirtschaftliche Softwarebibliotheken und Adaption. München 1994.

Hüllenkremer, M.: Rechnerunterstützte Arbeitsplanerstellung im CIM-Konzept. In: Krallmann, H. (Hrsg.): CIM – Expertenwissen für die Praxis. München, Wien 1990, S. 48-57.

ISO (Hrsg.): ISO/IEC 10027: Information Technology – Information Resource Dictionary System (IRDS) framework. Ohne Ortsangabe 1990.

Jablonski, S.: Workflow-Management-Systeme: Modellierung und Architektur. Bonn 1995.

Jablonski, S.: Workflow-Management-Systeme: Motivation, Modellierung, Architektur. In: Informatik Spektrum. 18 (1995) 1, S. 13-24.

Jacob, F.: Produktindividualisierung – Ein Ansatz zur innovativen Leistungsgestaltung im Business-to-Business-Bereich. Wiesbaden 1995.

Jacobson, I.; Ericsson, M.; Jacobson, A.: The Object Advantage - Business Process Reengineering with Object Technology. Wokingham et al. 1995.

Jansen, R.; Grünberg, R.: Trends in der Kommissioniertechnik. In: Zeitschrift für Logistik. (1992) 1, S. 4-15.

Jorysz, H. R.; Vernadat, F. B.: CIM-OSA Part 1: total enterprise modelling and function view. In: International Journal of Computer Integrated Manufacturing. 3 (1990) 3/4, S. 144-156.

Jorysz, H. R.; Vernadat, F. B.: CIM-OSA Part 2: information view. In: International Journal of Computer Integrated Manufacturing. 3 (1990) 3/4, S. 157-167.

Jost, W.: EDV-gestützte CIM-Rahmenplanung. Wiesbaden 1993.

Jost, W.; Keller, G.; Scheer, A.-W.: Konzeption eines DV-Tools im Rahmen der CIM-Planung. In: Zeitschrift für Betriebswirtschaft. 61 (1991) 1, S. 33-64.

Kagermann, H.: Perspektiven der Weiterentwicklung integrierter Standardsoftware für das innerbetriebliche Rechnungswesen. In: Horváth, P. (Hrsg.): Strategieunterstützung durch das Controlling – Revolution im Rechnungswesen? Stuttgart 1990, S. 277-306.

Kagermann, H.: Client/Server-Modelle: Chancen oder Risiko für ein effektives Controlling? In: Management und Computer. 1 (1993) 4, S. 273-280.

Kagermann, H.: Verteilung integrierter Anwendungen. In: Wirtschaftsinformatik. 35 (1993) 5, S. 455-464.

Keller, G.: Informationsmanagement in objektorientierten Organisationsstrukturen. Wiesbaden 1993.

Keller, G.: Dezentrales Informationsmanagement. In: Scheer, A.-W. (Hrsg.): Handbuch Informationsmanagement: Aufgaben – Konzepte – Praxislösungen. Wiesbaden 1993, S. 603-631.

Keller, G.: Eine einheitliche betriebswirtschaftliche Grundlage des Business Reengineering. In: Brenner, W.; Keller, G. (Hrsg.): Business Reengineering mit Standardsoftware. Frankfurt/Main, New York 1995, S. 45-66.

Keller, G.; Baresch, M.: Modulare CAD-Softwaresysteme auf Datenbankbasis. In: CIM Management. 6 (1990) 2, S. 17-22.

Keller, G.; Detering, S.: Process-Oriented Modelling and Analysis of Business Processes using the R/3 Reference Model. In: Bernus, P.; Nemes, L. (Hrsg.): Modelling and Methodologies for Enterprise Integration. London et al. 1996, S. 69-87.

Keller, G.; Kern, S.: Dezentrale Inselstrukturen in Planung und Fertigung. In: Scheer, A.-W. (Hrsg.): Fertigungssteuerung – Expertenwissen für die Praxis. München, Wien 1991, S. 105-125.

Keller, G.; Malt, D.: Gestaltung von Controllingprozessen mit SAP R/3. In: Controlling. 7 (1995) 4, S. 234-249.

Keller, G.; Meinhardt, S.: Business process reengineering auf Basis des SAP R/3-Referenzmodells. In: Schriften zur Unternehmensführung. Band 53. Wiesbaden 1994, S. 35-62.

Keller, G.; Meinhardt, S.: DV-gestützte Beratung bei der SAP-Softwareeinführung. In: Handbuch der modernen Datenverarbeitung. 31 (1994) 175, S. 74-88.

Keller, G.; Meinhardt, S.: SAP R/3-Analyzer – Optimierung von Geschäftsprozessen auf Basis des R/3-Referenzmodells. Walldorf 1994.

Keller, G.; Nüttgens, M.; Scheer, A.-W.: Semantische Prozeßmodellierung auf der Grundlage „Ereignisgesteuerter Prozeßketten (EPK)". In: Scheer, A.-W. (Hrsg.): Veröffentlichung des Instituts für Wirtschaftsinformatik. Heft 89. Saarbrücken 1992.

Keller, G.; Popp, K.: Gestaltung von Geschäftsprozessen als betriebliche Aufgabe. In: Management und Computer. 3 (1995) 1, S. 43-52.

Keller, G.; Popp, K.: Referenzmodelle für Geschäftsprozesse. In: Handbuch der modernen Datenverarbeitung. 33 (1996) 187, S. 94-117.

Keller, G.; Schröder, G.: Geschäftsprozeßmodelle: Vergangenheit – Gegenwart – Zukunft. In: Management und Computer. 4 (1996) 2, S. 77-88.

Kieser, A. (Hrsg.): Organisationstheorien. 2. Auflage. Stuttgart et al. 1995.

Kieser, A.: Managementlehre und Taylorismus. In: Kieser, A. (Hrsg.): Organisationstheorien. 2. Auflage. Stuttgart et al. 1995, S. 57-89.

Kieser, A.; Kubicek, H.: Organisationstheorien I / II. Stuttgart et al. 1978.

Kilger, W.: Industriebetriebslehre. Wiesbaden 1986.

Kilger, W.: Einführung in die Kostenrechnung. 3. Auflage. Wiesbaden 1987.

Kilger, W.: Flexible Plankostenrechnung und Deckungsbeitragsrechnung. 9. Auflage. Wiesbaden 1988.

Kimm, R.; Koch, W.; Simonsmeier, W.; Tontsch, F.: Einführung in Software Engineering. Berlin, New York 1979.

Kirchmer, M.: Geschäftsprozeßorientierte Einführung von Standardsoftware. Wiesbaden 1996.

Kirsch, W.: Betriebswirtschaftliche Logistik. In: Zeitschrift für Betriebswirtschaft. 41 (1971), S. 221-234.

Kleinaltenkamp, M.: Customer Integration – Kundenintegration als Leitbild für das Business-to-Business-Marketing. In: Kleinaltenkamp, M.; Fließ, S.; Jacob, F. (Hrsg.): Customer Integration – Von der Kundenorientierung zur Kundenintegration. Wiesbaden 1996, S. 13-24.

Klute, R.: Das World Wide Web. Bonn et al. 1996.

König, S.; Kundt, O.: Objektorientierte Systemanalyse. In: Krallmann, H. (Hrsg): Systemanalyse im Unternehmen – Geschäftsprozeßoptimierung, partizipative Vorgehensmodelle, objektorientierte Analyse. München 1994.

König, W.; Wolf, S.: Objektorientierte Software-Entwicklung – Anforderungen an das Informationsmanagement. In: Scheer, A.-W. (Hrsg.): Handbuch Informationsmanagement: Aufgaben - Konzepte - Praxislösungen. Wiesbaden 1993, S. 869-898.

Konrad, E.: Kostenplanung und -kontrolle. In: Management-Enzyklopädie. Band 3. München 1971, S. 1099-1118.

Kosanke, K.: CIM-OSA – Offene System Architektur. In: Scheer, A.-W. (Hrsg.): Handbuch Informationsmanagement: Aufgaben – Konzepte – Praxislösungen. Wiesbaden 1993, S. 113-141.

Kosanke, K.: Process oriented presentation of modelling methodologies. In: Bernus, P.; Nemes, L. (Hrsg.): Modelling and Methodologies for Enterprise Integration. London et al. 1996, S. 45-55.

Kosiol, E.: Organisation der Unternehmung. Wiesbaden 1962.

Kraemer, W.; Wiechmann, D.: BDE-gestützte Kosteninformationssysteme. In: CIM Management. 6 (1990) 3, S. 10-21.

Krcmar, H.: Bedeutung und Ziele von Informationssystem-Architekturen. In: Wirtschaftsinformatik. 32 (1990) 5, S. 395-402.

Krcmar, H.: Computerunterstützung für die Gruppenarbeit – Zum Stand der CSCW Forschung. In: Wirtschaftsinformatik. 34 (1992) 4, S. 425-437.

Kreikebaum, H.: Strategische Unternehmensplanung. 3. Auflage. Stuttgart et al. 1989.

Krickl, O.: Business Redesign – Prozeßorientierte Organisationsgestaltung und Informationstechnologie. In: Krickl, O. (Hrsg.): Geschäftsprozeßmanagement. Heidelberg 1994, S. 17-38.

Küffmann, K.: Software Wiederverwendung – Konzeption einer domänenorientierten Architektur. Braunschweig 1994.

Kuhlen, R.: Hypertext – Ein nicht-lineares Medium zwischen Buch und Wissensbank. Berlin et al. 1991.

Kuhlen, R.: Informationsmarkt – Chancen und Risiken der Kommerzialisierung von Wissen. Konstanz 1995.

Kühn, M.: CAD und Arbeitssituation. Berlin et al. 1980.

Küting, K.; Weber, C. P. (Hrsg.): Handbuch der Konzernrechnungslegung. Stuttgart 1989.

Kythe, D.: The Promise of Distributed Business Components. In: AT&T Technical Journal. March/April 1996.

Lederer, K. G.: EDV-gestützte Kommunikationssysteme in der Automobilindustrie. In: Fortschrittliche Betriebsführung und Industrial Engineering. 33 (1984) 1, S. 23-29.

Lewin, R.: Die Komplexitätstheorie – Wissenschaft nach der Chaosforschung. Hamburg 1993.

Luhmann, N.: Soziale Systeme. 4. Auflage. Frankfurt/Main 1991.

Lüscher, A.; Straubinger, A.: Objektorientierte Technologien – Eine Einführung. Zürich 1996.

Lutz, C.: Leben und arbeiten in der Zukunft. München 1995.

Macconaill, P.: Indroduction to the ESPRIT Programme. In: International Journal of Computer Integrated Manufacturing. 3 (1990) 3/4, S. 140-143.

Maier-Rothe, C.; Busse, K.; Thiel, R.: Computerverbundsysteme planen, steuern und kontrollieren den Produktionsprozeß. In: Maschinenmarkt. 89 (1983) 8, S. 106-109.

Malone, T. W.; Rockart, J. F.: How will Information Technology Reshape Organizations? – Computers as Coordination Technology. In: Bradley, S. P.; Hausman, J. A.; Nolan, R. L. (Hrsg.): Globalization, Technology and Competition – The Fusion of Computers and Telecommunications in the 1990s. Boston 1993, S. 37-56.

Malone, T. W.; Rockart, J. F.: Computers, Networks and the Corporation. In: Scientific American. September 3th 1991.

Männel, W. (Hrsg.): Integrierte Anlagenwirtschaft. Köln 1988.

Marca, D. A.; McGrowan, C. L.: SADT – Structured Analysis and Design Technique. McGraw - Hill 1988.

Martin, J.: Information Engineering Book I: Introduction. Englewood Cliffs 1989.

Martin, J.: Information Engineering Book II: Planning and Analysis. Englewood Cliffs 1990.

Martin, J.: Information Engineering Book III: Design and Construction. Englewood Cliffs 1990.

Martin, J.: Principles Of Object Oriented Analysis And Design. Englewood Cliffs 1993.

Martin, J.; Odell, J.: Object-Oriented Analysis and Design. New Jersey 1992.

Martin, J.; Odell, J. : Object-Oriented Methods – A Foundation. Englewood Cliffs 1995.

Martin, J.; Odell, J.: Object-Oriented Methods – Pragmatic Considerations. New York 1996.

Marr, R.; Stitzel, M.: Personalwirtschaft. München 1979.

Matzke, B.: ABAP/4 – Die Programmiersprache des SAP-Systems R/3. Bonn et al. 1996.

Mayer, C. F.: Bewertung von Rechnerinvestitionen durch den Vergleich von Wertschöpfungsketten. Berlin 1994.

Mayo, H.: The Human Problems of an Industrial Civilization. Boston 1946.

Meffert, H.: Marketing – Grundzüge der Absatzpolitik. 7. Auflage. Wiesbaden 1986.

Meinhardt, S.: Geschäftsprozeßorientierte Einführung von Standard-Software am Beispiel des SAP-Systems „R/3". In: Wirtschaftsinformatik. 37 (1995), S. 487-499.

Meinhardt, S.: Methodischer Rahmen für einen Projektverlauf. In: SAPInfo - Continuous Business Engineering. Walldorf 1996, S. 24-27.

Meinhardt, S.; Sänger, F.: R/3-Vorgehensmodell als methodischer Rahmen für einen erfolgreichen Projektverlauf. In: Handbuch der modernen Datenverarbeitung. 33 (1996) 192, S. 86-98.

Meinhardt, S.; Teufel, T.: Business Reengineering im Rahmen einer prozeßorientierten Einführung der SAP-Standardsoftware. In: Brenner, W.; Keller, G. (Hrsg.): Business Reengineering mit Standardsoftware. Frankfurt/Main, New York 1995, S. 69-94.

Meister, P.: Vernetztes Denken bei der Markteinführung neuer Produkte. In: Probst, G. J. B.; Gomez, P. (Hrsg.): Vernetztes Denken. Wiesbaden 1993, S. 145-161.

Melzer-Ridinger, R.: Materialwirtschaft und Einkauf. Band 1: Grundlagen und Methoden. 3. Auflage. München, Wien 1994.

Melzer-Ridinger, R.: Materialwirtschaft und Einkauf. Band 2: Qualitätsmanagement. München, Wien 1995.

Mercurio, V. J.; Meyers, B. F. ; Nisbet, A. M.; Radin, G.: AD/Cycle strategy and architecture. In: IBM Systems Journal. 29 (1990) 2, S. 170-188.

Mertens, P.; Wedel, T.; Hartinger, M.: Management by Parameters? In: Zeitschrift für Betriebswirtschaft. 61 (1991) , S. 569-588.

Meyer, B.: Objektorientierte Softwareentwicklung. München 1990.

Meyer, B.: The Reusability Challenge. In: IEEE Computer. 29 (1996) 2, S. 76-78.

Miles, R.; Snow, C.: Organizations – New Concepts for New Forms. In: California Management Review. 18 (1986) 3, S. 62-73.

Mili, H. et al.: Reusing Software: Issues and Research Directions. In: IEEE Transactions on Software Engineering. 21 (1995) 6, S. 528-561.

Myers, G. J.: Reliable software through composite design. New York 1975.

Nassi, I.; Schneiderman, B.: Flowchart Techniques for Structured Programming. In: ACM Sigplan. 12 (1973) 8, S. 12-26.

Nelson, T. H.: The Heart of Connection: Hypermedia unified by Transclusion. In: Communications of the ACM. 38 (1995) 8, S. 31-33.

Nierstrasz, O.; Meijler, T.: Research directions in Software Composition. In: ACM Computing Surveys. (1995) 2, S. 262-264.

Nordsieck, F.: Betriebsorganisation. 4. Auflage. Stuttgart 1972.

Nordsieck, F.: Die schaubildliche Erfassung und Untersuchung der Betriebsorganisation. Stuttgart 1932.

Nuppeney, W.; Raps, A.: Produktkosten-Controlling im System der Grenzplankostenrechnung. In: Männel, W.; Müller, H. (Hrsg.): Modernes Kostenmanagement. Wiesbaden 1995, S. 110-120.

Nüttgens, M.: Koordiniert-dezentrales Informationsmanagement. Wiesbaden 1995.

Nüttgens, M.; Keller, G.; Scheer, A.-W.: Hypermedia: Navigation in betriebswirtschaftlichen Informationssystemen. In: Die Betriebswirtschaft. 53 (1993) 5, S. 629-646.

Obbink, H.: System Engineering Environments of ATMOSPHERE. In: Endres, A.; Weber, H. (Hrsg): Software Development Environments and CASE Technology – Proceedings of the European Symposium (June 1991, Königswinter, Germany). Berlin et al. 1991, S. 1-17.

Oberweis, A.: Verteilte betriebliche Abläufe und komplexe Objektstrukturen: Integriertes Modellierungskonzept für Workflow-Managementsysteme. Karlsruhe 1994.

Ohno, T.: Toyota Production System – Beyond Large Scale Production. Cambridge, Massachusetts 1988.

Olle, T. W.: Hagelstein, J.; Macdonald, I. G.; Rolland, C.; Sol, H. G.; Van Assche, F. J. M.; Verrijn-Stuart, A. A.: Information Systems Methodologies: a framework for understanding. 2. Auflage. Wokingham et al. 1991.

Österle, H.: Business Engineering – Prozeß- und Systementwicklung. Band 1: Entwurfstechniken. 2. Auflage. Berlin et al. 1995.

Pagé, P.: Objektorientierte Software in der kommerziellen Anwendung. Berlin et al. 1996.

Pahl, G.; Beitz, W.: Konstruktionslehre. 2. Auflage. Berlin et al. 1986.

Panse, R.: CIM-OSA - Ein herstellerunabhängiges CIM-Konzept. In: DIN-Mitteilungen. 69 (1990) 3, S. 157-164.

Petri, C. A.: Kommunikation mit Automaten. Bonn 1962.

Pfähler, D.: IDES – die Musterfirma im System R/3. In: SAPInfo. Heft 48. Walldorf 1995, S. 20.

Pfeifer, T.: Tendenzen zur rechnergestützten Qualitätssicherung. In: Scheer, A.-W. (Hrsg.): CIM im Mittelstand. Fachtagung. Saarbrücken 1991, S. 131-153.

Pfohl, H.-C.: Aufbauorganisation der betriebswirtschaftlichen Logistik. In: Zeitschrift für Betriebswirtschaft. 50 (1980), S. 1201-1228.

Pfohl, H.-C.: Logistiksysteme – Betriebswirtschaftliche Grundlagen. 5. Auflage. Berlin et al. 1996.

Plattner, H.: Die Organisation eines interaktiven Planungssystems für die Kostenstellen-rechnung. In: Kilger, W.; Scheer, A.-W. (Hrsg.): Rechnungswesen und EDV. 4. Saarbrücker Arbeitstagung 1983. Würzburg, Wien 1983, S. 89-110.

Plattner, H.: Neue Wege für das Controlling in einem hochintegrierten Anwendungssy-stem. In: Scheer, A.-W. (Hrsg.): Rechnungswesen und EDV. 8. Saarbrücker Arbeitsta-gung 1987. Heidelberg 1987, S. 58-81.

Plattner, H.: Der Einfluß der Client/Server-Architektur auf kaufmännische Anwendungs-systeme. In: Schriften zur Unternehmensführung. Band 44. Wiesbaden 1991, S. 102-109.

Plattner, H.: Client/Server-Architekturen. In: Scheer, A.-W. (Hrsg.): Handbuch Informati-onsmanagement: Aufgaben – Konzepte – Praxislösungen. Wiesbaden 1993, S. 923-938.

Plattner, H.; Kagermann, H.: Einbettung eines Systems der Plankostenrechnung in ein EDV-Gesamtkonzept. In: Scheer, A.-W. (Hrsg.): Grenzplankostenrechnung – Stand und aktuelle Probleme. 2. Auflage. Wiesbaden 1991, S. 137-178.

Pomberger, G.; Blaschek, G.: Software Engineering. 2. Auflage. München 1996.

Porter, M. E.: Competitive Advantage – Creating and Sustaining Superior Performance. New York 1985.

Probst, G .J. B.: Vernetztes Denken für komplexe strategische Probleme. In: Königswie-ser, R.; Lutz, C. (Hrsg.): Das systemisch evolutionäre Management. Wien 1992, S. 22-41.

Probst, G. J. B.; Gomez, P.: Die Methodik des vernetzten Denkens zur Lösung komplexer Probleme. In: Probst, G. J. B.; Gomez, P. (Hrsg.): Vernetztes Denken. Wiesbaden 1993, S. 3-20.

Probst, G. J. B.; Gomez, P.: Vernetztes Denken für die strategische Führung eines Zeitschriftenverlages. In: Probst, G. J. B.; Gomez, P. (Hrsg.): Vernetztes Denken. Wiesbaden 1993, S. 23-39.

Rathwell, A. G.; Williams, T. J.: Use of the Purdue enterprise reference architecture and methodology in industry. In: Bernus, P.; Nemes, L. (Hrsg.): Modelling and Methodologies for Enterprise Integration. London et al. 1996, S. 12-44.

Regionales Rechenzentrum in Niedersachsen (Hrsg.): Internet – Eine Einführung in die Nutzung der Internet-Dienste. 2. Auflage. Hannover 1996.

Reisig, W.: Anforderungsbeschreibung und Systementwurf mit Petri-Netzen. In: Handbuch der modernen Datenverarbeitung. 23 (1986) 130, S. 81-96.

Richter, G.: Netzmodelle für die Bürokommunikation (Teil 2). In: Informatik Spektrum. 7 (1984) 1, S. 28-40.

Riehm, U.; Wingert, B.: Multimedia – Mythen, Chancen und Herausforderungen. Mannheim 1995.

Rockart, J. F.: The Changing Role of the Information System Executive: A Critical Success Factors Perspective. In: Sloan Management Review. 24 (1982) 1, S. 3-13.

Roethlisberger, F. J.; Dickson, W.: Management and the Worker. Cambridge 1939.

Rosenstengel, B.; Winand, U.: Petri-Netze – Eine anwendungsorientierte Einführung. Braunschweig, Wiesbaden 1982.

Ruffing, T.: Fertigungssteuerung bei Fertigungsinseln. Köln 1991.

Rumbaugh, J.; Blaha, M.; Premerlani, W.; Eddy, F.; Lorensen, W.: Object-Oriented Modelling and Design. New Jersey 1991.

Sänger, F.: Materialien und Leistungen beschaffen und verwalten. In: SAPinfo – Continuous Business Engineering. Walldorf 1996, S. 31-33.

SAP AG (Hrsg.): Funktionen im Detail – ABAP/4 Development Workbench. Walldorf 1995.

SAP AG (Hrsg.): Funktionen im Detail – Anlagenwirtschaft. Walldorf 1995.

SAP AG (Hrsg.): Funktionen im Detail – Das Instandhaltungssystem. Walldorf 1995.

SAP AG (Hrsg.): Funktionen im Detail – Das Vertriebssystem der SAP. Walldorf 1994.

SAP AG (Hrsg.): Funktionen im Detail – Die Branchenlösung für Banken IS-B der SAP. Walldorf 1995.

SAP AG (Hrsg.): Funktionen im Detail – Ergebnis- und Vertriebs-Controlling. Walldorf 1996.

SAP AG (Hrsg.): Funktionen im Detail – Gemeinkosten-Controlling. Walldorf 1996.

SAP AG (Hrsg.): Funktionen im Detail – Hauptbuchhaltung. Walldorf 1996.

SAP AG (Hrsg.): Funktionen im Detail – Investitionsmanagement. Walldorf 1995.

SAP AG (Hrsg.): Funktionen im Detail – Konsolidierung. Walldorf 1996.

SAP AG (Hrsg.): Funktionen im Detail – Krankenhausinformationssystem. Walldorf 1996.

SAP AG (Hrsg.): Funktionen im Detail – Materialwirtschaft. Walldorf 1996.

SAP AG (Hrsg.): Funktionen im Detail – Personalwirtschaft. Walldorf 1995.

SAP AG (Hrsg.): Funktionen im Detail – Personenkonten. Walldorf 1996.

SAP AG (Hrsg.): Funktionen im Detail – Produktionsplanung. Walldorf 1994.

SAP AG (Hrsg.): Funktionen im Detail – Produktionsplanung-Prozeßindustrie. Walldorf 1995.

SAP AG (Hrsg.): Funktionen im Detail – Produktkosten-Controlling. Walldorf 1996.

SAP AG (Hrsg.): Funktionen im Detail – Projektsystem. Walldorf 1994.

SAP AG (Hrsg.): Funktionen im Detail – Prozeßkostenrechnung. Walldorf 1996.

SAP AG (Hrsg.): Funktionen im Detail – Qualitätsmanagement. Walldorf 1995.

SAP AG (Hrsg.): Funktionen im Detail – SAP Business Workflow. Walldorf 1996.

SAP AG (Hrsg.): Funktionen im Detail – SAP R/3 Service & Support. Walldorf 1996.

SAP AG (Hrsg.): Funktionen im Detail – SAP R/3 Software-Architektur. Walldorf 1994.

Schäfer, E.: Der Industriebetrieb – Betriebswirtschaftslehre der Industrie auf typologischer Grundlage. Band 1. Köln, Opladen 1969.

Scharfenberg, H.: Von Taylor zum Team. In: Scharfenberg, H. (Hrsg.): Strukturwandel in Management und Organisation. Baden-Baden 1993, S. 9-28.

Schaschinger, H.: Objektorientierte Analyse und Modellierung. Wien 1993.

Scheer, A.-W.: Architektur integrierter Informationssysteme. Berlin et al. 1991.

Scheer, A.-W.: ARIS-Toolset: Von Forschungs-Prototypen zum Produkt. In: Informatik Spektrum. 19 (1996) 2, S. 71-78.

Scheer, A.-W.: CIM – Der computergesteuerte Industriebetrieb. 4. Auflage. Berlin et al. 1990.

Scheer, A.-W.: EDV-orientierte Betriebswirtschaftslehre - Grundlagen für ein effizientes Informationsmanagement. 4. Auflage. Berlin et al. 1990.

Scheer, A.-W.: Factory of the Future. In: Scheer, A.-W. (Hrsg.): Veröffentlichungen des Instituts für Wirtschaftsinformatik. Heft 42. Saarbrücken 1983.

Scheer, A.-W.: Wirtschaftsinformatik - Informationssysteme im Industriebetrieb. 3. Auflage. Berlin et al. 1990.

Scheer, A.-W.; Nüttgens, M.; Zimmermann, V.: Rahmenkonzept für ein integriertes Geschäftsprozeßmanagement. In: Wirtschaftsinformatik. 37 (1995) 5, S. 426-434.

Schmitt, G.: Methode und Techniken der Organisation. 9. Auflage. Gießen 1991.

Schneider, G.: Eine Einführung in das Internet. In: Informatik Spektrum. 18 (1995), S. 263-271.

Schneider, H.-J.: Lexikon der Informatik und Datenverarbeitung. München et al. 1991.

Schneeweiß, C.: Einführung in die Produktionswirtschaft. 5. Auflage. Berlin et al. 1993.

Scholz, C.: Virtuelle Unternehmen – Organisatorische Revolution mit strategischer Implikation. In: Management und Computer. 4 (1996) 1, S. 27-34.

Scholz, R.: Geschäftsprozeßoptimierung – Crossfunktionale Rationalisierung oder strukturelle Reorganisation. Bergisch Gladbach 1994.

Scholz, R.; Vrohlings, A.: Prozeß-Redesign und kontinuierliche Prozeßverbesserung. In: Gaitanides, M. et al. (Hrsg.): Prozeßmanagement – Konzepte, Umsetzungen und Erfahrungen des Business Reengineering. München 1994, S. 99-122.

Schroeder, P.: Isomorphismus. In: Sandkühler, H.-J. (Hrsg.): Europäische Enzyklopädie zu Philosophie und Wissenschaften. Band 3. Hamburg 1990, S. 425-432.

Schröder, G.: Industriespezifische Geschäftsprozeßmodellierung. In: SAPinfo – Continuous Business Engineering. Walldorf 1996, S. 19-22.

Schüller, U.; Veddeler, H.-G.: PC aufrüsten und reparieren. Düsseldorf 1996.

Schulte, C.: Konzepte der Materialbereitstellung. In: Corsten, H. (Hrsg.): Handbuch Produktionsmanagement. Wiesbaden 1994, S. 189-205.

Schulte-Zurhausen, M.: Organisation. München 1995.

Schulz, A.: Softwareentwurf – Methoden und Werkzeuge. In: Krallmann et al. (Hrsg.): Handbuch der Informatik. München et al. 1992.

Seeger, J.; Würth, H.: Integration sichert Leistungspotentiale. In: SAPInfo – Continuous Business Engineering. Walldorf 1996, S. 41-44.

Seubert, M.: Entwicklungsstand und Konzeption des SAP-Datenmodells. In: Scheer, A.-W. (Hrsg.): Datenbanken 1991 – Praxis relationaler Datenbanken. Fachtagung. Saarbrücken 1991, S. 87-109.

Seubert, M.; Schäfer, T.; Schorr, M.; Wagner, J.: Praxisorientierte Datenmodellierung mit der SAP-SERM-Methode. In: Informatik – Zeitschrift der schweizerischen Informatikorganisationen. 2 (1995) 1, S. 15-23.

Shlaer, S.; Mellor, S. J.: Object-Oriented Systems Analysis. New Jersey 1988.

Simon, K.: Effiziente Algorithmen für perfekte Graphen. Stuttgart 1992.

Sinz, E. J.: Das Entity-Relationship-Modell (ERM) und seine Erweiterungen. In: Handbuch der modernen Datenverarbeitung - Theorie und Praxis der Wirtschaftsinformatik. 27 (1990) 152, S. 17-29.

Smith, A.: Der Wohlstand der Nationen. 4. Auflage. München 1988.

Sommerville, I.: Software Engineering. 4. Auflage. Wokingham et al. 1992.

Spur, R.: Die Roboter verschwinden in der automatischen Fabrik. In: VDI-Nachrichten. 38 (1984) 52, S. 6.

Staehle, W. H.: Management – Eine verhaltenswissenschaftliche Perspektive. 6. Auflage. München 1991.

Stahlknecht, P.: Einführung in die Wirtschaftsinformatik. 7. Auflage. Berlin et al. 1995.

Starke, H.: Analyse von Petri-Netz-Modellen. Stuttgart 1990.

Steinmann, H.; Schreyögg, G.: Management – Grundlagen der Unternehmensführung. Wiesbaden 1990.

Steinmetz, R.: Multimedia-Technologie – Einführung und Grundlagen. Berlin et al. 1993.

Steinmetz, R.; Sabic, K.: Multimedia – Quo vadis. In: Handbuch der modernen Datenverarbeitung. 33 (1996) 188, S. 8-22.

Stotko, E. C.: CIM-OSA - Europäische Initiative für offene CIM-System-Architektur. In: CIM Management. 5 (1989) 1, S. 9-15.

Striening, H.-D.: Prozeß-Management – Versuch eines integrierten Konzeptes situationsadäquater Gestaltung von Verwaltungsprozessen. Frankfurt/Main 1988.

Svobodova, L.: Client/Server Model of Distributed Processing. In: Heger, D. et al. (Hrsg.): Kommunikation in verteilten Systemen I. Berlin et al. 1985, S. 485-495.

Syring, M.: Computerunterstützung arbeitsteiliger Prozesse – Konzipierung eines Koordinatensystems für die Büroarbeit. Wiesbaden 1994.

Taylor, D. A.: Business Engineering with Object Technology. New York et al. 1995.

Taylor, F. W.: The Principles of Scientific Management. New York, London 1911.

Teufel, T.; Ertl, F.: Prozeßorientierte Einführung mit dem R/3-Analyzer. In: SAPinfo – Business Reengineering. Walldorf 1995, S. 22-24.

Thome, R.; Hufgard, A.: Continuous System Engineering – Entdeckung der Standardsoftware als Organisator. Würzburg 1996.

Towers, S.: Business Process Reengineering – A Practical Handbook for Executives. Cheltenham 1994.

Ulrich, H.: Eine systemtheoretische Perspektive der Unternehmensorganisation. In: Seidel, E.; Wagner, D. (Hrsg.): Organisation – Evolutionäre Interdependenzen von Kultur und Struktur der Unternehmung. Wiesbaden 1989, S. 13-26.

Vaskevitch, D.: Client/Server Strategies – A Survival Guide for Corporate Reengineers. San Mateo 1993.

Venitz, U.: CIM-Rahmenplanung. Berlin et al. 1990.

Vernadat, F.: CIM business process and enterprise activity modelling. In: Bernus, P.; Nemes, L. (Hrsg.): Modelling and Methodologies for Enterprise Integration. London et al. 1996, S. 171-182.

Vernadat, F.: CIM-OSA – A European Development for Enterprise Integration. In. Petrie, C. J. (Hrsg.): Enterprise Integration Modelling. Cambridge 1992, S. 189-204.

Vester, F.: Neuland des Denkens. München 1980.

Vester, F.: Standpunkt – Die totale Information. In: Bild der Wissenschaft. Juli 1995, S. 14-15.

Vikas, K.: Controlling im Dienstleistungsbereich mit Grenplankostenrechnung. Wiesbaden 1988.

Ward, P. T.; Mellor, S. J.: Structured Development for Real-Time Systems. Englewood Cliffs 1985.

Weber, H. K.: Betriebswirtschaftliches Rechnungswesen. Band 1: Bilanz und Erfolgsrechnung. 3. Auflage. München 1988.

Weber, H. K.: Betriebswirtschaftliches Rechnungswesen. Band 2: Kosten- und Leistungsrechnung. 3. Auflage. München 1991.

Weihrauch, K.: Unterstützung aller Fertigungsarten. In: SAPInfo – Continuous Business Engineering. Walldorf 1996, S. 34-37.

Welz, G.: Byte Watchers. In: SAPInfo. Heft 50. Walldorf 1996, S. 14-15.

Wendt, S.: Nichtphysikalische Grundlagen der Informationstechnik – Interpretierte Formalismen. Berlin et al. 1989.

Wiegert, O.: Änderbarkeit durch Objektorientierung. Braunschweig 1995.

Wielinga, B.; Bredeweg, B,; Breuker, J.: Knowledge Acquisition for Expert Systems. In: Siekman, J. (Hrsg.): Advanced Topics in Artificial Intelligence – ACAI'87. Lecture Notes in Artificial Intelligence 345. Berlin et al. 1987, S. 96-124.

Wiendahl, H.-P.: Belastungsorientierte Fertigungssteuerung. München 1987.

Wildemann, H.: Das Just-in-Time-Konzept: Produktion und Zulieferung auf Abruf. 2. Auflage. München 1990.

Wildemann, H.: Einführungsstrategien für die computerintegrierte Produktion (CIM). München 1990.

Wintermantel, E.; Ha, S.-W.: Biokompatible Werkstoffe und Bauweisen – Implantate für Medizin und Umwelt. Berlin et al. 1996.

Wirfs-Brock, R.; Wilkerson, B.; Wiener, L.: Designing Object-Oriented Software. New Jersey 1990.

Wöhe, G. Einführung in die Allgemeine Betriebswirtschaftslehre. 19. Auflage. München 1996.

Wolff, M. R.: Computerunterstütztes Lernen in der wirtschaftswissenschaftlichen Hochschulausbildung – Status und Anforderungen. In: Dette, K. (Hrsg.): Multimedia, Vernetzung und Software für die Lehre: Das Computer-Investitions-Programm (CIP) in der Nutzanwendung. Berlin et al. 1992, S. 585-594.

Wolff, M. R.: Multimediale Informationssysteme. In: Handbuch der modernen Datenverarbeitung. 30 (1993) 169, S. 9-26.

Womack, J. P.; Jones, D.; Roos, D.: Die zweite Revolution in der Automobilindustrie. Konsequenzen aus der weltweiten Studie des Massachusetts Institute of Technology. Frankfurt/ Main, New York 1992.

Xu, Z.-Y.: Prinzipien des Entwurfs und der Realisierung eines Organisationsinformationssystems. Heidelberg 1995.

Zäpfel, G.: Entwicklungsstand und -tendenzen von PPS-Systemen. In: Corsten, H. (Hrsg.): Handbuch Produktionsmanagement. Wiesbaden 1994, S. 719-745.

Zencke, P.: Logische Erweiterung der R/3-Architektur. In: SAPInfo. Heft 50. Walldorf 1996, S. 19-24.

Zencke, P.: Modellgestützte R/3-Systemkonfiguration für eine Betriebswirtschaft des Wandels. In: SAPInfo – Continuous Business Engineering. Walldorf 1996, S. 6-9.

Zencke, P.: Softwareunterstützung im Business Process Reengineering. In: Schriften zur Unternehmensführung. Band 53. Wiesbaden 1994, S. 63-76.

Zendler, A.: Konzepte, Erfahrungen und Werkzeuge zur Softwarewiederverwendung. Marburg 1995.

Index

ABAP/4 99–100, 106–107, 203–204
accounting 68–75, 249–250
activity-type processing 322–325
application 59, 67, 100–104
architecture 64, 112–119
assembly manufacturer 280–282
asset management 243–244
automatic payment
   customer 748–757
   vendor 584–595

billing 732–741
billing document transfer and valuation
   742–747
business management science 1, 32
business process 54, 128–129, 145–149,
   179–183
business reengineering 51–53
business transformation 41–42
business workflow 104–105

client/server 9–11, 57–58, 64
componentware 58–62
computer 7, 8
Computer Aided Software Engineering 11
Computer Integrated Manufacturing 30,
   113–116
configuration 148–149, 156
Continuous System Engineering 48–51
contract release order 802–807
control flow 159, 164–167
controlling 73–75, 248–249
cost centre
   analysis 758–765
   plan closing 340–353
   planning with flexible standard costing
   326–339
   processing 316–321
cost/revenue processing 310–315
credit master data processing 518–527
customer contract

   processing 690–697
   release order processing 698–699
customer integration 4
customer master processing 726–731
cybernetics 42–44

data highway 8
data processing 7
database 13
decentralization 9
delivery processing 706–717
demand management 444–459
DNA 285–289, 797–781

encapsulation 12
engineering/design 30
enterprise 11, 109
enterprise planning 241–242
Entity Relationship Model 130–131
event-controlled process chain 150–167

Financial Accounting 68–71

goods issue
   for production order 636–641
   processing 718–725
goods movement, inspection lot completion
   for 568–577
goods receipt processing
   from production 652–657
   with PO reference 540–549
GRAI 135–136

HIPO 134
HTML 21
Human Resources Management 95–99,
   244–245
hypertext 16, 17, 18, 19

information broker 6
inheritance 12–13

inspection lot
  completion for goods movement 568–577
  creation for GR from purchase order 556–567
Internet 20–23
investment management 71–73
invoice processing
  with reference (posting) 528–539
  with reference (release) 578–583
Iterative Process Prototyping 189–273

Knowledge Acquisition 122–126

Lean Management 35–37
logistics 32–35, 72–94
lot-size manufacturer 277–279

manufacturer
  assembly 280–282
  lot-size 277–279
market 1, 2, 3
marketing 242, 243
material BOM processing 398–409
material master processing
  for costing 354–363
  MM 496–503
  PP 388–397
  QM 550–555
material planning – overall 468–487
Materials Management 79–81
metamodel 156–157
method 130–143, 150–153
model 109–111, 145, 158
model company 282–283
modelling 149
module 56–60, 156–157, 238–239, 250–251
MPS–single-item processing 460–467
multimedia 15–20

net value added chains 39–40, 145, 238, 272–273, 275–283, 285–289, 779–781
network 5, 9, 17

object orientation 11–15, 56–58, 126–129
order processing, standard 782–785
organization 1, 4, 14, 24–29, 244
  process-oriented 27, 138–142
  responsibility-oriented 27, 137–141
overhead calculation 658–667

Petri network 136–137
planned order conversion 596–601
plant maintenance 30, 88–91
position 139
preliminary costing with quantity structure 364–375
procedures 169–187
process 3, 56–58, 120–122, 145, 207–211
process analysis 252–271
process area 237–251
process module 238–239, 250–251, 285–289, 779–781
processing
  activity-type 322–325
  delivery 706–717
  MPS–single-item 460–467
process-oriented organization 27, 138–142
procurement 33–34, 245–246
product development 242–243
production 30, production 33–34, 81–85, 246–248
production order
  preliminary costing 616–621
  confirmation 642–651
  creation 602–615
  execution 628–635
  goods issue for 636–641
  release 622–627
  settlement 680–685
production variances, transfer of 686–689
production, goods receipt processing from 652–657
profit analysis 772–781
profit centre reporting 766–771
profit planning 376–387
programming 7, 13, 14, 30
project management 170–174
Project System 92–94

purchase order processing 510–517

quality assurance 30
Quality Management 85–87

R/3
    Customizing 200–203, 290, 214, 219,
        222–226, 228, 236
    Data Dictionary 203–205, 211, 216,
        221, 226, 231–236
    Object/Data Model 196–198, 210, 215,
        220, 225, 227–231, 234
    Organization Model 193–196, 208, 212,
        217–221, 224, 229, 233
    Prototyping 198–200, 207, 212–217,
        223, 230, 235
    reference process 145, 190–193, 207–
        211, 213, 218, 222, 227, 232
    Services 99–107
Reference Model 148
responsibility-oriented organization 27,
    137–141
results, transfer to demand management
    438–443
reusability 60–61
RFQ processing 488–495
routing processing 420–437

Sales & Operations Planning 298–309
Sales and Distribution 75–79, 247–248

sales planning 290–297
Semantic Object Model 119–122
server 9
Simultaneous Engineering 37–39
software
    development 174–178
    installation 179–187
    library 48–50
    standard 55, 56
standard order processing 782–785
standard software 55, 56
Structured Analysis 131–133
Structured Analysis and Design Technique
    133–134
system 27
task 27–29, 138–139, 145
Taylorism 3–4, 24–27
transfer of production variances 686–689

user interface 14

variance calculation 674–679
vendor master data processing 504–509
virtual corporation 4–6
WIP calculation 668–673
work centre processing 410–419
work scheduling 30
workflow management 45–48
World Wide Web 21